Encyclopedia of
GENDER
in MEDIA

Encyclopedia of
GENDER
in MEDIA

MARY KOSUT

Purchase College, State University of New York

EDITOR

$SAGE reference

Los Angeles | London | New Delhi
Singapore | Washington DC

Los Angeles | London | New Delhi
Singapore | Washington DC

FOR INFORMATION:

SAGE Publications, Inc.
2455 Teller Road
Thousand Oaks, California 91320
E-mail: order@sagepub.com

SAGE Publications Ltd.
1 Oliver's Yard
55 City Road
London, EC1Y 1SP
United Kingdom

SAGE Publications India Pvt. Ltd.
B 1/I 1 Mohan Cooperative Industrial Area
Mathura Road, New Delhi 110 044
India

SAGE Publications Asia-Pacific Pte. Ltd.
3 Church Street
#10-04 Samsung Hub
Singapore 049483

Publisher: Rolf A. Janke
Acquisitions Editor: Jim Brace-Thompson
Assistant to the Publisher: Michele Thompson
Managing Editor: Susan Moskowitz
Reference Systems Manager: Leticia M. Gutierrez
Reference Systems Coordinator: Laura Notton
Production Editor: Jane Haenel
Typesetter: Hurix Systems Pvt. Ltd.
Proofreader: Jennifer Thompson
Indexer: Scott Smiley
Cover Designer: Gail Buschman
Marketing Manager: Kristi Ward

Printed in the United States of America.

Library of Congress Cataloging-in-Publication Data

Encyclopedia of gender in media / editor Mary Kosut.

p. cm.
Includes bibliographical references and index.

ISBN 978-1-4129-9079-0 (cloth)

1. Sex role in mass media. 2. Women in mass media.
3. Men in mass media. I. Kosut, Mary.

P96.S5E53 2012

302.23081—dc23

2011052751

12 13 14 15 16 10 9 8 7 6 5 4 3 2 1

Contents

List of Entries

Reader's Guide

Biographies

Barthes, Roland
Berger, John
Bordo, Susan
boyd, danah
Doane, Mary Ann
Douglas, Susan J.
Ellul, Jacques
Fiske, John
Gamson, Joshua
Giroux, Henry
Guerrilla Girls
Hall, Stuart
Hanna, Kathleen
hooks, bell
Jenkins, Henry
Jervis, Lisa
Jhally, Sut
Kellner, Douglas
Kilbourne, Jean
Kruger, Barbara
Lasn, Kalle
McChesney, Robert
McLuhan, Marshall
Miller, Mark Crispin
Moyers, Bill
Mulvey, Laura
Radway, Janice
Rushkoff, Douglas
Steinem, Gloria

Concepts and Theories

Cognitive Script Theory
Critical Theory
Cultivation Theory
Desensitization Effect
Discourse Analysis
Encoding and Decoding
Feminism
Feminist Theory: Liberal
Feminist Theory: Marxist
Feminist Theory: Postcolonial
Feminist Theory: Second Wave
Feminist Theory: Socialist
Feminist Theory: Third Wave
Feminist Theory: Women-of-Color and
    Multiracial Perspectives
Gender Schema Theory
Hegemony
Ideology
Male Gaze
Mass Media
Media Convergence
Media Ethnography
Media Globalization
Media Rhetoric
Mediation
Patriarchy
Polysemic Text
Postfeminism
Postmodernism
Post-Structuralism
Quantitative Content Analysis
Queer Theory
Reception Theory
Scopophilia
Semiotics
Simulacra
Social Comparison Theory
Social Construction of Gender
Social Learning Theory
Televisuality
Textual Analysis
Transgender Studies
Transsexuality

Discrimination and Media Effects

Beauty and Body Image: Beauty Myths
Beauty and Body Image: Eating Disorders
Class Privilege
Heterosexism
Homophobia
Identity
Intersectionality
Minority Rights
Misogyny
Prejudice
Racism
Sexism
Sexuality
Stereotypes
Violence and Aggression

Internet and New Media

Avatar
Blogs and Blogging
Cyberdating
Cyberpunk
Cyberspace and Cyberculture
Cyborg
Electronic Media and Social Inequality
E-Zines: Third Wave Feminist
Hacking and Hacktivism
Hypermedia
Massively Multiplayer Online Role-Playing Games
Multi-User Dimensions
Online New Media: GLBTQ Identity
Online New Media: Transgender Identity
Second Life
Social Inequality
Social Media
Social Networking Sites: Facebook
Social Networking Sites: Myspace
Twitter
Viral Advertising and Marketing
Virtual Community
Virtual Sex
Virtuality
Web 2.0
Wiki
YouTube

Media Industry

Audiences: Producers of New Media
Audiences: Reception and Injection Models

Fairness Doctrine
Federal Communications Commission
Media Consolidation
Network News Anchor Desk
New Media
Telecommunications Act of 1996
Workforce

Media Modes

Advertising
Children's Programming: Cartoons
Children's Programming: Disney and Pixar
Comics
E-Zines: Riot Grrrl
Film: Hollywood
Film: Horror
Film: Independent
Graphic Novels
Men's Magazines: Lad Magazines
Men's Magazines: Lifestyle and Health
Music: Underrepresentation of Women Artists
Music Videos: Representations of Men
Music Videos: Representations of Women
Music Videos: Tropes
Newsrooms
Pornification of Everyday Life
Pornography: Gay and Lesbian
Pornography: Heterosexual
Pornography: Internet
Radio
Radio: Pirate
Reality-Based Television: *America's Next Top Model*
Reality-Based Television: Makeover Shows
Reality-Based Television: Wedding Shows
Romance Novels
Sitcoms
Soap Operas
Sports Media: Extreme Sports and Masculinity
Sports Media: Olympics
Sports Media: Transgender
Talk Shows
Textbooks
Toys and Games: Gender Socialization
Toys and Games: Racial Stereotypes and Identity
Tropes
Tween Magazines
Video Gaming: Representations of Femininity
Video Gaming: Representations of Masculinity
Video Gaming: Violence

About the Editor

Mary Kosut is an associate professor of Media, Society, and the Arts at Purchase College, State University of New York, and the coordinator of the Media, Society, and the Arts program. While her Ph.D. is in sociology, she teaches courses in a variety of academic fields, including gender studies, environmental studies, art history, and media studies. Her courses fuse cultural and social theory and inventive methodologies, encouraging a critical and creative investigation of mediated life and contemporary media culture(s). Her interdisciplinary research examines the intersections between embodiment, everyday practices, artworlds, and popular culture. She has published work on tattoo art, body modification, and academic life in journals such as *Deviant Behavior*, *Visual Sociology*, *The Journal of Popular Culture*, and *Cultural Studies-Critical Methodologies*. Her book, *The Body Reader: Essential Social and Cultural Readings* edited with Lisa Jean Moore, investigates embodied practices, regimes, and representations. She is currently working on a manuscript on the recent trend of urban beekeeping that explores how bees traffic within cultural, economic, and political systems, and interspecies relationships between insects and humans. She lives in Brooklyn, New York.

List of Contributors

Mary Alice Adams
Louisiana Tech University

Karley Adney
Butler University

Isra Ali
Rutgers University

Neil M. Alperstein
Loyola University Maryland

Patricia Amason
University of Arkansas

Rina Arya
University of Wolverhampton

Laura Barnes Ashley
University of Houston

Lucinda Austin
University of Maryland

Jay Baglia
Kutztown University of Pennsylvania

Lorin Basden Arnold
Rowan University

Judy E. Battaglia
Loyola Marymount University

Andrea M. Bergstrom
Franklin Pierce University

Derek Bolen
Wayne State University

Sarah E. Boslaugh
Kennesaw State University

Melissa Camacho
San Francisco State University

Jamie Capuzza
University of Mount Union

Amy M. Corey
Gonzaga University

Theresa Rose Crapanzano
University of Colorado, Boulder

Carolyn Cunningham
Gonzaga University

Jason Del Gandio
Temple University

Spring-Serenity Duvall
University of South Carolina, Aiken

Jennifer T. Edwards
Tarleton State University

Nahed Eltantawy
High Point University

Kathleen L. Endres
University of Akron

Erika Engstrom
University of Nevada, Las Vegas

Teri Fair
Suffolk University, Boston

Jesse Fox
Ohio State University

Julie Frechette
Worcester State University

Margaretha Geertsema
Butler University

Kim Golombisky
University of South Florida

Gloria Gómez-Diago
Rey Juan Carlos University, Madrid

Scott Gratson
Temple University

Brittany N. Griebling
University of Pennsylvania

Paul Grosswiler
University of Maine

Miles Groth
Wagner College

David Gudelunas
Fairfield University

Donna L. Halper
Lesley University

Megan Jean Harlow
European Graduate School, Switzerland

David S. Heineman
Bloomsburg University of Pennsylvania

Jason A. Helfer
Knox College

Stacey J. T. Hust
Washington State University, Pullman

Stacey O. Irwin
Millersville University

Robin Johnson
Sam Houston State University

Katherine N. Kinnick
Kennesaw State University

J. Meryl Krieger
Indiana University–Purdue University Indianapolis

Celeste C. Lacroix
College of Charleston

Jamie Landau
Keene State College

Rebecca LaVally
California State University, Sacramento

Brittney D. Lee
University of Arkansas

Micky Lee
Suffolk University, Boston

Ming Lei
Washington State University

Brett Lunceford
University of South Alabama

Susan Mackey-Kallis
Villanova University

Shaka McGlotten
Purchase College, State University of New York

Heather McIntosh
Boston College

Michelle Millard
Wayne State University

Shane Miller
St. John's University

Beth M. Olson
University of Houston

Natasha Patterson
Simon Fraser University, British Columbia

Lisa Pecot-Hebert
DePaul University

Kirsten Pike
University College Dublin

Karen C. Pitcher
Eckerd College

Gayle M. Pohl
University of Northern Iowa

Monika Raesch
Suffolk University, Boston

Bryce J. Renninger
Rutgers University

MJ Robinson
Marymount Manhattan College

Michelle Rodino-Colocino
The Pennsylvania State University

Lori Amber Roessner
University of Tennessee

Ryan Rogers
University of North Carolina, Chapel Hill

Stephen T. Schroth
Knox College

Read M. Schuchardt
Wheaton College

Rae Lynn Schwartz-DuPre
Western Washington University

Rachel E. Silverman
Embry Riddle Aeronautical University

Claire F. Sullivan
University of Maine

Chit Cheung Matthew Sung
Lancaster University

Shira Tarrant
California State University, Long Beach

Yarma Velázquez Vargas
California State University, Northridge

Wei-Chun Victoria Wang
Ohio University

Lynne M. Webb
University of Arkansas

Emily West
University of Massachusetts, Amherst

Susan Westcott Alessandri
Suffolk University, Boston

Robert Westerfelhaus
College of Charleston

Jeffrey T. Wickman
Knox College

Janice Hua Xu
Cabrini College

Introduction

The phrase *the media* is commonly employed both inside and outside the academy as a cultural and technological catchall. It is referenced to describe a range of media, both old and new. For example, I have heard college students use this generic term in relation to the content of Hollywood films and national newspapers, as well as social networking sites like Facebook. Often, when we think of the media, we consider the importance of the meanings of popular messages and images that are consumed by a mass audience. In this context, and at its most benign, mass media may be viewed as an outlet to provide us with information, or as a source of entertainment, pleasure, and escape. Conversely, "the media" has been criticized as politically liberal (or conservative), pornographic, superficial, and ultimately too influential in the daily lives of children and young adults. Intuitively, we know that all forms of media matter at the start of the 21st century, as they structure and saturate both the public sphere and the most personal aspects of our lives. As media scholar Douglas Kellner asserts, media culture provides the "materials out of which we forge our very identities, our sense of selfhood, our notion of what it means to be male and female, our sense of class, of ethnicity and race, of nationality, of sexuality, and of 'us' and 'them.'" Clearly, the relationship between gender and media is a significant subject within academia and in the everyday lives of women and men.

While this work examines mass media as a social institution and diverse media texts produced from within cultural industries, its focus is on *gender* in *media*. Over the last 30 years, technological changes have broadened our conception of, and relationship to, media in terms of both form and content. The advent of the Internet has ushered in a new relationship between media and user. As discussed in the articles on social networking sites, dating sites, and online video games, these platforms provide space for interaction, creativity, and what scholars have termed a "bleed" between real-world activities and those that occur within mediated environments. At this historical moment, more people not only use some kind of media everyday (from reading a magazine to searching for a word on Google) but also *produce* media in the form of texts, images, and videos. Given the ubiquity of cameras and video technology in cell phones and the interactivity made available via the Internet, there is a new generation of media users who are simultaneously media creators. People post updates of images on their Facebook walls and upload home videos onto YouTube. Others blog about their personal experiences, create online dating profiles, or debate whether or not we have entered an era of "postfeminism." Thus, media is a multifaceted rubric that includes not only forms of media—from cable television and college radio to multi-user online video games—but also the production, consumption, and creation of media content.

The Internet in particular has transformed how business is conducted in late-capitalism and has altered the way we obtain information. It has revolutionized communication, broadening the possibility of real-time interaction between people who live in different countries and time zones. In particular, e-mail and software programs such as Skype facilitate the potential for interconnectivity across cultural and geographical borders. Time and space have literally sped up, imploded, and virtually collapsed for those who have access to a computer with an Internet connection. Technological advances have radicalized the amount of information that may be available at the click of a key. While much of popular American mass media has been globally exported via print, film, video, records, and television for many decades, becoming familiar in numerous cultures, those living within developing countries have more opportunities not only to gather knowledge but also to create and transmit local media within a larger global media landscape.

Today the spectrum of mediated experiences often challenges binary boundaries, blurring how we conceptualize public and private, real and virtual, and old and new media. It is possible to participate in virtual sexual encounters in the online social world of *Second Life* via a laptop computer in a coffee shop. We can also stream television shows and read the *New York Times* on an iPhone. With this in mind, this volume explores the complexity of media across diverse platforms, technologies, and cultural, economic, and political landscapes. The ubiquity of mass media and the emergence of new media technologies have had a significant influence on culture (defined here in the broadest sense of the word), as well as our intimate daily experiences. Understandably, the relationship between gender and the media has become an increasingly salient subject within the last few decades.

As an agent of socialization, media has an enormous impact on how we make sense of the social world—from what occurs in the local community in which we live to our understanding of transnational politics. Media, whether in the form of text or technology, literally mediate our relation to social institutions that structure our lives, including educational, healthcare, and economic systems. For example, media content can provide knowledge of a financial crisis, and access to types of media determine how (or if) we may participate in the postindustrial global labor force. Yet, media content also shapes our self-identity and, in turn, our gender identity. In the articles that appear within this text, gender is delineated as a socially constructed system of classification that hinges on the binary categories of masculinity and femininity. As a result, certain behaviors, expectations, and subjectivities are attributed to that which is deemed masculine and that which is categorized as feminine. Within the context of patriarchy, characteristics and social roles associated with masculinity are more highly valued than those that are defined as feminine. Furthermore, it is important to stress that the social construction of gender is directly related to power, as men have more political, cultural, and economic power, broadly speaking, than women. For example, men disproportionately hold upper-level positions in media industries and are more often owners of major media outlets such as television broadcasting companies, advertising agencies, and social networking sites.

The history of mass media, both behind the scenes and in front of the camera/screen/microphone, has been a history of exclusion. In terms of media presence and participation, women, as well as nonwhite people and other minorities, have played limited roles, particularly in network television, Hollywood film, newspapers, and radio. For example, as discussed in this volume, within the history of network television news, women rarely held behind-the-scenes positions as reporters and writers, and only a few women sat behind the news anchor desk prior to the 1970s. Notably, in the 1970s Barbara Walters coanchored with Harry Reasoner, and later in the 1990s, Connie Chung coanchored with Dan Rather. However, it was not until 2006 that the coveted nightly news anchor position was given to a woman, Katie Couric. Before Couric, women had never anchored the news solo (that is, without a male coanchor). Until fairly recently, print newsrooms had a similar history of excluding women as key reporters. Historically, women have been relegated to covering "soft" news stories that are presumably of interest to female audiences. Female reporters and editors traditionally worked on articles and content centering on fashion, health, beauty, celebrity, entertainment, and human interest. The coverage of "hard" news, information that is culturally and politically significant, has been the domain of men. Implied within this tradition of exclusion and topical gender stereotyping is the idea that issues of great importance and seriousness "naturally" fall under male purview and authority.

Media representations contain veiled and explicit scripts pertaining to gender. These narratives edify audiences regarding social roles and personal characteristics that are accepted and valued for men and women, as well as those that are undesirable. For example, female characters are more likely to be shown in television and film as mothers and caregivers, as compared with male characters. Although it is a biological fact that women have children, this gendered televisual script reproduces the notion that women are innately better at child rearing. Although gender is based on the biological categories of male and female, gender differences are not a "natural" fact. Gender roles have been traditionally read as a given in popular culture, as illustrated in the popular maxim "boys will be boys and girls will be girls," but masculinity and femininity exist on a continuum and have never been static categories. Gender bending, drag, and even the recent arrival of the metrosexual male (thanks in part to the television show *Queer Eye for the Straight Guy*) are examples of how gender is performed, negotiated, and challenged.

The gender binary is directly connected to heteronormativity, as men or women who transgress gender boundaries may risk being identified as butch, fag, or queer (in the pejorative sense of these words). Recently, there have been more representations of transgender and homosexual people in the media, from transgender guests such as Susan Stryker and a very pregnant Thomas Beatie, who both appeared on *Oprah*, to television shows, such as *Queer as Folk* and *The L Word*, that feature mainly gay and lesbian characters. Although the inclusion of homosexual and transgender people in mainstream media has allowed for greater visibility within heteronormative popular culture, it is imperative to examine whether sexual and gender stereotypes are being reproduced or transgressed within media. Such representations, which increase the visibility of alternative gendered and sexual experiences, are never neutral and emanate from within a larger cultural framework that is predominantly heterocentric.

In addition to examining the role of media in enabling, facilitating, or challenging the social construction of gender in our society, this work acknowledges media and feminist theorists who have made significant contributions in the social sciences, humanities, and visual studies, including cinema studies and new media. The study of both gender and media as distinct areas of academic inquiry is a relatively recent phenomenon that reflects larger social and historical changes. Media and communication studies emerged as distinctive areas of inquiry within American universities and colleges within the late 1960s and 1970s. Not surprisingly, the study of media has become a progressively popular field of specialization across a range of disciplines, including not only communication and media studies programs but also sociology, anthropology, cultural studies, and the visual arts. While the output of media scholarship is currently unparalleled, many contemporary scholars have drawn from early theoretical works. For example, Canadian media theorist Marshall McLuhan, who placed emphasis on the specificities of television as a medium in *Understanding Media* (1964), has influenced current media scholarship. Additionally, media theory has been shaped by the work of European sociologists

and philosophers, notably French literary critic and semiotician Roland Barthes (1915–80), as well as German Frankfurt School theorists such as Theodor Adorno (1903–69), who considered the impact of the emergence of the "culture industries" in the 20th century.

The 1960s and the 1970s were a particularly important time not only for the burgeoning field of media studies but also for the institutionalization of feminist theory and women's studies programs. The women's rights movement of the 1960s ushered in what is commonly referred to as the "second wave" of feminism, an umbrella term for a divergent range of theoretical perspectives, including liberal, radical, Marxist, and socialist feminism. Notably, second wave feminists examined the connection between images of women in popular media, particularly magazines and advertisements, and the perpetuation of sexism and misogyny. Liberal feminist Betty Friedan's *The Feminine Mystique* (1963) analyzed the content of women's magazines, critiquing how advertisements and articles normalized and exulted women's place within the home. Friedan argued that media content reinforced the idea that all women were to fulfill their "natural" social roles as dutiful wives and mothers. Similarly, radical feminist Andrea Dworkin asserted that there is a direct relationship between pornographic images of women and the lived experiences of the women who work within the porn industry. She argued that pornographic media should not be protected as "free speech," as it is based on and contributes to the perpetuation of sexual assault and violence against women. While these feminist scholars problematize very different forms of mass media content, they both argue that there is a real link between the lives of men and women, and media representations. More contemporary, or third wave feminists, have continued to highlight and deconstruct media messages in popular culture. Notably, *Bitch* magazine, founded in 1996, is an independent quarterly devoted to providing a critical feminist response to mainstream media. A decade and a half later, *Bitch* continues to take a radical and oppositional approach, now offering a Website with video and interactive content.

In addition to examining feminist theoretical paradigms and theorists, this volume highlights contemporary scholars who have contributed to and expanded our understandings of how the media play a role in perpetuating not only gender inequalities but also those based on race, class, and sexuality. Included are biographies of cultural studies scholars such as bell hooks, who has underscored the connection between sexism, racism, and identity through a variety of popular media, including advertisements, film, and rap music, and Stuart Hall, whose encoding/decoding model of communication illuminates how mass media perpetuates dominant ideologies that are often accepted by audiences. It is significant that there are numerous individuals who have broadened our understandings of the power of media as an economic and political force, such as journalist and media reform activist Bill Moyers and writer/theorist Douglas Rushkoff, who has written extensively on digital media and cyberculture; both are included in this volume.

Feminist scholars have critically analyzed the negative impact of hegemonic representations of masculinity and femininity, both past and present. Susan Bordo's *Unbearable Weight* (1993) and media literacy documentaries produced by the Media Education Foundation, such as Jean Kilbourne's *Killing Us Softly* series, Sut Jhally's *Dreamworlds* films, and Jackson Katz's *Tough Guise: Violence, Media, and the Crisis in Masculinity* (1999), describe how gender binaries are reproduced in media texts, negatively affecting the bodies and subjectivities of men and women. For example, an idealized female body, one that is unattainably thin, beautiful, and typically white, has become a normative standard by which women judge themselves and in turn are judged by others. Low self-esteem, poor body image, and eating disorders such as anorexia and bulimia have been attributed to media representations that reify an unreachable standard of what constitutes an attractive, and by extension a feminine, body. Likewise, masculinity, as embodied in media texts is often drawn in binary opposition to that which is deemed feminine. Men often appear taller, more muscular, and powerful—physically, economically, and culturally—as compared to women. While women are portrayed as thin, weak, and sexually objectified, men take on the role of emotionally vacant, oversexed macho aggressor.

As noted above, our relationship with the media is complex, and scholars have debated the extent to which the media influences the ideological construction of gender and hegemonic understandings of masculinity and femininity. Media consumption studies have focused on how audiences interpret texts, attempting to assess the degree to which individuals critically and reflexively engage with media. Reception theories have purported that all people are not simply passive consumers when it comes to encountering media content. For example, as discussed within, Janice Radway's 1984 study of women's interpretation of romance novels—which typically perpetuate traditional gender roles vis-à-vis plotlines based on old-fashioned ideas of romance, marriage, and sexuality—showed how readers of such novels reinterpreted the narratives, viewing female characters as empowered and independent. Studies in this vein reject a naïve "injection" model approach to media—that is, one that views media consumption as simply unidirectional. Notwithstanding, even if individuals reflexively revise and reinterpret media narratives, these alternative readings do not challenge dominant social structures and institutions that reproduce gender-biased, heterosexist, and racist media content.

Given the fact that we live in an era that is more image-saturated and technologically mediated than at any other time, media scholars and activists have championed media literacy. As discussed in this volume, media literacy calls for reflexive engagement with media, including the ability to read, understand, evaluate, differentiate, and deconstruct media materials. Media literacy recognizes that media are forms of cultural pedagogy. In this vein, Kalle Lasn, author of *Culture Jam* (1999) and founder of *Adbusters* magazine, has advocated "culture jamming" as a means to critique and subvert media narratives and wage "meme warfare." Culture jamming, as discussed in this book, refers to social critique centered on the relationship between the rise of consumer society and what is commonly referred to as the mass-media spectacle. Culture jammers posit that the media-consumption nexus is slowly corroding the human psyche (we are free to resist, but it never occurs to us to do so) and that the mediated public sphere is not public, as it is not free and, by extension, not democratic. Rather, it is controlled by corporations, owned by a small cadre of individuals who profit from the production of media content that reiterates narratives that are predictably stereotypical and ultimately easily consumable given their simplicity. Culture jamming takes many forms, from tweaking advertisements, to subtly revealing a subtext, to staging anticonsumer demonstrations in Disney stores.

In addition to detailing the politics of media production and consumption, this volume addresses alternative media made by individuals, feminists, and media activists who have not only critiqued media but also created content that is subversive and oppositional. For example, the Riot Grrrls music and zine movement that was born out of a merger between punk and political activism in the early 1990s is an example of the do-it-yourself (DIY) approach to cultural creation. In addition to forming all-girl bands, such as the influential Bikini Kill, the Riot Grrrls spawned a generation of young women who took a personal and proactive approach to independent media production (before the ubiquity and accessibility of the Internet). Since then, zines—handmade, low-budget, self-distributed Xeroxed magazines—have continued to be an accessible alternative to mass-media messages and imagery. In an era of media convergence, both traditional zines and e-zines share a common culture online and off, circulating amid more dominant and hegemonic media forms and representations. As new media technologies continue to influence and structure our everyday lives, it is crucial to be reflexive consumers, users, and creators of media content.

Thanks to the women's liberation movement of the 1960s, in the past half century women and other minority populations have become a more integral part of the labor force and a more visible and vocal presence in public life. Women's participation, not only in media but also within the spheres of politics and education, has invariably influenced how we think about traditional gender roles and has led to shifting understandings of masculinity and femininity. As media owners, makers, and producers continue to become more diverse, including not only women but other ethnic and cultural minorities as well, underrepresented perspectives and experiences will both challenge dominant media representations and empower a new generation to participate actively in the increasingly heterogeneous media landscape.

Mary Kosut
Editor

Chronology

1792

The first women's magazine, *The Lady's Magazine*, begins publication in England. It creates the model for other popular women's magazines of the period by targeting upper-class women with a combination of fiction and articles focused on concerns such as fashion and etiquette.

1830

Godey's Lady's Book becomes the first fashion magazine published in the United States. It features sewing instructions as well as hand-colored plates exhibiting the latest fashions and, along with imitators such as *Peterson's Magazine*, is influential in creating the "cult of true womanhood," which advocates that women should concentrate their energies on the domestic sphere and be submissive, pious, and pure.

1863

The Delineator, a women's fashion magazine that features tissue-paper dressmaking patterns, begins publication. It will eventually reach a circulation of more than 2 million before going out of business in 1937.

1867

Harper's Bazar, a magazine devoted to women's interests, including fashion and household matters, begins publication. It is still in publication today (now titled *Harper's Bazaar* with two *a*'s), making it the oldest continuously published fashion magazine in the United States.

1892

Vogue is founded by Arthur Baldwin Turnure; in 1909 the magazine is purchased by Condé Nast, and it remains a leading fashion magazine today.

1896

Alice Guy-Blaché directs *La Fée aux Choux*, one of the first narrative films ever created. She will create more than 700 films in the course of her career in France and the United States.

1912

Sybil Herrold begins hosting a weekly radio program in San Jose, California; she is generally assumed to be the first woman radio announcer in the United States.

1924

The radio station WUMS, operated by David Thomas, begins broadcasting in Ohio. Thomas never obtains a license from the Federal Radio Commission, required after passage of the Communications Act of 1934, but manages to keep broadcasting until 1948.

1926

The National Broadcasting Company (NBC) becomes the first national radio network in the United States, with the Columbia Broadcasting System (CBS) following a year later.

1927

The Jazz Singer, starring Al Jolson, becomes the first feature film to include synchronized sound dialogue and ushers in the era of the "talkies" and the decline of the silent film industry.

1934

The Federal Communications Commission (FCC) is created in the United States to regulate domestic nonfederal use of the radio spectrum, including radio and television broadcasting.

Eleanor Roosevelt begins a weekly news commentary program on the radio, making her the first First Lady to have her own radio show.

1936

The Olympic Games in Berlin are broadcast to television parlors in several German cities, representing the first practical use of television.

Dorothy Arzner, who had been directing films in Hollywood for 10 years (including Clara Bow's first talkie, *The Wild Party*), becomes the first woman to join the Directors Guild of America.

Joe Weider begins publication of an early bodybuilding magazine, *Your Physique*, which in 1966 will be renamed *Muscle Builder* and in 1980 *Muscle and Fitness*.

1938

Jerry Siegel and Joe Shuster create the first Superman story, published by DC Comics, and usher in the era of the costumed superhero.

1940s

Talent search programs on American television and radio, such as Arthur Godfrey's *Talent Scouts* and Ted Mack's *Original Amateur Hour*, involve audience members in the programs by allowing them to vote on contestants.

1941

The Amazon warrior princess Wonder Woman first appears in a DC Comics issue, and one year later she first appears on the cover of a comic. Wonder Woman is remarkable both for her superhero attributes (which include martial arts expertise and possession of magic bracelets that can deflect bullets) and for her well-developed figure and revealing costume.

1946

Regular television broadcasting to the general public begins in the United States.

1949

The American mathematicians Claude Shannon and Warren Weaver publish *The Mathematical Theory of Communication*, which refines theories of how messages are communicated and received, adding concepts such as the possibility of corruption in delivery and the ability of the receiver to affect the producer of the message.

1953

Playboy magazine, founded by Hugh Hefner, begins publication. *Playboy* becomes noted not only for its nude centerfolds (Marilyn Monroe was an early model) but also for publication of contemporary fiction and interviews with cultural leaders.

1954

The nonprofit organization American Women in Radio and Television is founded with 282 members; today it has more than 2,300, employed mostly at television and radio stations.

1959

Mattel introduces the Barbie Doll, an adult-bodied doll designed by Ruth Handler after a German doll called Bild Lilli. Barbie's fictional boyfriend, Ken, is introduced in 1961.

1960s

Television begins broadcasting in color, and by the end of the decade color broadcasting has become the norm.

1963

Hasbro introduces G.I. Joe, an action figure based on members of the U.S. armed forces.

Betty Friedan's *The Feminine Mystique* criticizes role expectations for American women (including that they should forgo their own careers in favor of homemaking) and challenges contemporary images of the "ideal woman." Although criticized as addressing primarily the interests of middle-class white women, it becomes a galvanizing force in the feminist movement.

1964

In the United States, Title VII of the Civil Rights Act prohibits discrimination in employment on the basis of race or gender.

Sports Illustrated publishes its first swimsuit issue; it becomes phenomenally successful and evolves into an annual publication, relying on a formula featuring primarily supermodels posing in exotic locations but occasionally female athletes (including Steffi Graf, Anna Kournikova, Serena Williams, and Danica Patrick).

Marshall McLuhan publishes *Understanding Media: The Extensions of Man*, which advocates studying the media themselves because they affect society over and above any content they may carry; this gives rise to the popular formulation "the media is the message."

1965

The Equal Employment Opportunity Commission (EEOC) is created in the United States to investigate complaints of discrimination based on characteristics such as race and gender.

1966

Gloria Steinem, Shirley Chisholm, and colleagues found the National Organization for Women (NOW), currently the largest women's liberation organization in the United States.

That Girl, a television program starring Marlo Thomas, becomes the first American situation comedy to focus on an unmarried woman living alone.

Lawyer and civil rights activist Florynce Kennedy founds the Media Workshop to counter racist representations of minorities in the media.

1968

The Kerner Commission, created by President Lyndon B. Johnson to investigate the underlying causes of racial unrest in the United States, identifies in its report a lack of diversity among the staff of newspapers and television stations, leading to a lack of coverage of issues important to racial minorities.

1969

Gloria Steinem and Dorothy Pitman publish "After Black Power, Women's Liberation," which points out the inequalities within the civil rights movement and the New Left while taking on the issue that U.S. feminism was widely understood to be the concern of white women.

The Brady Bunch, an American television program created by Sherwood Schwartz, begins broadcasting. The show presents a "blended family" in which the parents both have children from previous marriages; the father (played by Robert Reed) is described as a widower; the reason that the mother (Florence Henderson) was not married is left open.

1970

Electronic versions of popular role-playing games such as *Dungeons and Dragons* are developed by users, often on mainframe university computers.

The videocassette recorder (VCR) presents a relatively cheap and easy way for people to watch movies at home at their convenience and also to record television programming for use on their own schedules.

The Mary Tyler Moore Show, created by James L. Brooks and Allan Burns, becomes the first American situation comedy to focus on a career woman who is not seeking a husband.

1971

The groundbreaking American sitcom *All in the Family*, produced by Norman Lear, begins broadcasting. Over its run (to 1979 in its original form, and from 1979 to 1983 as *Archie Bunker's Place*), this show addressed many controversial issues, including women's liberation, homosexuality, racism, menopause, and impotence, and was also one of the most popular shows of its era.

Ken Robinson directs *Some of Our Best Friends*, an early documentary featuring gay activists and other members of the community (some of whom appear in shadow).

1972

John Berger and four colleagues create *Ways of Seeing*, a British television series as well as the title of a book published to accompany it, which argues that power relationships based on gender and class are evident in both modern advertising and historical western European art. One famous example is Berger's observation that in European art "men act, and women appear" and that women in art were represented for the pleasure of men, an early formulation of the theory of the male gaze.

Maude, a situation comedy spun off from *All in the Family*, features Bea Arthur as a liberal, feminist woman who is the opposite of Archie Bunker in every way (in *All in the Family* Maude was the cousin of Archie's wife, Edith). The program incorporated serious themes such as alcoholism, drug addiction, and abortion.

Title IX of the Education Amendments of 1972 stipulates that girls and women in the United States must have equal opportunity to participate in educational programs. This is interpreted to include school sports teams, leading to a great expansion of organized sports for women at the high school and college levels.

Gloria Steinem cofounds *Ms.* magazine, the first major U.S. magazine to focus on women's issues from a feminist point of view.

The television drama *That Certain Summer*, which focuses on a teenage boy who learns that his father is gay, becomes the first television movie to deal with gay issues.

1973

Stuart Hall publishes *Encoding and Decoding in the Television Discourse*, which states his theory that media producers encode messages in media content, which is then decoded by audience members.

The Miller test (as developed by the U.S. Supreme Court while considering the case *Miller v. California*) becomes the standard for defining pornography: Pornography must appeal to the prurient interest (as defined by community standards), describe sexual conduct in a patently offensive manner, and lack serious literary, artistic, political, or scientific value.

1974

Molly Haskell publishes *From Reverence to Rape*, an early work of feminist film theory and one of the first books to focus on images of women as presented in the movies.

1975

Laura Mulvey publishes her groundbreaking essay "Visual Pleasure and Narrative Cinema" in *Screen*. This essay explicates her theory of the "male gaze," basically that the conventional Hollywood

movie is created to appeal to a male viewer and that story lines, shot selections, and other technical elements are governed by this male point of view.

Susan Brownmiller publishes *Against Our Will*, which attempts to redefine rape as a crime of violence (usually against women) rather than sex.

1976

Barbara Walters becomes coanchor (with Harry Reasoner) of the *ABC Evening News*.

1977

Word Is Out: Stories of Some of Our Lives is released by the Mariposa Film Group; this documentary features 26 gay men and lesbians willing to be interviewed on camera about their lives.

The American television comedy *Soap* features the bisexual character Jodie Dallas, played by Billy Crystal.

1978

In the United States, the FCC issues its *Statement of Policy on Minority Ownership of Broadcasting Facilities*, which attempts to remedy the underrepresentation of women and minorities as owners of broadcast licenses.

The Sundance Film Festival, originally titled the Utah/U.S. Film Festival, is held for the first time; it will go on to become a major showcase for independent American films.

1979

Tom Truscott and Jim Ellis create Usenet, a worldwide Internet discussion system that allows users to read and post messages to newsgroups.

1980s

The first participatory reality television programs are broadcast in the United States. The genre receives a strong boost in 1988 during a strike by the Writers Guild of America.

Cable television becomes popular in the United States, providing subscribers with access to more specialized programming than is available on the broadcast channels.

1980

The American Psychiatric Association recognizes transsexuality as an official disorder.

1981

The African American feminist bell hooks publishes *Ain't I a Woman: Black Women and Feminism*, which examines the portrayal of black women in the media, as well as a number of other issues relating to racism and sexism.

The maze video game *Ms. Pac-Man*, featuring a female protagonist, is released in North America and becomes one of the most popular video games of all time.

The prime-time soap opera *Dynasty* begins broadcasting. The show will stay on the air until 1989 and feature American television's first recurring gay character, Steven Carrington (played by Al Corley and Jack Coleman).

1983

Oprah Winfrey begins hosting the television program *AM Chicago*, which rapidly becomes the most popular talk show in Chicago. In 1986, the program begins national broadcast as *The Oprah Winfrey Show*, which soon becomes the most popular daytime talk show in the United States.

1984

The Times of Harvey Milk, a film about the gay politician directed by Robert Epstein and produced by Richard Schmiechen, wins the Academy Award for Best Documentary.

1985

The WELL (Whole Earth 'Lectronic Link), one of the oldest virtual communities in the world, is founded as a dial-up bulletin board system by Stewart Brand and Larry Brilliant.

The American Broadcasting Company (ABC) drama *An Early Frost*, starring Aidan Quinn and D. W. Moffett, becomes the first television movie to deal with acquired immune deficiency syndrome (AIDS).

Janice Radway publishes a book-length study of the audience for romance novels, which argues for reader response criticism (looking at how audiences receive and interpret a work) rather than the close readings (focused on the text itself), typical of New Criticism, to understand the impact of romance novels on their female readership.

1988

Murphy Brown, an American situation comedy starring Candice Bergen as a journalist and news anchor, begins broadcasting. In the show's 1991–1992 season, one story arc concerns Murphy becoming pregnant and choosing to raise the child as a single mother, a choice that becomes famous when Vice President Dan Quayle refers to it in a speech as emblematic of the decay of family values in America.

1989

Kimberlé Crenshaw coins the term "intersectionality" to emphasize how race, class, and other attributes together influence the unique experience of minority women.

1990s

Internet chat rooms such as those in the America Online (AOL) network become popular sites for social interaction, a practice celebrated in the popular 1998 feature film *You've Got Mail*. The potential in such chat rooms for people to assume an identity different from their own (changing gender, age, and other traits) led to the caption "on the Internet, no one knows you're a dog," featured in a *New Yorker* cartoon.

Many girl-oriented video games come on the market, including *Hawaii High: The Mystery of the Tikki*, *Barbie Fashion Designer*, and *Tomb Raider*, the latter featuring archaeologist Lara Croft.

Satellite broadcast companies such as the Dish Network offer television viewers an alternative to terrestrial broadcast and cable programming.

1990

A touring exhibition of photographs by Robert Mapplethorpe, funded by the National Endowment for the Arts, is shown at the Cincinnati Contemporary Arts Center. Because some of the photos are sexually explicit (although they have been exhibited elsewhere without fuss), the center and its director, Dennis Barrie, are both charged with promoting obscenity, although they are ultimately cleared of the charges. The episode is chronicled in the 2000 television movie *Dirty Pictures*, directed by Frank Pierson.

1991

With *Daughters of the Dust*, Julie Dash becomes the first African American woman to direct a feature film shown in general theatrical release.

1994

The U.S. Public Broadcasting Service (PBS) produces a miniseries based on Armistead Maupin's *Tales of the City*, which is popular but controversial because of its inclusion of homosexual characters, drug use, and explicit sexual situations. The conservative backlash against the program leads PBS to decline to produce the sequel, *More Tales of the City*, which is produced instead by the cable network Showtime.

1995

The television program *Xena: Warrior Princess*, a spin-off of *Hercules: The Legendary Journeys*, offers a new role model to women in the form of the leather-clad warlord, Xena (Lucy Lawless), and her best friend, Gabrielle (Renée O'Connor).

1996

The magazine *Bitch: Feminist Response to Pop Culture* begins publication; its particular focus is to respond to antifeminist messages in mainstream media for young adults and to provide alternatives for young women.

In the United States, the Telecommunications Act deregulates much of the media market, dropping rules against local monopolies (such as those that had prohibited a company from owning both a newspaper and a radio or television station in the same city) and allowing for consolidation of media ownership.

Tim Draper and Steve Jurvetson use the term "viral marketing" to describe their practice of attaching advertising (for Hotmail) to every e-mail sent through the Hotmail system.

1997

Popular actress and comic Ellen DeGeneres comes out (publicly declares her sexual preference as homosexual) on *The Oprah Winfrey Show*.

1998

Sex and the City, a television series loosely based on the book of the same name by Candace Bushnell, begins airing on HBO. The show focuses on four professional women in New York City (played by Sarah Jessica Parker, Kim Cattrall, Kristin Davis, and Cynthia Nixon) and includes frank discussion of issues such as female sexual fantasies and desires, promiscuity, and sexually transmitted diseases.

Will and Grace, a broadcast television situation comedy featuring two gay male characters (Will, played by Eric McCormack, and Jack, played by Sean Hayes), begins airing. The program is highly rated and wins numerous awards but is also criticized for reinforcing stereotypes through the superficial, flamboyant character of Jack.

1999

American soccer player Brandi Chastain makes media history when, after scoring on a penalty kick that won the championship game for the United States, she peels off her jersey and falls to her knees in celebration. The photo of Chastain in her sports bra is widely featured in the mainstream media, including on the cover of *Sports Illustrated*.

2000

Queer as Folk, an American gay soap based on a British series of the same name, premieres on the premium cable network Showtime. The program follows the stories of a group of gay men and is far more explicit than previous television programs, including numerous scenes of same-sex lovemaking and dramatic elements such as drug use and cross-generational romantic relationships.

Robert McChesney publishes *Rich Media, Poor Democracy: Communication Politics in Dubious Times*, which argues that consolidated corporate media ownership in the United States compromises journalistic integrity, creates conflicts between the public interest and the corporation's desire for profit, and reduces consumer choice, because the most profitable genres and formulas tend to be repeated and others ignored.

2002

Julie Powell blogs about her project of cooking all the recipes in Julia Child's *Mastering the Art of French Cooking*. This project becomes one of the first blogs to be adapted to book form (in 2005) and made into a film (2009), both titled *Julie and Julia*.

One of the first reality makeover television programs, *Extreme Makeover*, begins broadcasting on ABC. This program features extensive makeovers (sometimes including plastic surgery) of individuals (mostly female) who were presented as being transformed from ugly to beautiful.

2003

Niklas Zennström and Janus Friis create Skype, a software program that allows users to make voice calls and other forms of communication, including instant messaging and video conferencing, using the Internet.

The social networking site Myspace is founded to compete with sites such as Friendster, Xanga, and AsianAvenue; it becomes the leading social networking site by 2005 but in 2008 is overtaken by Facebook.

Second Life, a virtual world that uses three-dimensional modeling to allow users to create avatars that can interact with other avatars, engaging in many of the same activities common to the real world, including sexual relations.

The cable channel Bravo begins airing *Queer Eye for the Straight Guy*, a reality television show in which five gay men perform a makeover on a straight man, giving him advice about grooming, clothing, cooking, home decorating, and relationships. It became a popular hit and won an Emmy in 2004 and in later seasons included women and gay men as makeover subjects.

2004

The groundbreaking program *The L Word*, a Showtime series based on the lives of a number of lesbians, begins airing.

Mark Zuckerberg and several collaborators found Facebook, a social networking service originally limited to Harvard students but later expanded to other universities, then to high school students, and finally anyone age 13 or older.

2005

Logo, an American cable channel that focuses on gay, lesbian, transgender, and bisexual programming (including reality shows, original dramas, and travel programming and films) begins service.

The video-sharing Website YouTube, which allows individuals to upload their videos and watch the videos uploaded by others, begins operation.

The Huffington Post, a news-aggregation and opinion Website, is created by Arianna Huffington, Kenneth Lerer, and Jonah Peretti. It becomes extremely popular and influential, winning numerous awards, including a Webby Award for Best Politics Blog in 2006 and 2007, but is also criticized for its policy of relying on content created at other sites and for not paying many of those who create its unique content.

2006

The social networking and microblogging site Twitter is launched by the San Francisco–based company Twitter, Inc.

Internet pornography in the United States is reported to be a $2.8 billion business.

2009

Glee, a television drama about high school students participating in a glee club (show choir), begins broadcasting. The series, created by Ryan Murphy, Brad Falchuk, and Ian Brennan, is notable for featuring the out gay character Kurt Hummel, played by Chris Colfer, another character (Rachel Berry, played by Lea Michele) with "two gay dads," and guest appearances by gay icons including Kristin Chenoweth and Idina Menzel.

RuPaul's Drag Race, a reality television program featuring the drag queen RuPaul, begins airing on Logo.

2010

Kathryn Bigelow becomes the first woman to receive the Academy Award for Best Director, for her film *The Hurt Locker*.

Tyler Clementi, a freshman at Rutgers University, commits suicide by jumping from the George Washington Bridge. Clementi, who was gay, was videotaped by his college roommate, Dharun Ravi, during a sexual encounter. Although Ravi was not charged with Clementi's death, he was convicted in 2012 on a number of charges, including invasion of privacy, bias intimidation, and evidence tampering.

Dan Savage and Terry Miller found the "It Gets Better" project in response to teen suicides. Many celebrities (and non-celebrities) post videos speaking about the bullying and harassment they experienced in their childhoods and teenage years and the better lives they are currently enjoying as adults.

2011

Journalist Peggy Orenstein publishes *Cinderella Ate My Daughter: Dispatches From the Front Lines of the New Girlie Girl Culture*, detailing the cultural pressures on preteen girls to adopt sexualized clothing and appearances.

ESPN airs *Reneé*, a film about the transsexual tennis player Reneé Richards.

2012

In January, gay civil union laws go into effect in Delaware and Hawaii.

In March, Maryland becomes the eighth U.S. state to allow same-sex couples to marry.

Sarah E. Boslaugh
Kennesaw State University

ADVERTISING

Advertising is the act of drawing the attention of the public to a specific product or service. By employing methods of persuasion, advertisers endeavor to convince members of that public to purchase or otherwise acquire a product or service. In the United States and throughout the West at the beginning of the 21st century, advertising is pervasive—everywhere and incessant.

Gender-specific advertising involves creating persuasive messages expressly for men or women. Along with encouraging the acquisition of a concrete product or service, gender-specific advertising "sells" a social identity, albeit a largely abstract one. Frequently, the target of such an advertisement is asked to consider the ways in which purchasing a certain product fixes a problem. Gender-specific advertising also targets other demographic indicators within the larger categories of masculinity and femininity, including age, sexuality, socioeconomic status, race, and ethnicity. Despite the myriad ways in which these categories can be combined to target a specific social group—through an unprecedented variety of television networks and programs, magazines, Websites, radio stations, and other forms of mediated entertainment—most advertisements are still created to attract the majority of a targeted audience. As a result, masculine product advertisements are directed at men and feminine product advertisements are directed at women.

Cultural critics of gender-specific advertising call attention to how this kind of advertising perpetuates stereotypes, sexism, and objectification. From a feminist lens, gender-specific advertising represents evidence of how hegemonic portrayals of masculinity and femininity, misogyny, and homophobia are communicated and reproduced in media.

Drawing from feminist theory, several binaries surface in relationship to how women and men are depicted in advertisements, including active/passive, mind/body, and public/private. For example, researchers have demonstrated how men are overrepresented in advertising with a far larger range of options for their active, public participation (whether at work or, for automobile ads in particular, on the open road), whereas women are most frequently depicted in passive roles, often in the home. As John Berger asserts in *Ways of Seeing*, "men act, and women appear." Women are more likely to be depicted as inert and sexualized objects.

Gender-specific advertising reinforces traditional stereotypes of boys and girls, young adult men and women, and middle-aged men and women, as well as the elderly. Researchers have pointed out that in children's toy advertising boys are far more likely to be playing with a toy, whereas girls are more likely merely to be posing beside it. Furthermore, toy advertisements are far more likely to show boys rather than girls playing outdoors with their toys.

Stereotypes of men and women in gender-specific advertising include both positive and negative attributes. Beer commercials, in particular, frequently portray men as klutzy and/or combative while inevitably winning the interest of an easily duped woman, who succumbs to trickery. Meanwhile, in automobile ads, men frequently appear heroic, if not

A billboard of a scantily clad woman towering over Cologne, Germany, provides an example of the gender stereotyping that is prevalent in Western advertising campaigns. Women of all ages feel societal pressure to achieve unrealistic beauty standards, a desire aggravated by the images they see in the media. (Wikimedia)

mythic, in their ability to maneuver a sport utility vehicle to the top of a mountain. Women, on the other hand, when they do appear in car ads, appear mainly as competent moms who choose the "right" family vehicle to help them successfully manage their broods. Rarely is a woman featured in a car ad in which her primary goal as a consumer is escape and solitude.

Stereotypes of gendered aging adults are no less common. Ads for erectile dysfunction depict men in their 40s, 50s, and 60s as strong, silent types, incapable of discussing their sexual problems unless the condition formerly known as impotence is reframed as a physical, "organic" complaint rather than a psychological one. Conversely, menopause is something that is portrayed as not natural and a condition that, with the right treatment (the product), can be overcome.

The perception that the inevitable process of aging is a problem to be solved is what Julia Wood refers to as the pathologizing of the human body. Whether the "problem" is a lackluster sexual desire,

sagging breasts, graying hair, loss of skin tone, or the presence of an undesirable "spare tire," pathologizing is often gender-specific insofar as those parts that are in need of correction are tied to values and attributes that correspond with societal expectations of ideal gendered bodies.

Together, gender stereotyping and pathologizing have contributed significantly to objectification. In some ways, men are rapidly closing the gendered gap of objectification as they increasingly undergo cosmetic surgery in order to appear younger. Arguably, however, women pay a much larger price for their objectification, both individually and collectively. As individuals, women of all ages succumb to the societal pressure, encouraged by advertising, to achieve the ideal body type and adhere to unrealistic standards of beauty—often with disastrous results, both physical and psychological. The collective financial and professional cost of this emphasis on beauty is chronicled expertly by Naomi Wolf in her book *The Beauty Myth* and by Jean Kilbourne in her documentary film series *Killing Us Softly*.

Some companies have conducted advertising campaigns with an obvious eye to correcting these tendencies. Perhaps the Dove Soap Company's Campaign for Real Beauty is the best known. Employing women who were not size 8 or smaller in their ads, Dove scored major successes in sales. Similarly, a 2002 *More* magazine issue featured a "natural" Jamie Lee Curtis appearing without makeup and in an exercise outfit. Meanwhile, in 2010, Super Bowl ads—arguably the most watched advertisements in any calendar year—represented a backlash for those interested in eradicating dangerous gender stereotypes. Hence, although progress toward more positive gender-specific advertising has been achieved, negative stereotypes continue to be perpetuated, and media researchers continue to investigate gendered advertising patterns and trends.

Jay Baglia
Kutztown University of Pennsylvania

See also Berger, John; Gender Media Monitoring; Mass Media; Media Convergence; Stereotypes; Telecommunications Act of 1996; Viral Advertising and Marketing

Further Readings

Berger, John. *Ways of Seeing: Based on the BBC Television Series With John Berger*. London: British Broadcasting Corporation and Penguin Books, 1972.

Goffman, Erving. *Gender Advertisements*. Cambridge, MA: Harvard University Press, 1979.

Wolf, Naomi. *The Beauty Myth: How Images of Beauty Are Used Against Women*. 1991. Reprint, New York: HarperPerennial, 2002.

Wood, Julia. "Gendered Lives: Communication, Gender, and Culture." In *Gendered Lives*, 8th ed. Florence, KY: Cengage Wadsworth, 2009.

AFFIRMATIVE ACTION

Affirmative action—loosely defined as a set of policies, remedies, or requirements designed to overcome the effects of past discrimination against people of color and women—had its roots in the administration of President John F. Kennedy. It came to full flower after the U.S. Civil Rights Act of 1964 was signed by Kennedy's successor, President Lyndon B. Johnson, to ban discrimination based on race, ethnicity, or gender in workplaces, schools, and other venues. Its proponents argued that proactive steps to recruit and favorably consider members of underrepresented groups for hiring, promotions, or university admissions were necessary to counter practices, overt or subtle, that once systematically hindered advancement of these groups. Critics responded that affirmative action amounted to "reverse discrimination" that privileged some at the expense of others (especially white men).

Whether voluntarily pursued or compelled by government or the courts, affirmative action operated at its zenith from 1969 to 1980 with support from all three government branches. It began to wane, however, under skepticism from President Ronald Reagan and the Republican Party, an increasingly conservative U.S. Supreme Court, and doubting voters in California and some other states. In its heyday, affirmative action helped transform university campuses and countless workplaces—including those in the news media—from enclaves of white male dominance into more integrated environments that benefited from gender equity and multicultural diversity.

Unlike affirmative action, focused on alleviating past wrongs, the concept of diversity emphasizes the advantages of multiculturalism for all—employers, employees, corporations, consumers, students, and college campuses—without much heed to the past. In a modern era more attuned to diversity than affirmative action, then, it is easy to overlook the kinds of once common discriminatory practices that led the federal government to put the teeth of affirmative action into enforcing the Civil Rights Act.

Ingrained Discrimination in Workplaces

Gender bias was once so ingrained in the workplace that newspaper "help wanted" ads were segregated by sex, with high-paying managerial positions designated for men and low-paying clerical work earmarked for women. Many believed female workers ought to make less than male breadwinners.

Scholarship on the history of women journalists points to newsroom norms that routinely channeled hard news to male reporters—even coverage of women's suffrage after it moved to the front pages—while relegating female journalists to the women's pages and soft features. Jan Whitt writes that many editors believed women were inherently naïve or simply lacked the abilities of men. Women's sections, dating to the late 19th century, originally were aimed at wooing female readers for newspaper advertisers, given that women were more likely than men to make household purchases. Scholars note, however, that women's sections conveyed a message that the rest of the paper, with its emphasis on affairs in other spheres, was the province of males.

In the 19th century, as Dustin Harp has observed, female editors and publishers typically inherited their positions from deceased husbands or fathers. However, the changing role of women in industrialized society spawned women journalists in their own right. Some wrote columns, a culturally sanctioned pursuit for women. The 1920 Census reported 7,105 female reporters and editors, a tally that more than doubled to 15,890 in 1940. Most of these women, however, worked on women's pages, for magazines, or in book publishing, as Maurine H. Beasley and Sheila J. Gibbons report. Even into the 1960s, some journalism schools restricted enrollment of women students, subscribing to the belief that the field was limited for them.

A Wartime Surge of Newswomen

In a kind of early foray into affirmative action, Eleanor Roosevelt, wife of President Franklin D. Roosevelt, held 348 press conferences limited solely to women journalists, with the goal of encouraging newspapers to employ them, according to Beasley and Gibbons. During the Roosevelt administration, workplaces did open to women in a plethora of fields, including news reporting and editing, as male workers were drafted into military service. By 1943, two years before the end of World War II, nearly 100 women held credentials to cover the U.S. Congress. Even so, press associations often were segregated by gender, and the National Press Club banned women from covering political speeches delivered on its premises.

With the war's end came layoffs and demotions for many female staffers. Fewer than 5 percent of newspaper publishers surveyed in 1944 planned to retain all the women journalists who wished to keep their jobs, Beasley and Gibbons report. For example, Dorothy Jurney, acting city editor of the *Washington Daily News*, was told her gender prevented her from permanently holding that job. She was asked to train a male replacement before becoming women's editor for the *Miami Herald*.

When college-educated women of the baby-boom generation began entering the labor market in the 1960s, many discovered that little about newsroom culture had changed. Print and broadcast editors and news managers commonly assumed that women's demeanors, capabilities, voices, and bylines were insufficiently authoritative for the news business. Women held mostly lower-ranking, lower-paying, lower-visibility jobs in media organizations. At news magazines, they researched articles written exclusively by men. Women reporters seldom appeared on local or network television news. In radio, they handled program content that paralleled the women's pages. In 1972, 50 percent of more than 600 commercial television stations reported no women in management. Even when women and men did comparable work, women could expect smaller paychecks, report Beasley and Gibbons. A survey of 335 women's page editors in 1974 found that 15 of the 30 male editors made more than $17,000 annually, but only 11 of the 305 female editors had salaries that high.

Affirmative Action and the Feminist Movement

Into this environment, affirmative action and the second wave feminist movement arrived almost simultaneously, generating a sea change. Historian Terry H. Anderson explains that the term *affirmative action* as a discrimination remedy dates to a 1961 executive order by President Kennedy that created the President's Committee on Equal Employment Opportunity, chaired by Vice President Lyndon Johnson. Kennedy ordered it to recommend "affirmative steps" to promote nondiscrimination in hiring and employment in the executive branch. Two years later, Kennedy added federal contractors, state and local governments, and other entities which received federal funds, when complying with his order. Kennedy's instructions covered race and ethnicity but not gender. However, in 1961 he appointed the first Presidential Commission on the Status of Women, charging it with documenting discriminatory treatment of women in government, education, and employment. Among his appointees was Eleanor Roosevelt, a staunch proponent of equal pay for comparable work.

After Kennedy's assassination in 1963, President Johnson proposed sweeping legislation to end racial and ethnic discrimination in public places, workplaces, schools, and businesses. A southern congressman, believing it would help defeat the measure, added the word *sex* to the list of categories to be protected from discrimination. Although some considered its gender protections a political fluke, the hard-fought bill passed to become the Civil Rights Act of 1964. At a time when airline stewardesses could be fired for marrying or even aging beyond 32, prohibitions on sex discrimination in workplaces seemed revolutionary.

Johnson ordered the U.S. Equal Employment Opportunity Commission (EEOC), the law's enforcement agency, to investigate discrimination by private employers as well as federal contractors. Opening for business in 1965, the EEOC received thousands more complaints than had been anticipated. More than a third came from women who accused their employers of sex discrimination.

The Nixon Administration's Goals and Timetables

Democrats Kennedy and Johnson were cautious about setting milestones for achieving nondiscrimination; critics during congressional debate had heatedly argued that the Civil Rights Act could lead to hiring preferences and quotas. Republican president Richard Nixon, however, took a regulatory approach to implementing the law's nondiscrimination requirements, and his Labor Department imposed goals and timetables on federal contractors. Contractors with a combined workforce of

20 million or more were required to develop affirmative-action plans for making their workforces more representative of the general population. Despite controversy, the U.S. Supreme Court in *Griggs v. Duke Power Co.* (1971) backed the administration's approach without dissent. The high court was less concerned about the imposition of hiring preferences than with putting the onus on employers to show that they had not routinely discriminated against oppressed groups. The same year, the Federal Communications Commission (FCC) added gender to its affirmative-action policies governing the renewal of broadcast licenses. Television and radio stations were required to report to the FCC the affirmative steps they were taking to achieve population parity in their employment of women and people of color.

Thousands of private employers, including newspaper editors and publishers, developed affirmative-action policies in ensuing years. In the nation's newsrooms, however, women were not relying solely on federal pressures and employer largesse to bring about fair treatment, equal pay, and gender parity. Their own consciousness heightened by the feminist movement, they banded together to pursue legal actions under the nation's new laws and remedies. In complaints lodged with the EEOC or in lawsuits filed in federal court, women accused the Associated Press, the *Washington Post*, the *New York Times*, *Time*, *Newsweek*, the National Broadcasting Company (NBC), and other media outlets of inequitable practices and pay. Although some actions dragged on for years, they typically were settled with employer agreements to provide back pay and institute affirmative-action plans. Media scholars report that such pressures and actions—or corporate desires to avert them—helped advance the careers of television network journalists Catherine Mackin, Connie Chung, Lesley Stahl, Jane Pauley, and Diane Sawyer, among others.

Striking Gains for Newswomen

Gains for women were striking. The percentage of women on radio and television news staffs leaped from 10 percent in 1972 to 26 percent in 1979, reports media scholar Vernon Stone. Between 1968 and 1973, only two women were among the 60 journalists awarded Nieman fellowships to study at Harvard University; soon more than a third were

going to women every year. Front pages began featuring the bylines of women, and more women went on the air as reporters and local anchors. Barbara Walters joined Harry Reasoner as a coanchor of the *ABC Evening News*. Women's pages morphed into gender-neutral lifestyle sections. Beginning in the late 1970s, a majority of American journalism students annually were women. For all this, Shirley Biagi and Marilyn Kern-Foxworth report, affirmative action never really took hold in Hollywood. Federal monitoring of employment in the entertainment industry ended in the mid-1970s. Some 20 years later, according to Biagi and Kern-Foxworth, just 112 of 2,057 entertainment companies that contracted with the Writers Guild had programs for training underrepresented minorities to write for film and television.

Where affirmative action had made inroads, tensions were mounting. Remedying discrimination with favorable treatment—under a law that required nondiscrimination—was inherently paradoxical. The U.S. Supreme Court was growing conflicted, too. In a decision some found contradictory, it ruled 5–4 in 1978 in *Regents of the University of California v. Bakke* that universities could use race as a factor in admissions but that racial quotas were unconstitutional.

By the 1980 presidential campaign, the two major political parties were deeply at odds over affirmative action. The Democratic Party platform supported the practice outright, while the Republican Party said it opposed quotas favoring some groups over others. Republican Ronald Reagan, in his first news conference as president in 1981, suggested that affirmative action had devolved into an unconstitutional quota system. He appointed Clarence Thomas, an opponent of racial preferences, hiring goals, and timetables, to head the EEOC.

Backlash Against Affirmative Action

A backlash against the notion of reverse discrimination mushroomed during the Reagan years. The U.S. Supreme Court—which by 1992 would be dominated by appointees of Reagan and his successor, Republican George H. W. Bush—began curtailing use of affirmative-action remedies. In its 1989 session, the high court essentially reversed *Griggs*, Anderson writes, by requiring proof that individuals had actually faced discrimination in hiring or promotions. It would now be necessary to do more than simply show that groups were underrepresented in order to win a discrimination case. Opinion polls showing support for affirmative action nosedived when survey questions associated it with quotas or preferential treatment, echoing the rhetoric of Reagan, Bush, and other critics. Encouraged by Republican governor Pete Wilson, California voters in 1996 approved a state constitutional amendment that banned affirmative action from state and local government programs and public education. Voters followed suit in Washington, Nebraska, Michigan, and, in November 2010, Arizona.

Whatever the future holds for racial, ethnic, and gender parity, there is little doubt that affirmative action at its peak transformed U.S. cultural environments, from campuses to corporations. Today's widespread acceptance of the worth of gender equity and the value of diversity may be one of the policy's most enduring legacies.

Rebecca LaVally
California State University, Sacramento

See also Class Privilege; Diversity; Electronic Media and Social Inequality; Empowerment; Equal Employment Opportunity Commission; Feminist Theory: Second Wave; Minority Rights; Misogyny; Network News Anchor Desk; Newsrooms; Prejudice; Racism; Stereotypes; Workforce

Further Readings

Anderson, Terry H. *The Pursuit of Fairness: A History of Affirmative Action*. Oxford, UK: Oxford University Press, 2004.

Beasley, Maurine H. and Sheila J. Gibbons. *Taking Their Place: A Documentary History of Women and Journalism*. Washington, DC: American University Press, 1993.

Biagi, Shirley and Marilyn Kern-Foxworth. *Facing Difference: Race, Gender, and Mass Media*. Thousand Oaks, CA: Sage, 1997.

Harp, Dustin. "News, Feminist Theories, and the Gender Divide." In *Women, Men, and News: Divided and Disconnected in the News Media Landscape*, Paula Poindexter, Sharon Meraz, and Amy Schmitz Weiss, eds. New York: Routledge, 2008.

Stone, Vernon A. *Let's Talk Pay in Television and Radio News*. Chicago: Bonus Books, 1993.

Whitt, Jan. *Women in American Journalism: A New History*. Champaign: University of Illinois Press, 2008.

Audiences: Producers of New Media

The notion of audiences as producers of new media refers to a shift in the way that media have been not only consumed and distributed but also produced since the advent of digital communication technologies. New media have several dimensions, notably *convergence*, or the overlapping of traditionally separate media forms. New media replace the one-to-many (or broadcast) model of communication with a many-to-many (interactive) form of communication. In a mass-media, broadcast model of communication, audiences were seen as passive consumers of media content. Media companies, such as newspapers and television networks, acted as gatekeepers that controlled access to publishing and mass forms of communication. Instead, new media have allowed audiences to be active producers of content, referred to as user-generated content (UGC).

User-Generated Content

In general, UGC can be defined as content, made publicly available on the Internet, that is created outside professional routines and practices, often by nonprofessionals. UGC comes in many forms that have largely grown out of social media—those online tools that allow users to interact with other users in a variety of multimedia formats. Hence, UGC includes commentary on others' content as well as one's own content. In general, UGC can be understood by the amount of interactivity that the particular medium allows. For example, some UGC is controlled by mainstream news organizations, whereas other UGC is self-generated. Research on UGC examines the influence of UGC both on the business models of traditional media organizations and on social issues such as privacy and surveillance.

In 2006, UGC gained public recognition when *Time* magazine named the person of the year "You." This symbolic gesture was intended to draw attention to the public's important contribution to Internet content and to raise significant issues regarding the public domain. Social media applications, such as blogs and Twitter, allow audiences to create multimedia material in which they can comment on social issues. Additionally, the availability of smart phones, which allow users to access the Internet from a mobile device, has led to the proliferation of UGC. The inexpensive cost of communication technologies, such as digital cameras, reduces barriers to entry for those individuals who want to contribute content online.

Many scholars argue that it is important to question the assumptions behind the idea that UGC is a radically new concept. In the mid-20th century, scholars such as Marshall McLuhan and Charlotte Brunsdon challenged the notion that audiences are merely passive receivers of information. Several scholars point out that there is a long history of audiences actively creating content. For example, for decades alternative media, such as zines, have been printed and distributed outside mainstream media outlets. Additionally, reality television programs, which encourage audience participation in the construction of media content, have existed since the early days of television in the form of talent shows, game shows, and "candid camera" shows.

Citizen Journalism

One example of UGC is citizen journalism. *Citizen journalism* refers to the participation of citizens in the production of news stories. The goal of citizen journalism is to encourage citizens without professional training in journalistic practices to create, distribute, and check the facts of news stories. Although citizen journalism has been a tradition in the United States, new online tools make it easier to self-publish and have led to the proliferation of this use of media.

One example of citizen journalism is the *indymedia* movement. The Independent Media Center, also known as Indymedia or IMC, started in 1999 in response to the World Trade Organization (WTO) protests in Seattle, Washington. Activists believed that their perspectives would not be represented by mainstream media and instead created an online network for audiences to upload stories, pictures, and videos. Indymedia.org encourages audiences to "be the media" and has a global reach.

Mobile phones have led to the growth of citizen journalists. Mobile phones allow people to provide eyewitness accounts of breaking news. For example, during the September 11, 2001, terrorist attacks, there were many eyewitness accounts of the attacks on the World Trade Center. Citizen journalism via mobile phones becomes especially important when traditional journalists have limited access to certain events. For example, during the 2009 Iranian protests, a YouTube video of the death of a female activist, Neda Agha-Soltan, went viral, drawing the attention of the democratic movement there. Without the images and sounds recorded by mobile phones, little news of these events would have been available.

While some argue that citizen journalism allows for a shift in power relations among the gatekeepers of the news, others argue that citizen journalism is exploitative because it allows news organizations to acquire content for free. While citizen journalists have played an important role in the reporting of events, some argue that the amateur nature of this brand of journalism can lead to a lack of objectivity, which is a goal of professional journalists. As a result, citizen journalists often become activists, advocating for specific causes.

Video-Sharing Sites

Video-sharing sites such as YouTube allow users to create their own media. These sites create interactivity by allowing users to comment on videos or to post links to the videos to their social networking sites. In addition to citizen journalism, audiences engage in UGC through remixing culture or being curators of media content. *Remix culture* refers to how audiences take a popular cultural form, such as a movie clip, and edit it to create a different meaning. For example, a user might take a popular music video and add a different song. Users may also edit movie trailers to insert a different ending from the one put forward by Hollywood. In the viral video *Brokeback to the Future*, one user created a movie trailer combining the plots of two films, *Brokeback Mountain* and *Back to the Future*.

Video-sharing sites can become a resource for talent scouts. For example, some celebrities have been discovered based on their YouTube videos. Others have garnered the attention of Hollywood producers for their short videos.

Audiences' Curatorial Roles

Audiences can also be curators of media, by customizing and commenting on the type of Internet content that they prefer. For example, blogging sites such as Blogger and Tumblr allow users to follow other bloggers and share information they find useful. However, many scholars warn that it is important to pay attention to the accuracy of content. Just because a story was posted and then reposted on a blog does not make it true.

UGC brings up several issues related to copyright law. Many consider videos in which the creators have remixed culture to be in violation of copyright laws rather than extensions of fair use provisions. The concept of fair use within copyright law states that a limited amount of copyrighted material may be used for noncommercial or educational purposes, when such use does not abrogate the rights (such as infringing on the market) of the copyright holder. Internet sites such as YouTube have policies that discourage users from violating copyright laws. For example, in the case of YouTube, if a user is in violation of copyright law and the copyright holder makes a complaint to YouTube, the company will remove the questionable content. Scholars such as Lawrence Lessig argue that copyright laws should be relaxed to allow for cultural innovation.

New Business Models

UGC has led to the development of new business models as mass-media companies, the traditional gatekeepers of communication channels, have recognized that audiences are receptive to a range of content that is not professionally produced. Mass-media companies are increasingly integrating UGC as part of their business models. For example, in 2006 CNN launched iReport, which provides an online space for citizens to document and report on potentially important media events. Other news organizations followed CNN's lead, soliciting photographs and videos from their viewers.

However, critical scholars argue that it is important to examine how the owners of online platforms are using and controlling UGC. Thus it is important to consider how much interactivity different Websites allow for users as well as the extent to which media organizations control and edit content. For example, YouTube was developed in 2005 by entrepreneurs and sold to Google in 2006. This acquisition raised questions about the integration of a search engine with UGC, the role of advertising, and the integration of social networking sites. It is important to ask questions about how

economics and technological infrastructures impact the relationships among media companies, advertisers, and users.

Additionally, UGC can raise concerns about exploitation of labor. UGC can establish a dichotomy between professional content and amateur content, which can be used to justify why UGC is free and professional content is paid for. Much of the labor that goes into UGC relies on volunteerism, yet sites such as YouTube are profiting from this free labor by selling advertising space. Thus, it is important to ask questions about the commercialization of information.

Social Impacts

UGC has had a strong impact on society. Social impacts include the circulation of diverse ideas and opinions, increased debate and discourse over political ideas, increased watchdog functions of media (including accountability), and the heightened need to consider important questions about social and political issues.

UGC not only has drawn attention to the variety of cultural forms that audiences produce but also has raised awareness of social problems. For example, individuals have used their camera phones for surveillance, recording criminal behavior and later submitting these images to law enforcement authorities and broadcast media. The result may be a deterrence of crimes, from theft to sexual harassment to police brutality. This type of surveillance, however, raises questions about individuals' right to privacy.

Other privacy concerns include the use of personal data. Often, sites on which UGC is uploaded require that users register personal information, such as their names, e-mail addresses, and ages. This information becomes part of a database that can be mined for information, or metadata.

Researchers have studied users' motivations to create their own content. These motivations include the desire to connect with peers, attain celebrity status, develop prestige, and express oneself. While consumer-grade digital video cameras allow users to upload images and editing programs such as iMovie allow users to edit videos, some argue that it is important to be aware that inequality still exists in terms of who has access to these technologies. Indeed, the majority of Internet users are passive consumers of information. Thus, it is important to ask questions such as who is producing UGC, what are they producing, and for what purposes? For example, some have argued that representations of race, class, and gender in UGC are not diverse.

Carolyn Cunningham
Gonzaga University

See also Audiences: Reception and Injection Models; Blogs and Blogging; Electronic Media and Social Inequality; Media Convergence; New Media; Reality-Based Television: *America's Next Top Model*; Reality-Based Television: Makeover Shows; Reality-Based Television: Wedding Shows; Social Media; Twitter; Viral Advertising and Marketing; Web 2.0; Wiki; YouTube

Further Readings

Gilmor, Dan. *We the Media: Grassroots Journalism by the People, for the People*. North Sebastopol, CA: O'Reilly Media, 2006.

Keen, Andrew. *The Cult of the Amateur: How Today's Internet Is Killing Our Culture*. New York: Currency Books, 2007.

Lessig, Lawrence. *Free Culture: The Nature and Future of Creativity*. New York: Penguin, 2004.

Lievrouw, Leah and Sonia Livingstone, eds. *The Handbook of New Media*. Thousand Oaks, CA: Sage, 2002.

Organisation for Economic Co-operation and Development. *Participative Web: User-Generated Content*. OECD Committee for Information, Computer and Communications Policy Report, 2007. http://www.oecd.org/home (Accessed May 2011).

Tapscott, D. and A. Williams. *Wikinomics: How Mass Collaboration Changes Everything*. New York: Penguin, 2002.

van Djick, José. "Users Like You? Theorizing Agency in User-Generated Content." *Media, Culture and Society*, v.31/1 (2009).

AUDIENCES: RECEPTION AND INJECTION MODELS

In the history of media studies, there have been several trends in how to conceptualize the audience. In the mid-20th-century heyday of government-funded studies of media, media were studied as if they constituted a "hypodermic needle"—injecting the audience, the public, with information. In the hypodermic needle theory, audience members and national publics are affected by the messages sent out by the media. The conception of the hypodermic needle was facilitated by studies of propaganda during mid-20th-century historical events ranging from the world wars (especially the rise of fascism in Europe during World War II) to the Cold War.

As time went on, researchers realized that the effects of the media were not as severe and clear-cut as they once thought, and a "minimal effects" model replaced the standard model of the hypodermic needle. With the rise of the Birmingham School of British cultural studies, the understanding of the audience's relationship with the media became more nuanced. This school of thought asked media researchers to understand media from three perspectives: that of the producer, that of the text itself, and that of the audience.

As the fields of media studies and cultural studies have continued to evolve, various other paths have become available to understand the audience as meaning maker, citizen, consumer, and fan. These strands of audience research often understand communication as a one-way street in which one mass-media source communicates to many audience members. With the cultural studies shift to what is called reception studies, more focus has been placed on analyzing the audience as gendered.

Propaganda Analysis and the Hypodermic Needle Model

Studies of audiences began in the arena of propaganda analysis, a project of mid-20th-century media research and behaviorism, which seeks to understand human thoughts and actions as innate responses to stimuli. These early researchers did not place great emphasis on gender in their studies. Nonetheless, early mass-media researchers laid the groundwork for future audience researchers.

The *hypodermic needle*, or *magic bullet*, model of communication implies that the mass media inject or insert meanings into the audience members' consciousness. In this model, the viewing, listening, or reading publics all experience the information communicated (such as a radio program, a television show, a book, or a magazine article) in the same way. This model of audience behavior took hold in the period of time after World War I, as researchers were interested in analyzing how effective mass media's propaganda efforts were. These researchers, often funded by the U.S. government, were interested in how fascist and communist powers used media to indoctrinate their citizens.

Leading the field of propaganda research, Harold Lasswell made a case for the hypodermic needle model in his analysis of mass-media propaganda in the World War I, *Propaganda Technique in the World War* (1927). In this book, Lasswell asserted that mass communication during the war period could be characterized as national governments sending messages to an audience whose response was uniform. Lasswell's understanding of the one-way flow of communications is summed up in his distillation of how to break down all communication into a number of universal elements: "Who says what to whom in what channel with what effect?"

Working alongside Lasswell in the field of political mass communication, Paul Lazarsfeld studied audiences' responses to propaganda surrounding the political campaigns of Franklin Delano Roosevelt in the mid-20th century. Lazarsfeld and his fellow researchers found that interpersonal communication among a close network of people was a more important indicator of whom a person would vote for than was the content of the media they consumed. Lazarsfeld's studies began to put holes in the hypodermic needle theory, showing other ways that audiences came to their conclusions.

Challenges to the Hypodermic Needle Theory

By the time of World War II (1939–45), various challenges to the hypodermic needle theory of communication had been leveled. One of the most famous defenses of the theory had been found in audience reactions to Orson Welles's 1938 radio dramatization of H. G. Wells's 1898 classic *The War of the Worlds*. The radio broadcast was popularly believed to have duped large numbers of people into thinking that aliens had landed in New Jersey. However, public opinion researcher Hadley Cantril's study of the broadcast, published in 1940, shows that much of the audience found the broadcast to be an imaginative, creative use of the radio-show format for entertainment.

The hypodermic needle model depends on the transmission model of communication, which posits that a message is communicated from a transmitter and is received, unaltered, by the receiver, the audience. In Claude Shannon and Warren Weaver's landmark contribution to the mathematical theory of communication, they allowed for the formerly indestructible message to be corrupted between the sender and the receiver. In the transmission of content from transmitter to receiver, the message can encounter noise, which disrupts the communication process. Their model also allowed the viewer to provide a response to the producer, in the form of feedback.

Limited Effects Theory

Criticisms of the hypodermic needle approach led media effects researchers to develop the theory of *limited effects*, that is, a theory that consumption of the mass media had incremental effects on its viewers. Many researchers working within the paradigm of the hypodermic needle approach had noted the flaws in this research and adopted the theory of limited effects and the *uses and gratifications model* of an audience's approach to media. Under the uses and gratifications theory of mass communication, the emphasis is placed on the audience and frames mass-media consumption as the search for specially selected uses, which lead to gratification for the user.

Following the uses and gratifications model, George Gerbner, a longtime dean at the University of Pennsylvania's Annenberg School for Communication, noted in the 1960s that regular television viewers had a relatively gloomy vision of the world because they were regularly inundated with reportage on their communities' most violent events. This study focused less on how viewers were indoctrinated than on how the media they consumed affected them.

Reception Studies

The more explicit turn to reception studies began with Stuart Hall's 1973 essay explaining his encoding/decoding model of meaning-making in the mass media. According to Hall's model, the producer of a media message "encodes" the media content and sends it to the audience. Individual audience members then "decode" the media message. Hall's theory moves the study of audiences to a framework wherein the audience's interpretation of a text is less sure and less direct. Hall's framework allows for four "ideal types" for decoding mediated messages: the professional code (for messages that are already hegemonic), the dominant code (the message the producers prefer the audience to decode), the negotiated code (in which the decoded message is not taken at face value but some resistance affects the audience member's understanding of the message), and the oppositional code (in which the audience member understands the message in the code but rejects its greater meaning).

Inspired by Hall's theory, many studies followed using his formulation of the audience, the most famous of which is David Morley's 1980 study of young male students' reading of the British news program *Nationwide*. In this study, Morley divided the students into groups based on social class and had each group watch an episode of the program. Morley's study concluded that the different socioeconomic groups he later interviewed in focus groups fit fairly neatly into three categories based on their style of reading the program. He said that many of the students (banking students) developed a dominant reading of the program that took the producers' intent at face value; others (art students) had a negotiated reading of the program; and still others (black students) produced an oppositional reading of the program, actively disagreeing and responding against the message encoded by the show's producers. This study led to the theory of the active audience, one that actively produces a meaning unlike the one the producer intends. Since publishing this study, Morley has cautioned that interpreting his and other studies as proof of an active audience constitutes romanticizing the notion of the audience as always active.

Audience Studies Research

Shortly after Morley's *Nationwide* study, a number of studies attempted to do ethnographies on audiences, a term that Morley later used to describe his work on the *Nationwide* study. The majority of these first studies focus on audiences and fan communities of the romance genre, a genre targeted to and consumed by women.

In 1985, Janice Radway studied a group of women who regularly bought romance books from an independent bookstore in a small Pennsylvania town. Radway's book-length study, *Reading the Romance*, became one of the best-known studies of literary audiences and one of the best-known in a field called reader-response criticism. Her book looks at the genre of the mass-market romance novel, through analyses of the production, content, and audience for the books. Within her analysis, Radway advocates for reader-response criticism over the New Criticism that had previously dominated literary studies (New Criticism advocates close readings of texts and ignores or deemphasizes the text's audience, intended or real). Through interviews with the women who read romance novels, Radway found that women's act of reading is often resistant. First, women often take time usually devoted to domestic service to read these books; second, women find in the books characters who are outcasts from patriarchal culture.

The prime-time serial *Dallas* provided the impetus for several important studies of audiences. Ien Ang, in her 1985 study of the show, *Watching* Dallas, uses solicited letters from fans of the show to illuminate what made the show so popular, particularly among women. Ang explores the ways that audiences found themselves attached to the show as fans. Elihu Katz, who had been working on studies of media audiences for decades, and Tamar Liebes also wrote a book on *Dallas*, comparing audience responses in communities across the globe. Ang later wrote another book, *Desperately Seeking the Audience*, which explored how the television industry, specifically in the United States and Europe, imagines the audience in different ways. Barry Dornfeld explored this concept further in his book about the production of a PBS show, *Producing Public Television, Producing Public Culture*.

Scholars like Jacqueline Bobo, Sut Jhally, Justin Lewis, and Marie Gillespie have studied the responses of particular American ethnic communities to cultural texts. Bobo's study uses a group of middle-class African American women as an example to show that black readership provides meanings and perspectives not found by white audiences. Jhally and Lewis's book *Enlightened Racism* uses interviews of audiences of the popular sitcom *Cosby* in order to investigate how the show affected viewers' perceptions of race.

The focus of audience studies research on television programs was met with studies of television that placed the technology of television within the home. Scholars like Morley, Raymond Williams, and Lynn

Spigel have studied how television affects the home, including how the technology affects gender roles within the home.

As studies of the audience matured along with the discipline of media studies, our understanding of the audience has become less stable, more fractured, and more helpful in revealing and understanding the subjectivity of the audience.

Bryce J. Renninger
Rutgers University

See also Audiences: Producers of New Media; Cultural Politics; Encoding and Decoding; Hall, Stuart; New Media; Polysemic Text; Postmodernism; Post-Structuralism; Radway, Janice; Reception Theory; Romance Novels; Semiotics; Textual Analysis

Further Readings

Alasuutari, Petri. *Rethinking the Media Audience: The New Agenda*. Thousand Oaks, CA: Sage, 1999.

Ang, Ien. *Watching* Dallas. London: Methuen, 1985.

Brooker, Will and Deborah Jermyn. *The Audience Studies Reader*. New York: Routledge, 2003.

Cantril, Albert Hadley, et al. *The Invasion From Mars: A Study in the Psychology of Panic*. Princeton, NJ: Princeton University Press, 1940.

Dornfeld, Barry. *Producing Public Television, Producing Public Culture*. Princeton, NJ: Princeton University Press, 1998.

Hall, Stuart. "Encoding/Decoding." In *Culture, Media, Language*, Stuart Hall et al., eds. London: Routledge, 2002.

Jhally, Sut and Justin Lewis. *Enlightened Racism: The Cosby Show, Audiences, and the Myth of the American Dream*. Boulder, CO: Westview Press, 1992.

Lasswell, Harold D. *Propaganda Technique in the World War*. 1927. Reprint, *Propaganda Technique in World War I*. Cambridge, MA: MIT Press, 1971.

Morley, David. *The Nationwide Audience: Structure and Decoding*. London: British Film Institute, 1980.

Radway, Janice. *Reading the Romance: Women, Patriarchy and Popular Literature*. Chapel Hill: University of North Carolina Press, 1984.

Shannon, Claude Elwood and Warren Weaver. *The Mathematical Theory of Communication*. 1949. Reprint, Urbana: University of Illinois Press, 1978.

Staiger, Janet. *Media Reception Studies*. New York: New York University Press, 2005.

AVATAR

The word *avatar* is adapted from the Sanskrit for "descent," used to describe a Hindu god emerging from the heavens and bodily manifesting itself in order to intervene in human affairs. Generically, the term can refer to any representation of a person. Names, online profiles, and dolls can all be considered types of avatars by this broad definition. Neal Stephenson's science fiction novel *Snow Crash* popularized the use of the word, as it is commonly understood today, to describe a digital representation in a virtual environment. Commonly, avatars are used to represent people in Internet chat, video games, social virtual worlds, massively multiplayer online role-playing games, social networking sites, and other mediated contexts.

Avatars are distinguished from *agents*, another form of digital representation, by the element of control: Avatars are controlled by human users, whereas agents are controlled by computer algorithms. For example, in single-player video games, the player at the controls is represented by an avatar, whereas the other characters on the screen are agents controlled by the computer.

One function of avatars is to help the user parallel the virtual world with the familiar physical world. For example, a user may have a photographic avatar attached to a chat interface to approximate a face-to-face interaction or may use an avatar with a human form to navigate virtual space or engage virtual objects, agents, or other avatars. Avatars may also be used to facilitate communication. Whether through a simple smiley-face icon or a highly realistic virtual human, avatars may help virtual communication more closely resemble the richness of face-to-face communication by allowing users to convey nonverbal as well as verbal messages. When selecting an avatar for a virtual world, users can often demonstrate sex, gender, group affiliation, social identity, interests, goals, or personality traits through their choice of representation. Additionally, avatars may be manipulated to express and convey emotions.

Avatars also present users with the opportunity for an experience beyond mere exposure to mediated imagery. Users embody avatars, controlling the movements and interactions of the representation;

thus, the avatar becomes a proxy for the physical self in the virtual world. The ability to design and customize an avatar, combined with the time spent using the avatar, often leads users to develop a strong affinity for an avatar. Indeed, avatars have been shown to increase users' identification, or sense of being similar to someone, which has been linked to changes in beliefs, attitudes, and modeling behavior.

In some environments, users are constrained to choose among a set of avatars; in others, they are free to choose or customize their representation. In custom environments, users may choose an avatar of either biological sex or one that is androgynous. Regardless of the chosen sex, the avatar may be outfitted with clothing, weapons, or accessories that may or may not be gendered. The user may also determine how accurately the avatar reflects his or her physical appearance. Thus, the creation of an avatar enables a user to explore the spectrum of gender portrayals, whereas in forced-choice environments, users may be constrained to stereotypical representations.

Research has determined that virtual worlds mirror traditional media: Men typically outnumber women, with drastic disparities in video and online games. When women appear, they are often depicted in a highly sex-stereotypical fashion. Additionally, photorealistic depictions of women in video games are systematically thinner than the average American woman, perpetuating the body image myth. Women are typically portrayed as weak and in need of rescue (the damsel in distress motif) or as highly sexualized aggressors (the dominatrix motif). Although men are featured in a wider range of gender roles, the muscular, aggressive, hypermasculine representation is common.

Gender- or sex-swapping occurs when users represent themselves in a virtual environment in contrast to their biological sex. Users report a variety of reasons for gender-swapping, from seeking a competitive advantage in a game to attracting or deferring attention from others in a social virtual world. Lisa Nakamura considers this process a form of identity tourism, wherein users try out different virtual representations to see how they will be perceived socially. Some argue that this is a safe form of gender experimentation. Nakamura suggests that, rather than developing a deeper understanding or sympathy for the body they inhabit, people reinforce their own stereotypical beliefs by acting as they think the other sex would or should. The secondary impact is that the avatar then behaves as a stereotypical member of that sex and thus reinforces those stereotypes when others interact with the avatar in virtual worlds.

Current research is exploring the effects of encountering or embodying gendered virtual representations. Women playing a game as a sexualized female avatar reported significantly lower self-efficacy than women who played with a nonsexualized female avatar or men who played with either avatar. Men and women encountering stereotype-confirming women in a virtual environment expressed greater sexism and rape-myth acceptance (beliefs that a victim is to blame for her own rape). Women who embodied a photorealistic avatar that was sexualized and looked like them reported greater rape-myth acceptance than those embodied in nonsexualized avatars or those that did not look like them. Men and women who played a game as an avatar of their own sex with an ideal body type reported decreased body esteem. Future research will continue to investigate the social and psychological effects of inhabiting gendered avatars.

Jesse Fox
Ohio State University

See also Cyberspace and Cyberculture; Gender Embodiment; Massively Multiplayer Online Role-Playing Games; Multi-User Dimensions; *Second Life*; Stereotypes; Video Gaming: Representations of Femininity; Video Gaming: Representations of Masculinity; Virtual Community; Virtuality

Further Readings

Barlett, Christopher P. and Richard J. Harris. "The Impact of Body Emphasizing Video Games on Body Image Concerns in Men and Women." *Sex Roles*, v.59/7–8 (2008).

Boellstorff, Tom. *Coming of Age in Second Life: An Anthropologist Explores the Virtually Human.* Princeton, NJ: Princeton University Press, 2008.

Downs, Edward and Stacy L. Smith. "Keeping Abreast of Hypersexuality: A Video Game Character Content Analysis." *Sex Roles*, v.62/11–12 (2010).

Nakamura, Lisa. *Cybertypes: Race, Ethnicity, and Identity on the Internet.* New York: Routledge, 2002.

B

BARTHES, ROLAND

Roland Barthes (1915–80) was a French literary theorist whose work has profoundly influenced the fields of literary criticism, film and media studies, discourse studies, and photography. He contributed to intellectual debates on Marxism, semiotics, structuralism, and post-structuralism in France and abroad. His essays collected in *Mythologies* have shaped the British school of cultural studies. Although he did not specifically write on issues related to women and gender in the media, feminists have adopted his ideas to critique gender ideology (the most notable study is Angela McRobbie's reading of teenage girls' magazines). Barthes was a prolific writer. Twenty-six of his books have been translated into English. Among all, *Camera Lucida*, *Elements of Semiology*, *Empire of Signs*, *The Fashion System*, *Image-Music-Text*, *Mythologies*, and *The Pleasure of the Text* have been the most widely read and discussed among media scholars.

Barthes first advanced his theory of semiology in essays collected in *Mythologies*. The first part of the book is a collection of essays originally written for *Les Lettres Nouvelles*. The second part, "Myth Today," is a theoretical essay on the semiotics of contemporary culture. Barthes started to write about the "myths" of 1950s French society because of his impatience at seeing how ideology has been naturalized as the truth. One example that he gave was of a black soldier in French military uniform saluting the (unshown) French flag on a cover of *Paris Match*. While the literal image was nothing more than "a black soldier saluting the French flag," the reader may have understood the image as "France, as a great nation, is saluted by its citizens, regardless of their races." The ideology embedded in the cover image effectively hid French violence in North Africa and French colonialism worldwide.

In order to understand how myth works, Barthes updated Ferdinand de Saussure's theory of semiology. According to Saussure, there are many sign systems, and the linguistic system is only one of them. There are two components to a sign: the signifier (a sound, a word, a picture, or an image) and the signified (a concept). The word *tree* and a picture of a tree both evoke the concept of tree in one's mind. Barthes called this the first level of signification (or denotation). The concept of tree may evoke other meanings, such as "environmental protection," "forest," and "Vermont." Barthes called these the second level of signification (or connotation)— the "what goes without saying" meaning. Before the widespread concern about global warming, people did not associate the concept of tree with the concept of environmental protection. Once the ideology of environmental protection gained popularity, people assigned a new meaning to the concept of tree. Similarly, people who live in the U.S. state of Vermont may associate the concept of tree with their home state; people who live in other states may not make the association, because the relationship between the first and the second levels of signification is not natural (*arbitrary* using Barthes' term) but ideological.

After *Mythologies*, Barthes continued to work on the theory of semiology in *Elements of Semiology* and *The Fashion System*. In the latter, Barthes saw fashion as a meaning-making system. A woman can choose a blouse or a T-shirt to wear as a top and skirt or a pair of jeans for the bottom. The combination of T-shirt and jeans connotes a different meaning from that of blouse and skirt. Similarly, in a linguistic system, the subjects "woman" and "lady" connote different meanings. After his travel to Japan, Barthes wrote *Empire of Signs*. In this book, he "read" Japanese culture as a system of signs. This system is different from that in Western/French culture. Barthes used the elaborate gift-wrapping practice in Japan to illustrate how meanings are made in Japanese culture; in this instance, the gift needs to be wrapped in multiple layers, and the unwrapping of each layer elicits a new meaning.

In addition to his writings on structuralism, Barthes also wrote about the understanding of the meanings of texts. *Camera Lucida*, *Image-Music-Text*, and *The Pleasure of the Text* established some major groundwork for post-structuralist theories. *Camera Lucida* is a collection of sometimes poetic and sometimes theoretical essays on photography. He suggested that there are two levels of reading a photograph: first, *studium*—a general, educated level of reading; second, *punctum*—a personal, unexpected meaning that "pierces" the reader's consciousness. In *The Pleasure of the Text*, Barthes also suggested two ways of reading: pleasure and *jouissance* (this French word connotes sexual pleasure). Reading with pleasure is to read the dominant meanings of a text (similar to the dominant meaning in Stuart Hall's encoding/decoding model). Reading with *jouissance* is to make meanings unintended by the writer (similar to the negotiated and oppositional meanings of the encoding/decoding model). Last, Barthes coined the terms *readerly text* and *writerly text*. Readerly text has only one layer of meanings. Writerly text, on the other hand, can be read in multiple ways (similar to polysemic texts). Whereas news reports constitute mostly readerly text, modernist novels such as James Joyce's work can be seen as writerly text.

Barthes did not specifically write on women and gender in the media, but several of his books include women as subjects. In his essay "The Face of Garbo" (collected in *Mythologies*), Garbo's face is a text to be read. To him, Garbo's face is neither a person nor a mask, but an idea. In the autobiography *Roland Barthes by Roland Barthes* and the posthumously published *Incidents*, he wrote extensively about his close relations with his mother. The death of his mother as recorded in *Incidents* may give a glimpse into the early death of Barthes.

Micky Lee
Suffolk University, Boston

See also Encoding and Decoding; Hall, Stuart; Ideology; Polysemic Text; Post-Structuralism; Semiotics

Further Readings

Barthes, Roland. *Camera Lucida: Reflections on Photography*. London: Jonathan Cape, 1982.

Barthes, Roland. *Elements of Semiology*. London: Jonathan Cape, 1967.

Barthes, Roland. *Empire of Signs*. London: Jonathan Cape, 1983.

Barthes, Roland. *The Fashion System*. London: Jonathan Cape, 1985.

Barthes, Roland. *Image-Music-Text*. New York: Noonday, 1978.

Barthes, Roland. *Incidents*. Berkeley: University of California Press, 1992.

Barthes, Roland. *Mythologies*. London: Jonathan Cape, 1972.

Barthes, Roland. *The Pleasure of the Text*. London: Jonathan Cape, 1976.

Barthes, Roland. *Roland Barthes by Roland Barthes*. London: Macmillan, 1977.

McRobbie, Angela. *Jackie: An Ideology of Adolescent Femininity*. Birmingham, UK: Centre for Contemporary Cultural Studies, University of Birmingham, 1977.

BEAUTY AND BODY IMAGE: BEAUTY MYTHS

One of the most pervasive and profitable ideologies in mass media is the beauty myth. Feminist media scholars have used the expression *beauty myth* to denote the media's ability to create a powerful set of unrealistic ideals that keep girls and women preoccupied with femininity and beauty standards. Predicated upon bodily stereotypes of Anglo-European whiteness, thinness, buxomness, and curviness, the beauty myth creates what is called a "normative standard of beauty" that reduces the concept of attractiveness to a limited and exclusive set of age, race, and physical traits. Within mainstream media, Hollywood actresses and supermodels are heralded as cultural hallmarks of beauty and success, leading to a Western beauty ideology that values girls and women for their appearance over their intellect, ambition, personality, and unique traits. Through this exaggeration and glamorization of normative beauty standards, a popular cultural myth forms around the notion of what beauty is and, subsequently, how to attain it. Ironically, few can ever attain the beauty ideals held as the standard in mainstream media and advertisements, as models and celebrities undergo extreme makeovers, surgeries, and other beauty transformations before they are filmed and photographed. The postproduction techniques of airbrushing and computer-generated modifications "perfect" the beauty myth by removing any remaining blemishes or imperfections visible to the eye.

Economics

From an economic standpoint, studies indicate that the function of the beauty myth is capitalistic, enabling related industries to profit from consumers' anxieties about their bodies and appearance. While marketing strategies aimed at boys and men have been on the rise, girls and women remain the primary targets of the beauty myth. The myth's economic function is to perpetuate the idea that beauty can be attained by purchasing the right products and services. Each year, the beauty industry earns billions of dollars through business profits in diet, cosmetics, cosmetic surgery, and pornography. According to the *Economist*, the aggregate annual figure for the international beauty industry is projected at $160 billion. Financial analysts at Goldman Sachs estimate annual global profits of $24 billion in skin care, $18 billion in cosmetic makeup, $38 billion in hair-care products, and $15 billion in perfumes, with 7 percent annual growth figures, more than twice the rate of the developed world's gross domestic product. Americans alone spend approximately $60 billion a year trying to lose weight and $10 billion a year on pornography. Despite a global economic recession, the personal care products producer Unilever (which owns the Dove and Axe brands) posted a 39 percent increase in profits in its second quarter of 2010.

Politics

Within the political realm, the beauty myth serves as the means for judging women by a different standard from their male counterparts. Whereas men are judged according to their qualifications for political leadership, the beauty myth functions as a gatekeeper to remind women that they must adhere to normative standards of beauty and femininity in order to be electable or attain political power. A female politician's fashion, dress, makeup, hairstyle, legs, and overall body type are more likely to be subjects of media commentary, punditry, or polling data than her leadership, experience, and qualifications. In the 2008 U.S. presidential election, Democratic candidate Hillary Clinton was ridiculed by male news reporters and commentators for wearing pantsuits that symbolized masculine power. Combined with her fashion, her age was the subject of scrutiny rather than her level of professional experience. Photos of an exhausted-looking Clinton on the campaign trail appeared on the Matt Drudge Website and were used by politically motivated pundits to question her ability to lead the nation. Radio commentator Rush Limbaugh (as Maureen Dowd noted in her *New York Times* column on December 19, 2007) criticized Clinton's appearance, posing the question, "Will this country want to actually watch a woman get older before their eyes on a daily basis?" adding, "Men aging makes them look more authoritative, accomplished, distinguished. Sadly, it's not that way for women, and they will tell you." He noted that Hillary "is not going to want to look like she's getting older, because it will impact poll numbers, it will impact perceptions," and that "there will have to be steps taken to avoid the appearance of aging."

Although Republican vice presidential candidate Sarah Palin adhered to the feminine beauty ideal and was applauded by fashion reviewers and political pundits alike for her thinness, long hair, and skirtsuits, the beauty myth's "either/or" insistence—that women are either beautiful or smart (never both)—impeded her entry into the political realm. The monetary costs associated with Palin's wardrobe became subject to news scrutiny when figures related to her fashion expenditures were leaked to the press. According to the news leaks, the Republican National Committee spent roughly $150,000 on Palin's clothing, makeup, hair styling, and other "campaign accessories."

News

Female reporters and news anchors are also judged according to the beauty myth in mainstream media. Despite their levels of expertise and experience, women whose age, fashion, or body-type do not conform to the beauty myth are fired or pressured to undergo cosmetic surgery and beauty makeovers in broadcast news. In the 1980s, television news anchor Christine Craft filed a discrimination suit against KMBC-TV in Kansas City for allegedly applying the beauty myth based on her gender and age. Although the news station moved up in rank from third to first place in audience ratings after she became an on-air news anchor, Craft was demoted to reporter after research from a focus group indicated that she was, as reported in the August 11, 1983, issue of the New York Times, "too old, unattractive and not deferential enough to men." The jury awarded Craft $500,000 in damages, at which time the station's corporate owner, Metromedia, initiated an appeal. The retrial led to another victory in Craft's favor. However, Metromedia's third appeal led the 8th Circuit Court to throw out the second verdict, at which time the Supreme Court denied hearing the case.

In 2002, FOX News television reporter Greta Van Susteren received media publicity for undergoing a surgical face-lift designed to remove "bags" from beneath her eyes before appearing on the program On the Record with Greta Van Susteren. Although the public's reaction generated heated discussions about the news industry's practice of glamorizing entertainment stars rather than professional journalists, few analyses focused on the ways that the beauty myth systematically discriminates against female news reporters while holding men to a different standard. In a People magazine cover story about Van Susteren's makeover, veteran television writer Michele Greppi (quoted on the Website Mediaite in January 2010) said, "FOX hired a tomboy, and they got a babe," underscoring the culture's preoccupation with the female reporter's appearance over her credentials as an attorney and reporter.

Similar public scrutiny was applied to Columbia Broadcasting System (CBS) broadcast news correspondent and anchor Katie Couric, who in 2006 became the first female solo anchor of a weekday network evening news program. Prior to her debut on the station, CBS airbrushed 20 pounds off a public relations photo designed to promote Couric's new role on the station. Critics were quick to point out that this practice was not applied to American Broadcasing Company (ABC) anchor Charlie Gibson or National Broadcasing Company (NBC) anchor Brian Williams, thereby revealing inconsistent patterns of gender equity within broadcast news.

Reality Television

Cultural obsession with the beauty myth has manifested itself in other genres, such as reality television and game shows. The underlying premise within such programming is that beauty must be publicly judged and regulated in order for participants to win societal acceptance. The body ideal of thinness is projected on programs such as The Biggest Loser and Celebrity Fit Club. On these shows, the drama is predicated upon the trials and efforts of contestants striving to regain self-esteem and "a better life" by losing weight. Although these programs document the efforts of the contestants striving to achieve weight loss, the narrative reveals the shortcomings of those who cannot advance to the ultimate challenge, which enables them to win a sizable monetary prize and endorsements. While program producers praise these shows for helping people live a healthier lifestyle, critics point to the inconsistencies between the programming and advertisements that encourage viewers to eat unhealthy foods.

Full-body makeovers represent another programming trend. Popular shows such as Extreme Makeover, The Swan, and I Want a Famous Face maintain the belief that beauty is achievable through dieting, cosmetic surgery, hairstyling, and fashion transformations. This goal is closely associated with the economic function of the beauty myth.

Beauty Pageants

Another form of programming designed to encourage women to compete based on the beauty myth is the beauty pageant competition. The best-known pageants are the Miss America and Miss Universe contests. Like other forms of media programming, such contests subject young girls and women to competitions rooted in valuing the body over the mind. Although some pageants have added new scoring criteria, attached to categories such as talent and social causes, to help validate women's achievements, the underlying function of pageantry is to reinforce the beauty myth through sanctioned public scrutiny. Race and ethnicity continue to privilege Anglo-European features and light skin pigmentation. In the last 75 years of pageantry, only four African American women and one Jewish woman have won the Miss America title. Beauty competitions have also encouraged girls as young as 5 years old to receive coaching on their appearance, with reality

Popular reality shows *Toddlers and Tiaras* and *Little Miss Perfect* document infants and young girls competing in beauty pageants being coached, trained, and groomed to look and act like the Western ideal of beauty and perfection. (iStockphoto)

programs like *Toddlers and Tiaras* and *Little Miss Perfect* comparing infants and children to airbrushed models found in celebrity and women's magazines. This culture of beauty perfectionism has been linked to findings that show young girls' self-esteem plummeting after they are exposed to airbrushed images.

The Beauty Myth in the Globalized World

The communications revolution and globalization have both advanced and challenged the beauty myth. The United States remains the largest exporter of media products in the world, leading to growing concerns about the impact of the beauty myth in non-Western, or non-Anglo-European, nations. Studies demonstrate that since 2005, women of various socioeconomic and ethnic backgrounds in Seoul, Hong Kong, and Singapore have been experiencing a new form of self-starvation, and reports have appeared of anorexia spreading in the Philippines, India, and Pakistan. Experts studying the disorder are unsure whether the disease results from the globalization of Western media and fashion or the epidemic is a symptom of modernization and prosperity. Regardless of the cause, the effect has been to spread the influence of the beauty myth to developing nations around the globe.

Technology and Resistance

Developments in new technologies and their uses among younger generations have enabled media-savvy youths to challenge the beauty industry by creating their own Internet magazines, blogs, vlogs (video logs), and YouTube videos. Free from the restraints of editors, designers, photographers, videographers, makeup artists, and beauty experts, new media forms allow users to break free from the conventional boundaries of the beauty myth through their own media production. The outcome offers a fluid range of cultural criteria that open up the meaning of beauty across all ages, races, ethnicities, classes, genders, and body types.

Julie Frechette
Worcester State University

See also Advertising; Beauty and Body Image: Eating Disorders; Bordo, Susan; Film: Hollywood; Gender and Femininity: Single/Independent Girl; Kilbourne, Jean; Social Comparison Theory; Tween Magazines; Women's Magazines: Fashion

Further Readings

"Are We Turning Tweens Into 'Generation Diva'?" *Newsweek* (March 30, 2009). http://www.newsweek.com/2009/03/29/generation-diva.html (Accessed September 2010).

Bordo, Susan. *Unbearable Weight: Feminism, Western Culture, and the Body, Tenth Anniversary Edition*, 2nd ed. Berkeley: University of California Press, 2004.

Cummings, Jeanne. "RNC Shells Out $150K for Palin Fashion." http://www.politico.com/news/stories/1008/14805.html (Accessed September 2010).

Dines, Gail and Jean M. Humez, eds. *Gender, Race and Class in Media: A Text Reader*. 1995. Reprint, Thousand Oaks, CA: Sage, 2010.

Douglas, Susan J. *Where the Girls Are: Growing Up Female With the Mass Media*. 1994. Reprint, New York: Three Rivers Press, 1995.

The Economist. "The Beauty Business: Pots of Promise." http://www.economist.com/printedition/displayStory.cfm?Story_ID=1795852 (Accessed September 2010).

HealthyPlace.com. "Eating Disorders on Rise in Asia." http://www.healthyplace.com/eating-disorders/main/eating-disorders-on-rise-in-asia/menu-id-58 (Accessed September 2010).

Kilbourne, Jean. *Can't Buy My Love: How Advertising Changes the Way We Think and Feel*. New York: Free Press, 2000.

Marketplace from American Public Media. "Our Loss, Diet Industry's Gain." http://marketplace.publicradio.org/display/web/2007/05/30/our_loss_diet_industrys_gain (Accessed September 2010).

Marlane, Judith. *Women in Television News Revisited: Into the Twenty-First Century*. Austin: University of Texas Press, 1999.

Paul, Pamela. *Pornified: How Pornography Is Damaging Our Lives, Our Relationships, and Our Families*. New York: Owl Books, 2006.

Pipher, Mary. *Reviving Ophelia: Saving the Selves of Adolescent Girls*. Boston: Riverhead Trade, 2005.

Rhode, Deborah. *The Beauty Bias: The Injustice of Appearance in Life and Law*. New York: Oxford University Press, 2010.

Rouvalis, Cristina. "Female News Broadcasters Criticize Double Standard." Post-Gazette.com. http://www.post-gazette.com/pg/06248/719015-237.stm (Accessed September 2010).

Wolf, Naomi. *The Beauty Myth: How Images of Beauty Are Used Against Women*. 1991. Reprint, New York: HarperPerennial, 2002.

WWD.com. "Unilever Profits Climb 39 Percent." http://www.wwd.com/beauty-industry-news/unilever-profits-climb-39-percent-3204916 (Accessed September 2010).

BEAUTY AND BODY IMAGE: EATING DISORDERS

Body image is a multidimensional construct that refers to the mental picture people form of their bodies. That picture is influenced by one's own beliefs and attitudes about how they look, as well as socially constructed ideals of beauty. Negative body image (when a person has a distorted self-perception) is thought to be a risk factor for the development of eating disorders. An eating disorder is a psychological disorder centering on the avoidance, excessive consumption, or purging of food. Eating disorders affect a person's physical and emotional well being. The two most common eating disorders are anorexia nervosa and bulimia nervosa. Anorexia entered the medical literature in the late 19th century when it was described as a nervous disorder associated with young women. Today, anorexia and bulimia are understood to be psychosocial disorders that affect both genders and are often related to issues of low self-esteem, negative body image, and at times, a result of body dysmorphic disorder (a psychological disorder in which the affected person is excessively concerned about and preoccupied by a perceived defect in his or her physical features).

Anorexics severely limit their intake of food in an effort to avoid gaining weight, while bulimics partake in recurrent binge eating followed by compensatory behaviors such as purging (self-induced vomiting or excessive use of laxatives). Individuals with anorexia nervosa and bulimia nervosa evaluate themselves primarily on the basis of their body weight and shape. One method individuals use to assess their bodies is to measure them against the ideal body characteristics of a culture, which results in body satisfaction or dissatisfaction. Sociocultural variables, in particular social pressures regarding thinness and attractiveness, internalization of societal beauty ideals, and body dissatisfaction, play a role in how people view their bodies. Problems arise when there is a discrepancy between what the body looks like and what a person thinks the body should look like. Researchers have identified two conceptually distinct components of body image. The first, body-image evaluation, denotes individuals' evaluative thoughts and beliefs about their physical appearance. The second, body-image investment, refers to the behaviors individuals perform to manage or enhance the way they look. To meet societal expectations of an ideal body, individuals use appearance-management behaviors such as exercise, dieting, and surgery. Eating disorders enter the realm of possibility when a person's body does not approximate their definition of "ideal."

Many scholars who study the body focus their research on gender differentiation, citing a pervasiveness of body image concerns among women. While millions of people in the United States are affected by eating disorders each year, more than 90 percent of those afflicted are adolescent and young adult women between the ages of 12 and 25. Males account for only 5 to 10 percent of bulimia and anorexia cases. Researchers say one out of every two women is dissatisfied with her body and consistently find that males display much higher rates of body satisfaction than women. Men are significantly less likely than women to distort their perceptions of their own bodies and more likely to indicate that their ideal body type coincides with their current body type. Puberty is often a factor when discussing body image issues among teenage boys and girls. Breast enlargement and increased body fat for girls and muscle mass for boys have been cited as factors that contribute to body dissatisfaction. When a child goes through puberty can also determine if they will be more or less satisfied with their body. In studies done on teenage boys and girls, girls who matured early reported less body

An eating disorder can be triggered by social pressure to reach the definition of an "ideal" body, by low self-esteem, or from the onset of the psychological body dysmorphic disorder. Ninety percent of afflicted women in the United States are between the ages of 12 and 25. (Photos.com)

satisfaction and lower self-esteem with their bodies than girls who matured later. In contrast, boys who matured early rated their bodies as more satisfactory than boys who entered puberty later. These findings coincide with societal standards of attractiveness, which tend to favor a prepubertal look for females (lean and thin) and a postpubertal look for males (muscular, tall, and strong). Regardless of a person's gender, weight tends to be at the heart of body image issues. Some studies have indicated that underweight men have similar if not more negative self-views than overweight women. Thin males wanted to be more muscular, and overweight males wanted to be thinner.

Conversely, thin *and* overweight females expressed a desire to be thinner, thus identifying weight as a contributing factor for female body dissatisfaction. In sum, self-worth (and how one is viewed by others) is often determined by how one looks, what one eats, and how much one weighs.

Media images are also acknowledged as being among those factors contributing to the rise of eating disorders as they often help to create unrealistic cultural definitions of beauty and attractiveness. Researchers consistently find that women identify an ideal body as being similar to that suggested by the mass media (tall, thin, and young). Exposure to images of female attractiveness commonly presented in advertising and the broader media has been linked to body image disturbance. The media present a standard of female attractiveness that is quite exaggerated, using ultra-thin models and a host of artificial enhancements with respect to the photography and production of media images. Those who suffer from a negative body image are prone to buy into the mediated images as being the ideal and their own body as deviating from that ideal. Body image becomes problematized when comparisons occur between what one sees on television and in magazines to what one sees in the mirror. Social psychologists often use social comparison theory (comparing oneself to another individual in an effort to assess personal attributes against the attributes of another) when talking about the mass media, which studies confirm elicits greater pressure to conform to idealistic standards of attractiveness than comparisons made to friends and family.

While people of all races and ethnic backgrounds develop eating disorders, the vast majority of those diagnosed are white. Most research conducted on eating disorders and body image has been done with middle-class, Caucasian college-age women. In comparison, less research has been done on ethnic minorities or the gay and lesbian community. In studies conducted on African Americans, Latinos, and Asian Americans, researchers found an indirect correlation between ethnic identity and disordered eating, however more studies are needed before conclusions can be drawn. In general, ethnic groups who identify with Westernized ideals are likely to experience the same sociocultural risks as their Caucasian counterparts. Acculturation and cross-cultural differences ("ideal" body shapes differ within cultures) are all factors to consider when examining eating disorders and body image among ethnic minorities. Research over the last decade found that eating disorders exist among minority women and lower-income women. Increasingly, anorexia and bulimia are affecting all women regardless of ethnicity or race. Within the gay and lesbian community, numerous studies have found that, compared with heterosexual men, gay men have more behavioral symptoms indicative of eating disorders. In one study, the proportion of gay and bisexual men with symptoms related to eating disorders was 10 times higher than among heterosexual men.

There were no significant differences among heterosexual women, lesbians, and bisexual women in the prevalence of any eating disorders. The incidence of eating disorders among lesbians and bisexual women was comparable to that found in heterosexual women. Eating disorders are about much more than eating. They are about exerting control over the body through the manipulation of food, feeling a sense of low self-worth or self-esteem, and wanting to have a different body shape. Quantitative studies show that people who suffer from negative body image and subscribe to societal constructions of beauty, often fall prey to eating disorders. The increasing numbers of people afflicted by disordered eating show that more qualitative work is needed to probe the correlation between negative body image and eating disorders.

Lisa Pecot-Hebert
DePaul University

See also Advertising; Beauty and Body Image: Beauty Myths; Bordo, Susan; Film: Hollywood; Gender and Femininity: Single/Independent Girl; Kilbourne, Jean; Social Comparison Theory; Tween Magazines; Women's Magazines: Fashion

Further Readings

Bordo, Susan. *Unbearable Weight: Feminism, Western Culture, and the Body*. Berkeley: University of California Press, 1993.

Cash, Thomas, Jennifer Morrow, April Perry, and Joshua Hrabosky. "How Has Body Image Changed? A Cross-Sectional Investigation of College Women and Men From 1983–2001." *Journal of Consulting and Clinical Psychology*, v.72 (2004).

Castel, Davis and Katherine Phillips. *Disorders of Body Image*. Petersfield, UK: Wrightson Biomedical Publishing, 2002.

Groesz, L., M. Levine, and S. Murnen. "The Effect of Experimental Presentation of Thin Media Images on Body Satisfaction: A Meta-Analytic Review." *International Journal of Eating Disorders*, v.31/1 (2002).

Heaton, Jeanne and Claudia Strauss. *Talking to Eating Disorders: Simple Ways to Support Someone With Anorexia, Bulimia, Binge Eating, or Body Image Issues*. New York: New American Libraries, 2005.

Hendricks, Alexandra. "Examining the Effects of Hegemonic Depictions of Female Bodies on Television: A Call for Theory and Programmatic Research." *Critical Studies in Media Communication*, v.19/1 (2002).

Moradi, Bonnie and Adena Rotttenstein. "Objectification Theory and Deaf Cultural Identity Attitudes: Roles in Deaf Women's Eating Disorder Symptomatology." *Journal of Counseling Psychology*, v.54/2 (2007).

Morgan, John. *The Invisible Man: A Self-Help Guide for Men With Eating Disorders, Compulsive Exercise and Bigorexia*. London: Routledge, 2008.

Wood, Nikel and Trent Petrie. "Body Dissatisfaction, Ethnic Identity, and Disordered Eating Among African American Women." *Journal of Counseling Psychology*, v.57/2 (2010).

BERGER, JOHN

John Berger (1926–) is a British art critic, artist, and acclaimed novelist, best known among scholars of gender and media for the 1972 British television series and accompanying book he created, *Ways of Seeing*. In *Ways of Seeing* Berger argues that power relations, particularly related to gender, class, and capitalism, are visible in the history of western European art as well as in the advertising of his day. His work inspired scholarly attention to the media as central to gendered power relations.

Although *Ways of Seeing* is often attributed to Berger alone, it is a coauthored book, with Sven Blomberg, Chris Fox, Michael Dibb, and Richard Hollis. In both the book and the television series, Berger brings a Marxist critique to art history and criticism and compares fine art to contemporary advertising. What makes his critique Marxist is his attention to how European art, particularly oil painting, has been shaped by power relations in society, so he foregrounds who produced the paintings, for whom they produced these paintings, and how the resulting images reinforced the status quo. Berger is concerned that the conditions of production of these paintings have been obscured and are routinely ignored by both art critics and audiences, and therefore their ideological meanings have become naturalized.

Ways of Seeing is a short book containing seven essays, four of which are visual essays that feature series of images. The central argument of the book is that images are not benign; rather, they invite viewers to see the world in particular ways. Berger demonstrates that the ways of seeing promoted in western European art are very particular by pointing out patterns and conventions in how certain kinds of subjects, such as women or animals or possessions, are represented. Berger's observation that relations of looking, particularly through images such as paintings and photographs, are central to how power works in modern society is a key premise of many theories of visual culture.

The best-known phrase from *Ways of Seeing* is that, arguably, "men act, and women appear" (p. 47). Berger argues that this is the case because European oil paintings were produced by men, for men, and that women were represented for men's pleasure in looking at them, even possessing them. While this pattern of representation naturalizes the idea that women should be available for the pleasure of men, Berger argues that it also shapes the subjectivity of women. He writes, "Women watch themselves being looked at" (p. 46). Therefore, female subjectivity is split in two—a woman is aware of being surveyed by men, but she also surveys herself. Berger points out that in the tradition of western European art the female nude is often arranged in paintings for the pleasure of the male spectator (often the patron who commissioned the work), and further that she looks not at her environment but at the spectator, acknowledging and even inviting the spectator's gaze. Otherwise, Berger notes that the

female nude is often looking at herself in a mirror, thereby justifying the desire of the spectator to look at her. Berger argues that the nude is depicted as passive, which communicates that the female subject must submit to the desire of the spectator. In other words, European oil paintings objectify women, turning them into objects of pleasure for their male spectator-owners.

Berger's arguments about gender ideology in art resonated with second wave feminist theories of the era, in particular the second wave critiques of how social forces, including culture and norms, disempowered women. *Ways of Seeing* reinforces critiques of idealized femininity, including a focus on appearance and sexuality, and the notion that women ought to defer to male desire and authority.

Berger compares the historical examples of women in European oil paintings to 1960s and 1970s advertising images to demonstrate that gender ideology remains very much in place. In both the book and the film, he juxtaposes European oil paintings with commercial advertisements to draw attention to the similarities in poses and facial expressions. Women continue to be objectified in these images, arranged for the pleasure of an imagined male look. Berger points out that this is so even when the targeted

John Berger has written extensively about the relationship between the individual and society and posits that gender ideology in art resonates with second wave feminist theories of the time, particularly the critiques of how social forces, culture, and norms disempower women. (Wikimedia)

audience for the ads is women, because women have learned to survey themselves and other women through men's eyes. Publicity images then have a reason to persuade women to transform themselves in order to become enviable and glamorous. This Marxist critique of advertising was later taken up by other critical scholars of advertising, such as Sut Jhally, who pointed out that modern advertising does not try to promote actual products and services but fantasies about the future self.

Ways of Seeing was the first text in a series of studies that focused on the *male gaze*, a phrase that comes from a seminal essay by Laura Mulvey that influenced theories of spectatorship in film studies. Berger's work is cited in the influential book *Gender Advertisements*, by Erving Goffman, which analyzes how gender ideology is communicated through the gestures, positions, and gazes featured in ads. Today scholars debate whether, on one hand, the gender ideology that Berger and others observed in the 1970s continues to be reproduced in images or, on the other, changes in gender relations and ideologies, including greater awareness of queer and intersectional identifications, complicate these analyses.

Emily West
University of Massachusetts, Amherst

See also Feminist Theory: Second Wave; Jhally, Sut; Male Gaze; Mulvey, Laura; Scopophilia

Further Readings

Berger, John, Sven Blomberg, Chris Fox, Michael Dibb, and Michael Hollis. *Ways of Seeing: Based on the BBC Television Series With John Berger*. London: British Broadcasting Corporation and Penguin, 1972.

Goffman, Erving. *Gender Advertisements*. Cambridge, MA: Harvard University Press, 1979.

Mulvey, Laura. "Visual Pleasure and Narrative Cinema." *Screen*, v.16/3 (1975).

Sturken, Marita and Lisa Cartwright. *Practices of Looking: An Introduction to Visual Culture*, 2nd ed. New York: Oxford University Press, 2009.

BLOGS AND BLOGGING

Blogs, a shortened form of the term *Weblogs*, are frequently updated personal Websites where content (text, pictures, music, videos, and so forth) is posted on a regular basis and displayed in chronological order. Blogs typically allow readers to comment on posts; such interactive blogs hold the potential to facilitate the development of interpersonal relationships and a sense of community among bloggers and their readers. More than 12 million Americans report blogging, with men and women blogging in approximately equal numbers. Blog authors express their gender through both visual and discursive means, as they communicate their ideas and form relationships with like-minded individuals who read and post on their blogs.

Blogs display a combination of three characteristics unique across online venues: First, blogs display frequent, short posts. Regular contact between bloggers and readers can build close relationships and create a strong online identity by reinforcing identity portrayals. Second, blog posts blend mass and interpersonal communication in that they are written for a mass audience but promote one-on-one relationships between blog interactants. Bloggers write to a mixed audience that may include family, friends, and strangers. Readers become increasingly familiar and friendly with bloggers after reading their posts regularly and responding with their posted comments. Third, blogs tend to be highly interconnected via the "blogroll," a list of links that allows the user to add others' blogs to their list of recommended reading, creating a network of blogs sometimes called the "blogosphere." Blogrolls often feature reciprocal listings as bloggers tend to add one another's blogs to their blogrolls, when they approve of the blog. For example, many feminist blogs are interconnected via their blogrolls.

Enacting Gender on Blogs

In creating online identities, almost all bloggers reveal their gender, both by explicitly stating their sex and by employing various forms of nonverbal behaviors (such as colors, backgrounds, fonts, and pictures). For example, a self-proclaimed "girly girl" could select a pink background for her blog and a "macho man" might post pictures of weight lifters on his blog.

Bloggers also enact gender via language choices, including the announcement of biological sex and the use of masculine factual, emotionless language versus feminine expressive, inclusive language. Teen girls' diary blogs provide examples via statements such as "I am a woman, not a girl!" and "Since

I was a little girl . . . ." Also, women tend to employ more inclusive, expressive, passive, cooperative, and accommodating language than men. For example, a woman's blog may read, "I love seeing pictures of people's homes online. It gives us a tiny peek into their world. And it's a great way for us to get decorating ideas!" The use of "us" is inclusive and the words *love* and *tiny* are expressive, as is the exclamation point. A male blogger might post: "My fantasy football team is kicking butt. I'm gonna beat everyone in the league. You just wait and see." Here the "I" and "you" exemplify competitive language, typical of male language.

Gendered Use of Blogs

Most blog commentators recognize two broad categories of blogs: journal blogs and filter blogs. Journal blogs describe personal life with "internal" content typically known only to the blogger until he or she posts it. Filter blogs contain information that is primarily external to the author—for example, about news and political events; in these blogs, certain arguments, ideas, and information are included and others are excluded. Political filter blogs often link to the Websites of traditional media sources, such as newspapers. In turn, traditional media outlets often quote political filter blogs. Because filter blogs are typically written by men, quoting such blogs can highlight the words of men versus women. Likewise, academic research on filter blogs is more prevalent than research on journal blogs.

Filter blogs display multiple masculine stylistic features, such as statements and restatements of facts. In a study of British bloggers, men's blog content focused on sharing information, providing opinions, and highlighting links. A study of U.S. bloggers reported that male authors carefully avoid expressing emotion, focusing their blogs on information and ideas. Taken together, these findings paint a gendered picture of how males share information through blogging—a picture consistent with Deborah Tannen's descriptions of the typical ways males communicate in face-to-face (FtF) interactions: Men engage in report talk, giving information and opinions as a means of gaining or sustaining status.

Medical blogs serve as a prime example of how men perform masculinity on blogs. A study of blogs about health and medicine reported that 59 percent of medical bloggers were male; 74 percent of the bloggers reported posting to share knowledge and

skills, and 56 percent to gain insights from others. (Respondents could choose more than one motivation; therefore, when totaled, the percentages may exceed 100.) Two thirds of medical bloggers received attention from the news media about their blogs. Males may participate in medical blogs, in part, because the nature of these blogs aligns with a masculine communication style, allowing the authors to enact their gender through their blogs. Because men are more likely to write informational blogs, others view them as credible bloggers. In short, male bloggers are seen as information transmitters who form blogging relationships based on the sharing of credible information.

Women, on the other hand, are more likely to write journal, or diary, blogs. Unlike traditional diaries, however, journal blogs do not have the connotation of privacy and instead seek an online audience by encouraging readers to post comments. Journal bloggers invite their readers to identify with and share in a relationship with the author through reciprocal self-disclosure in responses and comments. Readers who habitually read these blogs are more likely to be female. Through journal blogging, reading blogs regularly, and leaving feedback, women engage in discourse that Tannen labeled "rapport-talk"— conversations that privilege confirmation, support, and consensus. The creation of these support networks on blogs is consistent with the more communal, relational communication often characteristic of women. When multiple readers share their life experiences and establish an emotional connection, they often develop multiple relationships on the same blog, building a virtual community.

Bloggers often employ hyperpersonal communication (extreme depth of interpersonal exchanges), as they share very personal information. Hyperpersonal communication can facilitate the development of relationships. Online relationships may take longer to develop than FtF relationships, because it takes longer for interactants to transmit, decode, and trust online messages. However, the longer the duration of an online relationship, the more it resembles an FtF relationship in terms of breadth, depth, understanding, and commitment.

Women's Movements on Blogs

Because females are misrepresented and underrepresented in traditional media, women bloggers can gain a voice through blogging. For example, some female authors of "blooks" (blogs turned into books) emphasize sexual openness, empowerment, and pleasure. These women redefine their sexuality and femininity by exploring their sex lives through blogging, writing about what many people would consider the most intimate and personal form of communication.

Blogs provide a vital venue for female self-expression in countries that limit women's freedom of expression. One study of female bloggers in Egypt, Saudi Arabia, and Jordan reported that women turn to blogs as a form of political activism and as a vehicle for self-expression, including the online publishing of prose, poetry, and short stories.

Female blogging is on the increase. BlogHer, one of the leading online networks for women, received more than 4.23 million unique visitors in the month of October 2007. The blogs in the BlogHer network cover a wide variety of topics, including parenting, health, food, career, money, and politics. The site's mission statement reflects the goal of creating opportunities for women who blog to pursue exposure, education, community, and economic empowerment. Such a blog community allows women to perform their femininity via socialization. BlogHer sponsors many "mommy blogs," journal blogs where women post about issues related to their families and personal lives. These blogging mothers also offer product reviews and shopping tips to readers. The mommy blogs have become a force in the business world; for example, Procter and Gamble incorporated 15 mommy bloggers into their 2008 national marketing strategy.

Vlogs: Video Logs

Video logs, or vlogs, contain videos accompanied by text-based comments that allow for ongoing interpersonal communication. Most vlogs focus on personal content and create social networks by allowing both text and video comments from viewers. Men and women employ vlogs quite differently. In a study on YouTube vlogs, males posted vlogs more than women; however, female vloggers were more likely to interact by asking questions and responding. Men created vlogs with better sound quality; women created more interactive vlogs with better image quality. Men tend to vlog about public and technology-related topics; women tend to vlog about

personal matters. Despite gender differences in the content and creation of vlogs, both men and women report feeling a part of the YouTube community. Vlogs may have more impact than blogs on interpersonal relationships, as authors both write and literally talk to viewers. Seeing and hearing the author may forge stronger relational bonds.

The blogosphere provides a space for both men and women to enact gender identity via gendered language, images, and blog format. These performances can take the form of gender liberation or traditional gendered behaviors. As a channel of communication, blogs are simultaneously empowering and value-neutral; their gendered use is up to the average blogger "on the street" of the information super highway of the 21st century.

Lynne M. Webb
Brittney D. Lee
University of Arkansas

See also Audiences: Producers of New Media; Cyberdating; Cyberspace and Cyberculture; Empowerment; Identity; New Media; Sexuality; Social Media; Twitter; Virtual Community

Further Readings

Hans, Mark L., Brittney D. Selvidge, Katie A. Tinker, and Lynne M. Webb. "Online Performances of Gender: Blogs, Gender-Bending, and Cybersex as Relational Exemplars." In *Computer Mediated Communication in Personal Relationships*, Kevin B. Wright and Lynne M. Webb, eds. New York: Peter Lang, 2011.

Herring, Susan C. and John C. Paolillo. "Gender and Genre Variation in Weblogs." *Journal of Sociolinguistics*, v.10/4 (2006).

Neff, Jack. "P&G Relies on Power of Mommy Bloggers." *Advertising Age*, v.79/27 (2008).

Stefanone, Michael and Chyug-Yang Jang. "Writing for Friends and Family: The Interpersonal Nature of Blogs." *Journal of Computer-Mediated Communication*, v.13/1 (2008).

Tannen, Deborah. *You Just Don't Understand: Women and Men in Conversation*. New York: William Morrow, 1990.

BORDO, SUSAN

Susan Bordo (1947–) is a professor of philosophy at the University of Kentucky and a noted feminist author focusing on culture and the body. Bordo is best known for her 1993 book *Unbearable Weight: Feminism, Western Culture, and the Body*. She has published several other books, including *The Male Body: A New Look at Men in Public and in Private* (1999) and *Twilight Zones: The Hidden Life of Cultural Images From Plato to O.J.* (1997). While most readers would agree that Bordo represents a feminist perspective, placing her work neatly into a "wave" of feminism is difficult. Her work has been highly influential in gender studies related to body and body image. Currently teaching English and women's studies at the University of Kentucky, Susan Bordo holds the Otis A. Singletary Chair in the Humanities. She received her Ph.D. from the State University of New York at Stony Brook in 1982, completing a feminist reading of René Descartes' *Meditations* for her dissertation.

In her best-known work, *Unbearable Weight*, Bordo makes an argument regarding the way in which expectations of female bodies in Western culture have contributed to body/eating disorders such as anorexia and bulimia, appearance practices such as plastic surgery and constant dieting, and a general feeling of inadequacy and self-hatred among women. While Bordo's work addresses how culture and social standards impact perceptions of the self and the body, she does not position the individual as helpless or victimized in the process. Rather, she argues that women are active participants in a patriarchal culture that promotes such views of the female body. While women are a part of the perpetuation of these physical expectations, they also participate in resistance to the system that objectifies the female body. In fact, it is partly in the effort to resist appearance expectations that "diseases" like anorexia and bulimia arise. The text is a best seller for the University of California Press and was nominated for a Pulitzer Prize.

Although Bordo is connected primarily with work regarding the female body, she has not limited her explorations of culture and physical standards to women. A 1999 book, *The Male Body: A New Look at Men in Public and in Private*, and a number of articles have addressed the connections between popular culture and men's understandings of their physical selves. In these works, Bordo argues that representations of the male body in media utilize stereotypes of men (both heterosexual and homosexual) and the male body to create anxieties and insecurities that promote consumption of products and result in bifurcated standards of masculinity that are impossible to meet.

In the collection of essays titled *Twilight Zones: The Hidden Life of Cultural Images From Plato to O.J.*, Bordo considers how cultural images impact (and even become) our realities—including those related to gender. She discusses the ways in which our understandings of perfection, race, gender, age, and even our historical and philosophical beliefs are built through our interactions with media. While noting the entertainment and relaxation value of media forms, Bordo argues that we need to cultivate our ability to engage in cultural critique so that we might more actively and thoughtfully participate in the creation of culture.

Bordo's work is connected to a variety of philosophical and theoretical perspectives relevant to feminist studies. Considering in her work the ways in which women engage in self-surveillance and correction to social norms, Bordo draws on writings by Michel Foucault and other post-structuralists. Her critical reflections on rationality and dualism are also consistent with the scholarship of Genevieve Lloyd and Susan Hekman. Because of her focus on the body, Bordo's work has also frequently been compared to that of Judith Butler.

Bordo's writing has been highly influential in gender and women's studies. She is widely considered a major contributor to the interdisciplinary field of "body studies." She has also been active in popular media, speaking about gender and the media in sources as diverse as *Bitch* magazine, *The Oprah Magazine*, and *People*.

Lorin Basden Arnold
Rowan University

See also Beauty and Body Image: Beauty Myths; Cultural Politics; Feminism; Feminist Theory: Second Wave; Feminist Theory: Third Wave; Gender Embodiment

Further Readings

Bordo, Susan. "Gay Men's Revenge." *Journal of Aesthetics and Art Criticism*, v.57/1 (1999).

Bordo, Susan. *The Male Body: A Look at Men in Public and in Private*. New York: Farrar, Straus and Giroux, 1999.

Bordo, Susan. *Twilight Zones: The Hidden Life of Cultural Images From Plato to O.J.* Berkeley: University of California Press, 1997.

Bordo, Susan. *Unbearable Weight: Feminism, Western Culture, and the Body*. Berkeley: University of California Press, 1993.

Jaggar, Alison M. and Susan Bordo, eds. *Gender/Body/ Knowledge: Feminist Reconstructions of Being and Knowledge*. Rutgers, NJ: Rutgers University Press, 1989.

BOYD, DANAH

American social media researcher danah boyd (1977–) is an activist and scholar and one of the first to study youths' everyday practices with social media and the various interactions between technology and society. She is also a researcher at Microsoft Research New England, a Fellow at the Harvard University Berkman Center for Internet and Society, and an Associate Fellow at the Tilburg Institute for Law, Technology and Society. She combines theory and ethnography in her in-depth study of young people's use of social media networks and practices like Facebook, Myspace, Twitter, tagging and blogging. *Fortune* magazine has dubbed boyd one of the "50 Smartest People in Tech," as well as the "Smartest Academic" in technology, while the *Financial Times* has described her as the "High Priestess of Internet Friendship."

Born in Altoona, Pennsylvania, boyd graduated in 2000 from Brown University with a degree in computer science. While studying at Brown, she focused on hypertext and gender studies and became interested in women's issues. She completed a master's degree in media arts and sciences at the Massachusetts Institute of Technology (MIT) in 2002. Her master's thesis at MIT, supervised by Judith Donath, focused on faceted identity and self-presentation in online environments.

While completing work on her master's degree, boyd began working at V-Day, a nonprofit organization that aims to end violence against women and girls across the globe. She worked at V-Day for five years and continues to volunteer there, where she has helped create an online global activist support community. She has also worked as an ethnographer and social media researcher for other nonprofit organizations and corporations, including Google, Yahoo! and Tribe.net.

In 2003, boyd moved to San Francisco, California, where she began to blog about her observations on the social media network Friendster. These blog

danah boyd spoke during the opening keynote of the 2010 ROFLCon II convention. boyd is a social media researcher who gained attention for her commentary on the use of social networking sites by young people. (Wikimedia)

posts helped turn boyd into an expert on the cultural dynamics of social media networks. Between 2003 and 2008, she worked on her Ph.D. at the School of Information at the University of California, Berkeley. Her dissertation, *Taken Out of Context: American Teen Sociality in Networked Publics*, examined American teenagers' use of social network sites such as Facebook and Myspace in daily interactions and social relations. She was specifically interested in how mediated environments impact structural conditions within which teens interact, forcing them to deal with complex dynamics such as invisible audiences, the convergence of public and private life, and context collisions.

The MacArthur Foundation funded boyd's dissertation as part of a larger grant on digital youth and informal learning. boyd worked with other members of the MacArthur Foundation grant on the 2009 book *Hanging Out, Messing Around, and Geeking Out: Kids Living and Learning with New Media*. The book examines the outcomes of a three-year ethnographic study on how teens use social media for learning and living in various settings such as the home, after-school programs, and online groups. This collaborative work on youth and social media integrates 23 case studies that include music sharing, Harry Potter podcasting, and online romantic breakups.

In 2007, boyd published "Why Youth (Heart) Social Network Sites: The Role of Networked Publics in Teenage Social Life" as part of the MacArthur Foundation Series on Digital Learning. In this research, boyd argues that social network sites, which she dubs "network publics," enjoy four properties that distinguish them from face-to-face public life: persistence, sociability, invisible audiences, and replicability. These four properties impact social dynamics and complicate online interactions between people.

At the Berkman Center, boyd codirected the Internet Safety Technical Task Force, which worked with private companies and nonprofit organizations on creating technical solutions for the safety of children online. She codirects the Youth and Media Policy Working Group, funded by the MacArthur Foundation. She conducts research on various social media topics that include digital backchannels, social visualization design, Internet interactions and sexting, and the use of artifacts for memory work. Her recent and forthcoming publications cover topics such as online harassment and cyberbullying, race and class in American youth's interaction on Facebook and Myspace, Twitter and imagined audiences, and Facebook and the invasion of privacy.

Nahed Eltantawy
High Point University

See also Audiences: Producers of New Media; Blogs and Blogging; Social Media; Social Networking Sites: Facebook; Social Networking Sites: Myspace; Twitter; YouTube

Further Readings

boyd, danah. Apophenia. http://www.zephoria.org/thoughts (Accessed February 2011).

boyd, danah. "A Bitty Auto-Biography/A Smattering of Facts." http://www.danah.org/aboutme (Accessed February 2011).

boyd, danah. danah boyd Website. http://www.danah.org (Accessed February 2011).

boyd, danah and N. B. Ellison. "Social Network Sites: Definition, History, and Scholarship." *Journal of Computer-Mediated Communication*, v.13/1 (2007).

boyd, danah, et al. *Hanging Out, Messing Around, and Geeking Out: Kids Living and Learning With New Media*. Cambridge, MA: MIT Press, 2009.

Fortune magazine online. "The Smartest People in Tech." http://money.cnn.com/galleries/2010/technology/1007/gallery.smartest_people_tech.fortune/26.html (Accessed July 2010).

Palfrey, John G., danah boyd, and Dena Sacco. *Enhancing Child Safety and Online Technologies: Final Report of the Internet Safety Technical Task Force*. Durham, NC: Carolina Academic Press, 2009.

CHILDREN'S PROGRAMMING: CARTOONS

Animated cartoons have been a dominant form of children's television programming since the mid-1960s. In keeping with broader concerns about media targeting young people, researchers and policy makers have focused sustained attention on violent content and promotion of consumerism in television cartoons. More recently, girls' studies scholars have also illuminated the complex gendering of content and audiences that takes place in programs such as *The Powerpuff Girls*, *G.I. Joe*, and other popular television cartoon franchises. Finally, the similarities and differences between television cartoons that are designed to be entertaining and those designated as educational allow for more nuanced understandings of the ways in which children are perceived as citizens and consumers. Cartoons convey complex social messages that young viewers may learn and carry into their adult lives.

Consumerism

A growing body of media research emphasizes the commercial aspect of children's cartoons as marketing tools that promote lifelong consumerism. Mainstream children's animated television brands young consumers by creating multimedia franchises that seamlessly use entertainment content to promote merchandise. In addition to developing toys from existing cartoon characters, the industry has transitioned to specializing in toy-driven content.

By developing "licensable characters" that could become lead characters in television cartoons, producers also ensured longevity of franchises that could engage in circular promotion, whereby demand for the cartoon enhances demand for products and vice versa. Toy manufacturers began developing product lines with marketable characters around which animated television content could be created. Program-length commercials such as *The Hot Wheels Show* (created by toy giant Mattel), *Transformers* (created by Hasbro), and *Strawberry Shortcake* (created in part by General Mills) spawned highly profitable merchandise lines and were able to skirt government regulations designed to limit advertising to children. Key to marketing cartoons and products to children is the advertising industry's practice of segmenting young audiences by age and gender in order to target branding efforts. By so doing, toy and production companies maximize profits while perpetuating gender stereotypes in content.

Gender

Cable television outlets such as Nickelodeon, Cartoon Network, and The Disney Channel have taken an active role in developing representations of female characters that are marketed as empowering for young girl viewers. In an analysis of children's media, "girl power," and consumerism, Sarah Banet-Weiser, in her 2004 article "Girls Rule! Gender, Feminism, and Nickelodeon," explains that the Nickelodeon network was one of the first outlets for progressive representations of young girls and remains an industry standard for producing television content that appeals to the latest generation of girls who have come to expect girl-power programming. Nickelodeon is Cartoon Network's closest competitor in both the children's television market and the commercial industry of accompanying products such as films, toys, Internet content, and clothing. The network has been lauded by many in the industry and in academia for its representations of strong, independent girls, in such shows as *Clarissa Explains It All* and *As Told by Ginger*. Through such shows, Nickelodeon acts as a conduit for girl-power culture. Moreover, by stepping into the arena of media production, Nickelodeon facilitates girls' production of their own culture. Banet-Weiser also points out, however, that, along with the production of girl power, Nickelodeon "produces its own kind of commodity feminism through its original programming" as it encourages consumption of signifiers of girl-power identity. Hence, animated programs such as *The Powerpuff Girls* and *Justice League* occupy a problematic space between empowering and exploiting young viewers, as do many of the television cartoon lineups that feature entertainment content encoded with gender norms and promotion of brand loyalty.

Nickelodeon was one of the first networks with programming that showed empowered, progressive representations of young girls. Early Nickelodeon "girl-power" productions focused on independent, "real" girls, but more recent shows feature animated girls with superhuman powers. (Wikimedia)

Early Nickelodeon productions that were characterized as girl-power programs featured independent, "real" girls, but more recent programs exalt superhuman powers that set animated girls apart. *My Life as a Teenage Robot* features a female lead character who is "metal on the outside and teenager on the inside," according to the program's Website. The XJ9 robot named Jenny has superpowers, but just as *The Powerpuff Girls* have to save the world before bedtime, Jenny struggles to defend Earth in time to get her homework done and attend her prom. Targeted at a teen audience, *My Life as a Teenage Robot* contains many of the same messages regarding friendship, loyalty, and doing the right thing when faced with difficult decisions that appear in *The Powerpuff Girls*. However, *The Powerpuff Girls* features close relationships among the three main characters, whereas *My Life as a Teenage Robot* offers an example of the more common lone female character. Thus, although *The Powerpuff Girls* is not alone in depicting strong, aggressive, and empowered female characters, it stands out as a rare cartoon program featuring an all-female superhero cast of characters, portraying strong female bonds, that targets a younger audience (all of the other aforementioned programs target young teen and older audiences).

Violence in Cartoons

Beginning with Senate hearings in the mid-1950s, policy makers have shown sustained interest in violence in children's television programming. By the mid-1980s, more than two thirds of children's programming was animated, as it was inexpensive to produce and profitable. It is evident from the overall content of the two main outlets of cartoon programming, Nickelodeon and Cartoon Network, that regardless of whether lead characters are male or female, violence remains prevalent in children's cartoons. *Samurai Jack*, *Dragonball*, *Dragonball Z*, and *Codename Kids Next Door* are all cartoon programs with high levels of violent content and virtually all-male casts.

Violent media content and its potential effect on young viewers have long been a focus of media researchers, and numerous content analyses and experimental studies have explored the violence in television programming targeted at children. As more cartoons that depict female characters and target female audiences become prominent conveyors of both prosocial and antisocial violence, debates have emerged over whether such content should be interpreted as empowering girl viewers or as detrimental to them in the manner that violent male-centered cartoons have often been understood. Researchers have examined the ways in which young girls interpret violence in cartoons both as atypical for feminine characters and as a moderately empowering source of identity for girls; such characters challenge gender norms by engaging in the kind of violence that is usually associated with boy heroes.

One common finding, noted in a 1997 study by J. Cantor and A. I. Nathanson, is that boys are more likely to prefer violent, action-oriented programming, whereas girls tend to prefer harmless, humorous programs. However, it is not just any violence that holds the interest of seemingly bloodthirsty youth. Media research that has studied how specific acts of violence are depicted and whether certain modes of violence have different effects on viewers suggests that adult audience reactions differ depending on whether the violence is "happy" or "justified" (that is, whether it serves a moral good, such as defending one's family). Another aspect of cartoon content that privileges heroic violence is an emphasis on patriotism in such programs as *Justice League*, *Captain America*, and other franchises based on comic book superheroes.

In the wake of volumes of studies on the relationship between adults and violent media, researchers have advanced the argument that children are also drawn to violence that promotes the restoration of justice and order, which might explain the popularity of superhero and crime-fighting cartoons. Cantor and Nathanson argue that older boys are most attracted to violent content that functions to restore justice (good versus evil), whereas girls are more likely to enjoy violence that occurs in the context of humor, as girls are traditionally taught to abhor violence but embrace humor. The indication that male violence is normal whereas female violence is deviant reinforces traditional gender-role stereotypes that demarcate assertiveness and aggression as male traits that girls have no business emulating. The finding

that gender and age are key determinants of media use is consistent across ethnicity and nationality.

Educational Cartoons

Although the Children's Television Act of 1990 was intended to stem some of the cross-promotion and negative content targeting young viewers and promote educational content, its focus on traditional broadcast television and lack of regulation of cable television outlets that had come to dominate children's cartoon programming meant the legislation was limited in scope and impact. Even as the Federal Communications Commission (FCC) mandated in 2004 that requirements for educational content continue as broadcasters switched to digital distribution, the cable television market was still excluded.

Building from the model pioneered by *Sesame Street*, animated programs also use educational goals to create content that targets children from preschool age through adolescence. The success of the Nickelodeon program *Blue's Clues* (which featured both animation and live-action content) on television and in toy stores led to a plethora of educational franchises such as *Super Why* and *Dora the Explorer*, produced for both the nonprofit Public Broadcasting Service and for-profit corporations. Current trends in programming include emphasis on positive socialization as well as promotion of science, reading, and math as fun. Branding and merchandising are vital components of animated education programming, as a source of profit for corporations and as a necessary revenue stream for nonprofit producers.

In addition to identifying gender differences in children's preferences for violent content, researchers have argued that children gender-stereotype the content that they consume. Research shows that, among the prosocial educational programs that appear primarily on public television stations, a disproportionate number feature male characters. A study by S. L. Calvert and others examined the significance of children's internalizing and reproducing male biases: Both girls and boys were more likely to remember and prefer male characters. An interesting exception was that girls and boys also were highly likely to recall and claim to enjoy "nontraditional" or "adventurous heroic" female characters. Girls and boys were, in effect, seeking out characters "similar to their perceptions of self." The researchers argued that the growth in children's television programs featuring nontraditional female characters "may alter traditional gender schemas, or support nontraditional schemas," thus having an impact on the individual viewers and social gender norms. Notwithstanding, it is important to keep in mind that nontraditional female characters appearing on educational programs still exhibit traditionally feminine behaviors, such as compromising.

Spring-Serenity Duvall
University of South Carolina, Aiken

See also Advertising; Children's Programming: Disney and Pixar; Comics; Desensitization Effect; Empowerment; Federal Communications Commission; Feminist Theory: Third Wave; Heroes: Action and Super Heroes; Reception Theory; Social Learning Theory; Television; Toys and Games: Gender Socialization; Violence and Aggression

Further Readings

Banet-Weiser, S. "Girls Rule! Gender, Feminism, and Nickelodeon." *Critical Studies in Media Communication*, v.21/2 (2004).

Bryant, J. Alison. "How Has the Kids' Media Industry Evolved?" In *Twenty Questions About Youth and the Media*, Sharon R. Mazzarella, ed. New York: Peter Lang, 2007.

Calvert, S. L., J. A. Kotler, S. M. Zehnder, and E. M. Shockey. "Gender Stereotyping in Children's Reports About Educational and Informational Television Programs." *Media Psychology*, v.5 (2003).

Cantor, J. and A. I. Nathanson. "Predictors of Children's Interest in Violent Television Programs." *Journal of Broadcasting and Electronic Media*, v.41/2 (1997).

CHILDREN'S PROGRAMMING: DISNEY AND PIXAR

Founded in October 16, 1923, the corporation now known as The Walt Disney Company (Disney) has grown to become the world's largest entertainment and media conglomerate, with a wide range of products that include amusement parks, books, collectibles, cruise ship vacations, DVDs, films, television shows, theatrical productions, and toys.

In 2008, Disney reported revenue of nearly $1.1 billion. From its beginnings as a small animation studio producing Mickey Mouse shorts (cartoons originally shown as preludes to feature films) to the multimillion-dollar diversified enterprise it is today, Disney has established itself as the most recognized purveyor of children's media as well as toys and other merchandise connected with the Disney brand. Disney's cultural influence stems at least in part from the synergistic marketing, or "total merchandising," of Disney products that Walt Disney pioneered.

History

In the 1950s, after making a name in the film industry with Mickey Mouse shorts and such signature feature-length fairy tales as *Snow White and the Seven Dwarfs* (1937) and *Cinderella* (1959), Walt (use of Disney's first name is in keeping with the folksy image he worked to project and avoids confusion between reference to the man and reference to the company) used a deal with American Broadcasting Company (ABC) television to finance the construction of Disneyland, his dream amusement park. In return, Disney produced a one-hour weekly anthology television program, *Disneyland*, for the network. Because the television show discussed past and upcoming Disney films and reported on the progress of the park's construction (later focusing on the larger Walt Disney World in Florida), it served as a constant reminder to the audience of other Disney products. At the park, attractions were built and continue to be updated to re-create classic and current Disney movie settings. Disney animated characters, played by costumed employees, populate the "Magic Kingdom." In addition to acting as a platform for promoting Disney films and parks, the original television program, *Disneyland* (which later became *The Wonderful World of Disney*), aired cartoons, films documenting nature and animals, live-action features, and miniseries dramatizations of historical figures, such as Davy Crockett. By the 1960s—thanks to its commercial success with *Disneyland*, *The Wonderful World of Disney*, *The Mickey Mouse Club*, signature feature-length animated films, live-action family films (such as 1961's *Swiss Family Robinson* and 1964's *Mary Poppins*), and amusement parks—Disney had established itself as the preferred media source for "family entertainment."

Today, the Disney corporation owns such well-known film industry subsidiaries as Walt Disney and Touchstone Pictures, Miramax Films, and Pixar; broadcast and cable television networks including The Disney Channel, ABC, ABC Family, ESPN, and Lifetime; and myriad music, radio, magazine, and other media entities. As a result, it is virtually impossible for a media consumer not to have been exposed to the cultural influence of Disney's programming, and other products, for children.

As the leading purveyor of family entertainment over the course of the last 80 years, Disney has offered audiences stories of princesses and princes, heroes and heroines, victims and villains. Gender plays a central role in these narratives. Scholars from a number of disciplines—including but not limited to psychology, film studies, communication, sociology, media studies, and cultural studies—have critiqued the various ways in which both classic and contemporary Disney film and television programming depicts masculinity and femininity. So-called classic Disney animated films (such as *Snow White and the Seven Dwarfs*, 1950's *Cinderella*, and *Sleeping Beauty*) arguably laid the groundwork for film treatments of established folk fairy tales. In doing so, the studio relied on traditional and stereotypical gender roles. Contemporary animated films from Disney and Pixar tend to offer more complex gender constructions, reflecting shifting cultural norms and consumer demographics. Similarly, Disney television programming, from the original *Mickey Mouse Club* to today's *Hannah Montana*, can also be seen as reflecting the same societal changes with regard to gender roles over the last 50 years. Although it has demonstrated a willingness to adapt to changing trends, Disney's successful commercial formula rarely veers far from or overtly challenges accepted gender norms.

Disney animated film production from the mid-1930s to the present can be divided into two fairly distinct "eras": the "classic" animated era that begins with the release of *Snow White and the Seven Dwarfs* in 1937 and ends around the time of Walt Disney's death in 1966, and the "contemporary" era, which begins after a near-disastrous 20-year "slump" experienced by the animation division from Disney's death until a newly appointed chief executive officer, Michael Eisner, brought producer Jeffrey Katzenberg and other creative talents on board in the mid-1980s. Thereafter the company began producing such box-office and critical hits as *Oliver and Company* (1988), *The Little Mermaid* (1989), and Academy Award Best Picture nominee *Beauty and the Beast* (1991). Disney continues to produce traditional animation with such productions as *The Princess and the Frog* (2009), but the studio also releases animated films produced in three-dimensional, or 3-D (such as 2010's *Tangled*) and computer-generated-image (CGI) formats, often released by Pixar. In the classic era, gender roles were overtly traditional—with women typically portraying princesses in need of rescuing or evil villainesses and men cast as gallant princes, rescuers, caring fathers, or adventurous boy heroes. Contemporary films have, at times, reflected changes in gender-role expectations by depicting both male and female characters in ways that can be seen as blurring the lines between traditionally masculine and traditionally feminine characteristics and behaviors.

Depictions of Gender Roles

From 1937's Snow White, the title character of Disney's first feature-length cartoon, to 2010's Rapunzel in *Tangled*, female protagonists have played an important, and often central, role in the distinctive narrative formula that has rendered Disney animated films popular worldwide. These characters are culled from fairy tales and other expressions of popular culture, from classic and contemporary literature, from history, and from the imagination of the studio's auteurs. Disney often depicts the historical and literary female characters included in its films in ways that differ, sometimes drastically, from the original source material. Many of these characters are now marketed as part of the "Disney Princesses" franchise, which includes heroines from both classic and contemporary films: Snow White, Cinderella, Princess Aurora, Ariel, Belle, Jasmine, Pocahontas, Mulan, and Tiana among them. In classic-era animated films, Disney princesses were, first and foremost, beautiful and young—drawn to appear delicate and graceful—and they share with one another kindness, innocence, and caring, nurturing natures as key qualities that serve to contrast them to the evil stepmothers, malicious queens, and other villainesses who seek to destroy them. Thus, in the Disney oeuvre a binary opposition constructs women as either young, innocent, beautiful, caring, and good or old, evil, selfish, vain, and ugly. In fact, the plots of these films often turn on the jealousy and resentment that older (albeit more powerful) women feel toward the young, innocent, and beautiful protagonists. In addition, narrative resolution in classic Disney films often relies on the rescue of the princess by her prince, with marriage as the actual or implied conclusion of the story. This narrative formula reflects and continues to perpetuate normative heterosexual monogamy as personally and socially desirable.

Contemporary Disney animated films are also populated with beautiful heroines—particularly those marketed as a part of the Princesses line, thus fitting in well with Disney's strategy regarding marketing synergy. However, beginning with *The Little Mermaid*, heroines often appear to possess greater agency than had previously been the case and are frequently depicted as adventurous, high-spirited, even physically strong and athletic, as in the cases of Pocahontas and Mulan. There are other changes in the traditional formula as well. For example, it is Pocahontas who saves the unlucky John Smith's life, reversing the usual gender roles whereby heroic males save hapless and helpless females.

Whereas there has been much critical examination of Disney's depictions of its female protagonists, relatively little critical scrutiny has focused on the studio's male characters, and much of that has been done in relation to feminist critiques of the studio's representation of females. This lack is due, in part, to the fact that in contrast to Disney's many famous female characters, fewer memorable male protagonists are included in the studio's animated feature-length films, especially when one exempts the animated anthropomorphized animals, for which Disney is famous, who occasionally appear in such films (such as Mickey Mouse in *Fantasia*, 1940). Indeed, during Disney's classic period most major male characters played bland supporting roles in relation to strong female leads in such films as *Snow White and the Seven Dwarfs*, *Cinderella*, and *Sleeping Beauty*. Indeed, the first of these films, *Snow White*, set the gender-relations formula followed by Disney for decades. In serving as cook and housekeeper for seven dwarfs, Snow White takes care of their emotional as well as material needs. Later, she is saved from a deep, deathlike sleep by the handsome Prince, who is known merely by his title and not his name and whose only function is to serve as her admirer and rescuer. Thus, women take care of men's needs in the domestic sphere, and men in turn protect and rescue women in the public sphere.

This formula helped drive Disney's commercial success and was not tampered with until the sociocultural changes that occurred during the 1960s and 1970s rendered it out of touch with the American mainstream. In order to remain commercially viable, and to market its products to an increasingly lucrative young girl and tween market, Disney was forced to revise the formula. This revision resulted in the more adventurous heroines described earlier, as well as relatively egalitarian relationships between the sexes, as illustrated by that of Princess Jasmine and Aladdin. This new treatment of gender is a feature of the so-called Disney Renaissance. Indeed, by the time *Beauty and the Beast* was released in 1991, Disney not only had abandoned the old formula regarding the treatment of gender but openly mocked it in its films as well.

Now a Disney subsidiary, Pixar, unlike its parent company, has produced a series of feature-length films that include complex male protagonists as central figures. Indeed, as Ken Gillam and Shannon R. Wooden argue, exploring what it means to be a man in contemporary culture appears to be one of Pixar's major themes. In such films as *Toy Story* (1995), *Monsters, Inc.* (2001), *The Incredibles* (2004), and *Cars* (2006), traditional alpha-male characters experience some crisis, the resolution of which requires them to follow as well as lead, to learn to depend on others rather than be always self-reliant, to negotiate complex male and female friendships, to navigate conflicting and sometimes disturbing attractions, and to tap into and develop their nurturing side. In *Monsters, Inc.*, for example, the main monster, Sulley, learns from a little girl important lessons that lead him to change the firm's mission from scaring children to making them laugh. During the course of each film's narrative, Pixar's male protagonists experience personal growth, and by film's end, they are transformed, rejecting the conventions of alpha masculinity in favor of a new conception of what it means to be a man, one that is more caring of and connected to others.

Celeste C. Lacroix
Robert Westerfelhaus
College of Charleston

See also Advertising; Children's Programming: Cartoons; Comics; Empowerment; Giroux, Henry; Heroes: Action and Super Heroes; Patriarchy; Reception Theory; Social Learning Theory; Stereotypes;

Television; Toys and Games: Gender Socialization; Violence and Aggression

Further Readings

Bell, Elizabeth, Lynda Haas, and Laura Sells, eds. *From Mouse to Mermaid: The Politics of Film, Gender, and Culture.* Bloomington: Indiana University Press, 1995.

Do Rozario, Rebecca-Anne. "The Princess and the Magic Kingdom: Beyond Nostalgia, the Function of the Disney Princess." *Women's Studies in Communication,* v.27/1 (2004).

Gillam, Ken and Shannon R. Wooden. "Post-Princess Models of Gender: The New Man in Disney/Pixar." *Journal of Popular Film and Television,* v.36/1 (2008).

Giroux, Henry. *The Mouse That Roared: Disney and the End of Innocence.* Lanham, MD: Rowman & Littlefield, 1999.

Wasko, Janet. *Understanding Disney: The Manufacture of Fantasy.* Malden, MA: Blackwell, 2001.

CLASS PRIVILEGE

Class privilege derives from an economic, wealth-based hierarchy in society. Like other forms of privilege (such as white privilege or male privilege), class privilege is a result of the power relationship that produces it. Karl Marx believed that a system of stratification is based on people's relationship to the economic process. Max Weber, however, pointed out that it was not the ownership of private property but life chances—access to basic opportunities and resources in the marketplace—that define one's class position in society. Racism, sexism, heterosexism, and class privilege are systems of advantage that provide certain individuals and groups with opportunities and rewards unavailable to others. These systems of oppression work in relation to one another, rationalizing and maintaining the prevailing distribution of power and privilege. In addition to tangible benefits, privilege brings individuals of a social group a sense of acceptance, inclusion, and respect, enabling them to set the agenda in a social institution and determine the rules and standards and how they are applied. It also grants these individuals the cultural authority to define reality, to have prevailing definitions of reality reflect their experience, to make judgments about others, and to ensure that those judgments stay unchallenged.

Class is not only an economic marker in society but also a symbolic and cultural marker. Pierre Bourdieu's theory of social distinction identifies three different types of capital in a society: economic, social, and cultural. Economic capital refers to money or assets that can be turned into money. Cultural capital is a means by which distinctions between social classes can be expressed and reinforced, encompassing such things as educational credentials, technical expertise, general knowledge, verbal abilities, and artistic sensibilities. For example, experiences of international travel, familiarity with exotic flavors, and appreciation of stylish architectures and gardens are regarded as part of cultural capital. Social capital constitutes the benefits of having a network of relationships and contacts that enables access to the capital of others. When these forms of capital are recognized to have value, they act as symbolic capital, a mark of distinction for the possessor. Bourdieu believed that a society's culture is as unequally distributed as its material wealth, and culture also serves to identify class interests and to promote and naturalize class differences. Bourdieu analyzed the phenomena of taste at elite, middlebrow, and popular levels of cultural consumption. Whereas economic capital is more powerful in general, cultural capital is always needed to transform good fortune into "legitimate" fortune. His theory is especially valuable in connecting the production, consumption, and valuation of cultural capital with the social practices of establishing hierarchies, maintaining distances, and legitimating differences between dominant and dominated groups.

In modern societies, many traditional class barriers and distinctions have been eroded. Without a clear boundary of identity and demarcation between classes, class takes a more fluid and indefinite meaning in social consciousness. Scholars note the dying of the old class and the rise of the new class that is composed of elites and professionals, equipped with technology and education. The presence or relevance of cultural capital is the basis of the new class; meanwhile, its relative absence or irrelevance contributes to the old class's loss of control. While the uneven distribution of economic, social, and cultural capital is a key feature of class, it is the ways in which different capitals are classified, valued, and judged that produce the lived experience of class. Scholars believe that inequality based on race, class, and gender is present in our commonsense knowledge and thus perpetuated through our daily interactions. Class might seem less visible than the other dimensions of privilege, because whereas our objective position in an economic order depends on empirically measurable criteria (income, occupation, education), class as an everyday experience rests on other people's evaluation of our presentation of self.

Class affects more than lifestyle and well-being. Research studies have found that wealthy people in general have fewer health problems than poor people and can live longer. The wealthy also find more fulfillment and satisfaction from their work than poorer people do. For those who are positioned as working-class, the lack of class privilege often leads to insecurity, self-doubt, resentment, and anger. In most middle-class careers, the professional or manager is granted certain autonomy in his or her work and is expected to be fairly self-directed much of the time. The middle-class and upper-class positions of privilege assume the possibility of self, individualization, reflexivity, choice, mobility, and entitlement. When entering the job market, young people from privileged backgrounds often search for employment that is seen as meaningful, challenging, and enjoyable, regarding employment as more than a source of income and knowing that they have other networks to rely on for safety and financial backing. Although members of the middle class need to work for a living, the perceived nature of their work creates a difference between them and the working class. Their privilege is reflected in the values and notions of success—such as freedom of expression and the pursuit of authentic passions. For members of the professional middle class, work is often characterized as intrinsically rewarding, creative, and important. For working-class people, work is often considered fatiguing, monotonous, and a source of no particular pleasure.

In the United States, there is generally a reluctance to discuss the issue of class differences, which is reflected in the lack of attention to the topic in mass media and public debate. Mass media play a role in the obscuring of middle-class advantage through discourses of "natural ability." The neoconservative ideology presumes that equal opportunities exist and that social and economic differences stem not from systems of inequality but rather from individual and group deficiencies in work ethics and cultural attributes. Because the majority of people prefer to consider themselves middle class, the issue of class privilege is muted, and the myth of the "American

dream" of upward mobility is depicted as reality. While mass media occasionally offer a glimpse of the lives of the upper class and the lower class, these depictions are designed mainly to satisfy the voyeuristic desire of the audience and are presented in a manner that obscures the class structure and denies any sense of exploitation. Some researchers also have found that entertainment media tend to exaggerate affluence and underrepresent working-class men and women. Working wives in television series tend to be middle-class women in pursuit of careers. Working-class wives are rarely portrayed in entertainment media. Working-class men tend to be shown as immature, irresponsible, inarticulate, and old-fashioned.

Dominant groups and institutions ensure that parents' class status is inherited by their children. This is largely accomplished through the education system, as well as opportunities to enroll children in enrichment activities outside school, such as music lessons and private sports teams. In the schooling process, working-class students who have ambitions usually experience conflicts and tensions involved in moving across social groups, having to engage in additional emotional labor in a college environment as they cope with an alienating social structure, which often conflicts with their home cultures. For students in an educational system in which school officials and course curricula reflect and affirm their social locations and perspectives, it is more likely that they will exhibit higher levels of entitlement, ownership, and confidence in the classroom. For example, studies indicate that when class discussion is encouraged, white males tend to speak more frequently and for longer periods of time than other students. Minority students may experience being treated as "native informants" who are asked to "educate" the class on the histories, experiences, or opinions of an entire group of people.

Although women in all social classes face gender-based discrimination, the class privilege experienced by middle-class and upper-class women confers certain advantages in terms of lifestyle choices—for instance, in educational opportunities and options for child rearing. Although the feminist movement in the United States has achieved much, critics point out that it has reflected the concerns of primarily white bourgeois women, without much consideration for the situations of poor and working-class women. For instance, on the issue of child rearing, the work of contemporary black feminist scholars argues that the intensive mothering ideology—the notion that mothers must lavish all their attention on their children—is based on the privileges available to middle-class white women. Thus, this mothering ideology devalues nonwhite and working-class women's child-rearing practices, which traditionally have been associated with sharing responsibilities among extended family members and the members of the community.

Janice Hua Xu
Cabrini College

See also Electronic Media and Social Inequality; Social Inequality

Further Readings

Bourdieu, Pierre. *Distinction: A Social Critique of the Judgement of Taste.* Cambridge, MA: Harvard University Press, 1984.

Johnson, Allan G. *Privilege, Power, and Difference.* Boston: McGraw-Hill, 2001.

Kendall, Diana. *Framing Class: Media Representations of Wealth and Poverty in America.* Lanham, MD: Rowman & Littlefield, 2005.

Pascale, Celine-Marie. *Making Sense of Race, Class, and Gender: Commonsense, Power and Privilege in the United States.* New York: Routledge, 2006.

Rothenberg, Paula S. *Race, Class, and Gender in the United States: An Integrated Study.* New York: St. Martin's Press, 1992.

Sayer, Andrew. *The Moral Significance of Class.* Cambridge, UK: Cambridge University Press, 2005.

Skeggs, Beverley. *Class, Self, Culture.* London: Routledge, 2004.

COGNITIVE SCRIPT THEORY

Cognitive script theory was posited by Roger C. Schank and Robert P. Abelson, from the fields of computer science and psychology, as a unifying construct for the field of psychology, including social, cognitive, learning, and developmental psychology. According to cognitive script theory, people organize their experiences in scriptlike formations they can refer to in the future to understand the same, or similar new, situations. Scripts contain instructions for how to behave, what is expected, and what to expect. Gender scripts, a dimension of cognitive scripts, organize instructions along the lines of who performs roles (masculine, feminine) within scripts, according to expectations. Scripts are acquired through experience, interaction, and observing. The media provide one mode of script acquisition.

Scripts

A script is a form of schema. Schemas work to organize and structure inferred sociocultural knowledge acquired through experience, interaction, and observation into a general structure of sequences pertaining to a context, situation, or event that can be recalled in the future. Cognitive scripts and social scripts are often used interchangeably; however, cognitive scripts should not be confused with social scripts. *Social script* refers to an overarching social construct of which any given individual may or may not be aware, whereas *cognitive script* refers to an individual's processes that result from interaction with social scripts.

Cognitive script theory describes the way that people, on an individual level, write scripts for how they should attend to situations in the future. The scripts comprise actors, actions, and props, and they generally dictate who the individuals are, what they should be doing, and how actions are ordered in a situation. Scripts help people to understand situations by virtue of previous experience, using inferential knowledge to work toward a goal. Scripts are acquired through participation and observation over the course of life. Abelson was clear that acquiring scripts through observation could be vicarious and gave the example of reading.

Scripts are activated through recognizing similarities between a situation and previous experience. Once activated, scripts work to organize, make sense of, predict the outcome, or offer expectations for a specific context, situation, or event using the associated inferences. Enacting a script provides direction as to how a situation should be processed toward the end goal. Scripts rely on inferences made from norms of typical or standard situations, events, or contexts. Because enacted scripts are based on experiences outside the new situation, the script can be wrong and enacting it can lead to a violation of expectations. Beyond understanding the expectations, sequences, and roles of a situation, behaving or performing a script refers to taking on a role-specific situation.

Consider this variant of Schank and Abelson's restaurant script. When one goes to a restaurant, one knows several things: For instance, one goes to restaurants to eat, there will be some choice as to what we eat, and one will have to pay for the food and service. One also knows that not all restaurants are the same. When one goes to a new restaurant, one looks for clues as to how it works, whether one is expected to order at a counter, wait to be seated, or seat oneself, for example. The restaurant script allows one to make inferences about how the new restaurant will work in consideration of other experiences at restaurants similar to the new one.

Gender, Media, and Cognitive Scripts

Although there are several examples of gender roles being explicitly taught and enforced, the position that gender is learned through everyday sociocultural experiences is most prevalent. Because gender is pervasive, the scripts that one acquires through life experiences are encoded with gendered inferences. Gender emerges as a dimension of scripts that accounts for direction regarding which sex performs specific roles within a given script—masculine roles and feminine roles. One then tends toward enacting the roles with which the appropriate sex is associated. For example, in school at recess, boys might tend toward physical activity while girls might tend toward conversationally focused activity. However, gender scripts are not gender roles; rather, they are subscripts that prescribe who performs specific roles within a larger, context-bound script. Furthermore, gender scripts should not be confused with gender schemas. *Gender schema* refers to a base of knowledge pertaining to understanding gender, whereas *gender script* refers to a specific type of script that organizes experiences in such a way as to direct action along the lines of sex. Gender schemas are concerned with information, while gender scripts are focused on actions and goals. The role of gender scripts in child development has been of particular interest in research. As means of constituting gender, gender scripts implicate variants of social learning theory and social cognitive developmental theory.

As Abelson noted, scripts can be acquired from observing the experiences of others as well as vicariously through text. In all forms, the media portray people as characters in situations ranging from fictional to nonfictional. Whether partaking in mundane tasks of everyday life, fulfilling the duties of governmental offices, or even exploring space, characters are depicted navigating experiences and working toward goals. Through observing characters portrayed in the media, people are vicariously made privy to experiences. These experiences have similar potential to one's own with regard to the acquisition of cognitive scripts. In that respect, one learns how to do things that one has never done. If one should ever find oneself in such a situation, one can activate scripts acquired through the experiences of characters.

As in life, gender is pervasive in the media. In acquiring scripts from the media, people encode dimensions of gender into the scripts they form. When one activates scripts acquired through media observation, one recalls roles within scripts that have gendered implications. Just as cognitive script theory has engendered concern over violence in the media, there is also cause for concern pertaining to gender and the media.

Much research is conducted on the representation of gender in the media. Male characters often carry out stereotypically masculine gendered behavior. For instance, in conflict a male character might be portrayed as more aggressive or violent than a female character, who might be portrayed as more emotional or empathic. The implications of conveying such experiences are of interest when the situations that viewers observe might be parlayed into the acquisition of cognitive scripts. The script of conflict is then encoded with gendered roles. The media provide a location where cognitive scripts, with gender dimensions encoded into the roles, are acquired.

Derek Bolen
Wayne State University

See also Gender Schema Theory; Sexism; Social Inequality; Social Learning Theory

Further Readings

Abelson, Robert. "Psychological Status of the Script Concept." *American Psychologist*, v.36/7 (1981).

Carroll, John and John Payne, eds. *Cognition and Social Behavior*. New York: Lawrence Erlbaum Associates, 1976.

Levy, Gary and Robyn Fivush. "Scripts and Gender: A New Approach for Examining Gender-Role Development." *Developmental Review*, v.13/2 (1993).

Schank, Roger and Robert Abelson. *Scripts, Plans, Goals and Understanding: An Inquiry Into Human Knowledge Structures*. Hillsdale, NJ: Lawrence Erlbaum Associates, 1977.

Comics

The traditional comic book consists of narratives told in text placed within a series of brightly colored panels the sequentially depict the plot's action. Traditionally, these narratives have been printed on cheap newsprint sandwiched between glossy covers published in magazine format. Historically, comic books have been produced and consumed primarily by males. Consequently, the narratives featured in comics and the characters that populate them reflect mainstream masculine tastes. This gender bias is significant, given that the sociocultural influence of comic books extends far beyond the printed page to include books, films, and television series, as well as lunch boxes, toys, video games, and other merchandise.

The comic book medium can be traced to the Great Depression as the brainchild of entrepreneur Max Gaines, who saw the social need for, and the commercial potential of, inexpensive escapist entertainment. Initially, "the comics" were cheaply reproduced collections of "funnies" that had first appeared in newspapers. These were popular enough to warrant the development of original material, as there were not enough recyclable funnies to satisfy demand. Initially, new material consisted of stories conforming to the conventions of popular genres, such as hardboiled detective mysteries and "shoot 'em up" westerns, adapted to the comic book format. In February 1935, Malcolm Wheeler-Nicholson published the first comic book to contain all-new material, *New Fun*. This venture proved successful enough to prompt him to publish others, including *Detective Comics*, which was launched in 1937. Although financial difficulties forced Wheeler-Nicholson out of the comic book business, *Detective Comics* continued to be published, with its publisher adopting the name Detective Comics, Inc. (which became DC Comics). This publisher went on to become one of the giants in the industry.

Rise of the Superhero

In June 1938, a new genre, one especially suited to the possibilities and limitations of the comic book format, was introduced when DC Comics published the first Superman story in *Action Comics* #1, written by Jerry Siegel and drawn by Joe Shuster. That story created an enduring sensation and a mythic character that has spawned numerous imitations.

Following up on Superman's surprising commercial success, DC Comics introduced Batman in *Detective Comics* #27 (May 1939). Soon, other comic book publishers were rushing to produce their own versions of the costumed superhero, and the superhero genre came to dominate the medium.

During this early period in the history of comics (late 1930s to mid-1950s), called the Golden Age by comic book enthusiasts, the key conventions that now define the superhero were developed:

By definition, superheroes must possess inhuman powers that set them apart from the average person, such as super speed or strength; elemental, magical, psychic, or supernatural powers; the ability to fly; X-ray vision; elasticity; invisibility; and invulnerability. In the case of some superheroes, their powers are not inhuman per se but rather exceptionally well developed: for example, Green Arrow's archery skills or Batman's acrobatic talents and martial arts prowess. Other powers are the result of gadgets or technological enhancements, such as Iron Man's suit of armor. By definition, therefore, superheroes must be heroic. They should fight for good and against evil, protect the powerless and defend the oppressed, promote justice and remedy injustices.

Superheroes often have an origin story that explains how they obtained their powers. Some are aliens from outer space or members of exotic races. Some derived their powers through magic or science, obtained them through accident, or developed them through hard work. Often a tragic event is involved, as when the baby who becomes Superman escapes the planet Krypton just as it explodes, or when the young boy who grows up to become Batman witnesses the brutal murder of his parents. Most superheroes have a secret identity that allows them to retire from their public persona. Finally, the typical superhero wears a costume that is tight-fitting and often brightly colored. These costumes emphasize their heroes' well-developed physiques.

Women as Superheroes

The first female costumed superhero, the Woman in Red, appeared in 1940. Short-lived, her character generated little in the way of interest or sales. For the most part, during the Golden Age women were confined to certain strictly defined roles within comic book narratives that both reflected and supported hegemonic masculinity. They were depicted as hapless victims awaiting rescue, as bumbling incompetents who often created the dangerous situations from which they needed to be saved, as aggressive romantic predators pursuing male superheroes, or as passive admirers impatiently pining for them. In playing such roles, these women served to paint male superheroes in positive terms, as protectors of the weak and helpless and as objects of female desire.

The superhero genre might have remained an exclusively male domain if not for the introduction of Wonder Woman by DC Comics in *All Star Comics* #8 (December 1941). In January 1942, Wonder Woman was featured on the cover of *Sensation Comics* #1. This placement is a mark of the character's recognized commercial success, as comic book covers drive comic book sales. Wonder Woman was created by William Moulton Marston,

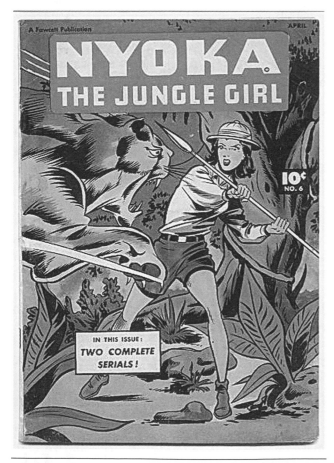

Nyoka the Jungle Girl, a character from the 1940's series *Jungle Girl*, was the frequent subject of comic books published by Fawcett. In 1940, the first female costumed superhero, the Woman in Red, made a brief appearance in comic books and was discontinued due to lack of interest. (Wikimedia)

a psychologist who argued that the comic book medium possessed unexploited educational potential. (Incidentally, Marston was also the inventor of the systolic blood-pressure measuring apparatus that was instrumental in the development of the polygraph, popularly referred to as the lie detector.) Like her male counterparts, Wonder Woman adheres to the conventions of the comic book superhero. She fights for good against evil. She possesses an impressive array of superpowers, including exceptional expertise in martial arts, the ability to deflect bullets with her Amazon bracelets, and skill in wielding her golden lasso, as well as super speed, stamina, and strength. In addition, Wonder Woman has her own origin story (she is an Amazon warrior, Princess Diana of Themyscira), a secret identity (Diana Prince), and a tight-fitting and brightly colored costume that is also quite revealing: The pants are short, and much cleavage is visible. In this respect, Wonder Woman established a salacious sartorial precedent followed by later female superheroes.

While enjoying enough commercial success eventually to merit her own comic title, Wonder Woman was not nearly as popular as other Golden Age comic book heroes, such as Batman, Captain America, Captain Marvel, and Superman. In part because of tepid consumer interest, she did not inspire many imitators. Although a rare female presence in a predominantly male world, she could claim a few female counterparts. During the Golden (late 1930s to mid-1950s) and Silver (mid-1950s to mid-1960s) Ages, female superheroes were mostly complementary companions to, and/or variations of, male popular superheroes, or they were members of superhero teams. Examples of complementary companions, who are related in some way to a male superhero, include superheroes' cousins (She-Hulk and Supergirl), daughters (Aquagirl), sisters (Mary Marvel), and wives (Hawkwoman), whereas variations include such obvious examples as Batgirl and the less well-known Batwoman.

The female superhero as a member of a mostly male team can be traced back to Wonder Woman, who in her long career belonged to several superhero groups, notably the Justice Society of America (from 1941) and the Justice League of America (from 1960). In the 1960s, Stan Lee, Steve Ditko, and other artists and writers working for Marvel Comics reinvented the standard comic book narrative by introducing complex superheroes, such as Spider-Man, who struggle with interpersonal and social problems in addition to fighting criminals. These included several female superheroes, most of whom were part of teams such as the Avengers (whose rotating roster has included, among others, Black Widow, Mockingbird, She-Hulk, Tigra, and the rehabilitated Scarlet Witch), the Fantastic Four (which included the Invisible Woman, wife of the team's leader, Mr. Fantastic), and the X-Men (whose original lineup included Marvel Girl). This strategy allowed for the inclusion of more female superheroes in comic book narratives without risking possible commercial failure by having them headline their own solo titles.

Female superheroes are not the only "super" women who inhabit comic books. The most enduring female comic book criminal, Catwoman, was introduced in *Batman* #1 (spring 1940). Catwoman is Batman's arch nemesis, a key love interest, and an occasional partner in fighting crime. Her character has enjoyed long-term popularity—so much so, in fact, that Catwoman has her own eponymous title, which is the mark of a top-tier comic character. Also suggestive of her popularity, she has not been confined to the pages of comic books but has appeared in film and on television, with iconic portrayals by such actresses as Eartha Kitt, Julie Newmar, Michelle Pfeiffer, and Halle Berry.

Superheroes Since the 1980s

The 1980s saw a significant shift in commercial comic book culture. Previously, comics had been mostly marketed as inexpensive impulse purchases in venues such as drugstores and newsstands, with only a few specialty stores focusing on their sales. As collectors began to pay substantial sums for rare older issues of their favorite comic books and adults with disposal incomes continued to purchase new issues, more comics shops entered the market. Consumer patterns indicated there was a market for comics with mature subject matter aimed at affluent and well-educated adults. As a result, established comics publishers reinvented traditional genres and popular heroes (as in Frank Miller's edgy *Dark Knight* version of Batman). In addition, new publishers entered the market offering subject matter and formats different from those previously available. A now classic example of this alternative comic trend is the black-and-white series *Love and Rockets*, created by Gilbert and Jaimie Hernandez and published

by Fantagraphics Books since 1982. Issues contain a mix of material, including stand-alone and serial stories, one of which, *Hoppers 13*, focuses on a recurrent cast of Chicano characters who inhabit a fictional town in southern California. This series has been nicknamed *Locas* (literally, "crazy women") because of the many eccentric women it features.

The first decade of the 21st century has seen the increased presence of female superheroes in comic book narratives, as well greater ethnic, linguistic, racial, and religious diversity among comic book characters. An example of this new diversity is the character of Dust, who is regularly featured in Marvel's *New X-Men: Academy X* series. She is an observant Sunni Muslim who wears a burka in public. The explicit expression of her Islamic faith is a radical departure from the conventional depiction of superheroes in the American popular media, whose religious affiliations, if any, play little role in defining them or driving plots.

The superhero genre has dominated comic book sales, reflecting the masculine bias noted previously. Although not nearly as commercially successful, other genres favored by males—horror, war, the western—have also tended to be popular. However, genres that appeal to female consumers have not proven as popular, such as romance comics, which emerged in the wake of World War II and continued to be published until the mid-1970s, when it became obvious to publishers that they could not compete with more mature treatments of romantic relationships then available to consumers in books, films, magazines, and television. Their inability to compete was due, in part, to self-imposed constraints placed on publishers in 1954 by the Comics Code Authority. The CCA was developed in response to criticism leveled against the medium by psychologist Fredric Wertham, author of the influential *Seduction of the Innocent* (1954), in which he claimed that the drug use, latent homosexuality, suggestive clothing, and violence depicted in comics were corrupting America's youth. As a result, the romance comic was rendered blandly pure and robbed of any emotional or sexual intensity, as is evident in the perennially popular titles featuring Archie and his Riverdale High School friends. In 2003, publisher Archie Comics obtained a cease and desist order to prevent an Atlanta-area theater company from mounting a play depicting Archie as gay. However, in 2010 the same publisher introduced an openly gay character,

Kevin Keller, indicating that comics continue to reflect and perpetuate the shifting biases and values of the culture in which they are printed and read.

Robert Westerfelhaus
Celeste C. Lacroix
College of Charleston

See also Children's Programming: Cartoons; Film: Hollywood; Gender and Masculinity: White Masculinity; Graphic Novels; Heroes: Action and Super Heroes; Patriarchy

Further Readings

Bongco, Mila. *Reading Comics: Language, Culture, and the Concept of the Superhero in Comic Books.* New York: Garland Publishing, 2000.

Pustz, Matthew J. *Comic Book Culture: Fanboys and True Believers.* Jackson: University Press of Mississippi, 1999.

Reynolds, Richard. *Superheroes: A Modern Mythology.* Jackson: University Press of Mississippi, 1994.

Robbins, Trina. *The Great Women Superheroes.* Northampton, MA: Kitchen Sink Press, 1996.

Wright, Bradford W. *Comic Book Nation: The Transformation of Youth Culture in America.* Baltimore, MD: The Johns Hopkins University Press, 2001.

CRITICAL THEORY

The Frankfurt School grew out of a group of political and cultural theorists that formed in the 1920s at the University of Frankfurt, Germany, which was called the Institute for Social Research. The leading Critical Theorists of this group include Theodor Adorno, Herbert Marcuse, Walter Benjamin, Max Horkheimer, and Erich Fromm. Later, Jürgen Habermas, who was Adorno's student, is identified as a second-generation Frankfurt School Critical Theorist. The Frankfurt School theorists referred to their cultural critique, which sought to change society, as Critical Theory. Critical Theory grew out of Marxism but abandoned the totalitarian turn of an economic determinist Marxism and infused Marxism with Freudian psychology and a focus on the culture industries. Many of the Frankfurt School theorists fled Germany in the 1930s after the Nazis seized their library. Adorno, Horkheimer, and others came to Columbia University in New York, where

they stayed until 1950. Fromm and Marcuse did not return to Germany. Benjamin committed suicide during an attempt to escape the Nazis from Paris to Spain in 1940.

Turning away from economic Marxism, the Critical Theory perspective studied the media and popular culture as economic forces that were central to creation and maintenance of the capitalist culture of consumption. When capitalized, *Critical Theory* refers to the Frankfurt School's particular brand of cultural, political, and economic critique, analyzing mass culture in order to challenge the status quo and change society. With lowercase letters, *critical theory* more broadly refers to all approaches to communication and culture studies that put forward a critique of the existing social system.

Critical Theory and Western Marxism countered the failed Marxism of the Soviet Union and responded to capitalism's increased monopoly structures and government intervention in the economy. Marx's theory of a revolutionary working class coming to power and the withering away of the state to create a socialist system had become unworkable after World War I created the opposite: international capitalism. The Frankfurt School theorized that culture industries had co-opted the working class. To counter this negative impact of mass culture, the Frankfurt School sought to liberate individuals from the use of reason as an instrument of domination. Critical Theory undertook the systemic study of society with the purpose of using social critique as a basis for praxis, or activist social change. Critical Theory also incorporated Freudian psychoanalysis into its social critique, as well as an attack on instrumental rationality.

At its heart, Critical Theory is concerned with ideology and false consciousness in relation to critical self-awareness. As Critical Theorists became concerned with cultural and ideological forces that thwarted revolutionary movements and furthered the system of domination, they turned to the problems of authority and mass culture. The Frankfurt School Critical Theorists were faced with the fact that capitalism had produced fascism and Nazism rather than a workers' revolution. Civilization had produced its opposite: barbarism. The Frankfurt thinkers argued that the dominated classes had been bought off by mass media. Their goal was to create radical philosophical consciousness against instrumental reasoning, commercialization, mass culture, and mass media as forms of political domination.

Horkheimer and Adorno introduced the concept of the culture industry in their seminal chapter, "The Culture Industry: Enlightenment as Mass Deception," in their classic work *Dialectic of Enlightenment*, first published in German in 1944 and in English in 1972. They wrote that art is degraded under capitalism, and the culture industry no longer needs to pretend to be art. The term *culture industry* reflected changes in communication technologies and capitalist economics in the 1930s and 1940s. The culture industry referred primarily to the merging of the capitalist entertainment and information industry and mass media to orchestrate the manipulation of production and consumption of goods. The culture industries are those social institutions that produce popular mass culture, such as television, books, radio, music, and movies. These media serve an ideological function, privileging capitalism and offering escapist trivialities. They also merge individuals with capitalism and produce consumer goods, so that the industries and ideologies are reproduced. In this grim assessment, which reflects a perspective of technological determinism, Horkheimer and Adorno showed how the culture industry influences ideology, how the management of leisure time manipulated individuals, and how individuals were encroached upon by mass culture.

Shaped by their experience under Nazism and Adolf Hitler, Adorno and Horkheimer focused on the dark side of the culture industry. They set themselves the task of discovering why humanity was sinking into a new barbarism. Material productivity offered the conditions for greater justice but allowed a minority to control and administer the technology, while most people were devalued. The authors described their theses as: Myth is already enlightenment and enlightenment reverts to mythology. The role of the culture industry, or the new media, was to aid the regression of enlightenment into myth and ideology.

For Horkheimer, mass communication was noncommunication, and the movie, book, and radio destroyed personal life. Adorno accused the culture industry of impeding the growth of independent individuals. Adorno also found that the culture industry transformed the critical negativity of art into shallow affirmation. The world was filtered through the culture industry and deadened, as mass media produced a retreat from enlightenment. The culture industry promised to universalize culture but instead led to the regression of civilization into barbarism. This negative assessment of the culture industry does not waver in Horkheimer and Adorno. Horkheimer attributed intellectual passivity to television and expressed resignation toward technology. Adorno found that television followed totalitarian creeds, even though the surface message was antitotalitarian. The members of the Frankfurt School emphasized the problems of the nearly universal false consciousness that they saw as the main product of the culture industries.

Art negates the influence of mass culture and offers the possibility of authenticity in individual life. In Marcuse's work, the media and mass culture are one factor that prevents the realization of utopia, where life is art. The media and mass culture justify the status quo and divert attention from the oppression exerted by the ruling class. This domination is largely psychological in Western democracies, where the media internalize false needs and false consciousness. The media and the culture industry threaten human liberation, as newspapers, film, radio, and television cut off communication, co-opt culture, and destroy subjectivity and privacy. Media also co-opt the aesthetic realm by making works of intellectual culture seem familiar, and high culture disappears. The media make radical thought and practice impossible. Genuine art is inaccessible to the public.

Benjamin was a German literary essayist whose idea of "technical reproducibility" of art was popularized in his seminal essay "The Work of Art in the Age of Mechanical Reproduction." Benjamin envisioned a more positive role for the culture industry in popularizing art, as well as a more negative role. Negatively, Benjamin argued that the age of mechanical reproduction had eliminated art's "aura" of "authenticity" because a reproduction lacks the art object's unique presence and its unique place. Benjamin further suggested that this destruction of tradition by removing the work of art from the original—he includes landscapes reproduced in photography and movies as examples—destroyed the historical aspect and authority of the artwork. More positively, the mechanical reproduction of art reactivates the artwork as it brings the work into the observer's own situation. Benjamin thought that the culture industry's mechanical reproduction and mass distribution of art could politicize art, making the culture industry a revolutionary force that could free mass culture. Younger Critical Theorists picked up on the hopeful side of Benjamin's analysis. Hans Enzensberger, for example, faults Critical Theorists for not being aware of the media's socialist possibilities as a challenge to capitalist culture.

A practicing psychoanalyst, Erich Fromm argued that the role of Critical Theory was to liberate individuals living in a capitalist society so that they overcome alienation and restore the capacity to relate fully to themselves, one another, and nature. Fromm follows Marx's understanding of labor as the expression of individuality. By opposing themselves to nature, individuals act on the world and change it, thereby changing and becoming themselves. Originally calling this function self-activity rather than labor, Marx later differentiated between free and alienated labor. Alienation develops as private property and the division of labor develops. Under capitalism, work loses the character of self-expression; labor and products assume an existence separate from the worker. People feel at home only in leisure time, which is more and more dominated by the culture industry.

Fromm was concerned with work that destroys individuality, making the individual a "slave of things." The alienated person who believes he or she has become the master of nature has become the slave of things. This alienation leads to the perversion of all values by making the economy the supreme aim of life. Through the culture industry, capitalism creates new needs in workers to exert an alien power over them. Fromm wrote that Marxism did not foresee the extent to which the vast majority of people would be alienated, especially the growing number of people who manipulate symbols and people rather than machines. "Symbol manipulators" are hired for "attractive personality packages" that are easy to control. In consumption, most people crave new things and are passive recipients, consumers alienated by things that satisfy false needs rather than true needs.

The task of Critical Theory was to make people aware of illusory false needs, which are as urgent and real as true needs from a subjective viewpoint. This will happen only when production serves people and capital ceases to create and exploit false needs. Unalienated people do not dominate nature but become one with it, are alive and responsive toward objects so that objects come to life, Fromm argues. In unalienated society, people would no longer be crippled by alienated modes of production and consumption, and people would begin to make living their main business rather than producing the means for living.

Paul Grosswiler
University of Maine

See also Cultivation Theory; Electronic Media and Social Inequality; Feminist Theory: Marxist; Ideology; Kellner, Douglas; Mass Media; New Media; Postmodernism; Radio; Social Media; Television

Further Readings

Benjamin, Walter. "The Work of Art in the Age of Mechanical Reproduction." In *Illuminations*, Hannah Arendt, ed. Translated by Harry Zohn. New York: Shocken Books, 1969.

Brantlinger, Patrick. *Bread and Circuses: Theories of Mass Culture as Social Decay*. Ithaca, NY: Cornell University Press, 1983.

Enzensberger, Hans. *The Consciousness Industry*. New York: Seabury Press, 1974.

Fromm, Erich. *Marx's Concept of Man*. New York: Ungar, 1961.

Horkheimer, Max and Theodor Adorno. *Dialectic of Enlightenment*. Translated by John Cumming. New York: Continuum, 1987.

Warren, Scott. *The Emergence of Dialectical Theory: Philosophy and Political Inquiry*. Chicago: University of Chicago Press, 1984.

Cultivation Theory

Cultivation theory is based on the belief that audience behaviors and attitudes are shaped by cumulative exposure to mainstream media, with an emphasis on television as a dominant social force in shaping public opinion. Developed by George Gerbner, the theory contends that perceptions about reality are the result of long-term, cumulative exposure to television. According to the theory, the process of socialization, or "acculturation," is largely influenced by television as a powerful storytelling medium that encourages viewers who watch it most gradually to accept the worldviews espoused on television as reality. As a result, viewers are encouraged to align their own attitudes, aspirations, and fears with the dominant themes and issues of the television world as they have been shaped and told by mainstream media producers. The hypothesis holds that the more audiences watch television, the more closely aligned their ideas and values are with those of television. Researchers have studied the extent to which television viewing alters the attitudes and behaviors in realms such as violence, politics, health, education, religion, sex roles, age roles, and more. Cultivation theory is particularly relevant to those interested in studying the long-term impact of mass-media exposure on gender attitudes and behaviors. The theory demonstrates the marginalization of women and minorities in television drama and the consistent victimization of women and minorities within the world of television violence.

The methodological approach to cultivation theory involves three main facets: (1) analyzing the institutional approaches that lead to the production of media messages, such as media ownership and production practices; (2) documenting the patterns that emerge from the stories and images that are represented in media content; and (3) correlating message exposure to the formation of audience beliefs and behaviors.

Although cultivation theory cuts across mainstream media genres and forms, research has focused primarily on news and on prime-time and daytime television drama. Television is viewed as an important socializing agent because it cuts across all ages, classes, and groups by offering a streamlined perspective on reality. The underlying reason for emphasizing the power of television over that of other mass media is that audiences continue to spend more time watching television than other media, and that the majority of people's leisure time is spent with this medium. Estimates indicate that on average, a television set is on for more than seven hours a day in the typical American household, and that individual family members consume four hours a day. In addition to its dominance in individual households, television provides the most widespread and influential ideological platform in a given society, thereby serving as a powerful cultivating force for learned attitudes and behaviors. In this regard, television is considered to be an important and persuasive audiovisual medium that reflects and distorts reality through its conventional storytelling. Cultivation theory argues that television's power comes from its ability to present a consistent and

unified set of cultural values and norms to a large viewing population.

Given television's importance in shaping attitudes and behaviors, cultivation analysis aims to analyze mass-media effects through a methodology that is different from that employed in other social scientific research. Unlike most effects research, which examines short-term behavioral changes in subjects who are exposed to isolated media messages in a clinical or lab setting, cultivation analysis aims to study the attitudinal and behavioral changes that emerge from cumulative, long-term television exposure within audience members' everyday lives. Whereas "stimulus-response" models of mass-media effects research encourage simple and linear relationships between media content and viewers, cultivation analysis seeks to analyze the cumulative consequences of television exposure in conjunction with the patterns that are representative of television content as a whole. Rather than isolate single programs, messages, episodes, series, or genres to see if they stimulate attitudinal or behavioral change, cultivation analysis analyzes the most recurring and stable patterns in television content by focusing on the themes, values, and issues that are consistently shown across media channels and genres. As such, the theory is predicated on observing consistencies in audience responses, such as maintenance of the status quo, inasmuch as it is interested in documenting shifts in the cultivation of common points of view as they correlate with mass media.

According to Nancy Signorielli and Michael Morgan, cultivation analysis tries to document whether variations in attitudes, values, and behaviors can be attributed to varied levels of television exposure independent of the social, cultural, and individual factors that distinguish light and heavy viewers. The goal is to provide evidence that high levels of exposure to television can significantly affect viewers' conceptions of social reality. Degrees of daily television exposure (light, medium, and heavy television consumption) are correlated with the beliefs and opinions expressed by audience members and then compared with the dominant views of the television world that have been documented. Variations in television exposure are assumed to generate differences in viewers' consciousness. That is, light viewers of television are more likely to be exposed to a variety of sources of information and experiences that shape their consciousness, whereas heavy television viewers are, by default, more likely to rely on television's influence to shape their perceptions.

Sexuality Stereotyping

Studies on sexuality stereotyping that use cultivation analysis validate concerns among feminist theorists that long-term exposure to misogynic or pornographic content cultivates and perpetuates a social system in which women's subjugation is tolerated and rendered inevitable. Findings indicate that college men who are heavily exposed to pornography are more likely to accept stereotypes associated with male and female sexuality. Likewise, males are more likely to agree with the notion that men have stronger and less controllable sexual urges than women. In contrast, women are perceived by men to be less likely to admit that they have sexual desires and are more likely to say "no" to sex when they do not really mean it.

Mean World Syndrome

Among its findings, cultivation theory has shown that audiences' perceptions of violence in their communities and the world are correlated with their intake of television culture. Described as the "Mean World Syndrome," the theory holds that the more viewers watch television drama and news, the more likely they are to believe that the world is a violent place. Explanations for this finding uphold cultivation's premise that consciousness is directly correlated with television's ability to amplify certain topics, issues, and genres over others. The Mean World Syndrome resonates with research that documents the steady increase in televised representations of violence over the past 40 years, leading to inflated and distorted public perceptions of real violence in response to violence shown on television. Social scientists have expressed concerns about the statistical disparity between real-world crime and televised crime, particularly since government figures have consistently reported a downward trend in societal violent crimes at the same time that representations of crime on television continue to rise. These disparities between real-life and televised violence have led to concerns about the political exploitation and public manipulation of the Mean World Syndrome, as politicians and authority figures allay public concerns about crime and safety through policy measures and legislation aimed at "fighting crime."

Women and minorities are particularly affected by this finding, as they are significantly more likely to be depicted on television as victims of crime who are reliant on authority figures to enact personal and societal safety by regulating crime.

Mainstreaming

In addition to the Mean World Syndrome, cultivation research has shown a connection between one's dependence on television for news and information and the adoption of "mainstream" or centrist political views. The mainstream of public opinion or thought refers to the common perspectives and values that television cultivates and that heavy television viewers develop after being exposed to a steady and consistent set of beliefs and images. According to this finding, differences in perspectives that would otherwise be attributed to variations in demographics, such as education, socioeconomic status, gender, race, and age, are diminished or missing from viewers who rely heavily on television content. This finding is important to those studying gender and media, as it correlates heavy viewing of television content with public opinion formation. Hence, if television content cultivates a patriarchal and misogynic view of women by marginalizing them from production and representation across genres and programming, it follows that heavy television viewers may develop negative perceptions about women and their role in society.

Julie Frechette
Worcester State University

See also Advertising; Audiences: Reception and Injection Models; Beauty and Body Image: Beauty Myths; Children's Programming: Cartoons; Critical Theory; Desensitization Effect; Electronic Media and Social Inequality; Film: Hollywood; Gay and Lesbian Portrayals on Television; Gender Media Monitoring; Mass Media; New Media; Reality-Based Television: *America's Next Top Model*; Reality-Based Television: Makeover Shows; Reality-Based Television: Wedding Shows; Sitcoms; Soap Operas; Social Construction of Gender; Telecommunications Act of 1996; Television; Televisuality

Further Readings

Gerbner, George. *Against the Mainstream: Selected Works of George Gerbner*, Vol. 1. New York: Peter Lang, 2002.

Gerbner, George. *Women and Minorities in Television Drama, 1969–1978: A Research Report*. Philadelphia: University of Pennsylvania, Annenberg School for Communication, 1979.

Morgan, Michael and James Shanahan. *Television and Its Viewers: Cultivation Theory and Research*. New York: Cambridge University Press, 1999.

Preston, Elizabeth Hall. "Pornography and the Construction of Gender." In *Cultivation Analysis: New Directions in Media Effects Research*, Nancy Signorielli and Michael Morgan, eds. Newbury Park, CA: Sage, 1990.

Signorielli, Nancy and Michael Morgan, eds. *Cultivation Analysis: New Directions in Media Effects Research*. Newbury Park, CA: Sage, 1990.

CULTURAL POLITICS

The term *cultural politics* refers to the milieu in which negotiations of power, dominance, and subjection take place. The theory addresses the ways in which culture is political and politics is cultural. As Stuart Hall clarifies, cultural politics is "the relationship between culture and power." The basis of cultural politics is a social constructionist perspective that views culture as created and sustained by everyday practices and representations. Culture is viewed as the entirety of human interactions and productions, rather than simply the "highbrow" notions of culture as elite artifacts and performances.

As Hall argues, politics is "decentered" in favor of analysis that views culture as an ongoing struggle between the dominant and subversive forces. Investigators of cultural politics interrogate power structures by arguing that individuals may subvert dominance through interpretations that create their own meanings but may still be subject to existing ideologies that limit their access, acceptance by mainstream culture, or ability to engage with political processes. Furthermore, politics is conceived of not as formal electoral processes but as the ongoing negotiations of power structures that determine representation, access, privilege, and agency.

Richard Maxwell argues that culture works in both formal political and institutional structures, as well as informal interactions. Through memory, economics, sport, geographic spaces, physical experiences, and material possessions, as well as cultural industries and mass media, culture may be produced for political ends. Culture may also be politicized through competing dominant and subversive narratives that negotiate hegemony. One challenge of studying cultural politics is to situate practices and representations in specific contexts, while also historicizing issues of power relations.

By conceiving of politics broadly as a negotiation between dominant and subversive forces, cultural politics, Hall argues, "is empowering and endangering, oppositional and hegemonic" in the sense that it is both practiced by individuals in collective interactions and prescribed by institutions. Cultural politics is therefore concerned with differences that allow for a diversity of interpretations and perspectives, but also as they are the basis for continued stereotyping and oppression.

Examinations of cultural politics are situated in cultural studies paradigms, particularly Marxist and/or Foucauldian theories and methods. Michel Foucault argues that power is disembodied, both everywhere and nowhere, and therefore does not repress but instead produces social structures, norms, and behaviors. The emphasis on understanding power relations when examining cultural politics is reflected in a rejection of traditional scientific research methods in favor of critical analysis, ethnography, and political economy. Critical analysis of media texts and other cultural artifacts and practices is wielded to illuminate representations of stereotypes, hegemonic norms, and inequalities in visibility. Reception studies and ethnographies allow for examinations of audiences' collective and individual identity formations as they negotiate dominant and subversive meanings in texts and in everyday practices. Finally, political economy is a lens through which institutional structures may be examined to trace the production of meanings that are influenced by economic forces, work relations, labor dynamics, and modes of distribution.

Cultural theorists also argue that the practice of exposing power structures through analysis of cultural politics also has political ramifications. The self-reflectivity often exhibited by scholars such as Foucault, Hall, Douglas Kellner, and many others represents an attempt to show the cultural politics of academia. Thus, investigations of cultural politics are often situated in the experiences and interpretations of the investigators themselves in efforts to foster transparency in research processes and the relationships between researcher and researched.

Mass Media

Scholarly attention has focused on the role of mass media in cultural politics. Cultural theory rejects binary distinctions between high and low culture, turning the critical lens toward mass media that had previously been dismissed as trivial. Advertising, popular entertainment, fandom, and virtual communities all constitute sites for the exploration of cultural politics. Investigators both focus minutely on the intricacies of specific texts and theorize more broadly about the interconnectedness of mass media and cultural politics.

On one hand, mass media often reinforce stereotypes and negative representations of race, gender, sexuality, ethnicity, and religion. For example, radical activism of all kinds tends to be marginalized in mainstream media, and feminism and female activists have historically received overwhelmingly negative media coverage. Media representations of identity serve to delineate cultural boundaries and define proper modes of political engagement, but these representations also mark certain peoples as being "better" citizens by virtue of embodying specific norms of hegemonic race, gender, class, nationality, and sexuality. On the other hand, scholars point to the potential for mass media to provide alternative images that might galvanize imagined communities or national unity, as may be the case with sports or images of patriotism in times of crisis. Collective sharing of media consumption may foster community, both interpersonally and virtually in cyberspace.

Mass media also promote capitalist consumerism, representing citizens as capable of participating fully in society by virtue of their purchasing power. As a result of this legitimization of consumerism as a vital form of political action, other forms of political engagement further marginalize traditional, public modes of social justice activism in favor of private consumer acts. Thus, promotion of consumerism and the act of consuming are politically motivated and constituting.

Personal and Political Dimensions

A central concern of cultural politics is to investigate the markers of inclusion that define citizenship and oppression. The daily practices and struggles in which people engage are subject to being politicized as well as capable of subverting dominant norms.

Cultural politics also addresses the ways in which private lives intersect with public discourses, thus rendering personal choices and behaviors political. In her exploration of Reagan-era national identity, Lauren Berlant argues that the cultural spaces have changed in recent decades to privilege private citizenship over public collective acts. Whereas feminists agitated for women's rights on the basis of bringing "personal" issues such as abortion and domestic violence into public discourses, Berlant argues that a backlash against progressive ideologies has provoked policing of family values and sexual relations in the name of protecting national interests. Berlant is concerned with the co-optation of private lives by conservative political powers as political terrain and the consequent interference of the state in those formerly private lives. The politicizing of what had previously been considered the domain of private lives comes full circle as private lives become expressions of political agendas and the lines between private, public, and political are obliterated.

Berlant examines the ways in which institutions are actively engaged in prescribing correct modes of living and being as involving personal consumption and habits that conform to hegemonic norms. Thus, access to full citizenship is dependent on sexual and familial choices as performances of civic duty. The result is a public sphere dominated by discourses wherein individuals' private lives become topics of public scrutiny and form the basis of political engagement.

The shift toward public political discourses of personal acts is also indicative of institutional pressures to marginalize and overlook activism that is defined as radical. Public protests are increasingly characterized in mainstream media as scary mob activity that misses relevant political issues and endangers the nation, whereas personal, private choices have become the "proper" outlet for pursuing political change.

Politicization of personal lives also extends to the politicization of emotions. As Sarah Ahmed points out, love may be used to support politics of exclusion and relies in part on socially constructed ideologies of ideal femininity, masculinity, and sexuality. Thus, the use of emotion to make political appeals to audiences seems to be effective in gaining at least implicit support, but does so by obscuring the hegemonic norms. Postcolonial critic Ann Stoler also expands Foucauldian analysis by considering sexuality, race, and power within the home (particularly the colonial home). Stoler argues that there were repeated, conscious efforts to maintain racial boundaries that would prohibit intimacy between colonizer and colonized. The interpersonal and institutionalized modes of racial discrimination also circulate in cultural artifacts and influence ideologies. It is worthwhile to note that Stoler draws on Foucault to define the domain of intimacy as a legitimate area of study, furthering the examination of personal lives and choices as political actions.

Spring-Serenity Duvall
University of South Carolina, Aiken

See also Empowerment; Hall, Stuart; Hegemony; Identity; Jhally, Sut; Kellner, Douglas; Mass Media

Further Readings

Ahmed, Sarah. *The Cultural Politics of Emotion*. New York: Routledge, 2004.

Berlant, Lauren G. *The Queen of America Goes to Washington City: Essays on Sex and Citizenship*. Durham, NC: Duke University Press, 1997.

Grewal, Inderpal. *Transnational America: Feminisms, Diasporas, Neoliberalisms*. Durham, NC: Duke University Press, 2005.

Jackson, Peter. "The Cultural Politics of Masculinity: Towards a Social Geography." *Transactions of the Institute of British Geographers, New Series*, v.16/2 (1991).

Maxwell, Richard. *Culture Works: The Political Economy of Culture*. Minneapolis: University of Minnesota Press, 2001.

Morley, David and Kuan-Hsing Chen. *Stuart Hall: Critical Dialogues in Cultural Studies*. New York: Routledge, 1996.

Stoler, Ann. *Race and the Education of Desire: Foucault's* History of Sexuality *and the Colonial Order of Things*. Durham, NC: Duke University Press, 1995.

Culture Jamming

Culture jamming, broadly defined, involves activist resistance to and rearticulation of cultural practices and media messages deemed detrimental in order to educate citizens and transform social practices. Adopting the practice of "detournement" (a French word meaning "turnabout"), culture jammers hoax corporate practices and products or spoof mass-media messages in a way that unveils hidden agendas or counteracts meaning in order to negate their impact or success. Jamming takes various forms, such as "subvertising" (parodies of advertising messages), product "reengineering," billboard resignification or "liberation," and public performance or protest. The latter is exemplified by the performance art collective Ant Farm, whose 1975 "Media Burn," a public event in which numerous television sets were simultaneously destroyed in order to critique the ubiquity of television in America, is widely credited as the first modern example of culture jamming.

The target of most jammers is cultural practices and media messages that support global capitalism, conspicuous consumption, and ecologically dangerous practices, but many culture jammers target racism and sexism as well. Barbara Kruger, for example, is a contemporary artist who uses multiple media elements to examine the links between gender and consumption. In one of her works, the slogan "Your Body Is a Battleground" was superimposed over media images in order to critique how the media and advertising perpetuate stereotypical representations of female beauty. More recently, culture jamming has been aimed at political parties and politicians, such as the group "Billionaires for Bush" which employs irony, spectacle, and counter-images to advance its critique of citizen-spectators while

The first modern example of culture jamming is thought to be collective art group Ant Farm's 1975 performance piece "Media Burn." The group created a pyramid of television sets, set it ablaze, and drove a car through the stack to critique the omnipresence of TV in the United States. (Photos.com)

agitating for political change. Cultural jammers have become increasingly sophisticated in their use of new media to both jam messages and disseminate their protests. Although jammers have mounted provocative and widely publicized campaigns against such major global corporations as Nike and Coca-Cola, more recently a number of critics have questioned the efficacies of culture jamming and its ability to effect cultural transformation.

The roots of the term *jamming* can be found in the historical practice of factory workers in Europe at the beginning of the 20th century, who, as a means of protesting working conditions or wages, would throw their wooden clogs, or *sabots*, into the machinery, thereby jamming, or *clogging*, the works in an act of *sabotage*. A more recent root of the word comes from amateur citizens' band (CB) radio operators who would illegally "jam" transmissions of fellow CBers, radio signals, and the audio tracks of television broadcasts.

Historically developed out of a critique of advertising, particularly advertising's depiction of women and minorities, organizations such as Adbusters, the internationally well-known Vancouver-based magazine, reinterpret brands to undermine meaning. For example, "Joe Camel" becomes "Joe Chemo," hooked up to an intravenous feed, or images of impossibly thin female fashion models are "skulled" to link them to disordered eating behaviors. One Manhattan-based feminist collective, the Barbie Liberation Organization (BLO), formed in 1989 in response to the increasingly sexist messages in media and culture. The BLO, in one highly publicized prank, purchased hundreds of best-selling Barbies and G.I. Joes, switched their voice boxes, and returned them to the stores, where they were purchased over one Christmas season by unsuspecting shoppers. When unwrapped and activated, the G.I. Joes girlishly exclaimed, "Math class is tough," "I love shopping," and "Let's plan our dream wedding," while Barbies gutturally intoned, "Eat Lead, Cobra" or "Vengeance is mine!"

The Guerrilla Girls, another New York–based group of media activists, comprises feminist artists and art world professionals who wear gorilla masks to protect their identities while engaging in feminist resistance to patriarchal representations of gender in art and the historical exclusion of women artists in the West. Formed in 1985, the group has more than 80 posters, public performances, and hoaxes to its credit,

many of which are detailed in its highly successful published manifestos, *Confessions of the Guerrilla Girls* and *The Guerrilla Girls' Bedside Companion to the History of Western Art*. The group, according to Gloria Steinem, "symbolizes the best of feminism in this country, . . . smart, radical, creative, funny and uncompromising and (I assume) diverse under those inspired gorilla masks, they force us to rethink everything from art to zaniness" (*Confessions of the Guerrilla Girls*, back cover, 1995).

While not explicitly feminist in their orientation, Adbusters, established in 1989, claims that its mission is "to advance the new social activist movement of the information age. Our aim is to topple existing power structures and forge a major shift in the way we will live in the 21st century." Adbusters is well known for trenchant jamming of the iconic Absolut Vodka advertising campaign, in which the product is depicted as everything from "Absolut Perfection" (the bottle pictured with a halo) to "Absolut Larceny" (broken chains with the bottle missing, presumably so desirable that it was stolen). Adbusters re-envisioned this campaign through such subvertisements as "Absolut Hangover" (the bottle pictured in the form of a noose) or "Absolut Impotence" (the bottle pictured with the neck in a flaccid or limp state). An Adbusters parody of Calvin Klein's "heroin chic" ads of the mid-1990s features a female model hunched over a toilet, vomiting, presumably to maintain her waifish figure. The ad tells viewers that women are dissatisfied with their own bodies because "the beauty industry is the beast."

Although perhaps the most well-known culture jamming collective, Adbusters' single-minded focus on anticonsumerism has come increasingly under attack for its failure to address how consumer culture is impacted by various hierarchies of power and privilege that shape articulations of race, class, gender, and sexuality. Failure to address these hierarchies, critics argue, makes these forces and their perpetuation incomprehensible while implicitly naturalizing them by "demonstrating" that the simple act of critique levels the playing field.

Since the World Trade Organization protests in Seattle in 1999, media activists have used new media not only as the site of media events but also as a means to coordinate their actions and build audiences for their protests. Web pages, e-mail lists, blogs, wikis (open-editing software), and sites such as YouTube have become central to sharing information, organizing protests, producing documents and artifacts, and disseminating results. Indymedia.org has been particularly influential as a Web-based clearinghouse and organizer of protest-related material and events for culture jammers.

Although potentially sympathetic to their goals, many critics of culture jamming note how the political agenda of jammers risks becoming either lost in the "counterculture fun" or co-opted by the very market forces—advertising companies and media messengers—that jammers spoof. Increasingly ironic in tone, modern mass media have a penchant for incorporating savvy, cutting-edge satire into its self-presentation. Conversely, the techniques employed by jammers do not always connect with larger political movements, such as feminism, and thus do not directly confront the power of the corporations and organizations that produce the messages being targeted by jammers. Finally, consumers may be satisfied with having "gotten the joke" and may feel, as a result, that their political activism need not extend to such activities as protesting, donating, voting, boycotting, or volunteerism.

Susan Mackey-Kallis
Villanova University

See also Guerrilla Girls; Hacking and Hacktivism; Kruger, Barbara; Lasn, Kalle; Postfeminism

Further Readings

Branwyn, G. *Jamming the Media: A Citizen's Guide to Reclaiming the Tools of Communication*. San Francisco: Chronicle Books, 1997.

Carducci, V. "Culture Jamming: A Sociological Perspective." *Journal of Consumer Culture*, v.6/1 (2006).

Chung, S. and M. Kirby. "Media Literacy Art Education: Logos, Culture Jamming and Activism." *Art Education*, v.62/1 (2009).

Demo, A. "The Guerrilla Girls; Perspective by Incongruity, and Feminist Resistance." *Women's Studies in Communication*, v.23 (2003).

Dery, M. *Culture Jamming: Hacking, Slashing and Sniping in the Empire of the Signs*. Westfield, NJ: Open Media, 1993.

Dunbar-Hester, C. "OurSpace: Resisting the Corporate Control of Culture." *Rhetoric and Public Affairs*, v.13/1 (2010).

Farrar, M. and J. Warner. "Rah-Rah-Radical: The Radical Cheerleaders' Challenge to the Public Sphere." *Politics and Gender*, v.2 (Fall 2006).

Guerrilla Girls. *Bitches, Bimbos, and Ballbreakers: The Guerrilla Girls' Illustrated Guide to Female Stereotypes*. New York: Penguin, 2003.

Guerrilla Girls. *Confessions of the Guerrilla Girls*. New York: HarperPerennial, 1995.

Guerrilla Girls. *The Guerrilla Girls' Bedside Companion to the History of Western Art*. New York: Penguin, 1998.

Harold, C. "Pranking Rhetoric: 'Culture Jamming' as Media Activism." *Critical Studies in Media Communication*, v.21 (2004).

Harris, A. "Jamming Girl Culture: Young Women and Consumer Citizenship." In *All About the Girl: Culture, Power, and Identity*, A. Harris, ed. New York: Routledge, 2004.

Lasn, Kalle. *Culture Jam: How to Reverse America's Suicidal Binge*. New York: Quill, 1999.

Raizada, K. "An Interview With the Guerrilla Girls, Dyke Action Machine (DAM!), and the Toxic Titties." *NWSA Journal*, v.19/1 (2007).

Sandlin, J. "'Mixing Pop (Culture) and Politics': Cultural Resistance, Culture Jamming, and Anti-Consumption Activism as Critical Public Pedagogy." *Curriculum Inquiry*, v.38/3 (2008).

CYBERDATING

Cyberdating, or online dating, has come to be understood as the use of particular Websites to find people for romantic or sexual encounters or relationships. These sites, commonly called dating Websites, allow users to search for others with whom they think they would be compatible. Dating Websites typically have users fill out a profile describing themselves for the benefit of other users who will come upon them while browsing or searching. New mobile technologies allow these and other technologies for dating and sex to be available wherever a mobile device travels and a network signal is available.

Dating Websites have their antecedents in the conceptions of cybersex, or computer dating on the early Internet. Even before users widely navigated through the online world through the World Wide Web, the Internet's architecture allowed for social uses of the medium. Multi-user dungeons, bulletin boards, chat rooms, Internet relay chat, and other ways for people to congregate and communicate on the early Internet allowed users to develop rapport with one another. Often, these interactions allowed users to develop computer-mediated attractions to

The Oxford Internet Institute surveyed 12,000 couples worldwide with access to the Internet to determine how many had used online services to look for their partner during the time period 1997 to 2009. The study showed that 30 percent of those people had used dating Websites in 2009, an increase from 6 percent in 1997. (Photos.com)

or relationships with other users. The early Internet allowed people to experience relationships and sex virtually, without touch or physical intimacy.

As the Web interface for the Internet became the standard way of experiencing the Internet, the medium began developing an emphasis on communicating information via visuality. Thus, cybersex has slowly eroded as the dominant way of thinking about the relationship between the Internet and dating and sex. Now, as social networking sites, scanning software, and amateur photography and videography allow people the opportunity to upload and share visual representations of themselves online, the dominant mode of social networking online is visually based.

Most dating Websites allow users to create a profile for themselves. Central to this is the profile picture, which is often part of a gallery of images that show the user in various situations and states. Dating Websites allow users to create profiles with pseudonyms, not unlike instant messaging handles or e-mail aliases. The dating Website profile usually allows users to describe themselves in a free-response section of the profile. Other fields may be available for users to describe more fully themselves, the type of relationship or sexual experience they are seeking, their ideal partner, their typical night out, or their favorite books, television programs, and movies. Often, there are questions that can be answered with predetermined choices, such as age, body type, height, marital status, sexual orientation, gender, smoking, drinking, attitude toward pets, "level" of relationship (long-term, friendship, or casual sex), and, sometimes, desired attributes in a mate. In the case of sites specifically designed for sexual pursuits, penis size, fetish types, human immunodeficiency virus (HIV) status, and other sex-related fields are made available. Often, these predetermined answers preclude the expression of bisexual and transgender identities.

Dating Websites, thus, are large databases of people looking for relationships or sex. Different sites allow these databases to be searched differently, and the database structures often are a symptom of what the perceived user wants out of the site and greatly affect the way that users browse or search for potential mates. Most sites allow for geographical searches based on gender and sexual orientation, but the other fields available for searching often differ from site to site.

Websites that have taken hold of the public imagination of dating and sex online are largely sites that charge for membership. Often this membership will allow for complete access to a site. Other times, membership will allow access only to most functions or simply the browsing functions of a site. For some sites, there is a fee to be able to contact other members, and membership will allow only greater search functionality and guaranteed placement of the member's profile in relevant search results.

As social networking and "connected" users are more accustomed to being constantly connected to a social network or, through mediated communication, with at least one other person at most times in their day, users on sites where nonmembers cannot communicate back are often misread as purposefully nonresponsive, when reasons for nonreply may be other than disinterest. The reason for this nonreply could be the relatively high cost of a membership for the user. The obvious ways to subvert this membership requirement for communication have led these sites to strip information from the free-response fields of user profiles that give other means of communication (such as e-mail) outright. Alternatively, the pay structures dividing members and nonmembers may differentiate how the database can be searched by the two groups, along with other limitations for nonusers, while communication possibilities remain intact.

Most sites present users with selections after using search parameters to limit the field of profiles to browse. When search results come back, they lead with a photo and some statistics. This is the model of sites like Match.com. The Internet classified ads megasite Craigslist.org allows for personal Websites that are chronologically arranged by time of posting and expire, similar to the personal ads in newspapers that allow users to place ads for limited amounts of times. The Craigslist personals allow users to attract other users with enticing headlines that encourage other users to click. On the ad's page, the user can upload photos. Ads are organized by gender of posting user and the type of responder the user is seeking, such as "long-term relationship." The site also lists "missed connections," which target specific people whom the posting user saw but did not follow through with in the physical world. Other sites, like eHarmony.com and Chemistry.com allow users to form a psychological profile. Users are connected based on the compatibility tests developed by psychologists. Other sites, like the database for online sex and relationships Nerve.com, are part of a syndicated dating Website network that allows one database to serve under a number of different domain-name banners.

As social networking sites like Myspace and Facebook began to take a hold of the market of online communication, both sites featured search mechanisms that allowed users, through an advanced search, to look for users with a relationship status, sexual orientation, or special interests that the searcher found desirable. As these social networking sites have matured, though, these advanced search features no longer allow for such easy uses of the search functions and database

structures of these Websites. This does not mean that social networking sites are no longer used for purposes of finding people for dating or sex, only that meeting people outside one's network of social ties and specified interests has become more difficult.

Not all sites are marketed to a general clientele or user base. As Larry Gross and others have noted, the Internet has allowed for much community and identity formation among lesbian, gay, bisexual, and transsexual/transgender (LGBT) people. Dating sites allow users looking for gay and lesbian relationships and sex to do so. As many scholars of queer studies have noted, dating sites often serve as an online gay bar, where users can be sure they are approaching queer users. Although lesbian and gay users can use sites like Match.com, some sites, like eHarmony, which was established by a Christian psychologist, have not allowed gay members in the past. Many gay sites, especially those for gay men, are gay-exclusive, and these sites often include a more sex-oriented database organization, where nude photos often proliferate. Some dating sites target communities for whom dating within is important. Thus, ChristianMingle.com and Jdate.com serve the Christian and Jewish singles communities, respectively, and Shaadi.com allows South Asian users and those in the diaspora to find mates with an interface that allows users to be arranged by their families.

Bryce J. Renninger
Rutgers University

See also Blogs and Blogging; Cyberspace and Cyberculture; New Media; Online New Media: GLBTQ Identity; Online New Media: Transgender Identity; Pornification of Everyday Life; Pornography: Gay and Lesbian; Pornography: Heterosexual; Pornography: Internet; Sexuality; Social Media; Social Networking Sites: Facebook; Social Networking Sites: Myspace; Virtual Sex

Further Readings

Arvidsson, Adam. "'Quality Singles': Internet Dating and the Work of Fantasy." *New Media Society*, v.8/4 (2006).

Campbell, John Edward. *Getting It On Online: Cyberspace, Gay Male Sexuality, and Embodied Identity*. New York: Routledge, 2004.

Heino, Rebecca D., Nicole B. Ellison, and Jennifer L. Gibbs. "Relationshopping: Investigating the Market Metaphor in Online Dating." *Journal of Social and Personal Relationships*, v.27/4 (2010).

CYBERPUNK

Cyberpunk is a term used to describe a subgenre of science fiction popularized in the mid-1980s by novels such as William Gibson's *Neuromancer* (1984) and films such as Ridley Scott's *Blade Runner* (1982). The word was coined in a short story by Bruce Bethke titled "Cyberpunk" and published in 1983. Cyberpunk fiction is marked by an attention to how digital and cybernetic technological innovation alters the human condition. This recurring theme is frequently explored via plots, settings, and characters that hark back to hard-nosed detective novels of the 1920s and 1930s as well as the noir films of the 1940s and early 1950s. Starting in the early 1990s, a cyberpunk subculture formed, in part in response to the intersection of ideas about technology found in cyberpunk fiction and real-world technological change.

Most cyberpunk fiction is dystopian and finds socially marginalized main characters addressing the consequences of technology run amok. Murder, drug use, prostitution, and war are all common tropes in the genre, as is technological enslavement, networked neurosystems, and urban decay. Popular examples of cyberpunk fiction include novels such as Gibson's *Sprawl* trilogy (1984–88); *Snow Crash* (1992), by Neal Stephenson; and *Islands in the Net* (1988), by Bruce Sterling. Cyberpunk fiction can also be seen in films such as *Tetsuo, the Iron Man* (1989), *Dark City* (1998), the *Matrix* trilogy (1999–2003), and *Hackers* (1995). Cyberpunk narratives are usually understood to be postmodern, in that they often deliberately blur the lines between reality and fiction, are presented in a fragmented manner, and make many references to popular culture. Most narratives are fast paced, complex, and full of technical jargon. In addition, because of its connection to classic crime stories and noir, characters often use language and engage in activities that are usually associated with culture from the first half of the 20th century, even though most cyberpunk plots take place in the future.

Gendered representations in cyberpunk fiction can be understood as fluid and ambiguous, since many characters choose to perform, define, or change their identities through technological means. However, although gender can be fluid, it is also common for characters to use technology to attain hypermasculine or hyperfeminine ideals of physical appearance or emotional character. For example, Dani Cavallaro

Costumes from the cyberpunk science-fiction film *Blade Runner* are on display at the Science Fiction Museum and Hall of Fame in Seattle. Cyberpunk plots are often set on Earth, and gender is generally ambiguous as characters can change or augment their bodies and gender using fictional technology. (Wikimedia)

has explained that the character of Molly in Gibson's *Neuromancer* undergoes both sexual and financial hardships in order to get visual implants and weapons grafted onto her body, making her an archetype for many other women characters in the genre. Women in cyberpunk are often placed in situations in which their reproductive or sexual qualities are threatened to be replaced by technology, so augmenting their natural bodies with cybernetics is seen as a pathway to attaining a culturally valued femininity.

Masculinity in cyberpunk is shaped by augmentation as well. In films such as *Terminator* (1984) and *Robocop* (1987), testosterone-fueled bodybuilders portray cybernetic machines that represent the pinnacle of masculine physicality, often driving human males to incorporate technology into their bodies in order to stand with or against them in combat. These human/machine hybrids are known as cyborgs, and they are prominently featured in cyberpunk fiction, usually functioning to address cultural anxieties about an increased reliance on technology across modern medicine. In addition, Samantha Holland has argued, cyborgs can be seen as a critique of the constructed, mechanical nature of both the body and ideas about gender in postmodern culture.

Outside fiction, cyberpunk culture has several defining characteristics. Like the "punk" music subculture referenced in the term, cyberpunk culture is usually understood as rebellious and critical of mainstream popular culture. Specifically, cyberpunks rebel against popular uses for technology, choosing instead to find alternative ways to use modern innovations. In this way, cyberpunks have much in common with hackers and crackers (though, unlike hackers, cyberpunks are not necessarily knowledgeable about how and why technology works as it does). Cyberpunks embrace a certain technophilia and will sometimes present themselves in a way that highlights their immersion in the culture. Technological implants, wearable electronics, and clothing, makeup, ornamentation, and hairstyles that mimic those found in visual forms of cyberpunk media are all part of cyberpunk culture. Cyberpunk culture has also at times been fairly and unfairly associated with techno and industrial music, raves, gothic dress, hacktivism, anarchistic politics, body modification culture, online role play, cybersex, and any number of other uncommon computer-based activities. The most famous cyberpunk culture publication was the magazine *Mondo 2000* (1989–98), which addressed many of these topics and regularly featured new cyberpunk fiction, fashion tips, cyberpunk film reviews, and other areas of interest to the subculture.

David S. Heineman
Bloomsburg University of Pennsylvania

See also Culture Jamming; Cyberspace and Cyberculture; Cyborg; Hacking and Hacktivism; New Media; Online New Media: GLBTQ Identity; Online New Media: Transgender Identity; Postmodernism; Video Gaming: Representations of Femininity; Video Gaming: Representations of Masculinity; Video Gaming: Violence; Virtuality

Further Readings

Cavallaro, Dani. *Cyberpunk and Cyberculture: Science Fiction and the Work of William Gibson*. London: Athlone Press, 2000.

Holland, Samantha. "Descartes Goes to Hollywood: Mind, Body, and Gender in Contemporary Cyborg Cinema." In *Cyberspace/Cyberbodies/Cyberpunk: Cultures of Technological Embodiment*, Mike Featherstone and Roger Burrows, eds. London: Sage, 1995.

Leblanc, Lauraine. "Razor Girls: Genre and Gender in Cyberpunk Fiction." *Women and Language*, v.20/1 (1997).

Rucker, Rudy, R. U. Sirius, and Queen Mu. *Mondo 2000: A User's Guide to the New Edge*. New York: HarperPerennial, 1992.

CYBERSPACE AND CYBERCULTURE

The concepts of cyberspace and cyberculture refer not only to the many types of communication and content that have developed by fusing the Internet with a variety of devices but also to their producers and users, as well as the values that are being built on line. The prefix *cyber* denotes "piloting" or "governing" and was originally used in the word *cybernetics*, defined by Norbert Weiner in 1948 as the science of control and communication in the animal and the machine. *Cyberspace* refers to the skeleton of the Internet, comprising new communication media, from its infrastructure to its social use, while *cyberculture* embraces the set of practices, attitudes, modes of thought, and values that have grown along with cyberspace.

Cyberspace

The term *cyberspace* was coined by William Gibson in his novel *Neuromancer* (1984), in which he envisioned it as a graphical representation of data abstracted from the banks of every computer in the human system. By referring to the new medium of communication that arose through the global interconnection of computers, cyberspace describes the nonphysical field created by computer systems and the users who navigate and nourish it.

Every day, an increasing number of people gain access to the Internet. According to Internet World Stats' "Internet Usage Statistics," as of mid-2011 the number of users had grown nearly 450 percent since the year 2000. Most Internet users were from Asia (44 percent), followed by Europe (22.7 percent) and North America (13 percent). The rest of the users were distributed between Latin America and the

Caribbean (10.3 percent), Africa (5.7 percent), the Middle East (3.3 percent), and Oceania/Australia (1 percent). In 2011, the Internet's penetration in the world was nearing 30 percent. Therefore, in a world population of nearly 7 billion persons, there are approximately 2 billion Internet users.

Although it is important to remember that many people still do not have a role in cyberspace, the spread of wireless communication technology around the world is provoking a surge of horizontal networks of interactive communication, whereby millions of people share messages both synchronous and asynchronous, via e-mails, chats, short message service (SMS, popularly called texting), blogs, video logs (vlogs), podcasts, wikis, and the like. By being part of networks and by acceding to the huge and diverse content available on the Internet, these people can share information. Access to the Internet has made it possible to purchase a variety of goods and services, study for a degree, and search for a job. These facilities offer both women and men more autonomy.

Cyberculture

Cyberspace has led to the establishment of a cyberculture that comprises both material and intellectual technologies, practices, attitudes, modes of thought, and values where people from many different geographic locales, cultures, and backgrounds, and hence with different values, can coexist and communicate. Cyberculture finds utterance through practices such as global sharing, distributed creation, social networking, streaming, mass collaboration, collaborative assessment, social bookmarking, and cloud computing. These routines encourage commitment, participation, and empathy, making us irrevocably involved with and responsible for one another and provoking experiences lived in cyberspace that influence the way we think, the way we form communities, and our very identities. By using social networks, by accessing virtual worlds, and by publishing their ideas on blogs or Websites, people share their thoughts, allowing others to know them. Therefore, users who are far from each other geographically can come closer by sharing a message through the multiple tools and devices available.

Pierre Lévy situates the core of cyberculture in the fact that it embodies a new universality not based on the fixity and independence of signification but instead built and extended by interconnecting messages through virtual communities, provoking the continuous renewal of the meanings and the performance of a collective intelligence whereby people share their individual expertise in order to meet shared goals and objectives.

It must be remembered, however, that many people are not engaged in cyberculture—not just because they do not have access to the Internet but also because the governments of the countries in which they live may impose restrictions on access to Internet content. Empirical research carried out by the OpenNet Initiative in 2006 found evidence of technical filtering in 26 of the 40 countries that were analyzed, with "women's rights" being one of the categories subject to this Internet filtering. Although users of the Internet tend to generate resources to face and counter such obstacles, designing tools to allow people access to forbidden Websites, the research is a reminder of the interplay between the virtual and physical/political worlds and the importance of taking into account the multitude of human agents who not only invent, produce, and use but also interpret technologies.

Cyberculture and physical culture are thus constantly feeding back to each other. Both dimensions continuously interact, not just because all cultures, people, organizations, and enterprises hold a stake in the construction of cyberculture but also because of the variety of the devices that allow us to have ubiquitous connectivity, making the Web present and accessible throughout our physical world, from our desktops to our pockets to our cars.

Construction of Gender in Cyberspace

Gender is a dynamic concept, constantly redefined by its performance in different contexts, and new technologies and their users have played a significant role in today's construction of gender. The lack of political boundaries in cyberspace facilitates and encourages conversations among people who belong to different cultures. With the ease of communication in cyberspace and the interactions of people who have different attitudes, behaviors, and customs, the concept of gender has broadened.

Women in particular have found ways to use the Internet to better their situations. For example, women who live in isolated regions can now access information and opportunities that, without the resources available through cyberspace, would not be possible. In 2000, research by the Pew Research Center for its Internet and American Life Project found that women use cyberspace to establish and maintain relationships, and a study by Brian Solis in 2009 found that online services such as Facebook, Flikr, FriendFeed, DocStoc, Myspace, and Twitter were used more often by women than by men.

The possibilities that women and men have for communicating, for creating groups related to their interests, and for addressing issues that concern them make cyberculture a revolutionary mode of communication in contrast to the dominant, one-way broadcast mode of the 20th century, in which few people had a voice. Different ideas and types of content now have visibility, and more people have access to a multitude of resources to inform and satisfy their varied interests. Cyberculture thus plays an important role in the pursuit of gender equality by allowing women and men from different places of the world to share their ideas, thoughts, and experiences.

Gloria Gómez-Diago
Rey Juan Carlos University, Madrid

See also Audiences: Producers of New Media; Empowerment; Gender Media Monitoring; Massively Multiplayer Online Role-Playing Games; Media Globalization; Minority Rights; Multi-User Dimensions; Social Construction of Gender; Social Inequality; Social Media; Social Networking Sites: Facebook; Social Networking Sites: Myspace; Twitter; Web 2.0; Wiki; YouTube

Further Readings

Bruneau, Tom. "Empathy." In *Encyclopedia of Communication Theory*. Thousand Oaks, CA: Sage, 2009.

Buzzanell, Patrice M., Hellen Sterk, and Lynn H. Turner. *Gender in Applied Communication Contexts*. Thousand Oaks, CA: Sage, 2002.

Castells, Manuel. "Communication, Power and Counter Power in the Network Society." *International Journal of Communication*, v.1 (2007). http://www.itu.dk/stud/speciale/specialeprojekt/Litteratur/Castells_2007%20-%20Communication%20power%20in%20the%20network%20society.pdf (Accessed October 2010).

Deibert, Ronald, John Palfrey, Rafal Rohozinski, and Jonathan Zittrain, eds. *Access Denied: The Practice and Policy of Global Internet Filtering*. Cambridge, MA: MIT Press, 2008.

Gibson, William. *Neuromancer*. New York: Ace Science Fiction, 1984.

Haraway, Donna. "A Cyborg Manifesto: Science, Technology, and Socialist-Feminism in the Late Twentieth Century." In *Simians, Cyborgs, and Women: The Reinvention of Nature*. New York: Routledge, 1991.

Internet World Stats. "World Internet Users and Population Stats." http://www.internetworldstats.com/stats.htm (Accessed October 2010).

Lévy, Pierre. *Cyberculture*. Minneapolis: University of Minnesota Press, 2001.

McLuhan, Marshall. *Understanding Media: The Extensions of Man*. New York: New American Library, 1964.

Pew Research Center. "Tracking Online Life: How Women Use the Internet to Cultivate Relationships With Family and Friends." May 10, 2000. http://www.pewinternet.org/Press-Releases/2000/Tracking-online-life-How-women-use-the-Internet-to-cultivate-relationships-with-family-and-friends.aspx (Accessed October 2010).

Solis, Brian. "Revealing the People Defining Social Networks." October 1, 2009. http://www.briansolis.com/2009/10/revealing-the-people-defining-social-networks/?utm_source=twitterfeed&utm_medium=twitter (Accessed October 2010).

Turkle, Sherry. "Looking Toward Cyberspace: Beyond Grounded Sociology—Cyberspace and Identity." *Contemporary Sociology*, v.28/6 (1999).

CYBORG

A cyborg is a cybernetic organism, an entity that is a hybrid of organic material and machinery or technology. Manfred Clynes and Nathan Kline first proposed the term *cyborg* in considering how to adapt humans to the environment of space travel, rather than adapting the environment to the needs of the body. In a sense, most living humans are already cyborgs, to the degree that they are technologically modified organisms. Individuals who use prosthetic limbs, pacemakers, pain pumps, and such commonplace enhancements as eyeglasses, contact lenses, and hearing aids would technically fall into this category. Few individuals today exist as purely organic individuals who have remained technologically and mechanically unaltered from the womb. However, there are other elements of cyborg life that have less to do with the physical embodiment of the cyborg than with the connection to information systems.

Feminists have challenged patriarchal and phallocentric ideals, calling attention to how the physical body (sex) is often presumed to be the defining factor in a person's gender. More recently, feminists have also drawn on the idea of the cyborg as a liberatory concept, suggesting that one way to escape issues of sexual inequality is to escape sex itself, assuming a posthuman, or cyborg, body that defies categorization into clear binaries. This has led to a strand of cyberfeminism that exults in the potential subversion of power structures through technology. The clearest incarnation of this stance is found in the often quoted final line of Donna Haraway's essay, "A Cyborg Manifesto: Science, Technology, and Socialist-Feminism in the Late Twentieth Century": "Though both are bound in the spiral dance, I would rather be a cyborg than a goddess." For Haraway, what makes the cyborg particularly useful is its postmodern nature, that it is neither male nor female, and that it challenges traditional binaries. Some have critiqued Haraway's notion of the cyborg, arguing that it assumes a privileged, Western, educated stance and that cyborg life is not necessarily a liberatory condition of being. Others observe that despite Haraway's celebration of the end of dualities, she instead reinforces other dualities.

Although often used metaphorically in feminist discourse, the notion of the cyborg has become almost commonplace in popular culture, especially in science fiction. Images of the Borg in *Star Trek: The Next Generation* (1987–94) and of Darth Vader in the *Star Wars* movies (1977–2005), as well as films such as *The Terminator* (1984), *Blade Runner* (1982), and *Robocop* (1987), depict a decidedly dystopian view of the cyborg as at once dangerous, murderous, and imbued with a deep disdain for weaker species such as completely organic humans. Indeed, many films, such as the *Matrix* series (1999–2003) and *The Terminator* depict technology's eventual war and victory over humankind—a notion that goes back to Fritz Lang's 1927 film *Metropolis*, complete with its own feminine robot.

Some films and television shows demonstrate a particularly feminine view of the dangers of cyborg existence, such as the Borg, with its queen and hive mind. Others depict female cyborgs, or gynoids, mainly as sex objects either for their creators' pleasure or for sale, as in the case of *Cherry 2000* (1987) and Pris in *Blade Runner* (1982). Perhaps the ultimate dystopian vision of the female cyborg is found

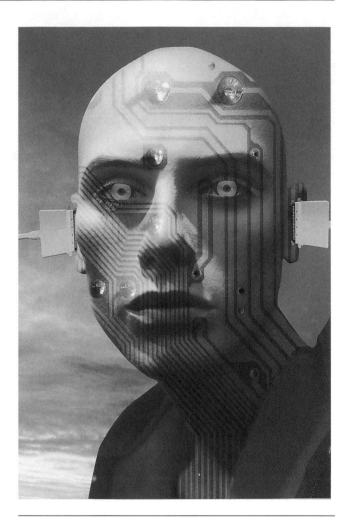

While the concept of a cyborg, a being composed of both human and artificial matter, is still a fictional creature, today's human beings are often technologically and mechanically altered from their original state. (Photos.com)

in *The Stepford Wives* (1975), in which intelligent, independent women are replaced by subservient, submissive gynoids. However, there are also strong feminine cyborgs in popular culture, such as Molly in William Gibson's cyberpunk novel *Neuromancer* (1984), T-X in *Terminator 3: Rise of the Machines* (2003), and the 1970s television series (reprised in 2007) *The Bionic Woman* (although the latter seemed mainly to be a spinoff of *The Six Million Dollar Man*).

Still, some cyberfeminists maintain a hope that technology can erase harmful social phenomena such as racism and misogyny. For example, Haraway argues that communication and biotechnologies can provide a means of restructuring existing social structures and power dynamics for women. By altering one's body, one can, in essence, alter one's world. Such an impulse can also be seen in other futurists. Stelarc, a performance artist whose work has explored the nature of the body as it relates to prosthetics and information technologies, declares that the body is "obsolete." Many of these futurists, including Haraway and Stelarc, observe that it is not merely the mechanical elements of cyborg existence that bear promise but also information technologies.

All of this points to a desire for a posthuman future in which the body is overcome through technology. This notion can be found in popular culture as well. For example, the protagonists in Gibson's cyberpunk novels profess a disdain for the "meat" and exult in the disembodiment of cyberspace, sentiments that are shared by the hacker community as seen in The Mentor's "The Conscience of a Hacker," commonly referred to as the "Hacker Manifesto." In other words, true liberation from the problems of the world can be found in the realm of cyberspace. Connection with individuals while removing the biological markers of race, sex, gender, and class is viewed as a potential means by which society can progress. This ambiguity is the hope of cyberfeminists who have adopted Haraway's vision of the cyborg. Still, despite the potential for individuals to exist in a world devoid of gender and physical identifiers, it is clear that even as individuals have become more connected through information technologies, such embodiment has not moved toward hybridity—as can be observed through the ubiquitous query in chat rooms, "a/s/l?" (What is your age, sex, and location?).

In short, the ideal of the cyborg is taking place, although perhaps not as some scholars would hope. To see the beginnings of cyborg existence, one need only look to the ubiquitous need for connection, the Bluetooth headsets that are continually at the ready for incoming information, the desire constantly to broadcast information about one's day through Twitter, Facebook, and other social media networks. People already willingly integrate technologies into their bodies through plastic surgery, joint replacements, and prosthetics. Perhaps such actions are not viewed as cyborg existence because they do not measure up to the complete integration found in popular media, but when carefully considered, many people have already become part machine and technology and part flesh. In other words, the technological embodiment of cyborg life seems already to be here. Whether or not such embodiment has the liberatory potential imagined by cyberfeminists, however, remains to be seen.

Brett Lunceford
University of South Alabama

See also Cyberpunk; Cyberspace and Cyberculture; Feminism; Identity; Postmodernism; Virtuality

Further Readings

Clynes, Manfred E. and Nathan S. Kline. "Cyborgs and Space." *Astronautics* (September 1960).

Graham, Elaine. "Cyborgs or Goddesses? Becoming Divine in a Cyberfeminist Age." *Information Communication and Society*, v.2/4 (1999).

Haraway, Donna Jeanne. "A Cyborg Manifesto: Science, Technology, and Socialist-Feminism in the Late Twentieth Century." In *Simians, Cyborgs, and Women: The Reinvention of Nature*. New York: Routledge, 1991.

Mentor, The. "The Conscience of a Hacker." *Phrack*, v.1/7 (1986). http://www.phrack.org/issues.html?issue=7&id=3#article (Accessed October 2010).

Millar, Melanie Stewart. *Cracking the Gender Code: Who Rules the Wired World?* Toronto, ON: Second Story Press, 1998.

Paffrath, James D. and Stelarc, eds. *Obsolete Body: Suspensions: Stelarc*. Davis, CA: J P Publications, 1984.

DESENSITIZATION EFFECT

The term *desensitization effect* has been used to describe numbing in response to repeated exposure to media and real-life violence. Research on desensitization shows that continued exposure to violence may result in the lessening of typical cognitive, emotional, behavioral, or biological responses to violence. Desensitization has been studied in relation to violence, specifically sexual violence, and in varying types of media such as television, film, music, advertisements, and video games. Continued exposure to sexually explicit and violent materials has been hypothesized to create a desensitization of traditional values, shifting them toward a cultural climate that is tolerant of sexual violence against women.

Systematic desensitization, or exposure therapy, has been used as a form of clinical treatment to encourage patients to become more comfortable with situations that would normally provoke anxiety. Unintentional desensitization, as it applies to media consumption, operates much the same way as clinical therapy; viewers of violence in media become desensitized over time to violence that would typically create anxiety or cause them to become uncomfortable. Intentional systematic desensitization may allow viewers to cope with repeated exposure to stimuli that otherwise may be too overwhelming; however, unintentional desensitization of gendered violence and abuse through media can be damaging to society and can reinforce negative gendered stereotypes. Desensitization can disrupt moral evaluation of sexualized violence, as viewers do not fully absorb that which they are viewing.

With repeated exposure, portrayals of domestic violence or sexual abuse that once may have seemed shocking to viewers become less startling and viewers become more accepting of them. Once desensitized, viewers may lose empathy for the victims of violence and believe that acts of violence are inevitable. Although both men and women are affected by desensitization, research has revealed gender differences in desensitization effects of sexual violence. Men exposed to stereotyped images of gender and sexuality in film, television, and advertisements have been shown to become more accepting of types of violence such as rape and domestic violence. Desensitization has also been shown to affect children and adolescents.

Desensitization is studied as either a short-term, immediate effect or a long-term, gradual effect after continuous or repeated exposure to violent media. Emotional desensitization has been studied by means of individuals' reports of concern or empathy for victims of violence. Cognitive desensitization has been studied by considering individuals' changes in attitude and perception about what is "violent." Behavioral effects have been examined by looking at individuals' own aggression and acts of violence or their willingness to take action to prevent real-world violence against others. Physiological changes have been measured by factors such as individuals' pulse and heart rate when viewing violent media.

Research in the 1970s and 1980s began to show that repeated exposure to violence displayed on television could lead to individuals' desensitization to subsequent exposures of violence. For example, a research study by Margaret Thomas and colleagues found that children and college students exposed to fictional violence were less responsive to subsequent viewings of real-life violence portrayed on news or in film. Erica Scharrer found that frequent consumption of local news, which often highlights violent acts, also led to desensitization in response to real-life violence.

Desensitization effects have also been found in violent film viewership, particularly regarding sexual violence against women. Daniel Linz and colleagues found that male viewers of a series of R-rated violent films were less sympathetic toward and more judgmental of alleged rape victims in a fictitious trial than were viewers of nonviolent pornographic films. Similarly, Carol Krafka, Linz, and other colleagues found that women who viewed violent or sexually violent films were less sensitive toward alleged rape victims and did not view the rape act as seriously.

Later research on desensitization effects has focused on the effect of rap music and music videos. For example, Linda Kalof at George Mason University found that exposure to sexually violent music videos and sexual stereotypes led to adversarial sexual beliefs, pitting partners against each other as opponents. Other research has shown that teenage girls exposed to rap music become more accepting of teen dating violence.

Researchers have focused on the desensitization effects of sex and violence in video games. For example, Nicholas Carnagey and fellow researchers found that individuals exposed to violent video games for a period of 20 minutes were less affected by scenes of real violence that followed immediately after. Brad Bushman and Craig Anderson extended this research to show that individuals exposed to violent video-game play were less likely to help actual victims of violence or perceive the violent act seriously. Jeanne Funk and fellow researchers found that the active nature of violence in video games created stronger desensitization effects than the effects experienced from other forms of media, such as television, movies, and the Internet.

Resensitization, the process whereby individuals regain sensitivity to violence, can occur after removing exposure to violent media. Less is known about the resensitization process. Charles Mullin and Daniel Linz found that individuals who had become desensitized to domestic violence through repeated exposure to sexual violence in films regained sensitivity for domestic violence victims after five days without exposure to sexually violent media.

Lucinda Austin
University of Maryland

See also Pornification of Everyday Life; Video Gaming: Violence; Violence and Aggression

Further Readings

Bushman, Brad and Craig Anderson. "Comfortably Numb: Desensitizing Effects of Violent Media on Helping Others." *Psychological Science*, v.20/3 (2009).

Carnagey, Nicholas, Craig Anderson, and Brad Bushman. "The Effect of Video Game Violence on Physiological Desensitization to Real-Life Violence." *Journal of Experimental Social Psychology*, v.43/3 (2007).

Funk, Jeanne, et al. "Violence Exposure in Real-Life, Video Games, Television, Movies, and the Internet: Is There Desensitization?" *Journal of Adolescence*, v.27/1 (2004).

Kalof, Linda. "The Effects of Gender and Music Video Imagery on Sexual Attitudes." *Journal of Social Psychology*, v.139/3 (1999).

Krafka, Carol, Daniel Linz, Edward Donnerstein, and Steven Penrod. "Women's Reactions to Sexually Aggressive Mass Media Depictions." *Violence Against Women*, v.3/2 (1997).

Linz, Daniel, Edward Donnerstein, and Steven Penrod. "Effects of Long-Term Exposure to Violent and Sexually Degrading Depictions of Women." *Journal of Personality and Social Psychology*, v.55 (1988).

Mullin, Charles and Daniel Linz. "Desensitization and Resensitization to Violence Against Women: Effects of Exposure to Sexually Violent Films on Judgments of Domestic Violence Victims." *Journal of Personality and Social Psychology*, v.69/3 (1995).

Scharrer, Erica. "Media Exposure and Sensitivity to Violence in News Reports: Evidence of Desensitization?" *Journalism and Mass Communication Quarterly*, v.85/2 (2008).

Thomas, Margaret, Robert Horton, Elaine Lippincott, and Ronald Drabman. "Desensitization to Portrayals of Real-Life Aggression as a Function of Exposure to Television Violence." *Journal of Personality and Social Psychology*, v.35/6 (1977).

DISCOURSE ANALYSIS

Discourse analysis is a commonly used qualitative research method in humanities and social sciences. Despite its common usage, there is not a single definition of discourse and there is not a single way to conduct a discourse analysis. However, precisely because there is not a rigid methodical parameter, discourse analysis offers the researcher flexibility, unlike other methods, such as the quantitative method content analysis and the qualitative method narrative analysis. In media studies, discourse analysis can be applied to analyze media contents from news reports to movie dialogues; it can also be used to analyze audience response gathered from interviews and online forums.

A traditional definition of *discourse* is a formal piece of spoken or written text on a certain topic. Two examples are an expository essay and an after-dinner speech. In linguistics, discourse is a unit of analysis, as in the discourse of vocabularies used by bilingual children. Discourse also refers to a body of texts of the same conventions, such as broadcast news discourse or sports discourse. In the 1980s, French philosopher Michel Foucault's notion of discourse (*discours* in French) heavily influenced the understanding of the term in Anglo-Saxon academia. Foucault argued that discourse has to be understood historically. Therefore, a news report about sexual assault is more than a three-minute news story. The news story has to be situated in the conventions of broadcast news (for example, the capacity of news anchors to sound authoritative and knowledgeable) and in the historical construct of the subjects, the attacker and the victim (for example, women of loose morality may be said to deserve sexual violence and attackers may be considered unable to help their sexualities).

Because of the different definitions of discourse, there are different ways to conduct a discourse analysis. Here three ways are reviewed. First, some applied linguists, such as Norman Fairclough, analyze the linguistic choice of a discourse in order to examine how the choices construct an ideology. For example, news reports often use passive voice in a sexual assault story: "A woman is attacked" is more commonly used than "A man attacked a woman."

The linguistic choice simultaneously reflects and constitutes a patriarchal ideology in which the language obscures a real gender relation. When a sentence lacks a subject, it is unclear who and which gender attacked the woman.

Second, some researchers draw on methods such as ethnomethodology and conversation analysis to analyze a discourse. Harold Garfinkel founded ethnomethodology to uncover social norms and conventions in daily interactions. In daily life, social actors respond to verbal interactions without questioning the meanings of words. For example, in response to a conventional "good morning," researchers would question what the interlocutors mean by "good morning." Conversation analysis examines the stylistics used in a conversation. Researchers record and transcribe a conversation and examine issues such as sequence and preference, interruption and silence. For example, in a conversation about sexual violence, one interlocutor may say, "News reports tend to give too many details about what the victim wears." The response can be, "I agree" (a preferred answer) or "I disagree" (a "dispreferred" answer). Research commonly shows that women tend to give preferred answers more than men do. Men also tend to interrupt others more often, and women tend to be silent after being interrupted.

Third, researchers who adopt Foucault's definition of discourse collect and analyze discourses that constitute the topic of sexual assault. For example, in addition to news reports about sexual assault, researchers look at court rulings, police reports, and sex education materials, as well as films, music, and literature about sexual violence. Researchers attempt to reach a contemporary meaning of sexual assault through history.

Despite the varieties of discourse analysis, analysts commonly recognize the importance of language in constructing a reality. When social actors actively make linguistic and stylistic choices in spoken and written discourses, they construct a form of reality. To discourse analysts, language is not merely a tool to reflect reality. Most often, social actors adhere to social norms and conventions, hence perpetuating the dominant ideology. Nevertheless, precisely because language has the power to construct reality, it can also be used to make transformative changes. For example, the adoption of the word *survivor* to replace "victim" is an example of how word choice may empower people who have been sexually assaulted.

The flexibility of discourse analysis allows researchers to uncover deeper meanings in media texts. This flexibility does not exist in rigorous methods such as content analysis. In the 1970s, content analysis was a popular method to examine gender stereotypes in media texts. However, this method tends not to problematize the relations between sex, gender, and meanings. Very often content analysis reinforces gender ideology by codifying gender as a limited set of characters (for example, femininity is expressed in certain professions and attires).

The boundary between discourse analysis and textual analysis is not clear cut. While some see "discourse analysis" as an umbrella term that includes textual analysis, some argue that "textual analysis" is the umbrella term in which discourse analysis is included. Suffice it to say that discourse analysis not only can be applied to a wide array of spoken and written discourses in the media but also can be used to analyze audience responses gathered through interviews and online forums. For example, by recording a conversation among college students about sexual assault in news reports, researchers may find out how social actors construct their sense of gender through linguistic and stylistic use. Discourse analysis is not effective to examine discourses that are visually rich. For example, an advertisement that prominently uses images may be better analyzed from a semiotic perspective.

Micky Lee
Suffolk University, Boston

See also Media Rhetoric; Post-Structuralism; Quantitative Content Analysis; Semiotics; Textual Analysis

Further Readings

Fairclough, Norman. *Discourse and Social Change.* Cambridge, UK: Polity Press, 1992.

Fairclough, Norman. *Language and Power.* London: Longman, 1989.

Fairclough, Norman. *Media Discourse.* London: Edward Arnold, 1995.

Foucault, Michel. *Discipline and Punish: The Birth of the Prison.* New York: Vintage, 1995.

Garfinkel, Harold. *Studies in Ethnomethodology.* London: Polity Press, 1991.

Gill, Rosalind. "Discourse Analysis." In *Qualitative Researching With Text, Image and Sound*, Martin W. Bauer and George Gaskell, eds. London: Sage, 2000.

Hutchby, Ian and Robin Wooffitt. *Conversation Analysis: The Study of Talk in Interaction.* Cambridge, UK: Polity Press, 1998.

DIVERSITY

Promoting diversity among those who work in the news media with the goal of fostering more inclusive coverage is a notion rooted in the civil turmoil of the 1960s, when mainstream media outlets were criticized for failing to cover African American neighborhoods adequately. The Kerner Commission, investigating urban violence in Detroit, Newark, and elsewhere, argued in 1968 that local newspapers and television stations were overlooking and underserving impoverished and frustrated citizens in their own communities. Decades later, the intrinsic value of diverse newsrooms and inclusive coverage is a media given, but the concept has taken on new urgency. Industry leaders say that it represents both good business sense and good journalism for the racial, ethnic, and gender composition of print and broadcast journalists to reflect the makeup of the communities they cover. Although a mountain of scholarship has long pointed to lags in the inclusiveness of media coverage of women and underrepresented racial and ethnic groups, professional organizations of newsroom executives and working journalists express a commitment to multicultural diversity—if not always gender parity—through initiatives, awards, and well-publicized tallies of the industry's employment figures. A host of associations of women journalists and journalists of color profess a dedication to closing the inclusiveness gap.

Since the 1970s, the American Society of News Editors (ASNE) and the Radio and Television News Directors Association (RTNDA) have separately monitored newsroom progress in employing journalists who are Hispanic, African American, Asian American, or Native American. RTNDA has tracked employment of women from the inception of these efforts, and its auxiliary foundation's Newsroom Diversity Project promotes recruiting and training aimed at bringing more women and people of color into, especially, broadcast news management. ASNE's diversity goals are focused on hiring, promoting, and retaining newspaper journalists of color; it has tallied employment figures for women journalists only since 2000. It urges that newsrooms become as diverse as the nation's population by 2025—a significant extension of the target date of 2000 that it initially set in 1978.

Percentages of Journalists of Color Declining

Employment ratios of journalists of color are slipping in both broadcast and print media amid waves of industry layoffs that have cost thousands of journalists their jobs. ASNE reports that the nation's full-time newsroom workforce has fallen by 25 percent since 2001. Television stations employ larger percentages of historically underrepresented journalists than do newspapers, yet, RTNDA acknowledges, its figures fall well below parity with the nation's estimated populations of color, 34 percent.

In 2009, 21.8 percent of television journalists were Hispanic, African American, Asian American, or American Indian, compared with 23.6 percent in 2008. The comparable drop in radio newsrooms was from 11.8 percent to 8.9 percent, RTNDA reports. On the other hand, women made record gains in television newsrooms in 2009 to represent 41 percent of the television workforce and 29 percent of news directors.

Among the nation's newspapers, journalists of color held an estimated 13.3 percent of the 41,500 full-time jobs in 2009 as editors, reporters, copy editors, and photographers—a ratio that has moved incrementally down from a high of 13.9 percent in 2005, ASNE figures show. The larger a newspaper's circulation, the larger its percentage of journalists of color; hundreds of papers with circulations below 50,000 have no journalists of color at all. The shrunken newspaper workforce is roughly equal to the number of full-time print journalists that ASNE tallied back in 1978, when only an estimated 4 percent of journalists were people of color. The organization reports that women in 2009 represented 36.6 percent of newspaper journalists, a ratio that has remained roughly stable. Some 16.3 percent of women staffers were journalists of color in 2009, compared with just 11.5 percent of male staffers. A small collection of online-only news operations appears to be more racially and ethnically diverse than mainstream newsrooms; about 20 percent of these staffs were minority-group journalists.

Although the figures lag behind parity with the nation's growing minority populations, newsrooms clearly are more self-consciously integrated today than when the Kerner Commission identified media disinterest in troubled urban neighborhoods and called for newspapers and broadcast stations to hire more African American journalists to generate insightful community reporting. Still occasionally citing the commission's tongue-lashing, industry executives have paid heed to the call to cover all Americans better. Some have sought, day-to-day, to make multiculturalism second nature in newsrooms and on airwaves. National Public Radio and its local stations regularly air shows with a multicultural bent, such as *Latino USA* and *Tell Me More*, hosted by Emmy Award–winning journalist Michel Martin, an African American. Since the mid-1980s, the Gannett company has required reporters at its now 100 newspapers, including *USA Today*, to seek out comments from members of underrepresented groups to quote in their daily stories. The company in 2006 reported that staffing at 39 of its newspapers matched the diversity of the populations they served; the number fell to 33 papers the following year as staffing shifted and populations grew.

Journalists Take Initiative to Promote Diversity

More than two dozen journalism associations specifically represent women, people of color, and gays and lesbians in the print and broadcast industries. Especially notable is UNITY: Journalists of Color, an alliance of 10,000 members that encompasses four major associations of Asian American, African American, Hispanic, and Native American journalists. UNITY's Website explains that the alliance is dedicated to fostering fair and accurate coverage of people of color, as well as "aggressively challenging the industry to staff its organizations at all levels to reflect the nation's diversity."

The big umbrella organizations—RTNDA in conjunction with UNITY, and ASNE in tandem with Associated Press Managing Editors—annually bestow awards recognizing leadership in diversifying newsrooms and content. ASNE also honors newspapers that achieve newsroom parity with their circulation populations. An annual ASNE journalism competition includes the category of "Diversity Writing," which generally attracts stories on issues of immigration, race, and ethnicity. Ilia Rodriguez, in examining stories written by winners and finalists in the diversity category, found that most strove to explain the concerns of other racial and ethnic groups to predominantly white audiences. Stories tended to document the struggles of individuals to align their lives with European American core values, Rodriguez found. Within this framework, journalists addressed social tensions and inequalities tied to class, race, and ethnicity and, to a lesser degree, highlighted gender and class conflicts. What was missing, reported Rodriguez, was a recognition that cultural values of nonwhites could conflict with an "American dream" norm or examinations of how established economic and political structures might perpetuate inequities. Perhaps in line with this, *Covering the Community*, a diversity handbook written by Leigh Stephens Aldrich primarily for print journalists, asserts that themes of multicultural coverage ought to support a sense of American unity. Aldrich urges reporters to avoid perpetuating stereotypes and story biases by asking themselves if they would have written about white males in the same way.

Americans Think the Poor and Muslims Get Unfair Coverage

Despite all the professional attention to notions of diversity, pluralities of Americans believe that coverage of impoverished people and Muslims has been too negative, the Pew Research Center for the People and the Press reported in 2010. Pluralities also think that coverage of African Americans and Hispanics is generally fair, yet many other respondents consider it unduly negative as well. Whereas 44 percent find the tone of African American coverage appropriate, 36 percent do not. Similarly, 41 percent think coverage of Hispanics is fair, but 35 percent believe it is too negative. On the other hand, 57 percent of respondents agree that whites receive generally fair coverage, and 56 percent think that the middle class does.

Although the twin goals of diverse newsrooms and diverse coverage have been linked since the days of the Kerner Commission, some scholars question how closely the two really match. Diverse employment in newsrooms may create only an "illusion of inclusion," some research suggests. Further, Kristina Widestedt in 2008 found that diversity policies of U.S. and foreign broadcasting companies emphasized racial and ethnic diversity while minimizing the desirability of gender parity. The two goals ought to be entwined, she asserts, noting that gender is shared within groups as well as between groups. Organizations such as Media Report to Women observe that even though women's bylines have approached parity with men's in some outlets, women remain underrepresented in the news, especially as experts and authority figures. Marjan de Bruin and Karen Ross explain that, despite a rising "body count" of women journalists, newsrooms have persisted in taking a macho approach to defining and gathering news, perhaps because long-standing newsroom values mesh with masculine norms. Still, a 2009 study, based on interviews with African American and Hispanic journalists at mainstream American newspapers, found that journalists of color could act as newsroom watchdogs to help ensure more representative stories, even though newsroom norms explicitly prohibit advocacy.

Rebecca LaVally
California State University, Sacramento

See also Network News Anchor Desk; Newsrooms; Prejudice; Racism; Radio; Sexism; Stereotypes; Talk Shows; Workforce

Further Readings

de Bruin, Marjan and Karen Ross, eds. *Gender and Newsroom Cultures: Identities at Work*. Cresskill, NJ: Hampton Press, 2004.

Lind, Rebecca Ann. *Race/Gender/Media: Considering Diversity Across Audiences, Content, and Producers*. Boston: Pearson, 2004.

Nishikawa, Katsuo A., et al. "Interviewing the Interviewers: Journalistic Norms and Racial Diversity in the Newsroom." *The Howard Journal of Communications*, v.20 (2009).

Rodriguez, Ilia. "'Diversity Writing' and the Liberal Discourse on Multiculturalism in Mainstream Newspapers." *The Howard Journal of Communications*, v.20 (2009).

UNITY: Journalists of Color. "Unity's Mission." http://www.unityjournalists.org/mission/index.php (Accessed October 2010).

DOANE, MARY ANN

Mary Ann Doane is an American film theorist whose work in feminist film criticism shifted the focus from representations of women in cinema to analyzing how filmic depictions of women target the female spectator. Working from the assumption that as an aspect of a patriarchal society, the Hollywood film bases its construction of the gaze as male, Doane examined the effects of filmic identification on women. Her prominent works in this area of film criticism, beginning in the early 1980s, thus moved the subject of the gaze from men to women, notably through her work in analyzing and categorizing women's films of the 1940s using analytic tools provided by psychoanalysis, namely, the theories of Sigmund Freud and the French psychologist Jacques Lacan. Of import to Doane's and other feminist film theorists' work is how femininity and the woman signify absence or negation in relation to the man.

In terms of subjects and objects of the gaze, the patriarchally based world of cinema and Hollywood film privilege men in both roles; women who appear serve only as objects of the gaze, as Laura Mulvey explicated in her influential essay on the male gaze, upon which Doane bases her departure from the male-spectator perspective. Scopophilia, the "love of looking" underlying the pleasure derived from voyeurism, had been reserved for men, namely in the context of men looking at women. Within the context of patriarchy, the insistence of looking on the part of women poses a threat. In *Femmes Fatales*, for example, Doane notes that because the intellectual woman, whose cognitive mastery becomes further underscored by the wearing of eyeglasses, looks and analyzes, she serves as countertype to the feminine object of the male gaze and thus threatens the established, patriarchal system of representation.

In Doane's collection of essays on female spectatorship and cinematic discourse, *The Desire to Desire: The Woman's Film of the 1940s*, she defines the woman's film and organizes its subgenres, using psychoanalysis as a method by which to interpret the psychical operations of the cinema and cultural conventions depicted in film as reflective of a gendered society during World War II, when women's incursion into the working world posed a threat to ideals of femininity. The woman's film as genre does not constitute one in a technical sense in terms of thematic content, iconography, or narrative structure; these films can include thrillers, films noirs, melodramas, or love stories. Rather, the woman's film attempts to engage female subjectivity by addressing the female spectator. The woman's film thus refers to movies about women created for women; they dealt

with a female protagonist contending with female issues—the family, children, and self-sacrifice. It is thus the ways in which the female viewer identifies with and approaches the active female character that provide the basis for Doane's treatment of the female viewer–female character relationship and its resultant forms within the woman's film genre.

Given the male-based structures of cinematic narrative, the lack of distance that results when a woman watches another woman creates several problems, which Doane outlines in terms of the subgenres reflecting psychoanalytic theories that define the feminine as pathological. Doane addresses four subgenres of the woman's film, each characterized by a corresponding psychoanalytic condition. Films of medical discourse replaced the erotic gaze with the medical gaze; the narrative involved a male doctor treating a female patient, whose external symptoms of disease or defect belie an internal, mental illness, corresponding to hysteria, wherein a woman is betrayed by her own body. The female body/object of gaze is framed as pathological, in the same way that disease and the feminine are socially devalued or undesirable. The maternal melodrama, which Doane refers to as the familiar "weepie," features the real or threatened separation of a mother and child, resulting in depictions of masochism. The classic love story centers on female desire and the consequences of desire for women in patriarchy; the instrument of closure in such films is the woman's death, especially if she commits adultery. Women waiting serves as a recurrent theme of the love story, symbolizing women's roles as outsiders, excluded from the active world of male-dominated politics and business. The gothic or paranoid woman's film features a female protagonist who has hastily married, only to suspect either correctly or incorrectly that her new husband is trying to murder her. Invoking elements of the gothic novel such as locked doors in a large, forbidding house and a secret involving family history or the husband himself, Doane utilizes the Freudian concept of paranoia, the conviction of being watched or delusions of observation, to elucidate how female exhibitionism becomes transformed into a fear of being looked at. This "ever-present sense of being on display for the gaze of a judgmental other is symptomatic of another condition within our culture as well—that of femininity" (p. 126). Through the woman's film and corresponding marketing strategies and product tie-ins aimed at female audiences, the Hollywood movie industry thus created an image of femininity targeted at women that reasserted the prewar status quo.

Erika Engstrom
University of Nevada, Las Vegas

See also Film: Hollywood; Male Gaze; Mulvey, Laura; Patriarchy; Scopophilia

Further Readings

Doane, Mary Ann. *The Desire to Desire: The Woman's Film of the 1940s.* Bloomington: Indiana University Press, 1987.

Doane, Mary Ann. *Femmes Fatales: Feminism, Film Theory, Psychoanalysis.* New York: Routledge, 1991.

Doane, Mary Ann, Patricia Mellancamp, and Linda Williams, eds. *Re-Vision: Essays in Feminist Film Criticism.* Los Angeles: American Film Institute, 1984.

DOUGLAS, SUSAN J.

Susan J. Douglas is a feminist cultural critic and award-winning author and columnist. She serves as the Catherine Neafie Kellogg Professor of Communication Studies at the University of Michigan. Her book *Where the Girls Are: Growing Up Female With the Mass Media*, received critical acclaim from media scholars and was selected as a 1994 top ten book by National Public Radio, *Entertainment Weekly*, and The McLaughlin Group. In the book, Douglas uses historical and cultural criticism to point out the contradictions and schisms within mainstream media's depictions of feminism. Douglas's book *The Mommy Myth: The Idealization of Motherhood and How It Has Undermined All Women* (with Meredith Michaels, 2004) describes how the media have pushed the ideology of "momism" in the wake of the women's movement by returning to postfeminist, conservative values and ideals. Her book *Enlightened Sexism: The Seductive Message That Feminism's Work Is Done* (2010) explains how contemporary mainstream media continue to marginalize feminist ideals and achievements through pseudo-empowerment fantasies of liberation and girl power.

A common theme within Douglas's work concerns the mainstream media's ambivalence toward feminist ideals across forms, channels, programming, and genres. While advertisers, editors, and producers seemingly champion women's gains and achievements in the culture at large, they also reify traditional sexist values and ideals, thereby perpetuating antifeminist ideologies. In her first book on women in media, *Where the Girls Are*, Douglas explains that historically, cultural critics and mass media have revered the impact of boys and men, honoring their achievements in rock music, popular film, and television, yet while men are held as the cultural exemplars of "transgressiveness" and revelry, history ignores the lasting impact of girls and women within mainstream media. Whereas male rock stars (Elvis, The Beatles, Jimmy Hendrix) have been canonized, female figures in rock (The Shirelles, Janice Joplin, Aretha Franklin) continue to be marginalized in a male-driven media culture. Likewise, Douglas argues that the impact of strong female protagonists in television and film (such as Lucy and Ethel in *I Love Lucy*) has been marginalized and replaced by programming and genres that pit women against each other through unrealistic expectations of body image and beauty.

In all realms, Douglas offers a complicated and comprehensive critique of the mainstream media's denouncement and exploitation of women's liberation. She documents how serious topics that came out of the feminist movement—such as equal pay, sexual freedom, abortion, family and marriage—are rarely prominently featured in media content and programming. Instead, the media entertain a pseudofeminism that seemingly empowers women while keeping them contained in traditional scripts and normative roles. For instance, feminist discourses around collective equality and power have been repackaged into the ideology of narcissism and capitalist selling campaigns. These new advertising strategies encourage women to associate liberation with issues within the beauty industry as a means to keep them preoccupied with beauty and individual needs over collective political empowerment. Douglas contends that today's pseudofeminism encourages women to take control of their bodies not for their own political or health reasons but to make themselves aesthetically pleasing for men. Media campaigns continue to depict women's equality inaccurately by patronizing the few women who enter the realm of politics or business. This kind of window dressing disguises the greater invisibility of women in male-centered realms. For young girls, Douglas argues that growing up with stereotypical images of femininity leads to a cultural schizophrenia whereby girls and women remain ambivalent toward femininity on one hand and feminism on the other. Females are told they are equal, yet they remain trapped by history and cultural depictions within popular media.

By exploring the love/hate continuum of women's relationship with the media, Douglas uses contemporary representations of women to show how girl and female power are reduced to sexist ideals and stereotypes, all in the guise of "fun" and comedy with the assumption that no offense is taken. While media depictions seem occasionally to poke fun at sexist ideologies, they also perpetuate stereotypes by overrepresenting women as sex and beauty objects rather than dominant equals who deserve their fair share of political and economic power. Whether the content is directed at men through "lad magazines" such as Maxim or is presented in shows like *Buffy the Vampire Slayer*, *Desperate Housewives*, and reality shows with strong female characters, women are nevertheless reduced to their lone powers and individual struggles. Moreover, women are often shown in isolation rather than in solidarity with other females and striving toward global feminist equality. Hence, Douglas argues that from the 1990s to present day, "girl power" has been a clever ruse to distract women from the remaining postfeminist work that needs to be done on a variety of sociocultural issues. As Douglas contends, contemporary programming's mixed messages on feminist ideology continue to create deep divisions across generations, leading to distrust and animosity between mothers and daughters, grandmothers and granddaughters. According to Douglas, if women are to challenge the force of patriarchy in today's culture, they need to understand the complicated ways that the media perpetuate stereotypes and reduce women's issues to clever slogans to sell products.

Julie Frechette
Worcester State University

See also Beauty and Body Image: Beauty Myths; Feminist Theory: Third Wave; Gender and Femininity: Motherhood; Patriarchy; Postfeminism; Radio; Sexism; Television

Further Readings

Douglas, Susan J. *Enlightened Sexism: The Seductive Message That Feminism's Work Is Done.* New York: Times Books, 2010.

Douglas, Susan J. *Listening In: Radio and the American Imagination.* Minneapolis: University of Minnesota Press, 2004.

Douglas, Susan J. *Where the Girls Are: Growing Up Female With the Mass Media.* 1994. Reprint, New York: Three Rivers Press, 1995.

Douglas, Susan J. and Meredith Michaels. *The Mommy Myth: The Idealization of Motherhood and How It Has Undermined All Women.* New York City: Free Press, 2005.

ELECTRONIC MEDIA AND SOCIAL INEQUALITY

Electronic media—including radio, television, and the Internet—have been historically male-dominated in their productions, developments, representations, and industries. Whereas the introduction of each new medium brings with it the hope that it will empower underrepresented groups and foster social equality, new media also deepen divisions between underrepresented groups and those in power. Electronic media enable new types of participation, including the development of identities, access to knowledge, and the building of communities for those with access. Notwithstanding, electronic media also have created challenges and concerns about media literacy, knowledge gaps, and the "digital divide" for those individuals without access to them. As a result, women with higher socioeconomic status in more industrially or postindustrially developed societies experience benefits from these technologies, whereas women of lower socioeconomic status from less developed parts of the world struggle to gain access to them.

Radio and Television

Early developments in radio created opportunities for women to engage in the new medium. Some women received training from the U.S. Navy as radio operators during World War I; other women participated as wireless amateurs, or hams, in clubs and Girl Scout activities. Entertainment programming on radio featured the comedic talents of Gracie Allen and Lucille Ball. Other programming targeted housewives, with shows featuring advice about housekeeping and consumer products. Before and during World War II, radio recruited women to join the workforce and support the war effort. After the shift from radio networks to formats in the 1950s and 1960s, much of the radio programming moved to television, and women's roles in radio shifted to on-air talent and production activities. Currently, about a dozen women run their own national radio programs, and about 20 percent of radio news directors are women. National Public Radio (NPR) offers more opportunities for hosting: Three of its five major shows feature women. Also, women have held top positions in NPR, including chief executive officer and head of news.

The segue from radio programming to television defined early possibilities for the representation of women. Like radio, television became a domestic medium. It attracted domestic audiences through shows such as *The Kate Smith Hour* (1950–54), which offered advice and product announcements. Shows such as soap operas—another carryover from radio—attempted to draw homemakers into watching during the afternoons. Evening programming such as situation comedies, or sitcoms, affirmed women's roles within the home or in secretarial positions subordinate to those of male authority figures.

Some women played important roles in early television. Lucille Ball changed the nature of television production with her show *I Love Lucy* (1951–57). She requested that the show be recorded on film

A member of the U.S. Navy updates an ouija board—a system used to track the movement of every airplane on a carrier—in Baltimore, Maryland. During World War I, the U.S. Navy trained women as radio operators, marking the first time women were accepted into certain branches of the armed forces. (Wikimedia)

instead of performed live for broadcast. The major broadcasters turned her down, so she and her husband, Desi Arnaz, funded the program's production through their own company, Desilu. In using film cameras, Ball created the opportunity for syndication, proving to the networks that reruns offered an additional source of income. Ball's innovation still defines the industry today.

Not until the 1970s did television programming begin to expand its representations of women beyond the domestic roles typical of earlier sitcoms. *The Mary Tyler Moore Show* (1970–77) and *Maude* (1972–78) showed strong women in leading roles, and shows such as *Murphy Brown* (1988–98) and *Ally McBeal* (1997–2002) continued the new tradition into the 1990s. Procedural dramas such as *CSI* and *Law & Order: SVU* included

women portraying key members of their investigative teams. Other shows, such as *Sex and the City* (1998–2004), *Living Single* (1993–98), and *The L Word* (2004–09), brought together all-women or women-dominated casts. Although the appearance of more women in nondomestic roles offered some positive representations, depictions of women in traditional marriages with children tended to reinforce gendered stereotypes. These depictions reinforced a world primarily for white women and rarely delved into non-middle-class issues. In crime and police procedural programs, however, women still tended to comprise the majority of victims.

Nevertheless, some programs broke new ground: *All in the Family* (1971–79) deliberately parodied and undercut domestic stereotypes by revealing the ignorance and ridiculousness of a traditional 1960s husband, Archie Bunker (Carroll O'Connor), whose submissive housewife (Maureen Stapleton) often, if unwittingly, foiled her husband's bigotry and chauvinism. In *Family Ties* (1982–89), a strong mother figure enjoyed an equal relationship with her husband, who together were ideologically at odds with a neoconservative Reaganite son; *The Cosby Show* (1984–92) for the first time depicted an upper-middle-class black family not as victims of racism but as social leaders; and *The Golden Girls* (1985–92) showed four aging women who debunked the grandma stereotype with active lives, rapier wit, and a healthy interest in dating and sex.

Changes in television also moved beyond representations in programming. In today's multichannel, multimedium television environment, niche programming and targeted channels attempt to address female audiences. Networks such as Lifetime and Oxygen market themselves specifically to women. The Learning Channel, HGTV, and The Food Network present programming about issues that they think appeal to women, such as makeover shows, home decorating ideas, and new recipes.

Women today also take on leadership roles in television production. Oprah Winfrey created and branded herself through her talk show, her television station, and her production company. Appointed head of HBO's documentary division in the late 1970s, Sheila Nevins earned much prestige for the premium cable channel. As of 2010, approximately 27 percent of those working in prime-time television production were women. During the 2009–10 television season, almost 40 percent of producers were women, including Wendy Walker, who spent many years with *Larry King Live* (1985–2010).

While women have enjoyed some improved and expanded representation on television and have gained more access to production positions, it is important to note that these changes have occurred within the context of major media conglomerate control. Those conglomerates focus on earning profits and sustaining advertising, so the possibilities for more radical social change in representation and production are limited. Public broadcasting still offers some opportunities through documentaries—many of them directed by women—aired on PBS to bring forward key women's issues. However, even PBS faces restrictions on showing more controversial material because of fears of losing sponsorship and possibly membership support.

The Internet

The Internet offers the most visible and expansive opportunities for women to create and maintain their own virtual communities and to connect with other women to discuss politics, health issues, activism, and other social issues. Developments in social networking—such as blogs, Twitter, and Facebook—encourage these connections. Several sites bring together multiple writers, such as feministing.com for contemporary feminism and HuffingtonPost.com for culture and liberal politics. Some sites, though, share potentially dangerous information, such as those that encourage anorexia nervosa and bulimia. Multiple scholars argue further that pornography sites continue to objectify and denigrate women.

While the Internet has created an opportunity for independent people to start sites and exchange ideas, multimedia conglomerates also use the Internet to advertise to their audiences. Many established women's magazines, for example, offer Websites where potential customers can blog about products and otherwise conduct approved interaction. These blogs sometimes cause controversy when they present unpopular views, such as when a writer for *Marie Claire* magazine expressed revulsion at an overweight couple on a television sitcom or when a writer for *Better Homes and Gardens* suggested that women who breast-feed should do so only in

bathrooms. Both sites offered apologies and retractions, but independent writers used their connections through social media to bring attention to these stories. Some media conglomerates hide their involvement altogether, aware that people prefer information and suggestions from trusted peers and individuals over traditional advertising. Several companies have therefore recruited women bloggers to write about the companies' products for compensation. "Mommy bloggers," for example, are paid to write about products for children and families in the hope that their readers will purchase the products.

In addition to the influence of the profit-driven corporate media, the concepts of the digital divide and the knowledge gap underscore issues of gender and social inequality in access to technology. Insufficient access occurs among those with lower socioeconomic status and those of certain ethnic backgrounds, and this lack of access leads to a digital divide between those who are able to use the Internet and those without access to it. As more information moves across media—with an unprecedented amount of material available on the Internet more than any other resource—those without access to these new technologies will find themselves with fewer opportunities to learn and grow. Without access to this information, the knowledge gap also creates challenges to participating in a democratic society and gaining access to agency and power.

An important overall consideration is that national governments and sociopolitical events wield great influence over whether women have access to these technologies. In countries where political and social unrest is occurring and widespread poverty and famine exist, the questions of digital divides and knowledge gaps become moot in the face of the struggle to survive.

Heather McIntosh
Boston College

See also Blogs and Blogging; Cyberspace and Cyberculture; Film: Hollywood; Film: Independent; Gay and Lesbian Portrayals on Television; Gender Media Monitoring; Media Consolidation; Radio; Soap Operas; Social Media; Talk Shows; Television

Further Readings

Byerly, Carolyn M. and Karen Ross. *Women and Media: A Critical Introduction*. Malden, MA: Blackwell, 2006.

Creedon, Pamela and Judith Cramer, eds. *Women in Mass Communication*, 3rd ed. Thousand Oaks, CA: Sage, 2006.

Ebo, Bosah, ed. *Cyberghetto or Cybertopia? Race, Class, and Gender on the Internet*. Westport, CT: Praeger, 1998.

Hilmes, Michelle. *Radio Voices: American Broadcasting, 1922–1952*. Minneapolis: University of Minnesota Press, 1997.

Media Report to Women. "Industry Statistics." http://www.mediareporttowomen.com/statistics.htm (Accessed December 2010).

Shade, Leslie Regan. *Gender and Communication in the Social Construction of the Internet*. New York: Peter Lang, 2002.

Walker, Wendy, with Andrea Cagan. *Producer: Lessons Shared From 30 Years in Television*. Nashville, TN: Center Street, 2010.

ELLUL, JACQUES

Jacques Ellul (1912–94) was one of the 20th century's most articulate critics of technological society. He was born and educated in Bordeaux, France, and spent his career at the University of Bordeaux. From 1944, he was a professor of the history and sociology of institutions in the Faculty of Law and a professor in the Institute for Political Studies. He was a prodigious writer who produced 58 books and more than 1,000 articles. His most famous sociological works are *The Technological Society* (1954) and *Propaganda: The Formation of Men's Attitudes* (1965). Ellul used the blanket term *technique* to describe "the totality of methods rationally arrived at, and having absolute efficiency (for a given stage of development) in every field of human activity." It was the efficiency and other characteristics inherent in technique that allowed Ellul to claim a natural progression that would ultimately enslave all of humanity in a "global concentration camp." Ellul wrote more theological books than sociological works, and his "pessimistic" views on technology and media are not fully understandable outside an engagement with his theology. Of his theological works, the most notable are *The Presence of the Kingdom* (1948), *The Politics of God and the Politics of Man* (1966), *The Meaning of the City* (1970), *The Ethics of Freedom* (1973), and *The Humiliation of the Word* (1981).

Ellul's key influences were Karl Marx and the Swiss theologian Karl Barth, who served as opposing touchstones of what became a dialectical interpretation of history, reality, and human purpose. In Ellul's phrase "*L'existence, c'est résistance*" (existence is resistance), we see the essence of both his dialectical worldview and his poetic sensibility.

In relation to gender, Ellul was deeply convinced that inherent in women lay the solutions to the problems created by men:

I feel that women are now far more capable than men of restoring a meaning to the world we live in, of restoring goals for living and possibilities for surviving in this technological world. Hence, the women's movements strike me as extraordinarily positive.

Specifically, he considered the nature of technology and electronic media as the domain of sight (as opposed to hearing) and thus the embodiment of male characteristics, which led to unavoidable consequences. Thus, for Ellul, the 20th century was simultaneously and inextricably (1) the century of the image, (2) the century of the masculine, and (3) the century that posed the greatest threat to the feminine. This paradoxical viewpoint is directly opposed to Leonard Shlain's position in *The Alphabet Versus the Goddess* (1998), for example, in which Shlain argues that the rise of the image and fall of the word (via television, film, and the Internet) signify a great re-equalizing of the sexes by bringing equity to the word-image ratio caused by printing press technology. Ellul's view was one in which he saw technique as ultimately embodying the masculine and as ultimately threatening the chances of human survival:

Since 1930 we have been witnessing the radical failure of that type of society—a failure manifested in totalitarian regimes, in the alarming dangers of technology, in the development of racism, of apartheid, of ruinous competition among business firms and nations, in the massacres which have taken place almost incessantly everywhere for the last half century, in the impotence to which excessive force has led us. I could multiply the signs of the failure of our world and one would easily see that they are all linked to the primacy of masculine values. . . . Above all, it is necessary to realize that what one calls Christian values (love, charity, preeminence of the meek, trust, nonviolence) are typically feminine values.

Ellul saw the 20th century situation as one that called for a dialectic response by women, since he saw the feminine as embodying those things that alone were capable of salvation for human culture:

> The necessity for a salvation based on feminine values does not imply that women assume political or economic power. If women wish to take power, if they triumph because women become heads of state or cabinet members, they will, deservedly, enter into the masculine hell, they will adopt masculine behavior. The worst error of women today is the desire to become men. . . . If women become like men, it will effectively be the end of our civilization. But if they succeed in penetrating their particular way of understanding life everywhere, in transforming values through education, if they succeed in subverting society from inside, then salvation is possible.

Although it is impossible to prove, several sources consider Ellul to be the coiner of the phrase, "Think globally, act locally." If nothing else, the literature and his life confirm that he was a great early adopter and popularizer of the phrase, as well as the commitments it implied.

Read M. Schuchardt
Wheaton College

See also Barthes, Roland; Critical Theory; Empowerment; McLuhan, Marshall; Patriarchy

Further Readings

Ellul, Jacques. "Anarchism and Christianity." *Katallagete*, v.7/3 (Fall 1980).

Ellul, Jacques. "Christianity, Morality, and the Victimization of Women." *The Other Side* (September 1987).

Ellul, Jacques. "Jacques Ellul." http://www.ellul.org (Accessed February 2011).

Ellul, Jacques. "Jacques Ellul: Answers From a Man Who Asks Hard Questions: An Interview With Jacques Ellul by David W. Gill." *Christianity Today*, v.28/7 (April 20, 1984).

Ellul, Jacques. "Women in the Future: A Summary Statement From Jacques Ellul." *Alternative Futures: The Journal of Utopian Studies*, v.4/2–3 (Spring/Summer 1981).

Fasching, Darrell J. *The Thought of Jacques Ellul: A Systematic Exposition.* Lewiston, NY: Edwin Mellen Press, 1981.

Greenman, Jeff, Read Mercer Schuchardt, and Noah Toly. *Understanding Ellul.* Eugene, OR: Cascade, 2011.

Jesus Radicals. "Jacques Ellul." http://www.jesusradicals .com/theology/jacques-ellul (Accessed February 2011).

Marlin, Randal. *Propaganda and the Ethics of Persuasion.* Peterborough, ON: Broadview Press, 2002.

Wheaton College Archives and Special Collections. Jacques Ellul Papers, 1936–99. http://archon.wheaton .edu/?p=collections/controlcard&id=13 (Accessed February 2011).

EMPOWERMENT

Defining empowerment is difficult, because the word has been used in very diverse ways. In general, *empowerment* refers to an increase in power. The nature of that power varies dependent on context; however we rarely speak of empowerment with regard to cultural groups already understood to be in a position of power. Women's studies and feminist scholars have often utilized concepts of empowerment in response to marginalization and limited power for women. Understandings of empowerment differ with regard to the type of empowerment, the "signs" of empowerment, and the process of empowerment.

Frequently, empowerment refers to the increased ability of an individual to make choices and take actions (personal empowerment). The term is often used in this way by those involved in therapeutic efforts. For example, in medical empowerment literature, scholars and practitioners focus on patients' access to information and control and their ability to utilize those resources in medical interactions and decision making. Many writers argue that the structures of traditional medicine are disempowering to patients and that steps should be taken to create openings for patient empowerment.

Empowerment can also refer to interactional change, in which participants attain greater equality in particular relationships. The term is utilized in this way by self-improvement texts and by therapy and counseling services. Organizations that work directly with women in abusive relationships can often use a relational empowerment approach. Though such organizations may attempt to help a woman feel personal empowerment as well (and thereby improve self-concept), they typically address the unique relational system rather than only the psychological state of the woman herself.

Finally, the term *empowerment* can be used to address the status of groups of marginalized individuals, along with efforts made to increase their social and political power in a particular cultural or societal milieu. Literature and scholarship that focus on so-called Third World countries and their relationships to world powers sometimes utilize this approach. The assumption is that empowerment is an issue of political and social positioning within a larger structure. When we hear the term *feminist empowerment*, it is likely to be used in this fashion, with an emphasis on the empowerment of women as a group, within larger cultural domains.

While these categories of empowerment may be definitionally distinct, the personal, relational, social, and political are completely intertwined. Thus, when we talk about gender empowerment or female empowerment, we could be thinking about the belief that individual women have in their ability to make choices and act. We could also be considering the extent to which women in relationships have access to power bases in those specific relational cultures, or we may be focusing on the extent to which women, as a demographic-social-political group, have power in a culture.

The term *empowerment* can also signify multiple qualities of an individual or group. In some cases, empowerment or empowered refers to a feeling of self-confidence or agency. Used this way, it principally addresses changes in self-cognition that may, or may not, have an impact on behaviors or relationships but would impact the individual's understandings and evaluations of self. Empowerment may also be used in the context of behavior, with the idea that what we are speaking of is the ability to make choices and enact them, to "act purposefully." In these instances, the focus is on the behavioral component, though there is an implicit understanding that changes in self-concept are necessary for behavioral change. Finally, empowerment can refer to the way groups or individuals are perceived and responded to by others. To consider empowerment in this way focuses not on the feelings or behaviors of the individual or group but on how the individual or group is assessed. Again, there is some underlying presumption of a relationship between changed feelings, behaviors, and assessments.

Empowerment process is a final area of difference that can be seen in the discourse. In some instances, empowerment is understood as something that can be provided or given to others. Discussions of social programs and their worth may revolve around the argument that we can empower people through the programs. In this way, we see empowerment as a "thing" that can be given to, or developed in, an individual by others. In other cases, empowerment is seen as something that happens through personal change (taken, not given). This view reflects the idea that it is through individual change in thoughts and behaviors that one becomes more empowered. Empowerment can also be seen as something that cannot be given or taken but that arises from larger social structures. Scholars who look at empowerment from a political position may assert that an individual cannot "become" empowered if he or she is part of a socially disempowered and marginalized group. In addition, one group in a culture or society cannot simply "give" power to another. There must be overarching social and political change that alters the position of one group vis-à-vis others.

Some scholars argue that women's empowerment happens through mutual, supportive, empathetic relationships. Empowering relationships could include those with close family and friends, as well as in larger community groupings (including those occurring online). Although this view of female empowerment reflects the importance of interpersonal relationships in the creation of self-concept and self-efficacy, it does hinge on a view of women as primarily relationally centered and focused (and may imply that such relationships are not empowering for men). Additionally, this view may redirect attention from needed larger social change. Those supporting this view of female empowerment argue that women are conditioned to be relationally focused. Thus, it is not surprising that they would gain empowerment from mutually supportive relationships that validate them and honor their efficacy. These scholars might argue that the personal is political, and through individual empowerment women gain the strength to come together for social change.

Regardless of the perspective of empowerment taken, communication is central to the concept, as it reflects the empowerment of individuals and groups, provides a mechanism for putting that empowerment into action, and is a foundational mechanism of efforts toward increasing empowerment. Control of and access to media outlets is thus interwoven with these understandings of empowerment. As noted previously, access to information is seen by many scholars as extremely important to personal and relational power. When access to media is restricted for particular individuals or groups, or the content is tightly scripted based on societal or political norms, knowledge required for choice making is reduced. For example, in cultures where women's rights are of low priority, information regarding family planning and contraceptives may be largely absent from available media. Without access to such information, women in these areas are not empowered to make sound decisions and take actions for their well-being. Similarly, when particular social groups are restricted from participation in media production and control, marginalization of voices and perspectives occurs, which has the recursive effect of continued disempowerment. Research on "radical media" channels, which provide access to production for typically unheard voices, has indicated the power that can be created in social and political processes via even nonmainstream media venues. As media continue to change and evolve and the power of production shifts from official production organizations to individual and group levels via blogs and citizen journalists, the opportunity for representation of marginalized voices is increased.

Empowerment can be defined distinctly based on the level of focus (individual, relational, social/political), qualities (feelings, cognitions, behaviors), and starting points for change (others, self, structure). While empowerment is a difficult concept to define succinctly, it is clear that considerations of empowerment, of whatever type, are important for our understandings of gender and social relationships.

Lorin Basden Arnold
Rowan University

See also Affirmative Action; Cultural Politics; Electronic Media and Social Inequality; Gender Embodiment; Patriarchy

Further Readings

Beteta, Hanny Cueva. "What Is Missing in Measures of Women's Empowerment?" *Journal of Human Development*, v.7/2 (2006).

Downing, John D. H. *Radical Media: Rebellious Communication and Social Movements*. London: Sage, 2000.

Esplen, E., S. Heerah, and C. Hunter. "Women's Empowerment: An Annotated Bibliography." *BRIDGE Bibliography*, v.14 (2006). http://www.bridge.ids.ac.uk/reports/bb14.pdf (Accessed September 2010).

Melcote, S. and H. L. Steeves. *Communication for Development in the Third World: Theory and Practice for Empowerment*. London: Sage, 2001.

Mosedale, S. "Assessing Women's Empowerment: Towards a Conceptual Framework." *Journal of International Development*, v.17/2 (2005).

Spreitzer, Gretchen. "Taking Stock: A Review of More Than Twenty Years of Research on Empowerment at Work." In *The Handbook of Organizational Behavior*, C. Cooper and J. Barling, eds. Thousand Oaks, CA: Sage, 2007.

Stein, J. *Empowerment and Women's Health: Theory, Methods, and Practice*. London: Zed, 1997.

Surrey, J. L. "The Self in Relation: A Theory of Women's Development." In *Women's Growth in Connection: Writings From the Stone Center*, J. V. Jordan et al., eds. New York: Guilford, 1981.

Encoding and Decoding

Audience studies include a range of perspectives, from those stressing the power of the media text to those stressing the active audiences' resistance to media messages and their ability to read against the grain. The encoding/decoding model is a representative part of the effort, originating with British cultural studies scholars during the 1970s, to examine the process by which media messages become meaningful to the audience. These researchers shifted the focus of media studies away from media text to examine the audience and the variety of ways that it might interpret and react to media content.

According to Stuart Hall, in the process of program production, meanings and ideas are encoded into the content as meaningful discourses. *Code* refers to a system of meaning that connects visual signs and spoken and written language to the different ideological positions. *Encoding* means that television producers select the codes that assign meanings to events and place events in a context that attributes meaning to them. The selection of codes, which are the preferred codes in the different domains and which seem to embody the "natural" explanations that most people in the society would accept, puts the problematic events within the range of the dominant ideologies. The process of *decoding* happens when audience members watch the programs and make their own readings of the text. Among television viewers, there could be different positions in the process of decoding of the television content. Hall suggests three hypothetical interpretation codes for audience of the text: dominant, negotiated, and oppositional readings. The dominant, or mainstream, ideology is generally the preferred reading in a media text, but the reader does not automatically adopt this. Negotiated readings are produced by those who inflect the preferred reading to take account of their social position. Oppositional readings are produced by those whose social position places them in direct conflict with the preferred reading.

It is necessary to point out that the essence of multiple readings here is different from some findings in cross-cultural studies, which indicate that people from various cultures would receive the same television program differently. Research work on television news found that audiences within a culture do not typically create a new meaning with each "reading," or encounter, with an encoded message. Instead, they are likely to criticize the content of the message in relation to another perspective, which they hold to be correct. They are therefore aware of the encoded meaning and the manner in which it has been constructed, though they disagree with it.

David Morley's important work *The* Nationwide *Audience: Structure and Decoding*, put Hall's model to test. As one of the earliest attempts at an "ethnography of reading" of television audience, it is a radical departure from the critical media theories preoccupied with an abstract text/subject relationship, in which the role of the audience is conceived as a position inscribed in the text. By showing tapes of the British Broadcasting Corporation (BBC) news magazine show *Nationwide* to groups of viewers from various social strata, and then recording the similarities and differences of their responses, Morley demonstrates how one text could be read in different ways by different groups of subjects. He suggests that the relationship between texts and viewers is a complicated encounter of a multiplicity of forces—some historical and social, but also other texts—that simultaneously act on the subject concerned. Morley therefore pointed to the need to develop a model of text-audience relations more flexible and of wider application than the decoding model.

Morley sees the audience as composed of certain cultural clusters of social individuals, whose individual readings will be framed by shared cultural formations and practices. Since then, there has been more communication research work aimed at finding out the conditions under which people accept or reject a perspective when they are aware of the range of alternatives. Some scholars suggest that subcultures can provide a pool of available meaning structures on which groups can draw to make sense of media messages. Thus, the negotiated or oppositional reading is not just one individual disagreeing with the preferred meaning but a specific strategy as a result of the meaning structures created within a particular culture or subculture.

The encoding/decoding model can also be applied to areas of culture other than television or film. For instance, Michel de Certeau explored the oppositional practices of marginalized groups in popular culture, such as the ingenious "tactics of consumption." Using the established vocabulary of media as their material, subversive groups are capable of sketching out new meanings to serve their *own* interests and desires. When removed from the original context, fragments lose their preferred meaning and gain a negotiated or oppositional meaning when combined in their new context. Therefore, the consumer is empowered in the process. Because marginalized groups do not have the power or financial resources to control media organizations, these groups must work with the offerings they can find within the world of media.

Communication scholars have started to apply the encoding and decoding model to new media forms, suggesting that audience studies can constructively be extended to the analysis of Internet use. By studying how teenagers decode Website content, Sonia Livingstone finds that there are communicative challenges for Website producers—in terms of subject matter, formal composition, and mode of address—that have to be overcome in order to engage young Internet users.

Janice Hua Xu
Cabrini College

See also Identity; Media Ethnography; Polysemic Text; Reception Theory

Further Readings

Brooker, Will and Deborah Jermyn, eds. *The Audience Studies Reader*. Abingdon, UK: Routledge, 2003.

de Certeau, Michel. *The Practice of Everyday Life*. Berkeley: University of California Press, 1984.

Hall, Stuart. "Encoding/Decoding." In *Culture, Media, Language*, Stuart Hall et al., eds. London: Routledge, 2002.

Livingstone, Sonia. "The Challenge of Engaging Youth Online." *European Journal of Communication*, v.22/2 (2007).

Morley, David. *The* Nationwide *Audience: Structure and Decoding*. London: British Film Institute, 1980.

Morley, David. *Television, Audiences, and Cultural Studies*. New York: Routledge, 1994.

EQUAL EMPLOYMENT OPPORTUNITY COMMISSION

The Equal Employment Opportunity Commission (EEOC) is a federal agency whose mission is to enforce federal laws that make employment discrimination illegal. Workplace discrimination is a serious problem, as indicated by the facts that more than 93,000 cases were filed in 2009 with the EEOC and discrimination often goes unreported. The five members of this bipartisan commission are appointed to five-year terms by the president and include a general counsel responsible for litigation. The EEOC's role has changed over the years because it is subject to varied influences, including the U.S. Supreme Court, the U.S. Congress, and the enforcement philosophies of its commissioners. The U.S. workplace has benefited in many ways from the EEOC's work; however, the agency has received strong criticism from various sources and must work to improve effectiveness.

Initially, the EEOC was created to implement Title VII of the Civil Rights Act of 1964. This act prohibited discrimination by private employers, labor unions, and employment agencies, typically with 15 or more employees, based on race, color, religion, sex, or national origin. Since its inception, other types of discrimination have been added to the act, including age, disability, and genetic information. As of 2010, the act does not protect lesbian, gay, bisexual, or transgendered people. The act forbids discrimination in a variety of forms, including hiring, firing, promotion, benefits, and compensation. It also is illegal to retaliate against employees who file complaints. Originally, the commission only investigated allegations and provided conciliation. In 1972, the commission was authorized to litigate cases. Relief for plaintiffs may include hiring, reinstatement, back pay with interest, promotion, and payment of attorney's fees and court costs.

Claimants must seek resolution through the EEOC before filing a lawsuit. Charges may be filed

The Equal Employment Opportunity Commission was initially formed in 1964 in order to implement Title VII of the Civil Rights Act and today is charged with enforcing federal laws that ban hiring discrimination. The overburdened agency plans to focus on systemic discrimination to increase its effectiveness. (Photos.com)

by individuals or by a commissioner. If the EEOC finds discrimination was present, attempts are made to remedy the complaint with the employer voluntarily. If this attempt is unsuccessful, the EEOC may sue or authorize claimants to do so. The EEOC successfully has filed class-action suits against large corporations, resulting in several multimillion-dollar settlements. In addition to litigation and conciliation, the commission provides education, outreach, and technical assistance.

Title VII has been amended several times and now prohibits discrimination by federal contractors, educational institutions, and state and local governments. Congress amended the act in 1978 to ban discrimination against pregnant women, and in 1986 the U.S. Supreme Court ruled that sexual harassment violated Title VII. As of 1991, courts ruled that compensatory and punitive damages may be awarded. The EEOC's mission has also been expanded to enforce other laws, such as the Equal Pay Act (1963), the Pregnancy Discrimination Act (1978), the Age Discrimination Act (1986), and the Americans with Disabilities Act (1990).

Civil rights and feminist organizations have criticized the EEOC. The agency's initial failure to take sex discrimination seriously was one catalyst for the creation of the National Organization for Women in 1966. The agency's reputation was seriously damaged in 1991, when Anita Hill testified, during congressional hearings to confirm the appointment of her EEOC supervisor, Clarence Thomas, to the U.S. Supreme Court, that he had sexually harassed her.

Most critiques focus on two issues: the agency's inability to manage its backlogged caseload and inconsistent application of laws to their fullest extent. Historically, the EEOC has been under-funded and understaffed. In the 1980s, the EEOC's effectiveness was drastically undermined by budget cuts and the appointment of commissioners hostile to the agency's mission. The EEOC's effectiveness did not improve during the 1990s. Performance reviews by the General Accounting Office (GAO) and congressional hearings indicated that there was an increase in the inventory of cases, an increase in time for investigations, and a decline in the quality of investigations.

In an effort to improve, a strategic plan was created and so-called "national and local enforcement plans" established agency priorities. The EEOC adopted a strategy of "alternative dispute resolution," typically mediation, to process more cases. The agency also plans to focus its resources on systemic discrimination cases rather than individual cases so as to have a broader impact. Until the U.S. workplace becomes less discriminatory and more resources are provided, it is unlikely that the strain on the EEOC will subside.

Jamie Capuzza
University of Mount Union

See also Affirmative Action; Diversity; Minority Rights; Workforce

Further Readings

American Bar Association. *American Bar Association's Guide to Workplace Law.* New York: Random House, 2006.

Cushman, Clare, ed. *Supreme Court Decisions and Women's Rights.* Washington, DC: CQ Press, 2011.

Giele, Janet Zollinger and Leslie Stebbins. *Women and Equality in the Workplace.* Santa Barbara, CA: ABC-CLIO, 2003.

U.S. Congress, House of Representatives. Oversight Hearing on the EEOC. 103rd Congress, 2nd session, 1994.

U.S. Equal Employment Opportunity Commission. http://www.eeoc.gov (Accessed February 2011).

U.S. General Accounting Office. *EEOC: An Overview.* GAO/T-HRD-93-30. Washington, DC: Author, 1993.

E-Zines: Riot Grrrl

The (under)groundswell of a movement that is now commonly referred to as "Riot Grrrl" had its origins in two cities simultaneously: Olympia, Washington, and Washington, D.C., in the early 1990s. Contextually, the movement began form-ing just after the riots in the Mt. Pleasant area of Washington, D.C., where bystanders witnessed a man being shot in the back by police and later heard police claim that the man was resisting arrest. After seeing this injustice, many started rioting. One of the "founders" of the Riot Grrrl movement, Kathleen Hanna, remembers how Jean Smith, a fellow femi-nist writer and musician, declared (after the Mt. Pleasant riots), "We need a girl riot, too." Thus the Riot Grrrl spirit was born. The shared vision at the time was that everyone should be rioting and ral-lying to free herself from the discrimination faced on a daily basis. Black, white, Jewish, Christian, Muslim, Buddhist, gay, straight, bisexual, transgen-dered, or otherwise, Riot Grrrl writers saw the need for women to come together to form communities and consciousness-raising groups in order to share and disseminate their ideas. They sought to spread their messages, not through the mainstream media (which are thought by many of the Riot Grrrls to commodify and colonize women, minorities, and their messages), but instead through zines that the Grrrls independently produced.

The reason these young women called themselves Grrrls is twofold. First, following Gloria Steinem and their second wave feminist foremothers, these women objected to being labeled as "girls" once they hit puberty. Like many feminists both before and after them, they see the word *girl* as a pejora-tive term when applied to teenage and adult women. However, since the Riot Grrrl movement grew out of the third wave of feminism, these young women were also starting to reclaim terms. They thought *grrrl* would be an interesting play on the word girl. By changing the spelling from "girl" to "grrrl," they were labeling themselves as angry young women who were fed up with the existing system and who were ready and willing to riot and roar.

In academic circles, feminist Riot Grrrl zines are often cited as examples of outsider journalism. *Outsider journalism* can be defined as comprising

Riot grrrl homemade zines covered a range of feminist topics, from sexism to stalking to homophobia. The Riot Grrrl movement waned by the mid-1990s, but the tradition continues through groups like the Guerrilla Girls. (Wikimedia)

oppositional expressions of meaning. It is a type of alternative media created by groups that are not only overlooked by mainstream media but also marginalized by society. This form of journalism often emerges from populations with a dramatic sense of alienation who see themselves as pariahs or outlaws. Outsider journalism creates alternative public spheres and forums to help give these marginalized people a voice. It helps people make sense of common experiences of adversity and outlaw status and is a form of feminist consciousness-raising. It insists on its own value, even though the mainstream may not value it. It privileges the lived experiences of its participants over other forms of knowledge. Outsider journalism, like zine production, offers its writers and creators a sense of agency and self-determination in the form of oppression and a collective or shared identity, as well as a connection to a similarly situated audience.

History of the Riot Grrrl, Third Wave Feminist Zines

Two women from the punk rock band Bratmobile, Molly Neuman (vocals, guitar, and drums) and Allison Wolfe (vocals and guitar), took the idea and the name Riot Grrrl and created the first "official" Riot Grrrl zine. Kathleen Hanna of Bikini Kill and Toby Vail of Jigsaw had already been circulating their thoughts in zines around the same time.

Neuman was working for a government official in Washington, D.C., and thus had easy access to photocopiers. There she made many copies of that first zine, which contained many "merry prankster" tips, such as how to get free postage, how to provoke the police, how to conflate "coolness" with a James Dean type of masculinity, and how that definition is constraining to both genders. Much of what the Riot Grrrls do is about humor. The authors of these zines wrote just as freely about French post-structuralist feminisms as they did about American punk rock music. In these zines such statements were literally right next to and aligned with one another: a concept commonly referred to as "textual splicing" or "textual poaching" by media studies scholars such as John Fiske. Fiske defines *defiance* as acts that go against an already maintained, reinforced, and legitimized system or social order. This was exactly what feminist Riot Grrrl zines did in the 1990s.

The creators of the zines utilized Situationist tactics to get their messages across. Such techniques as cultural and cognitive mapping, use of code words, quotations, and sketches functioned not only to stir up the system but also to create an insider-outsider alliance among the supporters of the zines. The zines called for women to write on their bodies and articles of clothing with black Magic Markers, so that when they saw one another or were photographed by the media they were able to identify one another. Thus, their messages were widely dispersed and circulated. Being a part of the third wave of feminism, the Riot Grrrls and the zine producers used the tools of the existing system to call that very system into question through its own means and its current modalities.

Many of the "founders" of the Riot Grrrl movement contest the label "leaders" and even the name Riot Grrrl as a unified or umbrella term. As Hanna explains to Andrea Juno (AJ) in Volume One of *Angry Women in Rock*:

Part of the point was to challenge hierarchies of all kinds. We did not have a statement we were all willing to agree with, and we did not even want to do that, because we did not want to be a corporation or a corporate identity. We never even called it Riot Grrrl; the media started calling it Riot Grrrl and then I guess we did, too.

Because of this issue of misrepresentation and reappropriation of voice on behalf of the media, many members of the movement engaged in a media block, whereby they simply would refuse to speak with the media to avoid co-optation or commodification. They held women-only meetings, and Riot Grrrl D.C. (RGDC) members organized a convention where they constructed their own zines and held punk rock shows, workshops, and discussions on sexism, racism, homophobia, and representation.

Many nonprofit, independent, and student-run groups still use zines to spread awareness about their work, including I Live Here, http://www.i-live-here.com, and the Guerrilla Girls, http://www.guerrillagirls.com.

Judy E. Battaglia
Loyola Marymount University

See also E-Zines: Third Wave Feminist; Feminist Theory: Third Wave; Guerrilla Girls; Hanna, Kathleen; Steinem, Gloria

Further Readings

Cogan, B. *The Encyclopedia of Punk*. New York: Sterling, 2008.

Fiske, J. *Television Culture*. New York: Methuen, 1987.

Foss, S. J. *Rhetorical Criticism: Exploration and Practice*, 4th ed. Long Grove, IL: Waveland Press, 2009.

Juno, A. *Angry Women in Rock*, Vol. 1. New York: Juno Books, 1996.

Marcus, Sara. *Girls to the Front: The True Story of the Riot Grrrl Revolution*. New York: HarperPerennial, 2010.

Monem, Nadine. *Riot Grrrl: Revolution Girl Style Now*. London: Black Dog, 2007.

E-Zines: Third Wave Feminist

Moving into the globalized, digitalized third wave of feminism, e-zines have become a popular method of transmitting information to a wide variety of audiences. Third wave feminist e-zines are digitalized newsletters that convey messages that seek to improve conditions for women, girls, and other marginalized individuals. An e-zine is very similar to a third wave feminist Riot Grrrl zine, in which the content is political, rhetorical, persuasive, artistic, and homemade. Some e-zines appear very do-it-yourself (DIY), with scanned-in sketches, while others use computerized graphics or "ready-mades."

With the advent of "new media" technologies, third wave feminist e-zines can now feature recordings, clips, sound and image bites, streaming video, live performances, and "behind-the-scenes footage," both historical and contemporary. They commonly feature the art of dissent or uprising. Some are also "fanzines" and function as tribute journals or updates for fans about a certain person in the third wave feminist scene.

Following in the U.S. American tradition of "Revolution Girl Style Now," many other countries are starting to use third wave feminist e-zines as a chief method of communication. For example, in the Philippines, Pinay zines have become popular. However, because zine making is no longer a response to a male-dominated punk rock music scene, some see the third wave feminist "zinesters" as mere "scenesters" who are "selling out" and becoming a mere trend. Some ask, Where is the revolution now? Where is the riot? and Why is it so quiet?

This is not to say, however, that third wave feminist e-zines are not prompting any kind of political change, because in fact they are. They have been used by both radical and liberal feminist girl groups to address issues within and surrounding the music industry, the clothing industry, homelessness, pornography, the crisis in the Middle East, the depiction of women in the media, women's health and reproductive rights, the idea of "going green," gay and lesbian marriage, and gays and lesbians in the military, among other issues.

E-zines are not designed to achieve financial success. They are preferred by some groups over paper zines because of their accessibility and because they are eco-friendly. However, in places where the power of the Internet is not widespread, many groups tend to have both an e-zine and a paper zine. Some e-zines, like their paper-zine predecessors, are similar to activity books, inviting reader input to fill in the blanks or help create the messages. They also often contain alternative comics, such as Alison Bechdel's *Dykes to Watch Out For* (1986).

Gender and media scholars have considered third wave feminist e-zines from a variety of different perspectives. Some see the e-zines as a logical outgrowth of the paper zines of the third wave feminist Riot Grrrl movement. Others see them as pure fun and fancy or as nonsensical or apolitical and utterly postmodern. Still others see them as similar to teen magazines in general, telling girls a different way to be, but nevertheless serving in a governing or controlling capacity for girls. Coming into effect in the context of neoliberal globalization, third wave feminist e-zines have also been seen as commodifying the ideas of the third wave of feminism, making them more candy-coated and palatable for a relatively homogenized readership and contributing to e-commerce. However, because those girls who create e-zines usually create them on a volunteer basis and do not get paid for their work, this argument has yet to be accepted by most gender and media scholars. In fact, Angela McRobbie notes that sociologists have "perhaps ignored this social dimension because to them the very idea that style could be purchased over the counter [goes] against the grain of those analyses which saw the adoption . . . of punk style as an act of creative defiance far removed from the mundane act of buying."

E-zine entrepreneurs (the creators of the e-zines) use the technological techniques and the language of the late capitalist market in order to challenge that very market and turn it on its head in a very third wave style of resistance. The girls barter and trade the e-zines rather then sell them. If they ever are sold, the earnings often go back into the project they seek to serve—for example, Mia Kirshner's *I Live Here* projects or Noemi Martinez's *La Tiendita*. Other contemporary examples include *Pisces Catalog*, *Frida Loves Diego*, and *Grrrl Style Distro*. Even popular feminist magazines, mostly known for their glossies, such as *Bitch*, *Bust*, and *Ms.*, have online versions of their publications.

Judy E. Battaglia
Loyola Marymount University

See also E-Zines: Riot Grrrl; Feminist Theory: Third Wave; Guerrilla Girls; Hanna, Kathleen; Pornography: Gay and Lesbian; Steinem, Gloria; Tween Magazines; Women's Magazines: Feminist Magazines

Further Readings

McRobbie, A. "Second-Hand Dresses and the Role of the Ragmarket." In *Postmodernism and Popular Culture*. New York: Routledge, 1994.

McRobbie, A. "Shut Up and Dance: Youth Culture and Changing Modes of Femininity." In *Postmodernism and Popular Culture*. New York: Routledge, 1994.

Nava, M. "Consumerism Reconsidered: Buying and Power." In *Feminism and Cultural Studies*, Morag Shiach, ed. Oxford, UK: Oxford University Press, 1999.

Fairness Doctrine

The fairness doctrine was formalized as policy in 1949 by the Federal Communications Commission (FCC) in its *Report on Editorializing by Broadcast Licensees*. After a controversial 40-year history marked by challenges to its constitutionality and problematic enforcement, the policy was repealed in 1987. Calls for reinstatement of the fairness doctrine cause it to remain a politically charged issue today.

The doctrine specified that, because the airwaves are a "scarce" public resource (there are a finite number of frequencies available in any geographic market), broadcast stations act as trustees of this public resource and must (1) present adequate coverage of controversial issues of public importance and (2) provide content reflecting opposing views on these issues. Broadcasters were required to meet this obligation at their own expense if sponsorship was unavailable.

When the fairness doctrine was developed, most communities had access to only a small number of broadcast outlets. The doctrine addressed concerns about placing such concentrated power in just a few broadcasters' hands. Although it was intended to ensure freedom of speech, the doctrine was the focus of multiple legal challenges that claimed it violated broadcasters' First Amendment rights. In its most significant constitutional challenge, *Red Lion Broadcasting Co. v. Federal Communications Commission* (1969), the U.S. Supreme Court upheld the right of the FCC to enforce the fairness doctrine in areas where public access to broadcast channels was limited.

The fairness doctrine did not require stations to provide equal time to opposing viewpoints, only reasonable opportunities for opposing viewpoints to be expressed. Broadcasters could present opposing views in any way they chose; they were not required to put advocates for those views on the air. Content within individual programs did not have to be balanced, so long as the station's overall content reflected opposing views.

The most severe penalty for violation of the fairness doctrine was revocation of a station's broadcast license, effectively putting the station out of business. Although every year the FCC received hundreds of thousands of complaints about potential violations, most were dismissed on procedural grounds for failure to meet high standards of proof. Complaints that survived the vetting process were sent to the broadcast stations, which were required to respond to the FCC. Broadcasters' defenses often characterized the issues as not of public importance. Because stations were allowed to determine what issues of concern were important to cover in their communities, only once did the FCC find that a station was in violation of the first requirement of the fairness doctrine, to devote adequate coverage to issues of public concern (Rep. Patsy Mink, 59 F.C.C. 2d 987, 37 R. R. 2d 744, 1974). In most cases, where the broadcaster was found to have violated the second requirement, to provide coverage of opposing views, the station was simply told to present additional content reflecting the slighted position. In the doctrine's 40-year history, only one broadcast station ever lost its license for failing to provide coverage of opposing views. However, the penalty in this case might have been due to the fact that the licensee, Brandywine-Main Line Radio, misrepresented facts to the FCC.

Criticisms of the fairness doctrine led to two reexaminations of the doctrine by the FCC. The first inquiry resulted in a 1974 report that supported its constitutionality. The second was launched in 1984 in an era of deregulation of business, under President Ronald Reagan's appointee, Mark Fowler. Fowler argued that a proliferation of new media channels had increased public access to information sources, undermining the premise of the scarcity doctrine. The inquiry concluded that the doctrine was an unconstitutional restriction on free speech. However, because Congress favored the fairness doctrine, the FCC did not abolish it, hoping the courts would make that politically difficult decision. In 1986, Congress adopted a bill to impose the fairness doctrine through an amendment to the Communications Act of 1934. Just before the bill reached President Reagan's desk in 1987, the U.S. Supreme Court declined to review an appeal of a case, *Telecommunications Research and Action Center v. FCC*, which might have upheld the fairness doctrine as a valid statute under the Communications Act. Reagan vetoed the bill, and the vote needed to override the veto did not materialize. With other avenues exhausted, the FCC repealed major aspects of the fairness doctrine in 1987, and a 1989 federal appellate court allowed it to expire.

Calls to reinstate the fairness doctrine continue, although they would result in inevitable legal challenges. The doctrine may be reinstated either through FCC policy or an act of Congress amending the Communications Act of 1934. In recent years, Congress has been split on the issue, along party lines, with Democrats supporting a return to the doctrine and introducing unsuccessful legislation to do so in 2005. Republicans responded with unsuccessful legislation to block the FCC from reinstating the doctrine in 2007 and 2009. A revival of the doctrine would challenge the dominance of conservative talk-radio programming, and proposals to do so have generated vigorous dissent from conservative activists and groups.

Katherine N. Kinnick
Kennesaw State University

See also Advertising; Children's Programming: Cartoons; Federal Communications Commission; Gay and Lesbian Portrayals on Television; Media Consolidation; Media Rhetoric; Network News Anchor Desk; Newsrooms; Radio; Radio: Pirate; Talk Shows; Telecommunications Act of 1996; Television

Further Readings

Aufderheide, Patricia. "After the Fairness Doctrine: Controversial Broadcast Programming and the Public Interest." *Journal of Communication*, v.40/3 (1990).

Federal Communications Commission. *Report Concerning General Fairness Doctrine Obligations of Broadcast Licensees*, 102 FCC 2d 142 (1985).

Federal Communications Commission. *Report on Editorializing by Broadcast Licensees*, 13 FCC 1246 (1949).

Hazlett, Thomas W. "The Fairness Doctrine and the First Amendment." *Public Interest*, v.96/2 (1989).

Inquiry Into the General Fairness Doctrine Obligations of Broadcast Licensees, 49 F.R. 20317 (1984).

Rowan, Ford. *Broadcast Fairness: Doctrine, Practice, Prospects: A Reappraisal of the Fairness Doctrine and Equal Time Rule*. New York: Longman, 1984.

FEDERAL COMMUNICATIONS COMMISSION

The Federal Communications Commission (FCC) is an independent U.S. government agency empowered to regulate communication industries and their content by the Communications Act of 1934. As the act is amended and technology advances, the FCC's role evolves. Minority and feminist organizations consistently urge the FCC to document discrimination in media industries and to promote diversity.

The FCC is a bipartisan group that comprises five commissioners appointed by the president for five-year terms. The agency processes license applications, conducts investigations, develops and implements regulations, and takes part in hearings. Specifically, the agency regulates interstate and international communications by radio, television, telephone, wire, satellite, and cable. Although the FCC is restricted from violating First Amendment rights of broadcasters, the agency is permitted indirectly to regulate content. For example, the FCC can fine violators of obscenity standards. The FCC is funded by

Congress, but most of its multimillion-dollar annual budget comes from fees paid by regulated industries and not tax dollars.

Perhaps the agency's most significant power is the ability to grant, revoke, renew, and modify broadcast licenses. Licenses are awarded or renewed using the "public interest, convenience, and necessity" standard. The original justification for licensing was the "scarcity rationale." The FCC claimed, since there are natural limitations to the electromagnetic spectrum, licensing would eliminate broadcast signal interference. The FCC also justified licensing as a means of avoiding monopolies, arguing that limitations on broadcast station ownership would provide a robust marketplace of ideas.

The FCC gains new responsibilities as the Communications Act is amended, usually in response to new technologies. For example, the advent of cable television necessitated FCC regulation. Additionally, FCC responsibilities increase when new acts, such as the Telecommunications Act (1996) and the Broadcast Decency Enforcement Act (2005), are passed.

Scholars hold different opinions about the FCC's effectiveness. One controversy surrounds prioritizing a "marketplace rationale" over the scarcity rationale. Starting in the 1980s, critics contended that the FCC had become too market-driven, often favoring business over educational or community needs in licensing decisions. Similarly, the move toward deregulation that began in the 1980s controversially resulted in more cross- and multiple ownership. The FCC now argues that removing ownership limits increases competition and lowers prices. Consumer advocates disagree, arguing that corporate mergers create large media empires, drive up prices, and reduce local news coverage.

Additionally, groups such as the National Organization for Women argue that consolidation creates difficulties for women and minority entrepreneurs. The number of women media company owners is meager. As of 2010, women owned approximately 5 percent of television stations and 6 percent of radio stations. Women of color own less than 1 percent of stations.

At times the FCC promoted a "diversity rationale," based on the assumption that diversity of ownership leads to greater diversity of viewpoints in broadcasting and, consequently, supports its public interest mandate. At other times, commissioners have not advanced this rationale.

Similarly, at times the courts have supported the FCC's diversity rationale and at other times they have not. In the *TV 9* (1973) case and in the *Garrett* (1975) case, courts ruled that there was a "reasonable expectation" of a link between minority ownership and program diversity. Moreover, in *Metro Broadcasting* (1990), the court upheld FCC policies designed to promote diverse media ownership. For example, in 1971, the FCC adopted a merit policy for minorities and extended it to women in 1978. This policy gave preferential status to minority and women applicants over similarly situated nonminority applicants. The FCC also created a program of tax certificates to provide incentive to sell stations to women or minorities. Additionally, the FCC created the distress sales policy in 1999, which ruled that out-of-market buyers, including minority broadcasters, must be given notice when a station is up for bid before it can be merged with an in-market station.

Such policies have not always been effective. There are few cases of distress sales resulting in minority ownership, and Congress sometimes does not fund tax incentives. Most significant, the courts have sometimes invalidated the FCC diversity policy. For example, in *Lamprecht* (1992), the court ruled that the FCC's gender merit policy was unconstitutional because it violated the equal protection clause of the First Amendment. Furthermore, in *Steele* (1985), the court held that the FCC had exceeded its authority when applying the merit policy to women, and it rejected the FCC's diversity rationale.

The FCC was unable to defend the diversity rationale because it failed to keep a record of past discrimination. In 1998, the FCC began collecting race and gender information about owners, and the agency has since highlighted studies that document discrimination and demonstrate government interest in developing programs that promote diversity.

In addition to collecting data and responding to litigation, the FCC addresses economic barriers related to diversity. In 2010, the agency chartered the Advisory Committee on Diversity for Communications in the Digital Age to identify ways of removing market entry barriers for women and minorities. Initial recommendations included outreach programs and facilitation of financing opportunities. Additionally, President Barack Obama created the position of FCC Chief Diversity Officer. While important strides toward diversity have been made, this issue is likely to challenge the FCC in the future.

Jamie Capuzza
University of Mount Union

See also Advertising; Children's Programming: Cartoons; Diversity; Fairness Doctrine; Gay and Lesbian Portrayals on Television; Media Consolidation; Media Rhetoric; Network News Anchor Desk; Newsrooms; Radio; Radio: Pirate; Talk Shows; Telecommunications Act of 1996; Television

Further Readings

Federal Communications Commission. *Re-Examination of the Commission's Comparative Licensing, Distress Sales and Tax Certificate Policies Premised on Racial, Ethnic or Gender Classifications*, 3 FCC Rcd 766 (1988).

Gauger, Timothy. "The Constitutionality of the FCC's Use of Race and Sex in the Granting of Broadcast Licenses." *Northwestern Law Review*, v.83 (1989).

Kleiman, Howard. "Content Diversity and the FCC's Minority and Gender Licensing Policies." *Journal of Broadcasting and Electronic Media*, v.35 (1991).

Veraldi, Lorna and Stuart Shorenstein. "Gender Preferences." *Federal Communications Law Journal*, v.45 (1994).

Wilson, Lisa. "Minority and Gender Enhancements: A Necessary and Valid Means to Achieve Diversity in the Broadcast Marketplace." *Federal Communications Law Journal*, v.40 (1989).

Zarkin, Kimberly and Michael Zarkin. *The Federal Communications Commission: Front Line in the Culture and Regulation Wars*. Westport, CT: Greenwood, 2006.

FEMINISM

Although there are many feminisms and feminist philosophies, *feminism*, defined broadly, is a commitment to improving the lives of women and the societies in which they live. Practicing this commitment, feminists around the world have organized women's movements for social, legal, economic, and cultural changes to benefit women. Since the modern feminism's origins in the 18th century, media technologies and mediated communication have been tools as well as targets of feminists. This especially became true in the 20th century with the development of new media technologies and the global expansion of corporate media.

Feminism and the Media

Feminists and the media have had a symbiotic though rarely friendly relationship. Representing the status quo controlled by men, mainstream media historically attempt to discredit feminism by demonizing or trivializing the issues, the movements, and the women leading them. Going back 200 years, mainstream media depictions of feminists and feminisms mostly are so negative that women hesitate to call themselves feminists. For example, news accounts of mid-20th century "women's libbers" (women's liberation advocates) led to the stereotype of the strident man-hater. Even so, media portrayals of feminists and feminisms helped circulate new ideas leading to change.

Indeed, the success of feminist movements has depended on a media-savvy leadership with a knack for publicity. Feminists in the 1960s and 1970s staged the marches, sit-ins, demonstrations, and "happenings" that became the image of feminism in the popular imagination, thanks to newspapers, magazines, movies, and television. A couple generations earlier, suffragists, in organizing their marches and demonstrations, also understood the value of spectacle in garnering the attention of newspapers and so newspaper readers. Many historically notable feminists were journalists. Mary Ann Shadd Cary founded the Canadian *Provincial Freeman* newspaper in 1853 to become the first black woman publisher in North America. A century later, Gloria Steinem was a freelance writer before she became a feminist and in 1972 cofounded *Ms.* magazine.

Outside media owned by women, however, women have been denied media positions of status and power. In response, feminists have targeted the media for reform. U.S. feminist organizers in the 1960s and 1970s refused news outlets access to feminist events unless women reporters were sent to cover the stories. Feminists also campaigned to end gender-segregated help-wanted advertising. Florynce Kennedy established the Media Workshop in 1966 to counter racism in the media. In 1970, a coalition of feminist groups, including Media Women and the

National Organization for Women, staged a sit-in at the *Ladies' Home Journal* (*LHJ*) to protest sexist management and content. The sit-in led to naming editor Lenore Hershey as *LHJ*'s publisher. Hershey was the magazine's first woman publisher since its founder, Louisa Knapp Curtis, stepped down in 1890. Ironically, during World War II, *LHJ* adopted what has been called a feminist slogan, "Never Underestimate the Power of a Woman," albeit a slogan yoked to, first, the war effort and, second, commodification and consumption.

Mainstream media do profit from feminism, including sensationalizing women's movements and capitalizing on feminist celebrities. Feminist books have become best sellers. The growth of women's studies, feminist scholarship, and feminist research methodologies on university campuses also legitimized feminist publishing and media. Moreover, as represented in the *LHJ* slogan, the media have a history of co-opting feminism for profit. The advertising and entertainment industries dilute feminist themes and issues to cash in on them with mass audiences. This includes persuading women that consuming household, fashion, and even cigarette brands is equivalent to declaring independence, a phenomenon that began with women's magazines in the 19th century.

For their part, feminists always have appropriated media technologies. By the mid-1800s, feminists were publishing journals all over Europe and North America. Today feminist media still bypass mainstream channels. Now on the Web, Feminist International Radio Endeavor is in its fourth decade of broadcasting in Spanish and English from Costa Rica. In 1990, the International Women's Media Foundation founded a network to promote women in and as the international press. The U.S. *Media Report to Women* has monitored media representations of women since 1972. Women's eNews packages multimedia news of interest to women.

Feminisms

Feminism is not monolithic. There are varieties of feminist thought, although they all attempt to explain the universal second-class status of women and then advocate change. Depending on their philosophical and theoretical foundations and commitments, however, different feminisms engage different media issues.

Transnational feminism focuses on the global status of women, monitoring the impact of communication technologies and multinational media conglomerates on social, political, and economic inequities worldwide. Postcolonial feminism opposes Western imperialist practices and ideologies that subjugate and obliterate indigenous peoples and cultures. Such practices include the export of Western media, as well as the West's appropriation and commodification of indigenous cultures. At the same time, gaining access to information and communication technologies (ICTs) becomes important for empowering women everywhere.

Third World feminism comprises both critique and celebration. The critique points to white U.S. feminists' failure to engage race, class, and ethnicity. The celebration gives voice to feminist women of color as well as the interests of nonwhite women in both so-called First World and Third World countries. In North America, multicultural and multiracial feminisms emphasize the ways gender intersects race, ethnicity, class, religion, nationality, age, disability, and sexuality to produce very specific forms of women's oppression. These feminisms scrutinize the quantitative and qualitative representation of women in media messages and careers.

Western liberal feminism mostly has worked to establish women's legal rights. Important liberal feminist media issues have been about the so-called glass ceiling, the obstacles to women's rise to the top of the corporate career ladder, including media professions. Marxist feminists blame capitalism and its accompanying gendered division of labor for higher rates of poverty among women. Marxist feminism reminds liberal feminism that some groups of women, out of economic necessity, always have worked outside the home doing the underpaid, low-status labor in what is now called the pink-collar ghetto, including low-paid media jobs overrepresented by women. Socialist feminists add male-controlled church and state to male-controlled capitalism's patriarchal oppression of women. Both Marxist and socialist feminists critique the advertising industry, which exploits women as consumers in order to underwrite capitalist media profits. Similarly, eco-feminists critique the media's disposable consumer culture for degrading the environment.

Laura Mulvey's concept of the male gaze, an influential media theory emerging from psychoanalytic feminism, describes *scopophilia*, meaning pleasure in watching. The male gaze is a gendered visual regime in which the one who looks, the masculine position, has power over the one who is the object of the gaze, the feminine position. Mulvey demonstrated how visual media reproduce these gendered power relations. Mulvey's work represents a rich late 20th-century tradition of feminist film and film theory.

Post-structuralist, deconstructionist, and postmodern feminisms argue that "woman" as a category does not exist outside the symbolic communication that produces it. Therefore, images and narratives, including mediated ones, literally construct our notions of gender, sexuality, women, and men. This is the social constructionist view of gender as nurture or learned culture, distinguished from nature as essentialist biology. Feminist and queer theorists now argue that gender is performative, meaning that gender is a socially enforced enactment of the body. Performativity accounts for the variability of gender across cultures and history but allows women to claim the subjectivity of their own gendered bodies.

Feminist Waves

Western women's movements also can be understood by three overlapping eras: the first wave, prior to women's winning the vote; the second wave, during the 1960s and 1970s; and the third wave, beginning in the 1980s.

First wave feminism in Europe and North America encompasses a period from the 18th century into the first half of the 20th century. First wave concerns included women's legal status, which left women powerless and totally dependent on not always benevolent male relatives. First wave issues included marital, property, voting, and educational rights. The first wave also advocated workers' rights, particularly for unmarried women. Barred from participating in official avenues of social change, first wavers organized their own clubs and associations to lobby for reform. First wave feminists circulated their agendas by writing periodicals, pamphlets, poetry, letters, books, and speeches. Many first wave feminists became great orators at a time when women were excluded from public speaking.

Feminists of the period also found affinity with other social movements, including labor unions, temperance, and the abolition of slavery. In the United States, first wave feminism was inspired by the egalitarian status of women in indigenous American cultures such as the Iroquois Nation. African American women's organizations also supported feminist causes. White feminists, however, were not always welcoming, because of racism and fears of weakening the cause politically. Sojourner Truth's 1851 speech "Ain't I a Woman?" marks the first time a black woman addressed a white women's rights convention. Ultimately, U.S. suffragists betrayed their alliances with African American women by opportunistically playing to white fears of a powerful black voting bloc.

Some locate the end of the first wave with women earning the right to vote, which, in the United States, came in the form of the Nineteenth Amendment in 1919. However, feminism did not hibernate between 1919 and the 1960s. Women in Quebec did not get the vote until 1940. Just a few years later, in 1949, the French existentialist Simone de Beauvoir published *The Second Sex*, which some mark as the beginning of the second wave. Coinciding with the beginning of the 20th century, rebellion against oppressive Victorian mores led to the "New Woman," who emerged during the flourishing literary and art scenes of the period. The development of photography, radio, telephones, cinema and movie palaces, gramophones and record players, and later television exponentially increased the speed with which new ideas spread. Meanwhile, women in the first half of the 20th century continued to organize via social, educational, political, athletic, and business and professional clubs, associations, and unions. Throughout the 20th century, U.S. women's press clubs networked women in journalism and broadcasting. Also important during the overlapping period between the first and second waves were birth control and family planning to give women control over their reproductive lives. By 1960, the U.S. Food and Drug Administration had approved the birth-control pill, which began the sexual revolution. Additionally, the Equal Rights Amendment (ERA) to the U.S. Constitution, giving women explicit constitutional equality, was introduced to Congress annually between 1923 and 1970.

Two world wars separated by the Great Depression distracted attention to the women's movement. During World War II, U.S. women participated in war-manufacturing jobs formerly reserved for men. After the war, these women—symbolized by the poster image of a woman factory worker, "Rosie the Riveter"—were sent home again. Successful war propaganda to persuade women to work outside the home during the war effort quickly retooled. Postwar discourse, including a booming advertising industry, severely restricted women's roles to those fitting an idealized domesticity in the suburbs. This was the unfulfilling lifestyle Betty Friedan critiqued in her 1963 best seller *The Feminine Mystique*. Enter the second wave.

U.S. second wave feminism participated in a synergy of social movements in the 1960s, from antiwar protests to civil rights for farmworkers, African Americans, the disabled, the elderly, and lesbians and gays. Second wavers went to school on 1960s agitprop, as less public consciousness-raising sessions in private homes initiated many women into the movement. The decade was not a campfire sing-a-long of solidarity, however. Black, radical, socialist, and lesbian feminist groups in particular criticized liberal feminism's white heterosexual, middle-class myopias. That the mainstream media seemed to give liberal feminists more legitimacy did not facilitate sisterhood.

Nevertheless, the U.S. second wave boasts seismic legal changes benefiting women—sometimes unintentionally—beginning with the 1963 Equal Pay Act. Title VII of the 1964 Civil Rights Act forbids race and gender discrimination in employment and was amended in 1978 with the Pregnancy Discrimination Act. Title IX of the 1972 Education Amendments protects women from educational discrimination. The Supreme Court in 1971 and 1973 ruled that women merit equal constitutional protections under the Fourteenth and Fifth Amendments. Also in 1973, the Supreme Court's decision in *Roe v. Wade* in effect legalized abortion. In 1972, Congress finally passed the ERA, although it died in 1982 without full states' ratification.

If the second wave motto, "Biology Is Not Destiny," spoke to women seeking employment and reproductive rights, then the second wave's other motto, "The Personal Is the Political," resonated with women fighting abuse. Sexual politics had always treated the sexual and the domestic as private instead of legal concerns. In the 1970s, however, women redefined rape as a form of violence against women, in part because of Susan Brownmiller's 1975 *Against Our Will*. The book did not, however,

In the 1970s, Eleanor Holmes Norton, chair of the U.S. Equal Employment Opportunity Commission and then head of the New York City Human Rights Commission, held the first U.S. hearings on workplace discrimination against women. (U.S. Congress)

deal with the U.S. social history of slavery and the rape of slave women. By 1975, women also had named a formerly invisible workplace phenomenon, "sexual harassment." Women of color take credit for filing the early lawsuits, a fact absent in a legal canon about gender, not race, according to Eleanor Holmes Norton. In her role as chair of the U.S. Equal Employment Opportunity Commission, Norton in 1980 first codified federal sexual harassment policy, including definitions of *quid pro quo* and *hostile environment*.

The third wave began with the first critique of second wave liberal feminism as predominantly white, Anglo, heterosexist, able-bodied, and economically privileged. By the time Alice Walker coined the term *womanist* to honor black feminism in 1983, the third wave was organizing on the principle of recognizing differences among women. Classic texts of the period include the 1981 books *Ain't I a Woman*, by bell hooks, and *This Bridge Called My Back*, edited by Gloria Anzaldúa and Cherríe Moraga. Then came *All the Women Are White, All the Blacks Are Men, but Some of Us Are Brave* (1982), edited by Gloria T. Hull, Patricia Bell Scott, and Barbara Smith. Audre Lorde published *Sister Outsider* in 1984, and Trinh T. Minh-ha published *Woman, Native, Other* in 1989. The phrase "white supremacist capitalist patriarchy," coined by hooks, underscores the "interlocking systems of oppression" that impact gender. Recognizing the intersectionality of one's multiple identifications and being reflexive about one's unique standpoint became key feminist concepts.

Part of the third wave is generational. Mainstream media tend to cast third wavers as young, attractive, sexually assertive feminist daughters rejecting old, unattractive, humorless second wave mothers. This undermines both generations by trivializing the third wave as hedonistic pleasure seekers and dismissing the second wave as irrelevant. Third wavers, however, embrace and recuperate popular culture's watered-down girl-power brands of feminism. The third wave also developed distinctive media practices, beginning with zines. In the 1980s, feminist zines were underground pastiche magazines reproduced on copy machines. In the 1990s, they evolved into Internet e-zines, which further evolved into blogs and LiveJournal Web communities after the turn of the century. Also in the 1990s, the Pacific Northwest produced the feminist punk Riot Grrrl scene, which inspired a movement of "girl" bands dedicated to empowering women and dealing with serious issues such as violence against women. Third wavers also embrace prankster and jamming activist practices, which interrupt and subvert mainstream media practices, often with irony and humor. The exemplar group remains the Guerrilla Girls, an anonymous group of gorilla-masked activists that began in the 1980s to critique women's exclusion from the art community. The Guerrilla Girls continue to use guerrilla tactics and amusing messages to shame the art establishment, including museums.

Concurrent with but distinct from the third wave is postfeminism, an antifeminism deployed from the political right. Postfeminists argue that feminism is passé and fault feminism for contemporary social ills. Postfeminists say that single mothers on public assistance should be working and, contradictorily, that career women have destroyed the traditional family. The origins of postfeminism lie in U.S. neoconservatism in the 1980s, which journalist Susan Faludi documented as feminist "backlash." Antifeminism continues, however, and mainstream media have been criticized for giving postfeminists more media presence than progressive feminists.

Postfeminism notwithstanding, most feminist thought is reducible to either equality or difference. Equality feminists argue that women deserve rights equal to those enjoyed by men. One problem with this approach is the assumption that men represent an unassailable ideal toward which women should aspire. Difference feminists argue that women are different. Some difference feminists characterize women's differences as rendering them superior to men. Arguments that women are "naturally" different or better at some things are susceptible to biological determinism or essentialism, which suggests women are preordained to their subordinate status. A pragmatic feminist approach to equality and difference examines issues on a case-by-case basis. Equality dictates that women earn equal pay for equal work, but difference demands that the workplace adjusts for pregnancy, a phenomenon unique to women.

Feminist Media Issues

No media topic, from ownership to audiences, is immune to feminist analysis and intervention. Key themes in this work are access, voice, representation, and power.

Regarding ownership, as media corporations in the last 30 years grew into global giants, their numbers decreased to a handful controlling the international agenda and flow of information. Continued open access to the Web may help counter such concerns, as do independent, alternative, feminist, and women-owned media, such as Oprah Winfrey's multibillion-dollar media enterprises. However, a digital divide remains for women, who are disproportionately impoverished and undereducated, while governments and corporations struggle to control the Web.

Feminists also critique the hiring, promotion, and retention of women and minorities in media industries. This includes the feminization of some fields, such as public relations, and the exclusion of women and people of color from others, such as creative departments in advertising. Overall, women remain rare in upper management. Furthermore, on the job, media practices and routines may be gendered and discriminatory. Gendered news beats concentrate women in fashion, food, and families. Men dominate sports media. All journalists quote men more than women as news sources. When women are serious news makers in, for example, politics, business, science, sports, and even the media, the news often focuses on their marital status and wardrobe. When Katie Couric became the first woman to anchor the Columbia Broadcasting System (CBS) evening news in 2006, sensationalized news accounts of her first weeks on the job were laden with sexist impressions of her professionalism, appearance, and family life. Kathleen Hall Jamieson describes the double bind women in leadership face because the cultural qualities valued in a good leader are at odds with those valued in a good woman.

Gaye Tuchman's 1978 concept *symbolic annihilation* refers to the absence, trivialization, infantilization, and sexualization of women in media content and messages. Media stereotypes of women's family and workplace roles persist, including in textbooks. Feminists criticize representations of ideal womanhood as young, white, heterosexual, able-bodied, unrealistically beautiful, financially secure, happily subordinate to men, and sexually available. Images of women frequently depict close-ups of tightly cropped sexual body parts, a practice that objectifies and dehumanizes. At the same time, women of color are underrepresented but routinely depicted as exotic, animalistic, and oversexed. Feminists link media emphasis on unattainable beauty with poor body image.

Some of the worst offenders are mainstream corporate women's media, which target women as audiences to garner advertising revenue. Women's media seem to celebrate womanhood, although often in restricted traditional forms tied to motherhood and domesticity. Thus, historically, women's media are marginalized as less important than men's or general interest media. Feminists argue that the media, including women's media, hail audiences to take up and enact heteronormative gender. Additionally, feminists are interested in audiences of women as interpretive agents who may resist and even subvert

media messages, as seen in Janice Radway's research on romance novel readers and Constance Penley's research on *Star Trek* slash erotica fans.

On college campuses, women have formed the majority of students in mass communications classrooms since 1977, although the implications of this have never been a focus of mass communications education. After Title IX, feminists in mass communications fought for student, faculty, research, and administrative positions formerly denied women in the academy. Feminist pedagogy accounts for women and minorities in teaching methods. Feminist historiography and feminist historians reexamine the canon and curriculum for absences of and erroneous information about women and gender. Feminist scholars conduct research that generates knowledge about women, gender, and media.

Kim Golombisky
University of South Florida

See also Empowerment; E-Zines: Riot Grrrl; E-Zines: Third Wave Feminist; Feminist Theory: Liberal; Feminist Theory: Marxist; Feminist Theory: Postcolonial; Feminist Theory: Second Wave; Feminist Theory: Socialist; Feminist Theory: Third Wave; Feminist Theory: Women-of-Color and Multiracial Perspectives; Gender and Femininity: Motherhood; Gender and Femininity: Single/Independent Girl; Heterosexism; Identity; Ideology; Male Gaze; Mass Media; Media Consolidation; Minority Rights; Patriarchy; Postfeminism; Prejudice; Racism; Scopophilia; Sexism; Social Construction of Gender; Stereotypes; Women's Magazines: Feminist Magazines; Workforce

Further Readings

Butler, Judith. *Undoing Gender*. New York: Routledge, 2004.

Byerly, Carolyn M. and Karen Ross. *Women and Media*. Malden, MA: Blackwell, 2006.

Collins, Patricia Hill. *Black Feminist Thought*, 2nd ed. New York: Routledge, 2000.

Hartsock, Nancy. "Standpoint Theory for the Next Century." *Women and Politics*, v.18 (1997).

Kolmar, Wendy K. and Frances Bartkowski, eds. *Feminist Theory*, 2nd ed. Boston: McGraw-Hill, 2005.

Rakow, Lana F. and Laura A. Wackwitz, eds. *Feminist Communication Theory*. Thousand Oaks, CA: Sage, 2004.

Sandoval, Chela. *Methodology of the Oppressed*. Minneapolis: University of Minnesota Press, 2000.

Schneir, Miriam. *Feminism: The Essential Historical Writings*. New York: Vintage, 1972.

Tong, Rosemarie. *Feminist Thought*, 3rd ed. Boulder, CO: Westview Press, 2009.

FEMINIST THEORY: LIBERAL

Feminism encompasses a wide variety of perspectives. The shared focus is on a belief that oppression or silencing of women—because they are women—has occurred and that this should be somehow rectified. It is difficult to divide feminist perspectives into a clear set of groupings; however, most scholars agree that one general category of feminism that can be examined is liberal feminism. Liberal feminism, sometimes called egalitarian feminism, rests on an assertion that men and women are similar in most ways and thus are equal. Differences between the sexes are products of social conditioning and cultural expectations, not inborn characteristics that differentiate men from women. Therefore, men and women should be afforded the same rights, roles, and responsibilities within a culture. If women are given these rights, they can individually maintain equality through their own actions, without wholesale changes to the society. Given this underlying concept, liberal feminist activity focuses on altering laws or political processes to promote equality, including voting rights, education, equal pay, reproductive rights, and domestic rights.

Liberal feminist efforts can be seen in the actions of suffragists from around the world, including British feminists of the 18th century. Fighting to obtain more equality in rights for women, Mary Wollstonecraft wrote *A Vindication of the Rights of Woman* (1792) in response to Thomas Paine's *The Rights of Man* (1791). Also in that time period, suffragists, including Millicent Fawcett (organizer of the National Union of Women's Suffrage Societies), Dame Ethel Mary Smyth, Emily Davison, and Emmeline Pankhurst (cofounder of the Women's Social and Political Union) fought with both peaceful protest and vigorous—some might say violent—action for the right to vote and be a part of the political process in Great Britain. British women (property owning and over 30) received the right to vote in the 1918 Representation of the People Act. In 1928, women received full voting equality. In that same time period, women in the United Kingdom were granted the same grounds for divorce as men (1923) and their exclusion from a variety of professions was reduced by the Sex Disqualification Act of 1919.

In the United States, we speak of feminism as having occurred (thus far) in three waves. The first wave of feminism was largely characterized by liberal feminist efforts, as the focus was on securing equal rights (specifically related to voting) for women. During that time, journalist Margaret Fuller published *Woman in the Nineteenth Century* (1845), considered the first major work of U.S. feminism to appear in print. In the same year, Lucretia Coffin Mott and Elizabeth Cady Stanton organized the 1848 Seneca Falls Convention for women's legal rights and wrote the Declaration of Sentiments, a document built from the Declaration of Independence but with a focus on the historical treatment of women and the need for a refashioning of women's legal and political positions. Groups such as the American Woman Suffrage Association and the National Woman Suffrage Association organized efforts to fight for women's role in the political process. Women gained the right to vote in the United States on August 26, 1920.

Unlike the first wave, which was primarily a liberal feminist effort, the second wave of feminism, during the 1960s and 1970s, had several different strands; however, the liberal perspective was still well represented in this period. During this time, liberal feminists worked to change the many institutionalized policies and laws that have prevented women from obtaining positions of influence. In 1966, the National Organization for Women (NOW) was launched, with the help of noted feminist Betty Friedan (author of *The Feminine Mystique*, 1963). The focus of NOW is on the political, professional, and educational equality of women. The women's liberation movement (WLM) was also established in that period, and their key spokesperson became Gloria Steinem (Steinem sometimes characterizes herself as a radical feminist but is often spoken of as a key player in liberal feminism). An activist for women's reproductive rights, Steinem was cofounder of *Ms.* magazine. While a variety of women's rights, including reproductive, relational, and workplace, were advocated by second wave feminists, during that period much liberal feminist attention was given to the passage of the Equal Rights Amendment (ERA).

The ERA was first introduced to Congress in the 1920s. The proposed amendment was authored by Alice Paul, an active member of the suffragist campaign. Its original wording stated that "men and women shall have equal rights throughout the United States and every place subject to its jurisdiction." The amendment languished in relative obscurity for more than two decades, being introduced almost yearly in Congress but never really gaining steam. It was voted on for the first time by the Senate in 1946 and was quickly defeated. It was adopted by the Senate in 1950, but with an added clause (the Hayden Rider), which maintained all protective legislation and thereby made the act void. In its entirety, it reads:

Section 1. Equality of rights under the law shall not be denied or abridged by the United States or by any state on account of sex.

Section 2. The Congress shall have the power to enforce, by appropriate legislation, the provisions of this article.

Section 3. This amendment shall take effect two years after the date of ratification.

The amendment was brought back to Congress multiple times by the National Woman's Party (NWP) in the next decade, but little happened until after the second wave created renewed attention to women's issues in the 1960s. In the early 1970s, pressure to pass the ERA was increased via the work of NOW and the NWP. The amendment passed in the House in 1971 and in the Senate in 1972, but over the next decade it failed to be ratified by the requisite number of states—it was three states short—and the deadline for ratification, which had been extended by three years to 1982, arrived without success.

A variety of critiques of the liberal feminist stance have been lodged over the years by feminists and nonfeminists alike. First, some argue that there is an internal contradiction in the liberal feminist belief that men and women are the same and that equality should be predicated on that standpoint, in effect extending male rights to women. Some feminist theorists have argued that this viewpoint runs counter to feminist goals, because efforts to "de-gender" culture tend to take the form of adapting masculine expectations for both men and women. One example of this can be seen in attempts to provide women more access to the upper echelons of business, based

on the view that they can be just as professional and capable as men. Critics charge that the very notions of "professional and capable" utilized in organizational rhetoric are masculine (unemotional, logical, efficient, hierarchical, powerful). Thus, these scholars argue, we have continued the prioritization of the male and devalued women's ways of being in the name of emancipation.

This relates directly to the second concern. Because the liberal feminist viewpoint begins from a standpoint of sameness between men and women, the real experiential differences of being in the male body and being in the female body are downplayed or ignored. Some scholars argue that it is more appropriate to think about how we can achieve equality in ends (opportunity, respect, power, and so forth) than sameness in means. An example of this might be in workplace policies or accommodations for nursing mothers. If men and women are the same, then women should not need special rooms or additional breaks for nursing or expressing breast milk. In this case, we need to understand that men and women have a fundamental bodily difference, and instead consider how the means (work hours or physical accommodations) can be adjusted to provide equality of opportunity and ends.

The third primary critique of the liberal feminist perspective is that it does not go "far enough" in its efforts to redress the problem. Because liberal feminist effort has been primarily focused on changing laws, policies, and enactments within the current structures of society, some feminists argue that it will never get to the root of the problem. These scholars state that the very social fabric of patriarchal culture and how it unfolds in relational, organizational, educational, legal, and political contexts needs to be disassembled in order to get at the fundamental causes of injustice.

A final criticism of liberal feminism is predicated on the belief that it has arisen largely from the perspective of white, heterosexual, middle-class women. As a whole, liberal feminism has not concerned itself with the intersections of race, ethnicity, sexual orientation, class, and gender. Critics argue that this limited viewpoint creates oppression or silencing of the diversity of female voices and experiences. The experience of being a white middle-class woman is fundamentally different, these theorists argue, from being a Hispanic woman in a low-income demographic. This attention to the particular perspectives from which women experience their gendered life course has been the springboard for third wave perspectives.

Lorin Basden Arnold
Rowan University

See also Empowerment; Feminism; Feminist Theory: Marxist; Feminist Theory: Postcolonial; Feminist Theory: Second Wave; Feminist Theory: Socialist; Feminist Theory: Third Wave; Feminist Theory: Women-of-Color and Multiracial Perspectives; Identity; Ideology; Minority Rights; Patriarchy; Postfeminism; Prejudice; Racism; Sexism; Social Construction of Gender; Steinem, Gloria; Stereotypes; Workforce

Further Readings

Castro, Ginette. *American Feminism: A Contemporary History.* New York: New York University Press, 1990.

Friedan, Betty. *The Feminine Mystique.* New York: W. W. Norton, 1963.

National Organization for Women. "Chronology of the Equal Rights Amendment, 1923–1996." http://www .now.org/issues/economic/cea/history.html (Accessed September 2010).

Stanton, Elizabeth Cady and Lucretia Mott. *The Declaration of Sentiments.* http://www.nps.gov/wori/ historyculture/declaration-of-sentiments.htm (Accessed September 2010).

Tong, Rosemarie. *Feminist Thought: A More Comprehensive Introduction*, 2nd ed. Boulder, CO: Westview Press, 1998.

Wollstonecraft, Mary. *A Vindication of the Rights of Woman.* Boston: Peter Edes, 1792. http://www.bartleby .com/144 (Accessed September 2010).

FEMINIST THEORY: MARXIST

Marxist feminism is a school of feminist thought that explains women's oppression by drawing on the 19th-century political philosopher Karl Marx's ideas on class relations and class struggle. Both Marxist and socialist feminists share concerns about women's oppression. For example, both schools of feminists believe that women's oppression is rooted in capitalism, whereby the owners of capital and means of production exploit workers. Both schools of feminists believe that women will end oppression only if capitalism is overthrown. Moreover, unlike liberal feminists, both Marxist and socialist feminists do not frame women's issues as rights and equality issues. They see the ultimate goal of feminism as the liberation of women and men from oppression and exploitation. Despite these similarities, Marxist and socialist perspectives do disagree: Marxist feminists tend to see capitalism as the sole factor in women's oppression, whereas socialist feminists believe capitalism and patriarchy both contribute to women's oppression.

Marx did not write explicitly on women workers' conditions in a capitalist society. Rather, he focused on workers as a whole. In his 1867 book *Capital: A Critique of the Political Economy* (often better known by its original German title, *Das Kapital*), he explained the formation and maintenance of class relations in a capitalist society. To Marx, the mode of production primarily determines other aspects of life, such as social, political, and intellectual life. In other words, the base determines the superstructure. In the 19th century, as English society transformed from a feudal society to an industrial society, the capitalist class emerged. In feudal society, the nobles had leased land to peasants for farming and animal rearing. The peasants did not own the land, but they owned the means of production (such as farming equipment and the farm animals), and they owned their own labor. Peasants transformed their own labor to produce means of subsistence such as crops and domestic animals. However, in an industrial society, workers owned neither the means of production nor their own labor. The capitalists owned both the means of production (such as factory machines) and the workers' labor. The forms of capital that the capitalists and workers brought to the market were different. The capital of the capitalists was money, whereas the workers' only form of capital was their own labor. Workers sold their labor to the capitalists in exchange for wages. Marx called this process *alienation*, because in the process of selling their labor, workers and their labor were in a sense alienated from each other—labor became something external to the workers. In the process of production, both the machines and the labor created surplus value because they transformed one form of commodity (such as cotton) into another form of commodity (such as cloth). However, the capitalists did not share the profit with the workers. Instead, surplus value was reinvested in capital. The capitalists used the capital to buy more machines and labor in order to make more profits.

As a consequence, workers worked harder (produced more commodities in the same amount of time), and they worked more (for longer hours), but they did not earn more money. Marx called this process *exploitation*. Both concepts, exploitation and alienation, are commonly used by feminists, Marxist or not, to describe women's status in society. For example, women are said to be exploited in a male-dominated society because their labor at home and at work is used by men to make a profit. Women are said to be alienated by society because they are not seen as full members of the society.

Marx documented in *Capital* the inhuman working conditions to which women and children were subject: Children as young as six years old were employed in factories; women lace workers labored for 16 hours a day in dimly lit rooms. Despite Marx's mention of women workers, he did not write about the producer and reproducer roles that women workers played at home. Moreover, Marx's analysis of the labor process is not gendered. He did not explain why women and children were more likely to be exploited by capitalists and why male workers were more likely to be the ones who revolutionized against the capitalist class.

Friedrich Engels, Marx's long-term collaborator, explained women's role in the family in *The Origin of the Family, Private Property, and the State* (1884). Engels saw the family as an economic unit; women's roles in the family changed when the broader society changed from an agricultural society to an industrial society. Engels believed that monogamy and patrilineage were results of private ownership of property. When men and women conquered nature by producing sufficient food for subsistence, men created the concept of private property to manage surplus economic resources. Private property came in the form of land, wives, and children. Men dominated their wives and children because they legally owned their family members. Women had no rights because they were owned by their husbands. Engels objected to the bourgeois family because the wives were nothing but possessions of the men. Bourgeois wives were likened to prostitutes because they earned their means of living through offering their bodies to their husbands. To Engels, marriage in the bourgeois class was only a form of economic exchange that did not involve love. He believed that true love was only possible among the proletarians, because proletarian women did not marry for money and comfort.

Based on Engels's idea of the family, Marxist feminists believed that women would be liberated from oppression only by rejecting capitalism. To them, as long as capitalism exists, women continue to be seen as possessions and commodities.

The former Soviet Union and Mao Zedong's China are two societies in which women's lives were shaped by Marxism. It is unclear, however, if both communist societies advocated for Marxist feminism. Both communist states aimed to liberate women from feudalism by granting women status equal to that of men. In Mao's China, women's equal status entailed women's rights to be educated, to have a job, to choose a spouse, and to get a divorce. Prostitution and pornography were banned because they were deemed bourgeois. However, equal status also meant that women and men would wear the same style of clothing and would do the same work. In Mao's China, feminine expressions and personal adornments were frowned upon because they were deemed feudal. The ideal woman in Mao's China would wear loose-fitting clothes (such as the Mao suit) and have short hair. In Mao's society, women were not to be viewed as sexual beings. Women and men were to take up hard, manual labor and to perform military work in the Red Army. The strong arms of women peasants were glorified in propaganda posters. Because women were asked to work on farms and in factories, they did not have time to take care of the home. To solve the problem of child rearing and other reproductive duties, the state provided communal canteens and child-care centers.

Although women's status in communist China was sometimes glorified by Western feminists such as Julia Kristeva and Simone de Beauvoir, contemporary feminists argue that a state-directed feminism was problematic in communist societies. The political leaders of the Soviet Union and Mao's China were more interested in class equality than gender equality; they used the rhetoric of gender equality only to encourage women to join the revolution and class struggle. In reality, the male was still the norm in those societies. Gender difference was erased because women were asked to act like men. The deep-seated gender ideology in both Russian and Chinese societies reemerged when both countries adopted capitalism. Not only did women in both societies embrace feminine expressions after the abandonment of communism; prostitution and pornography also reemerged in both societies.

Evelyn Reed, a member of the U.S. for the Socialist Workers Party in the 20th century, wrote "Women: Caste, Class or Oppressed Sex?" to illustrate that it is class, not gender, that oppresses women. She did not believe that all men oppress women. On the other hand, she believed that bourgeois women oppress working-class women as servants and workers. To Reed, the solution to women's oppression was for working-class women to join working-class men in order to wage a caste war.

However, the example of the Soviet Union proved that even in a classless society with a state-instilled gender equality program, women are still more oppressed than men. When the state assigned jobs to women, they were asked to perform repetitive, mundane tasks. In addition, women were still assumed to perform domestic and reproductive duties at home. Margaret Benston suggested that women's use value at home is not counted and that women form a class that is responsible for production in the household and the family. Maria Dalla Costa and Selma James called for a wage-for-housework campaign. They believed that one way to make women's productive work at home visible is to put a value on housework. Unlike Benston, they argued that women's housework has a surplus value, not merely a use value, because the productivity of male family members depends on a functional household. Hence, women add value to the formal economy indirectly.

Micky Lee
Suffolk University, Boston

See also Critical Theory; Empowerment; Feminism; Feminist Theory: Liberal; Feminist Theory: Postcolonial; Feminist Theory: Second Wave; Feminist Theory: Socialist; Feminist Theory: Third Wave; Feminist Theory: Women-of-Color and Multiracial Perspectives; Identity; Ideology; Minority Rights; Patriarchy; Postfeminism; Prejudice; Racism; Sexism; Social Construction of Gender; Steinem, Gloria; Stereotypes; Workforce

Further Readings

Engels, Friedrich. *The Origin of the Family, Private Property and the State*. London: Penguin, 2010.

Hershatter, Gail. *Women in China's Long Twentieth Century*. Berkeley: University of California Press, 2007.

Kristeva, Julia. *About Chinese Women*. London: Marion Boyars, 1977.

Marx, Karl. *Capital: A Critique of the Political Economy*. London: Penguin, 1990.

Reed, Evelyn. "Women: Caste, Class or Oppressed Sex?" *International Socialist Review*, v.31/3 (1970).

Tong, Rosemarie. *Feminist Thought: A More Comprehensive Introduction*, 2nd ed. Boulder, CO: Westview Press, 1998.

FEMINIST THEORY: POSTCOLONIAL

Postcolonial feminist theory considers the critical importance feminist politics play in the struggle against colonization while simultaneously racializing traditional feminist theory. As an academic discipline, postcolonial feminist theory is invested in revisioning, remembering, and critically interrogating colonialism through a feminist lens. Postcolonial feminist theory begins from an intersectional identity-based perspective, placing equal emphasis on the overlapping set of subject positions affected by colonization: gender, class, sexuality, race, caste, nationality, development, religion, and other identity markers. It rejects debates over whose interests should come first, those of anticolonization or those of feminist groups, suggesting that the two groups are linked because colonial dominances disproportionately impact women and feminist struggles, often ignoring the complexities of colonization while contributing to them. Furthermore, many women's experiences in patriarchy are similar to those of colonized subjects under imperialism; both patriarchy and imperialism exert dominance. Feminism and postcolonial theory actively resist this oppression. Thus, postcolonial feminist theory takes as its point of departure a theoretical perspective that is inclusive of multiple struggles embedded within the colonial system.

Postcolonial feminist theory is not just concerned with the conditions of people in territories formally or currently colonized; it is also greatly invested in past and contemporary struggles of colonial discourse. Colonial discourses, or ways of knowing, are critical to postcolonial feminist theorists because these theorists believe language and representation produce and maintain the power of both patriarchy and colonialism. Accordingly, postcolonial feminist theory is heavily invested in critically considering the role of language in representations and identity construction, bringing attention to ways in which discursive colonization adversely affects the material realities of women. Scholars with this perspective

Gayatri Chakravorty Spivak, speaking here at the University of London in 2007, often objects to being labeled as a postcolonial feminist; however, the views of Spivak and Chandra Talpade Mohanty are generally seen as signifying the emergence of the movement. (Wikimedia/Shih-Lun Chang)

understand not only that language is a tool of imperialism but also that language can be used as a means to resist and subvert patriarchal and imperial power. In efforts to break down linguistic colonization, feminist postcolonial scholars have used two main strategies: (1) abrogation, or the rejection of imperial cultural as central, and (2) appropriation, the reconstitution of colonial discourse.

The roots of postcolonial feminist theory are often attributed to black feminist theory and Third World feminism—both strands of scholarship that critique the centrality of the white Western brand of feminism that privileges "woman" as the foundational category of oppression. While there is no original movement leader or formal point of entry, postcolonial feminist theory was said to have emerged in the 1980s when feminists such as Chandra Talpade Mohanty and Gayatri Chakravorty Spivak (who, while often denying the title postcolonial feminist, tends to be the only feminist voice consistently mentioned in contemporary postcolonial studies) accused Western feminists of deploying universal feminist rhetoric while failing to recognize their Eurocentric biases. These early writings claimed that gender was always and already racialized and that the very popular Western slogan "Sisterhood Is Global" falsely assumed that white Western women's concerns were relevant to women worldwide. These scholars, writing on behalf of mostly women of color and Third World women, accused Western middle-class feminists of silencing the concerns of women who did not share their North American economic status. Any type of privileging of gender, postcolonial feminists argued, ignores women who face colonial conditions. Here the term *double colonization* proved useful to describe the experiences of women who face both patriarchal and colonial oppression. One particularly pervasive example of double colonization is the violent use of women's bodies as literal sites of struggle between male colonizers and the males colonized.

Principally, postcolonial feminist theorists reject Western feminism's representation of Third World women as a passive homogenous category of people who are universal victims of male violence, the family system, religion, tradition, economic development, and the colonial process. However, postcolonial feminists are also quick to caution against a direct reversal of representation—or any articulation claiming to find a more "accurate" image of non-Western women—stating that colonial women are heterogeneous and thus lack an authentic or appropriate illustration.

Because many postcolonial scholars emerged out of the discipline of comparative literature, it is not surprising that a great deal of postcolonial feminist writing calls for a revisioning of traditional Western canonical literature. Postcolonial feminist scholars have sought to introduce the writings of indigenous and non-Western women in the canon. Similarly, in an effort to counter the breadth of writing that pacifies and victimizes non-Western women, postcolonial feminists offer writings that document and celebrate feminist resistance movements (such as the Indian Chipko movement and more recently the work of the Revolutionary Association of the Women of Afghanistan).

While postcolonial feminist theory has attended to various topics relevant to women, a great deal of their work is focused on veiling, female circumcision, and reproductive rights. Each of these acts or practices demonstrates the heterogeneous nature of non-Western women and signifies how important it is to consider the unique circumstances of different women around the world. These issues demonstrate the postcolonial feminist extremes that privilege universal rights, on one hand, or protect the rights of cultural relativism, on the other. For example, female circumcision (or female genital mutilation, depending on one's perspective) is a topic that divides postcolonial feminists. One group of scholars argues that the practice is a violent infringement of women's bodies and sexual rights, while defenders hold up the practice as an important cultural tradition that uneducated Western feminist reformers fail to understand or respect. Similarly, discussions of the image of veiled Muslim women occupy a place in the postcolonial feminist debate because veiling, perhaps more than any other issue, highlights the Western preoccupation with stereotyping non-Western women without critical consideration of their status and privilege. Although the veil is condemned by scholars under the banner of universal rights, it is also defended under the name of religious and ethnic diversity. Debates such as these raise a question of critical importance for postcolonial feminist theorists: Who has the right to speak for whom, when, and where?

While the rejection of any foundational category of analysis has enabled postcolonial feminist theory to avoid a great many of the criticisms plaguing other genres of feminist theory, postcolonial feminist theory is not without its critics. The most prominent critique waged against postcolonial feminist theory condemns scholars for deploying a vocabulary laden with jargon and advanced theoretical terminology. This criticism is often countered by the claim that postcolonial feminist theory seeks to revision that which has yet to be seen, understood, and thus named. Still there remains dispute among scholars as to how much theoretical language is necessary to advance a progressive political agenda. The concern is that if the people cannot understand or participate in the discussion, they are unlikely to join the struggle.

Rae Lynn Schwartz-DuPre
Western Washington University

See also Critical Theory; Empowerment; Feminism; Feminist Theory: Liberal; Feminist Theory: Marxist; Feminist Theory: Second Wave; Feminist Theory: Socialist; Feminist Theory: Third Wave; Feminist Theory: Women-of-Color and Multiracial Perspectives; Identity; Ideology; Intersectionality; Minority Rights; Patriarchy; Postfeminism; Prejudice; Racism; Sexism; Social Construction of Gender; Steinem, Gloria; Stereotypes; Workforce

Further Readings

Lewis, Reina and Sara Mills. *Postcolonial Feminist Theory: A Reader*. New York: Routledge, 2003.

Mohanty, Chandra Talpade. "Under Western Eyes: Feminist Scholarship and Colonial Discourses." *Boundary*, v.2 (1984).

Spivak, Gayatri Chakravorty. "Can the Subaltern Speak?" In *Marxism and the Interpretation of Culture*, Cary Nelson and Lawrence Grossberg, eds. Urbana: University of Illinois Press, 1988.

Spivak, Gayatri Chakravorty. "Three Women's Text and a Critique of Imperialism." *Critical Inquiry*, v.12 (1985).

FEMINIST THEORY: SECOND WAVE

The terminology of *waves* as applied to feminism is generally used to describe periods of growth and mobilization within the movement for women's rights and corresponding higher degrees of public attention paid to the struggle. While some scholars and critics debate the nuances of the precise categorization of waves, the second wave is generally used to describe a period of activist movement from the mid- to late 1960s to the mid-1980s. Often referred to as the "women's liberation movement," second wave feminism was largely focused on identifying the subordination of women and ending discrimination.

The second wave emerged during a period of substantial social upheaval, drawing from cultural movements that questioned entrenched power, such as student, anti-Vietnam War, and race activism. However, while it held commonalities with other counterculture movements at the time, second wave feminism was itself a break with other leftist movements, which were criticized for being male dominated, with a lack of female leadership and expression. While multiple strains of feminist theoretical thought underscored the movement, second wave activism was largely focused on righting inequality. Documenting both the contemporary and historic marginalization of women, second wave feminists worked to promote equal pay and equal access to education and employment. One of the overarching notions of the second wave is reflected in the often quoted phrase, "The personal is political." While many campaigns were focused on forging more opportunities for women in the public sphere, this saying is emblematic of the movement's corresponding focus on the private, lived experiences of women, with discussions of sexual relations, motherhood, violence, and reproductive rights taking precedence. Activists and theorists likewise focused a great deal on the cultural representation of women and gender, forwarding notions about the ways in which gender inequality in both public and private spheres is perpetuated through media and offering opportunities and models for resistance.

Overarching Approach

Central to much second wave feminist theory are critiques of patriarchy, conceptualized as an oppressive system of male domination that is enacted at institutional, social, cultural, and personal levels. Second wave feminists argued that patriarchy is not natural or inevitable but rather a result of social construction. Media are theorized as major contributors to the establishment and maintenance of this social system. Many feminist theorists tackled popular culture in particular, identifying it as a space where gender inequalities were reflected and upheld. They theorized that media have powerful effects, training women (and men) and keeping them in their prescribed, and profoundly unequal, roles. Linking their studies to the personal experiences of women, studies often focused on demonstrating the ways in which media construct gender roles and how stereotypical portrayals are linked to women's participation in public life and their feelings about themselves.

Key Studies

Betty Friedan's book *The Feminine Mystique* (1963) is often credited with sparking the second wave and contributing greatly to the movement's analysis of media and gender. In the book, Friedan theorizes about her mediated society, where advertising, magazines, and other media create a definition of womanhood based on being a wife and mother and where commercial forces work to manipulate women into consumption based on these domestic roles. Women's striving and ultimate inability to conform fully to this idealized image is, Friedan argues, the source of a great unhappiness and lack of personal fulfillment for women in postwar America. Likewise, in 1978 Gaye Tuchman voiced concern about young girls modeling their beliefs and expectations on repeated portrayals of women as housewives on children's television. Tuchman forwarded a notion, building on the work of George Gerbner, that women are "symbolically annihilated" by mass-media products, which show them primarily in traditional, gendered roles, if they represent them at all. These portrayals, in effect, teach females that they "should direct their hearts toward hearth and home," rather than pursuits in the public sphere, and train women to be passive, submissive, and dependent on men. Feminists working in the area of film studies offered similar critiques of their subject. Laura Mulvey's groundbreaking 1975 article "Visual Pleasure and Narrative Cinema," which uses Freudian and Lacanian psychoanalysis to forward a notion of the "male gaze," theorizes that Hollywood films create an imbalance of power between the viewer and viewed, objectifying the women portrayed in film and putting the audience in the role of the heterosexual male gazing upon the female.

This concern with depictions of mediated portrayals of sexuality and power is also reflected in the second wave's concern with pornography. The late 1970s and early 1980s saw an increase in debate in the movement around issues of sexuality and sex, in what came to be termed the "Sex Wars." Andrea Dworkin's 1981 book *Pornography: Men Possessing Women* is typically cited as one of the foundational texts in the radical feminist antipornography movement. In this and other works, Dworkin links pornography to rape and violence against women. The antipornography campaigns heightened conflicts within the feminist movement, leading to a "pro-sex" wing in feminism, which positioned arguments against pornography as indicative of censorship and a stifling of sexual expression. These schisms, around issues such as transwomen and lesbianism, pornography, sadomasochism, and representations of sexuality, are often thought to have contributed to or marked the end of the second wave feminist period.

Making Media

While much of the theory that emerged from the movement attended to examining harmful portrayals and their strong effects, there was also a growing examination of the ways in which women participated with popular culture. Spurred, in part, by the growing influence of cultural studies in academia, feminist scholars focused their attention on both women's production of media and the ways in which active female audiences resist and rewrite dominant, repressive media depictions.

In many ways, second wave feminists demonstrated an uneasy relationship with mass media. Mass media were thought to constitute an extremely negative force in the lives of women. However, in recognizing the influence of media on popular understandings of gender and behavior, some feminists also advocated harnessing the tools of mass media and using them to empower women. If a major goal of feminism was to make women more aware of the shared concerns they experienced, then media could be used to break down this isolation. It was thought that popular culture could be used to create positive portrayals of women while also making women aware of their oppressed state through media-based consciousness-raising.

Perhaps one of the most famous examples of this is *Ms.* magazine, the first commercial feminist magazine in the United States. Founded in 1972 by Gloria Steinem and Letty Cobin Pogrebin, the magazine often struggled to balance its desire to be an open forum for feminist dialogue with survival in the commercial, mass-media environment. Australian feminist Helen Reddy's 1970 song "I Am Woman" is another example of this popularizing of feminism. The song became a mainstream success, rising to number one on the U.S. charts in October 1972 and number two on the Australian charts in 1973, and became a touchstone for the women's movement. While some feminists were critical of participation with mainstream media, others argued that these efforts helped the feminist movement reach people who might not have as readily identified with feminism, making the movement's ideas and goals more accessible to a wider audience.

Impact

Although it was often promoted as a radical movement open to everyone, regardless of class, race, or sexuality, the second wave has been criticized for promoting the concerns of the more mainstream elements of feminism, in some cases becoming the province of white, heterosexual middle-class women. The overall movement has been criticized both by feminists at the time and by later feminists for not being appropriately attuned to the differences among women or considering the nuances of oppression based on other conjoining factors, such as race, sexuality, class, ethnicity, and national or ethnic background. The second wave's ideas about media have likewise been critiqued for being tied to mass-culture theories that assume singular, uniform effects on groups of people. Despite these problems, however, the movement produced some of feminism's most significant and lasting contributions to our understanding of the relationship between media and gender, forming the basis of much academic critique by feminists working today within various intellectual traditions.

Theresa Rose Crapanzano
University of Colorado, Boulder

See also Cultural Politics; Empowerment; Feminism; Feminist Theory: Liberal; Feminist Theory: Marxist; Feminist Theory: Postcolonial; Feminist Theory: Socialist; Feminist Theory: Third Wave; Feminist Theory: Women-of-Color and Multiracial Perspectives; Gender Media Monitoring; hooks, bell; Identity; Ideology; Mass Media; Media Literacy; Minority Rights; Misogyny; Mulvey, Laura; Patriarchy; Postfeminism; Prejudice; Racism; Sexism; Social Construction of Gender; Social Inequality; Steinem, Gloria; Stereotypes; Television; Women's Magazines: Feminist Magazines; Workforce

Further Readings

Arrow, Michelle. "'It Has Become My Personal Anthem': 'I Am Woman,' Popular Culture and 1970s Feminism." *Australian Feminist Studies*, v.22/53 (2007).

Farrell, Amy Erdman. *Yours in Sisterhood:* Ms. *Magazine and the Promise of Popular Feminism.* Chapel Hill: University of North Carolina Press, 1998.

Friedan, Betty. *The Feminine Mystique.* 1963. Reprint, New York: W. W. Norton, 2001.

Hollows, Joanne. *Feminism, Femininity and Popular Culture.* New York: Manchester University Press, 2000.

Luckett, Moya. "A Moral Crisis in Prime Time: *Peyton Place* and the Rise of the Single Girl." In *Television, History, and American Culture Feminist Critical Essays*, Mary Beth Haralovich and Lauren Rabinovitz, eds. Durham, NC: Duke University Press, 2002.

Millett, Kate. *Sexual Politics.* Urbana: University of Illinois Press, 2000.

Morgan, Robin, ed. *Sisterhood Is Powerful an Anthology of Writings From the Women's Liberation Movement.* New York: Random House, 1970.

Mulvey, Laura. "Visual Pleasure and Narrative Cinema." *Screen*, v.16/3 (1975).

Nicholson, Linda, ed. *The Second Wave: A Reader in Feminist Theory.* New York: Routledge, 1997.

Rosen, Ruth. *The World Split Open: How the Modern Women's Movement Changed America.* New York: Penguin, 2001.

Tuchman, Gaye. "The Symbolic Annihilation of Women by the Mass Media." In *Hearth and Home: Images of Women in the Mass Media*, Gaye Tuchman, Arlene Kaplan Daniels, and James Benet, eds. New York: Oxford University Press, 1978.

FEMINIST THEORY: SOCIALIST

Socialist feminism examines different women's experiences by explaining how women have been historically oppressed and exploited by capitalism and patriarchy, or male domination. It acknowledges that most women are oppressed, both as members of the working class and by patriarchal social relations. Although socialist feminists agree that a full analysis of women cannot exclude the economic relations of production and the social relations of reproduction (as well as other social divisions based on race, ethnicity, and nationality), major debates lie in the nature of the relationship between capitalism and patriarchy.

One approach to socialist feminism is to describe capitalism and patriarchy as dual systems of oppression. This approach argues that there is no fixed relationship between capitalism and patriarchy. Patriarchy does not determine the social relations of production and reproduction in the final instance, but neither does capitalism. Thus, the two systems can work in tandem, move independently, or develop in contradiction. The socialist feminist analysis of the development of the family wage as a settlement between working-class men and capitalists in the 20th century is one example of the use of dual systems theory. The family wage paid to some men was large enough that they could support a wife and children. This excluded some women and children from the labor market. Men obviously benefit from this arrangement because it renders women economically dependent on men making the family wage. However, this arrangement is not logical from the perspective of capital, because capital benefits from having a large labor pool to keep wages low. In this case, patriarchal relations intervened in the realm of economic relations. Although the family wage is not logical from the standpoint of capital, providing a means for men to control women decreased the likelihood of an economic revolution.

Another approach to socialist feminism is to argue that there is an integrated system of women's oppression. Capitalism has historically always had a gender bias, so there cannot be separate or independent systems of power. In the example of the family wage, an integrated analysis suggests that keeping women as a secondary labor force is only one of several ways in which capitalism has exerted a gendered form of discrimination. Analyzing the gendered division of labor moves beyond class analysis and determines why women are treated unequally in terms of lower wages or no wages for domestic work, are excluded from certain types of jobs and occupations, are restricted in terms of access to positions of authority, and are sexually harassed in the workplace.

Socialist feminism has been influential in critical inquiries into gender in the media. Socialist feminism offers a framework for addressing women's oppression in communication, how mass media are produced, media artifacts, and audiences. Particularly in the study of media artifacts (such as literature, film, and television), socialist feminism, influenced by psychoanalysis, has revealed important insights, such as the male gaze, which objectifies women. Other socialist feminist studies of the media show how media representations, such as the valorization of the heterosexual, nuclear family, reinforce the capitalist and patriarchal status quo.

Socialist feminist theory was first articulated in the 1970s as a corrective to Marxist analysis that did not fully engage with the entirety of women's experiences. Marxism had come to focus too narrowly on the production of goods and services and not on the reproduction of people. Marxist analysts focused primarily on wage labor, ignoring unpaid labor traditionally allotted to women, such as childbearing, child rearing, and household chores and management. Additionally, Marxism understood women's oppression as a form of class oppression. The argument against Marxist theory as it developed in the West in the 20th century was that it assumed gender equality would follow workers' liberation from the capitalist mode of production. Socialist feminists, however, point out that women's subordination to men developed before the advent of capitalism and that women's inequality persisted in noncapitalist countries such as China and the Soviet Union.

Socialist feminism also arose as a critique of liberal and radical feminist theories. According to socialist feminism, liberal feminism's call for individual equality would not end working-class women's oppression by capitalism. Moreover, the idea that individuals are autonomous agents whose needs are different from those of other individuals derives from patriarchal philosophy. The critique of radical feminism is that it sees men and women as essentially different and the relation of oppression between men and women, with men as the oppressors, cannot be changed. Socialist feminism expresses the idea that the differences between men and women are historically contingent and socially constructed. Additionally, the relationship between men and women is arranged through the production of things and the production of people.

Robin Johnson
Sam Houston State University

See also Critical Theory; Empowerment; Feminism; Feminist Theory: Liberal; Feminist Theory: Marxist; Feminist Theory: Postcolonial; Feminist Theory: Second Wave; Feminist Theory: Third Wave; Feminist Theory: Women-of-Color and Multiracial Perspectives; Heterosexism; Identity; Ideology; Intersectionality; Minority Rights; Patriarchy; Postfeminism; Prejudice; Racism; Sexism; Social Construction of Gender; Steinem, Gloria; Stereotypes; Workforce

Further Readings

Ehrenreich, Barbara. "What Is Socialist Feminism?" *Monthly Review*, v.57/3 (2005).
Eisenstein, Zillah. "Constructing a Theory of Capitalist Patriarchy and Socialist Feminism." *Critical Sociology*, v.25/2 (1977).
Hansen, Karen and Ilene Philipson, eds. *Women, Class, and the Feminist Imagination: A Socialist-Feminist Reader*. Philadelphia, PA: Temple University Press, 1990.
Jaggar, Alison. *Feminist Politics and Human Nature*. Totowa, NJ: Rowman & Allanheld, 1983.
Rowbotham, Sheila. *Women, Resistance and Revolution*. New York: Random House, 1973.

FEMINIST THEORY: THIRD WAVE

Third wave feminism refers to feminist philosophy, writings, and activism dating from approximately the mid-1990s through the present. Third wave feminism can indicate a variety of perspectives, including intersectional feminism, Third World and diasporic feminism, and what is known as postfeminism. Commonly, however, third wave feminism refers to U.S.-Anglo writings, popular-culture texts, and, to a lesser degree, activism that focus on issues of concern to younger people living in highly mediated, wealthy societies in an age of neoliberalism and globalization.

Unlike earlier generations of feminists, members of the third wave take for granted that the overwhelming majority of women will, because of economic necessity, participate in the workforce. They also expect women to have equal access to educational opportunities. In fact, part of the challenge for third wave feminists is defining feminism's goals in the wake of its successes in improving many women's life opportunities. In an era when women are earning more college degrees than men and discrimination in the workplace is outlawed, some people argue that there is no further need for feminist activism. Compounding the challenges wrought, paradoxically, by feminism's qualified successes are profound cultural and intellectual shifts since the 1970s. For example, not only do third wave feminists need to account fully for issues of race, class, and sexual orientation in forging their agenda; they must also contend with those who question the fundamental identity of "women."

The character of third wave feminism, its core issues, and the controversies around its purpose and goals are best understood through the viewpoint of its progenitor, second wave feminism. In the late 1960s, spurred by the energy and achievements of the civil rights movement, many women with experience in leftist political activism banded together to work for "women's liberation." Second wave feminism was characterized by conflicting strains—radical, liberal, and cultural—that worked toward somewhat different ends; however, feminists in this era did share key concerns. For example, all second wave feminists desired liberation from patriarchy. Sexist treatment—often symbolized by women's sexual subjugation to men in the law, in romantic relationships, and in pornography—was a shared target of activism and consciousness-raising. Second wave feminists worked for women's collective and individual empowerment through a variety of means, including legal protections from sexual harassment and workplace discrimination, reformed rape laws, increased protection from domestic violence, equal education, the celebration of women's achievements in the arts and sciences, acknowledgment of women's unpaid domestic contributions, and greater respect for women in their role as mothers.

Third wave feminism continues its predecessor's legacy in some respects and departs from it in others. Third wave feminists continue to promote women's substantive equality with men, though they may differ among themselves as to what, exactly, this entails. The majority of feminists influenced by the third wave support reproductive rights, equal treatment in the workplace, and lesbian, gay, bisexual, transsexual/transgender, queer/questioning (LGBTQ) rights. Third wave feminists face different challenges from those faced by second wave feminists. For example, third wave feminism must find ways to engage people who are allied with feminist concerns but who do not feel much political urgency regarding women's rights. In wealthy, English-speaking countries, much of the most obvious and egregious oppression, such as blatant sexual discrimination, is outlawed and routinely prosecuted. Women have access to legal remedies and some degree of cultural support in seeking redress from those who engage in misogynic behavior. Moreover, although abortion rights in the United States have been under nearly constant attack since the 1973 *Roe v. Wade* Supreme Court ruling, abortion is legal and various forms of effective birth control are widely available. These developments have made the fight to secure women's reproductive rights seem less pressing, despite the reality that poor and rural women still find it almost impossible to secure a timely and affordable abortion.

Perhaps the most notable difference between the second and third waves is feminists' divergent attitudes toward sex, particularly the portrayal of women as sexual objects and sexual subjects in popular-culture texts. The distinction between the two traditions' analyses of sexuality can be somewhat simplistically reduced to an emphasis on power versus an emphasis on pleasure. Second wave feminists focused more on the political realities of men's power over women in the realm of sex and intimacy. In the 1970s and 1980s, feminists fought against the sexual double standard and the widespread acceptance of men's sexual violence toward women; they transformed social and legal norms. In contrast, third wave feminists tend to highlight women's agency and choice in intimate relationships. They frequently insist on the complexity of sexual relationships and representations.

There are important philosophical differences behind this discrepant take on sexuality. The first is many feminists' concern that the second wave's emphasis on the negative aspects of sex—abuse, rape, discrimination, and unequal treatment in medicine and the law—reinforced the message that sex was bad and that "good" women did not actively pursue it. Some members of the second wave, and most third wave feminists, advocate "sex positivity," or having an inclusive, pleasure-oriented perspective on the sexual activities of consenting adults. Third wave feminists are unlikely to view heterosexual marriage as sexist per se or to advocate "political lesbianism"; they defend the performance of inequality (such as sadomasochism) in the realm of sex. Many members of the third wave have even come out in favor of strip clubs, pornography, and prostitution, arguing that these can be sites of women's empowerment and pleasure.

Another philosophical difference is that third wave feminism has been affected by the movement toward individualization and "choice" that characterizes industrialized countries at the beginning of the 21st century. Instead of proscribing certain behaviors or beliefs as sexist, many third wave feminists argue that women should be free to choose how they wish to live their lives. They argue that empowering women means making more choices available and then being able to understand that each person will have different ideas about what constitutes a good or successful life path. This rhetoric makes third wave feminism more inclusive; however, it also makes it more difficult to adopt a single stance toward controversial issues ranging from cosmetic surgery to the subordination of women in many world religions.

The prominence of choice in third wave rhetoric is one of several features that alienate feminists more influenced by second wave principles. Some detractors of third wave feminism have even termed it "postfeminist." In this understanding, third wave feminists do little more than apologize for, or even celebrate, gender inequality, particularly when it comes to the sexual objectification of women and girls in popular culture. Additionally, because of its attention to issues of sexual representation and its "girl power" image, third wave feminism, some argue, is simply another movement whose concerns are most relevant to white, middle-class, heteronormative women. Such criticism is important as an opportunity for reflection on the meaning and goals of feminism in the 21st century.

Third wave feminism, with its unwavering support of reproductive rights, activism against domestic abuse and rape, and engagement with problems of representation in a highly mediated world, demonstrates the continuing relevance of feminist critique. Though considerable advancements have been made, serious gender inequalities continue to limit women's opportunities around the world. Lower pay for equal work, limited and expensive childcare, and violence against women remain major problems almost everywhere. Sexist treatment also affects men, as well as gays, lesbians, and those with nonnormative gender identifications. Particularly in its more expansive and subtler take on sexuality, the third wave has made significant new contributions to our understanding of issues such as intimacy, power, love, and the erotic. Third wave feminism is still evolving and promises to offer new insights into gender, sex, the family, work, life balance, and many other issues in the years to come.

Brittany N. Griebling
University of Pennsylvania

See also Empowerment; E-Zines: Riot Grrrl; E-Zines: Third Wave Feminist; Feminism; Feminist Theory: Liberal; Feminist Theory: Marxist; Feminist Theory: Postcolonial; Feminist Theory: Second Wave; Feminist Theory: Socialist; Feminist Theory: Women-of-Color and Multiracial Perspectives; Identity; Ideology; Intersectionality; Minority Rights; Patriarchy; Postfeminism; Prejudice; Racism; Sexism; Social Construction of Gender; Steinem, Gloria; Stereotypes; Workforce

Further Readings

Gillis, Stacy, Gillian Howie, and Rebecca Munford, eds. *Third Wave Feminism: A Critical Exploration.* New York: Palgrave Macmillan, 2004.

Haywood, Leslie and Jennifer Drake, eds. *Third Wave Agenda: Being Feminist, Doing Feminism.* Minneapolis: University of Minnesota Press, 1997.

Shugart, H., et al. "Mediating Third-Wave Feminism: Appropriation and Postmodern Media Practice." *Communication Abstracts*, v.24/6 (2001).

FEMINIST THEORY: WOMEN-OF-COLOR AND MULTIRACIAL PERSPECTIVES

Within feminist theory there is a rich and important stream of intellectual thought produced for and by black feminists and women-of-color activists and scholars that challenges the ethnocentricity of the women's movement. Black feminist theory grew out of the racism experienced in the mainstream feminist movement as well as the sexism black women experienced through their participation in the black liberation movements. Although important figures such as Sojourner Truth were critical of white women during the first wave of feminism, the mass political movements of the mid- to late 20th century primarily facilitated the production of this body of work.

Black feminist theory illustrates the ways in which women's experiences of subordination and oppression are informed by a matrix of race, class, and gender rooted in legacies of slavery and colonialism. Black feminist theory and multiracial feminism continue to play a crucial role in interrogating and making sense of women's roles and representations within media culture.

A Movement Divided

While the second wave feminist movement can claim many successes, it was not immune from internal strife. Black feminists and many women of color called out white feminists for their role in perpetuating racist and other oppressive behaviors. They called on white feminists to consider the ways in which their racial privilege informed their perspectives as well as the kind of political strategies devised. In ignoring or downplaying their collusion with oppressive behaviors, white women effectively marginalized and silenced the experiences of black women and women of color. White feminists exacerbated racial tensions by insisting that the cause of women's oppression and inequality was sex- and gender-based. This placed black women and women of color in an untenable position wherein they felt pressured to place sex and gender issues ahead of race differences, which was problematic and only fueled tensions with the men in their communities.

As a result, many black women began to question the very meaning of "feminism," "sisterhood," and "women's culture," recognizing that these terms might reflect only the experiences of white women. Black feminists also rejected the strategy of "separatism"—the idea that women should voluntarily remove themselves from patriarchal society—because it failed to account for the ways in which black women and women of color have shared oppression with the men in their communities. These growing divisions within the movement led many black women and women of color to begin exploring, debating, and strategizing ways to address their particular concerns rather than work on the "problems of white women."

These debates continued to flourish with the institutionalization of women's studies and black studies in higher education in the wake of second wave feminism, as a number of key thinkers—such as Angela Davis, Audre Lorde, bell hooks, and Patricia Hill Collins—came to prominence within academia. Black feminist theory challenges the "gatekeepers" of theory production—white, middle-class women and men—by writing into existence the stories, histories, and experiences of black women and women of color. Black feminist scholars argue that articulating the collective standpoint of black women is necessary in order to resist the dominant culture's attempt to speak for and define them. Black feminist works attend to the multipositionality of women as racial, classed, sexual, and gendered subjects and refute the notion that one identity or form of oppression is more important than another. Rather, scholars like bell hooks refer to "interlocking systems of domination." Intersectional analysis offers an alternative approach to understanding women's oppression and exploitation by moving beyond binary thinking and instead attending to these fluid and complex structures and how they shape women's everyday lives.

Black feminists not only are concerned with theorizing the constraints imposed on women through structures of domination but also focus on the ways in which black women and women of color have resisted such oppressive structures—for instance, through the formation of alternative kinship structures and cultural practices and forms rooted in Afrocentric traditions. Collins similarly writes about the "outsider within status," revealing the ways in which black women throughout American history have had to cultivate their own ideals and understandings about black womanhood in a society that has historically tried to deny their personhood by restricting "access" to the privileges and rights accorded to white, middle-class, heterosexual women. Black feminist theory reveals the ways in which black women and women of color have always been positioned as the "racial other" through the construction of harmful stereotypes, such as the welfare queen and mammy.

Interrogating Media Culture

Black women and women-of-color feminists also utilize theory to explore, investigate, and deconstruct the ways in which black women are represented in media, whether as racist stereotypes, purveyors of resistance, or entrepreneurs. For instance, black feminist scholar Tricia Rose has explored the role of black women within hip-hop culture and how their participation as rappers revealed a form of cultural resistance informed by antiracist feminism. Female rap artists, through their lyrics and music, explore hetero-relations, sexism, domestic violence, and rape but also seek to empower black women by celebrating their history, culture, and achievements. This brand of rap music not only confronts sexism in their communities but also challenges the racism of the dominant culture through such ethics as "Black is beautiful."

Media pose new challenges for black feminist theorists in other ways, especially as a handful of black women—such as Oprah Winfrey and African American supermodel turned media mogul Tyra Banks—have emerged as prominent public figures who have become the focus of much critical debate. On one hand, Banks is held up as a resistant feminist figure; on the other hand, she espouses (post)racial and (post)feminist discourses that render notions of inequality and oppression as passé. Such depoliticized discourses, in turn, enable the reproduction of problematic images of black women, such as the "bitch" and the "welfare queen," with few consequences. Figures like Banks remain controversial because their successes overshadow the ways in which black women and women of color continue to be affected by systemic racism and other forms of social and economic oppression that have roots in historical legacies of slavery and colonialism.

Natasha Patterson
Simon Fraser University, British Columbia

See also hooks, bell; Intersectionality; Patriarchy; Prejudice; Racism; Reality-Based Television: *America's Next Top Model*; Stereotypes

Further Readings

Collins, Patricia Hill. *Black Feminist Thought: Knowledge, Consciousness, and the Politics of Empowerment.* New York: Routledge, 1991.

Davis, Angela. *Women, Race, and Class.* New York: Random House, 1981.

hooks, bell. *Black Looks: Race and Representation.* Toronto, ON: Between the Lines, 1992.

Joseph, Ralina L. "'Tyra Banks Is Fat': Reading (*Post-*) Racism and (*Post-*) Feminism in the New Millennium." *Critical Studies in Media Communication*, v.26/3 (August 2009).

Lourde, Audre. *Sister Outsider.* New York: The Crossing Press, 1984.

Rose, Tricia. *Black Noise: Rap Music and Black Culture in Contemporary America.* Hanover, NH: University Press of New England, 1994.

FILM: HOLLYWOOD

Every week, Hollywood releases a bevy of films in various genres, meant to relieve viewers from their everyday lives for a few hours while entertaining them. This entertainment, however, sends countless messages about gender—about females, males, and even members of the transgender community. Overall, the Hollywood film industry, in dramatic, action, western, science fiction, fantasy, horror, and comedy movies, supports traditional depictions of gender.

The drama genre ultimately represents women and men in situations that reflect contemporary gender pressures and stereotypes. For instance, many dramas emphasize women's struggles with expectations for their gender; most other well-known dramatic films starring women center on romance, doomed love, or love gone wrong. On the other hand, male-dominated dramas emphasize stories about corruption, loyalty, and war. Dramas with male-centered stories tend to be more championed by critics than are female-dominated dramas; this pattern may result from the fact that dramas about women focus on feelings (playing off the cultural stereotype that women are more emotional and intuitive), whereas dramas about males usually incorporate some romantic element but balance this aspect with a wealth of action.

Movies like *Kramer vs. Kramer* (1979) and *Revolutionary Road* (2008) show women battling stereotypes and the drastic measures some women take to escape the oppression of these expectations. In *Kramer vs. Kramer*, Meryl Streep plays Joanna Kramer, a wife and mother who abandons her family, stifled by the expectations placed on her by late 1970s America. She returns months later and asks for her son, but in the end she leaves the boy to live with his father. This film in particular toys with traditional notions about gender in America (including commentary on men as successful single parents). In *Revolutionary Road*, April Wheeler (played by Kate Winslet) struggles with the pressures faced by women in 1950s America. April and her husband, longing for a life more adventurous than the one they lead, concoct a plan to relocate to Europe. April feels unfulfilled raising her children and attending to the house. April unexpectedly becomes pregnant, however, and enters a downward spiral, ending ultimately with an abortion she performs on herself and her own death. Both of these films represent the inner turmoil many women experience in relation to traditional expectations about gender in American society. A subgenre of drama, romantic dramas tell stories about lost love, doomed love, or love gone wrong. Films such as *Casablanca* (1942), *An Affair to Remember* (1957), *Gone With the*

Wind (1939), *Love Story* (1970), *The Lake House* (2006), and *The Notebook* (2004) represent this subgenre. In the film *Titanic* (1997), for instance, upper-class girl Rose Dewitt meets the working-class Jack Dawson aboard the infamous ship, and though fiery passion (and love) ensue, Dawson dies while Dewitt must live on without him. Hollywood romantic dramas reinforce the idea that women are hopeless romantics or entirely dependent on their male lovers.

Male-centered dramas focus on action over emotion. Popular male-dominated dramas include films like *The Godfather* (1972) and its sequels (1974, 1990), *The Departed* (2006), *The Boondock Saints* (1999), *Goodfellas* (1990), and *Fight Club* (1999). Each of these films incorporates a wealth of action and fighting between men (either with weapons or in hand-to-hand combat). Films like *The Godfather*, *Goodfellas*, and *The Departed* also treat the theme of crime and ultimately imply that men are responsible for corruption but also that they are the only people who can restore order in a corrupt society (like the MacManus brothers of *The Boondock Saints*, who both cause chaos but who also restore order in their neighborhood). These male-centered dramas also emphasize the role of men as warriors, with a hunger for physical combat. Similarly, dramas about war, such as *All Quiet on the Western Front* (1930), *Das Boot* (1981), and *Saving Private Ryan* (1998), stress how men are expected to be soldiers and fight, all while keeping a brave face.

Action films, like dramas, often emphasize contemporary stereotypes about gender. In general, Hollywood action films portray men as adventurous, intelligent, and central characters, whereas women play characters with secondary status or love interests for the hero. Main characters in most popular action films are men. Film series like the *Indiana Jones*, *Die Hard*, *Crank*, and *National Treasure* franchises all have male protagonists who are intelligent, adventurous, and charming. The men in these films are also presented as deft and indestructible. Indiana Jones, for example, solves the riddles presented him on his quest for the Holy Grail in *Indiana Jones and the Last Crusade* (1989), and Chev Chelios in the *Crank* series is resuscitated multiple times to attack those who have thwarted him. The women in these films serve as love interests for the protagonists, temptresses, or sidekicks (with physical and mental capacities secondary to those

of the protagonist). Action films centered on superheroes also, largely, have male protagonists. Films or film series like *Superman*, *Batman*, *Spider-Man*, *Iron Man*, *Hellboy*, and *X-Men* support this pattern. Although there are several superhero films with women as central or supporting characters—including *Elektra* (2005), *Catwoman* (2004), and *Lara Croft: Tomb Raider* (2001)—the action/superhero genre remains dominated by men, and these films imply that men are indestructible and intelligent, while females in action films usually have subservient status.

Closely related to the action film genre are westerns, a category of film that upholds strictly traditional notions about gender. One of the most famous western stars is John Wayne, who was often paired with Maureen O'Hara as leading lady. In films like *Rio Grande* (1950), *The Quiet Man* (1952), *The Wings of Eagles* (1957), *McLintock!* (1963), and *Big Jake* (1971), Wayne stars as the macho, strong, adventurous cowboy with O'Hara as the woman in need of rescue or a source of tension and animosity. Though these films represent westerns from the 1950s, 1960s, and 1970s, even more recent films perpetuate conventional ideas about gender, including *Legends of the Fall* (1994) and *No Country for Old Men* (2007). In *Legends of the Fall*, three brothers fight in wars and conquer the wilderness, but all meet destruction by the same woman; this film casts men as soldiers and pioneers, and women in the stereotypical role as temptress. *No Country for Old Men* focuses on the battle between very violent men, either searching for or trying to preserve a large amount of money, thus painting men as angry, aggressive, and greedy. Women in the film are portrayed as unintelligent, slack-jawed victims. One of the few westerns to experiment with representations of gender is *Brokeback Mountain* (2005), which chronicles the love affair between two cowboys. The majority of westerns, however, support traditional ideas about both men and women.

Other film genres deserving analysis include fantasy and science fiction. Science fiction and fantasy films are designed primarily with a male audience in mind, but scholars demonstrate that the number of female viewers has grown steadily and continues to do so. Regardless of changing viewer demographics, science fiction and fantasy movies rarely experiment with gender expectations and instead portray women as sex symbols or peace weavers, while men hold the role of hyperintelligent beings and world saviors. In science fiction films like the *Star Trek* series (1996's *Star Trek: First Contact*, for instance), women hold roles of importance, like Dr. Beverley Crusher or Commander Deanna Troi. Even so, these women's professions emphasize stereotypically feminine traits; Crusher, as a doctor, exemplifies caring and nurturing, while Troi, the ship's counselor, is applauded for her empathic ability to understand what others are thinking and feeling. In contrast, men on the ship, even the noble and revered Captain Picard, are guided by logic. That is not to say the men on the starship *Enterprise* are without feeling; filmmakers do not emphasize these characteristics in male characters. Instead, Picard, first officer Will Riker, and especially the android and sentient being Data are known for their mental prowess and quick thinking, which allow them to save countless species from themselves or enemies. While all the members of the *Enterprise* show understanding of difficult scientific concepts designed for space travel and survival, the men on the ship excel in comparison to the women. Likewise, in the *Star Wars* universe, filmmakers portray women more as sex symbols and temptresses than as warriors. Padmé Amidala may be a queen and member of the intergalactic senate, but she is also the downfall of Anakin Skywalker, who disregards Jedi rules to pursue his love for her. Leia Organa, though independent and witty, also serves as a distraction for Han Solo. When Jabba the Hut takes her prisoner, filmmakers created one of the most well-known sexy and iconic images, with Leia in her maroon and gold bikini top and skirt, chains shackling her neck. In contrast, the fate of the world depends on the talents of men like Luke Skywalker, Obi-wan Kenobi, and Darth Vader. These major science fiction franchises affirm gender stereotypes through film.

Related to the genre of science fiction films is the fantasy film genre. Some of the most popular fantasy film series remain *Lord of the Rings*, *Harry Potter*, and *Twilight*. Each of these film series relays messages about gender to viewers. In the *Lord of the Rings* films, the fate of Middle Earth hinges on a fellowship constituted entirely of men. The task of destroying evil plaguing the world is left to them, while the women in the films function primarily as romantic interests. Arwen, with her soft, soothing voice, attends to the injured Frodo and saves his life by racing him to Rivendell; Éowyn disguises herself as a man to fight in battle, then nurses Faramir back

to health and eventually marries him. These women both represent and revise expectations for females. When Arwen faces the ring wraiths on her own, risking her life to save Frodo's, she proves herself independent, strong, and fearless. Unlike most empathetic female figures, she does not hesitate to destroy her opponents, conjuring a wrathful river to wash the wraiths away. Similarly, in a scene beloved by many female fans, Éowyn enters battle and destroys the king of the Nazgül (the ring wraiths): When the king says he cannot be destroyed by a man, Éowyn tears off her helmet, her long, blond locks tumble down, and states, "I am no man." She successfully destroys her enemy. Both Arwen and Éowyn confirm traditional ideas about the female gender with their gentleness in times of sorrow, willingness to cater to the needs of others, and the desire for love, but both also refuse to conform to the traditional expectations for women.

Another successful fantasy film franchise, *Harry Potter*, conforms more rigorously to beliefs about gender. In *Harry Potter*, women like Molly Weasley and Petunia Dursley are both stay-at-home mothers, while their husbands daily leave the house for jobs outside the home. Teachers like Sybil Trelawney, Minerva McGonagall, and Dolores Umbridge behave in ways stereotypical for women. Trelawney wears a lot of jewelry and practices the art of divination (a subject in which intuition and feeling are critical, both which are elements closely associated with women). McGonagall serves as a stern mother figure and teaches transfiguration, a type of science course, but not a "hard" science like potions, which involves a great deal of chemistry. Umbridge's love for the color pink and her affection for cats cast her as the stereotypical lonely old maid. Hermione, the most important female in the series, is highly intelligent and loyal to her friends, but she is also hyperfeminized in the films and morphs into more of a sex symbol in later films than the average-looking but brilliant student she is in the books on which the films are based. The most important figures in *Harry Potter* are men (Harry, Dumbledore, Voldemort), and, as in the *Lord of the Rings* series, the fate of the world depends on the actions of men. In sum, with a few exceptions, such fantasy films send traditional messages to viewers about gender: that women are meant to comfort others and become the wives of men, while men's actions determine the fate of a nation or an entire world.

Hollywood horror movies also reproduce traditional views about gender. In almost all cases, monsters are male, insinuating that men are more aggressive and violent than women. Men in horror movies are also presented as masterful manipulators, capable of outsmarting not only their victims but anyone hunting them as well; consider, for instance, Hannibal Lecter of *The Silence of the Lambs* (1991). Filmmakers also represent men as antagonistic in horror movies, suggesting that men in general seek out and revel in confrontation (like Micah in *Paranormal Activity* (2007), who taunts the demon that haunts his home). Women usually play the role of victim, and quite often the violence they experience is sexual. It is not unusual for today's horror films to include scenes in which women arc at least implicitly abused sexually or raped by predators, as in the film *The Last House on the Left* (2009). Some horror films, such as *Hostel II* (2007), depict women in positions of power, but on the whole, horror movies imply that men are strong, intelligent, and aggressive, while women are victims.

Comedy films, on the whole, represent men as bumbling idiots and women as desperate for romance. The most famous comedies star men, implying that men are both funnier and more immature than women. A keen example of this pattern occurs in the film *Knocked Up* (2007), in which a woman, impregnated after a one-night stand, immediately confronts the reality of her situation while the man who impregnated her indulges in drugs and alcohol, ignoring the situation. In *Tommy Boy* (1995), Chris Farley plays Tommy, an immature and unintelligent man who saves his deceased father's business only with the help of his love interest, the mature and beautiful Michelle. In comedy movies in which the lead is played by a woman, Hollywood films represent women as willing to go to any lengths, no matter how much of a fool they make of themselves, to obtain love. In *Bridget Jones's Diary* (2001) and the sequel *Bridget Jones: The Edge of Reason* (2004), Bridget makes a fool of herself repeatedly, all in the quest for love, which she eventually obtains and then nearly loses completely because of her insecurities. Many romantic comedies follow the story of a single, independent woman looking for love who, by the close of the film, is on her way to wedded bliss. One keen example of this pattern occurs in the film *Sex and the City*, in which the ultimate single girl, Carrie Bradshaw, marries Mr. Big. In romantic comedy films like *Moonstruck* (1987) and *Working Girl* (1988), abandoned women (the widow Loretta Castorini, played by Cher in *Moonstruck*, or the upwardly mobile Tess McGill, played by Melanie Griffith, whose boyfriend in *Working Girl* is threatened by her successs), suddenly find love again, promising them bright futures and faithful, loving companionship. Films such as these suggest that women seek love above all else and reaffirm the message that, for women, love is the best definition of success.

The Hollywood film industry also offers various representations of transgender people. One of the first mainstream films to represent the transgender community was *Dog Day Afternoon* (1975), in which Sonny Wortzik (played by Al Pacino) robs a bank to obtain enough money to pay for his lover Leon's sex reassignment surgery. Leon is a nervous man who attempts suicide to escape his lover. More recent films, however—including *Normal* (2007) and *Transamerica* (2005)—chronicle the struggles of both men and women pursuing sex reassignment surgery and emphasize the strength these characters have, in contrast to earlier depictions of weak and unlikable characters.

With diverse story lines, characters, and themes, Hollywood films entertain viewers of all demographics; no matter the genre, though, certain patterns appear. Filmmakers consistently place women in secondary roles, or in positions that emphasize their sexuality, weaknesses, or desperation. Men, on the other hand, typically assume roles of great importance and depict characters who are adventurous, charming, and strong. Although exceptions to these patterns exist, for the most part Hollywood films continue to support traditional ideas of gender and cultivate similar ideologies.

Karley Adney
Butler University

See also Beauty and Body Image: Beauty Myths; Children's Programming: Disney and Pixar; Desensitization Effect; Film: Horror; Film: Independent; Gender and Femininity: Motherhood; Gender and Femininity: Single/Independent Girl; Gender and Masculinity: Black Masculinity; Gender and Masculinity: Fatherhood; Gender and Masculinity: Metrosexual Male; Gender and Masculinity: White Masculinity; Heroes: Action and Super Heroes; Male Gaze; Mass Media; Media

Rhetoric; Misogyny; Racism; Sexism; Sexuality; Stereotypes; Television; Tropes; Violence and Aggression

Further Readings

Andris, Silke and Ursula Frederick. *Women Willing to Fight: The Fighting Woman in Film*. Newcastle Upon Tyne, UK: Cambridge Scholars Publishing, 2007.

Benshoff, Harry M. and Sean Griffin. *America on Film: Representing Race, Class, Gender, and Sexuality at the Movies*. Oxford, UK: Blackwell, 2004.

Clover, Carol. *Men, Women, and Chain Saws: Gender in the Modern Horror Film*. Princeton, NJ: Princeton University Press, 1993.

Codell, Julie F., ed. *Genre, Gender, Race, and World Cinema*. Oxford, UK: Blackwell, 2007.

Ferriss, Suzanne and Mallory Young. *Chick Lit: Contemporary Women at the Movies*. New York: Routledge, 2007.

Gabbard, Krin and William Luhr, eds. *Screening Genders*. Piscataway, NJ: Rutgers University Press, 2008.

Grant, Barry Keith, ed. *The Dread of Difference: Gender and the Horror Film*. Austin: University of Texas Press, 1996.

Lehman, Peter. *Masculinity: Bodies, Movies, Culture*. London: Routledge, 2001.

Matthews, Nicole. *Comic Politics: Gender in Hollywood Comedy After the New Right*. New York: Manchester University Press, 2000.

Pomerance, Murray. *Ladies and Gentlemen, Boys and Girls: Gender in Film at the End of the Twentieth Century*. Albany: State University of New York Press, 2001.

Powrie, Phil, Ann Davies, and Bruce Babington, eds. *The Trouble With Men: Masculinities in European and Hollywood Cinema*. London: Wallflower Press, 2004.

Rehling, Nicola. *Extra-Ordinary Men: White Heterosexual Masculinity in Contemporary Popular Cinema*. Lanham, MD: Lexington Books, 2009.

Rowe, Kathleen. *The Unruly Woman: Gender and the Genres of Laughter*. Austin: University of Texas Press, 1995.

Schleier, Merrill. *Skyscraper Cinema: Architecture and Gender in American Film*. Minneapolis: University of Minnesota Press, 2009.

Tasker, Yvonne, ed. *Action and Adventure Cinema*. New York: Routledge, 2004.

Willis, Sharon. *High Contrast: Race and Gender in Contemporary Hollywood Film*. Durham, NC: Duke University Press, 1997.

FILM: HORROR

Critics often attack horror films for the way in which they capitalize on gender stereotypes of men and women. In the horror genre, men typically assume roles of the monstrous, the mastermind, the madman, or the antagonizer. Writers often assign women to roles of the possessed, the victim, and the figure ripe for sexual assault. Several recent horror films disregard the stereotypes supported and furthered by the rest of the genre, but in sum, horror films reinforce stereotypical messages about gender for their viewers.

Many of the classic horror films, such as *Frankenstein*, *Dracula*, and *Dr. Jekyll and Mr. Hyde* (all three originally appearing in 1931), are based on novels and carry the ideological slant of the original author. Most of the monstrous lead characters are men, a pattern common in contemporary horror. Monsters like the Fly, Chucky, Leatherface of *The Texas Chainsaw Massacre* (1974), Michael Meyers of the *Halloween* series (since 1979), Freddie of *Nightmare on Elm Street* (1984), and Jason Voorhees of the *Friday the 13th* franchise (since 1978) are all male. Many horror movies incorporate monstrous women, but most often the scariest monsters are male. This pattern suggests that men remain more dangerous and capable of greater destruction than women or that they are more inclined to acts of terror. Females are just as capable of horrific acts, yet the stereotype of placing men in the role of monster consistently portrays males negatively.

Men also often assume the role of mastermind. Characters like Hannibal Lecter of *The Silence of the Lambs* (1991) and Jigsaw of the *Saw* movies (beginning in 2004) typify the extremely intelligent male; these men outsmart the women who study them or with whom they work. Clarice Starling follows Lecter's trail, and while she solves many of his riddles and seems to partake in mental banter with him, she cannot catch him. Some viewers and critics suggest that Starling does not catch Lecter because she finds herself sexually attracted to him and allows him to escape; this scenario, however, also portrays Starling as the weaker of the two, the one more inclined to act on emotion rather than logic. Likewise, the main character in the *Saw* films, Jigsaw, continually outsmarts his victims and even his assistant, Amanda.

Another common role that men play in horror films is the antagonist. A wealth of examples exists to demonstrate this point. Consider, for instance, Micah in *Paranormal Activity* (2007). A demonic presence has haunted Katie, Micah's girlfriend, for most of her life. The presence accompanies her into Micah's home. Though Katie begs him not to antagonize the demon, Micah repeatedly provokes the demon, acting as if he feels unthreatened. Similarly, in movies like those in the *Halloween* series, men often insult or irritate Michael Meyers without considering how he might react. These examples cast men as rash, unthinking, and antagonistic, perpetuating negative stereotypes about males.

In the horror genre, women most often appear weaker than men. To begin, in films about possession, the possessed is almost always female. Consider films involving exorcisms: *The Exorcist* (1973), *The Exorcism of Emily Rose* (2005), and *The Last Exorcism* (2010). Those possessed in the films are all women. In *Paranormal Activity*, the female is ripe for demonic possession and abuse. Similarly, in films like *Rosemary's Baby* and *The Omen*, women are used to perpetuate evil by either bearing or raising the son of the Devil. While logistically women are chosen for this role because of their childbearing or child-rearing capabilities, women like Rosemary Woodhouse (*Rosemary's Baby*, 1968) and Katherine Thorn (*The Omen*, 1976) also either succumb to the charms of their satanic child, like Rosemary, or die at the hands of the child instead, like Katherine. All of these women subjugated because of demonic forces to possession, childbearing, or child rearing are incapable of saving themselves. In turn, women are often cast as victims, a decision that emphasizes a traditional stereotype about gender.

Women are often the victims of highly sexualized violence in horror films, while men are not. *Rosemary's Baby* shows the Devil raping Rosemary while a group of people, including her husband, watch. In the Australian film *Woolf Creek* (2005), filmmakers show the serial killer Mick Taylor sexually abusing some of his female victims and threatening them with rape. Perhaps the most controversial example of sexualized violence occurs in the 2009 remake of the classic horror film *The Last House on the Left*. In the film, Mari Collingwood finds herself captured by a gang of crooks. One of the men brutally rapes her, and the movie follows the rape in detail, capturing all of Mari's suffering. Most horror

The horror film genre has historically been labeled male-driven and male-centered, portraying women as victims ripe for possession or sexual assault. Late 20th-century projects began to depict vicious, violent women in films like *Hostel, Hostel II,* and *Hard Candy*. (Photos.com)

movies desensitize viewers to brutal violence, but films like *Rosemary's Baby*, *Wolf Creek*, and *The Last House on the Left* desensitize viewers to sexual violence and send messages to viewers that violence can be arousing, especially when that violence has beautiful women as its target.

Although critics often fault horror for its tendency to victimize women, several contemporary horror films revise that depiction and instead empower women. The film *The Wicker Man* (1973) was remade and released again in 2006. The original includes a character named Lord Summerisle, the leader of a cult. The cult eventually sacrifices a man, hoping that the ritual will cause the group's crops to flourish. In the 2006 remake (starring Nicolas Cage), the cult is composed entirely of women who use men as their slaves; the cult leader is Sister Summerisle. When they sacrifice the man, the cult rejoices. The remake of the original film places women in power and living in a society where men are unnecessary except as a means of reproducing. Furthermore, the title of "sister" rather than "lord" hints at a more peaceful society in which the women work together, instead of a patriarchal society like the one depicted in the original film.

The film *Hard Candy* (2005) also experiments with gender roles of both men and women. An adult male, Jeff Kohlver, meets a teenage girl at a restaurant after talking with her online. The teenager, Hayley Stark, goes with Kohlver to his home.

Stark drugs Kohlver and when he awakens, Stark questions him about a missing teen (presumably a friend of hers). Eventually Kohlver confesses that he watched the missing teen die. Stark threatens to castrate Kohlver and, after numbing his crotch, proceeds with the operation, which he watches performed since Stark sets up a camera to project the procedure on his own television. Kohlver eventually realizes that Stark has not really castrated him (she played a recording of a castration for him instead). Stark psychologically torments Kohlver and tells him that she has called his ex-girlfriend and will reveal that Kohlver was a pedophile. Stark taunts Kohlver relentlessly, and eventually he commits suicide. She leaves, victorious. The film hinges on the victimization of a woman (the missing teenage girl) but places a woman in the role of mastermind, a role usually assigned to men (like Lecter or Jigsaw).

The most criticized and strongest example of female empowerment in a horror film concerns Eli Roth's *Hostel II* (2007). The concept of both *Hostel* and *Hostel II* involves teenagers traveling abroad and being kidnapped. The teens are taken to a mysterious warehouse, where they are killed by members of Elite Hunting, a group of people who place bids on the teenagers in order to be able to kill them. The first *Hostel* film follows the adventures of several young men. The sequel, however, chronicles the travels of some young women, all of whom are murdered in the warehouse save one, Beth Salinger. The man who won the bid to kill Beth, Stuart, is emasculated by his wife and wants to kill a woman to feel more confident. Beth manages to manipulate Stuart and straps him down in the chair in which he had been holding her captive. She cuts off his genitals and throws them to a dog, which eats them happily. Viewers and critics alike labeled *Hostel II* as misogynic, but other viewers championed the film for placing a woman in a position of power and simultaneously revising the stereotypical messages about gender typical of most horror films.

The horror film genre has long been attacked for these stereotypical representations of gender, especially those concerning women and the troublesome messages involving sexualized violence. Although filmmakers still indulge in this tradition and continue to portray men as more intelligent and dangerous than women, some contemporary films, such as those described above, revise these gender roles and award women more complicated roles than that of helpless victim.

Karley Adney
Butler University

See also Desensitization Effect; Film: Hollywood; Film: Independent; Mass Media; Media Rhetoric; Misogyny; Racism; Sexuality; Stereotypes; Television; Tropes; Video Gaming: Violence; Violence and Aggression

Further Readings

Berman, A. S. *The New Horror Handbook*. Duncan, OK: BearManor Media, 2009.

Carolyn, Axelle. *It Lives Again: Horror Movies in the New Millennium*. Denbighshire, UK: Telos Publishing, 2008.

Clover, Carol. *Men, Women, and Chain Saws: Gender in the Modern Horror Film*. Princeton, NJ: Princeton University Press, 1993.

Grant, Barry Keith, ed. *The Dread of Difference: Gender and the Horror Film*. Austin: University of Texas Press, 1996.

Skal, David. *The Monster Show: A Cultural History of Horror*. London: Faber and Faber, 2001.

FILM: INDEPENDENT

The meaning of the term *independent film* or *independent cinema* has evolved since the birth of film and will continue to do so as the industry changes and adapts to new technologies and production procedures.

In regard to gender, Sofia Coppola is one of the female directors who most commonly comes to mind, as her film *Lost in Translation* (2003) was nominated for three Academy Awards in 2004. As a woman working in a male-dominated industry (whether independent or Hollywood big-studio), she had little chance of winning. For example, of the 55 independent film directors Donald Lyons documented in the filmographies for his 1994 book *Independent Visions*, 47 were male. Data available on employment in the United Kingdom film industry show that, in 2002, 67 percent of the total workforce was male. To this day, the industry is often considered to be highly male dominated regardless of official workforce statistics. This perception will not change until the percentage of women in high profile roles, such as directing, increases. Although Kathleen Kennedy is a successful Hollywood producer, her name is not widely recognizable. This example magnifies the issue for independent cinema, where names are even less familiar. Linda Ellman, for instance, produced and directed the documentary *On Native Soil* (2006), distributed by Lionsgate. Overall, the median age of independent filmmakers was estimated to be 25 years old in the 1990s, with only about 50 percent of the directors having attended film school or having received some other type of training in the field via higher education.

Most commonly, the term implies independence from studio control; in the case of the U.S. film industry, it means independence from Hollywood, both in the way films are produced and in narrative content. One envisions ambitious filmmakers who work with a very small budget and create their film against all odds, with the movie becoming an expression of the filmmaker's personal vision. Such a film is often summarized as a "low-budget indie." Robert Rodriguez's *El Mariachi* (1992) exemplifies this notion: It was shot on a $7,000 budget, which the director earned as a medical research subject. However, such a definition does not illustrate the complexity of the term, and when asking filmmakers to define independent film, they also do not agree on a definition. For some, the content has priority—the film needs to position itself against the dominant ideology and/or represent a filmmaker's personal message—while for others classifying a film as independent requires the movie not to have a distributor. From a historical perspective, the term can also be understood in various ways.

Looking back to the early stages of cinema, before the corporate film industry was established, every film could have been labeled an independent film. Different entrepreneurs, such as Georges Méliès and Auguste and Louis Lumière, were exploring the new technology and financing their films in different ways. Once the studio system began to emerge in the 1920s, directors lost control, and films had to adhere to rules and emerging codes and conventions. For instance, Marshall "Mickey" Neilan was a director from the silent era who enjoyed considerable authority over his pictures. He not only directed but also wrote, acted, and produced. Neilan, who began directing motion pictures in 1913, completed production on *Tess of the D'Urbervilles* (1924)

without studio interference, but the film that would eventually be distributed and exhibited at theaters was not the director's cut, which did not adhere to emerging studio guidelines. Eventually, many of the silent directors who could not transition into studio control, including Neilan, would leave the studios and the Hollywood industry.

From the 1920s until the late 1940s, *independent* meant that a film did not follow established studio guidelines. This implied to audiences that such a film was not produced by one of the big Hollywood studios (also known as the "majors" and the "minors") but by one of the "poverty row studios." These studios included, among others, Hollywood Pictures, Metropolitan Pictures, and the Ideal Pictures Corporation. Hollywood Pictures was located in New York and focused on the distribution of independent productions. It also invested in some feature film production. Metropolitan Pictures, which formed following the collapse of Reliable Pictures in 1937, produced Bob Steele films, starting with *Feud of the Range* (1939). In 1940, the company merged with Monogram, which originated in 1931. The Ideal Pictures Corporation was founded in 1920 and by the late 1940s had become the largest distributor of 16-millimeter films in the United States. It specialized in nontheatrical ventures at first but started theatrical distribution in 1933. Eventually, the Ideal Pictures Corporation would revert to nontheatrical distribution, continuing in that business into the 1970s. These companies were able to exist parallel to the larger studios, partially because they did not attempt to compete with those studios but also because they created and focused on their own niche market.

Today, some consider financing to be the main determinant of whether a film is an independent movie. This interpretation of the term emerged in the 1970s. It defines the independent film as one that is not financed by a Hollywood studio. This raises the question of whether one can classify *Star Wars: The Phantom Menace* (1999) as independent, because the director, George Lucas, raised the money by himself. Although no studio assisted in the financing, Lucas used the Hollywood distribution system to exhibit the film. Some define independent to exclude the use of distributors that are affiliated with a Hollywood studio. Small, independent distribution companies include Savoy, October, Trimark,

Fine Line, New Line, and Goldwyn. The film releases from these distributors can be described as ranging from nonconformist to classical Hollywood cinema and can tackle sociological and political subject matter that is either too sensitive or entirely taboo for the big studios.

Also challenging the current definition of independent film is the emergence of sister studios, created by the big studios to produce so-called independent film. These smaller studios are part of conglomerates, such as Fox Searchlight, which belongs to FOX and Disney-owned Miramax. Lionsgate Entertainment, while it formed independently in 1997, has acquired Artisan Entertainment, Trimark Holdings Ltd., Redbus Film Distributors, Debmar-Mercury, and Mandate Pictures. During November 2010, Lionsgate was in talks with both Metro-Goldwyn-Mayer (MGM) and Carl Icahn to merge the two studios. This company has integrated itself into the modern film business, and the meaning of its being independent and producing independent films has changed significantly.

Because the term lacks a precise definition, independent film also overlaps with other commonly used film classifications, including art-house cinema and specialty films, two terms with equally vague definitions. Furthermore, independent film can be understood as its own genre, and independent film usually means U.S. film, because other countries have different film business structures and their films are usually classified as foreign or world cinema or as belonging to a certain film movement, such as neorealism. This movement brings together Italian, Brazilian, and Iranian films, regardless of their modes of financing, overall budgets, the filmmakers' personal visions, and distribution approach.

In the evolving film business, it is debatable how truly independent directors such as Richard Linklater (*Slacker*, 1991; *The School of Rock*, 2003; *Me and Orson Welles*, 2008) still are. These filmmakers have created their own brands. Every consumer holds certain expectations of a Quentin Tarantino film (*Reservoir Dogs*, 1992; *Pulp Fiction*, 1994; *Inglorious Basterds*, 2009; the *Kill Bill* series, beginning in 2003). This branch of filmmakers, given their success with mass audiences, could establish their own businesses and are not equivalent to independent filmmakers. Instead, these filmmakers have found a way to establish themselves in the existing system by carving out a niche audience for themselves. Also, independent cinema increased in popularity in the 1990s, as many Hollywood stars participated in films for little or no salary, thus expanding audience attention beyond films produced solely by the big studios.

Probably the best-known film festival for independent film is the Sundance Film Festival, which originated as the Utah/U.S. Film Festival in 1978. The name changed in 1991, the same year Linklater's *Slacker* was part of the festival's program. Throughout the 1990s, the festival would become known as the premier U.S. event for independent film. The festival's 1998 report shows that more than 1,200 films were submitted for 150 screening slots, illustrating the growing popularity of independent work. In 2009, more than 3,600 films were submitted for 120 slots. To qualify for the festival, a film has to be independently produced and it must have a minimum of 50 percent American financing.

The Independent Spirit Awards take place annually, prior to the Academy Awards in March. Errol Morris's *The Fog of War* (2003) won the award in the Best Documentary category in 2004. The Independent Spirit Awards were the brainchild of the Independent Feature Project (IFP)/West, which was founded in 1981. In 2005, it changed its name to Film Independent. By mid-2010, the not-for-profit organization had approximately 4,000 members.

Documentary is a key subgenre of independent film. Especially with the success that Michael Moore (*Roger & Me*, 1989; *Bowling for Columbine*, 2002; *Fahrenheit 9/11*, 2004), Morgan Spurlock (*Super Size Me*, 2004), and Morris (*The Thin Blue Line*, 1988; *The Fog of War*) have had over the previous decades, independent documentary film has become known for criticizing U.S. capitalism, whether the focus is the food industry, the penal system, or the laws on firearms possession. The independent documentary that may have challenged the Hollywood system the most over the past two decades is *Hoop Dreams* (directed by Steve James, 1994), which critics continue to rank as the most important film of the 1990s. Its absence from the Academy Award nominees focused negative attention on the Hollywood system; it is rumored that the film was not nominated because it would have won the documentary award and would have diverted attention away from Hollywood-produced documentaries.

Thus, the film resulted in social commentary not only on inner-city housing, schooling, and the overall lifestyle of the lower class but also on the Hollywood system and its treatment of a successful independent film.

With the rise of lightweight and affordable film-making technology, independent filmmaking has become a possibility for the masses. The Internet functions as a distribution and exhibition platform. Thus, a YouTube movie can be considered an independent film, as it has not been funded or distributed via Hollywood. Whether the term *independent film* is valuable in this application is another matter. Generally, the variety of definitions of the term calls its value into question: Its meaning has evolved and continues to change with the development of the film industry and related technology, and it is becoming increasingly difficult to determine if a film "qualifies" as an independent work. The term has its most stable definition among film scholars, historians, and critics. For the consumer, an independent film signifies that the movie treats content outside the established norms set by Hollywood at the time of the film's production and release. In reality, such a film is most likely a "hybrid," showcasing a director's personal vision but often assisted by studio financing or distribution.

Monika Raesch
Suffolk University, Boston

See also Film: Hollywood; Film: Horror; Workforce

Further Readings

Holm, D. K. *Independent Cinema*. Harpenden, UK: KameraBooks, 2008.

Horsley, Jake. *Dogville vs. Hollywood: The Independents and the Hollywood Machine*. London: Marion Boyars, 2005.

Levy, Emanuel. *Cinema of Outsiders: The Rise of American Independent Film*. New York: New York University Press, 1999.

Lyons, Donald. *Independent Visions: A Critical Introduction to Recent Independent American Film*. New York: Ballantine, 1994.

Martin, Reed. *The Reel Truth: Everything You Didn't Know You Need to Know About Making an Independent Film*. New York: Faber and Faber, 2009.

Merritt, Greg. *Celluloid Mavericks: A History of American Independent Film*. New York: Thunder's Mouth Press, 2000.

Parks, Stacey. *The Insider's Guide to Independent Film Distribution*. Oxford, UK: Focal Press, 2007.

Pitts, Michael R. *Poverty Row Studios 1929–1940*. Jefferson, NC: McFarland, 1997.

Rodriguez, Robert. *Rebel Without a Crew: Or How a 23-Year-Old Filmmaker With $7,000 Became a Hollywood Player*. New York: Plume, 1996.

Ryan, Maureen A. *Producer to Producer: A Step-by-Step Guide to Low-Budget Independent Film Producing*. Studio City, CA: Michael Wiese Productions, 2010.

FISKE, JOHN

John Fiske (1939–) is a cultural theorist best known for his advancement of television studies, critical analysis of popular culture, and cross-cultural investigations of the production of meaning and the creation of publics. With books such as *Reading Television* (coauthored with John Hartley), Fiske became established as one of the most influential media scholars of the late 20th century.

Fiske received his B.A. and M.A. from Cambridge University in England. After teaching communications and cultural studies in the United Kingdom, Australia, and the United States, he retired as professor emeritus of communication arts from the University of Wisconsin, Madison, in 2000. In addition to having written numerous book chapters and journal articles, Fiske is the author of both his own books and coauthored works with Graeme Turner, John Hartley, and Bob Hodge. He was the founding editor of the journal *Cultural Studies* in 1987, and he served as the editor of the book series Studies in Communication and Culture.

Situated in an interpretive paradigm, Fiske's works exemplify the interdisciplinary critical analysis of popular culture that deconstructs latent meanings and the social construction of culture and consumers. A source of inspiration to practitioners of the emerging discipline of cultural studies, Fiske's work critiques power structures in media representations of gender, race, and class that influence collective understandings of reality.

Fiske's critiques of popular culture specifically focus on the characteristics of Western, patriarchal, capitalist societies. He illustrates the ways in which popular culture is not simple entertainment but is integral to power relations. His work views popular culture as a constant struggle between dominant and subordinate forces, and agency and resistance. Fiske's analysis of English-language popular culture is an extension of the work of European theorists such as Pierre Bourdieu, Michel de Certeau, Roland Barthes, Stuart Hall, Mikhail Bakhtin, Louis Althusser, and Michel Foucault. Fiske turns the lens of European analysis on cultural artifacts that circulate in the United States and Australia.

In the book *Media Matters: Race and Gender in U.S. Politics*, Fiske advances the argument that there can be no distinction between "real" events outside media. Rather, media events such as the O. J. Simpson trial defy traditional binaries between news and entertainment, highbrow and lowbrow culture, or public and private realms. Instead, they exist across the media sphere and are constructed through and by media and consumers as they travel through culture. Fiske investigates the ways in which low-tech communications are used by marginalized peoples to negotiate and counter mainstream, dominant messages.

Fiske on Feminism

Fiske's work represents a significant contribution to cultural studies, in part because of his recognition of the influence of feminist theory. Taking seriously the work of feminist scholars, Fiske also examines the cultural influences of advances in women's rights. For example, he critiques the ways in which television genres shift and blur to account for the rise of feminism and the backlash of masculine power. Fiske argues that feminism achieved the naming of patriarchy as a dominating cultural force in much the same manner as Marxist theory illuminates the complex influences of capitalism.

Fiske extends his analysis to singer and dancer Madonna's practice of sampling earlier cultural iconography in her performances. She constructs postmodern identities in order to subvert gender norms while contributing to the memory of Marilyn Monroe and creating new performances of femininity. By arguing that Madonna simultaneously deploys both virgin and whore images, as well as religious iconography, Fiske advances the argument that strict binary categories that define "good" and "bad" womanhood must be abandoned in favor of understanding the ways in which young audiences interpret celebrities and incorporate cultural knowledge into their own identities.

Material and Method

The breadth of Fiske's source material reflects the influence of theorists such as Barthes, as each is known for advancing critical engagement with a variety of cultural texts in order to illuminate ideology that is performed broadly and not confined to any institution or genre. By conducting multimedia, cross-cultural analysis, Fiske joins other critical theorists in promoting the study of topics and artifacts previously deemed trivial. Like Barthes, Fiske demonstrates the ability to critique popular culture in broad terms—from advertising to shopping malls, commodities to celebrities, and entertainment media to journalism.

Furthermore, Fiske advanced the practice of audience research from the perspective that audiences are active players in the formation of culture rather than simply consumers of information. He conceived of audiences as active, and his use of ethnographic methods was integral to his argument that individuals are agents whose interpretive behaviors contribute to productions of meaning and the subversion of dominance.

Fiske is actively engaged with a consideration of audiences, both as they are constructed as publics by media texts and as they interpret media based on their own ideologies. Fiske conceives of audiences as interacting with media texts, interpreting them in personal ways that reflect their ideologies and bring them pleasure. Drawing on de Certeau's use of military metaphors, he has discussed popular culture as guerrilla warfare.

Fiske Matters

A key characteristic of Fiske's writing is a self-reflectivity and recognition that his own subject position influences his theory and analysis. Not only does Fiske discuss his own experiences as a product of white-male, European-educated scholars, but also he provides transparency into his own research methods, teaching experiences, the reasons for his interests in certain cultural texts, and his travels and colleagues.

In 2010, Fiske was the subject of a conference entitled "Fiske Matters: A Conference on John

Fiske's Continuing Legacy for Cultural Studies." The conference provided an occasion for critical engagement with his theories as well as for extending his notions of active audiences and negotiations of meaning.

Spring-Serenity Duvall
University of South Carolina, Aiken

See also Audiences: Reception and Injection Models; Barthes, Roland; Critical Theory; Feminism; Polysemic Text; Reception Theory; Semiotics; Television

Further Readings

Fiske, John. *Media Matters: Race and Gender in U.S. Politics*. Minneapolis: University of Minnesota Press, 1996.

Fiske, John. "Popularity and the Politics of Information." In *Journalism and Popular Culture*, Peter Dahlgren and Colin Sparks, eds. Newbury Park, CA: Sage, 1992.

Fiske, John. *Television Culture*. London: Routledge, 2002.

Fiske, John. *Understanding Popular Culture*. Boston: Unwin Hyman, 1989.

Fiske, John and John Hartley. *Reading Television*. London: Methuen, 1978.

G

GAMSON, JOSHUA

Joshua Gamson is a sociologist and cultural scholar best known for his work concerning fame and celebrity. Gamson earned his B.A. from Swarthmore College and his M.A. and Ph.D. in sociology from the University of California, Berkeley. His academic posts have included instructor and lecturer in sociology at the University of California (1992–93); assistant professor (1993–98) and associate professor of sociology (1998–2002) at Yale University; and associate professor of sociology (2002–05) and professor of sociology (2005–) at the University of San Francisco. He was named a Guggenheim Fellow in 2009.

After publishing the article "The Assembly Line of Greatness: Celebrity in Twentieth-Century America" while he was still a doctoral candidate, Gamson began to establish himself as a renowned cultural scholar. His works may be understood in relation to theories of celebrity, fame, gender and sexuality, commercial culture, social movements, and visibility. His use of multiple methods, including textual analysis and ethnographic research, defines the broad scope and purpose of his research.

As Gamson argues, celebrity is produced by and reproduces "fresh" celebrities and situations that may incorporate and reinvigorate "stale" scripts of sexuality and gender. According to Gamson's analysis of American celebrity, invitation into the "real lives" of celebrities contributes to the 20th-century shift toward promotion and visibility and away from any reliance on talent or democratic process to determine who becomes famous and who does not. Gamson discusses a complex media and celebrity environment wherein celebrities' personal lives become vital aspects of their fame, so his ideas are especially useful for analyzing celebrities who intentionally direct publicity toward their personal lives for political ends. The phrase "assembly line of greatness" refers to what Gamson sees as the mechanized manner in which cultural industries produce celebrity through both explicit and implicit narratives in popular culture.

Gamson expands his analysis of celebrity in the book *Claims to Fame: Celebrity in Contemporary America*. Historicizing the production of celebrity, Gamson argues that there have been three eras of celebrity. First, early notions of celebrity viewed people who rise to high levels of fame as possessed of special merit and therefore deserving of fame. Next, as media production of celebrity became steadily more widespread and consumers began to understand the cultural production of fame, marketing techniques emerged to manage the promotion not only of the public images but also of the private lives of celebrities. As a result, the distinctions between private and public lives became blurred as marketing efforts strove to establish the authenticity of celebrities' claims to fame. Finally, in the contemporary era, audiences are aware that they consume staged marketing efforts, regardless of their efforts to distinguish authentic from inauthentic celebrity.

In the article "Jessica Hahn, Media Whore: Sex Scandals and Female Publicity," Gamson expands his engagement with celebrity to show that visibility has traditionally been gendered to privilege men in public spaces and that women's publicity is dependent on some adherence to gender and sexual norms. The ability for women to access visibility and fame then requires reproduction of existing stereotypes and archetypes.

In the biography *The Fabulous Sylvester: The Legend, the Music, the Seventies in San Francisco* (winner of the Stonewall Book Award and finalist for a Lambda Literary Award), Gamson traces the life and career of gay disco icon Sylvester James. The book is a departure of style from his previous work, yet relates intensely detailed research about James, as well as about the music and culture of San Francisco in the 1970s. His work focuses on fame, sexuality, and politics.

Gamson has also been a significant voice in the study of queer identity in media. In addition, his appearance in the Media Education Foundation documentaries *Off the Straight and Narrow* and *Further Off the Straight and Narrow* provides insights into his critical perspective that are easily accessible introductions to undergraduate audiences. Gamson dissects queer media representations in the documentary, voicing over images of news, talk shows, and reality television. He argues that homosexuality was first an occasional topic of moral debate on news programs and talk shows, but then traces the normalization of same-sex relationships on talk shows as suffering from the same dysfunctions as heterosexual relationships. He argues that visibility of homosexual characters is in a new era as they have become a staple for reality television programming.

The inclusion of gay, lesbian, bisexual, transsexual/transgender (GLBT), and other nonconforming identities on daytime talk shows produces a variety of images and interpretations that have no uniform impact, according to Gamson. In the book *Freaks Talk Back: Tabloid Talk Shows and Sexual Nonconformity* (winner of both the Kovacs Book Award from the Speech Communication Association and the Culture Section Book Award from the American Sociological Association), Gamson takes a cultural studies approach by examining production, consumption, and media texts. By using textual analysis, Gamson advances an argument that talk shows provide transgressive narratives that challenge existing cultural norms. Furthermore, audiences also

react to and interpret the talk shows by questioning representations, contradicting experts, and challenging the images of nonconformity they see.

Spring-Serenity Duvall
University of South Carolina, Aiken

See also Queer Theory; Reception Theory; Textual Analysis

Further Readings

Gamson, Joshua. "The Assembly Line of Greatness: Celebrity in Twentieth-Century America." *Critical Studies in Communication*, v.9 (1992).

Gamson, Joshua. *Claims to Fame: Celebrity in Contemporary America*. Berkeley: University of California Press, 1994.

Gamson, Joshua. *Freaks Talk Back: Tabloid Talk Shows and Sexual Nonconformity*. Chicago: University of Chicago Press, 1998.

Gamson, Joshua. "Jessica Hahn, Media Whore: Sex Scandals and Female Publicity." *Critical Studies in Media Communication*, v.18/2 (2001).

GAY AND LESBIAN PORTRAYALS ON TELEVISION

Throughout much of its history, television's treatment of gay and lesbian characters mirrored the same mainstream cultural attitudes that preached and legislated against queer sexuality. The last decade of the past millennium and the first decade of the present witnessed radical changes in the way that gays and lesbians are portrayed on American television. These changes reflected, and often prompted, rapidly shifting sociocultural attitudes regarding sexuality. Currently, gay and lesbian main and supporting characters populate a wide range of broadcast, cable, and satellite series. They can be found in dramas, sitcoms, game shows, reality shows, talk shows, and other genres.

This open and pervasive presence was not always the case. Indeed, for much of television history gays and lesbians were conspicuous by their absence. When present, they were most often depicted as psychologically sick, as predator or prey, as the objects of humor and ridicule. In this respect, television's traditional treatment of gays and lesbians has much in common with the treatment of gays in film, as described in Vito Russo's classic work of queer criticism, *The Celluloid Closet* (1987). In part, this treatment reflected rules imposed by network censors responding to commercial pressures to appeal to the broadest possible audience, and in part it reflected the need to adhere to the laws regulating decency on the public airwaves.

For much of broadcast television's history, the presence of gay and lesbian performers was tolerated as long as they did not openly acknowledge their sexual orientation. They were, however, permitted to hint at it, especially when doing so with a degree of humor, preferably self-deprecating. Such hints were mostly subtle, but they could occasionally be bold, as was the case with the popular semiclassical pianist Liberace (1919–87), whose iconic over-the-top, camp performances included elaborate entrances and exits, exaggerated effeminate gestures, and frequent changes of gaudy costumes decorated with sequins, rhinestones, ostrich feathers, and capes. Liberace did not openly acknowledge that he was gay and in fact fought such rumors, even going so far as to sue those who claimed he was for libel. Although Liberace's sexuality was something of an open secret, social convention compelled him to deny he was gay in order to protect his career and preserve the interest of his core female audience.

A comic staple of mid-century American television was the male performer or character of ambiguous sexuality, whose subtle or overtly effeminate demeanor could be read as stereotypically gay. A classic example of this type is Paul Lynde, who played the recurring role of Uncle Author on the American Broadcasting Company (ABC) sitcom *Bewitched* (1964–72). He later became a fixture on the syndicated game show *Hollywood Squares* (between 1966 and 1979 and in 1980–81), where his unapologetically effeminate demeanor, camp humor, and sexually charged double-entendres won him a regular seat among the show's roster of has-been celebrities.

During the 1970s, television exhibited a growing openness regarding sexuality with respect to heterosexuals. The same decade saw the introduction of a sympathetically portrayed and openly gay recurring character in the person of Jodie Dallas, played by Billy Crystal, on *Soap* (ABC, 1977–81). More common were sitcoms featuring jokes made at the expense of gays, as illustrated by ABC's *Three's Company* (1977–84). The series' male lead, Jack

Tripper (played by John Ritter), is a single man who is permitted to live in a rented apartment with two attractive, single women only because he pretends to be gay and is thus considered heterosexually harmless by the apartment's landlords: Stanley Roper (Norman Fell, seasons 1–3) and Ralph Furley (Don Knotts, seasons 4–8). Often, Jack's manhood was mocked by the landlords, who made derisive references to "your kind" and to his being a "Tinker Bell" and a "fairy."

During the 1990s the television closet began to open wide with such series as ABC's groundbreaking sitcom *Ellen* (1994–98), starring comedienne Ellen DeGeneres. In 1997's two-part story "The Puppy Episode," the series' lead character, bookstore owner Ellen Morgan, inadvertently comes out of the closet to when she blurts "I am gay" into an airport intercom microphone she had not noticed. (DeGeneres had publicly come out on *The Oprah Winfrey Show*.) Announcing that the sitcom's central character was gay generated controversy and criticism from some quarters and won the series accolades and awards from others. Another ABC sitcom, *Roseanne* (1988–97), featured several openly gay characters, including Nancy (Sandra Bernhard) and Leon Karp (Martin Mull). In one episode, the series' lead character, Roseanne Conners (Rosanne Barr), accompanies her friend Nancy to a gay bar, where she receives a surprise kiss from Nancy's girlfriend.

Gays and lesbians also enjoyed an increased presence on television dramas during the 1990s. One prominent example is police administrative aide John Irvin (Bill Brochtrup) on ABC's *NYPD Blue* (1993–2005). To date, Irvin remains the longest-running gay character on network television. NBC's *Law & Order* franchise routinely includes gay and lesbian characters in a variety of roles large and small: as the victims and perpetrators of crimes (many of which having little if anything to do with their sexual orientation), as bystanders and witnesses, and as defense lawyers and district attorneys. Assistant district attorney Serena Southerlyn (2001–05), played by Elisabeth Röhm, came out as a lesbian in her very last appearance on the series. After the district attorney tells her she is fired, she asks him, "Is this because I'm a lesbian?" Southerlyn's sexual orientation played very little role in defining her character or shaping narratives. Indeed, many *Law & Order* fans were unaware of her sexual orientation, and many complained on chat lines and in

A group of street costumers parades during the 1999 New Orleans Mardi Gras festival, making fun of conservative fundamentalist Reverend Jerry Falwell who had denounced the children's television show *Teletubbies* for containing a character named Tinky Winky, who Falwell alleged to be a gay role model. (Wikimedia)

other fan forums that the announcement came out of nowhere.

During the 1990s, gays and lesbians were not limited to fictional television series. RuPaul, an openly gay African American drag queen, hosted his own VH1 talk show in 1996. The show attracted many top-tier celebrity guests. Earlier, in 1993, RuPaul generated controversy when he and Milton Berle appeared in drag at the MTV Video Music Awards. The two had a heated impromptu exchange, reflecting in part radical differences in worldview between Berle, a television pioneer for whom dressing in drag was just a gag, and RuPaul, for whom drag was a lifestyle to which he was seriously committed.

The 2000s continued the trend toward greater inclusion of gays and lesbians on mainstream television series. NBC's *Will and Grace* (1998–2006) put a new spin on the familiar trope of the gay man as a female's best friend and confidant, with its depiction of the relationship between lawyer Will Truman (Eric McCormack) and interior designer Grace Adler (Debra Messing), who met while in college at Columbia and have remained best friends since their student days. Just as significant as this continued trend toward mainstream inclusion, the first decade of the 21st century saw the

proliferation of television channels made possible by cable and satellite. The freedom such channels enjoyed from the confining regulations of the Federal Communications Commission allowed for the development of commercially viable niche programming designed to appeal specially and unapologetically to lesbian, gay, bisexual, transsexual/transgender (LGBT) viewers and others open to narratives and characters long marginalized by mainstream media. The basic cable network Bravo (owned by NBCUniversal), while not a gay network per se, has featured much gay-friendly programming, such as *Boy Meets Boy* (2003), *Gay Weddings* (2002), *Queer Eye for the Straight Girl* (2004–05), and *Queer Eye for the Straight Guy* (2003–07). The latter became a popular-culture phenomenon and generated high ratings for a few seasons. The series also garnered praise for showing straight and gay men in easy camaraderie with each other and drew criticism for perpetuating stock gay stereotypes. *The L Word* (2004–09), aired on Showtime, depicted the lives and loves of its lesbian, gay, and transgender lead characters and their relationships with friends, families, and neighbors. The series did so with a frankness regarding lesbian and gay romance and sexuality that had not been seen before in an

American television series. This is especially true with respect to the series' lesbian characters. In contrast to gay men, lesbians have historically received very little airtime. Another Showtime series, *Queer as Folk* (2000–05), focused on the lives of five gay men, as well as a lesbian couple, living in Pittsburgh.

Logo, part of Viacom's MTV stable of cable networks, debuted in June 2005. The network features new, repackaged, and syndicated gay- and lesbian-themed programming, airing a wide range of products, including such standard television genres as advice shows, documentaries, news, reality shows, stand-up comedy, and talk shows. Programming original to Logo includes *Shirts & Skins* (about an all-gay basketball team), *RuPaul's Drag U* (in which biological women receive drag makeovers), and *The Arrangement* (which presents competitive flower arranging). The network is advertiser supported. Some advertisements are aimed directly at gay and lesbian consumers, whereas others are commercials for the general audience.

If the recent past is any indication, American television will see an increasing number of openly gay and lesbian performers and characters in both the mainstream media and niche venues. The increased visibility, highlighting the breadth and diversity of the queer community, will certainly have cultural, political, and social implications in the years to come.

Robert Westerfelhaus
Celeste C. Lacroix
College of Charleston

See also Diversity; Empowerment; Federal Communications Commission; Film: Hollywood; Gender Media Monitoring; Heterosexism; Homophobia; Identity; Mass Media; Media Ethnography; Online New Media: GLBTQ Identity; Online New Media: Transgender Identity; Pornography: Gay and Lesbian; Queer Theory; Sexuality; Sitcoms; Soap Operas; Social Construction of Gender; Sports Media: Transgender; Talk Shows; Television; Transgender Studies; Transsexuality

Further Readings

Avila-Saavedra, Guillermo. "Nothing Queer About Queer Television: Televized Construction of Gay Masculinities." *Media, Culture and Society*, v.31/1 (2009).

Dines, Gail and Jean M. Humez, eds. *Gender, Race and Class in Media: A Text Reader*. 1995. Reprint, Thousand Oaks, CA: Sage, 2010.

Elledge, Jim. *Queers in American Popular Culture*. Santa Barbara, CA: Praeger, 2010.

Raley, Amber and Jennifer Lucas. "Stereotype or Success? Prime-Time Television's Portrayals of Gay Male, Lesbian, and Bisexual Characters." *Journal of Homosexuality*, v.51/2 (2006).

Russo, V. *The Celluloid Closet: Homosexuality in the Movies*, Rev. ed. New York: Harper & Row, 1987.

Gender and Femininity: Motherhood

While feminists have long championed women's professional ambitions and sexual desires, critics contend that mainstream media often depict moral-ethical conflicts between work, sex, and mothering. The result has been to create media imagery and narratives that promote a nostalgic return to, and sentimentalizing of, the nurturing qualities of women. Reflecting this double bind, critics charge that women are represented as either nurturing or sexual, leading to a conflict of mothering. E. Ann Kaplan argues that this outcome is part of patriarchy's response to women's newfound sexual freedom and professional rise in the workplace.

A significant challenge to traditional femininity comes from the fact that childbirth and childcare no longer exclusively relegate women to the home. As a result, contemporary motherhood is no longer predicated on the traditional notion that women must stay at home to raise children in marriages or sexually monogamous relationships. Feminist media scholars theorize that this profound sociocultural shift has led to a patriarchal backlash whereby women's sexuality and professional ambition are depicted as a moral dilemma. The conflict is established as one in which female desire is at odds with traditional family values predicated on good mothering.

As part of this conflict, representations of single motherhood operate within a mode different from those of the traditional family. When a single mother is shown to have sexual and professional desires in mainstream media, she is denounced as a threat to the moral order of traditional mothering. Just as the film noir shunned the femme fatale for her sexual "deviance," single mothers are similarly eschewed within contemporary media depictions for having sexual and professional desires. According to Susan

Faludi, many films in the 1980s and 1990s depicted the tension between traditional good mothering and liberal female sexuality through extreme violence, suggesting the psychological tension in society regarding women's changing roles in the home, work, and sex. For instance, the film *Fatal Attraction* upholds the ideal of the nuclear family by dichotomizing one woman's sexual and professional independence with that of the wife and mother. Feminists have expressed concerns over media depictions that ostracize women for their sexual desire by relegating them to the nuclear family instead of showing them as capable of succeeding in both realms.

In the 1960s, Betty Friedan posited "the feminine mystique," an ideological image of women as naturally positioned within the home, which presented a narrow and unfulfilling social script that led to psychic distress. She argued that women were culturally defined by their social roles as wives, mothers, and keepers of the hearth and home. She noted that the dominant male society defined "true" women as achieving fulfillment through the performance of such domestic duties and relationships. In this context, motherhood is the embodiment of femininity and serves as a means of regulating women within the safe confines of the nuclear family. Feminist media scholars correlate stereotypical representations of motherhood with the patterns of social movements. For instance, early on, the women's movement often ignored the professional and sexual needs of mothers, focusing instead on maternal issues related to concerns associated with day care, reproductive freedoms, and relieving women from the domestic duties associated with marriage and child rearing. By focusing on these early feminist concerns over those associated with workplace or sexual equity, media representations of motherhood often return to the safety of the domestic sphere.

In the 1980s and 1990s, the cultural icon of the "supermom/superwoman" symbolized the evolving feminine mystique. While supermoms were shown to be in control of their familial and work domains, sitcoms rarely ever showed mothers equally at work and home. The 1980s and 1990s did, however, offer many long-running programs about working mothers, several of whom were single. Their names gave these television programs their titles: *Alice* (1976–85), *Roseanne* (1988–97), *Cybill* (1995–98),

Betty Friedan's 1960s protest of what she called "the feminine mystique"—the idea that women's role is defined by their identity as wives, mothers, and keepers of hearth and home—is still being played out in the 21st century through media debates and the personal struggles of women trying to balance motherhood and careers. (Photos.com)

Murphy Brown (1988–98), and *Grace Under Fire* (1993–98). Critics have argued that television programs need to do a better job of representing women engaging in both professional activities at work and domestic management of the home and family, with all their complexities. Such images remain virtually absent from traditional network sitcoms, as cable and network television in general have turned to less expensive "reality" programs.

In the 2000s, working mothers remain marginalized on television, leading to an inaccurate dichotomization of mothers as either virtuous housewives or child-neglecting workaholics. Whereas women were judged according to their familial roles and professional ambitions in previous decades, beauty and sexuality have become the new standards by which working women and mothers are judged within media representations and the culture. Real-life working moms have been replaced by attractive "single gals" (in *Ally McBeal*, 1997–2002, or HBO's *Sex and the City*, 1998–2004) who have careers. In the family, the shift from domestic nurturance to sexual fulfillment is best embodied in the new-media iconography of "hot mamas" and "trophy wives" whose sexuality affords husbands libidinal satisfaction within domestic realms and sanctioned heterosexual marriages. The term *trophy wife* conjures up the image of a powerful man's wife who is young, beautiful, and sexual, while retaining the successes of the superwoman/supermom inculcated during the previous generation. Along with other ideals of gender and femininity, images of motherhood in mainstream media continue to be defined by beauty and thinness. Reality shows and dramas continue to overrepresent mothers who acquiesce to normative beauty standards along with other traditional markers of femininity. Programs like *Desperate Housewives* have been criticized for casting excessively thin and beautiful wives and mothers in their 40s, while new magazines such as *Shape Fit Pregnancy* reinscribe the ideology of labor through pre- and postdelivery body workouts.

In contrast to the ideology of the feminine mystique within media and culture, some contemporary media scholars have identified a "feminist mystique," an ideology that identifies the feminist movement as the cause of women's unhappiness and unfair predicament in society. According to Elizabeth Kaufer Busch, the feminist mystique's problems are attributed to three sources. First, by promoting sexual and professional liberation over traditional roles, it forces women to adopt unfulfilling and problematic ideals of masculinity rather than live by a new set of values. Second, although feminism blames culture/nurture rather than biology/nature for gender inequalities, it does not offer an alternative paradigm for achieving freedom. Third, feminist liberation theory inevitably creates an either/or binary for women in the public and private spheres, making it difficult for women to choose freely between a feminist view of sexual and professional liberation and traditional values associated with femininity, motherhood, and housewifery. Debates between career women and stay-at-home moms are often dramatized through emotionally driven media content, such as "mommy wars" and "infertility crises," designed to exacerbate the feminist mystique. For example, when Hillary Clinton was First Lady, the media turned her into a polarizing figure by sensationalizing comments she made in interviews that she followed her professional ambitions rather than stay home and bake cookies and have teas. The

media seized on the comments to launch a morally charged debate between high-achieving professional women and stay-at-home moms. This pattern of pitting women against each other for their personal and professional choices exemplifies the feminine-feminist conflict at the core of media stories about women's identity and search for fulfillment in the realms of work, sex, and motherhood.

Julie Frechette
Worcester State University

See also Beauty and Body Image: Beauty Myths; Douglas, Susan J.; Feminism; Feminist Theory: Second Wave; Film: Hollywood; Gender and Femininity: Single/Independent Girl; Media Convergence; Patriarchy; Postfeminism; Sexism; Sitcoms; Social Inequality; Steinem, Gloria; Television; Women's Magazines: Lifestyle and Health

Further Readings

Blades, Joan and Kristin Rowe-Finkbeiner. *The Motherhood Manifesto: What America's Moms Want—and What to Do About It*. New York: Nation Books, 2006.

Busch, Elizabeth Kaufer. "*Ally McBeal* to *Desperate Housewives*: A Brief History of the Postfeminist Heroine." *Perspectives on Political Science*, v.38/2 (2009).

Douglas, Susan J. and Meredith Michaels. *The Mommy Myth*. New York City: Free Press, 2004.

Dworkin, Shari L. and Faye Linda Wachs. "'Getting Your Body Back': Postindustrial Fit Motherhood in Shape Fit Pregnancy Magazine." *Gender and Society*, v.18/5 (2004).

Elshtain, Jean Bethke. *Public Man, Private Woman: Women in Social and Political Thought*. Princeton, NJ: Princeton University Press, 1981.

Faludi, Susan. *Backlash: The Undeclared War Against American Women*. New York: Three Rivers Press, 2006.

Friedan, Betty. *The Feminine Mystique*. New York: W. W. Norton, 1963.

Kaplan, E. Ann. "Sex, Work and Motherhood: The Impossible Triangle." *The Journal of Sex Research*, v.27/3 (1990).

Peskowitz, Miriam. *The Truth Behind the Mommy Wars: Who Decides What Makes a Good Mother?* Emeryville, CA: Seal Press, 2005.

Steiner, Leslie Morgan. *Mommy Wars: Stay-at-Home and Career Moms Face Off on Their Choices, Their Lives, Their Families*. New York: Random House, 2007.

GENDER AND FEMININITY: SINGLE/ INDEPENDENT GIRL

Media representations of single and independent women reflect the way gender roles are defined in everyday society. The second wave feminist movement of the 1960–70s sought to redefine the role of single women in the private sphere of the home and the public sphere of the workplace. Television and film serve as cultural benchmarks that identify and reflect these changes. However, these depictions also reveal how single women negotiate their independence within a society that still acknowledges traditional patriarchal norms.

Early Television

Early television representations of single women reflect traditional gender roles. Series like *Our Miss Brooks* (1952–56), *Private Secretary* (1953–57), and *How to Marry a Millionaire* (1957–59) featured single women as teachers and secretaries and in other positions considered appropriate for women at the time. These characters are often depicted as ditsy and/or incapable of doing their jobs efficiently. Much of their time is spent looking for an eligible man to marry. When they are successful, they willingly give up their job and their independence to take up traditional domestic roles. Later series like *That Girl* (1966–71) and *Julia* (1968–71) reflect limited changes in the way women are depicted on television by expanding the professional roles to include acting and nursing. However, single women's relationships with men still remain central to the show.

The Mary Tyler Moore Show (1970–77) is the first successful series featuring a woman capably working in a field traditionally designated for men. Its portrayal of Mary Richards, a young single female who moves to Minneapolis to pursue a journalism career, was in step with the second wave feminist call for women to be educated and independent, and to be given equal access to male-dominated fields. Her single status, as well as her decisions about men, dating, and marriage, also correspond with the second wave feminist call for independent choice. However, Mary's polite demeanor, occasional childlike behavior, and secretarial-type duties in the newsroom create a nonthreatening, domesticated image of a female professional. While this does not undermine her single, independent status, it simultaneously endorses a more traditional role for women.

Television action series' portrayals of single women often revolve around women whose careers are central to their identities but whose appearance and behavior mimic stereotypical gender roles. For example, characters like Sergeant Pepper Anderson of *Police Woman* (1974–78) and the private detectives of *Charlie's Angels* (1976–81) depict capable professionals who have the power to fight crime but who are sexually objectified. The cinematic remake of *Charlie's Angels* (2000) also capitalizes on this sex appeal. Later shows, like *Cagney and Lacey* (1981–88), avert the male gaze (voyeuristic male viewing of women as erotic objects) by offering a grittier, nonsexualized portrayal of female police officers. However, Cagney's personal struggle with addiction and various failed romantic relationships are consistently juxtaposed to partner Lacey's successful and stable role of wife and mother, thus sending conflicting signals about the advantages of single womanhood.

Divorced and Single

The growing social acceptance of divorce as a day-to-day reality in the 1970s allowed media producers the opportunity to explore plotlines featuring female characters negotiating their position as newly single, intellectual, and sexual beings. Series like *Rhoda* (1974–78) and the short-lived *Fay* (1975–76) underscore the second wave feminist notion of female liberation by featuring female protagonists who end their marriages and set out to explore their newfound freedom from their domestic roles. Later series like *One Day at a Time* (1975–84), *Kate and Allie* (1984–89), *Grace Under Fire* (1993–98), and *Reba* (2000–07) feature women who are free of their traditional marriages but who are limited in their personal and professional explorations of singlehood by the expectations placed on them to financially and emotionally support their children and, in some cases, members of their extended families. Media representations such as these reflect changes in the way society defines the traditional nuclear family while simultaneously upholding patriarchal images of motherhood.

Single Women and Social Groups

Media portrayals of female-centered social groups offer a modern and somewhat nonthreatening alternative to conventional portrayals of single women. These groups act as substitute families that offer the financial and emotional support that would be traditionally given by their parents or their husbands. Comedies like *Laverne and Shirley* (1976–83), *Kate and Allie*, and *The Golden Girls* (1985–92) portray single women at various stages in their lives living together in order to maintain economic independence while negotiating their roles as single and independent women. *Designing Women* (1986–93) offers a slightly different arrangement, featuring four single friends grouped together within a professional setting. Despite a consistent focus on the female characters' relationships with men in these programs, the characters' decisions to find a way to survive on their own characterize them as independent feminist women. The end to these arrangements usually occurs when a member of the group chooses to marry and relinquish her single status.

Issues like abortion and single motherhood remain a controversial subject in the media, despite the recognition of women's reproductive rights. Widowed characters like *Julia* and Alice Hyatt's character in Martin Scorsese's film *Alice Doesn't Live Here Anymore* (1974) are nonthreatening and socially accepted because they became mothers while they were married. Early portrayals of single women having children out of wedlock were almost nonexistent, and those who did were either married off or punished. The success of *Murphy Brown* (1988–98) reflects changes in these standards. Murphy, an edgy, award-winning journalist and self-proclaimed feminist, chooses to keep her child and raise it on her own rather than end the unexpected pregnancy. She personifies the struggle to define a single woman's desire to enter motherhood in a feminist context. Shows like Lifetime's *Oh, Baby!* (1996–2000) and *Ally McBeal* (1997–2002) continue to negotiate this definition of motherhood through their portrayals of single women opting to have children (either through artificial insemination or adoption) on their own.

Postfeminist Interpretations

Contemporary postfeminist portrayals of single women reflect the inability to contextualize the changing roles and desires of women in a second wave feminist context. Films like *Bridget Jones's Diary* (2001) and television series like *Ally McBeal* and *Sex and the City* (1998–2004) emphasize the existence of a social equality where a woman's attitudes toward sex, career opportunities, and reproductive choices are not limited by her gender. These women are more educated, unapologetically sexual, and financially independent. However, these portrayals also reveal an underlying sense of dissatisfaction with their role as single women, particularly when it comes to building and preserving successful relationships with men. These media depictions of single women suggest a desire to enter traditional domestic relationships that second wave feminists sought to abate. They reflect yet another renegotiation of the role of single women in society, as women explore ways of remaining independent without being single.

Melissa Camacho
San Francisco State University

See also Beauty and Body Image: Beauty Myths; Douglas, Susan J.; Feminism; Feminist Theory: Second Wave; Film: Hollywood; Gender and Femininity: Motherhood; Media Convergence; Patriarchy; Postfeminism; Sexism; Sitcoms; Social Inequality; Steinem, Gloria; Television; Women's Magazines: Lifestyle and Health

Further Readings

Busch, Elizabeth Kaufer. "*Ally McBeal* to *Desperate Housewives*: A Brief History of the Postfeminist Heroine." *Perspectives on Political Science*, v.38/2 (2009).

Dow, Bonnie, and J. Murphy Brown. *Postfeminism Personified in Prime-Time Feminism: Television, Media Culture, and the Women's Movement Since 1970.* Philadelphia: University of Pennsylvania Press, 1996.

Haralovich, Mary Beth and Lauren Rabinovitz, eds. *Television, History and American Culture: Feminist Critical Essays.* Durham, NC: Duke University Press, 1999.

GENDER AND MASCULINITY: BLACK MASCULINITY

Academic inquiries into masculinity as a field of study have grown since the 1980s. Discussions of black masculinity are often premised on the notion that both gender and race are social constructs, rather than biological determinants. Therefore, the characteristics associated with both of these constructs are part of a system of cultural representation, with media operating as one of the social institutions that creates, reflects, shapes, and upholds dominant views on race and gender. These cultural representations are far from static over time and vary among different groups of men. Correspondingly, many scholars prefer the term *masculinities* to denote that there is great variance in conceptualizing manhood, taking into account different time periods, races, classes, ethnicities, and cultural backgrounds. Critical race theorists and scholars of masculinities studies have positioned different masculinities and femininities in a hierarchical structure that places masculinity in a greater position of power than femininity. Within this structure, particular types of masculinity are more valued than others.

The term *hegemonic masculinity* refers to the most culturally dominant or valued expression of masculinity. The ideals of hegemonic masculinity are theorized to center on notions of power, dominance, strength, aggressiveness, authority, and heterosexism, and it is these types of traits to which men are thought to be encouraged to conform. Ultimately, like idealized notions of femininity, this hegemonic masculinity, many scholars argue, is something that most men will never fully achieve and has the potential to do serious harm to men and women both individually and in their gender relations.

Many of the current mediated portrayals of black masculinity are plagued by a tendency to demonize black men, constructing them as "others" who are to be feared. Some scholars note that early Hollywood portrayals of black men often portrayed them as seemingly docile, feminized, or Uncle Tom versions of black manhood. Frank Rudy Cooper (2009) articulates this dichotomy as "bipolar black masculinity," whereby black men are represented in media as one of two extremes: the "good black man" or the "bad black man." However, while the Uncle Tom trope is still commonly employed, many scholars argue that what has often come to dominate is a hypersexualized and violent concept of black manhood. While these original stereotypes were typically employed by a white, racist culture, it is important to note that they have been prominently taken on in media produced by members of the black community as well. Ultimately, however, these cultural representations, independent of the race of the creator, are rooted in an imbalance of power based on signifiers such as race, class, and gender. As many

critics discuss, these images, whether intentionally or subconsciously, can reflect attempts at social control.

Historians and theorists point to developments in the late 19th century as fostering growth in the image of black masculinity as violent and sexually predatory. The end of slavery ushered in a period of fear, fostered by white supremacist movements that resulted in depictions of black males as a dangerous threat to the social order and the economic livelihood of white men of the working class. The 1915 silent film *The Birth of a Nation* is often cited as one of the first prominent mass-media portrayals of this violent black masculinity. The widespread mainstream success of the film and its influence on public sentiment make *The Birth of a Nation* an important object of study in chronicling the history of media and black masculinity. While often recognized for its groundbreaking use of film technology, *The Birth of a Nation* is heavily criticized for its depiction of black men as aggressive sexual beasts in pursuit of white women. Historically, the release of the film correlates with an upsurge in public violence, including riots in major U.S. cities, gangs of whites attacking blacks, and at least one murder (of a black teenager by a white man). The film is likewise thought to have contributed to the resurgence in the 1920s of the Ku Klux Klan, whose members used *The Birth of a Nation* as a recruitment tool as late as the 1970s.

As Herman Gray (1995) has written, popular representations situate black masculinity "as the logical and legitimate object of surveillance and policing, containment and punishment." This is particularly true in news reporting, which has been found in studies to overemphasize black deviance or laziness, especially in stories concerning issues such as crime, welfare, gun control, affirmative action, and poverty. Some scholars, for instance, have examined news coverage of the trial of O. J. Simpson, the black former football star who was accused of murdering his white ex-wife and her friend. Much of the public discourse and the media attention were heavily focused on issues of both race and class, using Simpson's childhood in lower-income housing projects, past gang activity, and blackness as a means to explain his current situation. *Time* magazine's altering of Simpson's mug shot for a cover story to make him appear darker has been cited repeatedly as a particularly egregious example of some of the racist undertones in the coverage. More recently, critics have pointed to the 2005 coverage of Hurricane Katrina in New Orleans. One of the most commonly cited examples concerns two different Associated Press photographs, one of a black man and the other of a white couple, of people wading through water in the aftermath and carrying supplies. The caption under the black man refers to the man "looting" a grocery store, while the white couple is "finding" food at a local store.

Crucially, in order to achieve power and favorable media attention in the white-dominated social structure, black men need to avoid any appearance of anger or menace. Cooper's study of masculinity and news coverage of President Barack Obama's election examines this point in depth, arguing that a prominent media discourse emerged on Obama's "femininity" as he tried to avoid the stereotype of the angry black man.

Scholars studying marginalized groups, such as women, blacks, and working-class white men point to ways in which the body becomes a locus of authority for those who lack social, political, or financial power. Consequently, many media portrayals of black men suggest that it is primarily through hypermasculine displays of physical or sexual strength that black men are able to achieve any semblance of status. This notion of the power of the black male body, at the expense of the mind, is exemplified in the professional sports culture, where white athletes are often praised for their dedication and cleverness, while black athletes are praised for their strength and style. Black men, as an "other" to white men, must use physical prowess to achieve power, while white men are portrayed as able to use their intelligence.

Likewise, in hip-hop culture, authenticity has come to be defined by a connection to violence, crime, and heterosexual conquest. Consequently, both homophobia and sexism are aspects of this struggle to conform to the stereotypes of black masculinity. Anthony B. Pinn (1996) notes that, in hip-hop, "manhood is often defined in opposition to womanhood." While some critiques are careful to note that the objectification of women and, in particular, black women, happens at the hands of all different races, hip-hop videos, which have historically been produced by black men, reflect how some elements of black-mediated culture have taken on the stereotypes put on them by the dominant culture. The construction of rampant sexuality for both men and women, is, many scholars argue, just another way in which blacks are "othered" by the white, hegemonic culture. Director Byron Hurt, in his film *Hip-Hop: Beyond Beats and Rhymes* (2006), chronicles the shift within hip-hop from the expression of a politics of resistance to a focus on violence and sexual conquest. As he explores through interviews, the movement toward gangster hip-hop is linked with major record companies acquiring smaller labels. The image of the black gangster has become a successful marketing tool, sold both to those who wish to emulate the portrayal and to those who are fearful of it. This commodification by white-owned record labels and corporate radio ensures that the definitional power of black masculinity rests within the white power structure.

Running contrary to other mediated representations, studies of television show a perceptible shift in the representation of black men during the 1980s. Herman Gray (1986) and others have pointed to an increasing depiction of middle-class blacks, particularly in situation comedies. This image of the "new black man," as Gray terms it, can be viewed as reflective of an assimilationist and individualist approach to black culture that ignores the political struggles and barriers to equality in its attempt to make black males less frightening to whites. This conflict is further articulated in discussions surrounding the popular and long-running television show *The Cosby Show* (1984–92). Whereas the program is seen as progressive by some—who point to the positive portrayal of a professional, caring, and involved upper-middle-class black father as having changed white perceptions of black men—it has been criticized by others, who see the show's attempt at counter-stereotyping as a form of color-blindness that ignores the lived experiences and politics of black culture.

Recent studies point to some changing images of black masculinity in popular texts. For instance, in a 2004 study of Spike Lee's *Clockers* and the television show *Homicide: Life on the Street*, Erin MacDonald finds that the depictions of masculinity have become more nuanced and fully engaged with notions of how manhood is influenced by and intersects with other factors, such as race, class, age, education, and religion. Black film writer and director Lee has likewise worked to create movies that portray black men in a different light while tackling issues involving racism. However, he has been criticized by scholars and feminists who find that his work engages in an overt sexualization of black females.

Regardless of the race of the cultural producer, many scholars, such as bell hooks in *We Real Cool* (2003), argue that the power of representation is never fully in black hands. Long-standing negative stereotypes of black masculinity ensure that it is only in replicating and conforming to these tropes that black males can achieve visibility and success, even when this same conformation keeps them from achieving actual power. What is needed, hooks and others suggest, is a healing process that confronts and resists the dominant masculinity and a culture that promotes sexism while acknowledging the pain and anger associated with discrimination. As the space where these struggles often play out, media can offer opportunities for challenging and rewriting stereotypical portrayals, thereby playing an important role in this healing.

Theresa Rose Crapanzano
University of Colorado, Boulder

See also Bordo, Susan; Class Privilege; Critical Theory; Feminist Theory: Women-of-Color and Multiracial Perspectives; Gender and Masculinity: Fatherhood; Gender and Masculinity: Metrosexual Male; Gender and Masculinity: White Masculinity; Hegemony; Heterosexism; Homophobia; hooks, bell; Music Videos: Representations of Men; Music Videos: Representations of Women; Music Videos: Tropes; Prejudice; Racism; Social Construction of Gender; Video Gaming: Representations of Masculinity

Further Readings

Abdel-Shehid, Gamal. *Who da' Man? Black Masculinities and Sporting Cultures*. Toronto, ON: Canadian Scholars' Press, 2005.

Boyd, Todd. *Am I Black Enough for You? Popular Culture From the 'Hood and Beyond*. Bloomington: Indiana University Press, 1997.

Cooper, Frank Rudy. "Our First Unisex President? Black Masculinity and Obama's Feminine Side." *Denver University Law Review*, v.86/3 (2009).

Gray, Herman. "Black Masculinity and Visual Culture." *Callaloo*, v.18/2 (1995).

Gray, Herman. "Television and the New Black Man: Black Male Images in Prime-Time Situation Comedy." *Media, Culture and Society*, v.8 (1986).

hooks, bell. *We Real Cool: Black Men and Masculinity*. London: Routledge, 2003.

Hurt, Byron, director. *Hip-Hop: Beyond Beats and Rhymes* [film]. Northampton, MA: Media Education Foundation, 2006. http://www.mediaed.org (Accessed February 2011).

Jackson, Ronald L., II. *Scripting the Black Masculine Body: Identity, Discourse, and Racial Politics in Popular Media*. Albany: State University of New York Press, 2006.

MacDonald, Erin. "Masculinity and Race in Media: The Case of the Homicide Detective." In *Race/Gender/Media: Considering Diversity Across Audiences, Content, and Producers*, Rebecca Ann Lind, ed. Boston: Pearson, 2004.

Pinn, Anthony B. "'Gettin' Grown': Notes on Gangsta Rap Music and Notions of Manhood." *Journal of African American Men*, v.1/4 (1996).

Whitehead, Stephen M. *Men and Masculinities: Key Themes and New Directions*. Cambridge, UK: Polity Press, 2002.

Gender and Masculinity: Fatherhood

The figure of the father as depicted in media has had a varied career in American popular culture. Over time, several stock father figures have emerged. These include cold and remote authority figures, wise and caring parents, lovable but bumbling and often imposed-upon buffoons, psychologically and physically abusive monsters, and absent fathers. The stock figure of the father that tends to dominate popular-culture texts differs from one decade to another, reflecting cultural shifts and changing social concerns. There are also significant differences in the stock figures of fathers by type of medium (print, film, television) and genre (comic strip, film drama, television sitcom, animated series, and so forth).

Traditionally, newspaper comic strips have tended to offer positive portrayals of fathers. Reflecting the commercial constraints and comedic conventions of the genre, the fathers featured on the funny pages are typically flawed but likable characters. An early example of the type is Jiggs, a socially ambitious nouveau riche Irish immigrant lampooned in the long-running strip *Bringing Up Father* (1913–2000). The perennially popular Dagwood Bumstead from *Blondie* (1930–) is another classic example. Recent examples of the type are more nuanced, with less emphasis on physical comedy and social missteps and more focus on the myriad challenges of maintaining interpersonal relationships, as is the case with Jon Patterson of *For Better or Worse* (1979–).

In contrast to newspaper comic strips, films offer a wider variety of stock father figures, ranging from the loving and lovable fathers often featured in light comedies to the morally monstrous fathers who abuse their children—and others—physically, psychologically, and sexually. A father of the first type is featured in Bob Clark's *A Christmas Story* (1983), in which Darren McGavin plays a curmudgeon whose gruff demeanor and ready use of rough language cannot mask his genuine affection for his family. Roman Polanski's neo-noir *Chinatown* (1974) includes a classic example of the abusive father in the person of Noah Cross (John Huston), whose granddaughter/daughter was the product of his sexually abusing his daughter Evelyn (Faye Dunaway). The absent father also figures prominently in films. David Fincher's cult classic *Fight Club* (1999) includes several diatribes deriding physically absent and psychologically remote fathers. Filmmakers are willing to portray unsympathetic fathers in part because, unlike television producers, they do not have to develop characters that attract long-term audience loyalty.

During the 1950s, television replaced film as American popular culture's dominant medium. Televised depictions of fathers have great cultural weight because of the medium's popularity, pervasiveness, market penetration, and the parasocial relationships viewers enter into with characters in established, long-running series. Such enduring relationships often have greater immediacy and personal and collective cultural impact than those developed in response to a character featured in a single book or film. For this reason, televised depictions of fathers form a useful cultural barometer. The preferred portrayal of fathers during the 1950s is best summed up by the title of the popular sitcom *Father Knows Best* (which during its run, 1954–63, moved from the Columbia Broadcasting System, CBS, to the National Broadcasting System, NBC, and back again). Wise and knowing fathers from that era include Ward Cleaver (Hugh Beaumont) of *Leave It to Beaver* (which debuted on CBS in 1957, then was aired by the American Broadcasting Company, ABC, until 1963) and Ozzie Nelson, the sweater-wearing dad of *The Adventures of Ozzie and Harriet*

(ABC, 1952–66). The early to mid-1960s continued to depict televised sitcom fathers as beloved and respected authority figures in such series as *The Andy Griffith Show* (1960–68) and *My Three Sons* (1960–65 on ABC, then on CBS until 1972).

Television dramas and sitcoms of the 1970s reflected the nation's social unrest. No series illustrates this better than Norman Lear's groundbreaking sitcom *All in the Family* (1971–79), whose central character, Archie Bunker (Carroll O'Connor), was a likable bigot who fought constantly with his wife, daughter, son-in-law, and neighbors. He is loud, proud, and unapologetically racist, sexist, homophobic, and xenophobic. The critical and popular success of the series led to the development of such ethnically diverse and socially engaged Lear sitcoms as *Maude* (1972–78), *Chico and the Man* (1974–78), *Good Times* (1974–79), *Sanford and Son* (1972–77), and *The Jeffersons* (1975–85), which depicted an upwardly mobile African American family headed by George Jefferson (played by Sherman Hemsley), a combative character who originally appeared in *All in the Family* as a bigoted African American counterpart to Archie Bunker.

Fathers were treated relatively well by television during the 1980s, especially those featured in popular sitcoms. During that decade, two of the most prominent fictional father figures in American popular culture were Dr. Heathcliff "Cliff" Huxtable (Bill Cosby) of *The Cosby Show* (1984–92) and Steven Keaton (Michael Gross) of *Family Ties* (1982–89). Both were devoted family men. *The Cosby Show* was praised by some social critics for its positive portrayal of an African American family, while others noted that the series was unrealistic in depicting an upper-middle-class professional family at a time when few African American families fit that profile.

During the 1990s the main character in *Murphy Brown* (1988–98) generated a culture-war controversy when she decided to have a baby as a single mother without the participation of the child's biological father. This decision famously drew the ire of U.S. Vice President Dan Quayle. The 1990s also saw renewed interest in television police-procedural dramas depicting good fathers and bad. *Law & Order, Special Victims Unit* (NBC, 1999–), which focuses on sexually based crimes, includes graphic stories about sexually abusive fathers in its narrative repertoire. Televised depictions of father during the 2000s range from the irreverent to the reverent.

Alan Harper (Jon Cryer) of *Two and a Half Men* (CBS, 2003–) is an example of the former treatment, while Francis "Frank" Reagan (Tom Selleck) of *Blue Bloods* (CBS, debuted in the fall of 2010) illustrates the latter, as well as the tendency to valorize "traditional" masculinity in general, and fathers in particular, found in many popular-culture texts following the terrorist attacks of September 11, 2001.

In the past, popular-culture texts were populated predominantly by white, heterosexual fathers. This exclusionary convention changed during the last two decades of the 20th century, when an increasing number of African American and Hispanic fathers began to be featured, although not in numbers corresponding to their percentage of the general population. This trend toward demographic inclusion is illustrated by such comic strip fathers as Greg Wilkins of *Curtis* (1988–) and Sergio "Papi" Bermudez of *Baldo* (2000). During the same period, broadcast and cable television networks also became more inclusive, with series featuring African Americans, such as *Family Matters* (ABC, 1989–97; CBS, 1997–98), becoming regular fixtures on network schedules. The commercial success and popularity of these series paved the way for similar future series, such as *My Wife and Kids* (ABC, 2001–05) and *Tyler Perry's House of Payne* (TBS, 2006–). The commercial success also prompted the development of broadcast and cable networks with programming content aimed at African American viewers.

With such series as the eponymously titled *George Lopez* (ABC, 2002–07), Hispanic fathers have also enjoyed an increased presence on mainstream television, but not in numbers reflecting their growing demographic strength and cultural influence. This might be due, in part, to the widespread availability of such Spanish-language networks Azteca América, Telemundo, and Televisa. To date, depictions of Asian fathers remain relatively rare in mainstream media.

Fathers have played a prominent—even dominant—role in American animated television series. The early 1960s saw the development of the animated cartoon series, with the introduction of such Hanna-Barbera offerings as *The Flintstones* (ABC, 1960–66) and *The Jetsons* (originally aired on ABC during the 1962–63 season). While ostensibly set in different time periods, the former in an imaginary Stone Age past and the latter in a high-tech future, these series actually celebrate the nuclear families, working dads, and stay-at-home moms of post–World War II suburban American commuter culture. The success of *The Simpsons* (FOX, 1989–) sparked renewed interest in animated television series. The father in the series, Homer (voiced by Dan Castellaneta), is depicted as culturally crude, socially inept, and intellectually impoverished. This same unflattering constellation of characteristics defines other animated fathers, such as Peter Griffin (voiced by Seth MacFarlane) of *The Family Guy* (FOX, 1999–). In contrast, Hank Hill (voiced by Mike Judge) of *King of the Hill* (FOX, 1997–2010) is a decent, hardworking man who loves his job, family, friends, and country and is fiercely loyal to them. Homer and Hank are emblematic of the contemporary popular-culture tendency, noted previously, to treat fathers irreverently or reverently.

Robert Westerfelhaus
Celeste C. Lacroix
College of Charleston

See also Film: Hollywood; Gender and Femininity: Motherhood; Gender and Masculinity: Black Masculinity; Gender and Masculinity: Metrosexual Male; Gender and Masculinity: White Masculinity; Gender Embodiment; Gender Media Monitoring; Heroes: Action and Super Heroes; Patriarchy; Stereotypes

Further Readings

Broughton, Trev Lynn and Helen Rogers. *Gender and Fatherhood in the Nineteenth Century*. New York: Palgrave Macmillan, 2007.

Dowd, Nancy E. *The Man Question: Male Subordination and Privilege*. New York: New York University Press, 2010.

Gavanas, Anna. *Fatherhood Politics in the United States: Masculinity, Sexuality, Race and Marriage*. Urbana: University of Illinois Press, 2004.

Stacey, Judith. "Gay Parenthood and the Decline of Paternity as We Knew It." *Sexualities*, v.9/1 (2006).

GENDER AND MASCULINITY: METROSEXUAL MALE

The term *metrosexual male* or *metrosexuals* is an amalgamation of the words *metropolitan* and *heterosexual* that originally was used by journalist Mark Simpson in a story in the British newspaper *The Independent* and subsequently was used by

Simpson in a widely quoted and reproduced article appearing on Salon.com in 2002. The term was widely reproduced and recirculated in the popular media as a way of talking about shifting gender identity in the late 20th century. Today, a metrosexual refers to a heterosexual male who exhibits cultural tendencies stereotypically associated with homosexual men, namely a heightened concern with appearance, keeping physically fit, popular culture, and fashion. Metrosexual males are a representation of shifting gender norms more so than a distinctive sexual identity, as the name may imply. The term metrosexual male came about at a time when gay male cultural practices were gaining increasing attention in popular media and culture and were being adopted by heterosexual men. The term is significant; it challenges strict dichotomies between male and female gender identity, gay and straight sexual orientation, and related cultural differences, as well as the traditional gendered roles of men and women in relationships. The term ultimately points to the fact that stereotypically male and female qualities have more to do with culture than with biology and may signal a larger cultural shift in terms of gender attributes as much as a distinctive identity.

This construction of the metrosexual identity is used to describe a new type of urban male who is less stereotypically masculine and because of his geographical location has access to gyms, salons, fashion retailers, style cues, and other resources that influence his identity and appearance. In short, metrosexual males can care about their shoes and haircuts and still be interested in sports and automobiles. Metrosexual also describes men who are confident and secure in their sexuality and typically are well groomed, well educated, and well cultured. Though the term does not imply any specific level of socioeconomic status, it does imply that men considered metrosexual are more likely to spend their economic resources on consumer goods that directly benefit their immediate appearance and needs. While still heterosexual, metrosexual males are thought to be less concerned with spending their income on wives or girlfriends and more interested in using their income on themselves.

Celebrities, including movie icon Brad Pitt, soccer star David Beckham, and television personality Ryan Seacrest are often heralded as prototypical metrosexual males because they have demonstrated an overt concern with appearance and are not afraid to appear less stereotypically masculine. Magazines

A metrosexual can be described as a man who frequents gyms and salons and is more likely to invest in fashion and appearance than the stereotypical male. (Photos.com)

such as *GQ*, *Details*, and *Men's Health* are considered to be metrosexual bibles with their mix of stories and features on traditionally male topics, like bodybuilding and sports, and female topics, such as fashion and beauty (the latter written for a male audience). Other popular-culture artifacts, such as the films *Fight Club* (1999) and *American Psycho* (2000), exploited this metrosexual identity and made it acceptable for male audiences to enjoy seeing stylish and muscular actors without this appreciation bringing into question their own sexual identity. The Bravo television program *Queer Eye for the Straight Guy* helped popularize the idea of the metrosexual by having a team of gay stylists make over a straight man to improve his appearance, level of cultural sophistication, and overall confidence. The program ultimately helped popularize the genre of straight male makeovers, the idea of which is quintessentially metrosexual in and of itself.

The metrosexual male identity also represents a shift in traditional gender identity norms. The category opens up a space for heterosexual men to embrace more stereotypically feminine concerns without altering perceptions of their sexual orientation. Some argue that metrosexual as a category exists independent of sexual orientation. That is, both homosexuals and heterosexuals can be identified as metrosexuals as long as they share the same lifestyle cues and consumer habits. Others, however, maintain that metrosexual is a term that applies specifically to heterosexual men who are simply comfortable with and not threatened by homosexual identity, if not practice. Regardless, the label is not about sexual orientation as much as it is a lifestyle category. Metrosexuals, often defined as narcissists, are mostly interested in themselves as sexual objects and correspondingly spend time and money to make themselves attractive and stylish in their own eyes. They are described as enjoying being the center of attention and the object of both male and female gazes and desires.

Not a label that would likely be used by many men themselves, the category of metrosexual was largely developed in the popular media and by advertisers. Marketers and advertisers in particular are interested in cultivating the metrosexual identity in order to build a market and target it as a distinctive consumer segment interested in purchasing products such as moisturizers, fashion accessories, expensive label clothing, and other nonessential items that previously were marketed primarily to women. This metrosexual consumer, at least in the eyes of marketers, wants to spend his disposable income on himself for immediate gratification as opposed to saving or trusting his wife or girlfriend to make purchases on his behalf. Thus, the label metrosexual male is largely about men joining women as the primary consumers, and thus expanding the potential market for items ranging from designer fashions to hair care.

There seems to be some cultural impetus in the late 20th century for the development of the metrosexual label other than marketing concerns alone. As more women entered the workforce, as marriage between men and women happened later rather than sooner in life, and as social acceptance of

sexual minorities, including gay men, increased and was even celebrated in popular media, the conditions were in place for less rigid definitions of male and female gender identity. As women gained more power and wealth, they demanded more stylish, well-groomed partners. Men, for their part, relied less on women for tasks like picking out clothing and thus had more time to cultivate an identity that suited themselves first and not necessarily their partners. Ultimately the term metrosexual has to do with men adopting social and cultural concerns related to fashion, personal appearance, and grooming typically associated with women, raising larger questions about how culture constructs and reinforces gender norms.

David Gudelunas
Fairfield University

See also Advertising; Beauty and Body Image: Beauty Myths; Gender and Masculinity: Black Masculinity; Gender and Masculinity: Fatherhood; Gender and Masculinity: White Masculinity; Gender Embodiment; Identity; Men's Magazines: Lifestyle and Health; Queer Theory; Reality-Based Television: Makeover Shows; Social Construction of Gender; Stereotypes; Toys and Games: Gender Socialization

Further Readings

Coad, David. *The Metrosexual: Gender, Sexuality and Sport.* Albany: State University of New York Press, 2008.
Cova, Bernard, Robert V. Kozinets, and Avi Shanker. *Consumer Tribes.* Burlington, MA: Butterworth-Heinemann, 2007.
Flocker, Michael. *The Metrosexual Guide to Style: A Handbook for the Modern Man.* Cambridge, MA: Da Capo Press, 2003.
Simpson, Mark "Here Come the Mirror Men." http://www.marksimpson.com/pages/journalism/mirror_men.html (Accessed September 2010).
Simpson, Mark "Meet the Metrosexual." http://www.salon.com/entertainment/feature/2002/07/22/metrosexual (Accessed September 2010).

Gender and Masculinity: White Masculinity

Gender refers to social ideas and cultural expectations about behavior, emotion, fashion, and public or interpersonal interactions. The terms *sex* and *gender* are often used interchangeably; however, this is a misuse of the terms. Sex refers to biological conditions—for example, genitalia, genes, and hormones. Gender refers to constructed ideas about self-presentation, stereotypes, and behavioral expectations that are commonly associated with the biological body—for instance, aggression, fearlessness, or competitiveness. While there may be particular links between biological and cultural factors in regard to behavior and personality traits, biology does not necessarily cause behavior. Stereotypes, learned practices, and variations in access to power and resources impact human behavior. This is the focus of the term gender. We tend to associate expectations of masculinity with male bodies.

Ideas and expectations about social behavior are created through a variety of institutions and everyday practices. These include religious belief systems, family hierarchies, laws, books, television, music, and other forms of popular-culture media.

Social Constructions of White Masculinity

Ideas about gender and masculinity vary over time and across cultures. For instance, although tights and heels were considered masculine in 17th-century France, this fashion would not uphold 21st-century expectations of masculinity. Gender identity is impacted by sociopolitical, cultural, and economic factors, including ethnicity, religion, sexual orientation, transgender status, and class status. Gender refers to the complex web of social meanings—qualities like "pretty," "tough," and "reckless"—that are attached to biological sex. This process gets started early, sometimes before birth. When parents decide on decorating a baby's nursery in pink or blue or when they choose a baseball theme for baby-shower invitations instead of ballerinas, the process of gender differentiation is constructed and reinforced. Even though culture constantly creates and identifies gender roles, we do not tend to think about it if we are not taught to recognize the social dimensions of gender construction. Likewise, because "whiteness" is a position of relative power, it is often a default setting that is not questioned.

Masculinity is historically contingent, but so is the linking of gender expectations and stereotypes to ethnicity and class. References to the generic term *masculinity* often involve the invalid or unspoken assumption that when we say "men" we are talking about white, heterosexual, American, able-bodied, and middle-class males. This unexamined default setting reinforces privilege by making entire groups of men invisible. We often also assume that masculinity equals dominance and aggression, yet this invokes unrealistic expectations that men are by nature stoic, unemotional, aggressive, and interpersonally detached.

Popular culture is a powerful source of the stories we are taught about masculinity. Contemporary social meanings about white masculinity are conveyed through various media outlets, such as video games, sports, magazines, pornography, advertising, and music videos. The image of working-class white men as bumbling idiots or as hyperaggressive or criminal is a routine component of movie lines and sitcom plots. Sports culture often promotes the stereotypes of dominant masculinity, especially by establishing masculinity as distinct and different from gay men and all women. At the same time that these media constructs reinforce hegemonic ideology, such images can restrict white masculinity to what is called the Man Box.

The Man Box is a conceptual framework developed by violence-prevention educators Allan Creighton and Paul Kivel to understand the dominant standards and norms of masculinity. The boundaries and limitations of dominant masculinity include familiar traits or stereotypes: Men and boys do not cry, they are tough, and they are sexual and powerful. Restricting human qualities to a narrow range keeps men trapped, cutting them off from traits such as creativity, kindness, and attentiveness, which must be rejected to maintain the posture of dominant masculinity.

White men are featured in the majority of front-page news stories, sports reports, op-eds, headlining music acts, and box-office stars. The predominance of white men featured in newspapers and other media sources reinforces the imagery of white masculinity as generally powerful, dominant, and entitled. This relative position of power is offset by class status, physical ability, and sexual orientation or gender affect. White men can turn on the television or look at the front page of the newspaper and generally assume to see people of their race and gender widely represented. In addition, white men can turn on the radio or watch music videos knowing that it is unlikely they will encounter lyrics or visual images that refer to them in sexually degrading or objectifying ways. These media factors contribute to what is called white masculine privilege.

Popular-culture media send powerful messages about men's sexual access to women's bodies. For instance, music videos and lyrics are a central part of our popular culture, and they routinely portray women's bodies in hypersexualized, sexually available ways. Because teaching media literacy skills is not a widespread practice, we tend to see these images as "just entertainment" instead of understanding that popular culture also reinforces significant messages about sexuality, relations between women and men, and our cultural understandings about white masculinity.

Privilege and White Masculinity

White masculinity generally affords what is called unearned privilege. Those who are white and male yet do not hew to middle-class, heteronormative stereotypes of masculine style are at risk of becoming subjects of ostracism or even violence. This is often portrayed in popular culture and media. Moreover, although masculinity is tied to the male body, anyone can express masculine traits and masculine self-performance. White women who display characteristics or traits associated with masculinity may also face danger or ostracism. Media constitute a powerful source of stories that teach us about masculinity. White men receive power in society that is reinforced through media sources, although not all white men benefit equally from the privileges of race and gender.

Males who feel powerless in the broader society—particularly men of color and working-class white men—often turn to their own bodies as a source of power. Media tend to reinforce associations between sports like boxing and basketball, jobs like construction, and street-level drug dealing with poor men or men of color. Wealthier, privileged—and often white—men have access to economic, social, and political forms of power that do not require this kind of physical posturing.

At the same time, contemporary media entertainment also presents alternative versions of white masculinity that are limiting in other ways: Instead of acknowledging the diversity and complexity of masculinity, popular culture has recently given us a version of manhood that revels in escape. Movies, advertisements, and television shows in the "failure-to-launch" genre—such as *Superbad* (2007), *The Simpsons* (1989–), *Pineapple Express* (2008), *The 40 Year Old Virgin* (2005), *Knocked Up* (2007), and *Zack and Miri Make a Porno* (2008)—portray men languishing in a perpetual adolescent state without much responsibility.

These slacker assumptions are at odds with the take-charge version of dominant masculinity that is also imposed on men. These images present competing cultural messages to boys and men to take on a stoic hypermasculine pose *and* remain eternally irresponsible, coyly helpless, childlike "kidults." Both versions of masculinity are extreme and unrealistic, and neither serves men and boys well. Men are also told that they have power over others—and while as a group they have power over women, many men lack power in other areas of their lives.

Critical media studies investigate the sexism and rigid ideas about white masculinity that run rampant in movies, music, sports, and video games. This work analyzes books, videos, workshops, and Websites and holds conferences on media and gender politics to expose conflicting cultural messages and to expand gender options, in part by taking on popular-culture media with the understanding that gender is political and that social resources and power are not zero-sum games.

In her essay "White Privilege: Unpacking the Invisible Knapsack," Peggy McIntosh famously exposes invisible patterns and practices to promote critical thinking about the links between gender privilege, skin privilege, racism, and sexism. One way this privilege operates is in how we are taught to understand sexism and racism as individual acts of meanness. In fact, white masculine privilege is supported by systems that perpetuate and maintain dominance for light-skinned men *as a group*.

Backlash and White Masculinity

The media can sometimes be a source of critical investigation into the assumptions of white masculinity. Mainstream media often perpetuate stereotypes about white masculinity. Mainstream media also participate in what is known as backlash politics by reporting alarmist stories about academically underperforming white boys and how white men are allegedly falling behind in the economy.

The fact is that boys—specifically white, suburban, affluent boys—are scoring higher in school performance than ever before. At the very least, any boy-girl differences assessed in verbal, math, and reading skills are small. National Education Association figures place aggregate college enrollments at 51 percent female and 49 percent male, with men still outnumbering women at Ivy League schools. The high rate of unemployment among men, spurred by the great recession that began in 2008, has had a serious impact on labor issues and has prompted additional questions about what masculinity means or represents. However, white men still hold a disproportionate amount of power across business, entertainment, and media sectors, and white masculinity remains closely tied to hegemonic ideology.

Shira Tarrant
California State University, Long Beach

See also Class Privilege; Critical Theory; Feminism; Gender and Masculinity: Black Masculinity; Gender and Masculinity: Fatherhood; Gender and Masculinity: Metrosexual Male; Gender Embodiment; Identity; Men's Magazines: Lifestyle and Health; Queer Theory; Reality-Based Television: Makeover Shows; Social Construction of Gender; Stereotypes; Toys and Games: Gender Socialization; Video Gaming: Representations of Masculinity

Further Readings

Kahn, Jack S. *An Introduction to Masculinities*. Malden, MA: Wiley-Blackwell, 2009.

Katz, Jackson. *Tough Guise: Violence, Media, and the Crisis in Masculinity*. Sut Jhally, executive producer and director. Northampton, MA: Media Education Foundation, 1999.

Keith, Thomas, director. *The Manual for Building Dysfunctional Men*. Northampton, MA: Media Education Foundation, 2011.

Kimmel, Michael. *Guyland: The Perilous World Where Boys Become Men*. New York: Harper, 2009.

McIntosh, Peggy. "White Privilege: Unpacking the Invisible Knapsack." http://www.fjaz.com/mcintosh.html (Accessed November 2010).

Tarrant, Shira. "Guy Trouble: Are Young Men Really in Crisis, or Are These Boys Done Just Being Boys?" *Bitch: Feminist Response to Popular Culture*, Spring 2009.

Tarrant, Shira. *Men and Feminism*. Berkeley, CA: Seal Press, 2008.

GENDER EMBODIMENT

Regarding feminine embodiment, this essay examines the literature related to the "thin ideal," "objectification theory," "body-ism," "sexual objectification," "body surveillance," and the power dynamics of gendered body portrayals in media, along with research that demonstrates the impact of these messages on women's gender perceptions, self-esteem, pursuit of the thin ideal, distorted perception of body type, dissatisfaction with body, and predisposition toward eating disorders. In regard to masculine embodiment, literature is reviewed regarding recent trends in male objectification in advertising and media, depictions of the "metrosexual" man, and discussion of the "crisis in masculinity," viewed by some scholars as a backlash against feminism and depictions of the new, "softer" or objectified male.

The centrality of gender embodiment has animated recent debates in media studies about the relationship among gender representations in media, gendered bodies in virtual space, and gender as performance. This debate has been informed by such theoretical disciplines as post-structuralism, feminist theory, cyberfeminism, queer theory, semiotics, performance studies, and transgender studies. Key figures invoked in the conversation range from Sigmund Freud, Jacques Lacan, Plato, and Luce Irigary to Antonio Gramsci, Judith Butler, Michel Foucault, and William Gibson. The essay ends with a discussion of whether essentialist or materialist definitions of gender hinder or advance feminist and democratic causes, using the writing of Butler and performance studies scholars to offer some middle ground to this question of gender and embodiment.

Gender and Femininity: Female Embodiment

In media and culture, women, more so then men, have been defined or self-define in terms of their bodies. Whether this involves replicating or comparing oneself to the thin ideal presented in modern mass media (despite the looming specter of anorexia and bulimia) or altering one's body to heighten perceived sexuality, desirability, or youthfulness (through cosmetic surgery, exercise, or eating) or conforming to definitions of femininity (through fashion and cosmetics), the body has often been culturally signified for women as a source of power (usually sexual, aesthetic, or virginal) or shame (either sexual or nonnormative). In media, the female body is frequently a source of power or shame, constructed as either sexually attractive (bombshell or vamp) or sexually dangerous (siren or femme fatale), as either a prize to be honored and protected (the fashion icon, virgin, or mother/homemaker) or an object of sexual desire (lover), conquest (damsel in distress), punishment (bad girl/whore), or excess needing discipline (bitch or fat lady). Whether threat or promise, desirable, dangerous, or shameful, a woman's presence and meaning in media, and possibly in life to the extent that media shape identity and the perceptions of others, have historically been shaped by her body. From this perspective, for women, embodiment matters.

Despite the historical centrality of the female body and feminine embodiment as a frequent source of power or shame in media representations, feminist theorists and critics, particularly as influenced by post-structuralism and new media studies, have been torn over the following questions: Does the physical female body (as spectator/gamer/media producer) still matter? Should control over the female body as promoted in the media (through, for example, plastic surgery, diet, exercise, and body adornment) remain a source of political struggle? Is sexual objectification, as inscribed in the media, a personal choice or a problematic projection for women?

Female embodiment is often examined in studies of the thin ideal in media representations of women. Numerous studies have examined both the prevalence and the impact of this ideal on setting unrealistic expectations for women and as a source of body dissatisfaction and disordered eating. Women suffer disproportionately from eating disorders, with some statistics claiming that women account for close to 90 percent of the affected population. Despite general agreement on the prevalence of this thin ideal, the evidence that it does not reflect actual or healthy body size for young women, and the growing gap between the ideal and the real, some studies have found that this ideal has had little or no impact, whereas others have found, to the contrary, that images of overweight women actually have a positive impact on women's body image. However, one study, a meta-analysis of 25 different studies on this topic that controlled for (among other factors) age, preexisting body image problems, and research

The self-objectification theory is based on the concept that a woman is a "sight," meaning that seeing and judging her body as she thinks others see her is significant to her self-perception. (Photos.com)

design, found that "body image was significantly more negative after viewing thin media images than after viewing images of either average size models, plus size models, or inanimate objects." Not only does mass media promulgate the thin ideal but comparisons to that ideal and the ability to discipline the female body in terms of size remain central measures of positive self-concept for women and girls.

Objectification theory asserts that media, by articulating the centrality of women's bodies and appearance to identity, socialize self-objectification while contributing to feelings of anxiety and shame. This self-objectification involves adopting a "viewer's consciousness" wherein a woman is a "sight" and where body surveillance—seeing and judging her body as she thinks others see her—is significant to a woman's self-concept. John Berger refers to this phenomenon as a woman's "split consciousness," whereby a woman walking or talking or making love is a woman always watching herself walk, watching herself talk, and watching herself make love. The media constantly highlight bodies and body parts (promulgating "body-ism"), often coupling this practice with sexual objectification. One study, an examination of television shows popular with adolescents, found that the second most common sexual theme is that women are judged on their physical appearance.

Some studies have explored the extent to which audience members are predisposed to seek out or avoid sexually objectifying media based on factors such as anxiety over appearance or body shame as well as self-objectifying tendencies. Other studies have examined plastic surgery designed to enhance sexuality and attractiveness either as a source of increased self-confidence, satisfaction, and interpersonal influence or as a dangerous transcription of the cultural objectification of women.

Hundreds of studies of the representations of gender in media, from advertising to entertainment television to film and the Internet, have found that the sexual and the passive/vulnerable body is central to depictions of feminine identity, whereas the aggressive and active body is a significant marker of masculine identity. Research into gender depictions in video games and gamer magazines has replicated these findings. Male video-game characters, for example, are much more likely to be portrayed as aggressive and active than female characters, while female characters are much more likely to be portrayed as passive, sexual, and scantily clad. Other studies have shown that, although male and female gamers will often create cross-gendered identities in cyberspace, they still adhere to sexist stereotypes in life.

Gender and Masculinity: Male Embodiment

While body-ism, sexual objectification, the thin ideal, and a focus on the importance of passivity and physical attractiveness have been central to depictions of women in the mass media, men have increasingly become the target of such objectifying media messages.

Starting in the mid-1980s, the media began reinterpreting traditional gender roles. This trend mirrored the blurring of these roles in American culture due, in part, to the move from a production-based to a service- and consumption-based economy, the impact of 1960s and 1970s feminist consciousness-raising, and the entry of more women into the workforce and the assumption of child-care and household duties by men. This move toward the "softer" or more sensitive man was accompanied by a reverse trend in the depictions of more muscular and aggressive women, such as Lara Croft from the *Tomb Raider* video game and film franchise. The arrival of this softer man was also heralded by marketers' discovery of the male consumer of health and beauty products. He found himself increasingly targeted by products designed to make him look better, which often meant increasing muscle mass and overall body leanness, and perform better, which often meant physical performance in sexual and sports-based arenas. Since advertising often works by demonstrating the need for a product aimed at correcting the potential consumer's lack or inadequacy in comparison to some ideal model's possession of these qualities, men were increasingly objectified in the media and male audiences were invited to self-objectify by focusing on body development and maintenance as central to their self-concept.

This trend in advertising was accompanied by the birth of the "metrosexual" in culture and the entertainment media. The metrosexual was a somewhat androgynous man who embraced fashion and the importance of body sculpting and intensive grooming, including the use of products traditionally purchased by women, such as exfoliants and bronzers. The metrosexual not only was evident in fictional programming but also was represented by such significant sports figures as British soccer star David Beckham, the subject of the highly successful wide-release film *Bend It Like Beckham* and the most highly paid soccer player in the history of the sport until 2004. Beckham not only married a fashion model and cultural icon, Victoria "Posh Spice" Beckham, but also became one, selling such products as sports apparel, underwear, and cologne. Beckham seemingly embodied a blend of a more traditional definition of masculinity as physically accomplished with the new definition of masculinity as physically beautiful (articulated through a youthful, toned, muscular, stylish, and fashionable body), attractive to women both in and out of clothes, and requiring intensive surveillance and maintenance. Regardless of focus, however, a man's definition of self-worth, as depicting in the media by the late 1990s, increasingly resided in his body rather than in, for example, more traditional assets such as intellectual prowess, financial clout, or social and family connections.

Critics raised a number of questions about this new male in culture and the media. Were these gender messages transgressive? Was this new objectification of men in the media a refreshing change from the media's single-minded focus on female objectification? Did the advent of reverse objectification, in a visual culture that seems to thrive on the body as object, mark a sad day for both men and women? Was it a market bid by advertisers for the gay male consumer, historically already socialized to accept the importance of embodiment and possibly identifying with or attracted to the more androgynous metrosexual male as both consumer and objects of consumption? Finally, were these messages a response to a seeming "crisis in masculinity" articulated in films and the media more generally by the late 1990s?

Critics examined the media backlash against this objectified metrosexual male and the potential crisis in masculinity he represented by pointing to such extremely successful films as the perennial cult favorite *Fight Club* (1999). Starring the 1990s icon of hegemonic masculinity, Brad Pitt, the film reasserts a more traditional notion of masculinity as physical toughness, rather than physical beauty, and the ability to "take it like a man," or male masochism, as even more important than winning. This critique extends in the film to satirizing the "feminized" corporate culture and the lifestyle of conspicuous consumption so attractive to Pitt's counterpart in the film, played by Ed Norton, which, the film claims, contributed to his and all men's emasculation. Other films, such as those in the *Terminator* series, offered an ironic, self-conscious critique of muscular masculinity through an over-the-top parody of it.

Questions remained for critics, however, regarding whether these reflexive critiques of an objectified, essentialized, and impossible definition of masculinity invited self-awareness of the performative nature of gender or instead fed a nostalgic hankering for a return to a supposedly simpler, more prescriptive and stereotypical definition of masculinity. For example, critics pointed to the popularity of such television shows such as *Monster Garage* and *American Chopper* as responses to men's desire to return to traditional, "hegemonic" notions of masculinity based neither in the body as aesthetic sexual object nor in the importance of body maintenance.

Gender as Performance

Although sex and gender are not the same, critics like Judith Butler, in her influential book *Gender Trouble* (1990), pointed to the extent that feminist theory, despite its rejection of biology as destiny, has implicitly assumed an essentialist position (sex = gender) regarding the relationship between the two. Doing so, she argues, has reinforced a binary understanding of gender relations, where gendered identities must necessarily be built on male and female bodies. Second wave feminism, dedicated to liberating definitions of gender—through criticizing media stereotypes and gender-based career and life choices as well as stereotypically gendered understandings of media audiences—may have unwittingly rescribed gender-normative definitions of identity and relationships by assuming such an essentialist perspective.

This is done at the expense of allowing individuals to resist normative definitions, celebrate differences, and choose and construct their gendered identity (or identities). Rather than seeing gender as fixed, Butler views it as a fluid social construct that potentially changes with context, cultures, and time periods. Gender is best seen as a way of doing the body in performance. However, this is not simply a matter of choosing to perform gender; she argues that we perform gender every day, whether consciously or not. The types of unconscious performances that are normative in Western culture and media, however, support hegemonic ideals. Butler therefore calls for conscious performance, or "gender trouble," as a way of subverting normalized notions of gender identity. Since the mass media offer the central sites where normative or potentially nonnormative definitions of gender operate, Butler calls for and admires the type of gender trouble invited by cultural icons such as Madonna, famous for her reflexive, fluid, and often disruptive constructions of gender and sexuality.

In her book *Bodies That Matter*, Butler extends the examination of normative gender performance to show how it supports hegemonic heterosexuality. She once again argues that biological sex, by being problematically linked in culture to gender, shapes desire toward the opposite gender and thereby inscribes normative heterosexuality. Drawing on Lacan, Irigary, Foucault, and Freud, her theory has implications not only for feminism but also for queer theory.

Queer theory has adopted Butler's antiessentialist notion of gender. If identities do not express some inner authentic core but rather are expressed as a dramatic effect of performance, then queer identity, which is by definition at odds with the dominant or hegemonically constructed "normal," is also an identity without an essence only expressed and experienced performatively.

Support for Butler's understanding of gender also comes from cyberfeminism and new media studies, which have explored how gendered identity in the posthuman and cyborg realm, and in virtual reality and cyberspace generally, can be a source of gender and sexual anonymity, experimentation, and freedom. A number of media critics and theorists have examined what it means to experience fleshly gendered bodies in an age of media screens—from identification with gendered fictional media characters to constructing one's gender-mediated self in do-it-yourself media such as Facebook and YouTube to virtually gendered bodies, such as avatars constructed in video-game play and sites such as *Second Life*. Although embodiment currently constitutes a nonnegotiable prerequisite for human life (despite the claims of those who examine the possibilities of the posthuman in the laboratory), new technologies seem to discredit or undercut the centrality of fleshly existence in favor of the disembodied. They favor discussion of "telepresence" versus "presence" in interactions with digital media screens. In examinations of Internet relay chat (IRC) platforms, bulletin boards, multi-user domains (MUDs), object-oriented MUDs (MOOs), and other electronic communication forums, cyberspace theorists have suggested that the lack of the physically present body may be reshaping consciousness while allowing for more fluid and negotiable experiences of not only gender but also race, ethnicity, class, and sexual orientation.

This raises the question—given the possibilities of free-floating signification in virtual space and the predispositions of current American culture and media—of whether feminine-gendered bodies are likely to disappear and, if so, whether this will matter. Implicitly addressing this question, cyberfeminism tries to walk the fine line of embracing the possibilities of new media while both continuing to critically engage with women's position vis-à-vis these new technologies and still emphasizing the embodied nature of existence.

Theorists and critics grounded in neo-Marxist philosophy, such as the feminist political economy of media scholars and critical race theorists like bell hooks, support the notion that physical bodies still matter and that ignoring women's bodies and the material conditions that unequally shape them (poverty, famine, disease, rape, genital mutilation, and women's obstetric, sexual, and gynecological health) sets a dangerous precedent that reinforces patriarchal systems of power and dominance already prevalent around the globe. The post-structuralist turn in critical/cultural studies of media, in other words—by its focus on semiotic freedom, textual play, and active audiences—has contributed to undermining ideological critique. This results, in part, from examining how existing material inequalities associated with race, class, gender, and sexual orientation are continually reinscribed into media and culture. Some have even argued that the post-structuralist articulation of identity as an isolated, fragmented, and free-floating (con)textually constructed signifier inadvertently benefits the expansionist global capitalist project while undermining democracy.

As a final wrinkle in the debate, many performance studies scholars argue that bodies (whether performed as masculine, feminine, or transgendered), as well as embodied experience, matter now more than ever. The Cartesian split, "I think, therefore I am," that dominated Western thought for centuries and valorized mind over body while associating the male with mind and the female with body (elevating the former and denigrating the latter) has given way to a new awareness of the body as a site of performance. This focus returns us to fleshly bodies doing gender in performance without reducing gender to the biologically sexed body. Although these scholars, usually invoking phenomenology, privilege bodies, particularly the performer and audience bodies as experienced in the moment of live performance, many performance studies scholars incorporate media into their performance work and have extended discussion of performance into virtual (mediated) spaces and bodies as experienced, for example, in *Second Life*.

Susan Mackey-Kallis
Villanova University

See also Avatar; Beauty and Body Image: Beauty Myths; Beauty and Body Image: Eating Disorders; Berger, John; Bordo, Susan; Class Privilege; Critical Theory; Cultural Politics; Cyberspace and Cyberculture; Cyborg; Feminist Theory: Marxist; Feminist Theory: Socialist; Feminist Theory: Third Wave; Gender and Masculinity: Metrosexual Male; Hegemony; hooks, bell; Identity; Male Gaze; Mass Media; Massively Multiplayer Online Role-Playing Games; Media Rhetoric; Multi-User Dimensions; Post-Structuralism; *Second Life*; Simulacra; Social Construction of Gender; Video Gaming: Representations of Femininity; Video Gaming: Representations of Masculinity; Virtual Sex; Virtuality.

Further Readings

Butler, J. *Bodies That Matter: On the Discursive Limits of "Sex."* New York: Routledge, 1993.

Butler, J. *Gender Trouble: Feminism and the Subversion of Identity.* New York: Routledge, 1990.

Byrd-Bredbenner, C. and J. Murray. "A Comparison of the Anthropometric Measurements of Idealized Female Body Images in Media Directed to Men, Women, and Mixed Gender Audiences." *Topics in Clinical Nutrition*, v.18/2 (2003).

Cruikshank, L. "Avatar Dreams: Theorizing Desire for the Virtual Body." *Michigan Feminist Studies*, v.15 (2001).

Dill, K. and K. Thill. "Video Game Characters and the Socialization of Gender Roles: Young People's Perceptions Mirror Sexist Media Depictions." *Sex Roles*, v.57/11–12 (2007).

Foster, T. "Trapped by the Body? Telepresence Technologies and Transgendered Performance in Feminist and Lesbian Rewritings of Cyberpunk Fiction." *Modern Fiction Studies*, v.43/3 (1997).

Fredrickson, B. L. and T. Roberts. "Objectification Theory: Toward Understanding Women's Lived Experiences and Mental Health Risks." *Psychology of Women Quarterly*, v.21 (1997).

Gagne, P. and D. McGaughey. "Designing Women." *Gender and Society*, v.16/5 (2002).

Groesz, L. M., M. P. Levine, and S. K. Murnen. "The Effect of Experimental Presentation of Thin Media Images on Body Satisfaction: A Meta-Analytic Review." *International Journal of Eating Disorders*, v.31 (2002).

Holmstrom, A. J. "The Effects of the Media on Body Image: A Meta-Analysis." *Journal of Broadcasting and Electronic Media*, v.48 (2004).

Karen, H., G. Rosalind, and C. Mclean. "The Changing Man." *Psychologist*, v.15/4 (April 2002).

Saco, D. "The Gendered Bodies of Cyberspace." *Feminist Collections*, v.19/2 (2006).

Tragos, P. "Monster Masculinity: Honey, I'll Be in the Garage Reasserting My Manhood." *Journal of Popular Culture*, v.42/3 (2009).

GENDER MEDIA MONITORING

Gender media monitoring is the practice of analyzing how gender is represented and enacted throughout various media content, ranging from news to fictional portrayals and advertising. Groups of varying sizes engage in gender media monitoring on local, national, and international levels, concerning themselves with questions of content as well as the structure of media organizations. They conduct both short, targeted campaigns and long-term studies, identifying areas of concern and devising strategies for improvement. They come at their studies from various political perspectives and cultural outlooks, but what typically unites these efforts under the umbrella of gender media monitoring is a focus on an analysis of media content and institutional power coupled with activism.

Vital to these efforts is the active, informed participation of citizens; correspondingly, monitoring groups place a strong focus on using the tools of media literacy to equip the public with the ability to analyze media content, power structures, and audience effects. In addition to fostering public education, many groups strive to work directly with media organizations, supporting women and other underrepresented groups within the workforce and encouraging greater diversity within the industry. However, they also acknowledge that changing media is not simply about increasing the number of women in power but also about promoting a broader social, political, and cultural shift that recognizes the ways in which women and others are oppressed and works to right inadequacies in both media and society at large.

Contemporary movements in gender media monitoring stake their origins in the concerns expressed by the women's movement in the 1960s and 1970s. The representation of women (or lack thereof) was a source of critique for many feminists and academics, who tied mediated portrayals of gender to the status of women in society. They argued that media content was often dominated by male voices, resulting in poor or stereotypical representations of women—or the lack of representation entirely. These representations, in turn, had a social effect—contributing to a society that saw women as powerless and kept them in a subordinate position. Theorists such as George Gerbner (1972) and Gaye Tuchman (1978) popularized the term *symbolic annihilation* to describe the manner in which media content trivializes, condemns, and excludes women and other disenfranchised groups.

The United Nations International Decade for Women (1975–85), which focused on studying both media content and the underrepresentation of females in media institutions, was one of the first globally minded activist projects. Spurred in large part by the international development of satellite communication and deregulation, monitoring movements increased dramatically during the 1990s. In 1995, the Global Media Monitoring Project (GMMP) produced the first comprehensive, multicountry analysis of women's representation in media content, analyzing newspapers, radio, and television in 71 countries. The comparative study, involving the participation of a wide variety of people—including teachers, lobbyists, activists, and media professionals—found that women were news makers or interviewees in only 17 percent of news subjects internationally. As part of the project, researchers also analyzed how news stories covered certain issues concerning women. GMMP now releases a report on women and news media every five years and has begun to include studies of online news sources.

Other groups target media using various points of inquiry, including politics, violence, sexuality, and beauty or physical appearance, paying special attention to women who are most often marginalized based on their color, class, sexuality, disability status, ethnicity, or age. Engaging in both qualitative and quantitative analyses of content that range from basic studies (that, for instance, tally the appearance of female bylines and sources in news) to more elaborate coding and categorization schemes, groups today incorporate analyses of the structure of mediated messages, the employment of women in media organizations and patterns of representation, and audience studies that examine how consumption of particular media content influences behaviors and beliefs about gender. There is also a growing need for research and activism that better account for stereotyping of men and portrayals of masculinity.

As part of their advocacy efforts, groups engage a number of strategies, including hosting workshops and advocacy seminars, participating in street protests and letter-writing campaigns, creating alternative media, and producing directories of women experts who can be used as sources. The Internet has become a powerful tool for groups, who use it to produce their own content and publicize their message as well as provide a virtual space for the public to discuss issues of gender and media. For example, the Women's Media Center (WMC), a nonprofit founded in 2005 by Jane Fonda, Robin Morgan, and Gloria Steinem, has developed multiple Internet-based campaigns targeting sexism in media. During the 2008 presidential election, WMC released a video entitled "Sexism Sells but We're Not Buying It," featuring 30 examples of gendered media content, focusing largely on discriminatory coverage of Hillary Clinton's presidential campaign. The video, distributed on YouTube, received widespread attention. In December 2010, WMC hosted a virtual Facebook "watch-in" to show support for the MTV special *No Easy Decision*, which featured stories of teens who had had abortions.

Over the years, media monitoring efforts have grown partly because of the participation of organizations not explicitly focused on media, such as nongovernmental organizations, religious institutions, civil society groups, the United Nations Educational, Scientific and Cultural Organization (UNESCO), and other advocacy groups, which recognize the centrality of issues of gender and media to their missions. For instance, the National Eating Disorders Association launched a "Media Watchdog" program, which uses volunteers nationwide to monitor media content as it relates to body image.

Gender media monitoring efforts can count numerous achievements, such as the development of codified policies and indicators for evaluations of progress as well as partnerships with media organizations. While few comprehensive studies identify how media content has specifically changed as a result of their work, advocates point to the greater exposure their efforts receive and a growing awareness about the importance of critically analyzing media and gender.

Theresa Rose Crapanzano
University of Colorado, Boulder

See also Diversity; Hegemony; Ideology; Media Literacy; Quantitative Content Analysis; Racism; Sexism; Steinem, Gloria; Stereotypes; Textual Analysis

Further Readings

Gallagher, Margaret. *Gender Setting: New Agendas for Media Monitoring and Advocacy.* New York: St. Martin's Press, 2001.

Gerbner, George. "Violence and Television Drama: Trends and Symbolic Functions." In *Television and Social Behavior.* Vol. 1, *Content and Control*, George A. Comstock and Edward Rubinstein, eds. Washington, DC: U.S. Government Printing Office, 1972.

International Network for Gender Media Watchdogs. http://www.mediawatchdogs.gendersquare.org/ NetworkMore.htm (Accessed February 2011).

Media Watch. http://www.mediawatch.com (Accessed February 2011).

Tuchman, Gaye. "The Symbolic Annihilation of Women by the Mass Media." In *Hearth and Home: Images of Women in the Mass Media*, Gaye Tuchman, Arlene Kaplan Daniels, and James Benet, eds. New York: Oxford University Press, 1978.

Who Makes the News? http://www.whomakesthenews.org (Accessed February 2011).

WomenAction. http://www.womenaction.org (Accessed February 2011).

Women's Media Center. http://www.womensmediacenter. org (Accessed February 2011).

Gender Schema Theory

Gender schema theory describes the development of gender identity by combining aspects of cognitive learning theory with sociocultural elements of social learning theory. Gender identity is influenced by persons observing others and learning their actions, ultimately accomplishing different culturally specific cognitive tasks particular to males and to females. Children are active agents in the creation of their own gender identities, creating mental categories through cognitive maturation and environmental observation of behaviors identified as either male or female. Children follow culturally prescribed attributes by adjusting their own behaviors and norms according to their own sex.

Drawing from the cognitive developmental theory described by Jean Piaget, these mental categories or frameworks are labeled as schemas and serve as ways in which information is organized and stored for later use. Schemas are relationships between information and social experience that constantly undergo change. Their use enables persons to evaluate information efficiently, consistent with what already is known; to process new information on the basis of its similarity to the known; and to assess the relevance of inconsistent information. Schemas become more elaborated through a complex set of processes. Information is observed and (a) is internalized into existing schemas housing similar information, (b) is viewed as not relevant and ignored, or (c) is deemed relevant but inconsistent with known information and thus is placed into new schemas where similar information attained in the future will be housed. In addition to influencing information processing, schemas impact problem solving and memory as well as serve to regulate personal behavior.

Gender schemas are described by Sandra Bem as the mental frameworks in which persons organize information concerning those attributes associated with being masculine or male and being feminine or female. Piaget believed that the first social categories children learn are based on sex. Thus, children learn whether they are boys or girls. Gender schema theory asserts that what follows is learning behaviors, attributes, and roles associated with those sex differences. For example, a boy who has acquired the gender schema of being male and masculine might say, "I am a boy. Boys do not play with baby dolls. I play with action figures."

With increasing observation of culturally appropriate attributes, children develop understandings about how one acts and believes as a male or as a female within their culture. Gender schemas organize knowledge about one's own and others' behaviors and include information about attitudes, values, behaviors, and emotions. Gender schemas focus on personality features and moral qualities associated with males and females and influence which gender roles persons choose to play and how they respond to and play those roles based on what is considered appropriate role play for males and females. With exposure to more information, the schemas and role expectations expand. Hazel Markus contends that the categories of male and female are fixed. Once children learn these categories and identify the one into which they fit, placement in these categories never changes. Therefore, once a child identifies himself as a boy, he always sees himself as a boy—never possessing female attributes.

Bem describes gender classification in broader terms: people are either gender schematic or gender aschematic. Gender schematics are more inclined to categorize behavior or psychological attributes in terms that are distinctively masculine or feminine and see the world in culturally derived, stereotypical terms, regardless of how other persons may differ from mainstream views of masculinity and femininity. Among gender schematics, the drawing of distinct lines between groups according to gender is highly valued and heavily reinforced in the culture. The result is that children learn clear lessons about what is and what is not considered masculine and feminine. Gender schematics view their social world from a lens of what roles and psychological attributes are appropriate for females, such as caretaking and nurturance, and roles that are appropriate for males, such as decision making and self-assertion. Gender schematics then select roles deemed appropriate for their own sex and play those roles, displaying the characteristics society dictates as acceptable, and expect others to do accordingly.

Although seeing the world as gender schematic is heavily influenced in the culture, Bem asserts that some persons are gender aschematic, possessing a weak sense of categorization according to culturally derived and stereotypical gender norms. Attributes and behaviors associated with particular genders are blurred. Thus, persons are more psychologically androgynous or able to possess both culturally designated masculine and feminine characteristics and see the potential of androgynous characteristics in others.

While the conventional culture produces schematic children, it is possible to raise aschematic children. To do so, Bem contends that parents must serve as role models to teach their children distinctions between biological sex and psychological gender. This requires reinforcing unique individual differences both in choosing personal appearance and dress and in developing interests and skills, rather than relying on the gender-schematic dictates based on biological sex. The result is to demonstrate to children that differences according to biological

sex can contrast with individual differences, and thus limit the effects of sex-linked stereotypes.

Patricia Amason
University of Arkansas

See also Children's Programming: Cartoons; Cognitive Script Theory; Gender Embodiment; Gender Media Monitoring; Identity; Social Construction of Gender; Stereotypes; Toys and Games: Gender Socialization; Tween Magazines

Further Readings

Bem, S. "Gender Schema Theory: A Cognitive Account of Sex Typing." *Psychological Review*, v.88 (1981).

Fagot, B. I. and M. D. Leinbach. "The Young Child's Gender Schema: Environmental Input, Internal Organization." *Child Development*, v.60 (1989).

Fagot, B. I., M. D. Leinbach, and R. Hagan. "Gender Labeling and Adoption of Sex-Typed Behaviors." *Developmental Psychology*, v.22 (1996).

Markus, H. "Self-Schemata and Processing of Information About the Self." *Journal of Personality and Social Psychology*, v.35 (1977).

Markus, H., M. Crane, S. Bernstein, and M. Siladi. "Self-Schemas and Gender." *Journal of Personality and Social Psychology*, v.42 (1982).

Martin, C. A. and C. F. Halverson. "The Effects of Sex-Typing Schemas on Young Children's Memory." *Child Development*, v.54 (1983).

Martin, C. A. and C. F. Halverson. "A Schematic Processing Model of Sex Typing and Stereotyping in Children." *Child Development*, v.52 (1981).

Martin, C. L., D. N. Ruble, and J. Szkrybalo. "Cognitive Theories of Early Gender Development." *Psychological Bulletin*, v.128 (2002).

GIROUX, HENRY

Henry Giroux (1943–) is a North American critical theorist and public intellectual specializing in critical pedagogy, cultural studies (particularly film studies and youth studies), educational reform, and contemporary debates about war, terrorism, and neoliberalism (neo-laissez-faire economics). Giroux is influenced by various thinkers and traditions, including but not limited to Karl Marx, Antonio Gramsci, John Dewey, Stuart Hall, Zygmunt Bauman, Stanley Aronowitz, and, most of all, Paulo Freire. Freire's work with critical pedagogy in marginalized

Brazilian communities helped establish Giroux's own educational philosophy: Education exists at the center of the social landscape and thus constitutes a site of cultural, political, and economic contestation; rather than perpetuating traditional "banking models" of learning, education should be a liberatory and transformative experience of personal growth, political resistance, and democratic citizenship.

Giroux's personal background influences his philosophy and intellectual endeavors. He grew up in a Providence, Rhode Island, working-class neighborhood where basketball, odd jobs, racial tensions, and class barriers were common. He earned basketball scholarships to two junior colleges. He dropped out of the first school but successfully finished at the second. He went on to earn a master's degree in history at Appalachian State University. This enabled him to teach secondary school in a small town outside Baltimore, Maryland. He became a community organizer after witnessing racial segregation and gender and class injustices in the school system. This led to his eventual dismissal. He moved back to New England and taught high school in a white, upper-class Rhode Island suburb. Local conservatives publicly condemned his courses on "society and alienation" and "race and feminism." Giroux eventually left, earning a doctorate at Carnegie Mellon University in 1977. His first professorship was in education at Boston University. Despite an impeccable record of publications and endorsements, he was denied tenure for political reasons. He went on to establish a stellar career, teaching education and cultural studies at Miami University, Penn State University, and McMaster University in Hamilton, Ontario.

Giroux's critical pedagogy focuses on both critiquing and offering alternatives to prevailing educational norms. Borrowing an idea from educational philosopher John Dewey, Giroux argues that education should not be approached as a function of an already existing society; instead, society should facilitate an open-ended, experimental, exploratory education. Schools too often center their efforts on job preparation, standardized testing, instrumental reasoning, and unquestioned obedience to authority. Students are then inculcated into accepting and perpetuating such injustices as racism, sexism, classism, homophobia, violence, and economic inequality. Giroux's critical pedagogy counters this tendency by strengthening students' skills in democratic citizenship—students should learn to think critically

about, analyze, and debate pressing political issues, speak back to authority, and change social injustice. The overall educational experience should enable students to discover, create, and pursue their own passions, imaginations, and intellects in ways that counter (rather than conform to) the already existing society.

Essential to developing a critical, democratic education is Giroux's notion of teachers as transformative intellectuals. According to Giroux, teachers must resist the myth of absolute objectivity and the urge to teach to the test or apply one-size-fits-all approaches that ignore or exclude students' diverse learning styles, wants, and needs. Teachers must recognize the implications of their own labor: Students, teachers, administrators, and entire schooling systems do not simply exchange or disseminate objective knowledge but instead reflect and, more important, produce knowledge, experiences, values, beliefs, relationships, norms, and subjectivities. Teachers should thus seek to expose, critique, and alter the various power relations that exist within their schools and classrooms. Such transformative, intellectual work becomes a form of cultural politics that precedes and exceeds the narrow confines of traditional education. Borrowing the feminist notion of "the personal is political," Giroux argues that teachers have the opportunity—and even the obligation—to work at the micro level of face-to-face immediacy: student-to-student and student-to-teacher interactions are imbued with a transformative potential that enables both self and other to reconceptualize, reorient toward, and thus alter the wider world.

Giroux goes a step further and argues that teachers should move outside the classroom and take up the call of public pedagogy. Family dynamics, playgrounds, doctor's offices, places of worship, television programs, video games, films, presidential campaigns, and economic systems involve teaching and learning—each legitimizes or invalidates particular ways of knowing and being that shape individual and collective choices, desires, and practices. Teachers, fashioning themselves into committed, oppositional public pedagogues, are uniquely positioned to expose these discourses and to advocate for alternatives. Giroux's turn to cultural studies since the early 1990s demonstrates this oppositional vocation. He has, among other things, critically interrogated the racial, gendered, and sexually oriented codifications of Disney films; the homogenizing, depoliticized cultural representations of the Benetton fashion company; the cinematic depictions of youth, race, and violence in Hollywood films; the conservative backlash against political correctness; the social Darwinian philosophy of neoliberal economics; and contemporary educational reforms that criminalize and punish, rather than nurture and counsel, K–12 students.

Jason Del Gandio
Temple University

See also Children's Programming: Disney and Pixar; Cultural Politics; Film: Hollywood; Hall, Stuart

Further Readings

Giroux, Henry. *America on the Edge: Henry Giroux on Politics, Education, and Culture*. New York: Palgrave Macmillan, 2006.

Giroux, Henry. *Breaking In to the Movies: Film and the Culture of Politics*. Malden, MA: Blackwell, 2002.

Giroux, Henry. *Fugitive Cultures: Race, Violence, and Youth*. New York: Routledge, 1996.

Giroux, Henry. *Ideology, Culture and the Process of Schooling*. Philadelphia, PA: Temple University Press, 1981.

Giroux, Henry. *Teachers as Intellectuals: Toward a Critical Pedagogy of Learning*. London: Bergin & Garvey, 1988.

GRAPHIC NOVELS

Although the scope of the term is frequently contested, in the broadest sense *graphic novel* is used to define sequential art that is published in bound volumes. Specifically, the self-contained illustrated narratives found in graphic novels are usually differentiated from those found in the majority of comics, which are published in a serial format as part of a continuing story. Generally speaking, when compared to comics, graphic novels are longer, address more mature themes, have more sophisticated prose, feature higher-quality art, and are given greater attention as serious literature by academic, artistic, and literary critics. Gendered representations in graphic novels have varied significantly across history and geography.

In the United States, graphic novels as such date back at least to the late 1970s, when they represented a fairly niche but emerging medium for publishing illustrated fiction. Although collections of bound and illustrated stories have existed for several centuries, the contemporary graphic novel was shaped in the late 1970s by the work of pioneers like Will Eisner (*The Spirit*), as well as publications by the likes of Alan Moore and Dave Gibbons (*Watchmen*), Frank Miller (*Batman: The Dark Knight Returns*), Art Spiegelman (*Maus*), and Englishman Neil Gaiman (*Sandman*) in the mid-1980s. Often marketed to adults, graphic novels are more likely than most mainstream comic books to include heavy usage of profanity and explicit depictions of sex and violence. In addition, many award-winning graphic novels have eschewed comic book conventions such as the inclusion of superheroes or superpowers, a reliance on rigidly defined gender roles to drive character development and romantic relationships, and an adherence to the traditional fantasy tropes of adolescent male readers.

Japanese manga should be considered one important influence on contemporary graphic novels, and many manga publications fit the basic definition given above. Manga, like graphic novels, are self-contained illustrated narratives often published in a book format. Popular since the 1940s and 1950s with Japanese children and since at least the 1970s with Japanese adults, the manga industry now accounts for just under half of all annual publishing sales in Japan. Because manga are typically directed to specific audiences, over time several tropes for representing gender have emerged across these publications. For example, manga are one of the primary forms of media in Japan for carrying stories about homosexual male relationships. Gay men are often depicted in manga as androgynous, sharing many of the same physical characteristics as female manga characters, such as large eyes and small hands. In addition, homosexual male relationships are often portrayed as mutually loving and nurturing, in sharp contrast to heterosexual relationships in manga, which depict relationships as male-centered and, at times, abusive. As Mark McLelland has noted, the largest audience for this genre is not homosexual men but rather heterosexual women, who are often overly sexualized (if young and single) or desexualized (if mothers) in the majority of Japanese manga.

In the mid-1990s, Japanese manga sales surged in the United States, reflecting an increased market for Western graphic novels. Like manga in both countries, graphic novels have a wider purchasing demographic than comic books. Unlike Japanese manga, however, Western graphic novels do not portray primarily stereotyped gender roles, even if abusive sex and violence against women are still common. For example, Frank Miller's popular *Sin City* series (1991–2000) frequently featured murders in the red light district, sadomasochistic protagonists, strippers, and other sexual content that shares some of the same characteristics of gender as presented in Japanese manga and most comic book franchises. However, other popular graphic novels have featured more progressive and positive depictions of women, such as those found in *Persepolis*, by Majane Satrapi, and in the Hugo Award–winning *Girl Genius* series, created by Phil and Kaja Foglio. These critically acclaimed publications have strong female protagonists who rely on their intelligence and personal values, rather than their sexuality, to solve crises and drive the narrative forward. It is worth noting that, compared to the comic book industry, women authors and illustrators are better represented in graphic novel publishing.

Since the mid-1990s, graphic novels have enjoyed increasing success not only on bookstore shelves but in other contexts as well. Part of the resurgence in graphic novels in the United States has been due to a concerted effort by librarians to acquire and suggest graphic novels to their young adult and adult patrons (despite occasional debates about violent or sexual content). A string of well-received Hollywood adaptations—such as *The Spirit* (2008), *300* (2006), *V for Vendetta* (2006), *Sin City* (2005), *Watchmen* (2009), and *Persepolis* (2007)—have bolstered this trend. Because of this growth in popularity, depictions of masculinity and femininity in graphic novels are increasingly influential in shaping contemporary perceptions of gender.

David S. Heineman
Bloomsburg University of Pennsylvania

See also Comics; E-Zines: Third Wave Feminist; Heroes: Action and Super Heroes; Video Gaming: Representations of Femininity; Video Gaming: Representations of Masculinity

Further Readings

Lopes, Paul Douglas. *Demanding Respect: The Evolution of the American Comic Book*. Philadelphia, PA: Temple University Press, 2009.

Madrid, Mike. *The Supergirls: Fashion, Feminism, Fantasy, and the History of Comic Book Heroines*. Ashland, OR: Exterminating Angel Press, 2009.

McLelland, Mark J. "The Love Between 'Beautiful Boys' in Women's Comics." In *Male Homosexuality in Modern Japan: Cultural Myths and Social Realities*. Richmond, VA: Curzon, 2000.

Rothschild, D. Aviva. *Graphic Novels: A Bibliographic Guide to Book-Length Comics*. Englewood, CO: Libraries Unlimited, 1995.

GUERRILLA GIRLS

Established in 1985, the Guerrilla Girls are a grassroots feminist group seeking to raise awareness about sexism and racism in art, politics, and popular culture. They are artists and activists who wear gorilla masks and adopt the names of deceased female artists as pseudonyms in order to remain anonymous. They engage in various forms of culture jamming in order to expose institutions and individuals in power who actively exclude women and artists of color from exhibitions, funding, and other opportunities in culture and media. Based in New York City, the Guerrilla Girls have launched hundreds of art assault campaigns to raise awareness and work toward more inclusion and diversity in the creative arts. They are known for using satire, irony, and shocking statistics as weapons of cultural critique. Provocative imagery and catchy slogans are also among the tools they use. They have found humor to be an effective weapon against discrimination and use it to draw people into their messages, provoke a response, and then prompt them to think critically about inequality. The Guerrilla Girls are considered to be the feminist conscience of the art world. They have used posters, billboards, postcards, and sticker campaigns as ways to publicize prejudice, racism, and sexism. The Guerrilla Girls also give lectures and conduct workshops for feminist activists.

Strategies

The group originally adopted the name Guerrilla Girls as a way to liken sexist politics to guerrilla warfare. Rather than employing direct confrontation, they use strategies of anonymity, mobility, and ambush. Instead of violent protest or military warfare, they engage in culture jamming aimed at

Wearing gorilla masks and using pseudonyms of deceased female artists during their art assaults disguise member identities, keeping the focus of their grassroots feminist campaigns on the issues at hand as opposed to the individuals protesting. (Wikimedia)

sabotaging the overwhelmingly white, male, heterosexual power bloc.

They also play on the term *guerrilla* by wearing gorilla masks during their campaigns. The masks disguise the members' identities, a strategy used to keep the focus of their campaigns on issues of inequality as opposed to their individual personalities. The Guerrilla Girls also adopt the names of deceased female artists and authors to protect their identities. This strategy pays homage to the talents of artists such as Frida Kahlo, Lee Krasner, Käthe Kollwitz, Anaïs Nin, Georgia O'Keeffe, and Gertrude Stein, among others.

In addition to securing anonymity, the gorilla mask displaces stereotypical definitions of feminine beauty. In many of their awareness campaigns, the Guerrilla Girls re-figure classical works of art, especially female nudes, with gorilla masks. The Guerrilla Girls themselves have also been pictured wearing the masks while also wearing stockings, high heels, or short skirts as a way to confound people's stereotypes of ideal feminine beauty. The Guerrilla Girls even consider the masks to play with the conception of manhood. In a comic move, they believe the masks bring a sense of "mask-ulinity" to their agenda.

"Reclaiming" is another important concept for the Guerrilla Girls. They actively seek to reclaim the "F word" (feminism), the "G word" (girl), and public space itself. Feminism holds a contentious place in the popular imagination. As part of an antisexist agenda, the Guerrilla Girls proudly use the F word in order to promote the ideals of feminism: equal opportunity, equal access to healthcare and education, freedom from harassment and sexual exploitation, reproductive rights, and human rights for women everywhere. They also use the G word to reconfigure the ways in which women are infantilized and marginalized. Finally, the Guerrilla Girls seek to reclaim public space for women. Because women have been historically excluded from full participation in public spaces, it is particularly significant that the Guerrilla Girls conduct most of their awareness campaigns in the city streets and other public sites.

Awareness Campaigns

The Guerrilla Girls' first awareness campaign was held in 1985 in New York City. They came together in response to the International Survey of Painting and Sculpture, an exhibit at the Museum of Modern Art (MOMA). They found that the exhibit, intended to be a comprehensive survey of the contemporary art world, represented only 13 women among the 169 artists featured. All of the artists were white. As a result, the Guerrilla Girls launched a campaign in which they plastered hundreds of posters on buildings, kiosks, and construction sites around New York City to publicize the large-scale exclusion of women and artists of color.

Intended to shame the art world into thinking critically about sexism and the politics of exclusion, the campaign was an immediate sensation and cast the Guerrilla Girls into the limelight. Since then, they have launched hundreds of poster, billboard, and sticker assaults. Some of their most notable campaigns include a poster asking, "What's fashionable, prestigious, and tax-deductible? Discriminating against women and non-white artists." Another asks, "Do women have to be naked to get into the Met. Museum? Less than 5 percent of the artists in the Modern Art sections are women but 85 percent of the nudes are female." They have also suggested an anatomically correct Oscar, with the slogan "He's white and male, just like the guys who win!"

In addition to issues of sexism, the Guerrilla Girls have conducted campaigns on a range of issues, from the Gulf War and abortion rights to feminine beauty ideals, rape, and even homelessness. Their campaigns have been translated into dozens of languages and have appeared worldwide. They have been featured in numerous publications, including the *New York Times*, the *London Times*, the *New Yorker*, and *Bitch* magazine. The Guerrilla Girls have published several books and have been featured on National Public Radio and programs aired by the British Broadcasting Corporation.

Amy M. Corey
Gonzaga University

See also Culture Jamming; Diversity; Gender Media Monitoring; Racism; Sexism; Stereotypes

Further Readings

Guerrilla Girls. *Bitches, Bimbos, and Ballbreakers: The Guerrilla Girls' Illustrated Guide to Female Stereotypes.* New York: Penguin, 2003.

Guerrilla Girls. *Confessions of the Guerrilla Girls.* New York: HarperPerennial, 1995.

Guerrilla Girls. *The Guerrilla Girls' Bedside Companion to the History of Western Art.* New York: Penguin, 1998.

HACKING AND HACKTIVISM

Hacking is generally defined as the unauthorized use or entry into a computer or computer system. Hacktivism bridges computer-hacking techniques with political or social protest action. Such actions are sometimes referred to as electronic civil disobedience (ECD). In hacktivism, the hacker is not interested in personal gain but in the dissemination of a particular message. That message may be directed at a particular organization, such as the case in which

A programmer scans code to determine the location of a system virus. Hackers and hacktivists enter into others' computer systems and perform Website defacement, send e-mail bombs, or cause denial-of-service attacks to demonstrate civil disobedience or to make a statement that information should be free and that authority should not be trusted. (Photos.com)

an anti-fur activist hacked the Website of a furrier, or the Website itself may be inconsequential, serving only as a means of reaching viewers. There are many means by which hacktivism takes place. Common methods include Website defacement, e-mail bombs, and electronic sit-ins or denial-of-service attacks, but these techniques are not universally accepted as ethical within the hacker community.

Website Defacement

In Website defacement, the goal is to break into the system and upload a new version of the page that has been modified by the hackers. However, there is sometimes more to this effort than simply uploading a new web page. If the hackers gain complete access to the system (or "root") they may be able to alter user identification codes and passwords such that the page cannot be taken down until the system administrators are able to break into their own system. This prolongs viewer exposure to the modified page. There are varying degrees of sophistication within the hacker community, and this is reflected in Website defacements. Many defacements are simple messages consisting of the hacker's name and a short note or perhaps a graphic. These are often mass defacements, done by simply scanning networks for servers with open ports or looking for unpatched systems. These hackers seem more interested in disseminating their message as widely as possible, with little consideration of the site itself. On the other hand, some defacements are clearly targeted to send a message to the owner of the Website.

Denial-of-Service Attacks and Electronic Sit-Ins

As the name implies, electronic sit-ins are similar to physical sit-ins: Both seek to deny access by occupying space. Rather than occupying space physically, as in a traditional sit-in, electronic sit-ins occupy space in the form of connections and bandwidth. Servers can handle only as many connections as bandwidth allows. When this connection limit is exceeded, others attempting to access material on that server will be denied access until those who are already connected are no longer accessing material. This is why these kinds of actions are called denial-of-service (DOS) or distributed-denial-of-service (DDOS) attacks. Such attacks are simple to implement and require little skill to enact; some groups, such as Electronic Disturbance Theater, have even automated the process. At its most basic level, a DOS attack can be enacted merely by going to a Web page and continually hitting the refresh button. Most servers can handle this kind of action, but if hundreds or thousands of computers do this, even powerful servers may be brought down.

Because many network attacks are more efficiently mounted using many computers, it is in the interest of the attacker to gain access to many machines—whether through a collective united in the attack or by commandeering the machines of unwitting accomplices. One poorly publicized danger of spyware and viruses has to do with the creation of "zombie networks." Many types of spyware allow for both reception of messages and the transmission of data. If a person has spyware on his or her machine, it is possible to create an exploit that will use the existing spyware to send data to a different server—the target of the attack. This is also a problem of various kinds of viruses, which can install a backdoor into the system that can be used to take over the machine's computing resources, such as bandwidth, processing power, and e-mail send capabilities. A person whose computer is infected with spyware or certain viruses may unknowingly participate in a DOS attack.

E-Mail Bombs

Like DOS attacks, e-mail bombs overload e-mail servers so that legitimate e-mail cannot be received. Most e-mail servers have a set amount of space allocated to each user, and once this limit is reached, no new messages can be delivered. The sender receives an error message and must resend the message later. E-mail bombing is done by sending the recipient many large messages or a very large number of small messages. Some servers limit the size of messages that can be received, thus limiting the tactic to the e-mailing of small messages. Like DOS attacks, e-mail bombs can easily be automated by distributing the resources necessary for the attack.

Hacktivism can take place both on an individual level and through organized "hacktions." One of the most prominent politically active hacker organizations, Cult of the Dead Cow (cDc), claims to have coined the term *hacktivism* through one of its members, Omega. In 1999, cDc began to draw explicit links between activism and computer technology by forming Hacktivismo. Other politically motivated hacking organizations include the Chaos Computer Club (CCC) in Germany; the electro-hippie collective, a hacktivist group in the United Kingdom that staged a DOS attack against the World Trade Organization's meetings in 1999; and Electronic Disturbance Theater, whose members used a program called Floodnet to engage in DOS attacks in 1998 on behalf of the Zapatista movement in Mexico.

Although hacktivism seems extremely technical, many hacker tools are readily available online, meaning that one need not actually be a hacker to do the work of the hacktivist. Because hacktivism can be automated, one need not be present to conduct an attack, allowing individuals to protest from another continent if desired. This removes some of the risks inherent in traditional protest actions, which may lead to arrest or injury. However, hacktivism is not without serious risks, not least among which is the potential to incur criminal charges, especially if the act is defined as cyberterrorism. There is also the question of long-term efficacy, especially against a technologically well-defended organization.

Despite its seeming egalitarian nature, there remains the question of access to information technologies to engage in hacktivism. Moreover, the ability to acquire hacking tools does not imply that one has the skills required to use these tools. From a gender perspective, some scholars note that the hacker subculture is largely male-dominated and others have likewise argued that cyberspace itself is largely masculine space.

Brett Lunceford
University of South Alabama

See also Culture Jamming; Cyberpunk; Cyberspace and Cyberculture; Electronic Media and Social Inequality; New Media

Further Readings

Jordan, Tim and Paul A. Taylor. *Hacktivism and Cyberwars: Rebels With a Cause?* New York: Routledge, 2004.

Lane, Jill. "Digital Zapatistas." *TDR: The Drama Review*, v.47/2 (2003).

Ruffin, Oxblood. "Hacktivism, From Here to There." http://www.cultdeadcow.com/cDc_files/cDc-0384.html (Accessed October 2010).

Taylor, Paul A. "Maestros or Misogynists? Gender and the Social Construction of Hacking." In *Dot.Cons*, Yvonne Jewkes, ed. Portland, OR: Willan Publishing, 2003.

Thomas, Douglas. *Hacker Culture.* Minneapolis: University of Minnesota Press, 2002.

Wray, Stefan. "On Electronic Civil Disobedience." *Peace Review*, v.11/1 (1999).

HALL, STUART

Stuart Hall (1932–) is a British cultural theorist, critic, and political strategist whose work centers on intersections between culture, society, and power and the resultant meanings within texts that members of a culture consider as common sense. Hall is one of the most influential theorists responsible for the definition and institutionalization of cultural studies as a separate academic discipline and one of the key figures of the Birmingham Centre for Contemporary Cultural Studies (CCCS) at the University of Birmingham, England, where work in this area was pioneered notably during the 1970s. Hall argues that cultural forms, articulated as texts in mass-media artifacts, convey a preferred or dominant meaning, notably regarding representations of race, culture, ethnicity, and, related to these, gender. Hall sees the technological and social changes of the late 20th century combined with the development of global information and media systems as making

even more important the study of their effects on cultural difference and identity.

For Hall, there is no separation between power, culture, and the self. Meanings conveyed by advertisements, film, and television are encoded by their producers as a discourse based on assumptions of what a culture considers important and correct. How these meanings become inculcated into the media products consumed by audiences serves as the foundation for Hall's encoding/decoding model of the communication process, his treatment of cultural hegemony as a process whereby dominant viewpoints become so, and the underlying concept of self versus the "Other" as the basis for stereotyping.

In *Encoding and Decoding in the Television Discourse*, Hall proposes that the mass communication process reflected in television production—and which defines the elements of cultural studies—involves the creation of a message (encoding), which he terms a *sign-vehicle*, and the reception of that message by audience members (decoding). Borrowing from past theorists, Hall notes that the audience serves as both the source and the receiver of a message, because the creators of that message already are members of the same culture as those they are targeting; for shared meaning to occur, the "cultural circuit" must be completed so that the meaning encoded by a message sender is decoded correctly by the receiver. In this sense, the dominant, or "preferred," meaning of a signifying element (either visual or linguistic) is that suggested by the encoder (who works within an institutional structure), although not the one necessarily always decoded by the receiver.

Hall's encoding/decoding model positions meaning—within cultural forms and artifacts—as a product of power and domination, of ideology, popular consciousness, and common sense. The latter two reflect hegemony, which Hall defines as the taken-for-granted knowledge of social structures. Rather than depending on a monolithic, permanent means of control by those in power, hegemony is grounded in a combination of force and consent and remains open to contradictory ideologies (or counterhegemony) and resistance. For Hall, cultural hegemony has to be actively won and secured; it does not result in pure victory or domination, but rather concerns the shifts in the balance of power in relations within a culture. Thus, within the cultural circuit, mass media tend to reproduce a society's ideological field and, in so doing, its structure of domination.

Hall's personal background as a native of Jamaica and immigrant to Great Britain has informed his work on cultural and racial difference in terms of representation in media messages. In *Representation: Cultural Representations and Signifying Practices* (1997), he addresses the intertexuality, the interweaving of texts with others from disparate sources, present in messages that convey meanings regarding race, gender, and sexuality. Representation, as the production of meanings through language, discourse, and image, relies on viewing persons (their gender and sexuality), cultures, and races in terms of binary opposition and the power relation between opposites. The representation of the racial Other as a "spectacle" also can apply to the way media represent sexual difference. Hall notes that difference, while necessary for the production of meaning and social and sexual identity, also creates a sense of hostility and aggression toward the Other. Stereotyping sets up "a symbolic frontier" between the normal and deviant or pathological, between the acceptable and the unacceptable. By showing the "opposite" race, culture, or sex as the Other, media products that forward stereotypical portrayals thus help to maintain a symbolic order of social and political power. Thus, the cultural circuit completes itself, thereby continually reflecting the hegemonic notions within a particular society at a particular moment in history. In terms of fostering in media consumers, and indeed in message creators, a desire for critical reflection of media messages and the cultural work they encode, Hall challenges what audiences take for granted. As Lawrence Grossberg noted in his 1986 article on Hall's contributions to the field in the *Journal of Communication Inquiry*, Hall's theoretical advances are offered "not as the end of a debate, but as the ongoing attempt to understand the complexity, contradictions, and struggles within the concrete lives of human beings."

Erika Engstrom
University of Nevada, Las Vegas

See also Audiences: Reception and Injection Models; Barthes, Roland; Cultural Politics; Encoding and Decoding; Hegemony; Identity; Ideology; Kellner, Douglas; Mass Media; Reception Theory; Textual Analysis

Further Readings

Barrett, Michèle. *Imagination in Theory*. New York: New York University Press, 1999.

Grossberg, Lawrence. "History, Politics and Postmodernism: Stuart Hall and Cultural Studies." *Journal of Communication Inquiry*, v.10 (1986).

Hall, Stuart. *Encoding and Decoding in the Television Discourse*. Birmingham, UK: Centre for Contemporary Cultural Studies, University of Birmingham, 1973.

Hall, Stuart, ed. *Representation: Cultural Representations and Signifying Practices*. Thousand Oaks, CA: Sage, 1997.

Morley, David and Kuan-Hsing Chen, eds. *Stuart Hall: Critical Dialogues in Cultural Studies*. New York: Routledge, 1996.

HANNA, KATHLEEN

Kathleen Hanna (1968–), a third wave feminist musician, writer, and activist was born in Portland, Oregon. She is one of the cofounders of the Riot Grrrl band Bikini Kill and later, Le Tigre (both of which have disbanded). In 1998, she released one solo album under the name Julie Ruin, and later she founded and performed in a band called The Julie Ruin, with bandmate Kathi Wilcox of Bikini Kill. She is a feminist activist, musician, zine writer, and key figure in the Riot Grrrl movement of the early 1990s. Her albums include Bikini Kill's *Revolution Girl Style Now!* (1991), *Kill Rock Stars* (1991), *Yeah Yeah Yeah Yeah* (with Huggy Bear, 1993), *Pussy Whipped* (1993), and *Reject All American* (1996). Her other projects include *Suture*, *A Wonderful Treat*, *Real Fiction*, and *Viva Knieval*. She has also collaborated with feminist music icon Joan Jett.

Hanna recalls "becoming" a feminist at the age of nine, when her mother took her to a rally in Washington, D.C., where they heard Gloria Steinem speak. She and her mother enjoyed reading and making montages and collages with pictures and statements that they felt empowered women. They often took inspiration and material from Steinem's *Ms.* magazine. In rare interviews, Hanna has stated that her father disapproved of her and her mother's associations with the feminist movement for solidarity, possibly a source of dispute that caused her parents to divorce when she was still young.

Hanna is also known for her other associations, which include the *Fakes* zines, such as *Grrrl Power* and *Girl Gems*. Hanna was involved with a women's cooperative and eventually opened her own gallery space, Reko Muse. While working at the co-op, she met the musicians from the popular band Nirvana, who would come to play benefit shows for the co-op. Hanna and the band developed a close working relationship, for which the members of Nirvana extended their gratitude by using Hanna as the inspiration for their hit song "Smells Like Teen Spirit."

Hanna's work at the co-op inspired her to start playing music. She also worked at one time as a stripper and at a shelter with a group of teenage victims of sexual assault. Reflecting on her experiences, Hanna states, "I want to talk about power and privilege in complex ways, recognizing that there is such a thing as privilege that's just given to certain people. There's also earned privilege." Hanna and her friends quickly became bored with the male-dominated music industry, in particular the punk rock scene, which privileged boys and men and objectified and commodified the girls and women. Speaking out on this, Hanna has stated that she felt "completely left out of the realm of everything that is so important to me. And I know that this is partly because punk rock is for and by boys mostly and partly because punk rock of this generation is coming of age in a time of mindless career-goal bands."

Forming their own band called Bikini Kill (named after a zine the members had created), Hanna and her bandmates found the perfect place to begin creating their own music with their own tone, musicality, performances, shows, and lyrics. Soon after the formation of Bikini Kill, the group became associated and incorporated into the infamous Olympia, Washington, music scene. At the time, this scene was known for its grassroots political activism, local support, and do-it-yourself (DIY) attitude, which also largely characterized feminist punk music in the early 1990s. Bikini Kill also included Billy "Boredom" Karren on guitar, Tobi Vail on drums and vocals, and Kathi Wilcox on guitar and bass. However, Bikini Kill was against the process of "specialization" in their music—all members tried to trade off on instruments and vocals to avoid elitism in the band.

Hanna has used rhetorical strategies, including humor, humiliation, ridicule, as well as different forms of attire to great effect. Like earlier feminists, Hanna sees no distinction between the fashionable and the feminist. Much as she practices splicing and poaching in her music and zine writing, she manages to do the same in her style of dress. During the punk rock movement of the 1990s, Riot Grrrls such as Hanna could be seen combining grunge rock and rave styles. It was not rare to see Hanna and her bandmates decked out in combat boots or Converse shoes, with baby-doll dresses, schoolgirl skirts, kneesocks, and tight-fitting T-shirts. The mismatched items reflected the women's take-what-you-want, leave-what-you-don't attitude toward culture in general. Riot Grrrls utilized similar tactics in their zine writing, making use of photocopied playbills, collage, juxtaposition, and other techniques inspired by the New Left.

Hanna went on to study photography at Evergreen State College and has taught at New York University (NYU) and Parsons School of Design, lecturing at both college and high school campuses. She and other Riot Grrrls have been mentioned and celebrated in such popular cultural artifacts such as the television programs *Roseanne*, *Quincy*, and *The L Word* (2004–09). Hanna has also published an essay in Robin Morgan's third anthology, *Sisterhood Is Forever* (2003), and is active in the slam poetry and spoken word scene.

Judy E. Battaglia
Loyola Marymount University

See also E-Zines: Riot Grrrl; E-Zines: Third Wave Feminist; Steinem, Gloria; Women's Magazines: Feminist Magazines

Further Readings

Cogan, B. *The Encyclopedia of Punk: Music and Culture.* New York: Sterling, 2008.

Juno, A. *Angry Women in Rock*, Vol. 1. New York: Juno Books, 1996.

Morgan, R. *Sisterhood Is Forever: The Women's Anthology for a New Millennium.* New York: Washington University Press, 2003.

HEGEMONY

The concept of hegemony (derived from the Greek *hegemon*, meaning "leader") describes the process by which the beliefs, values, ideologies, and practices of a particular social class come to dominate the wider society. The beliefs of that particular class become hegemonic when alternative or competing beliefs are excluded, ignored, or repressed. This can occur through conscious or unconscious processes.

For example, a particular institution of power (a government, schooling system, or mass-media outlet) may consciously promote or exclude particular viewpoints. However, groups of people may develop patterns of thought or behavior that unconsciously valorize or demonize particular views. In either case, the hegemonic beliefs become the "common sense" of a society. Those beliefs are common, first, because a majority of people adopt them as their own and, second, because the beliefs appear to be natural, inherent, inevitable, and unchangeable. People then lack motivation to question and challenge those beliefs, thus enabling the beliefs to remain hegemonic.

The concept of hegemony is most often associated with Antonio Gramsci, an Italian Marxist theorist of the early 20th century. In an attempt to understand the possibilities of socialist revolution, Gramsci investigated the relationship between culture and capitalist domination. He argued that there are two basic forms of domination: physical force and cultural consent. The first refers to police and military repression, often waged by fascist and dictatorial regimes. The second refers to ideology often found within liberal democracies where notions of freedom, liberty, and rights create a false sense of political agency. Although citizens of liberal democracies are "free to choose" between various and even competing ideologies (between, for instance, liberal and conservative political parties or between different corporate brands), all choices are restricted to the perpetuation of the dominant capitalist ideology. Anyone who questions and seriously challenges that ideology is marginalized by the wider society. This occurs because a majority of citizens are inculcated with, and never think to question, the ideology that shapes their self-understanding. People thus "consent" to their own class oppression. This ideological superstructure depends on and is perpetuated by various institutions—schools, governments, newspapers, court systems, professional sports, organized religions, and even nonprofit organizations that operate according to the dominant ideology. Gramsci argued that committed cultural workers who have sufficiently developed a critical class-consciousness must infiltrate these institutions. These cultural workers are then in a position to work against the dominant ideology, develop and disseminate alternative viewpoints, and establish the cultural conditions for a socialist revolution.

In the latter part of the mid-20th century, cultural critics began investigating the relationship between mass media and hegemonic understandings of gender. Critics like Stuart Hall, bell hooks, and Judith Butler focused on the relationship between mediated representations and the social construction of gender (as well as race, class, and sexuality). For instance, the relationship between biological bodies and performances of gender are normalized and essentialized by continual images of men as physically superior, aggressive, and emotionally stoic and of women as physically inferior, passive, and emotionally supportive. Critics argue, however, that there is no inherent relationship between particular body types and enactments of masculinity and femininity. Homogeneous representations also ignore the gender diversity that exists in the world. Gender identities and rituals vary according to ethnicity, culture, age, historical time period, personal experience, family upbringing, and individual predisposition. The media's failure to recognize and represent such diversity not only establishes social expectations that are often unattainable but possibly contributes to low self-esteem, internalized self-hatred, social ridicule, and punishment.

A greater range of gender representations currently exist within mass media, but this fact does not dissolve the issue of gender hegemony. For example, 24-hour news channels, Hollywood and Disney films, television talk shows, celebrity gossip blogs, and advertising industries might discuss, debate, and disseminate discourses about "bromance movies," metrosexuality, emotionally vulnerable men, queer culture, female action heroes, and female politicians. However, this increased diversity does not necessarily equalize all representations or undermine gender hegemony. Bromance movies and popular discourses of metrosexuality can be interpreted as latently homophobic and heterosexist; depictions of emotionally vulnerable men might be diminutive and humorous rather than validating and serious; representations of queer culture, such as the reality-based makeover program *Queer Eye for the Straight Guy*, often perpetuate base stereotypes of effeminate men; the bodies of female action heroes are often hypersexualized, thus perpetuating the objectification of the female body; and female politicians are often caught within a double bind of being either too masculine or too feminine. Also, within a Gramscian framework, the expanded range of gender could be understood as economically motivated—it opens new markets, expands profit, and thus maintains rather than challenges capitalist domination.

The concept of hegemony has been both celebrated and critiqued. It is celebrated for advancing a theoretical understanding of ideology, but it is also critiqued for being too narrow in scope. For instance, Gramsci's original formulation inscribes an implicit hierarchy between self-aware agents of social change and unaware perpetuators of dominant ideology. The first group becomes the cultural vanguard, while the second group awaits direction. The concept of hegemony has been further theorized in order to work past its initial shortcomings. Feminist scholars Inderpal Grewal and Caren Kaplan argue, for instance, that modern mass media have undeniable hegemonic effects. However, the relationship between mass media and consumers is not unilateral. Reception of messages, images, and representations is always filtered through the unique biases of each individual. Such localized reception resists the possibility of a single, overarching ideology. What arise, instead, are "scattered hegemonies," ideologies that are simultaneously hegemonic and plural. The notion of scattered hegemonies maintains the critique of hegemonic ideologies but also recognizes that such critiques are waged by unique individuals with different predispositions.

Similar issues are addressed by R. W. Conwell's concept of "hegemonic masculinity." Conwell, a sociologist, developed this concept in order to better understand how different forms of masculinity emerge and then influence the construction of gender hierarchies. According to Conwell, hegemonic masculinity establishes a normative range of possible masculinities; it sits at the top of the gender hierarchy and thus acts as a cultural guide for masculine performance. Hegemonic masculinity is not transhistorical; what constitutes a hegemonic masculinity changes with social and historical conditions. In fact, a hegemonic masculinity could be less aggressive, less oppressive, and more humane and empathetic and could even undermine the entire structure of gender hierarchies. Hegemonic masculinities may also exist without an actual referent in the real world. Hegemonic masculinities might be constructed, for instance, from fairy tales, novels, movies, television shows, and music videos rather than the lives of actual people. When approached from this perspective, hegemonic masculinity helps us understand the relationships among discourse, gender, and power.

Jason Del Gandio
Temple University

See also Critical Theory; Hall, Stuart; hooks, bell; Ideology; Social Construction of Gender

Further Readings

Conwell, R. W. and James W. Messerschmidt. "Hegemonic Masculinity: Rethinking the Concept." *Gender and Society*, v.19/6 (2005).

Forgacs, David, ed. *The Antonio Gramsci Reader: Selected Writings 1916–1935*. New York: New York University Press, 2000.

Gramsci, Antonio. *Selections From the Prison Notebooks of Antonio Gramsci*. Quintin Hoare and Geoffrey Nowell Smith, eds. and trans. New York: International Publishers, 1971.

Grewal, Inderpal and Caren Kaplan, eds. *Scattered Hegemonies: Postmodernity and Transnational Feminist Practices*. Minneapolis: University of Minnesota Press, 1994.

HEROES: ACTION AND SUPER HEROES

Media presentations of heroism reflect a cultural understanding of men's and women's given roles in perpetuating what is good and fighting what is bad in a particular society. They also reflect and contradict traditional gender roles.

Action Heroes

Popular early male action heroes, such as Ringo Kid, Dirty Harry, and James Bond, are depicted in film as active, aggressive, and, most important, masculine in both physique and behavior. They are not necessarily young or handsome, but they are both strong and savvy when it comes to overcoming their enemies. Violence is their primary means of fighting the antiheroes who confront them. Male heroes' sexual prowess is often evidenced by their ability to capture the romantic interest of the women they are assisting. While they may exhibit moments of sensitivity or even tenderness, they do not wholly give in to these feelings. Their masculinity is also underscored by their rejection of traditional marriage, parenthood, and in some cases the establishment. Television action heroes such as *The Six Million Dollar Man* in the eponymous series (1974–78) also reproduce these male gender types. In the 1980s, male action heroes like Indiana Jones in *Raiders of the Lost Ark* (1981), John Cutter in *Passenger 57* (1992), and John Matrix in *Commando* (1985) also reflected these gender norms. Other male heroes, however, began to reflect a more modern version of masculinity. John McClane (*Diehard*, 1988) manages to maintain his masculine persona even though he is a husband and father. The television show *MacGyver* (1985–92) depicts an action hero who prefers science and ingenuity to guns. In *Walker, Texas Ranger* (1993–2001), Cordell Walker uses a combination of guns and martial arts to fight off criminals but also offers moral lessons about life and engages in community service. These activities are not offered as contradictions to their masculinity but as enhancements to their roles as men.

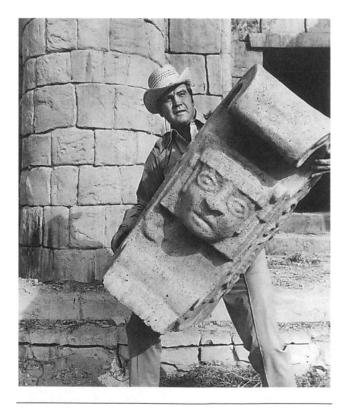

Lee Majors starred in the popular television show *The Six Million Dollar Man* from 1974 to 1978. Majors's role followed the stereotypical gender tradition of depicting a hero as an aggressive, powerful male. (Wikimedia)

Action Heroines

Female action heroes, or heroines, offer a negotiated representation of gender. They reflect feminist notions of womanhood by possessing stereotypically masculine traits such as strength and aggressiveness while maintaining their feminine youth, beauty, and sexuality. Female action heroes often depict women playing traditionally masculine roles while operating within traditional gender expectations that reflect male power. Figures like Sarah Connor in *The Terminator* (1984), Ellen Ripley in *Aliens* (1986), and Charli Baltimore in *The Long Kiss Goodnight* (1996) are physically strong, aggressive, and unapologetically violent in defense of themselves and others, using guns and other weapons. However, they negotiate their heroism with the expectations placed on them to take care of their natural or adopted children. Meanwhile, heroines like Foxy in *Foxy Brown* (1974) and Jane in *Mr. & Mrs. Smith* (2005) also take on traditionally male characteristics, but their image is highly eroticized in order to appeal to male sexual desire.

Television heroines also negotiate patriarchal notions of femininity. Emma Peel of *The Avengers* (1966–69) possesses outstanding fighting and fashion skills. The women working as *Charlie's Angels* (1976–81) are physically strong and able to defend themselves using martial arts, guns, and other weapons, but they also reinforce male power by acting under the orders of a faceless male voice and by being sexually objectified in their occasional ditzy behavior and low-cut, cleavage-revealing outfits. After receiving surgical implants, Jamie Sommers becomes *The Bionic Woman* (1976–78), a government secret weapon thanks to her speed, strength, and enhanced hearing. Nevertheless, she is weaker than her counterpart in *The Six Million Dollar Man* and works for a male-dominated government agency.

Since the 1990s, female action heroes have been depicted as superhuman but within the constraints of stereotypical gender roles. They are also characterized by feelings of ambivalence about their powers. In *La Femme Nikita* (1990), Nikita, a troubled teenage girl who is recruited against her will to become a government assassin, becomes a femme fatale by using seduction to lure her intended targets. She eventually abandons the agency and disappears. The 1997 television series of the same name and the 2010 series titled *Nikita* offer variations of the troubled heroine, and both turn against the agency that gave them their powers. The 1992 film and the 1997 television version of *Buffy the Vampire Slayer* (1997–2003) feature a young and attractive teen whose ability to enjoy cheerleading and boys is inhibited by the power and responsibility bestowed on her. *Alias* (2001–05) features young and pretty college co-ed Sydney Bristow, who struggles to hide her role as a double agent for the Central Intelligence Agency from friends and family.

Xena: Warrior Princess (1995–2001) features a warrior queen who is dedicating her life to making amends for her past sins as a power-hungry warlord. Her tall frame, muscular physique, and aggressive fighting style are juxtaposed to her tight, cleavage-revealing outfit. In contrast, her protégé Gabrielle, who often acts as her moral compass, is younger, smaller, and slightly weaker. The sexual ambiguity resulting from their close friendship offers an alternative to patriarchally defined roles fulfilled by other heroines in the media at the time but does not eliminate other gendered characteristics, including their beauty and their willingness to seduce, and be seduced, by men.

Comic Book Adaptations

A large number of media representations of superheroes are adapted from early comic book series. Action Comics (later DC Comics) generated a variety of superheroes endowed with super strength, robust muscular physiques, and good looks. Media representations of these characters emphasize not only these qualities but also their need to hide these specific gender-defined qualities in order to keep their identities secret. For example, radio, television, and film incarnations of 1938 comic book hero Superman feature him pretending to be Clark Kent, a passive and awkward crime reporter whose bespectacled face and clumsiness contrast greatly with his hypermasculine body and help to conceal his identity and super powers. Television and film depictions of Batman, the superhuman identity of the wealthy playboy Bruce Wayne, emphasize his image as Gotham City's most eligible bachelor to hide his secret identity. The television version of *Wonder Woman* (1975–79) disguises the heroine's voluptuous Amazonian physique and female sexuality (showcased by her skin-revealing outfit) in her

daily identity as the serious and rather uptight Diana Prince.

Marvel Comics' launch of *The Avengers* series in 1963 included superheroes like the Fantastic Four, The Incredible Hulk, Iron Man, and later Spider-Man and members of the X-Men. These characters struggle with inner demons and their ambivalence about their powers. Television and film adaptations of these characters continue to underscore the gender differences between the male and female members of this group. Although they all possess superpowers, male superheroes possess notably larger muscular physiques while women offer well-toned, voluptuous figures. Depictions of superheroines like *Fantastic Four*'s (2005) Invisible Woman and *X-Men*'s (2000) Rogue offer strong but still stereotypically feminine characteristics, including beauty and sensitivity. *X-Men*'s Wolverine, *Fantastic Four*'s The Thing, and multiple film and television versions of The Hulk and Spider-man feature brute strength and skills that underscore their masculinity, while heroines like Storm use violence only when it is absolutely necessary.

Heroines, Body, and Technology

Film and television action heroes and superheroes reflect a cultural interest in technology. The way technology is used also fulfills traditional gender expectations. Men like James Bond, Batman, and Iron Man use technologically innovative cars, weapons, and other devices to enhance their masculinized power. Meanwhile, the Bionic Woman's body is compromised by the insertion of cyborg-like parts so that she can serve men of authority. Lara Croft, a film heroine who first appeared in the video game *Tomb Raider* (1996), was developed to invite men's gaze (voyeuristic viewing of women as erotic objects) with her voluptuous physique and skin-tight outfits while still possessing all the strength and skill of a male action hero. These women challenge traditional gender expectations thanks to the technological reconstruction of their bodies. However, the way they are presented and used reinforces traditional male power.

Animated Superheroes

The Hanna-Barbera animated series known collectively as the *SuperFriends* (1973–84) featured child-friendly versions of superheroes like Superman, Batman, Wonder Woman, and Spider-man. These characters also possessed the same gender-specific qualities as the adult-oriented media adaptations. Later animated action series, such as *The Powerpuff Girls* (1998–2004), *Kim Possible* (2002–07), and *Ben10* (2005–08), offered limited variations of traditional gender roles. A survey conducted by Kasey Baker and Arthur A. Raney reveals that, whereas male heroes in animated children's programming continue to play traditionally masculine roles, heroines shed some traditional gender-role stereotypes, taking on aggressive, powerful, and self-sufficient characteristics. They still maintain traditionally feminine traits such as good looks and emotionality. These findings suggest that, like adult-oriented male and female heroes and superheroes, female characters are continuing to negotiate their roles as both young women and heroines.

Melissa Camacho
San Francisco State University

See also Comics; E-Zines: Third Wave Feminist; Film: Hollywood; Graphic Novels; Television; Video Gaming: Representations of Femininity; Video Gaming: Representations of Masculinity

Further Readings

Baker, Kasey, and Arthur A. Raney. "Equally Super? Gender-Role Stereotyping of Superheroes in Children's Animated Programs." *Media and Society*, v.10/1 (2007).

Bingham, Dennis. *Acting Male: Masculinities in the Films of James Stewart, Jack Nicholson, and Clint Eastwood.* New Brunswick, NJ: Rutgers University Press, 1994.

Schubart, Rikke. *Super Bitches and Action Babes: The Female Hero in Popular Cinema, 1970–2006.* Jefferson, NC: McFarland, 2007.

HETEROSEXISM

Heterosexism is the assumption that there are only two genders, male and female, and that people are attracted only to members of the "opposite" sex. Dichotomous gender roles are naturalized, with the world consisting of masculine men and feminine women. Gender stereotypes—men as intelligent, brave providers and women as nurturing, vulnerable dependents—are essential to heterosexism. Heterosexual romance and the creation of nuclear families are perceived as universal norms. In this worldview, every healthy, right-minded person wants a life organized around the practices and privileges of heterosexual intimacies. Consequently, people who perform sexualities and genders that challenge this worldview are often marginalized, ridiculed, and even subject to physical violence.

In the media, heterosexist representations are characterized by either blindness or hostility to non-heterosexual identities and lifestyles. The prevalence of heterosexism means that gay, lesbian, transgender/transsexual, and intersexual characters and relationships are often ignored or demeaned in popular media texts. Even straight men and women who defy gender stereotypes can be subject to ridicule and discrimination. Identifying, understanding, and disrupting heterosexism are therefore necessary not only for academics and teachers but for every media-literate person as well. To that end, it is important to examine both the history of heterosexist imagery and contemporary challenges to heterosexism as a framework for portraying gender and sexuality.

Heterosexual attraction and love have long been central to Western storytelling traditions; with the advent of consumer culture and the strengthening ideology of individualism over the past century, heterosexual romance has perhaps become an even more important theme in popular culture. In the United States, popular film and television shows provide especially salient examples of heterosexist representations, although magazines, novels, comics, video games, and other texts also portray heterosexual relationships as natural and universally desirable. Since the advent of film and radio in the early decades of the 20th century, numerous genres have featured plots that rely on heterosexual relationships and institutions (such as courtship, marriage, and the nuclear family) to fuel their narrative arcs. Romantic comedies, domestic dramas, and soap operas revolve around heterosexual intimacies, but romance is also frequently inserted, with varying degrees of fit or appropriateness, into other genres, such as adventure stories, science fiction, political dramas, and thrillers. Often, the addition of a heterosexual relationship helps offset and "straighten out" relationships that might otherwise be easily interpreted as queer. This occurs, for example, when the men who share a close same-sex friendship in a buddy movie are both depicted as having girlfriends or wives. The ubiquitous representation of straight romance helps to naturalize heterosexuality and to reduce the possibility that queer love and desire might be read into the relationships featured in media texts. However, heterosexism does not only mean the normalization and promotion of male-female romance; it also refers to the negative depiction of queerness.

Negative portrayals of queerness range in severity. Some depict queer people and relationships as insignificant or humorous. This kind of heterosexism occurs when gay and lesbian characters play second fiddle to straight couples or when queer (usually gay male) characters function primarily to provide comic relief. Casting gay and lesbian characters as "funny" frequently desexualizes them and helps defuse the threat of queer desire. In this vein, drag is occasionally deployed for comic effect. Many theorists observe that through its depiction of feminine men and masculine women as comical and bizarre, drag reasserts heterosexist gender norms; however, theorists also argue that drag unsettles assumptions about the naturalness of gender and straight sexuality. Very negative representations cast queer intimacies and characters as pathetic, miserably unhappy, antisocial, or evil. Within some texts, suicide or murder can function symbolically to punish queer characters for their transgressions against the heterosexual social order. In this way, the menace of nonnormative genders and sexualities can be contained. Despite their frequent negativity, heterosexist representations are also polysemous, and many lesbian, gay, bisexual, transsexual/transgender, intersexual, queer/questioning (LGBTIQ) people enjoy and identify with queer characters from television, film, novels, and other media by "reading against the grain" and understanding these texts differently from the way producers, actors, and writers may have intended.

Despite the hegemony of heterosexist media representations, alternative and dissenting images have always been around. Especially since the late 1990s and early 2000s, more positive—that is, more complex, diverse, and inclusive—representations of nonnormative sexualities have become available in the mainstream media. Changes in the depictions of romantic and sexual relationships on prime-time television, premium cable channels, and the Internet—particularly as evidenced in Internet pornography—have rendered queer intimacies more visible and normalized, even if such intimacies are still outnumbered by heterosexist representations.

Similar changes have occurred in other media as well. Magazines, music, and advertising often target gay and lesbian consumers, advocate the inclusion of LGBTIQ people at every level of society, and portray queer intimacies and nonnormative gender identities as healthy and sexy. It should be noted that some movement toward more positive representations does not mean that heterosexism is no longer a problem in media representations; nevertheless, it is undeniable that important changes are occurring.

Brittany N. Griebling
University of Pennsylvania

See also Gay and Lesbian Portrayals on Television; Online New Media: GLBTQ Identity; Online New Media: Transgender Identity; Pornography: Gay and Lesbian; Queer Theory; Sexism; Sexuality; Transgender Studies; Transsexuality

Further Readings

Benshoff, Henry M. *Queer Images: A History of Gay and Lesbian Film in America*. Lanham, MD: Rowman & Littlefield, 2005.

Clarke, J. N. "Homophobia Out of the Closet in the Media Portrayal of HIV/AIDS 1991, 1996 and 2001: Celebrity, Heterosexism and the Silent Victims." *Critical Public Health*, v.16/4 (2006).

Dines, Gail and Jean M. Humez, eds. *Gender, Race, and Class in Media: A Critical Reader*. 1995. Reprint, Thousand Oaks, CA: Sage, 2010.

Gross, Larry. *Up From Invisibility: Lesbians, Gay Men, and the Media in America*. New York: Columbia University Press, 2002.

HOMOPHOBIA

Although the exact definition of homophobia remains elusive, it has ranged from discomfort when in close proximity to homosexuals (part of its original definition) to a deeply seated revulsion toward homosexuals ensconced within antigay attitudes. Primarily, the term appears to suggest the manifestations of ideologies that are extensions of heterosexism. That is, the undergirding mentality concerning homophobia is that gayness is inherently contrary to the supposedly positive nature of heterosexuality and that heterosexuality should therefore be accepted as a positive prescriptive view toward sexual and affectional orientation.

Increasingly, media depictions of homophobia are grounded not only in questioning heterocentric paradigms but also in critically analyzing the communicative messages that underscore the creation of homophobia. For example, mediated depictions of homophobic utterances have been critiqued for underlying assumptions of behavioral expectations and psychological assessments. Additionally, media news outlets have covered the presence of organized homophobia, particularly related to legislative events such as California's anti-marriage-equality proposition, Proposition 8. Because of an increase in media exposure, orchestrated efforts both to promote and to curtail homophobia have been covered, while mediated attacks against homophobia have also been instrumental in ensuring the distribution of homophobic messages.

In relation to new media, homophobia continues to be present within numerous social networking sites, prompting consideration of the impact of such electronic communication on participants. With a growing number of Americans considering pervasive antigay and homophobic messages from organized religious and political entities, increasing counterefforts are being used to combat such discourse. Examples include numerous social networking sites but also mediated counterattacks to remedy the influence of homophobia, particularly in terms of messages geared toward youth.

Although originally homophobia was assumed to be primarily a psychological phenomenon, its additional influence within political and social spheres is becoming more apparent. In consideration of the rash of protests and media appearances of the staunchly homophobic Westboro Baptist Church, the intersection of homophobia and religious doctrine may have reached a cultural zenith. Homophobia was assumed to be an undercurrent to legislative actions taken to ensure a forestalling of marriage equality. These efforts were coupled with political polemics suggesting that homophobia was linked with political opportunity. Examples of such events include mediated reactions to hearings on "Don't Ask, Don't Tell" (the measure designed to forestall service by openly gay and bisexual members of the military), the Employment Nondiscrimination Act (ENDA), the Matthew Shepard Hate Crimes Prevention Act, and California's Proposition 8. By 2011, only the hate crimes bill had become law;

There was no mistaking this California citizen's stance on gay marriage when Proposition 8 was on the 2008 ballot. A "yes" vote supported the statement that "only marriage between a man and a woman is valid or recognized in California" and eliminated the rights of same-sex couples to marry. (Wikimedia/Jessie Terwilliger)

progress on each of the other bills was stalled at the legislative level. Increasingly, mediated depictions of homophobia may underscore the motivation behind these legislative actions.

With increased attention to the role of hate crimes that are underscored by homophobia, including the murder of Matthew Shepard and attacks in the Bronx, homophobia has been identified as an underlying motivation for not only vitriolic but also corporal attacks. The intersection between homophobia and the likelihood of physical assault is becoming more pronounced. As a result, homophobia may also be linked to the masking of lesbian, gay, bisexual, and transsexual/transgender (LGBT) characters in media. For example, mediated depictions of openly gay characters have traditionally been either stereotypical, affixed to societal scorn or ridicule, or simply nonexistent. Some mediated depictions included illustrations of the negative impact of both homophobia and acquired immune deficiency syndrome (AIDS). Thereafter, an increasing number of openly gay, permanent characters were featured in mediated depictions, as were considerations of the emergent role of homophobia within social settings.

Concerns over homophobia have risen as larger numbers of young people admit to widespread homophobia within educational settings. These are coupled with concerns over the frequency of anti-GLBT (gay, lesbian, bisexual, transsexual/transgender) bullying in American public schools. Bullying has been exhibited not only by students but also, at least tacitly, by the teachers and staff who permit it. Beyond the exclusionary tactics that undergird such sentiments, ongoing social and psychological damage may result from long-term exposure to homophobia. Pedagogical concerns have been matched by an increased effort on the part of numerous media groups to ensure that homophobia is countered in educational settings. Examples of such efforts include Dan Savage's It Gets Better Project, a viral mediated campaign that features adult GLBT participants who explain to youth that eventually the levels of homophobia they encounter in educational settings will dissipate. Other organizations, such as the Gay, Lesbian Straight Education Network (GLSEN) and the Trevor Project, have coupled such efforts with mediated efforts to curtail GLBT teen suicide.

From a critical perspective, efforts are also being considered that would highlight the different exigencies between homophobia and other extensions of heterosexism. Bi-, trans-, and queerphobias may be grounded in reactions that are very different from those experienced through homophobia. Moreover, each of these constructs may also be reviewed through lenses related to gender and gender identity. The communication of homophobia may entail a reaction to the motif of a gay contagion, an argument furthered through mediated depictions of gayness as a social ill or contaminant. This motif may be grounded in the perception of homophobia as a positive counteragent to gay behavior. With increased awareness of GLBTQ issues, the amount of positively regarded homophobia—particularly outside many religious organizations—has begun to dissipate. However, homophobia remains deeply rooted not only in anti-GLBTQ-inclusion efforts but also in the ongoing debate over the definition of sexual identity and experience.

Scott Gratson
Temple University

See also Diversity; Gay and Lesbian Portrayals on Television; Hegemony; Heterosexism; Prejudice; Stereotypes

Further Readings

Fone, B. *Homophobia: A History.* New York: Picador, 2001.

Herek, G., ed. *Stigma and Sexual Orientation: Understanding Prejudice Against Lesbians, Gay Men, and Bisexuals.* Thousand Oaks: Sage, 1998.

Kantor, M. *Homophobia: The State of Sexual Bigotry Today.* Santa Barbara, CA: Praeger, 2009.

HOOKS, BELL

Born in 1952, bell hooks (the pen name of Gloria Watkins) is one of the most celebrated African American black intellectuals of her generation. She is a social activist and prolific author who is committed to the goals of fair representation, gender equality, social justice, and the preservation of African American culture.

Her first major book, *Ain't I a Woman: Black Women and Feminism* (1981), is about the marginalized position of the black female who is doubly oppressed by the racism of feminism and the sexism of the black liberation movement. Unlike many of her contemporaries, hooks does not call for a separate black feminist movement but instead uses the unique position of black women to expose the dangers of universalizing discourses of the aforesaid movements. She thereby draws attention to the "invisible" and "silent" others who lie on the margins. She undertakes a three-pronged attack that exposes the issues of inequality, identifies the marginalized groups, and then creates the platform for these oppressed groups. In her recovery of black female identities, hooks creates a forum for black women to articulate their experiences.

hooks's writings are characteristically critical and accessible. Beyond that, there is variation in her writing and speaking styles. She often draws from her own personal experiences as a black working-class woman in order to emphasize the importance of life experiences as an important tool for empowering black women as well as the problematics faced by the black intellectual. For example, hooks identifies the needs for solitude and withdrawal from other responsibilities, such as family and community—practical needs that may be met for the privileged male writer but that the black feminist must fight to fulfill. In her writing, hooks combines her theoretical interest with her relentless activism. She also presents her work using a number of different media, including academic texts, popular journals such as *Artforum*, and film. She also represents her work in dialogue with other black intellectuals, such as Paul Gilroy.

hooks's critique traverses many different fields, from feminism to popular culture, the visual arts, and pedagogy. Her scholarship addresses a number of cultural practices, from representations of race and gender in popular culture to power dynamics in the academy. She believes that race and gender are used in numerous ways to subordinate women and non-white people in different spheres. Although she is renowned primarily as a feminist thinker, her multiple interests in gender, race, identity, the role of the media, and teaching are interconnected and mutually enlightening, adding to the wide readership for her work. hooks's criticism of the mass media is that it promulgates and develops invidious relationships between whites and blacks. She argues that the media constitute a white-dominated industry that inculcates the capitalist and patriarchal mind-set. She uses examples from popular culture, such as gangsta rap, to reveal the demonization of black youth culture.

Two books that exemplify hooks's critique of the relationship between race, gender, and the media are *Black Looks: Race and Representation* (1992) and *Reel to Real: Race, Sex, and Class at the Movies* (1996). In the former, hooks examines representations of "blackness" in advertising, fashion, and popular culture. She discusses the personal and political ramifications of the commodification of "the black other" and exposes the ideological manipulation of a white supremacist culture that seeks to dominate, marginalize, and stereotype blackness. In turn, marginalized communities may end up internalizing the negative stereotypes about them, thus reinforcing the dominant position. In the latter book, hooks turns to the medium of film and offers a criticism of culture viewed through film. She discusses how film operates as a pedagogical tool that teaches people about experiences and how this was pertinent in the context of her teaching, where she claimed that her students learned more about race, class, and gender from film than they did through theoretical texts.

Although bell hooks is known for her feminist views, her writings also cover gender, race, teaching, and the effect of media on modern culture. hooks is thought of as one of the leading intellectuals of her generation. (Wikimedia)

hooks's response to the pervasiveness of ideological indoctrination through media calls for a critically informed cultural analysis. One of her guiding principles is encapsulated in the command to "talk back," which is taken from the title of her volume of essays *Talking Back: Thinking Feminist, Thinking Black* (1989). hooks expresses the importance of speaking out against racism, sexism, and other forms of injustice that are manifested in political and social inequality. One way that this can be achieved is for politics to advocate a democracy that works for justice and the reform of the educational system, so that schools can empower children to open their minds and be receptive to learning. In *Teaching to Transgress: Education as the Practice of Freedom* (1994), hooks argues for a pedagogy that empowers and impresses on educators the social responsibility of enabling people through literacy. By "literacy" hooks is referring not simply to reading and writing but also to the powers of critical thinking that are existentially transformative. In her writing, hooks expresses the need for readers to become responsible members of a community of learners, thus advocating the importance of critical thinking and thinking more widely about the potential that ideas hold for social and political transformation.

hooks is a leading public intellectual and prolific writer who is engaged with equality in different spheres, from the academy to the streets. She has also taught at a number of different academic institutions, including Yale University, and since 1995 has been Distinguished Professor in English at City College of New York.

Rina Arya
University of Wolverhampton

See also Diversity; Electronic Media and Social Inequality; Feminism; Feminist Theory: Second Wave; Feminist Theory: Women-of-Color and Multiracial Perspectives; Gender and Masculinity: Black Masculinity; Gender Embodiment; Hegemony; Intersectionality; Misogyny; Racism; Stereotypes

Further Readings

hooks, bell. *Ain't I a Woman: Black Women and Feminism.* Boston: South End Press, 1981.

hooks, bell. *Black Looks: Race and Representation.* Boston: South End Press, 1992.

hooks, bell. *Feminist Theory From Margin to Center.* Boston: South End Press, 1984.

hooks, bell. *Reel to Real: Race, Sex, and Class at the Movies.* New York: Routledge, 1996.

hooks, bell. *Talking Back: Thinking Feminist, Thinking Black.* Toronto, ON: Between the Lines, 1989.

hooks, bell. *Teaching to Transgress: Education as the Practice of Freedom.* New York: Routledge, 1994.

Namulundah, Florence. *bell hooks' Engaged Pedagogy: A Transgressive Education for Critical Consciousness.* Westport, CT: Bergin & Garvey, 1998.

Hypermedia

Hypermedia is a term often used synonymously with *hypertext*, which is defined as the nonlinear media of information. Hypermedia and hypertext allow for the creation of multilinear narratives. George P. Landow defines hypertext as text that is based on groups of images and words that are electronically connected through many paths. Hypertext can be described using the terms *link*, *node*, *network*, *web*, and *path*. Hypermedia extends the notions of text in hypertext to multimedia forms of content, including images, video, and sound.

Hypertext theory came of interest in the 1960s, when academics were searching for ways to displace the traditional narrative structure. Critical theory can be embodied within hypertext. Hypertext promises to embody and thereby test aspects of theory, particularly those concerning textuality, narrative, and the roles or functions of readers and writers. This form of text has arguably been described by Roland Barthes as an "ideal text." One of the main issues at play in discussions of hypermedia is the disappearing role of the author. As reader and writer become indistinguishable, text is freed from traditional notions of ownership. Such free-playing text provides unique opportunities for the realization of post-structuralist theories on writing. Text freed from the author may allow readers a sense of agency as they navigate and create the meanings of texts through their choices of hyperliterature. Often hypermedia or hypertext narratives exist only as digital media. Through the use of linking, text can flow in a nonlinear format, giving room for feminist practices of narrative writing. Feminist writing often uses different forms of rationality and logic to allow feminine subjectivity to come to light. Nonlinear writing is particularly effective for feminist politics because of the challenges it poses to male-dominated models of narrative.

Hypermedia also provides the possibility for new individual political responsibility and subjectivity. Because the reader plays an active role in the creation of hypertext, much of the responsibility for the narrative lies in the reader's hands. Such self-empowered use of information provides new possibilities for expression and reading. The reader of hypertext is free from the confines of traditional textual structures.

Traditional forms of argument and writing rely on linear knowledge and logic to create a convincing argument. This system of writing and logic is tied to a male-dominated mode of communication that has excluded alternative perspectives. The strict rules of logical argumentation have been assigned as the privilege of a patriarchal system. Hypertext provides radical potentials that challenge and expand notions of narrative. As hypertext demands a nonfixed center with no boundaries or beginning or end, we begin to see information in matrices. Cybertheorist Donna J. Haraway points to the relationship between human and machine as a place for a gender-based struggle against the domination of information. Through the figure of the cyborg, she advances a new subjectivity that articulates the oppression females experience in a culture that is determined by a male-dominated system.

Women have played a crucial role in the development of hyperliterature. Using nonlinear formats, writers are using a whole new array of possibilities in the creation of narrative structures. Shelley Jackson's *Patchwork Girl* (1995) is an example of hypertext literature. *Patchwork Girl* is a modern feminist reinterpretation of Mary Shelley's *Frankenstein* (1818). Making use of available media technologies, *Patchwork Girl* weaves a narrative of the displaced female body, and by "clicking" through the narrative the user weaves a story that reunites the broken pieces of what Jackson refers to as the body made hysterical female form. Her text demands an engaged reading that in turn gives meaning to her text.

Critiques of hypermedia's liberatory potential point to the reliance of hypermedia on logocentric technologies. Although hypertext may be free of hierarchal narrative structure, it is not free of systematic, logical relationships. Its reliance on technological mediation keeps it dependent on the technological structures that dictate its formation. It may form new connections, but it is still connected through a system of regulated language that places it within the larger context of the militaristic and capitalist systems. These critiques say that, despite possibilities for multiplicity, there is no freeing of the text from the larger cultural systems from which it was written. The conflict here lies between techne and a discourse of liberation. Techne limits our abilities to realize a true form of emancipation, but working within techne, hypertext may provide opportunities to generate new discourses that provide alternatives to traditional modes of thought and communication technologies. Other critiques of the liberatory potential of hypermedia point to the reduction of choice to a set of consumer choices. Instead of taking real action, individuals feel a sense of agency that is manifested in a way that is beneficial only to commerce.

Hypertext markup language (HTML) is the language used to write hypermedia. Currently HTML5 is a way of simplifying and opening the generation of hypermedia audio and video without reliance on proprietary technologies such as Adobe Flash or Apple Quicktime. Semantic Web offers an approach that can extend the capabilities of hypermedia by adding new features based on machine-processable relationships between nodes/entities. Semantic Web is where future Web development is heading. By changing the ways in which computers and applications interpret links, the Web is opened to new possibilities for connections, and thus doors open in the creation of hypermedia that go beyond simple HTML links. Semantic Web allows for the possibility of generating new social networks that can create intelligent connections between networks and friends of friends (FoF). Current uses include the feature on Facebook that suggests adding friends based on other friends' associations. Semantic Web allows for more dynamic and real-time connections as machines process information on demand. A semantic Web is a more social Web that allows for new connections across the entire Web while allowing people to have more control over their privacy.

Research shows that gender plays a crucial role in perceptions and uses of hypermedia. As Semantic Web and future uses of hypermedia are explored, attention to gender is crucial. Despite new opportunities for publishing and relationships made possible by new technologies, it is essential that we pay further attention to the differences between male and female modes of navigation. Gender needs to be examined as a factor crucial to adaptability within hypermedia systems.

Megan Jean Harlow
European Graduate School, Switzerland

See also Audiences: Producers of New Media; Barthes, Roland; Cyberspace and Cyberculture; Cyborg; Feminist Theory: Postcolonial; New Media; Patriarchy; Polysemic Text; Postmodernism; Post-Structuralism; Reception Theory; Social Media; Social Networking Sites: Facebook; Social Networking Sites: Myspace; Textual Analysis; Twitter; Web 2.0; Wiki

Further Readings

Haraway, Donna. "A Cyborg Manifesto: Science, Technology, and Socialist-Feminism in the Late Twentieth Century." In *Simians, Cyborgs, and Women: The Reinvention of Nature*. New York: Routledge, 1991.

Jackson, Shelley. *Patchwork Girl*. 1995. http://www .eastgate.com/catalog/PatchworkGirl.html (Accessed February 2011).

Joyce, Rosemary A. and Ruth E. Tringham. "Feminist Adventures in Hypertext." *Journal of Archaeological Method and Theory*, v.14 (2007).

Landow, George P. *Hypertext Theory*. Baltimore, MD: The Johns Hopkins University Press, 1994.

Lowe, David and Wendy Hall. *Hypermedia and the Web: An Engineering Approach*. New York: John Wiley and Sons, 1998.

Protopsaltis, A. and V. Bouki. "Does Gender Matter in Hypertext Reading?" In *Proceedings of World Conference on Educational Multimedia, Hypermedia and Telecommunications 2008*, J. Luca and E. Weippl, eds. Chesapeake, VA: AACE, 2008.

IDENTITY

Identity is a term widely used in various disciplines in the social sciences, including gender and media studies. Broadly speaking, identity refers to our sense of who we are and our relationship to the world. It describes a person's conception of "self" and the expression of her or his individuality or group affiliations, such as national, ethnic, and cultural identities.

Specifically, the term identity can be conceptualized with respect to two different aspects, namely, personal identity and social identity. Personal identity refers to the idiosyncrasies that make a person unique, including personality traits, personal values, opinions, physical characteristics, and career and lifestyle choices. On the other hand, social identity refers to the collection of group memberships that define the individual, including one's social roles, such as gender, racial, religious, political, ideological, and national. In general, these social roles involve establishing ways that a person's identity is similar to others, such as sharing a physical characteristic, speaking the same language or dialect, enjoying a similar social class, and practicing the same religion. However, the two uses of the term *identity* are not mutually exclusive, and some disciplines may combine both concepts when discussing one's identity. Also, in some cases, *subjectivity* and *identity* are used interchangeably by some researchers, whereby the former refers to the conscious and unconscious thoughts and emotions of the individual, including one's sense of self.

An important concept related to identity is identity construction, which is an ongoing process of negotiation between the individual and the social context and environment, particularly cultural and power relations. It is believed that through communications and interactions with others, people negotiate and co-construct their conceptions of themselves and the world around them. In particular, the activities and contexts are imbued with and represent certain values and ideologies that privilege particular practices over others, and these activities constantly shape the dynamics of the interactions through which people display who they are to one another. Despite the dynamic nature of interactions, identity construction involves the development of a sense of sameness, continuity, and unity. In philosophical terms, personal identity refers to the extent to which an individual's characteristics remain unchanged over time. In other words, identity is seen as establishing a set of conditions that define a person's stable uniqueness. As such, most social science researchers accept that identity is something that develops over time, necessitates certain levels of organization and integration, and is achieved through the resolution of certain personal or social conflicts. On the other hand, the inability to accomplish some degree of identity coherence is thought to be an indication of psychological, social, or cultural problems.

Identity construction is also thought to involve an individual's commitment to a set of values and goals associated with specific characteristics. For instance, much of personal identity entails identifying one's unique features and establishing the value of those features. Social identity, on the other hand, presumes an awareness of one's group memberships, as well as a certain degree of commitment and emotional attachment to those groups. Indeed, people can either claim or resist membership of certain social groups. They can also choose to define who they are by deciding whether or not to construct themselves as credible members of a particular social group. In short, identity development is closely tied up with how people think about themselves and how they determine which aspects of their lived experiences are most significant as they define themselves.

Since the 1990s, much of the research on identity in sociology and psychology has moved away from a relatively static, essentialist paradigm to a more dynamic social constructionist approach that emphasizes the ways in which individuals construct their identities in interaction. As a highly complex and multifaceted issue, identity is seen as something we actively and publicly accomplish through discourse and other everyday activities. Specifically, identity is seen as a social performance that is achieved by making use of appropriate discursive and material resources. In the field of gender studies, for example, instead of assigning women and men to predetermined biological or social categories, researchers have focused on the ways in which people "do" gender—the ways in which they move, dress, and speak. Each individual is thought to constantly negotiate the norms, behaviors, and discourses that define masculinity and femininity for a particular community at a particular point in history. In short, gender identity is not seen as a given, but as an accomplishment; it is not conceptualized as something we are born with, but something we do and perform. It should be noted, however, that while performance of gender identity is available to everyone, there are constraints on who can perform which personae with impunity, since society always matches up certain gendered ways of behaving with the biological sex assignment.

Chit Cheung Matthew Sung
Lancaster University

See also Avatar; Cyborg; Empowerment; Gender and Femininity: Motherhood; Gender and Femininity: Single/Independent Girl; Gender and Masculinity: Black Masculinity; Gender and Masculinity: Fatherhood; Gender and Masculinity: Metrosexual Male; Gender and Masculinity: White Masculinity; Gender Embodiment; Gender Media Monitoring; Gender Schema Theory; Online New Media: GLBTQ Identity; Online New Media: Transgender Identity; *Second Life*; Sexuality; Social Construction of Gender; Stereotypes

Identity is not thought of as something we are born with but as an ongoing process of definition and examination of oneself in one's environment and in comparison to others. (Photos.com)

Further Readings

Blair, Maud and Janet Holland (with Sue Sheldon), eds. *Identity and Diversity: Gender and the Experience of Education*. Bristol, PA: Multilingual Matters, 1995.

Brockmeier, Jens and Donal Carbaugh. *Narrative and Identity: Studies in Autobiography, Self and Culture*. Philadelphia, PA: John Benjamins, 2001.

Butler, Judith. *Gender Trouble: Feminism and the Subversion of Identity*. New York: Routledge, 1990.

Du Gay, Paul, Jessica Evans, and Peter Redman, eds. *Identity: A Reader*. London: Sage, 2000.

Weedon, Chris. *Identity and Culture*. New York: Open University Press, 2004.

Woodward, Kath. *Questioning Identity: Gender, Class, Ethnicity*. London: Routledge, 2004.

IDEOLOGY

Ideology is one of the most discussed concepts in critical theory and in social sciences in general. The concept of ideology is highly contested: While classical Marxists argue that ideology is an objective reality that results from unequal class relations, neo-Marxists argue that ideology is created and maintained in superstructure institutions, such as schools, prisons, and media. Cultural studies scholars are interested in understanding how languages are used to create and to maintain ideology. Drawing on cultural studies theorists, feminists aim to find out how the media construct gender ideology for the audience and how the audience uses gender ideology to extract meaning from media texts.

The word *ideology* was first coined by the French philosopher Destut de Tracy in 1796 to describe the study of ideas. He believed that all ideas are derived from a perception of the physical world. His science of ideas is composed of three parts: ideology, general grammar, and logic. Napoleon later used the word *ideologues* to ridicule intellectual opponents during his regime, hence giving ideology a negative meaning. De Tracy's concept of ideology, however, did not influence the contemporary understanding of the term.

In *German Ideology*, Karl Marx and Friedrich Engels argued that ideology is used as a mask to distort real social relationships that emerged within the context of industrial capitalism. For them, the mode of production differentiated the ruling class from the working class. The working class sold their labor to capitalists in exchange for wages. Labor was said to be the only capital that the working class had in the market. The capitalists did not share the profits with the workers, instead, they reinvested the profits to buy more labor and machines. Marx saw the market as a sphere of appearances. For workers who sold their labor, the market was a reality because it dictated how much the labor was worth. Marx did not think that the ruling class deliberately "duped" the working class into a false reality, but the objectivity of the market created a false sense of reality. Engels used the term *false consciousness* to describe the beliefs that the ruling class and the working class had about social relations. The working class believed that they were subordinated because the only capital they had was their own labor. They did not believe that their intellect could be a form of capital. At the same time, the belief of the ruling class—that they were destined to rule because they had greater intellect and skills—also was a form of false consciousness.

Marx's concept of ideology was later modified by neo-Marxists, such as the French philosopher Louis Althusser and the Italian philosopher Antonio Gramsci. In the face of rising fascism in Europe, Althusser and Gramsci re-conceptualized Marx's economic determinist notion of ideology. Neo-Marxists rejected the idea that the economic sphere (the base) determines other spheres in the superstructure, such as society, politics, and religion. They believed that ideology is created and maintained in the superstructure. Althusser used the term *ideological state apparatuses* to explain how ideology works. Althusser agreed that the army, the police, and the prison are institutions that stabilize society by controlling social disorder. However, it cannot be overlooked that the school, the society, and the church are also institutions that maintain social order. By spreading the dominant ideology through an "apparatus" like the media, the state can control the society more successfully than it could merely by relying on repressive force. Althusser also coined the term *interpellation* to explain the process of understanding an ideology. In the process of interpellation, the subject recognizes that he or she is being addressed by an authority figure. For example, if a teacher asks a student to stand up in the classroom and the student does so, the student has recognized himself or herself as the subject of the address. The student thus understands the ideology that the teacher is the authority and hence should be obeyed. If a fellow student asks the same student to stand up in the classroom, the student probably will not acknowledge the request and hence deny being the subject of the address. Similarly, when audience members recognize that an advertisement addresses them, they acknowledge themselves as the subject of the ideology.

Gramsci, another neo-Marxist, coined the term *hegemony* to explain how the dominant ideology works. Gramsci differentiated the state from the civil society in the superstructure. Whereas the state maintains ideology through instruments such as laws and regulations, the civil society maintains ideology by circulating ideas and values in venues such as schools, arts, and the media. Gramsci believed that the ideology of the state and that of the civil society reinforce each other. As a result, ideology appears to be "common sense." For example, homosexuality used to be considered a mental illness, so it was a "common sense" for homosexuals to be cured in mental institutions.

Althusser's and Gramsci's definitions of ideology were popularized by the Centre for Contemporary Cultural Studies at the University of Birmingham in the 1970s. In the wake of Margaret Thatcher's neoliberal economic policies (which adhered to a philosophy that the state should open up more markets in which the private sector could compete), critical media scholars such as Stuart Hall and David Morley wanted to understand how the media reinforced the dominant ideology of Thatcher's Tory government. In addition to borrowing concepts from neo-Marxists, they borrowed concepts from structuralists (such as Claude Lévi-Strauss), post-structuralists (such as Roland Barthes and Michel Foucault), and psychoanalysts (such as Jacques Lacan). Hall believes that language is essential to maintain and to stabilize a particular form of power and domination. Hall rejected Marx's economically deterministic notion of ideology. He believed that ideas cannot be reduced to economic contents. It is only through language, Hall argued, that thoughts can be represented. Precisely because language has the transformative power to reinforce a dominant ideology, it also has the power to critique and overturn that ideology. For this reason, Hall found Foucault's notion of power useful. Foucault believed that power does not always work from a top-down direction; it instead circulates in multiple directions. For example, it is not only the state that has the power over its people; individuals in society can also assert power over one another.

Critical scholars use textual analysis (such as semiotic analysis), discourse analysis (such as narrative analysis), and interviewing (including ethnography) to uncover the ideology of the media. One famous study is Judith Williamson's *Decoding Advertisements* (1978). Drawing on structuralism and Marxist concepts of use value and exchange value, Williamson argues that advertising is a superstructure that creates a structure of meanings. She suggested that in the advertising system, an object becomes a certain kind of person. For example, a bottle of Chanel No. 5 perfume *is* Catherine Deneuve. Consumers are made to believe that by using Chanel No. 5, they will be as elegant as Deneuve. The problem arises when individuals come to identify themselves as consumers rather than as producers in the market. The ideology that "a working-class woman who uses Chanel perfume would instantly be like Deneuve" perpetuates unequal social relations because workers will no longer focus on unfair working conditions and will care only about what they can buy with their wages. The use value of advertising in a capitalist society is then to fulfill social needs for individuals, to give them a sense of belonging. However, this sense of belonging is false; although workers may buy brand-name products, they will not be economically powerful as a result of their consumption. In addition, they are less likely to struggle against the ruling class because they falsely believe that they can possess the same things the ruling class possesses.

Feminists of different schools of thought commonly agree that gender ideology exists. However, they cannot agree on what the definition of ideology is, what the roots of ideology are, and how to end ideology. Marxist and socialist feminisms are both grounded in Marxism. Marxist feminists believe that women are oppressed in a capitalist society because men see women as property. On the other hand, socialist feminists see both capitalism and patriarchy as oppressing women. Women's oppression will not end until both capitalism and patriarchy are abolished. Michele Barrett argues that the function of ideology is to legitimize unequal social relations. For example, women are told that their quantitative aptitude is less than men's; girl children are told by the media that only unattractive girls are good at mathematics and sciences. As a result, women are less likely to be in the high-paying STEM (science, technology, engineering, and mathematics) professions. Hence, women will earn less than men even though, in the United States, more women than men attend colleges.

Liberal feminists do not usually highlight gender ideology in their discussion of gender inequality. They believe that laws and regulations can be enacted to ensure equal opportunities for women in education and in the workplace. However, Betty Friedan, one of the founding mothers of liberal feminism in the United States, did recognize the gender ideology that upper-class, white housewives faced in the United States in the 1960s and the 1970s. She talked about the isolation that housewives felt and the depression from which they suffered. The belief that women's place is the home was a gender ideology that worked to subordinate women to men.

In feminist media research, gender ideology is one of the most often discussed and contested areas. Since the 1970s, a plethora of studies have quantified gender stereotypes in the media (particularly in advertising). These studies imply that gender ideology resides in the media texts. The audience is supposed to be influenced by the media to a similar degree. Therefore, these studies advocate for fairer and more balanced gender representation. It is believed that reality will be altered if there is a change in media representation. The growing popularity of audience research and post-structuralist feminism since the 1990s has prompted scholars to examine audiences' subjectivity in consuming media. Those scholars believe that audience members bring in their own gender ideology to understand media texts. Whereas some audience members may use the dominant ideology to read, "Blonds have more fun," other members may oppose the dominant ideology by rejecting the false association between hair color and personalities. To post-structuralist feminists, social change is possible only if the audience critically reads media texts.

Micky Lee
Suffolk University, Boston

See also Advertising; Audiences: Reception and Injection Models; Barthes, Roland; Critical Theory; Cultivation Theory; Feminist Theory: Liberal; Feminist Theory: Marxist; Feminist Theory: Socialist; Hall, Stuart; Hegemony; Patriarchy; Post-Structuralism; Semiotics; Social Inequality; Textual Analysis

Further Readings

Althusser, Louis. *For Marx*. London: Verso, 1976.

Barrett, Michele. *Women's Oppression Today: The Marxist/ Feminist Encounter*. New York: Verso, 1988.

Barthes, Roland. *Mythologies*. London: Jonathan Cape, 1972.

Eagleton, Terry. *Ideology: An Introduction*. New York: Verso, 2007.

Foucault, Michel. *The Archaeology of Knowledge*. New York: Harper and Row, 1976.

Friedan, Betty. *The Feminine Mystique*. 1963. Reprint, New York: W. W. Norton, 2001.

Gramsci, Antonio. *Prison Notebooks*. New York: Columbia University Press, 1996.

Hall, Stuart. "The Problem of Ideology: Marxism Without Guarantee." In *Stuart Hall: Critical Dialogues in Cultural Studies*, David Morley and Kuan-Hsing Chen, eds. London: Routledge, 1996.

Hall, Stuart. "The Television Discourse—Encoding and Decoding" *Education and Culture*, v.25 (Summer 1974).

Lacan, Jacques. *The Language of the Self: The Function of Language in Psychoanalysis*. Baltimore, MD: Johns Hopkins University Press, 1968.

Larrain, Jorge. "Stuart Hall and the Marxist Concept of Ideology." In *Stuart Hall: Critical Dialogues in Cultural Studies*, David Morley and Kuan-Hsing Chen, eds. London: Routledge, 1996.

Lévi-Strauss, Claude. *The Elementary Structures of Kinship*. Boston: Beacon Press, 1969.

Marx, Karl and Friedrich Engels. *German Ideology, Part 1, and Selections From Parts 2 and 3*. New York: International Publishers, 1970.

McRobbie, Angela. *Jackie: An Ideology of Adolescent Femininity*. Birmingham, UK: Centre for Contemporary Cultural Studies, University of Birmingham, 1977.

Morley, David. *The* Nationwide *Audience: Structure and Decoding*. London: British Film Institute, 1980.

Williamson, Judith. *Decoding Advertisements*. London: Marion Boyars, 1978.

INTERSECTIONALITY

Intersectionality is a theoretical response to traditional feminist claims that a single analytical category, that of "woman," is a lens through which all women can politically and socially unite. Feminists often argue that women have shared experiences and thus should rally around the category. Advocates of intersectionality reject the notion that women share a single experience, contend that identity politics frequently conflate or ignore intragroup differences, and highlight the limits of "woman" as a single point of convergence.

Intersectionality, as an analytical tool, was first articulated by African American women as a means to correct the omissions of historians in feminism theory. It is premised on the notion that identity categories do not act independently of one another but rather interconnect. While originally theorized in the interest of women of color, intersectionality is a reconceptualization of identity that has been expanded to include a variety of marginalized identities. Thus, socially constructed dimensions of identity, including, but not limited to, gender, race, class, sexuality, and nationality, are understood as interconnected components that make up individuals. While gender and race, for example, are often read as independent markers, intersectionality theorists critically consider how and what ways these social, political, and culturally constructed categories interact. Contemporary feminist theorists, such as Leslie McCall, argue that intersectionality is the most important theatrical contribution to the field of women's studies to date.

Intersectionality as a concept gained traction in the 1960s and 1970s, when black women found themselves divided between, and often ignored by, the antiracism and antipatriarchy movements. While black feminist scholar bell hooks gestures back to black female speakers like Anna Copper (1893) and Sojourner Truth (1851), women of color fighting for civil rights found themselves left out of agendas of both women and men of color. Intersectionality originated as an effort of black feminists in the United States to theorize their experiences and identity. Black women's social and political life could not be differentiated into race and gender but rather needed to be considered holistically as those of black women. Women of color highlighted the racism embedded in many women's movements and the patriarchal politics of the antiracism organizations. They argued that white, often middle-class, women were not serving the interests of black women and that black men did little to address the issues of black women. Intersectional agendas that addressed the unique concerns of women of color claimed to re-envision feminism in a way that critically considered the matrixes of oppression with and among both race and gender. It was not enough to act simultaneously by adding together the concerns of women and race. Rather, intersectionality encourages theoretical considerations of the spaces between and within groups.

While the civil rights era played an important role in the development of intersectional politics, *intersectionality* as a term was coined by Kimberlé Crenshaw in 1989. Crenshaw highlights the fact that women's race and class play an interconnected role in their experiences. Thus, rather than ignoring the differences between women, a tactic that often results in conflict, theories of intersectionality resist relegating experiences as either racist or sexist and accept that each black woman's experience is unique, distinct, and different. Furthermore, the political agendas of women and race are often at odds with one another. Racism is experienced differently by women, and patriarchy affects race in unique ways. Advocates of intersectionality argue individuals' lives cannot be explained by adding up theories of oppression (racism and patriarchy, for example), but rather need to be explained through an intersectional perspective. These promoters believe that if intersectionality is ignored, groups' emancipatory agendas will be undermined. Since oppression cuts across identity categories, antiracism groups that ignore the interests of women of color, for example, will serve only to subordinate members of their constituency. Likewise, if feminists do not account for intersectional experiences, their agenda is likely to be plagued with racist politics. Intersectionality rejects "doubling" or "tripling" discourses that claim that understanding queer Latina women, for example, is possible by adding together the experiences of Latina and queer women. Instead, intersectionality is premised on the belief that identity is created through fluid matrixes of privilege and domination—yet it is this very conceptualization of identity that grounds its harshest critics.

Intersectionality faces at least two strands of criticism. The first pushes for more categorization, whereas the second aims to abolish categorization altogether. First, critics of intersectionality argue that privileging difference rather than similarities will splinter and weaken political and social groups. Too much splintering, they argue, will leave people alone, without allies to support them. These first critics contend that if each social position is relegated to its own axis, there will be no effective group coalescence. The second group of intersectionality critics pushes in the other direction, arguing that a consideration of intersections does not go far enough, because it maintains and may even reinforce identity politics. Identity politics, these critics argue, rests on the presumption that there is a norm or center from which the disenfranchised identity group emerges as Other. That group, by opposing itself to a center, is thus only strengthening its oppressor. The second group of critics calls for a rejection of categories altogether.

Efforts to move beyond both strands of intersectionality criticism have been waged by post-structural scholars who argue on behalf of maintaining political categories of identity, while recognizing that identity is neither stable nor foundational. In this perspective, contingent groups can still rally around commonalities while recognizing the limits of their categorical agenda. The antifoundational group viewpoint considers context, recognizing that hierarchies, positions of privilege, and oppression may be more politicized in some environments than in others.

McCall, in her 2005 article "The Complexity of Intersectionality," suggests moving beyond the challenges of intersectionality by offering three categorical approaches: anticategorical, intercategorical, and intracategorical. The anticategorical complexity aims to deconstruct analytical categories and is premised on the belief that social life is too complex and fluid to use fixed categories. Fixed categories only simplify identity and produce further inequalities by focusing on difference. Instead, this perspective focuses on a holistic method of studying intersectionality without categories. The intercategorical complexity recognizes that inequality exists and aims to study how it functions and moves by using categories and studying them over time. Finally, the intracategorical complexity, like the anticategorical, rejects categories but, like the intercategorical, uses them strategically while always accounting for the fact that categories are ever-changing. The approach recognizes that categories change and are always and already in a state of flux yet aims to critically consider the categories strategically at any moment in time.

In the end, the debate over how best to recognize the multidimensionality of identity, while contingently deploying inclusive categories of experience as a rallying point for change, continues. Yet the contributions of intersectional theorists have moved feminists well beyond the limitations of single-axis frameworks.

Rae Lynn Schwartz-DuPre
Western Washington University

See also Cultural Politics; Feminist Theory: Women-of-Color and Multiracial Perspectives; hooks, bell; Identity; Minority Rights; Patriarchy; Racism; Social Construction of Gender

Further Readings

Crenshaw, Kimberlé. "Demarginalizing the Intersection of Race and Sex: A Black Feminist Critique of Antidiscrimination Doctrine, Feminist Theory and Antiracist Politics." *University of Chicago Legal Forum*, v.122 (1989).

hooks, bell. *Ain't I a Woman: Black Women and Feminism*. Boston: South End Press, 1981.

McCall, Leslie. "The Complexity of Intersectionality." *Signs: Journal of Women in Culture and Society*, v.30/3 (2005).

Jenkins, Henry

Henry Jenkins (1958–), a media studies scholar and self-proclaimed aca-fan (academic/fanatic), is best known for his concept of convergence culture, which describes the late 20th- and early 21st-century phenomenon of old media living alongside new or digital media. Throughout his academic career, Jenkins has focused largely on studying audiences, fans, and participatory culture. Jenkins is a proponent of media education and encouraging media literacies, and he is an advocate for video games, countering the much-publicized discussion of media effects that puts the blame on violent media (especially video games) for such events as the Columbine massacre. Nearly central to his questions surrounding media are questions of gender and sexuality, which guide many of his research projects.

Jenkins received his M.A. in communication studies from Iowa State University and finished his Ph.D. in communication arts at the University of Wisconsin–Madison. He was for many years the codirector of the comparative media studies program at the Massachusetts Institute of Technology (MIT), which he helped create. In 2009, Jenkins became provost professor of communication, journalism, and cinematic arts at the University of Southern California's Annenberg School for Communication and School of Cinematic Arts.

One of Jenkins's first important interventions in the field of media studies was his breaking down of the barrier between text and reader/audience/fan.

In his 1992 book *Textual Poachers: Television Fans and Participatory Culture*, Jenkins noted that fans wanting more story lines and content within their favorite franchise or set of texts would often produce their own stories in various genres that extended the narrative arc of certain episodic texts, seasons, or the entire franchise. Fan cultures produced texts based on the gaps or abandoned story lines found within a franchise. Jenkins, in this book and in other essays, has noted how fans have latched onto these lapses in media storytelling and have produced their own media products that extend the original narrative while following certain rules established by the original narrative. Jenkins uses the term *world-making* to note the creation of a fictional world that allows all of these texts, along with the canonical source material, to live within a logical, harmonic fan ecosystem. Thus, the worlds that fans create allow for contradictory narratives to coexist, as long as the canonical narrative stays intact and drives the logic of the fan productions. Jenkins examines the ways that fans interact with texts based on their expectations of genre, narrative, and franchise content. He also notes the wide variety of media that are used for fans' productive energies: fan fiction, music videos, music, and more. He explores the ways in which these productive acts have allowed for fans to consider themselves as a strong community.

Much of Jenkins's work has centered on the texts that have attracted large fan communities and the various ways these texts can be read and reappropriated by these communities and individual fans. In his analysis of participatory culture, Jenkins notes the

Henry Jenkins in a 2008 photo. Jenkins studies media and created the concept of convergence culture—the intersection of old and new media, grassroots and corporate media, and the dual powers of media producers and consumers. (Wikimedia/Joi Ito)

prominence of women participants and the trend of "slash fiction," the imagining of a text's characters in same-sex romantic or sexual situations that are not found in the canonical text. Jenkins also noted the importance of fan interaction with producers in his pre-Internet study of the queer community's demands for queer story lines in *Star Trek*, which the producers made concessions to by including implicitly queer story lines.

Though much of his early research on fan communities was based on old media and predigital methods of communicating, Jenkins has noted the great effect the Internet and new media have had on fan communities. He has noted that the early Internet, which networked only research laboratories primarily on university campuses, allowed for mostly male fan communities within those arenas to gather and talk about media texts such as *Twin Peaks*. He has also been concerned by the ways fan communities have created a collective knowledge of media texts and franchises, which could be seen in the early Internet era with *Twin Peaks*, where videocassette recorders were used to find small details in the television text. This phenomenon was epitomized in the fan-created wiki pages for several media texts, especially the television show *Lost*. In *Convergence Culture* (2006), Jenkins notes how, as new media have come to live next to old, media producers have begun to realize the importance of or potential profit

to be made in creating large transmedia worlds, where the narrative of the story is explored, much as in fan fiction, in various ways and in various media. Jenkins is a part of the Convergence Culture Consortium, which intends to make inroads between media scholars and the media industries.

In 1998, Jenkins published with Justine Cassell a collection of essays and interviews about gender and computer games, *From Barbie to Mortal Kombat*. These essays did much to expand the scope of critical attention of video games to girl and women gamers. Jenkins, who has testified on behalf of video games in the face of their criticism from the news media and lawmakers, writes about the gendered spaces of video-game worlds in this collection. At MIT, Jenkins worked on the Education Arcade, which explored ways to use video games in educational ways.

Jenkins has become increasingly fascinated by the ways that new media offer the public new modes to become involved in a participatory culture within the context of political activism and democracy writ large. He frequently blogs about these and other issues on his blog, Confessions of an Aca-Fan.

Bryce J. Renninger
Rutgers University

See also Audiences: Producers of New Media; Media Convergence; New Media; Online New Media: GLBTQ Identity; Online New Media: Transgender Identity; *Second Life*; Social Media; Twitter; Video Gaming: Violence; YouTube

Further Readings

Cassell, Justine and Henry Jenkins, eds. *From Barbie to Mortal Kombat: Gender and Computer Games.* Cambridge, MA: MIT Press, 1998.

Jenkins, Henry. *Convergence Culture: Where Old and New Media Collide.* New York: New York University Press, 2006.

Jenkins, Henry. *Textual Poachers: Television Fans and Participatory Culture.* New York: Routledge, 1992.

JERVIS, LISA

Lisa Jervis (1972–) is a prominent writer and feminist activist, widely acknowledged for her work in the areas of media advocacy and reform and her work in independent media. She is perhaps best known as the founding editor and publisher of the zine-cum-magazine *Bitch: Feminist Response to Pop Culture*. She also has served as a founding board chair of Women in Media and News, a group targeting media analysis, education, reform, and outreach, as a member of the advisory board of outLoud Radio, as the finance and operations director at the Center for Media Justice, and as an editor at large for *LiP: Informed Revolt*, an alternative magazine that started as a zine in Chicago. Her commentary has appeared in numerous print and online publications, including *Ms.*, the *San Francisco Chronicle*, *Mother Jones*, *Bust*, *Utne*, and *Salon*. Her work has been published in books such as *Body Outlaws* (2000), *The Bust Guide to the New Girl Order* (1999), *Tipping the Sacred Cow* (2007), and *Yes Means Yes: Visions of Sexual Power and a World Without Rape* (2008). Jervis has also coedited both *Young Wives' Tales: New Adventures in Love and Partnership* (2001), a collection of contemporary, personal feminist writings on love and relationships, and *Bitchfest: Ten Years of Cultural Criticism From the Pages of* Bitch *Magazine* (2006), which was published in honor of the tenth anniversary of *Bitch*. Both Jervis and commentators situate her as an active participant in the movement toward a type of protest that operates outside the confines of traditional activism. Using popular culture as the locus of action, she sees her work in media literacy and reform as inherently political.

Jervis was born in Boston in the early 1970s and spent a portion of her childhood in Los Angeles before moving to New York City at the age of eight. She graduated from Oberlin College in 1994, with a major in English and a minor in creative writing, and interned with her *Bitch* cofounder Andi Zeisler at the now defunct but much-heralded teen magazine *Sassy*. Chronologically, she is part of feminism's third wave, a term Jervis herself notes is helpful in situating herself as part of a movement at a particular time but that falls short in conceptualizing the scope and nuance of beliefs and approaches among feminists of her generation.

Jervis's work is an outgrowth of her belief in popular culture as an important site of feminist activism and emblematic of "indie" movements within progressive communities. It is in her work with *Bitch* that both of these notions collide. Attempting to engage in a more public way with their self-defined love/hate relationship with popular culture, high

school friends Jervis and Zeisler (with Benjamin Shaykin signing on to design) founded *Bitch* in 1996 in the San Francisco Bay Area, distributing the first 300 copies from the back of Jervis's station wagon. Inspired by various other outlets such as *Ms.* and *Sassy* and the burgeoning zine culture, the magazine was designed to be a feminist critique of mediated products, featuring columns, interviews, and reported pieces that analyzed representations of gender and feminist politics in various media.

Both Jervis, who stepped down as publisher in 2006, and Zeisler state that *Bitch* was born out of their own desire to read critical feminist engagements with popular culture that were accessible and fun. They also sought to dismantle the notion that popular culture is too ephemeral to be the subject of serious feminist criticism. Following in the footsteps of other do-it-yourself (DIY) movements, the creation of *Bitch* was based in the notion that if one cannot find what one is looking for in the culture, one should create it. Embracing a zine ethos in content and wrapped in a shiny magazine package, *Bitch* still stands out from other zine-like creations in its layout and overall look, which over the years has appeared slicker and more mainstream and magazine-like than its contemporaries. The magazine has grown to 50,000 readers and maintains a strong Web presence, with 8,000 daily visits to the Website http://www.bitchmedia.org.

While *Bitch* is perhaps her best-known foray into the world of independent media as political protest, Jervis has carried a similar outlook to her other work with independent media and advocacy organizations. Through these projects, she has continued to support and create content that operates outside corporate media structures and advocates for disenfranchised voices and perspectives not normally accounted for in mainstream news or popular culture. As with *Bitch*, Jervis is a staunch advocate of both interrogating media power and creating media to fill the voids she sees, which, for her, is a personal project as well as a larger political one. In much of her work, Jervis has stated that her goal is to reach a larger audience, which has placed her somewhat at odds with some other members of progressive communities, who situate mainstream success as "selling out" and a rejection of the politics of DIY.

Jervis published *Cook Food: A Manualfesto for Easy, Healthy, Local Eating* in 2009. This DIY guide to eating sustainable, healthy food she describes as part vegan cookbook and part dissection of the politics of food.

Theresa Rose Crapanzano
University of Colorado, Boulder

See also E-Zines: Riot Grrrl; E-Zines: Third Wave Feminist; Feminist Theory: Third Wave; Gender Media Monitoring; Media Literacy; Women's Magazines: Feminist Magazines

Further Readings

Bitch Media. http://www.bitchmagazine.org (Accessed February 2011).

Corrall, Jill and Lisa Miya-Jervis, eds. *Young Wives' Tales: New Adventures in Love and Partnership*. Seattle, WA: Seal Press, 2001.

Jervis, Lisa. *Cook Food: A Manualfesto for Easy, Healthy, Local Eating*. Oakland, CA: PM Press, 2009.

Jervis, Lisa and Andi Zeisler, eds. *Bitchfest: Ten Years of Cultural Criticism From the Pages of* Bitch *Magazine*. New York: Farrar, Straus and Giroux, 2006.

Piepmeier, Alison. *Girl Zines Making Media, Doing Feminism*. New York: New York University Press, 2009.

Spencer, Amy. *DIY: The Rise of Lo-Fi Culture*. London: Marion Boyars, 2008.

Women in Media and News. http://www.wimnonline.org (Accessed February 2011).

JHALLY, SUT

Satvider "Sut" Jhally (1955–) is professor of communication at the University of Massachusetts at Amherst and is the founder of the Media Education Foundation. He is known for his research, publications, and films on gender, race, and identity construction through the advertising and public media.

Jhally was born in Kenya, raised and educated in England at the University of York, and moved to Canada, where he earned both his second master's degree and his Ph.D. in communications. In 1985, he became a professor of communication at the University of Massachusetts at Amherst, and in 1991 he founded the Media Education Foundation (MEF), an organization of which he became the executive director. Jhally has focused his career on media criticism and the construction of identity—gendered, racial, sexual, and national—as it is presented through popular culture and the media.

Known as a third wave gender scholar, Sut Jhally is known as an expert on cultural studies, advertising, media, and consumption. (Wikimedia/Chris Moriarty)

Much of his work began as material to use in his own classes at the University of Massachusetts, yet his impact has stretched beyond that to engage with scholars specializing in a multitude of foci in gender and identity construction.

Jhally's early publications focus specifically on advertising, grounded in semiotic analysis and particularly the work of Roland Barthes, Judith Williamson, and notably Erving Goffman. Goffman became a mainstay of Jhally's theoretical framework in later work; Jhally was interested in both Goffman's work in his 1979 *Gender Advertisements*, an analysis of advertising, and Goffman's lifelong focus on the performativity of meaning. This sociological approach is based in the symbolic interactionist school, which articulates an approach to the study of individual/institutional interaction from the perspective that individuals create meaning from the events they see and in which they participate. Jhally's own first monograph, published in 1987, takes his concern with advertising as one of understanding the relationship between culture and economy. This interaction brings in what would become his increasing concern for media as a locus for representing popular culture within Western societies.

As Jhally's work at the Media Education Foundation progressed through the 1990s, he produced, and frequently wrote and directed, documentaries with other media scholars analyzing the construction of meaning in advertising. The analysis of gender became the clear focus of this work in the *Dreamworlds* films produced in 1990, 1995, and 2007. Two films, *Slim Hopes: Advertising and the Obsession With Thinness* (1995) and *Red Moon: Menstruation, Culture and the Politics of Gender* (2009), are part of MEF's media and health series of documentaries, many of which focus on the impact of gender construction on health issues as related to self-image, the stigma attached to menstruation, eating disorders, and the impact of tobacco and alcohol advertising on both men and women. In the films *Killing Us Softly: Advertising's Image of Women III* (2000) and *IV* (2010, both with gender scholar Jean Kilbourne) and *The Codes of Gender: Identity + Performance in Pop Culture* (2009), Jhally as the driving force addresses the representations of women in media, specifically advertising, music videos, and film. He is equally concerned with the construction of sexuality in the films *Off the Straight and Narrow* (1998) and *Further Off the Straight and Narrow* (2006), both concerning the gay, lesbian, bisexual, transsexual/transgender (GLBT) community, as well as gender constructions that work against social and cultural norms in the film *Playing Unfair: The Media Image of the Female Athlete* (2002). Both of these issues are also undercurrents throughout his films addressing gender constructions.

Jhally, like many third wave gender scholars, demonstrates equal interest in the study of masculinity and its constructions and representations, as seen in his films *Tough Guise: Violence, Media, and the Crisis in Masculinity* (1999), and *Wrestling With Manhood: Boys, Bullying and Battering* (2002), which is concerned with WWE professional wrestling. *Tough Guise* focuses on the relationship between gender representation and state-sponsored violence, combining Jhally's longtime concerns with both gender representations and politics. Jhally also considers alternative constructions of sexuality, as in his *Off the Straight and Narrow: Gays, Lesbians, Bisexuals and Television* (1998), and of race and religion, both in their stereotyped manifestations through advertising and in their more complex representations in politics.

While Jhally spent most of the 1990s devoting his energies to MEF, he also published many articles during that decade, which expanded on issues presented in his films, as well as a single monograph focusing on the role of race in the media (1992), an analysis of *The Cosby Show* as an opportunity to explore contemporary conceptions of racism as presented on television. In the first decade of the 21st century, he returned to publishing books (both monographs and edited volumes), continuing his focus on the role of media in public life, notably his 2004 edited volume examining the impact of the September 11, 2001, bombing of the World Trade Center in New York City and an updated collection (2006) of his essays and research into the relationship of media, popular culture, and politics. Throughout his career, Jhally has consistently explored issues related to both female and male identification, leading him to be identified by Chris Boulton as one of the leading contemporary "male feminists" whose work is frequently cited by radical feminists as a mechanism for reconstructing media spaces. Through his work as producer, writer, and director on MEF films, his approach to the study of gender representation in media is actively used by scholars in disciplines ranging from sociology and gender studies to anthropology, communications, and media studies, in part because of his use of the work of Goffman and its relevance to these disciplines.

J. Meryl Krieger
Indiana University–Purdue University
Indianapolis

See also Audiences: Reception and Injection Models; Berger, John; Cultural Politics; Gender and Masculinity: Black Masculinity; Gender and Masculinity: White Masculinity; Kilbourne, Jean; Media Literacy; Music Videos: Representations of Men; Music Videos: Representations of Women; Music Videos: Tropes; Tropes

Further Readings

Boulton, Chris. "Porn and Me(n): Sexual Morality, Objectification, and Religion at the Wheelock Anti-Pornography Conference." *The Communication Review*, v.11 (2008).

Chaney, David. "Review of William Leiss, Stephen Kline and Sut Jhally: *Social Communication in Advertising: Persons, Products and Images of Well-Being. 1986.*" *Theory, Culture and Society*, v.5 (1988).

Gates, Anita. "Review of Hijacking Catastrophe: A Plan to Create a New World Order." *New York Times* (September 20, 2004). http://movies.nytimes.com/2004/09/10/movies/10HIJA.html?_r=1 (Accessed November 2011).

Jhally, Sut. http://www.sutjhally.com (Accessed October 2010).

Media Education Foundation. http://www.mediaed.org/cgi-bin/commerce.cgi?display=home (Accessed October 2010).

Price, Vivian H. "War, Sex, and Resistance." *Radical History Review*, v.93 (2005).

"A Professor's Class Video Runs Into an MTV Protest." *New York Times* (May 18, 1991).

Wernick, Andrew. "Review of Sut Jhally: *The Codes of Advertising: Fetishism and the Political Economy of Meaning in the Consumer Society. 1987.*" *Theory, Culture and Society*, v.4 (1987).

KELLNER, DOUGLAS

Douglas Kellner (1943–) has blended German critical theory, French postmodernism, and British cultural studies in a syncretic mix applied to late 20th-century and early 21st-century American media and culture issues in more than 30 authored, coauthored, and edited books since the 1980s. Born in 1943 in New York City, Kellner earned a Ph.D. in philosophy from Columbia University in 1973. He was a philosophy professor at the University of Texas, Austin from 1973 to 1997 and thereafter held the George Kneller Philosophy of Education Chair at the University of California, Los Angeles. While conducting his dissertation research on the work of phenomenologist Martin Heidegger, Kellner spent two years in Germany, where he also became steeped in the work of the Frankfurt School theorists, especially Theodor Adorno, Max Horkheimer, and Herbert Marcuse, and where he attended the seminars of Ernst Bloch. Kellner then spent a year in Paris, studying the work of postmodernist thinkers Jacques Derrida, Michel Foucault, and Jean Baudrillard, among others. He became involved with British cultural studies in the 1970s, and his later work has taken a pluralistic approach drawing on all three traditions.

Kellner's books on critical theory include *Herbert Marcuse and the Crisis of Marxism* (1984) and *Critical Theory, Marxism, and Modernity* (1989). His postmodern works include *Jean Baudrillard: From Marxism to Postmodernism and Beyond* (1989) and *The Postmodern Turn* (1997, with Steven Best). Kellner's participation in a Marxist studies group in Texas led to the study of television from a Frankfurt School perspective and to a weekly public access television program, *Alternative Views*, as well as two books on television, *Television and the Crisis of Democracy* (1990) and *The Persian Gulf TV War* (1992). In these books, he intended to apply critical theory to analyze how television failed to inform the public or misinformed the public, thereby impeding democracy. He further combined cultural studies, philosophy, and critical theory in *Media Culture: Cultural Studies, Identity, and Politics Between the Modern and the Postmodern* (1995). He has described his work as the application of philosophical approaches from Marxism to feminism to the study of cultural and political issues through development of critical and political cultural studies. He has published research on new technologies and education in various venues from journals to books. His stated goal in this area is to mediate between the technologically sublime and technological horror in evaluating the impact of new technologies on education. His balancing includes basing education on book media as well as computer and multimedia material. Building on traditional print literacy, Kellner argues for adopting new technology skills in addition to those from past media cultures.

After the election of President George W. Bush in 2000, Kellner turned his attention to what he considered a major crime of the century in *Grand Theft 2000: Media Spectacle and a Stolen Election* (2001). In this and subsequent works about media in the early 21st century, Kellner analyzes how media contribute to the assault on democracy and, at the same time, how democratic media can help improve democracy. Applying a cultural studies model introduced in *Media Culture*, Kellner studies the 2000 election as a postmodern media spectacle and a traditional power struggle. He views media spectacle as entrenched in politics and culture as part of a media environment awash in a blending of information and entertainment as infotainment. In the wake of the terrorist attacks of 2001, Kellner analyzed the Bush administration's rhetoric of fear and attacks on civil liberties in the Patriot Act as examples of the politics of lying, which were, however, limited and reversible in the light of future events. Kellner also focused his media criticism on television coverage of the U.S. invasion of Iraq in 2003; he analyzes the government's propaganda, which the media duly channeled to the public, including the assertion that Iraq was concealing weapons of mass destruction. Dialectically, however, while the media helped advance President Bush's agenda, the media spectacle created by President Bush's "Mission Accomplished" slogan aboard an aircraft carrier ultimately negated the war rationale. Writing about the media and presidential election of 2004 in *Media Spectacle and the Crisis of Democracy* (2005), Kellner argued that corporate media control, the rise of infotainment and media spectacle, the emergence of conservative media propaganda, and the Bush administration media attacks and manipulations endangered democracy. Elaborating on the Frankfurt School's critique of the culture industries, Kellner identifies media spectacles as pivotal in organizing all aspects of political and cultural life. As part of a computer-networked system that sells communities and entrances consumers, media culture merges entertainment and information forms. Multimedia forms also combine radio, film, and television to create spectacles of technoculture in a symbiosis of political life and media spectacle.

Kellner has turned his attention to issues of gender as one of a complex of media issues, including ethnicity, race, class, sexuality, and power, that are not dealt with individually. He has identified feminist theory as a major contributor to media literacy, citing Carmen Luke, who links a feminist political commitment to change, and addressing media stereotypes and misrepresentations. Feminist media criticism provides a way to study subordinated people to reveal oppressive structures, as well as hegemony. Gender issues are one avenue for gaining an understanding of marginalized groups.

Paul Grosswiler
University of Maine

See also Critical Theory; Cultural Politics; Electronic Media and Social Inequality; Feminist Theory: Marxist; Hall, Stuart; Hegemony; Media Rhetoric; Postmodernism

Further Readings

Kellner, Douglas. *Grand Theft 2000: Media Spectacle and a Stolen Election*. Lanham, MD: Rowman & Littlefield, 2001.

Kellner, Douglas. *Herbert Marcuse and the Crisis of Marxism*. Berkeley: University of California Press, 1984.

Kellner, Douglas. *Jean Baudrillard: From Marxism to Postmodernism and Beyond*. Palo Alto, CA: Stanford University Press, 1989.

Kellner, Douglas. *Media Culture: Cultural Studies, Identity, and Politics Between the Modern and the Postmodern*. New York: Routledge, 1995.

Kellner, Douglas. *Media Spectacle and the Crisis of Democracy*. Boulder, CO: Paradigm Press, 2005.

Kellner, Douglas. *The Persian Gulf TV War*. Boulder, CO: Westview Press, 1992.

Kellner, Douglas. "Philosophical Adventures." http://gseis .ucla.edu/faculty/kellner/essays/philosophicadventures .pdf (Accessed December 2010).

Kellner, Douglas. *Television and the Crisis of Democracy*. Boulder, CO: Westview Press, 1990.

Kellner, Douglas and Steven Best. *The Postmodern Turn*. New York: Routledge, 1997.

KILBOURNE, JEAN

Jean Kilbourne (1943–) is a widely recognized and highly regarded feminist scholar, lecturer, and media activist who is dedicated to raising awareness about the relationship between gendered media messages, notably advertising, and a variety of public health issues, including the connection between sexualized female images and eating disorders as well as violence against women and addiction. Kilbourne began voicing her critical perspective against the objectifying representations of the female body in advertising in the late 1960s, before many other scholars and critics had begun to understand the complex relationship between media messages and audiences' conceptions of the social world. The connections Kilbourne first saw between her personal experiences and the impact of advertising messages launched her lifelong crusade to raise awareness about the effect of media messages on society, especially the ways in which society thinks and feels about women. Her work has contributed to mainstream awareness of the impact and power of media as well as a national movement intended to foster media literacy.

Kilbourne's crusade to raise awareness began when very few people took the impact of advertising seriously. She started sharing her findings by lecturing mainly on college campuses about the ways women were portrayed in the media, especially in advertising, and she began to alert audiences to the public health problem posed by media. This aspect of her work was recognized when Kilbourne was named the top campus lecturer in the country for two years in a row. Kilbourne then expanded her lectures to film through the production of educational videos. Her first film, *Killing Us Softly*, produced by the Media Education Foundation in 2000, became one of the best-selling educational videos in history, exposing thousands of students across the country to her critiques of the advertising industry's representations of gender. Kilbourne has periodically updated her groundbreaking film to keep her analyses and examples current. *Killing Us Softly IV: Advertising's Image of Women* was released in 2010.

Kilbourne and her cultural examination have also inspired the production of other educational films, including her early films *Slim Hopes: Advertising and the Obsession With Thinness* (1995), which examined the connections between advertising images and the epidemic of eating disorders among women in America, as well as *Pack of Lies* (1992), which examined the tobacco industry and its misleading advertising techniques targeted at girls and women. In addition to these, Kilbourne has been featured in films critiquing the advertising practices of the alcohol industry, including *Advertising Alcohol* (1991) and *Spin the Bottle: Sex, Lies, and Alcohol* (2004). Kilbourne also hosted the film *The Killing Screens: Media and the Culture of Violence* (1994), a critical analysis of the relationship between mediated images of violence and their impact on society with cultivation scholar George Gerbner.

In addition to her lectures and films, Kilbourne's work has also expanded into the realm of print. Her first book, *Deadly Persuasion: Why Women and Girls Must Fight the Addictive Power of Advertising* (1999), was first published in hardcover and then rereleased in paperback as *Can't Buy My Love: How Advertising Changes the Way We Think and Feel* (2000). This adept critique of the advertising industry considers the methods advertising messages use to make audiences feel as though they have connections with various products and the ways in which these relationships leave consumers feeling unfulfilled and empty. Her second book, *So Sexy So Soon: The New Sexualized Childhood and What Parents Can Do to Protect Their Kids* (2008), was coauthored by scholar Diane Levin and combines Kilbourne's earlier analyses with the work of Levin to extend into the arena of girlhood and the ways in which media messages socialize young girls into today's highly sexualized and commercial culture.

Kilbourne earned her doctorate of education from Boston University and is also an alumnus of Wellesley College, where she has been in the honorary position of visiting scholar since 1984, at the Wellesley Centers for Women. Kilbourne has also served as an adviser to Surgeons General C. Everett Coop and Antonia Novello and has testified before Congress regarding the impact of media messages on American culture. Moreover, Kilbourne has been granted numerous awards and recognitions by various organizations throughout her career, including the Academy for Eating Disorders, Planned Parenthood, and Action Coalition for Media Education (ACME). Additionally, Kilbourne has made numerous television appearances, including on *The Today Show* and *The Oprah Winfrey Show*, and has been featured in an array of mainstream publications, including the *New York Times,* the *Wall Street Journal,* the *Washington Post*, and *USA Today.* Westfield State College in Massachusetts awarded her an honorary doctorate.

Andrea M. Bergstrom
Franklin Pierce University

See also Advertising; Beauty and Body Image: Beauty Myths; Beauty and Body Image: Eating Disorders; Cultivation Theory; Gender and Femininity: Single/ Independent Girl; Jhally, Sut; Misogyny; Pornification of Everyday Life; Sexism; Social Comparison Theory; Social Construction of Gender; Toys and Games: Gender Socialization

Further Readings

Kilbourne, Jean. *Can't Buy My Love: How Advertising Changes the Way We Think and Feel*. New York: Simon & Schuster, 1999.

Kilbourne, Jean. "Jean Kilbourne." http://www .jeankilbourne.com (Accessed February 2011).

Levin, Diane and Jean Kilbourne. *So Sexy So Soon: The New Sexualized Childhood and What Parents Can Do to Protect Their Kids*. New York: Ballantine, 2008.

KRUGER, BARBARA

Barbara Kruger (1945–) is an American conceptual artist, a curator, a writer, a film critic, an editor, and a political agitator. She is also a professor at the University of California, Los Angeles. The startling nature of Kruger's signature work is its simplicity: Her large-scale back-and-white photographs are overlaid with red rectangular slashes embedded with short, aggressive phrases in a futura bold font. Kruger's art can be found in museums and on the sides of buses, billboards, T-shirts, book covers, shopping bags, and political posters. Her highly recognizable work addresses social power struggles, feminism, gender-based consumption, individual autonomy, and desire within a consumer culture and a system dependent on stereotypes.

Born in 1945, in Newark, New Jersey, to a lower-middle-class family, Kruger attended Syracuse University until her father died, when she dropped out of college to return home. Kruger then went to Parsons School for Design, where she worked with and was inspired by Diane Arbus and Marvin Israel. Arbus's work, which explored the grotesque underbelly of suburban life, was an early influence on Kruger, as was Arbus's position as a female role model to Kruger. Israel encouraged Kruger to create a portfolio before she left Parsons, and it was he who helped her get a position with magazine publisher Condé Nast. Whether her inability to finish either degree was a sign of restless and impatient intellect or a lack of commitment, her achievements in the magazine world are undeniable. By the age of 22, Kruger was *Mademoiselle* magazine's chief designer. Working in the magazine industry taught Kruger to have a sharp eye for images; she was trained to scan and select pictures, gauge their rhetorical potential, and then crop and edit them to focus their impact.

An installation by Barbara Kruger displayed at the Australian Center for Contemporary Art in Melbourne, Australia. Kruger's work has appeared in films, videos, on outdoor media like billboards and posters, and on a train station platform in Strasbourg, France. (Wikimedia)

Kruger learned about the manipulative and seductive possibilities images had on viewers and applied these lessons to her own work. In 1976, after designing a few book covers and becoming involved with New York City's performance art and narrative scene, Kruger left the east coast for California and began to teach at the University of California, Berkeley.

While in California, Kruger was drawn to semiotics, the "science of signs," and European cultural theorists such as Jean Baudrillard and Roland Barthes. In 1978, she published a book called *Picture/Readings*. The book placed images alongside texts to play contrapuntally with the meanings of each. Text, she believed, could make audible the elements of the images that remained unseen and unheard in the photograph. Kruger was fascinated by the ways in which social relations are experienced in the everyday world and began to explore the global etiquette of power—a concept she derived from French philosopher Michel Foucault. The source of social and cultural power, she understood, is anonymous and cannot be centralized. Power exists less as a singular body than as a network of relations working to unify social apparatuses and institutions; for Kruger, power is inscribed through the stereotype, the pose.

Kruger believes stereotypes produce docile and submissive subjects by the way they are arbitrarily imposed. Kruger uses text in conjunction with images to expose the stereotype as the prime instrument of submission, particularly for women. Her work intercepts the stereotype in the hope of suspending the identification that is afforded by the gratification of the image. Kruger implicates viewers of her art by using inclusive pronouns such as "you," "I," "we," and "they." Her infamous piece *You Invest in the Divinity of the Masterpiece* cuts text across Michelangelo's iconic image of God giving life to Adam. The "double address" constructs the viewer twice over by mimicking and arresting the conventional reception of images. Because Kruger believes that coercion happens through receivership, in which people consume images and codes, she contradicts the conventions of the media by combining images and words. Kruger uses her art to explore the ways in which consumption, gender, and sexuality are intrinsically linked and socially constructed. Her work plays with preponderant imagistic and textual conventions to mash up meanings and create new ones.

One of her best-known pieces, *I Shop Therefore I Am*, plays with our social knowledge of René Descartes' cognitive self-identification to humorously suspend the viewer between the fascination of the image and the indictment of the text. Another infamous piece, *Your Body Is a Battleground*, was designed for the 1989 march on Washington in support of abortion rights. The piece invokes a well-known slogan from the 1960s and juxtaposes it to a stereotypical image of a 1950s woman. The image is split on its vertical axis to summon up conventions of good versus evil and address the ways in which women's bodies are incorporated rather than corporeal. In both of these pieces, as in all her work, Kruger reminds us that language reinforces the interests and perspectives of those who control it.

Rachel E. Silverman
Embry Riddle Aeronautical University

See also Audiences: Reception and Injection Models; Barthes, Roland; Cultural Politics; Ideology; Media Rhetoric; Patriarchy; Postmodernism; Semiotics

Further Readings

Goldstein, Ann. *Barbara Kruger*. Cambridge, MA: MIT Press, 1999.

King, Stephen and Barbara Kruger. *My Pretty Pony*. New York: Knopf, 1989.

Kruger, Barbara. "Barbara Kruger." http://www .barbarakruger.com (Accessed February 2011).

Kruger, Barbara. *Money Talks*. New York: Skarstedt Fine Art, 2005.

Kruger, Barbara. *Picture/Readings*. [n.p.], 1978.

Kruger, Barbara. *Remote Control: Power, Cultures and the World of Appearances*. Cambridge, MA: MIT Press, 1993.

Kruger, Barbara and Phil Mariani. *Remaking History*. Seattle: Bay Press, 1989.

Linker, Kate. *Love for Sale: The Words and Pictures of Barbara Kruger*. New York: Harry N. Abrams, 1990.

LASN, KALLE

Popular legend has it that Kalle Lasn (1942–) was in a shopping center parking lot and came upon a coin-operated shopping cart dispenser. Frustrated and angry that he would have to pay simply to use a store's shopping cart, he jammed a coin into the slot, rendering the machine inoperable. This incident of activist vandalism is rumored to be the origin of "culture jamming," a worldwide activist movement, with Lasn at the media helm, that has a broad and ambitious objective of stopping the spread of commercial culture and consumerism. Although some attribute the origin of the concept of culture jamming to a 1993 *New York Times* article by Mark Dery, Lasn has undoubtedly become a highly visible figure in the culture-jamming movement—and one of the movement's media darlings.

Lasn was born in 1942 in Estonia. At the end of World War II he left, spending time in a German refugee camp with his family before being resettled in Australia. Lasn then lived in Japan, where he founded a market research firm, before moving to Vancouver, Canada. For 20 years Lasn worked as a documentary filmmaker for PBS and Canada's National Film Board. Today he oversees the Adbusters Media Foundation, the multimedia organization that serves as the predominant voice of the culture-jamming movement.

The Adbusters Media Foundation describes itself as a "global network of artists, activists, writers, pranksters, students, educators and entrepreneurs who want to advance the new social activist movement of the information age. [Its] aim is to topple existing power structures and forge a major shift in the way we will live in the 21st century." The most visible media vehicle of the Adbusters Media Foundation is *Adbusters* magazine, which was founded in 1989 and today states that it is "concerned about the erosion of our physical and cultural environments by commercial forces." Perhaps the best-known feature in every issue is the spoof advertising campaigns that aim to focus a critical eye on consumer culture. Joe Camel, the former and long-suffering mascot for Camel cigarettes, became "Joe Chemo," complete with hospital gown and intravenous drip. The super-skinny supermodels featured in Calvin Klein Obsession perfume ads are shown in the spoof spots to be hovering over a toilet as if they are purging their last meal. In spoofs of the Absolut Vodka campaign, chairs are arranged in the formation of the iconic Absolut bottle, with body copy that states, "Absolut AA," a juxtaposition of the vodka brand with the arrangement of chairs in an Alcoholics Anonymous meeting. Another, grimmer Absolut spoof shows a chalk outline, of the type found at a murder scene, in the shape of the vodka bottle, with "Absolute [*sic*] End" as the copy.

In addition to its magazine and Website, the Adbusters Media Foundation sponsors a series of activist campaigns, including TV Turnoff Week and Digital Detox Week. The most famous of these campaigns are likely the Buy Nothing Day and Buy Nothing Christmas campaign, which parallel Black Friday and the Christmas season, respectively, to persuade consumers that going without is more fulfilling than accumulating packaged gifts. Other culture-jam efforts include the December 2010 worldwide boycott of Starbucks.

Although it is difficult to determine the exact effect of the culture-jamming movement, the Adbusters Website boasts a "global network of culture jammers" more than 87,000 strong. The activist movement has also spread beyond the Website and magazine to Lasn's books *Culture Jam: How to Reverse America's Suicidal Consumer Binge—and Why We Must* (2000) and *Design Anarchy* (2006), a manifesto against the marriage of commerce and design for corporate profit.

Some might argue that, in his quest to rid the world of marketing, Lasn has branded himself and his culture-jamming movement using the very marketing tools that he and the movement decry, but he has gained an admirable level of notoriety in his grassroots attempt to subvert corporate America. During the 1990s, the European edition of *Time* magazine named Lasn one of its "People to Watch." His profile highlighted Lasn's belief that

he is conducting—and thrives on—a daily fight to regain control of our "mindscape" from corporate interests.

Susan Westcott Alessandri
Suffolk University, Boston

See also Advertising; Beauty and Body Image: Beauty Myths; Beauty and Body Image: Eating Disorders; Culture Jamming

Further Readings

Branwyn, Gareth. *Jamming the Media*. San Francisco: Chronicle Books, 1997.

Dery, Mark. "Culture Jamming: Hacking, Slashing, and Sniping in the Empire of Signs." Open Magazine Pamphlet Series, 1993. http://project.cyberpunk.ru/idb/culture_jamming.html (Accessed December 2010).

Klein, Naomi. *No Logo*. New York: Picador, 2000.

Lasn, Kalle. *Culture Jam: How to Reverse America's Suicidal Consumer Binge—and Why We Must*. New York: Harper Paperbacks, 2000.

Lasn, Kalle. *Design Anarchy*. Vancouver, BC: Adbusters Media Foundation, 2006.

MALE GAZE

Jonathan Schroeder describes how "the gaze" is more than a visual perception; it is more than just "a look" and is construed within a relationship of power. The "male gaze" is a trope that refers to the visual power dynamics set up across a gender axis between a (male) subject or viewer and the (female) object of the gaze. The term is used to describe viewing positions in the visual arts, film, and other media.

The feminist film theorist Laura Mulvey introduced her theory of the male gaze in an influential essay, "Visual Pleasure and Narrative Cinema" in *Screen* magazine in 1975. Taking her examples from conventional Hollywood films of the 1950s, Mulvey describes cinematic viewership and discusses how subject positions are constructed. Mulvey's study is not empirically based but is derived from psychoanalysis. Mulvey argues that women on the screen are objectified and reduced to stereotypes. There are three main ways that Mulvey suggests are responsible for the objectification of women. First, the camera takes on a voyeuristic role. Since many film directors are male, the "male" camera is responsible for framing the position of women on the screen. Second, the gaze exists within the dynamics of relationships in the film itself, which demonstrate an asymmetric power relationship. The male protagonist is active and differs from the female (and passive) object of his gaze. Third, there is the gaze of the viewer, who is assumed to be male. Hence, there are three instances of the male gaze within cinematic

viewing, each of which privileges the male, as the looker, over the female, who is looked at.

Mulvey's notion of the gaze is developed from Freudian and Lacanian psychoanalysis. Freudian scopophilia discusses the pleasure involved in looking at other people's bodies, and Mulvey develops this idea within the confines of the darkened cinema space where audience members can look without being seen. "The gaze" is also a term that is associated with Michel Foucault's notion of surveillance (which, however, does not have the gendered connotations and refers to ways of seeing and interpreting the social realm).

Originating in Mulvey's essay, "the male gaze" refers to the representation of women by a male subject. The female body is traditionally submissive, eroticized, and objectified. Pleasure is split between the active/male and the passive/female. The viewer identifies with the male protagonist (in a process of narcissism), and the female is treated as a passive object of desire, both in the narrative of the film and in the audience. Women are disallowed from being sexual subjects, and they are defined solely by their male counterparts.

The foregoing model can be applied to other spheres of culture to explain the inequality of gender roles. Retrospectively, the male gaze can be used as a framework to interpret many revered works in the history of art, such as Titian's *Venus of Urbino* (1538) and Paul Gauguin's images of Tahitian women. The male gaze is also pronounced in the advertising industry, where strategies of identification and objectification appeal to both male and female viewers. This is an expansion of Mulvey's interpretation. In outline, the male viewer buys the product that will then help him "get the girl of his dreams," who is featured in the advertisement (identification). The female viewer buys the product because she wants to be the female in the advertisement (she identifies with her objectification).

Although the influence of Mulvey's essay on the intersection between film theory and psychoanalysis cannot be understated, it has been critiqued for its limitations. Mulvey's focus on the male protagonist can be explained by her focus on films in the Hollywood era, when the protagonists were typically male. However, this does not explain why she assumed the viewer was male, thereby neglecting the existence of the female viewer entirely. Other assumptions include the conflation of masculinity with activity and of femininity with passivity.

In contemporary Western culture, with the development of the third wave of feminism, the male gaze is no longer regarded as normative. The positions assumed by Mulvey are no longer regarded as conventional or typical. There are more female directors and female protagonists and the simple division across the gender axis is problematic and inadequate. The fluidity, variation, and plurality of gender and sexual identities render it impossible to homogenize male or female experience, or indeed to assume heterosexist identification. Furthermore, the focus on gender and sexuality alone does not provide a sufficient picture of what is constituted in viewing relations. Other variables, such as race and class, play a part in the construction of viewing. The gaze still has currency as a conceit in viewing strategies. However, it is not necessarily prefaced with *male*. The term *female gaze* has been used to refer to the growing emphasis on the sexualization of the male body in film, television, and advertising since the 1980s, although this is often regarded ironically. The male gaze is useful as a hermeneutic for uncovering patriarchal structures within art history, but it does not reflect contemporary debates on gender and queer theory.

Rina Arya
University of Wolverhampton

See also Advertising; Film: Hollywood; Mulvey, Laura; Scopophilia; Social Construction of Gender

Further Readings

Mulvey, Laura. *Visual and Other Pleasures.* Bloomington: Indiana University Press, 1989.
Rose, Gillian. *Visual Methodologies: An Introduction to the Interpretation of Visual Materials.* London: Sage, 2001.
Schroeder, Jonathan E. "Consuming Representation: A Visual Approach to Consumer Research." In *Representing Consumers: Voices, Views and Visions,* Barbara Stern, ed. London: Routledge, 1998.

Mass Media

Mass media is the umbrella term used to describe the communication outlets that deliver information to a mass audience. Traditionally, these entities have included books, newspapers, magazines, telephones, motion pictures, radio, television, and cable. Currently, there is much debate regarding whether or not such new media forms as the Internet, video games, and cellular phones should also be included. Regardless of the entity's classification as traditional or new, mass media have played an integral and obvious role in the transmission and dissemination of both culture and ideology in society for nearly 200 years.

As a result of the industrialization and urbanization of society, traditional socializing agents such as families, churches, and schools were unable to fully integrate members of the public into society in a systematic and uniform manner because of the diverse nature of the populace. What was needed, then, were alternate socializing entities that could successfully unify the public, thus creating a culturally homogeneous sociocultural group. Because the traditional agents of socialization were unable to promote the dissemination of culture adequately in an increasingly urban and industrialized society, mass media—possessing a wide reach and appealing to a broad base of individuals—became the new cultural transmitters.

In sharp contrast to families, churches, and schools, mass media could address the multitudes in a quick and efficient manner. For example, schools and churches were physically limited in their space. Mass media, however, were not physically bound and, for all practical purposes, were omnipresent, meaning that they were everywhere at all times. Whereas one had to be physically present at a school or a church to hear the message being transmitted, mass media could be and were attended just about anywhere at any time; newspapers could be purchased on street corners; movie theaters are a familiar site in most cities; and radios, televisions, and eventually the Internet, video games, and cellular phones are, in some combination or other, to be found in nearly every home. This ubiquitous nature of mass media enables mass media to create a mass public that possesses a shared consensus about culture and society. As a result, the members of the public turn to media to learn about themselves and society, thus solidifying the homogenizing effect of the socialization process.

Newspapers

The mid-19th-century newspaper was the first mass medium. Although newspapers had existed since at least the 1700s, they were not considered a mass medium because they were directed at the affluent and educated members of society. The reasons that early newspapers were directed at elite audiences were simple. The non-elite members of society could not subscribe to these early papers because of their prohibitive cost, and many were illiterate. The elite's stranglehold on newspaper readership was steadily challenged throughout the 19th century as literacy rates increased to more than 75 percent of the population by the middle of the century.

Increased literacy rates combined with innovations in printing technology and distribution of newspapers, along with additional advertising revenue, helped to drive down the costs of the papers, thus popularizing the so-called penny press among members of the public. Also, the use of illustrations, photographs, color, splashy headlines, and tabloid-style writing drove up circulation numbers as well as newspaper sales during the latter half of the 19th century. Consequently, inexpensive daily newspapers continued to dominate the media market until the dawn of the 20th century.

As the 20th century progressed, there was a fairly rapid increase in the consolidation of newspapers as newspaper chains published numerous individual newspapers and thus could minimize costs. Another change in newspaper production occurred in 1982, when *USA Today* debuted. *USA Today* brought splashy graphics and charts, easy-to-read stories, and color not only to its pages but also to the pages of newspapers across America that chose to imitate the *USA Today* style. In the 1990s, in an effort to increase a rapidly declining readership in addition to luring a much younger demographic, newspapers began to create an online presence, with Websites that not only were interactive but also could be updated on a continual basis. Thus print and online media began to merge.

Film

The dawn of the 20th century brought with it the popularization of film, which eventually came to challenge the newspaper's domination of the media market. Unlike newspapers, which required that the public be literate in order to disseminate their message, film could be enjoyed by the both the literate and the illiterate members of the public because it was a visual and eventually an audiovisual medium.

Early films were short vignettes of daily life that were shown in nickelodeons that charged a nickel for admission. These were storefronts that had been turned into makeshift theaters with folding chairs, benches, and a piano player to accompany the (then silent) films' action. These brief and fairly inexpensive films soon morphed into well-developed narratives such as 1902's *A Trip to the Moon*, 1903's *The Great Train Robbery*, and 1915's *The Birth of a Nation*. Early film studios, called film factories, soon sprang up to cater to the ever-increasing cinematic demands of the public.

The first major technological innovation in film occurred in 1927 with the release of *The Jazz Singer*, which brought sound and music to the silver screen. The next innovation, Technicolor, debuted in 1935. To compete with the nascent television industry, film turned to such novelty formats as three-dimensional (3-D) and Cinerama, which covered the screen with images from three projectors.

With the debut of the videocassette recorder (VCR) in the late 1970s, viewers not only were able to prerecord movies airing on television (in order to watch them at a later time) but also were able to rent prerecorded videocassettes of films to view at their leisure in the comfort of their own homes. Consequently, viewers often made copies of the prerecorded videocassettes to watch at home as well. The late 20th century brought further innovations to the film industry as computer-generated images became commonplace in films. In the 21st century, when the digital video recorder, DVR, replaced the VCR, more individuals opted to watch movies at home on their televisions. Also, the digital distribution of films to an individual's home was established with companies such as Netflix, which allowed individuals to download movies from the Netflix Website to watch on their home computers.

Radio

Film was not the only new mass medium vying for the attention of the American public during the first few decades of the 20th century. The creation of a vacuum tube that could receive radio signals as well as the invention of a high-speed continuous wave generator that could broadcast voice and music brought radio to life. Legal battles over radio patents hampered early radio, and it was not until after World War I that radio began to grow.

The first radio station, Pittsburgh's KDKA, started broadcasting in 1920. During the 1920s, radio became a commercial medium as stations began to sell advertising to cover broadcast operating costs. Additionally, networks developed as stations began to share the costs of programming by agreeing to air the same show on all of the stations in the network. This allowed advertisers' marketing reach to expand exponentially, thanks to the increased geographic coverage of the various networks. In 1927, the first network, the National Broadcasting Company (NBC), debuted. The Columbia Broadcasting System (CBS) arrived in the following year.

The passage of the Radio Act of 1927 was a direct result of the tremendous growth of radio throughout the 1920s. The act established the Federal Radio Commission (FRC), which was the precursor to the Federal Communications Commission (FCC). This act also defined the AM radio band, standardized channel designations, minimized channel interference, and abolished portable stations. Seven years later, the Communications Act of 1934 was passed, establishing the FCC and consolidating the regulatory functions of the communication industry.

After World War II, the third radio network, the American Broadcasting Company (ABC), was established. Around the same time, the FCC established the FM broadcast band. By the late 1940s, radio serials and soap operas had migrated to television, which forced radio to turn to music as its new source of programming. Radio stations then began to specialize in particular genres of music, such as Top 40, country, and rock, in order to cater to specific segments of society. The dawn of the 1980s saw FM radio finally overtake AM radio in popularity. Consequently, musical programming remained on FM radio while AM radio shifted to a news and talk format. The 21st century saw both Internet radio, which enabled broadcasters to stream programming to anyone with an Internet connection, and satellite radio, courtesy of companies like XM and Sirius, which gave consumers the opportunity to pay for premium content not found elsewhere and thus alternatives to the traditional radio broadcasts.

Radio had a relatively short-lived supremacy in the broadcasting arena, thanks to the advent of television, which threatened not only the wireless but also the silver screen. The combination of an iconoscope, a primitive camera tube, with an image dissector created television. While television "debuted" at the 1939 World's Fair in New York City, it did not begin to capture the imagination of the American public until after World War II, when technology improved and networks began to become prominent. The rapid growth of television caught the FCC off guard and it instituted a freeze on television station applications in the late 1940s so that it could study station interference and overcrowding. The freeze was lifted in the early 1950s as the FCC allocated 12 VHF, very high frequency, channels and 70 UHF, ultra high frequency, channels to television. Additionally, certain channels were set aside for community and educational purposes.

Television

Early television was modeled on radio, with game shows, sporting events, comedies, and dramas forming the bulk of the network programming. Prime-time network programming was produced by advertisers, who controlled not only the content of the shows but also the length and placement of advertisements. In the 1960s, after a scandal involving a quiz show, networks and independent production companies assumed control of television programming.

The technological innovations of videotape and color broadcasting also began to make an impact during the 1960s. With the creation of videotape, shows no longer needed to be aired live. Rather, they could be videotaped for broadcast at a later time. Color broadcasts slowly started to increase throughout the decade; by the end of the 1960s, almost all television programming was in color. Additionally, the nightly newscast expanded in length from 15 to 30 minutes in the 1960s, as television brought President Kennedy's assassination and funeral, the civil rights movement, and the Vietnam War into the homes of the American public. In the late 1960s, the Public Broadcasting Service was established as a noncommercial alternative to the American commercial television networks.

The following decade saw film finally embrace television when made-for-television movies appeared on the small screen. Also, cable, which began as a way to distribute terrestrial television programming to remote locales, began to pose a serious threat to traditional broadcast entities during the 1980s as many viewers tuned into various cable channels at the expense of traditional terrestrial broadcast channels. The decline in viewership of the traditional terrestrial broadcast channels was heightened by the introduction of the videocassette recorder. VCRs allowed viewers to time-shift programs, meaning that viewers were not bound to watch a program at the time specified by the network. Viewers could watch programs on their own schedule as opposed to the network's schedule. Additionally, commercials were either zapped out or zipped over during playback, thus diminishing the commercial reach of advertisers.

In the 1990s, direct broadcast satellite companies, such as the Dish Network and DirecTV offered a new form of competition, allowing satellites to beam programming directly to home satellite dishes. This posed a significant threat to cable television. Other technological innovations, such as digital video recorders (DVRs), have allowed for greater time-shifting and zapping of commercials. Additionally, the Internet enabled television signals to be streamed or downloaded from various broadcast and Internet sites to an individual's computer. Streaming and downloading also allowed audience members to watch niche or specialized programming that they might not have had the opportunity to view elsewhere.

Analog television broadcasting ended in the United States in 2009, when networks were required to stop broadcasting analog signals and switch broadcast production to the digital format. This shift from the analog aspect ratio of 4:3 to the digital aspect ratio of 16:9 allowed for the superior resolution and increased clarity of high-definition (HD) television. As a result, broadcasters were able to subdivide digital channels and offer numerous standard-definition programs in the same space.

New Media

In the early 21st century, there has been much debate regarding what constitutes the media, because new media outlets such as the Internet, video games, and cellular phones jockey for positions of primacy in the electronic landscape with such stalwarts as television, cable, and film. For example, the Internet and cellular phones have exponentially expanded individuals' ability to communicate through e-mail and online telephone services such as Skype and various cellular phone voice and messaging packages that include Internet and texting options. Additionally, the Internet and cellular phones have enabled film, radio, and television to continue to stay relevant in the ever-shifting mediated environment. This is possible because of the Internet and cellular phones' ability to broaden the distributional outlets of motion pictures, radio, and television. As a result, audience members are now able to circumvent traditional media outlets in order to download, stream, and view or listen to films, television, and radio programs or podcasts on personal computers and cellular "smart" phones.

The issues at the heart of the argument regarding whether or not new media sources are the logical extension of traditional media outlets are the consumer's ability to manipulate new media sources and the dramatic shift in the modes of production and distribution of the media. The consumer's ability to manipulate new media sources and the dramatic shift in the modes of production and distribution of the media are diametrically opposed to the traditional media outlets' vaunted roles as primary producers and replicators of culture. The advent of new media has meant that elite media conglomerates are no longer the only creators and controllers of cultural products. Now, members of the public can create and disseminate their own cultural artifacts via e-mail, videos, and even virtual reality.

This radical shift in the means and modes of cultural production has democratized the media landscape. Unlike the traditional mass media, new media outlets allow audience members to interact and react instantaneously to the mediated messages to which they are exposed on a daily basis. The audience members' ability to respond to mediated messages stands in sharp contrast to their passive role when interacting with traditional mass-media outlets. Prior to the advent of new media, traditional media outlets created mediated products, which then were distributed for public consumption. Audience members' ability to give feedback regarding the mediated messages was limited at best. In the new media landscape, audience members are not only consumers but also creators of mediated messages; in this environment, messages can be tailored and targeted to particular segments of the public. A prime example of this is the ability of any person with a digital camera and access to the Internet to create and upload video content to the YouTube Website, which can be accessed at any time by anyone anywhere.

Online user-generated content runs the gamut from entertaining viral videos on YouTube to text and images about history and current events, which can be created and revised through submissions to the online "free" encyclopedia Wikipedia. Blogs afford individuals the opportunity to report, reflect on, and assess various aspects of news, sports, and popular culture.

In addition to reshaping how consumers relate and react to news and information, new media have also enabled individuals to immerse themselves in a digital world where the individual can manipulate sound, vision, and personal identity to create a "second self" in an alternate reality. Because of new media's ability to formulate a virtual reality, people can now traverse time and geographic boundaries in the effort to slay beasts and achieve mythical status in games such as *World of Warcraft* or try on new identities in *Second Life*. In these virtual realms, they can live out their fantasies or experiment with ideas for new modes of living.

Finally, thanks to the interactivity of new media, members of the public are no longer passive consumers of mediated products; they are now empowered and even challenged to transform not only their own lives but also the lives of other members of society.

Mary Alice Adams
Louisiana Tech University

See also Advertising; Audiences: Producers of New Media; Blogs and Blogging; Federal Communications Commission; Film: Hollywood; Film: Horror; Film: Independent; Gender Media Monitoring; Graphic Novels; Hypermedia; Massively Multiplayer Online Role-Playing Games; Media Consolidation; Media Convergence; Media Ethnography; Media Globalization; Media Literacy; Media Rhetoric; Network News Anchor Desk; New Media; Newsrooms; Radio; Radio: Pirate; *Second Life*; Sitcoms; Soap Operas; Social Media; Talk Shows; Telecommunications Act of 1996; Television; Televisuality; Twitter; Video Gaming: Violence; Viral Advertising and Marketing; Virtual Community; Web 2.0; Wiki; YouTube

Further Readings

Baran, Stanley J. *Introduction to Mass Communication: Media Literacy and Culture*, 6th ed. New York: McGraw-Hill, 2010.

Dennis, Everette E. and Melvin L. DeFleur. *Understanding Media in the Digital Age.* New York: Allyn & Bacon, 2010.

Dominick, Joseph R. *The Dynamics of Mass Communication*, 11th ed. New York: McGraw-Hill Higher Education, 2011.

Jowett, Garth and James M. Linton, eds. *Movies as Mass Communication.* London: Sage, 1980.

Lister, Martin, et al. *New Media: A Critical Introduction.* London: Routledge, 2003.

Rodman, George. *Mass Media in a Changing World*, 3rd ed. New York: McGraw-Hill, 2010.

Sloan, W. David and James D. Startt. *The Media in America: A History*, 3rd ed. Northport, AL: Vision Press, 1996.

Starr, Paul. *The Creation of the Media: Political Origins of Modern Communications.* New York: Basic Books, 2004.

Vivian, John. *The Media of Mass Communication*, 10th ed. New York: Allyn & Bacon, 2011.

Massively Multiplayer Online Role-Playing Games

Massively multiplayer online role-playing games are a genre of computer games developed in the 1990s and made popular in the 2000s by games such as *World of Warcraft*. MMORPGs are characterized by virtual narrative environments in which players must create avatars and collaborate with other players to achieve goals. MMORPG is a genre that represents specific technological and social histories that often carry stigmas for gamers. The genre has inspired sustained debates about such topics as the ways in which players may become addicted to virtual communities, the economic ethics of the gaming environments, the real-world practices associated with game play, and the extent to which the genre represents "new worlds" or perpetuates existing modes of dominance. MMORPGs have inspired acute attention from researchers, who investigate the gaming environment, the technical aspects of the software, the formation of virtual communities, and the real-world experiences of players.

MMORPGs, like other digital media, have been promoted and heralded by some as "new worlds" or "frontiers" that exist simultaneously with, yet apart from, the offline world. Edward Castronova is a leading investigator of MMORPGs, arguing that the genre comprises unique new frontiers that offer participants fully developed worlds in which players perform complex identities. Increasingly the distinction between online and offline is becoming impossible to define, and the marketing of MMORPGs often includes promises of ownership and the ability for players to redefine reality in a virtual setting. However, as David Gunkel and Ann Hetzel Gunkel argue, programs such as *Second Life* perpetuate individualism and colonialist ideologies of discovery and expansionism by promising players opportunities to re-create themselves online; therefore, the gamer is hailed as an active agent with the ability to manifest whatever identity he or she chooses.

History of MMORPG Genre

Although genre distinctions often become blurred in digital media, it is important to note the history of MMORPGs as having descended from real-world role-playing games (RPGs). MMORPGs are situated culturally in the interpersonal RPG genre, which formed the inspiration for and logistical basis of computer RPGs that later evolved to include online multiplayer platforms. Games became "massively multiplayer" as Internet access expanded and game-hosting capabilities grew.

There is some debate about what the MMORPG genre includes, specifically regarding programs such as *Second Life*, which are virtual communities but do not necessarily involve gaming. A narrow interpretation of MMORPGs may consider games such as *World of Warcraft* to involve virtual communities that are distinct from those of *Second Life*, because the latter does not share the evolutionary track of fantasy RPGs. However, *Second Life* is often discussed in popular and research discourses as a MMORPG, with the emphasis being on the fact that *Second Life* is "massively multiplayer" and does involve the use of avatars and role playing. Nevertheless, the development of MMORPGs such as *Ultima Online* and *World of Warcraft* in a specific cultural context informs the treatment of MMORPGs in gaming communities and publications, as well as explaining stigmas often attached to participants.

Addiction

MMORPGs have spawned cultural controversies regarding the practices of players both within the virtual-gaming interface and in the real world. First, the role-playing aspect of the genre involves players controlling avatars and creating characters that exist in the game environment. Evidence shows that some avid players may develop addictions to the gaming environment, playing so continuously that they damage their health, interpersonal relationships, or careers. The common colloquialism "*Warcraft* widows" refers to partners of MMORPG enthusiasts feeling abandoned by players who spend immense amounts of time in the game environment. Gaming addiction has been of growing concern in the developing field of cyberpsychology, with researchers arguing that young adolescent players who believe their online avatars are superior to themselves or who wish to emulate their avatars are most likely to develop addictions to MMORPGs.

Economies of MMORPGs

Ethical debates have arisen from the practice of buying and selling characters, accounts, or items in real life. The real-world secondary economy of MMORPGs involves people playing the game in order to create advanced or elite characters, amass gold, or find special items for the purpose of then selling them as products to other players in real life. The practice has become a cottage industry of sorts. Not only may individuals profit, but there are also businesses that employ people solely to play MMORPGs in order to generate virtual products that are sold for high profits. The debate that arises in gaming communities is whether the practice, while legal, is unethical or a form of cheating. Some supporters insist that the practice is no different from using strategy guides or online information sites as a way of advancing through the game, while others argue that the practice may be comparable to buying any other gaming accessories. It has become a ubiquitous aspect of MMORPGs that allows players to advance quickly through the game by purchasing elite characters or items rather than having to devote the necessary time or skill to advancing individually.

The practice of gold farming in MMORPGs such as *World of Warcraft* represents one area in which pursuit of affluence in the virtual environment may re-create inequality offline. Gold farming has elicited critiques from within gaming communities and in academic discourses. The practice involves people playing the game in order to acquire virtual currency that is then sold for profit to other players using real-world currencies. Gold farming, like selling characters or items, has divided gamers, who view the practice variably as cheating or as a legitimate exchange. Players who are employed in real life to farm gold may be paid nominal wages to generate profits for real-world businesses, so an element of real-world exploitation is taking place. Furthermore, the institutionalization of gold farming is usually associated with companies in China. Some evidence suggests that players in the gaming environment may rely on Asian stereotypes to target avatars they believe to be operated by people employed to gold farm. The perpetuation of stereotypes and prevalence of hate speech toward avatars (and therefore the gamers controlling them) reflects the contradictions between the utopian promise of MMORPGs and the problematic practice of online communities where players are anonymous.

Stereotypes and Hate Speech

In keeping with the history of RPGs, the majority of MMORPG participants are white males, and much of the marketing and promotion of the genre is targeted toward young male consumers. Although some identity shifting takes place in which players may adopt opposite-sex avatars, the genre has been heavily criticized for creating hostile gaming environments in which homophobic, ethnocentric, misogynic rhetoric and behaviors are normalized. Gaming companies and server maintainers have repeatedly faced pressures to monitor and control the use of hate speech in MMORPG environments but have had limited success in doing so.

The debates surrounding performance of gendered identity and sexuality in MMORPGs suggest the potential for breaking down stereotypes, as male players sometimes choose to play female avatars and vice versa, but the prevalence of prostitution, in which real-world currency may be exchanged for virtual sex acts, suggests a virtual exploitation of female characters that relies on and perpetuates stereotypes of feminine submissiveness.

In addition, MMORPGs often revolve around campaigns that are specifically violent in nature, including battles between groups and individuals. Research on the effects of media violence argue that players who control avatars may experience the act of inflicting violence in a more visceral way than less interactive gaming genres.

Virtual Communities and Identities

RPGs have long carried stigmas of being dangerous for young players, in the sense that participants often enact violence and "try on" alternate personalities. Traditional stereotypes of RPG gamers have been applied to MMORPG players, and there has been a concern that it is dangerous for people to play games that may alter their sense of self. However, theorists point out the continual negotiation of self that takes place in the gaming environment is an extension of the ongoing negotiation of self in which people engage throughout their lives. Thus, whereas opponents of MMORPGs point to a possible fracturing of identity for players, cultural theorists argue that performances of identity in the gaming environment can allow for empowering gender-bending, sexual experimentation, and fantasy play.

MMORPGs have also inspired heated scholarly and popular debates about the nature and meanings of community in virtual worlds. On one hand, MMORPGs have been hailed for offering players the potential to create utopian virtual communities and have repeatedly been identified by players as offering fulfilling social relationships. On the other hand, the secondary economies of virtual worlds are exclusionary, in that players must possess real-world affluence to participate, and the gaming environments can be hostile to players whose avatars are marked as "others" on the basis of race, gender, nationality, or sexuality.

Spring-Serenity Duvall
University of South Carolina, Aiken

See also Avatar; Cyberdating; Cyberpunk; Cyberspace and Cyberculture; Electronic Media and Social Inequality; Heroes: Action and Super Heroes; Identity; Misogyny; Multi-User Dimensions; *Second Life*; Simulacra; Social Media; Video Gaming: Representations of Femininity; Video Gaming: Representations of Masculinity; Video Gaming: Violence; Virtual Community; Virtual Sex; Virtuality

Further Readings

Bates, Marlin. "Persistent Rhetoric for Persistent Worlds: The Mutability of the Self in Massively Multiplayer Online Role-Playing Games." *Quarterly Review of Film and Video*, v.26/2 (2009).

Castronova, Edward. *Synthetic Worlds: The Business and Culture of Online Games*. Chicago: University of Chicago Press, 2005.

Gunkel, David J. and Ann Hetzel Gunkel. "Terra Nova 2.0*The New World of MMORPGs." *Critical Studies in Media Communication*, v.26/2 (2009).

McChesney, Robert

Robert McChesney is an American college professor, activist, and public intellectual who works on issues of media democracy. His work focuses on the history and the political economy of the media. He argues that since the 1990s, the consolidation of media corporations has been undermining democracy in the United States and abroad. Because of his public criticism of corporate America, critics from the political right label him as an "anti-American" Marxist. Although McChesney does not write about issues of women and gender in the media, his concerns with media ownership and consolidation have a direct impact on women and gender. For example, ownership and consolidation can lead to a reinforcement of stereotypical gender images in the media, unequal distribution of wealth between the two genders, and obstacles to women entrepreneurs entering the business.

McChesney obtained his Ph.D. from the University of Washington before teaching at the School of Journalism and Mass Communication of the University of Wisconsin, Madison. He moved to the University of Illinois at Urbana-Champaign in 1999. In 2007, he became the Gutgsell Endowed Professor in the Department of Communication.

McChesney's earlier work focused on the history of sports media and radio broadcasting in the United States before World War II. The political economic work of Paul Baran and Paul Sweezy had a profound impact on McChesney's conceptualization of the mass media. Their 1966 book *Monopoly Capital* argues that the American economy is not a competitive economy, with many buyers and sellers in the market. Instead, the market is oligopolistically controlled by a few hundred corporations. The Fortune 500 companies play an important role in the American economy and social life. These companies not only have a direct impact on the economy but also determine consumer preferences in the United States and abroad. Hence, the failure of a Fortune 500 company (such as General Motors, which underwent bankruptcy in 2009) would have a long-term impact on the American economy and would change how Americans view the economy in relation to lifestyle.

McChesney argues in his work that the U.S. media are owned by only a handful of global companies. These companies behave similarly to other corporations. However, unlike companies that sell consumer goods, the media have the power to sway public opinion. In order to be competitive in the market, media companies employ a number of strategies, such as acquisitions and mergers. Bigger companies buy smaller companies to eliminate competition in the market (an example is Disney's acquisition of Pixar in 2006). Big companies merge with other big companies to become megacompanies (an example is the merging of America Online [AOL] and Time Warner in 2000). Big companies buy companies whose businesses are related but different (an example is General Electric's acquisitions of NBC television and Universal Studios) or whose businesses are completely similar (an example is Viacom, which owns MTV and bought Black Entertainment Television, BET). Acquisition and merging of media companies are unhealthy to democracy in at least three ways. First, journalistic integrity may be compromised because of ownership. News reports on NBC may be less likely to report critically on energy issues because NBC's parent company is General Electric. Second, media become more commercialized because big corporations are responsible for shareholders' interests more than the public interest. For example, advertisers pay the media to secure product placement in programming (not merely in separate advertisements), which further commercializes the media content. Third, a reduction in consumer choice may result from mergers, because the media tend to repeat genres and formulas that have proved their profitability and avoid experimenting on forms and content that may require time to develop an audience and reap profits. For example, reality-based programming, which is relatively inexpensive to produce, has exploded since 2000 as dramas, which are relatively expensive to produce, have declined.

Because of his critical stance on big corporations, McChesney is inclined to publish with independent, nonacademic presses such as the New Press, the Seven Stories Press, and the Monthly Review Press. From 2000 to 2004, he was a coeditor of *The Monthly Review*, a socialist publication started by Sweezy. McChesney also attempts to reach a wider audience by writing for trade and popular magazines and for *The Nation*, the *Los Angeles Times Online*, and *The Washington Post*. He has also prepared reports for policy groups, such as the Center for American Progress, and for politicians and activists, such as Representative Dennis J. Kucinich and Ralph Nader. In addition, McChesney has appeared in media education videos produced by Sut Jhally of the Media Education Foundation (MEF).

In 2002, McChesney began to host a one-hour radio program, *Media Matters*, produced for National Public Radio in the Urbana, Illinois, area. He invites academics, journalists, politicians, and public intellectuals to appear on his show. Scholars who have appeared include Jhally of MEF and the University of Massachusetts at Amherst, Noam Chomsky of the Massachusetts Institute of Technology, Mark Crispin Miller of New York University, the late Howard Zinn of Boston University, and Lawrence Lessig of Stanford University. Journalists who have appeared include Naomi Wolf, Naomi Klein, and Amy Goodman.

Because of McChesney's public stance on media reform, he has attracted attention from politically right-leaning critics. He was named one of the most "dangerous" college professors in the United States by David Horowitz, in Horowitz's list of 101 American college professors whom he claimed to be anti-American, socialist, and communist.

McChesney is also a cofounder and the former president of the Free Press (not to be confused with the publisher of the same name), a nonprofit lobbying group in Washington, D.C. The group's interests reflect many of McChesney's interests, such as media consolidation and media ownership.

Micky Lee
Suffolk University, Boston

See also Federal Communications Commission; Jhally, Sut; Media Consolidation; Miller, Mark Crispin; Moyers, Bill

Further Readings

Baran, Paul A. and Paul M. Sweezy. *Monopoly Capital: An Essay on the American Economic and Social Order*. New York: Monthly Review Press, 1966.

Free Press. http://www.freepress.net (Accessed February 2011).

McChesney, Robert W. *Corporate Media and the Threat to Democracy*. New York: Seven Stories Press, 1997.

McChesney, Robert W. *Rich Media, Poor Democracy: Communication Politics in Dubious Times*. New York: New Press, 2000.

McChesney, Robert W. "RobertMcChesney.com." http://www.robertmcchesney.com (Accessed February 2011).

McLuhan, Marshall

Marshall McLuhan (1911–80) was a Canadian English and media professor who spent the majority of his career at the University of Toronto. He has been called the "oracle of the electric age" and the "high priest of popcult" for his groundbreaking studies of media as they interact with language and environments. He began as an English Ph.D. student at the University of Cambridge and moved to the United States, teaching at the University of Wisconsin at Madison and at Saint Louis University before heading back to his native Canada. During these early teaching years, McLuhan discovered that his students were less interested in English and poetry than they were in media products such as comics, advertisements, and radio programs. Using his skills in New Criticism, which he had learned from F. R. Leavis and I. A. Richards, he began to analyze and teach media as new forms of literature.

McLuhan's work was cumulative and borrowed heavily from his predecessors. His 1962 book *The Gutenberg Galaxy* was a "footnote" to the insights of Harold Innis. His 1964 book *Understanding Media* offered a media poetics based on the template set by Cleanth Brooks and Robert Penn Warren in their work, *Understanding Poetry* (1938, rev. 1950). McLuhan's other works relied heavily on his deep knowledge, acquired during his dissertation research on the trivium, of the classical rhetorical tradition. He referred to himself as a grammarian, an artist, and many things other than a scholar or an academic, seeing the latter as restricting labels, "wonderful buffers for preventing people from confronting any form of percept." He was one of the first celebrity professors and perhaps the first media professor made famous by the media itself.

McLuhan is most famously known for two sound-bite phrases: "The medium is the message" and "the global village." The former refers to the ways in which the formal qualities of a given communication shape the perception and understanding of that communication as much or more than the content itself. Thus, in the example of this medium (a SAGE Reference book), the inclusion of an entry on McLuhan within the medium of an encyclopedia conveys his importance far more than the content of this entry can. The medium (encyclopedia) is the message (that McLuhan is important). "The global village" refers to the idea that, with electronic media, all of the world can now know everything about everyone everywhere else, the way one can know the intimate details of people in one's small tribal village. Thus, "the global village" is used to refer to the fact that the world is getting perceptually smaller, which is quite different from the perception that it was getting larger during, for example, the age of exploration. This phrase is also connected to the phrase "Think globally, act locally," which Jacques Ellul popularized, and to the contemporary term *glocal*, a conflation of *global* and *local* usually used to signify the excellence of locally grown produce.

Work on and about McLuhan has been in a resurgent mode with the birth of the Internet and with the help of the institutions, groups, and cultural events he inspired, such as the Media Ecology Program at New York University, established by Neil Postman in 1971; *Wired* magazine, which named McLuhan as its "patron saint" upon its founding in 1993; and the Media Ecology Association, founded in 1998 by five of Postman's former students. *Media ecology*, a phrase coined by McLuhan's son Eric in 1968, is the term most frequently associated with McLuhan's ideas, although other terms associated with his influence include *media theory, media studies, information ecology,* and *digital ecosystems.* In these and many other areas of media scholarship, McLuhan is considered a canonical figure, if not *the* canonical figure.

McLuhan saw pornography as a fragmentation of the wild body in its first nature: "The word 'sex' is wrong to begin with because it is fragmentation. It automatically creates pornography. If you want to create pornography you just separate some aspect of sex and life from everything else. That is pornography. It is fragmentation."

As he neared the end of his life, McLuhan saw the threat of disembodiment, or disincarnation, as one of the greatest dangers posed by electronic media, since on the air or on the phone man had no "body"

to speak of. Thus, in a confluence of his Catholic beliefs and his media theory, he also saw theology of the body, or the Catholic Church's teachings on embodiment in love, marriage, sex, and family, as one of the strongest antidotes to the spirit of the age of disembodiment. If electronic media by their inherent biases tended to fragment man and woman from themselves and each other, then McLuhan saw Catholic social teaching as a key to their reintegration. New scholarship on McLuhan continues to dig more deeply into his archival material, unearthing some of his subtler interpretations, including the connections he made between sex, gender, and media.

Read M. Schuchardt
Wheaton College

See also Audiences: Producers of New Media; Cyberspace and Cyberculture; Ellul, Jacques; Media Rhetoric; Mediation; Rushkoff, Douglas; Scopophilia

Further Readings

Coupland, Douglas. *You Know Nothing of My Work.* 2010.

Marchand, Philip. *Marshall McLuhan: The Medium and the Messenger.* Toronto, ON: Random House of Canada, 1989.

McLuhan, Marshall. "Education in the Electronic Age." In *The Best of Times/The Worst of Times: Contemporary Issues in Canadian Education,* Hugh Alexander Stevenson, J. Donald Wilson, and Robert M. Stamp, eds. Toronto, ON: Holt, Rinehart and Winston of Canada, 1972.

McLuhan, Marshall. *The Gutenberg Galaxy.* Toronto, ON: University of Toronto Press, 1962.

McLuhan, Marshall. *The Medium and the Light: Reflections on Religion,* Eric McLuhan and Jacek Szklarek, eds. Toronto, ON: Stoddart, 1999.

McLuhan, Marshall. *Understanding Media: Lectures and Interviews.* Stephanie McLuhan and David Staines, eds. Toronto, ON: McClelland and Stewart, 2003.

McLuhan, Marshall. *Understanding Media: The Extensions of Man.* New York: McGraw-Hill, 1964.

McLuhan, Marshall and Eric McLuhan. *Laws of Media: The New Science.* Toronto, ON: University of Toronto Press, 1988.

Molinaro, Matie, Corinne McLuhan, and William Toye, eds. *Letters of Marshall McLuhan.* New York: Oxford University Press, 1987.

MEDIA CONSOLIDATION

Media consolidation, also known as *media conglom-eration*, is the term used to refer to the concentration of ownership in the media—more specifically, to the series of policies that have facilitated ownership of the majority of the major media outlets by a small number of corporations. In the field of communication, political economists look at the role of the media in promoting capitalism, the circulation of commodities, and consumerism. Political economists examine issues related to the production (ownership and structure) and distribution (what is selected and where is it seen) of media. They argue that media industries are important because they contribute to the national economy in promoting ideas and products and may contribute to democracy by influencing contemporary public discourse. This latter role is vital, because a functioning democracy depends on the people being informed: People must be able to understand the messages, afford to use the media, and have geographic access to the technologies through which media are disseminated. However, it has been argued that media conglomeration negatively affects the comprehensiveness, accessibility, and balance of media messages. An important aspect of the concentration of power is the consolidation of media outlets into conglomerates. Looking at conglomeration gives insight into the economic aspects of ownership and their effects on the content and structure of media.

The Radio Act of 1927 constituted the first attempt by the federal government in the United States to regulate and nationalize the airwaves. The Federal Radio Commission (FRC) was in charge of regulating a growing number of radio stations and took control of the airwaves. After passage of the Communications Act of 1934, the commission was renamed the Federal Communications Commission (FCC), and its role was expanded. The new agency was charged with regulating the public airwaves, administering licenses, regulating standards, and imposing penalties for infringements of those standards. As a requisite for granting licenses to broadcasters, the Communications Act of 1934 also established that broadcasters must reflect the public interest by providing news programming.

The Telecommunications Act of 1996 reduced and deregulated the media market. The act provided concessions that allowed the consolidation of the media and the mergers of large companies. In 2003, the FCC approved the elimination of the restrictions to limit ownership of media within a local area, a decision that, after some court rulings, was upheld by the Supreme Court in 2004. In 2007, the FCC expanded the deregulation of the media by passing legislation that eliminated media ownership rules that prevented a single company from owning both a newspaper and a television or radio station in the same city.

In 1978, the FCC approved the "Statement of Policy on Minority Ownership of Broadcasting Facilities." This policy attempted to remedy the underrepresentation of women and minorities by recognizing that most of the broadcasting licenses were originally awarded during a historical time when the nation lived under segregation. The Telecommunications Act of 1996 contained measures aimed at increasing female and minority ownership of broadcast licenses. However, the FCC has done very little to promote female and minority broadcast ownership. As a result of the 2003 changes in policies, the FCC has relinquished its responsibility to monitor and foster increased minority and female broadcast ownership.

Ben H. Bagdikian's work has dealt extensively with the topic of corporate consolidation. In his 2004 book *The New Media Monopoly*, he contends that the media landscape is composed of five media conglomerates (Time Warner, the Walt Disney Company, News Corporation, Viacom, and Bertelsmann) that have control over most newspapers, radio stations, book publishers, motion-picture studios, television stations, cable networks, and magazines. Since the publication of the book, a new major player has emerged with the acquisition by General Electric (owner of the National Broadcasting Corporation, NBC) of Universal in 2003. These corporations have been able to influence public policy and gain control of the market. Since 1996, the U.S. government, represented by the FCC, has consistently approved policies that allow corporate giants to gain control of most outlets of mass communication under the rationale that consolidation is necessary to ensure competition in a capitalist system. Here the idea is that concentration is needed in order to be competitive in an international market. However, great criticism of these policies has come from many scholars and media activists.

Critics of conglomeration point out that the current configuration of the media contributes to the notion that people must support the structures of power that finance the media market. Scholars see the concentration of media ownership in the contemporary media environment as a problem because it affects media messages, it solidifies the power of advertisers by allowing a few companies to control messages, and it reduces diversity.

First, conglomeration results in media messages that work to ensure the reproduction of the system by producing a form of consciousness that makes people believe that it is in their best interest to support those in power. Those with the control of the media outlets can create and distribute messages that support the ideological apparatus and economic system that keep them in a privileged position. For example, if the companies dominating a media market choose to avoid stories that do not serve their interests or those of their sponsors, members of the public suffer, because they are not adequately informed of some crucial issues that may affect them. If one happens to live in a small town, it is possible that all media channels (newspaper, radio, television) are owned by one outlet, thus giving the owners full editorial control of that market. The owners of that outlet may have political, racial, or economic motivations to support some causes and have the power to control and edit the information to which that community will have access.

Second, the consolidation of media affects the power advertisers have over media content. The media market structure is supported financially by the revenue of advertising sales. If a media market chooses to edit news stories and messages that will hurt advertisers, it is in fact protecting the interests of the business instead of the rights of audiences to be informed.

Robert McChesney, in his 1997 book *Corporate Media and the Threat to Democracy*, explains that corporate interests affect media content in various ways. First, corporations are constantly looking to maximize revenues by increasing exposure to their messages. For example, a high percentage of media and news coverage is produced by public relations professionals, whose job is to generate messages that meet the commercial interests of their employers. News outlets publish this coverage because corporations provide the material free of charge, thus saving time and resources for the news programs.

The result is that audiences have less access to news stories that present neutral or critical messages. Second, media conglomerates and joint ventures among these conglomerates affect content as they use cross-promotional strategies and synergies to promote their interrelated events and programming. Media content in these cases serves as a promotional agent for products. Third, media content affects the debates over policy, and the views represented favor those with economic interests in the area. Thus, the content focuses on the views of the political and business elites. Content that is critical of the establishment or those in power is avoided. When corporate interests control the diffusion of information, corporations can affect public policy, public perceptions, and the overall political agenda for their own benefit.

The media behave like all other businesses: Their goal is to be profitable, and therefore advertisers, the primary source of revenue for media outlets, have the most control over content. The dynamics of the media, and more specifically television, are then to serve their primary client, advertisers, and provide them outlets to reach the greatest number of people. Producers in turn generate profits and audiences by replicating formats and formulas that have proven effective. Because advertising is the primary funding system for television, producers ensure that content meets the needs of marketers. Big media companies shun controversial or strong content that can negatively affect audiences, ratings, and consequently revenues—advertising dollars. The problem is that, unlike other business, the media use the resources of the nation, which belong to all Americans, to provide audiences commercial messages that affect the public discourse. Ultimately, for many of the critics, the problem lies in the disparity between the way the media have been conceptualized and their actual function. When the commercial pursuit of maximizing profits is the main goal of a media outlet or corporation, its role in society is compromised.

Finally, critics of deregulation argue that the consolidation of media affects several aspects of diversity. Concerns of diversity in the media include issues of media ownership by females and minorities. The consolidation of the media into large conglomerates has had a negative impact on minority ownership, indirectly or directly contributing to the loss of stations that were owned by women and other minorities.

Consolidation also affects diversity in content, which is important because competing ideas in the media are vital to an informed decision-making process. Conglomeration reduces the diversity of information that is provided to the public. The ultimate consequence of consolidation, critics argue, is a poorly informed public, restricted to a reduced array of media options that offers only information that does not harm the media's growing range of interests. Conglomeration is used to push internal promotion efforts to ensure the success of their intellectual properties. The media landscape affects the creation and distribution of cultural products; formats that have been proven to be profitable are replicated and reproduced in the form of sequels and spin-offs. For example, if one reality television program proves to be successful, then that media outlet will produce more reality programs with a similar format, theme, or hosts. This is problematic for media critics, because the implications of such practices are that audiences view only several versions of the same program (six reality shows that feature the lives of housewives in the country, one dating show every season) or one story line (an emergency room or a police drama), instead of programming that reflects the stories and diversity of the country.

The concentration of media ownership also reduces the diversity of in media channels. Increased concentration of media ownership can lead to the censorship of a wide range of critical thought and local content. Many communities have expressed concern that consolidated media do not have the structural flexibility and staffing to serve local communities in case of emergency. A negative consequence of conglomeration is that most media content is received through automatic feeds from large cities and corporate headquarters. In emergencies, therefore, local media outlets are slow to respond to changes in programming.

Yarma Velázquez Vargas
California State University, Northridge

See also Advertising; Children's Programming: Disney and Pixar; Critical Theory; Cultural Politics; Federal Communications Commission; Mass Media; McChesney, Robert; Media Convergence; Media Ethnography; Media Globalization; Media Literacy; Media Rhetoric; Network News Anchor Desk; Newsrooms; Telecommunications Act of 1996; Television; Viral Advertising and Marketing

Further Readings

Bagdikian, Ben H. *The New Media Monopoly.* Boston: Beacon Press, 2004.

McAllister, Matthew P. *The Commercialization of American Culture: New Advertising, Control and Democracy.* Thousand Oaks, CA: Sage, 1996.

McChesney, Robert W. *Corporate Media and the Threat to Democracy.* New York: Seven Stories Press, 1997.

MEDIA CONVERGENCE

Media convergence is an overarching term that describes a number of developments in the field of mass communication. The term has several connotations, and it is important to understand its different meanings and uses and their implications. In general, media convergence refers to the technological, industrial, and cultural changes brought on by digital technologies. From a technological perspective, the merging of video, audio, and text into a single platform has impacted the production and consumption of media content. From an industrial perspective, media convergence is the result of the merging of media industries that were previously unrelated. From a cultural perspective, media convergence has allowed audiences to participate actively in cultural production. Media convergence has therefore had a widespread impact on social, economic, and political life.

The term *convergence* was popularized in the 1980s by Ithiel de Sola Pool in his 1983 book *Technologies of Freedom*, in which he predicted that technological innovation would lead to a convergence of modes of communication, reconfiguring media policy frameworks related to the First Amendment. In the 1990s, Nicholas Negroponte predicted in his book *Being Digital* that media convergence would significantly transform the media landscape. Broadcasting would be replaced by "narrowcasting" to niche markets.

The most common use of the term *media convergence* is a technological one. Technological convergence refers to the shift from analog to digital technology, which provides the digital delivery of information. Technological convergence allows for the intermixing of audio, text, and video content, resulting in multimedia forms of communication. Previous modes of communication tended to be medium-specific. For example, television was broadcast in a one-to-many form of communication. Instead, technological convergence allows for media content to be delivered in multiple forms. The *New York Times*, for example, can deliver its journalistic content in several forms, including video, text, photos, and interactive material, on its Website.

Media convergence has increased users' mobility and interactivity. For example, smart phones allow users to make phone calls but also access Websites, download information, and take photos and videos and upload them to social networking sites.

Technologically, media convergence has had an impact on content creation, distribution, and consumption. Convergence requires that media content be delivered and accessible in digital formats. In addition to influencing content creation, convergence has affected how users receive information. More households receive information via the Internet than other traditional forms of communication, such as print or radio. Finally, technological convergence has an impact on the way audiences consume information. Technological convergence allows users to access content in different platforms. Users can access the specific media content in which they are interested, in the forms they prefer.

Convergence also refers to the merging of media industries that were previously unrelated. Historically, media industries in the United States were governed under distinct regulatory models. Each medium had its own function and market. The broadcast regulatory model, for example, saw the airwaves as a scarce resource that should be used to promote the public interest. Regulations discouraged cross-ownership as a way to maintain localism and diversity. For example, a 1975 rule barred a single company from owning a newspaper and a broadcast station in the same market. However, the trend toward deregulation in the 1980s loosened media ownership rules. Deregulation was intended to spur technological innovation and promote competition. The most significant policy change was seen in the Telecommunications Act of 1996, which removed many of the previous ownership restrictions, allowing for cross-ownership. The act led to media consolidation and the formation of media conglomerates.

One of the most visible examples of industrial convergence was the 2000 merger between America Online (AOL) and Time Warner. AOL, an Internet service provider, merged with Time Warner, a broadcasting and publishing giant. The merger drew attention to the synergy that occurred when bringing together content providers and distribution channels.

Industrial convergence has led to both horizontal and vertical integration. Horizontal integration refers to one company owning several firms within the same industry. For example, Clear Channel is horizontally integrated, because it owns more than 900 radio stations throughout the United States. Vertical integration refers to owning the means of production, distribution, and exhibition. Disney is vertically integrated because it produces its content through its movie studios and distributes that content through its media outlets, such as the American Broadcasting Company (ABC).

Many warn that consolidation of ownership, whereby a small number of companies control the majority of outlets for news and entertainment, can lead to a lack of diversity in content and opinion and can be antidemocratic. Media activists such as Robert McChesney argue for increased restrictions on media ownership.

Industrial convergence has impacted media workers. Convergence requires that journalists acquire proficiency in audio, video, and print communication. Increasingly, journalists are expected not only to investigate stories but also to present them in multimedia formats. There is a trend toward "backpack journalism," in which journalists present audio, video, visual, and text content related to their stories.

Industrial convergence has also impacted advertising. Advertisers have to design integrated marketing campaigns that can air on television, in print, and online.

A less common but important use of convergence refers to a cultural phenomenon. *Cultural convergence* is a term used to explain a shift in power in how users interact with media. Broadcasting assumed audiences passively consumed media. Instead, one of the distinctive characteristics of convergence is interactivity. Audiences have more control over the content they want to access, the way in which they want media presented to them, and the order in which they want it presented to them. Convergence has led to more active audiences, where users have multiple channels for accessing information that is presented in multiple modes of communication.

In his 2006 book *Convergence Culture*, Henry Jenkins describes how media convergence leads to a participatory culture in which audiences are active producers of cultural content. Convergence allows users to participate in cultural production, through user-generated content, such as blogs and video file-sharing sites like YouTube. User-generated content can draw attention to multiple perspectives and ideas. Cultural convergence allows users to remix culture, creating, for example, their own endings to popular movies or fan cultures to discuss popular television shows. Audiences can also participate in cultural production through commenting on news stories, linking ideas together through blogs, or creating video responses to current events. Smart phones allow users to take movies and upload the content quickly to different Websites as a way to draw attention to social movements. For example, a cell phone video of the death of a female protester in Iran during the 2009 presidential election there drew worldwide attention to the democratic uprising in Iran.

Cultural convergence can lead to what Pierre Lévy termed "collective intelligence," in which audiences collaboratively create and produce information. Social bookmarking, in which users create their own organizational systems for online resources, and crowdsourcing, in which large groups of people work collaboratively on tasks, are two examples of collective intelligence enabled by convergence.

Despite the ability of media convergence to facilitate user-generated content, media activists argue that it is important to pay attention to media consolidation as a result of industrial convergence. Media companies still act as gatekeepers of information. Convergence can decrease barriers to users' participation in culture, but users still do not have as much control as media conglomerates, which own certain sites and charge a premium for accessing content. Additionally, search engines such as Google can determine how users access content.

Media convergence has had a number of social, economic, and political impacts. Media convergence has raised concerns over how to protect private information, especially because there is an increased amount of information collected and stored about individuals as they create digital footprints throughout their lives. Feminists have discussed the implications of convergence for gender equality. On one hand, convergence provides a forum for women's and girls' voices to be heard. Females can create communities of interest and use social networking tools for social change. Media convergence has led to a rise in female-oriented content, such as blogs that discuss issues related to motherhood. Viral videos allow for quick responses from feminists to comment on social inequality. However, feminists are concerned with issues raised by media convergence, including cyberbullying, privacy, and sexist representations of women.

Carolyn Cunningham
Gonzaga University

See also Audiences: Producers of New Media; Blogs and Blogging; Cyberspace and Cyberculture; Federal Communications Commission; Hypermedia; Jenkins, Henry; McChesney, Robert; Media Consolidation; New Media; Social Media; Telecommunications Act of 1996; Twitter; Viral Advertising and Marketing; Web 2.0; Wiki; YouTube

Further Readings

Dwyer, Tim. *Media Convergence*. New York: McGraw-Hill, 2010.

Gordon, Rich. "The Meaning and Implications of Convergence." In *Digital Journalism: Emerging Media and the Changing Horizons of Journalism*, Kevin Kawamoto, ed. Lanham, MD: Rowman & Littlefield, 2003.

Jenkins, Henry. *Convergence Culture: Where Old and New Media Collide*. New York: New York University Press, 2006.

Lawson-Borders, Gracie. *Media Organizations and Convergence: Case Studies of Media Convergence Pioneers*. Mahwah, NJ: Lawrence Erlbaum Associates, 2006.

Lévy, Pierre. *Collective Intelligence: Mankind's Emerging World in Cyberspace*. Cambridge, MA: Perseus Books, 1997.

McChesney, Robert. *The Problem of the Media: U.S. Communications Politics in the Twenty-First Century*. New York: Monthly Review Press, 2004.

Negroponte, Nicholas. *Being Digital*. New York: Vintage Books, 1995.

Pool, Ithiel de Sola. *Technologies of Freedom*. Cambridge, MA: Belknap Press, 1983.

MEDIA ETHNOGRAPHY

Media ethnography as a field of study is influenced by both humanistic and social scientific inquiry. In general, media ethnography refers to the application of theories, concepts, and research methods from the field of cultural anthropology to the study of media texts. The field of media ethnography encompasses two broad areas, including ethnographies of production and audience ethnographies. Ethnographies of production examine the dynamics that take place in the making of media texts. Ethnographies of production are used in the study of journalism, film, television, and online content. The second broad area of study involves audience ethnographies, also called reception studies. Audience ethnographies examine how people consume media, in which contexts, and how their understandings of media have changed over time. Media ethnographers tend to prefer qualitative rather than quantitative research methods to investigate questions of the influence of media and culture. Ethnographic methods, such as participant observation and interviews, may provide what Clifford Geertz calls a "thick" description of how individuals and groups understand media, integrate media into their everyday lives, and form communities based on their media consumption. While there are several critiques of media ethnography, most notably that media ethnography is limited in terms of its scope, it is a growing field.

Media ethnography emerged as a response to dominant media effects research that supported a transmission view of media. The transmission view argues that media have direct, linear effects on audiences. Media effects research emphasized social and cognitive psychology, studying audiences' changes in attitudes and behaviors as a result of media exposure. Media ethnographers were critical of media effects research because it did not account for the contexts in which audiences consumed media. Ethnographic methods require researchers to study people's engagement with media in their own settings. Questions that are explored by media ethnographers include how audiences make meaning of media texts, the situations in which people view media, and the uses of communications technologies in the home.

The first broad area of study is ethnographies of production. Ethnographies of production examine how different forms of media, including news, film, television, and online content, are produced. For example, Michael Schudson's study of the newsroom used a sociological lens to better understand the occupational routines of journalists, the relationships between reporters and their subjects, and the

ways reporters understand the professional rules and values in the newsroom. More recent research has examined the production of news in new media environments, such as blogs.

Ethnographies of film and television are a newer area of research and fall under the general heading of production studies. Production studies shift focus away from an analysis of the product of media to better understand the processes that media producers encounter as they create media. Production studies scholars argue that creativity is not an isolated experience but instead is embedded in a complex web of economics, politics, and culture. Influenced by cultural studies, production studies scholars look at the ways in which culture both constructs and reinforces power relations. Areas of inquiry include organizational practices and the political economy of media production, or how economics have influenced the context of production. For example, production studies scholars are interested in how outsourcing of labor might influence media teams or how media ownership might influence the content of media.

Audience ethnographies, or reception studies, examine how audiences interact with products of cultural industries, such as films, music, and television shows. Reception studies researchers examine how the context of consuming media texts influences audiences' reactions. Similar to production studies, reception studies are influenced by the field of cultural studies. British cultural studies scholars such as Stuart Hall were influential in the development of reception studies. Hall was critical of media effects theories that framed audiences as homogeneous rather than heterogeneous. Hall argued that media texts were encoded with meaning. For example, certain ideologies were inscribed in the way that characters were portrayed. However, there are several different ways that audiences can decode messages. Audiences may accept these representations, negotiate them, or actively resist them.

Later research into audience analysis argued that media texts are not viewed in isolation but instead are social. For example, in his study of family television viewing, David Morley found that there were significant gender differences in the ways in which television viewing occurred in the household. In her study of the global impact of the American television show *Dallas*, Ien Ang recorded the ambivalent reactions that viewers had to the show.

Reception studies also examine how audiences create "interpretive communities," or how people create shared meaning from viewing the same media texts. For example, in her book *Reading the Romance*, Janice Radway conducted an ethnography of a bookstore, investigating the many reasons women read romance novels. She found that romance novels helped women to escape the everyday realities of their lives. Applications of the concept of interpretive communities have been applied to study a variety of groups, such as fan communities and video-game players.

Although media ethnography can be a useful way to study media audiences and the production of media texts, there are several critiques of this field of study. First, ethnographers should consider power relations between researchers and subjects. Many media ethnographers have addressed this critique by reflecting on their personal experiences and explaining their subject position.

Others critique media ethnography for narrowly relying on interview data and not employing long-term, in-depth ethnographic methods. From this perspective, the way that qualitative researchers use the term *ethnography* is problematic, because many of the methodologies used are interviews, focus groups, and case studies that do not offer descriptions as "thick" as when the researcher is embedded in a particular context for a long period of time. These critics suggest that media ethnography, while influenced by the field of cultural anthropology, differs significantly in terms of scope.

Carolyn Cunningham
Gonzaga University

See also Audiences: Reception and Injection Models; Encoding and Decoding; Gay and Lesbian Portrayals on Television; Gender and Masculinity: Black Masculinity; Hall, Stuart; Mass Media; Media Consolidation; Newsrooms; Radway, Janice; Reception Theory

Further Readings

Ang, Ien. *Watching* Dallas. London: Methuen, 1985.

Bird, S. Elizabeth. *The Audience in Everyday Life: Living in a Media World*. New York: Routledge, 2003.

Geertz, Clifford. *The Interpretation of Cultures*. New York: Basic Books, 1973.

Hall, Stuart. "Encoding/Decoding." In *Culture, Media, Language*, Stuart Hall et al., eds. London: Hutchinson, 1980.

Mayer, Vicki, Miranda Banks, and John Thornton Caldwell, eds. *Production Studies: Cultural Studies of Media Industries*. New York: Routledge, 2009.

Morley, David. *Family Television: Cultural Power and Domestic Leisure*. London: Comedia Publishing Group, 1986.

Paterson, Chris and David Domingo, eds. *Making Online News: The Ethnography of New Media Production*. New York: Peter Lang, 2008.

Radway, Janice. *Reading the Romance: Women, Patriarchy and Popular Literature*. Chapel Hill: University of North Carolina Press, 1984.

Schudson, Michael. *The Sociology of News*. New York: Norton, 2003.

Seiter, Ellen. *Television and New Media Audiences*. New York: Clarendon Press, 1998.

MEDIA GLOBALIZATION

Transnational media can be defined as media that are produced, distributed, and consumed across national boundaries through the new communication and information technologies that became available at the end of the 20th century. These technologies include satellite television and the Internet. Transnational media appeared in the era of globalization, an era characterized by an increased connectivity, interconnectedness, or interdependence. Transnational media are most often studied from an economic or cultural perspective. An economic perspective focuses on the concentration of power in the hands of only a few global media giants that aim to enrich themselves and their owners, potentially at the cost of consumers and citizens. For women, this increasing media concentration means a smaller number of media outlets worldwide and less diversity of ideas in the marketplace. A cultural perspective focuses on the impact of imported cultural products on local cultures as well as the reception of these products by various audiences. The flow of cultural products across nations is of specific interest to women, as ideas about appropriate gender roles are often quite nation-specific. Global news agencies, for example, often exclude voices of women in their news reports and typically represent women as victims. Third World, postcolonial, and transnational feminists are working to point out problems of access and representation of women in the media, especially of those in developing countries. Media activism groups around the world engage in activities such as the Global Media

Globalization and advances in technology have led to an era of more connectedness and interdependence, including the ready availability of transnational news. (Photos.com)

Monitoring Project, which is taking place every five years, to gather information about the participation of female journalists in the news media as well as the inclusion of female sources and the representation of women in the news. This research is used to lobby media houses for the inclusion of women in all aspects of the newsmaking process and to demand more gender-sensitive representations of both men and women.

Globalization

Media globalization can be seen as part of the more general phenomenon of globalization, which refers to an increased global connectivity, interconnectedness, or interdependence that results in the shrinking of the world and the compression of time and space. Globalization is often defined in terms of global capitalist markets, but Arjun Appadurai suggested that globalization and global cultural flows could be described in terms of five "scapes," or dimensions: ethnoscapes, mediascapes, technoscapes, finanscapes, and ideascapes. These *scapes* refer to the flow across borders of, respectively, people, media, technologies, money, and ideas. Of most interest to media scholars is the flow of media and ideas across

national boundaries. A result of globalization is deterritorialization, where the relationship between culture and space becomes destabilized. Feminist scholars have pointed out that "grand theories," those focusing on the macro level, typically ignore gendered dimensions of globalization. The globalization of media has been studied primarily from an economic and a cultural perspective.

The Economic Perspective

The economic perspective on media globalization uses the approach of a critical political economy to study structures of media ownership. According to this approach, media reflect the interests of powerful elites, including media owners and advertisers. In patriarchal societies, men are those in powerful positions, and media owners are typically men. These elites are often seen as politically conservative. As a result, media serve the conservative interests of (male) media owners.

Over the last 30 years, media ownership has become increasingly concentrated in the hands of a few powerful companies. This means fewer and fewer companies own more and more media outlets. Today, the most powerful media companies are considered to be Time Warner, Disney, Sony, Bertelsmann, Viacom, News Corporation, and Vivendi. Each of these companies is a conglomerate that exists of several subsidiaries. For example, the media giants often own television channels, film companies, newspapers, magazines, radio stations, book publishers, music groups, and Internet businesses. To maximize profit, media conglomerates use one company subsidiary to complement and promote another, a strategy that is known as synergy. These conglomerates are also maximizing economies of scale, whereby the cost of a company's output declines as its size grows.

The increasing concentration and conglomeration of media ownership result in a handful of media giants that control global information flows. These media giants are considered to be more interested in increasing their profits than in serving the public interest, and they may sacrifice the quality of content to keep expenses low or advertisers satisfied. For women, the concern is that media globalization results in fewer ideas in the marketplace. As the number of sources of information that are available for citizens and consumers declines, the number of available points of view also diminishes.

The Walt Disney Company provides a good example for feminist concerns related to media concentration and conglomeration. Critiques have pointed out that Disney is one of a few powerful media companies that exports entertainment for children across the globe. However, Disney's representations of women, people of color, and other nations in film are often stereotypical and degrading. Because of the dominance of Disney, these images reach children and reinforce stereotypes in young audiences. Disney's power is enhanced by its theme parks, toys, and television shows.

The Cultural Perspective

Media globalization is also studied from a cultural perspective, where the focus is on the impact of imported cultural products on cultures as well as the reception of these products by various audiences. The imbalance in power between the developed countries of the North and the undeveloped countries of the South has led to accusations of cultural imperialism, or the invasion of one culture by another through the media. For example, the United States dominates media exportation in several industries. These problems of unequal cultural flows were discussed at the United Nations Education, Scientific and Cultural Organization (UNESCO) in the 1970s, when representatives from Third World countries argued for a New World Information and Communication Order (NWICO). The developing world argued that an open marketplace simply did not allow for an equal flow of information and that governments should take special steps to protect and promote their nations' own cultural works. This idea was strongly opposed by representatives from especially the United States and United Kingdom. Today, new media technologies and a growing sense of nationalism have resulted in a limited contraflow, or the flow of media and information from the South to the North. This contraflow, however, is unequal, and the relationship between countries exchanging media in this way is therefore referred to as asymmetric interdependence. Examples of contraflow include the export of films from India's film industry (Bollywood) and broadcasts from news outlet Al Jazeera, which is based in Qatar.

The work of sociologist Jan Nederveen Pieterse is often drawn upon to consider issues of globalization and culture. He argues that cultural globalization will result in one of three scenarios: a clash of civilizations, McDonaldization, or hybridization.

In the first scenario, a clash of civilizations, cultures will remain separate from one another but ideological conflicts will increase. In the second scenario, McDonaldization (a term coined by sociologist George Ritzer to refer to the assumption by a culture of the characteristics of a fast-food chain), a global, homogeneous world culture may develop, as proponents of cultural imperialism have argued. In the final scenario, new hybrid cultures may develop because of cultural mixing and borrowing.

When media globalization is studied from a cultural perspective, one of the most important questions is how cultural products from one part of the world would be received in other parts of the world. The theory of cultural proximity states that nations that share cultural attributes—language, for example—more easily relate to each other's cultural products. Those studying media exports are interested in how programs can be adjusted through the processes of regionalization, localization, and glocalization. Media content can be tailored to fit particular regions, especially if these regions, called geolinguistic regions, share a language. Media content can also be adapted for a local market through a blend of the local and the global, called glocalization. An example of glocalization is the successful adaptation of the British program *Who Wants to Be a Millionaire?* to markets in more than 100 countries around the world. A variety of aspects were changed, including the host, participants, questions, and prize money. The result of glocalization is often hybridized media content. In this field of study, media audiences are typically seen as active in their decisions about media content.

Of interest to gender scholars is how media representations of women are received in various cultures. For example, the British show *Pop Idol* was adapted for the American market as *American Idol*, and then to the Afghan market as *Afghan Star*. In a country where music and dancing were forbidden under Taliban rule, *Afghan Star* created quite a controversy when a female finalist's head scarf fell to her shoulders while she was dancing. The woman received death threats and had to go into hiding after her performance.

Global News Agencies

Global news agencies are organizations that act as global news wholesalers to retail news outlets. These agencies collect and distribute news around the world, and they are often studied as part of media globalization. Where national news agencies focus on national concerns such as nation building and development, the focus of global news agencies is more on global concerns. Because of their global reach, they have much power over images and news that people around the world receive. Some of these news agencies—for example, Agence France-Presse (AFP), Reuters, and the Associated Press (AP)—have existed since the first half of the 19th century. In an era of globalizing media, news agencies are often blamed for cultural homogenization because of their focus on Western news and adherence to Western news values. In fact, some media scholars argue that globalization is the same as Westernization to global news agencies, because of their Western news ideologies and unequal attention to world regions.

Research has shown that women are seldom included in news content from mainstream global news agencies. However, research in this area is scarce. When women are included in international news more generally, they are most often represented as victims of disasters. In news about women from "other" countries, stereotypes abound. For example, Arab women are often portrayed as culturally inferior and repressed. These news representations seldom take specific historical contexts and circumstances into account. Because of the lack of representation of women in global news content, women have developed their own news networks, notably the Women's Feature Service (WFS) and WIN News. Between 1994 and 1999, the Inter Press Service (IPS), an alternative news agency that focuses on news from the developing world, implemented a gender-mainstreaming policy to hire more women and to include more women in the news. To mainstream gender in the news, IPS aimed to integrate issues of gender, equality, and women's rights into all its editorial coverage. While the project was not completely successful, IPS continues to work on gender equality through its *Gender Wire*, a free weekly newsletter.

Third World, Postcolonial, and Transnational Feminisms

The theoretical perspectives developed through Third World, postcolonial, and transnational feminisms have been used to inform scholarship on media globalization and transnational media. Third World feminism gives voice to women from the developing world and argues for the recognition of the histories and struggles of Third World women through inter-secting forms of oppression. Postcolonial feminism focuses on the effects of racism and colonialism on women, and it is also critical of cultural imperialism by Western feminism. Transnational feminism refers to the movement of feminism across national borders through networking, conferences, and new media technologies. Feminist scholars have used these theories to study various aspects related to gender, culture, and the media in a global perspective.

Global Media Activism

Feminist media groups around the world are engaging in media activism to demand better access for female journalists to the media and more gender-sensitive representations of both men and women. Media activists worked to include the media as one of 12 areas of concern in the "Platform for Action," which emerged from the United Nations' Fourth World Conference on Women in Beijing, China, in 1995. Strategic objectives related to women and the media were included in Section J of the document and specifically addressed the continuing problems that women face with regard to access and representation in the news media. Governments and other groups were urged to mainstream gender into all policies and programs. Media scholar Margaret Gallagher published *Gender Setting: New Agendas for Media Monitoring and Advocacy* in 2001, and it became an essential guide for those interested in gender and media activism on a global scale. Perhaps the best example of global media activism is the Global Media Monitoring Project, which was launched in 1995 to coincide with the fourth World Conference on Women in Beijing. The project has been repeated every five years since then: in 2000, 2005, and 2010. A total of 108 countries participated in the most recent study, which showed that only 24 percent of people who are heard or read about in print, radio, and television are female. This is considered to represent a significant improvement over that of 1995, when only 17 percent of people in the news were women. The study also found that female reporters wrote 37 percent of stories reported on television, on radio, and in newspapers.

Margaretha Geertsema
Butler University

See also Class Privilege; Cultivation Theory; Cultural Politics; Feminist Theory: Postcolonial; Feminist Theory: Women-of-Color and Multiracial Perspectives; Gender Media Monitoring; Mass Media; Media

Consolidation; Media Convergence; New Media; Newsrooms; Postmodernism

Further Readings

Appadurai, Arjun. *Disjuncture and Difference in the Global Cultural Economy.* Middlesbrough, UK: Theory, Culture and Society, 1990.

Byerly, Carolyn M. and Karen Ross. *Women and Media: A Critical Introduction.* Malden, MA: Blackwell, 2006.

Gallagher, Margaret. *Gender Setting: New Agendas for Media Monitoring and Advocacy.* London: Zed Books, 2001.

Media Education Foundation. "Mickey Mouse Monopoly: Disney, Childhood and Corporate Power." Video. Northampton, MA: Author, 2002.

Pieterse, Jan Nederveen. *Globalization and Culture: Global Melange.* Lanham, MD: Rowman & Littlefield, 2004.

Tkach, Andrew. "Fight for Future of Afghanistan's Culture Plays Out on TV." http://www.cnn.com/2009/WORLD/asiapcf/08/06/generation.islam.afghan.star/index.html (Accessed October 2010).

World Association for Christian Communication. "Who Makes the News?" http://www.whomakesthenews.org (Accessed October 2010).

MEDIA LITERACY

At the 1992 National Leadership Conference on Media Literacy, a rough consensus emerged from U.S. scholars—from such diverse fields as media studies, media production, literature and language arts, library information science, and educational theory and practice—regarding the importance of media literacy, its definition, and significant concepts for teaching it. Media literacy was defined as "the ability to access, analyze, evaluate, and communicate messages in a variety of forms." A media-literate person "can decode, evaluate, analyze, and produce both print and electronic media." Scholars could not agree on a list of goals or instructional practices for teaching media literacy; however, by using models developed by educators in Australia, Canada, and Great Britain, they did agree on the following conceptualizations:

> Media are constructed and construct reality; media have commercial implications; media have ideological and political implications; form and content are related, each of which has a unique aesthetic, codes, and conventions; and receivers negotiate meaning in media.

Thus a comprehensive definition of media literacy involves the ability to locate multimedia resources (research skills); to analyze them critically (possibly using various models of analysis); to evaluate them in the social, economic, political and historical contexts in which they are created and interpreted; and to interpret them in light of the grammatical logics (textual and visual) that shape them. For some scholars, media literacy also involves the ability to create media messages in print, audio, video, and multimedia formats, such as are found on the Web. For others, it involves not only acquiring cognitive skills but also aesthetic, emotional, and moral development.

Although media literacy is primarily taught in K–12 curriculums, it is also taught in institutions of higher education around the globe. In North America, the term often used is *media literacy*, whereas in the United Kingdom and other English-speaking countries it is often called *media education*. Teachers of media literacy use diverse pedagogical techniques, including close textual analysis, contextual analysis of specific media texts such as films or television shows, genre analysis, cross-media comparisons, and macroanalysis of media industries, such as advertising. They often employ techniques as diverse as role playing and media production.

The interdisciplinary field of media literacy studies has been informed by various conceptual models, such as media effects/inoculation theory, uses and gratifications, cultivation theory, cultural/critical studies, and semiotics. The conceptual foundations drawn upon result in very different kinds of media literacy education programs. American media studies tend to reflect the effects/inoculation and uses and gratifications paradigms, whereas Latin American and European countries draw primarily from cultural/critical studies and semiotics.

Types of Media Literacy

Media ecology theorist Joshua Meyrowitz argues for the importance of developing multiple media literacies in students. Specifically, he enumerates three media literacies; content literacy, media grammar literacy, and (drawing on the American media ecology tradition) medium literacy. He explains that each type is linked to a different conception of what counts as media.

The notion that media are conduits that carry messages points to the need for media content literacy. This is the most common understanding of media literacy, often espoused by those outside the discipline of communication. Content literacy involves being able to access and analyze a variety of types of media messages for both manifest (obvious or denotative) and latent (implicit or connotative) meanings. It also involves understanding how the conventions of various genres—for example, documentaries, broadcast news, or western films—shape construction and interpretation. It also involves awareness of how various commercial, cultural, or institutional forces shape both, which messages are constructed (agenda-setting), and how they are constructed (framing). Finally, it involves examining how different audiences—for example, women or working-class white males—might "read" messages differently. Meyrowitz argues that an explicit or implicit focus on media content dominates most media literacy debates and is the view held by such diverse advocates as ministers condemning the immoral content of television; activists protesting the limited or distorted portrayals of gays, women, and minorities; and qualitative and quantitative media researchers studying manifest and latent content in news and entertainment programming.

The idea that media are distinct languages suggests the need for a second type of literacy; media grammar literacy. Meyrowitz explains that this involves understanding how the production variables of each medium, often called the "aesthetic aspects," interact with content to shape meaning. How, for example, does a close-up of a female film star in a romantic comedy "read"? How, for example, does editing operate to create excitement and intensify conflict in television's competition-based reality shows? These grammars are often specific to the medium examined. More advanced grammar literacy would then involve teaching the ability to use medium grammars to create media productions.

Finally, examining media as an environment would invite a literacy of medium effects. In other words, this "media ecology" conception of media requires teaching the ability to examine how the nature of the specific medium—for example, print versus film—shapes key aspects of messages, both on the micro, single-situation level and on the macro, societal level. Meyrowitz asserts that each medium has a relatively fixed character and thus can be examined as a constant in its impact on diverse messages and cultures. For example, medium literacy could involve an examination of how the advent of the telegraph—which for the first time provided almost real-time messaging over vast distances, effectively collapsing both space and time—had an impact not only on the type and shape of messages conveyed but also on society's understanding of communication generally. This third type of media literacy is the least well known in media literacy programs, which tend to emphasize, in this order, content literacy, grammar literacy, and then medium literacy.

History of Media Literacy Studies

A brief history of the development of the interdisciplinary field of media literacy shows a number of shifts in emphasis. The 1970s and early 1980s focused on training and criticism from a moralistic or religious perspective. Organizations as diverse as churches and public interest groups, usually concerned with portrayals of sex and violence, often advocated for protecting children from television's negative influences and for media censorship generally. By the mid-1980s, researchers and educators, drawing from the uses and gratifications and media effects traditions, gradually began shaping the discussion in a way that claimed greater objectivity in offering nondirective and pluralistic approaches to media. Another group of scholars from Europe, in part responding to divisive social and economic conditions around the globe, injected a differently value-laden perspective on media. Taking a political economy of communication orientation, they focused on how governments, international organizations, and media institutions, often working together, shaped media policy and media content in ways that supported dominant ideologies. More recently, responding to the "active audience" paradigm in media studies scholarship, media literacy programs have stressed audience responsiveness, responsibility, and freedom in reaction to media structures and messages. Thus, media literacy has been treated as an issue of morality, public policy, and political activism, as well as a set of pedagogical tools for K–12 teachers, critical skills for student self-expression, guidelines for parents, and a topic of scholarly inquiry from diverse disciplinary traditions.

Debates in Media Literacy

Renée Hobbs, in "The Seven Great Debates in the Media Literacy Movement," summarizes a number of the debates about media literacy among K–12 educators and scholars. Although her article was published in 1998, several of the debates she highlights are still central to the field of media literacy, particularly those addressing the assumptions and goals of media literacy, the features of media literacy programs, where they should be taught, and whether or not they should be underwritten or supported by media institutions.

Should media literacy education aim to protect children and young people from negative media influences? Because they are shaped by diverse sociopolitical and cultural contexts and research traditions, media literacy projects differ widely between First World and Third World countries. Hobbs argues that U.S. programs tend to be defensive and protectionist in orientation. Based on the inoculation model of media effects, the focus is on "vaccinating" students in order to protect them from an array of diverse and potentially damaging media messages. This approach to media literacy, referred to as "impact mediation," often organizes content around problem areas such as materialism, high-risk behaviors, sexuality, nutrition and body image, stereotyping (by race, class, gender, sexual orientation), violence and aggression, and adolescent identity development. This approach has been criticized for promoting teaching methods that turn teachers into preachers and students into vulnerable and passive audiences in need of protection. Critics assert that such an approach fails to acknowledge the pleasures of media consumption and audiences' emotional engagement with it. In educational settings, students are invited to "parrot" the correct answers for teachers without truly engaging as active media audiences, critics, and producers.

Drawing on a cultural/critical studies model, British and Latin American literacy programs, by contrast, invite an activist ethical perspective. Here the focus is on examining media in their social, economic, and political contexts while training students as citizens to be able to influence media messages and organizations through diverse mechanisms.

The focus is on self-examination, social critique, and cultural transformation. Some programs, as Hobbs points out, even "strive to develop alternate media forms to counter established media systems."

Should media production be an essential feature of media literacy education? Some critics and educators argue that truly media-literate students should also know how to create media in diverse formats. This assertion is based on the assumption that producing media demystifies the production process to result in reflexive and critical insights. Whether it involves storyboarding, writing scripts, doing photography, constructing Web pages, or performing in front of a camera, creating media allows for self-reflection and critical inquiry through creative expression. Media production, for example, is an essential component in assessing media literacy in both British and Canadian schools. Educators note that production programs usually fall into one of two categories, media production as expressive or as vocational. Expressive media production tends to emphasize production as a "laboratory" for developing both creative and critical abilities while discovering one's own voice. Vocational training, by contrast, emphasizes learning all aspects of production from planning to editing to performing and directing, with a focus on developing industry professionalism and technical competency in media production skills. Herbert Zettl, author of *Television Production Handbook* (11th edition, 2012), argues that production is an important way of knowing the world and provides a model that helps frame production questions. For Justin Lewis and Sut Jhally, however, teaching production could be detrimental to heightening student awareness because, if taught as a set of decontextualized skills, production techniques may work simply to replicate and validate the dominant codes of media industries without allowing for reflexive examination that might create more critical messages. As vocational training, teaching production skills also may take time away from students' learning more culturally valued skills, such as print literacy.

Should media literacy have a more explicit political and ideological agenda? Linking to the previous debate, some educators have argued that teaching media literacy supports a range of politically progressive ends, from challenging and changing students' attitudes about racism, homophobia, sexism, and violence to promoting change in public schools' rigid institutional practices; from eliminating the use of commercially sponsored messages in public schools to promoting alternative media arts education; and from increasing advocacy for public-access television to challenging regulations of the Federal Communications Commission (FCC) regarding cable and broadcast ownership.

In a different publication, Hobbs asserts that it is inappropriate to conflate media literacy with media activism, arguing instead that media literacy should promote autonomy by developing students' skills in communication, reasoning, analysis, and self-expression. Others, such as Lewis and Jhally, feel that media activism and the transformation of media institutions should be a critical component of media literacy. Media literacy, they assert, should create sophisticated citizens rather than sophisticated consumers. In order to do so, classes in media literacy must convey that the mass media are to be "understood as more than a collection of texts to be deconstructed and analyzed so that we can distinguish or choose among them. They should be analyzed as sets of institutions with particular social and economic structures that are neither inevitable nor irreversible."

More recently, the interdisciplinary field of media literacy studies, following Hobbs's view, has shifted from a focus on *media* to a focus on *literacy*, deemphasizing the ideological and/or political role of the media in favor of increasing emphasis on audiences and the dynamic context of people's personal media experiences. Influenced, in part, by ethnography and phenomenology, this orientation observes and interviews media audiences in naturalistic settings in order to understand media habits, interactions, experiences, and perceptions.

Should media literacy be focused on school-based K–12 educational environments? Most literacy programs have traditionally been aimed at children and youth and the parents and educators who work with them. Such efforts range from weekend workshops to literacy retreats to curricular segments in various K–12 classroom settings. Although the vast majority of programs have been geared toward primary and secondary education, a number have more recently targeted higher education. Some scholars, however, note the tension between the goals of liberal arts and humanities-based media literacy education and the goals of a departmental program in journalism and/or media production in which the university's broad-based literacy efforts

might conflict with the focus on training students for specific jobs as media practitioners. This is not an issue in K–12 programs, because employment training is rarely a focus for university-bound students. In the United States, many media programs point with pride to their links with media professionals, claiming that professionals have much to offer students beyond simply internship opportunities. For some educators, however, this raises such questions as "Do media educators in higher education really want local news broadcasters coming in and telling their students how to perpetuate the status quo in local newscasts?" or "Should someone who will explain the regulatory environment that has allowed certain companies to flourish and others to wither be asked to speak?"

Should media literacy initiatives be supported financially by media organizations? The previously discussed debate regarding media criticism and practice is linked to debates about the role of profit and nonprofit media organizations that financially support media technology in the classroom and work with educators to develop media literacy programs. A well-known example is the Family and Community Critical Viewing Project, a program supported by the National Parent Teacher Association and the National Cable Television Association. This parent education workshop, which has reached more than 100,000 participants, links key ideas in media literacy to issues of media violence. Some educators applaud media industries and organizations for providing teachers with tools, technology, and training, acknowledging the long history of educators working with local cable access to develop community-interest programming; some critics, however, argue that recent trends in this area are troubling. Such a relationship may take advantage of underfunded education programs in need of such technology in order to provide free public relations to the sponsoring companies. The most egregious impact may be that such programs might effectively co-opt the media literacy movement to make it media-industry-friendly rather than critical.

Successes and Prospects

Regardless of the debates regarding where and how to teach media literacy, there is clear consensus on its increasing importance. Media literacy has been shown to be an effective tool for addressing a variety of social concerns, ranging from decreasing children's acceptance of violence on television to reducing adolescent alcohol and tobacco use. Programs in Canada, Australia, and the United States have shown success in alleviating the negative consequences of media on women's body image. One study found a media literacy program more successful than a self-esteem program for reducing teens' risk factors for eating disorders. Other studies have demonstrated that media literacy has a positive impact on knowledge about nutrition and its effect on dieting. In sum, although results in some areas are mixed, such as interventions related to self-objectification and body image, media literacy has demonstrated substantial success in a number of areas.

There is also a clear realization that media are inundating people with information at an exponential rate. We now live in a media-saturated, technologically dependent, and globally connected world. Citizens increasingly receive information from diverse, complex, multimedia formats on multiple media platforms. Currently, five major international media conglomerates control most of the world's media output. Also new is the rise of fairly inexpensive media-production tools that allow users to produce and disseminate their own content via YouTube and other video-sharing Websites. These rapid and major changes call for a critical media literacy that empowers students to read and produce media messages while understanding the various contexts that shape the institutions that produce media, the messages they create, and the audiences that interact with them. Despite this, most educators have not kept up with technological advances or educational research on this topic. Adding to the urgency is the reality that media literacy assessment measures, although advocated for by parents, administrators, accrediting institutions, and legislators, are not well developed and are often unevenly applied. Questions regarding what should be assessed remain. Should we assess knowledge? attitudes? behaviors? values? media-production skills? Although the National Communication Association has developed learning-outcome assessment standards in communication, some of which apply to media literacy, it is not clear to what extent these voluntary standards are employed in K–12 education, let alone higher education, which has been slower to adopt outcome assessment measures generally. Despite the debates that animate the field and the difficulties of dialoging across

disciplines with diverse theoretical and pedagogical foci, Hobbs points out that there is a sense—as a recent special issue of *American Behavioral Scientist* and the yearbook of the National Society for the Study of Education (NSSE) series suggest—that "media literacy is shaping up to be an emerging topic at the intersection of the fields of communication and education that may continue to gain momentum during the early years of the 21st century."

Susan Mackey-Kallis
Villanova University

See also Audiences: Producers of New Media; Audiences: Reception and Injection Models; Beauty and Body Image: Beauty Myths; Blogs and Blogging; Culture Jamming; Desensitization Effect; Electronic Media and Social Inequality; Encoding and Decoding; Gender Media Monitoring; Hacking and Hacktivism; Hypermedia; Mass Media; Media Consolidation; Media Convergence; Media Ethnography; Media Globalization; Media Rhetoric; Mediation; New Media; Polysemic Text; Postmodernism; Quantitative Content Analysis; Reception Theory; Semiotics; Social Comparison Theory; Social Learning Theory; Social Media; Textual Analysis; Tropes; Virtual Community; Virtuality; Web 2.0; Wiki; YouTube

Further Readings

Brown, J. A. "Media Literacy Perspectives." *Journal of Communication*, v.46 (1998).

Brown, J. D. and S. R. Stern. "Mass Media and Adolescent Female Sexuality." In *Handbook of Women's Sexual and Reproductive Health*, G. M. Wingwood and R. J. DiClemente, eds. New York: Kluwer Academic/Plenum, 2002.

Buckingham, D. *Media Education: Literacy, Learning and Contemporary Culture*. Cambridge, UK: Polity Press/Blackwell, 2003.

Foster, M. "Use of Objectification Theory to Examine the Effects of a Media Literacy Intervention on Women." *Sex Roles*, v.56/9–10 (2007).

Goodman, S. *Teaching Youth Media: A Critical Guide to Literacy, Video Production and Social Change*. Teachers College Press, 2003.

Hobbs, R. "The Seven Great Debates in the Media Literacy Movement." *Journal of Communication*, v.46 (1998).

Hobbs, R. and A. Jensen. "The Past, Present, and Future of Media Literacy Education." *Journal of Media Literacy Education*, v.1 (2009).

Irving, L. M. and S. R. Berel. "Comparison of Media Literacy Programs to Strengthen College Women's

Resistance to Media Images." *Psychology of Women Quarterly*, v.25 (2001).

Kellner, D. and J. Share. "Critical Media Literacy, Democracy, and the Reconstruction of Education." In *Media Literacy: A Reader*, Donaldo P. Macedo, ed. New York: Peter Lang, 2007.

Lewis, J. and S. Jhally. "The Struggle Over Media Literacy." *Journal of Communication*, v.46 (1998).

Livingstone, S. "What Is Media Literacy?" *Intermedia*, v.32/3 (2004).

Meyrowitz, J. "Mutiple Media Literacies." *Journal of Communication*, v.46 (Winter 1998).

National Telemedia Council. "About Media Literacy." http://nationaltelemediacouncil.org/aboutml.htm (Accessed 2004).

Potter, W. J. *Theory of Media Literacy: A Cognitive Approach*. Thousand Oaks, CA: Sage, 2004.

Rogow, F. "Shifting From Media to Literacy." *The American Behavioral Scientist*, v.48/1 (2004).

Vande Berg, L. R. "Media Literacy and Television Criticism: Enabling an Informed and Engaged Citizenry." *The American Behavioral Scientist*, v.48/2 (2004).

Wade, T. D., S. Davidson, and J. A. O'Dea. "A Preliminary Controlled Evaluation of a School-Based Media Literacy Program and Self-Esteem Program for Reducing Eating Disorder Risk Factors." *International Journal of Eating Disorders*, v.33 (2003).

Wenner, L. "Media Literacy and Television Criticism." *The American Behavioral Scientist*, v.48/2 (2004).

MEDIA RHETORIC

Rhetoric is, perhaps, one of the most abused words in the English language. Politicians dismiss one another's statements as "mere rhetoric" or demand that an opponent "get past the rhetoric and discuss real solutions." Such usage portrays rhetoric as empty, pompous speech with little substance behind it, but that is an unfair depiction. Before one can delve into the topic of media rhetoric, one must have a clear understanding of rhetoric itself. This can be perplexing because the phenomenon of rhetoric is often defined in different ways by different disciplines. For example, in sociology and media studies, when one talks about the ways in which a message is framed, the underlying issue is actually a question of how a movement or media outlet engages in rhetorical processes.

Aristotle defines rhetoric as "an ability, in each [particular] case, to see the available means of persuasion." However, there is more to rhetoric than simply persuasion. Kenneth Burke observes that a key function of rhetoric is to foster identification. People use rhetoric to make sense of the world linguistically and symbolically; through rhetoric, people define themselves and their relationships to others, cast blame or praise on individuals and groups, ascribe motives for actions, and interpret events. In other words, empirically observable phenomena are the province of the sciences, but phenomena that are perceptible only through our symbolic representation of them (such as nation-states, political identity, and religious ideologies) are firmly in the domain of rhetoric.

Rhetorical theory has long been based on traditional oratory, but as media have become an increasingly important part of society, rhetorical scholars have paid closer attention to how the medium shapes the message. This is not a new idea, of course. Marshall McLuhan famously proclaimed that "the medium is the message," meaning that the medium is by no means a neutral conduit, but rather an integral part of how we perceive the message. The 1960 Kennedy-Nixon presidential debates provide an excellent illustration of how rhetors can benefit from or be thwarted by the medium. Many who watched the debates on television thought that Kennedy won, largely because of the nonverbal cues that made Nixon appear sickly, untrustworthy, and sinister. However, many of those who listened to the debates on the radio felt that Nixon had won the debates. In essence, what changed was how one draws on *ethos*, or that credibility that is drawn from the speaker him- or herself, that entices one to believe him or her. However, the means by which one persuades in general had also changed as a result of the shift in the media environment (the Kennedy-Nixon debates were the first presidential debates to be televised). Other scholars, such as Kathleen Hall Jamieson, suggest that Ronald Reagan understood well the power of the visual medium, giving him a rhetorical edge over those who were less gifted at drawing on the resources of that medium.

Gender scholars have examined the difference between sex and gender, suggesting that sex is biologically constructed while gender is socially constructed. Although family plays a considerable role in how norms of gender performance are shaped, the media also play a significant role in shaping and perpetuating these constructions. Some of the concerns often raised by media effects scholars include body image and eating disorders, adolescent sexual behavior, the influence of the consumption of sexually explicit or violent media, and the creation or reinforcement of potentially damaging gender norms.

Some media effects scholars have argued that the ways in which the media portray the world shape individuals' views of the world. Cultivation theory, put forward by George Gerbner and his colleagues, suggests that heavy consumers of media, specifically television, begin to see the real world as a reflection of the mediated world. They found, for example, that individuals who watched crime dramas and reports of violent crime on the nightly televised news reported feeling that the world was a far more dangerous place than would be warranted by an objective view of crime statistics. What this means is that the media play a significant role in helping individuals make sense of their environment.

As it relates to gender and media, perhaps the area that has received the most interest is how the mass media shape one's perception of beauty and body image. Rhetorical scholar Edwin Black observed that rhetorical discourses ask individuals not only to do something but also to become something. When this concept is applied to the mediated messages that bombard us concerning what constitutes beauty, for example, one is faced with an impossible imperative. One can never look like the models in a fashion magazine or on a billboard, because even the models do not look like that. In an age when digital image manipulation is the norm, people are given a completely unrealistic view of what one should become. However, understanding this manipulation does not negate the imperative to become like these models. Some scholars have therefore argued that unrealistic images of beauty, especially those directed at young women and girls, play a role in the development of eating disorders and pathological self-body images.

Another area in which media plays a considerable role in shaping perceptions is gender roles. Many scholars have noted that gender is performed rather than simply biologically based. Because media is a part of one's socialization, how these gender performances are portrayed in the media has significant implications for how one enacts his or her own gender. Some have argued that television shows that portray women as largely subservient, passive sex objects and men as bumbling idiots held up for ridicule can be damaging for both sexes. Moreover,

some have argued that television shows and movies model family and intimate relationships in ways that may provide unrealistic expectations.

Although it seems that media are something directed at the individual, some individuals take aim at the media as well in order to reach large audiences quickly and simultaneously. For example, social movements have long recognized the importance of gaining media attention and sometimes create protest actions and demonstrations designed specifically to get the attention of the news media. People for the Ethical Treatment of Animals (PETA) is an excellent example of how this strategy can be employed through "die ins," seemingly intentionally provocative advertising campaigns that can become news items in themselves, and spectacles such as the "running of the nudes" in Pamplona Spain prior to the traditional bullfights. By giving the media something interesting to cover, such organizations are then able to use the media to disseminate their messages.

There is also the potential that, with the advent of new media, one's innermost thoughts and actions

PETA members in White Plains, New York, protest the use of fur by the clothing manufacturer Burberry, carrying signs and painted in the trademark Burberry plaid. People use rhetoric to define themselves and others, cast blame or praise on individuals and groups, explain their actions, and interpret events. (Wikimedia)

can be transmitted to an audience that would be impossible to reach previously. It seems that Andy Warhol's prediction that everyone would be famous for 15 minutes is now within reach. A renaissance of interpersonal communication appears to be taking place as media continue to evolve. No longer are the channels directed only one way; now content producers actually pay attention to their audiences, and the mediated environment in new media can seem more like a dialogue than a monologue. This phenomenon has implications for how one behaves rhetorically in such an environment.

With an understanding that rhetoric is the means through which people alter and reinforce their socially constructed world, it becomes clear that media are an integral part of that process. The music to which one listens, the movies and television shows one watches, and the digital content one consumes all contribute to one's understanding of how the world behaves and how it ought to behave. As such, media cannot be relegated simply to the realm of mere entertainment, because they serve a normative function. One must look at media not as something outside the sphere of rhetoric but rather as a part of the system by which we define who we are, what we should value, and how we should behave.

Brett Lunceford
University of South Alabama

See also Audiences: Producers of New Media; Audiences: Reception and Injection Models; Beauty and Body Image: Beauty Myths; Beauty and Body Image: Eating Disorders; Blogs and Blogging; Cultivation Theory; Gender and Femininity: Motherhood; Gender and Femininity: Single/Independent Girl; Gender and Masculinity: Black Masculinity; Gender and Masculinity: Fatherhood; Gender and Masculinity: Metrosexual Male; Gender and Masculinity: White Masculinity; Gender Embodiment; Gender Media Monitoring; Gender Schema Theory; Identity; Kilbourne, Jean; McLuhan, Marshall; Media Literacy; Mediation; New Media; Online New Media: GLBTQ Identity; Online New Media: Transgender Identity; Pornification of Everyday Life; Reception Theory; Social Construction of Gender; Social Media

Further Readings

Aristotle. *On Rhetoric: A Theory of Civic Discourse.* Translated by George Alexander Kennedy. New York: Oxford University Press, 1991.

Black, Edwin. "The Second Persona." *Quarterly Journal of Speech*, v.56/2 (1970).

Burke, Kenneth. *A Rhetoric of Motives*. New York: Prentice-Hall, 1952.

Gerbner, George, et al. "Growing Up With Television: Cultivation Processes." In *Media Effects: Advances in Theory and Research*, Jennings Bryant and Dolf Zillmann, eds. Mahwah, NJ: Lawrence Erlbaum Associates, 2002.

Jamieson, Kathleen Hall. *Eloquence in an Electronic Age: The Transformation of Political Speechmaking*. New York: Oxford University Press, 1988.

McLuhan, Marshall. *Understanding Media: The Extensions of Man*. 1964. Reprint, Cambridge, MA: MIT Press, 1994.

Medhurst, Martin J. and Thomas W. Benson, eds. *Rhetorical Dimensions in Media: A Critical Casebook*, 2nd ed. Dubuque, Iowa: Kendall/Hunt, 1991.

MEDIATION

For decades, media theorists have extolled Marshall McLuhan's statement that "the medium is the message." Humanistic scholars of media studies interpreted McLuhan to mean that the personal and social consequences of any medium or technology in a culture alter the way members of that culture communicate with their world. Karl Marx defined mediation as the reconciliation of two opposing forces within a given society by a mediating object, which can be cultural or material (such as print materials). Therefore, many media thinkers combine McLuhan and Marx and say that media mediates the message, especially from cultural, economic, political, and sociological perspectives. After considering both Marx and McLuhan, other media thinkers defined mediation as a process of cultural production and gatekeeping by media institutions that intervene in the relationship between people's everyday experience and a "true" view of reality or false consciousness.

Marxist cultural analysis emphasizes that the masses are manipulated and exploited by the ruling class. The Marxist method seeks to explicate the manifest and latent reflections of modes of material production, ideological values, class relations, and structures of social power—racial or gender as well as politicoeconomic or the state of consciousness of people in a historical or socioeconomic situation. The Marxist method provides an analytic tool for studying the political signification in every facet of contemporary culture, including popular entertainment in television and films, music, mass-circulation books, newspaper and magazine features, and comics, as well as acculturating institutions, whether educational, religious, familial, societal, or cultural. The most prevalent theme in Marxist cultural criticism is the way the mode of production and the ideology dominate in American culture, along with the way the rest of the world and American business and culture have colonized. This domination is perpetuated both through overt propaganda in news reporting, advertising, and public relations and through the often unconscious absorption of capitalistic values by creators and consumers in all aspects of the culture of everyday life.

The mass media and popular culture are centrally important in the spread of false consciousness, in leading people to believe that "whatever is, is right." From this perspective, the mass media and popular culture constitute a crucial link between the institutions of society and individual consciousness. Marxist media analysis reasons that media are tools of mediation. There is no such thing as unmanipulated writing, filming, or broadcasting. The question is therefore not whether the media are mediated, but who mediates them.

Marxism and Conflict

For Marx, history is based on unending class conflict—unending, that is, until the establishment of a communist society, in which classes disappear and, with them, conflict. The classes that Marx considered were the bourgeoisie, who own the factories and corporations; the ruling class; and the proletariat, the huge mass of workers who are exploited by the ruling class and whose condition becomes increasingly more desperate.

The bourgeoisie avert class conflict by indoctrinating the proletariat with ruling-class ideas, such as the notion of the self-made man and the idea that the social and economic arrangements in a given society at a given time are natural and historical. If social arrangements are natural, they cannot be modified; thus, one must accept a given order as inevitable. Marxists argue that the social and economic arrangements found in a given time are historical—created by people and therefore capable of being changed by people. The bourgeoisie try to convince everyone that capitalism is natural and therefore eternal, but this idea, say the Marxists, is false. People who live in bourgeois capitalist societies live in a state of

psychological terror. In our lives, we are under constant "attack" by print advertisements, radio and television commercials, and the programs carried by mass media, even though we may not recognize that we are being besieged or may not be able to articulate our feelings. The media mediate the conflict and terror. For example today's attacks may include being a woman in a male-dominated culture or being a woman manager who earns less than her male counterpart who performs the same job.

Marxism and the Consumer

Advertising is an institution in a capitalist society because it is necessary to motivate people to work hard so that they can accumulate money, which they can then use to buy material items. People must then be driven to consume, must be made crazy to consume, for it is consumption that maintains the economic system.

Media, in the form of advertising, mediates the consumer culture in a capitalistic society to generate anxieties, create dissatisfactions, and feed on alienation of those consumers. There is little that advertising will not do, use, or co-opt to achieve its goals. If it needs to debase the women's rights movement, debase sexuality, or terrorize the masses, it will. Advertising diverts people's attention from social and political concerns and directs that attention toward narcissistic self-concerns. Advertising is more than a merchandising tool; it takes control of everyday life and dominates social relationships. It also leads people to turn inward and separates them from one another. It imposes on society a collective form of taste. To sell goods, advertising has to change attitudes, lifestyles, customs, habits, and preferences while maintaining the economic system that benefits from these changes. To mediate human response to advertising, the appearance of the goods is manipulated to stimulate a desire for them. People have the illusion that they make their own decisions about what to purchase and what to do, but according to Marx, these decisions are made for them. Their acts turn out to be almost automatic responses to stimuli generated by advertisers and the commodities themselves.

In Marxism it is important to mediate people's consciousness by giving them certain ideas; in this way the wealthy, who benefit most from the social arrangements in a capitalist country, maintain the status quo. For example, women, who in the 1960s were second-class citizens, were virtually excluded from media representations, and that exclusion maintained their status quo. In 1978, Gaye Tuchman and George Gerbner called this "symbolic annihilation" that led to the marginalization of women's issues. When women were depicted in the media, they were relegated to domestic roles that accorded them no social power.

New Media and Mediation

Thinkers who grew up with online interaction, information seeking, and self-expression have found that the cultural views of mediation have shifted. The participatory and performative nature of digital culture and online interaction departs in key aspects from the production-consumption logic of mass media typified by television. It has been suggested that the term *connected presence*, referring to "always-on" technologies such as Blackberries and iPhones, describes the non-mass flow of communication exchanges. The ordinariness of new media and the recognition among new media thinkers that society and technology are mutually codetermining have redirected views of mediation from one of technological intervention between experience and reality to one in which the ongoing mutual reshaping of communicative action and communication technology constitutes experience.

A new media theory has emerged that rejects Marx's determinism. Domestication theory by Roger Silverstone states that people consume and appropriate new media technologies in their everyday lives and practices. The technology appropriation affects new technological developments. This view not only rejects technological determinism; it also rejects social-constructivist views that reduce media to mere reflections of existing cultural practices and formations. Domestication sees individual households as networks of people, practices, meanings, and objects. It shows how technologies move back and forth across the boundary between the home and the public and private spheres. Domestication emphasizes the meanings that people attribute to technologies, as well as how they use them—that is, both the material and the symbolic aspects of technology. Media systems are unique among other technologies because they are commodities in themselves, consumed and appropriated from

the public world beyond the home; their content promotes and reinforces consumption. The meaning of the technologies is worked out and negotiated within the private sphere of the home, as the members of the household make sense of and use the technology.

Mediation, Gender, and New Media

Sociologists suggest that media is functional when it contributes to the maintenance and stability of society and dysfunctional when it destabilizes an entity in society. Television, for example, is functional when it provides consumptive information about breast cancer prevention. It is dysfunctional when it depicts women as "just" housewives who do not have the capacity to enter the workforce.

Examining the function of the intent of the broadcasted depiction determines if the media want to inform the audience through a manifest function or indoctrinate the audience with specified beliefs through a latent function. Viewers of films and television programs often identify with the characters in the scripts and incorporate what they see in creating their own identities. Many observers believe that the mass media mediate a type of social teaching. The media often place women in demeaning roles. All too frequently, women are treated as sexual objects, used for display, or are portrayed as dummies who get excited about some brand of paper towel. They are much less often shown as professionals or productive citizens who should be taken seriously. Such roles give audience members images of what women are like and how they should be treated that can have negative consequences.

Ever-changing technology and media's significance allow for the promotion of oppressive gender roles not predicated on the strict duality of biological attributes of male and female bodies. Media influence can deconstruct this strict physiological view and open it up to a discussion based on a sociocultural analysis. Cyberfeminists, for instance, argue that the gender anonymity of the Internet and its relative disconnection from actual physical bodies provide a unique terrain on which to build a new, more fluid definition of gender.

Gayle M. Pohl
University of Northern Iowa

See also Advertising; Critical Theory; Feminist Theory: Marxist; Film: Hollywood; McLuhan, Marshall; New Media; Sexism; Television

Further Readings

Berger, A. *Media Analysis Techniques*. Thousand Oaks, CA: Sage, 2005.

Boczkowski, P. and L. Lievrouw. "Bridging STS and Communication Studies: Scholarship on Media and Information Technologies." In *New Handbook of Science, Technology and Society*, Edward J. Hackett et al., eds. Cambridge, MA: MIT Press, 2007.

Bolter, J. D. and R. Grusin. *Remediation: Understanding New Media*, Cambridge, MA: MIT Press, 1999.

Licoppe, C. "Connected Presence: The Emergence of a New Repertoire for Managing Social Relationships in a Changing Communications Technoscape." *Environment and Planning D: Society and Space*, v.22/1 (2004).

MEN'S MAGAZINES: LAD MAGAZINES

Inspired by the success of lad magazines in the United Kingdom, U.K.-based Dennis Publishing launched *Maxim* in the United States in April 1997. The magazine's debut encouraged what has been called the "lad magazine" genre, targeted to young men. Lad magazines parallel women's lifestyle magazines such as *Cosmopolitan*. The lad magazine genre also includes U.S. magazines *FHM: For Him Magazine*, which was launched by Emap in 2000, and *Stuff*, which was launched by Dennis Publishing in 2001. Shortly after their launches, these lad magazines experienced significant circulation growth and quickly became viable competitors to long-standing men's magazines like *Esquire* and *GQ*. *Maxim*, the oldest and most popular lad magazine, claimed it was the best-selling lifestyle magazine in the world in 2004. For years it boasted a 2.5 million circulation rate. In 2008, however, the circulation rates of all lad magazines, including *Maxim*, were on the decline. Despite this decline, *Maxim* remains one of the top 50 best-selling magazines in the United States.

Lad magazines differ from more general men's magazines in important ways. Lad magazines are more greatly focused on sexual interests and include more overt depictions of sex than men's lifestyle magazines. This difference is perhaps most noticeable when considering the magazines' covers. A recent content analysis found that every single issue of *Maxim* has featured either a three-quarter shot or an upper-body shot of a scantily clad woman. In 2003, Wal-Mart stopped selling lad magazines in its stores, in part because of complaints it had received about their racy covers. At the time, such pictures were rare on mainstream men's magazine covers. In this way, lad magazines are similar to pornographic magazines like *Playboy* and *Penthouse*. An important difference, however, is that lad magazines do not visually show women's nipples or genitalia. Given that full frontal nudity is avoided, these magazines are available for purchase by teens of all ages (hence the term *lad*). In contrast, readers must be at least age 18 to purchase either *Playboy* or *Penthouse*.

Despite their popularity, lad magazines have received little attention from academic scholars. Most of the existing research has focused primarily on cataloging the content of various lad magazines; only a handful of studies focus on the effects of exposure to such content. Most of the existing research has been narrowly focused on the sexual content in these types of magazines, which makes sense, given that sex is a major focus of the magazines. These studies have found that the genre promotes hegemonic masculinity and traditional gender roles. These magazines emphasize that men must attain sexual prowess and female domination. Women are portrayed as sexual objects on display for the male reader.

The most common topic of the sexual content that studies have found is that women like sex. Discussions of unorthodox sexual behaviors or positions and how to improve one's sex life were the second and third most common topics respectively. Although superficially it seems that lad magazines have promoted consideration of women's pleasure, with the most common secondary topic being how to improve one's own (the reader's, or man's) sex life, it seems clear that content focusing on what women enjoy sexually is essentially about how men can have more frequent and better sexual intercourse if they please women.

Sexual intercourse is largely portrayed as adventurous and fun, with little or no risk involved. Sexual articles were found to emphasize a variety of sexual positions and discussed sexual intercourse occurring in a variety of physical locations (such as outdoors or in public places). Discussions about sexually transmitted diseases or unplanned pregnancies, on the other hand, are virtually nonexistent. Furthermore, lad magazines do not include prescriptive sexual content at the same rate as women's magazines.

Mentions of marriage or engagement were found to be wholly absent from the articles about sex. Instead, the articles primarily discussed sexual intercourse among individuals in committed relationships, followed closely by discussions of sex among strangers. When relationships are discussed in lad magazines, sexual prowess is depicted as the top priority.

Overwhelmingly, women in these magazines are seen as objects of sexual conquest. In an illustrative example, in June 2002, *Maxim* published "*Maxim's* Guide to North American Girls." The story parodied a trophy hunt, including images of women walking through a jungle. Each woman was identified as a "species" and was characterized with descriptions of habitat and behavior patterns.

It was found that articles about sex were typically accompanied by photos of a sexualized woman, often with the woman in a state of disrobing. Furthermore, when men and women were shown together in photos accompanying sexual articles, they were shown in intimate contact. Women were not only shown as sexual objects in articles about sex, however. Three fourths of the advertisements featuring women in all men's magazines (including more mainstream magazines such as *GQ* and *Esquire*) were found to portray women as sex objects. In 13 percent of these ads, women were also presented as victims, and in 9 percent of these ads women were featured as both sexual objects and targets of violence, aggression, or bondage.

The magazines rarely focus on sexual minorities, and portrayals of gay men are largely absent. Lesbianism, in contrast, is mentioned somewhat frequently, although it is rarely the primary focus of an article. The mentions of lesbianism are really about women having sex together while a man or men observe the sexual act. Thus, lesbianism is mentioned within the context of the male fantasy and lesbians are included purely as objects of the male gaze.

Only a handful of studies have tested the effects of exposure to lad magazines, and results are not entirely consistent. Experimental studies have found that exposure is positively related to attitudes about male dominance. In contrast, survey research has not supported this finding. Survey research has found a relationship between reading the magazines and endorsing permissive sexual attitudes independent of sexual behavior. Readers of lad magazines

also have greater expectations for sexual variety and lower levels of romantic commitment. Finally, readers exhibit a more aggressive sexual self-schema than nonreaders.

Stacey J. T. Hust
Washington State University, Pullman

See also Beauty and Body Image: Beauty Myths; E-Zines: Riot Grrrl; E-Zines: Third Wave Feminist; Gender Embodiment; Heterosexism; Men's Magazines: Lifestyle and Health; Pornification of Everyday Life; Pornography: Heterosexual; Pornography: Internet; Sexism; Sexuality; Social Construction of Gender; Virtual Sex; Women's Magazines: Fashion; Women's Magazines: Feminist Magazines; Women's Magazines: Lifestyle and Health

Further Readings

Aubrey, Jennifer Stevens and Laramie D. Taylor. "The Role of Lad Magazines in Priming Men's Chronic and Temporary Appearance-Related Schemata: An Investigation of Longitudinal and Experimental Findings." *Human Communication Research*, v.35/1 (2009).

Coy, Maddy and Miranda Horvath. "Lads' Mags, Young Men's Attitudes Towards Women and Acceptance of Myths About Sexual Aggression." *Feminism and Psychology*, v.21/1 (2011).

Taylor, Laramie D. "All for Him: Articles About Sex in American Lad Magazines." *Sex Roles*, v.52/3–4 (February, 2005).

MEN'S MAGAZINES: LIFESTYLE AND HEALTH

During the last few decades, the number of popular periodicals devoted to men's fitness, well-being, and self-image has increased in response to the changing status of men and boys in society. Once considered to be only the source of the "gaze," males are now also its object. Concern about body shape and personal style now has the attention of young males beginning as early as middle school.

The first mainstream magazines marketed to men were devoted to soft pornography (*Playboy*), sports (*Field and Stream, Sports Illustrated*), and bodybuilding. The latter were published as early as the late 1930s by Josef "Joe" Weider. By the 1980s, his *Muscle and Fitness* and other physical culture magazines were purchased by many young men who emulated the physique of professional bodybuilding competitors, including Arnold Schwarzenegger. Currently, fitness and lifestyle magazines for men are even more popular than those devoted to bodybuilding. They have taken their place along with men's fashion magazines pioneered by *Gentleman's Quarterly* and *Esquire*. The popularity of these publications can be traced to the eroticization of the (especially young) male body in film and on television that began in the 1950s. Film and television performers and professional athletes are among the most prominent representatives of the new male, who both looks at and enjoys being looked at. Media personalities, including actors, have often started their careers as clothing models.

A youthful prototype of the male is emulated by men into early middle age and beyond. Certain parts of the body have been fetishized, especially the arms ("guns"), chest ("pecs") and abdomen ("six-pack"). A thin, mesomorphic body type is coveted. So is a body of certain proportions that are in fact fundamentally dependent on genetic makeup. While the boyish body is more popular, the big muscular ("buff") build remains the signature male prototype. These magazines contain advertisements selling nutritional supplements, along with exercise equipment and workout clothing. The sources of increasing attention to the male body include underwear advertisements (especially for briefs). Some magazine layouts feature a subtext suggesting sexual tension.

It has been noted that body dysmorphia (displeasure with one's physique, especially concern over not being sufficiently muscular) is a common topic in counseling sessions with men. Psychologists also claim an increase in the number of male clients seen for eating disorders, which had been the province of women. These trends may be a response to the new ideal of the masculine body promoted by the media, not only in men's magazines but also on television, on billboards, and in film. Such bodies are regularly associated with sexual prowess, wealth, and success, as well as with health.

As the male body itself has become an object to be sculpted and enhanced, highlighting its features with cosmetic procedures has also become more common. Removing facial and body hair either temporarily (waxing) or permanently is now an accepted practice

Natural bodybuilder Steve Jones poses after winning the 2007 Australasian Classic Physique title. Jones owns Powerzone Nutrition and owns and edits *Australian Natural Bodz* magazine. (Wikimedia)

among many males beginning in the college years. Body hair is said to obscure the finer contours of muscles that have been arduously exercised in the gym. Fitness magazines regularly feature sections on grooming as well as nutrition and healthcare. Several peer-reviewed professional journals on men's health have appeared since 2000, but they have a limited audience and are concerned more with illness (for example, obesity and prostate cancer).

Among the most influential of the popular magazines promoting the image of the new male is *Men's Health*. While catering to the full range of men's interests, its primary focus from the start has been the cultivation of an ideal version of the (usually young) male body, pursued not only by teens and men through the third decade of life, however, but also by middle-age men, especially those who hope to refashion their bodies in the image of the sexually attractive and healthy young man they once were or hoped to be.

Readers of all ages are likely unaware of the sophisticated methods of photographing (lighting and choice of angle) and "editing" (air brushing) the images of models produced. Unrealistic expectations of success in approximating the ideal are therefore formed. A random sampling of cover images suggests that the centerpiece of the male body is his midsection, which has become the emblem of male health and sexual attractiveness. While strength may have been the goal of the early magazines, a lean "aesthetic" look is now to be emulated and accomplished. Nearly every issue contains a feature that presents yet another way of losing weight and toning the "abs," which are iconic for the perfectible male body.

Miles Groth
Wagner College

See also Beauty and Body Image: Beauty Myths; Beauty and Body Image: Eating Disorders; Bordo, Susan; Gender and Masculinity: Metrosexual Male; Gender Embodiment; Identity; Male Gaze; Men's Magazines: Lad Magazines; Scopophilia; Women's Magazines: Lifestyle and Health

Further Readings

Brunner, B. R. and L. R. Brunner Huber. "101 Ways to Improve Health Reporting: A Comparison of the Types and Quality of Health Information in Men's and Women's Magazines." *Public Relations Review*, v.36/1 (2010).

Dworkin, Shari L. and Faye Linda Wachs. *Body Panic: Gender, Health, and the Selling of Fitness*. New York: New York University Press, 2009.

Friedman, D. B., J. N. Laditka, S. B. Laditka, and A. E. Mathews. "Cognitive Health Messages in Popular Women's and Men's Magazines, 2006–2007." *Preventing Chronic Disease*, v.7/2 (March 2010).

Jackson, Peter, Nick Stevenson, and Kate Brooks. *Making Sense of Men's Magazines*. Malden, MA: Blackwell, 2001.

MILLER, MARK CRISPIN

Mark Crispin Miller is a professor of media, culture, and communication (sometimes referred to as media ecology) at New York University (NYU) and a widely quoted and published media critic, political commentator, and blogger. He earned a B.A. from Northwestern University in 1971 and then went to The Johns Hopkins University, where he spent several years earning a master's degree in 1973 and a Ph.D. in English, with a focus on Renaissance literature, in 1977. Miller also served as director of film studies at Johns Hopkins before leaving for his post at NYU.

Since the 2000 U.S. presidential election, Miller has been an outspoken critic of former President George W. Bush and the two elections that elevated him to the White House. He has published three related books: *The Bush Dyslexicon: Observations on a National Disorder* (2002), *Cruel and Unusual: Bush/Cheney's New World Order* (2005), and *Fooled Again: The Real Case for Electoral Reform* (2007). Miller also edited *Loser Take All: Election Fraud and the Subversion of Democracy, 2000–2008* (2008).

Although Miller is widely known for his work on Bush policy and election mismanagement, he also teaches classes related to advertising and society as well as mass persuasion and propaganda. In 2011, Miller was at work on a new book, on the history and phenomenon of Marlboro cigarettes, *The Marlboro Man: An American Success Story*. Miller's research interests are also quite varied, ranging from the history and tactics of advertising to media ownership and sex education. In addition to writing books on these topics, he has edited two book series, Icons of America, published by Yale University Press, and Discovering America, published by the University of Texas Press.

Perhaps because he has such a variety of teaching and research interests, Miller has been a much sought-after interviewee for a number of documentaries, including *Hijacking Catastrophe: 9/11* (2004), *Fear and the Selling of American Empire* (2004), *The Fall of America and the Western World* (2009), and two Frontline documentaries for the Public Broadcasting Service (PBS) examining marketing, marketing research, and the industry known as trend spotting: *The Persuaders* (2004) and *The Merchants of Cool* (2001). Miller's credits on the Internet Movie Database (IMDb) also include an appearance as himself on a January 2006 airing of the popular and highly rated *The Daily Show With*

Jon Stewart. Other mainstream media appearances include *The Newshour*, FOXNews Channel's *The O'Reilly Factor*, and National Public Radio's *All Things Considered.*

In addition to appearing on mainstream television media, Miller has performed on the New York stage. In 2004, he developed and starred in *Patriot Act: A Public Meditation.* His performance was billed not as a work of theater but as "a provocative, funny, and scary exposé of threats to our American democracy and freedom." During six weeks' worth of performances, Miller walked audience members through a multimedia presentation, with each performance slightly different from the previous one because it incorporated the newest information and media reports.

Miller's appearance on *The Daily Show* and his stint on the New York theater scene are two ways in which he has successfully integrated his academic and professional work into the mainstream. Another way in which Miller educates the mainstream is through his blog, "News From Underground." The blog is a daily news feed and e-mail service that aims to keep readers up to date on issues affecting democracy and political life in the United States and abroad. Readers can also follow Miller on Twitter and Facebook, and the blog has a YouTube channel as well as an RSS feed to provide a multimedia view of the news.

According to his statement on his blog, Miller believes that "academics, like reporters, have a civic obligation to help keep the people well-informed, so that American democracy might finally work."

Susan Westcott Alessandri
Suffolk University, Boston

See also Blogs and Blogging; Cultural Politics; McChesney, Robert

Further Readings

Miller, Mark Crispin. *Boxed In: The Culture of TV.* Evanston, IL: Northwestern University Press, 1988.

Miller, Mark Crispin. *The Bush Dyslexicon: Observations on a National Disorder.* New York: W. W. Norton, 2002.

Miller, Mark Crispin. *Cruel and Unusual: Bush/Cheney's New World Order.* New York: W. W. Norton, 2005.

Miller, Mark Crispin. *Fooled Again: The Real Case for Electoral Reform.* New York: Basic Books, 2007.

Miller, Mark Crispin. *Loser Take All: Election Fraud and the Subversion of Democracy, 2000–2008.* Brooklyn, NY: Ig, 2008.

Miller, Mark Crispin. "News From Underground." http://markcrispinmiller.com.

Miller, Mark Crispin. *Seeing Through Movies.* New York: Pantheon, 1990.

Miller, Mark Crispin. *Spectacle: Operation Desert Storm and the Triumph of Illusion.* New York: Poseidon Press, 1992.

MINORITY RIGHTS

Historically stereotyped, diminished, or overlooked by the media, women and members of cultural minorities are pushing to heighten their own visibility, identities, and causes in myriad ways, from staging roadside dramas in isolated villages to demanding clearer voices in news outlets around the globe. Social media, where technologically accessible, have emerged as powerhouses to connect the disadvantaged or repressed in common causes, notably in the wave of "Arab Spring" uprisings across the Middle East and North Africa in 2011. Television images shown around the world depicted women joining or even leading protests against some Arab regimes, showcasing tensions between an age-old subordination of women and a 21st-century drive for fairer treatment. Regional and global organizations are systematically monitoring the progress of women as news gatherers and news makers, with the twin goals of promoting gender parity for women within the news industry and advancing women as the subjects of important stories.

Relevant to the intersection of personal rights and media attention was the mob attack on Columbia Broadcasting System (CBS) network correspondent Lara Logan in February 2011 in Cairo's Tahrir Square, where she was covering a massive rally by Egyptians who were, for the most part, celebrating the ouster of Hosni Mubarak's regime. Logan's landmark recounting of the prolonged sexual assault against her on the CBS news program *60 Minutes* focused new attention on the dangers to women reporters, especially in covering conflict.

A rich history of ethnic media has long given voice to those who are culturally marginalized, underscoring the enduring role of media messages in raising the consciousness of both the oppressed and their oppressors. In the United States, the first African American newspaper, *Freedom's Journal*, was founded in 1827, and the first Latino newspaper, *El Misisipi*, dates from 1808, report Clint C. Wilson II and his colleagues. They write that *Freedom's Journal* in its first issue declared, on the front page, that it sought to overcome misrepresentations of black Americans conveyed by the dominant press. In 1911, the researchers report, a Spanish-language weekly, *La Cronica* of Laredo, Texas, campaigned against movies shown across Texas that it believed demeaned Mexicans and Native Americans. The first Native American newspaper, the *Cherokee Phoenix*, was launched in 1828 to counter the federal government's plan to remove the people of the Cherokee Nation from their own lands. *The Golden Hills' News*, established in San Francisco in 1854 as the first Asian Pacific American newspaper, published news for Chinese immigrants as well as English-language editorials seeking improved treatment of Chinese workers in California.

Moroccan citizens participate in demonstrations calling for political change during the "Arab Spring" uprisings in 2011. The press-monitoring organization Freedom House reported that 95 percent of people in North Africa and the Middle East reside in areas where media are tightly controlled. (Wikimedia)

Autocratic Regimes Suppress Journalists

Autocratic regimes—and sometimes pervasive criminal elements—retain their power partly by seeking to intimidate and control the press. Correspondents assigned to tell the stories of repressed groups, from Mexico in North America to Thailand in Southeast Asia, have been subjected to grave personal risks from authorities and others. The independent press-monitoring organization Freedom House reports that just one of six people worldwide lives with a free press. For instance, it finds that 95 percent of the population in North Africa and the Middle East reside where the media are tightly controlled; some Western journalists who covered the Arab uprisings were detained, interrogated, and beaten. Morocco resurrected an article of law in 2001 that permits it to suppress publications considered a threat to its political and religious institutions, leading to the confiscation of newspapers and jailing of editors. In 2000 alone, Iran closed more than 20 publications, imprisoning and even executing journalists, report media scholars Gholam Khiabany and Annabelle Sreberny. *Zanan*, a popular women's magazine in Iran, was shut down in 2008 as socially detrimental. Among the 196 countries rated by Freedom House in 2010, those with the least-free media were Burma, Equatorial Guinea, Eritrea, Libya, North Korea, Somalia, Sudan, Turkmenistan, and Uzbekistan.

The Internet seems ideal for circumventing publication bans and even overcoming gender, ethnic, and geographical distinctions. Research shows, however, that many more men than women use the Internet; a 2006 study, for instance, found that women represented only 4 percent of Internet users in the Middle East. In seeking to quell the Arab uprisings, regimes employed measures ranging from Egypt's cutoff of Internet access and expulsion of journalists to Syria's blackout of foreign coverage and slaughter of hundreds of street protesters. China has long blocked access to Websites it deems suspect, and repressive governments everywhere are stepping up efforts to control technology ranging from satellite television to mobile phones.

War and conflict bring particular sets of challenges for those seeking gender rights. In Palestine, for instance, feminists must compete for their cause with Palestine's overarching drive for sovereignty against Israel. Benaz Somiry-Batrawi in a case study detailed the efforts of a nonprofit media institute in Palestine to create and distribute film documentaries on gender issues before its donated equipment was destroyed during an Israeli incursion.

Alternative Means of Finding Voices

In less developed regions, such as Bangladesh, grassroots workshops teach women to find and amplify their voices through videos. In villages in the Philippines, activists have used such basic techniques as roadside theater, blackboard newspapers, and folk literature to communicate the goals of social mobilization. Florangel Rosario-Braid reports that in the mid-1990s many Filipino women became risk takers by challenging the country's autocratic rule in letter-writing campaigns. Community broadcasting movements from Australia to Wales have sought access to radio waves for groups that otherwise might be excluded. Researcher Margaret Gallagher writes that village women in Kenya have been empowered by a community radio station that enables them to discuss topics, such as sexual abuse, that would be taboo in other forums.

In countries where women have risen to leadership, journalistic changes may—or may not—come as well. The female form of "chancellor" was unused in Germany's lexicon before Angela Merkel won the office in 2005, observes political communication scholar Christina Holtz-Bacha. She writes that the German media initially focused on perceptions that Merkel lacked experience as the first woman chancellor but that the novelty of her gender had become passé by her second term. In Chile, Michelle Bachelet's election as the first woman president in 2006, along with her decision to name a cabinet composed equally of women and men, put women squarely in the realm of political news making. However, scholars found that journalists tended to treat Bachelet's campaign for office in stereotypical ways. While her leadership and competency were portrayed negatively, those qualities were covered more positively in her male rivals.

Powerlessness Affects Media Coverage

Contrasting with the news-generating status of these leaders, the women of Mexico, as in many other developing nations, generally lack economic, political, or social power. When they do appear in the news, reports scholar Maria Flores, they typically are depicted as victims, sex objects, or mourners, with "victim" the most prevalent frame. In Jamaica, Women's Media Watch since 1987 has monitored how journalists cover violence against women, especially domestic abuse, while also striving to raise the visibility of women as legitimate subjects of other kinds of stories. Just 3 percent of surveyed political news reports prior to Jamaica's inauguration of its first female prime minister in 2006 included a woman as a news subject, notes Sharon Meraz. Yet women were subjects of 42 percent of the crime stories. Striving to promote women as news makers in their own right, Women's Media Watch circulates lists of female sources for journalists to call as experts and opinion givers. Blogging, adds Meraz, can fit into the lives of busy women writers while bypassing a need for male approval.

Young brides may fall victim to a mercenary brand of domestic violence in South Asian countries such as Pakistan, Bangladesh, and India, where thousands lose their lives each year over the size of their marriage dowries. The National Crime Records Bureau in India reports that as many as 8,000 Indian women a year are killed by their spouses or in-laws or are driven to suicide by torture and harassment, in dowry deaths. In the absence of a particularly sensational case, these deaths typically are treated as routine by the press, researchers report. Although women in India have modern constitutional rights, writes Sonia Bathla, they remain culturally subordinate in social structures that date to ancient notions of patriarchy. Within such systems, "private" issues, including violence against girls and women, may be overlooked in media and public debates.

Male Domination and Gender Rights

Fundamental rights and freedoms—and press attention to them—can come slowly in countries where women live with overt male domination. Although Kuwait has a partially free press and occasionally robust debates, it did not, for example, grant suffrage to women until 2005. Islamist activists for decades have advocated greater freedoms for women, yet some observers question whether feminist ideals can be compatible with Islamic principles. At the same time, media scholars raise concerns over negative stereotyping of Muslims in the Western media, especially in the aftermath of the September 11, 2001, terrorist attacks in the United States.

At their most rigid, Islamic tenets mandate that women live secluded lives and cover themselves to avoid arousing men. Women may require permission from male relatives for pursuits such as travel, work, and marriage. Rape victims and others thought to have violated sexual norms may become victims of "honor" killings for bringing shame to themselves and their families. Serra Gorpe reported in 2008 that Turkey was the only Muslim country with equal rights of inheritance and divorce for women, yet Turkish women still risked death at the hands of relatives for disobedience that included out-of-wedlock pregnancy or running away with an unapproved man. Gorpe cited a Turkish government study that found nearly 1,100 murders committed in the name of moral traditions between 2000 and 2005.

An independent assessment of personal security in Arabic-speaking countries sponsored by the United Nations Development Programme (UNDP) reports that the constitutions of many Arab nations allow violations of personal rights in favor of national ideologies. The report, titled *Arab Human Development Report 2009* and available online, found legal discrimination against women in some countries. Ingrained male dominance, it reported, exposes many girls and women to harmful practices ranging from genital mutilation, which remains a widespread custom although some countries ban it, to child marriage—which had not been outlawed by any Arab country at the time of the 2009 study. Because violence against women is a taboo subject and sexual crimes are shameful for both victim and family, the prevalence of such acts is hard to gauge. However, on the subject of child marriage, the study observed that United Nations Children's Fund (UNICEF) has estimated the proportion of women in their early 20s who were married by age 18 was 45 percent in Somalia, 37 percent in Yemen, and 27 percent in Sudan.

In mid-2011, a group of Saudi women attracted international attention when they used Facebook, Twitter, and YouTube to attempt to organize a protest against one of Saudi Arabia's most visible manifestations of male dominance: its ban on women driving.

Findings of the Global Media Monitoring Project

On an international level, the Global Media Monitoring Project (GMMP) periodically examines how women appear in print and broadcast news by reviewing simultaneous news coverage on a single day. It reports that women accounted for less than a quarter of news subjects on November 10, 2009, in media outlets across 130 countries. Still, this was a significant improvement over women's status as news makers in 1995, when the figure was just 17 percent. Only 16 percent of surveyed news stories in 2009 focused *specifically* on women. Nearly half of all stories reinforced gender stereotypes, while just 8 percent challenged them, the GMMP reported. Women in the news were five times more likely than men to be identified as parents or spouses. Fewer than one in five experts interviewed was female.

Although women outnumber men in many journalism schools around the world, newsrooms typically employ more men than women. Research is mixed on the effects that women journalists have on overall news reporting, given the norms of the profession, but there is evidence that women reporters quote women more often than do their male counterparts. Stories by women reporters more frequently challenged gender stereotypes than those by men, the GMMP found.

Women's presence in print and broadcast newsrooms is monitored by the International Women's Media Foundation (IWMF), which in 2011 released its *Global Report on the Status of Women in the News Media*. The study, available online, found that among the 522 news companies surveyed in 59 countries, women were underrepresented in all seven regions of the world except eastern Europe. Overall, just a third of full-time journalists were women. Men held nearly three quarters of the top management jobs.

News companies tended to have policies of gender equity in countries that had gender-equity laws, the study reported. For instance, it said, no national laws prohibited workplace discrimination in North Africa and the Middle East—where only about a quarter of the 38 companies surveyed had policies promoting sex equity. Groups such as Gender Links, a media-monitoring organization based in South Africa, were credited with encouraging news companies to adopt equity policies in their regions. For instance, the report said, sex-equity policies were common at companies surveyed in Kenya, where a strong women's movement has existed since the 1970s. Over time, such policies appear to lead to greater representation of women in newsrooms. On the issue of sexual harassment, however, companies in many nations had no policies at all—even though other nations had 100 percent showings.

Recognizing Courageous Newswomen

In the aftermath of the well-publicized attack on Logan and abuses against other women correspondents who have come forward, some journalists noted that the Committee to Protect Journalists (CPJ) keeps records on how many reporters have lost their lives on assignments but not on the numbers who have been sexually harassed or assaulted. Responding to this, CPJ has begun surveying its members to document attacks on female reporters and photographers in war zones and other regions of conflict.

In line with this, too, the IWMF recognizes women journalists who risk their lives to cover the news. Its Courage in Journalism awards in 2011 went to Adela Navarro Bello of Mexico, who has been targeted by drug cartels for her coverage of violence and corruption; Parisa Hafezi of Iran, who has been beaten, harassed, burglarized, and detained for covering government opposition; and Chiranuch Premchaiporn of Thailand, who has been repeatedly arrested and faces up to 70 years in prison for anti-government remarks on her Website.

Rebecca LaVally
California State University, Sacramento

See also Affirmative Action; Diversity; Electronic Media and Social Inequality; Empowerment; Feminist Theory: Women-of-Color and Multiracial Perspectives; Gender Media Monitoring; Hegemony; Misogyny; Network News Anchor Desk; New Media; Newsrooms; Patriarchy; Prejudice; Racism; Sexism; Social Inequality; Social Media

Further Readings

Gallagher, Margaret. "Women's Human and Communication Rights." *Media Development*, v.57/1 (2010).
Khiabany, Gholam and Annabelle Sreberny. "The Politics of/in Blogging in Iran." *Comparative Studies of South Asia, Africa and the Middle East*, v.27/3 (2007).
Poindexter, Paula, Sharon Meraz, and Amy Schmitz Weiss, eds. *Women, Men, and News: Divided and Disconnected in the News Media Landscape.* New York: Routledge, 2008.

Sakr, Naomi, ed. *Women and Media in the Middle East: Power Through Self-Expression.* London: Tauris, 2004.
Wax, Emily. "For Newswomen Abroad, Risks Abound." *Washington Post* (April 15, 2011).
Wilson, Clint C., II, Felix Gutierrez, and Lena M. Chao. *Racism, Sexism, and the Media: The Rise of Class Communication in Multicultural America*, 3rd ed. Thousand Oaks, CA: Sage, 2003.

MISOGYNY

Deriving from the Greek *misogynia* (*misein*, "to hate," and *gyne*, "woman"), *misogyny* means the hatred, dislike of, or prejudice against women. Misogyny supports patriarchy, systematic male dominance, and female subjugation. In practice, misogyny objectifies women (especially sexually), limits women's economic and political power, and causes violence against women. Media critics study whether misogynic media contributes to women's lower pay, depression, eating disorders, rape, mutilation, and murder.

Misogyny is culturally contingent across centuries and continents. Greek philosopher Plato argued that women are inferior to men because women are closer to animals. Sigmund Freud employed Aristotle's notion that women are deviant, "mutilated males." Buddhist, Christian, Hebrew, Hindu, and Muslim texts imagine women as inferior, wicked, lustful, and inducing men to sin. These texts reduce women to body parts, especially sex organs. Anthropologists found the men in New Guinea and the Amazon Basin used gang rape and male-only homosocial spaces to avoid the polluting influences of women, especially their genitalia and menstrual blood. Renaissance-era French employed gang rape to discipline women who transgressed sexual codes. Today, the World Health Organization estimates that between 100 million and 140 million females worldwide have endured genital mutilation.

Media promote misogyny in several ways. Media often represent women and girls as inadequate unless they conform to Western standards of beauty that are expensive, labor-intensive, painful, unhealthy, and unattainable. Beauty standards become means to discriminate against women, who, even as athletes and news anchors, must conform or risk their reputations and careers. Because misogyny is a cultural norm, women in media may embrace feminine

Anheuser-Busch uses "Bud girls" to promote their Budweiser beer at the 2008 Canadian Grand Prix. Misogyny perpetuates female subjugation and objectifies women, usually in a sexual manner. (Wikimedia)

standards of beauty and sexual objectification and experience them as empowering. However extreme or subtle, misogynic media often depict women as sexual objects for men's pleasurable consumption. Blatant misogyny appears in television's *The Man Show*; in Howard Stern's, Eminem's, and Snoop Dog's multimedia content; in advertisements for beer and hard liquor; in hardcore pornography featuring painful, degrading sexual acts on women; and in "soft-core" content like *Girls Gone Wild*. Subtler, perhaps, is the misogyny in Disney's *Beauty and the Beast* (1991), which features a courtship between the angry, abusive Beast and Belle (whose name means "beautiful"), who overcomes maltreatment with her beauty and love. Belle's faith is rewarded with heterosexual union with the wealthy, reformed, handsome Beast-prince. Such narratives glamorize

intimate partner violence, which kills more than 1,000 women and 300 men annually in the United States. The World Health Organization reports that between 40 and 70 percent of female murder victims in Australia, Canada, Israel, South Africa, and the United States were killed by husbands or boyfriends, compared to 4 percent of United States and 8.6 percent of Australian male homicide victims. Misogynic media may carry paradoxical messages that feature violence against women yet enable critique of patriarchy; feminist media scholars find both tendencies in the films of Alfred Hitchcock.

Misogynic media and its critique frequently carry additional messages that reflect hate or dislike of nonwhite, lesbian, gay, bisexual, transgender, poor, and disabled "others." Feminist scholars argue that academic and popular critiques of misogynic rap music enact a racist double standard that criticizes black men for sexually objectifying women and ignores white men's routine objectification and victimization of women. Such critiques also ignore violence against women in military and occupied zones. During wars and terrorist attacks, when masculinity appears threatened, media portray women as weak victims and men as strong heroes who repair white heterosexual patriarchal order. Research on misogyny and homophobia suggests each has agency; they may act together or mask each other as social forces.

Ending misogyny is an ongoing feminist project. Scholar-activists working to end misogyny and media that promote it include bell hooks, Byron Hurt, Jean Kilbourne, and Jackson Katz. Resources for feminist media activists include Bitch Media, Feministing, the Media Education Foundation, *Ms.* magazine, the National Organization for Women (NOW), Off Our Backs, and Women in Media & News (WIMN).

Michelle Rodino-Colocino
The Pennsylvania State University

See also Beauty and Body Image: Beauty Myths; Beauty and Body Image: Eating Disorders; Empowerment; Feminism; Heterosexism; Patriarchy; Sexism; Workforce

Further Readings

Adams, Terri and Douglas B. Fuller. "The Words Have Changed but the Ideology Remains the Same: Misogynistic Lyrics in Rap Music." *Journal of Black Studies*, v.36/6 (2006).

Beres, Laura. "Beauty and the Beast: The Romanticization of Abuse in Popular Culture." *European Journal of Popular Culture*, v.2/2 (1999).

Bristow, Joseph. "Homophobia/Misogyny: Sexual Fears, Sexual Definitions." In *Coming on Strong: Gay Politics and Culture*, Simon Shepherd and Mick Wallis, eds. London: Unwin Hyman, 1989.

Clack, Beverly. *Misogyny in the Western Philosophical Tradition: A Reader*. New York: Routledge, 1999.

Dworkin, Andrea. *Woman Hating*. New York: E. P. Dutton, 1974.

Enloe, Cynthia. *Bananas, Beaches and Bases: Making Feminist Sense of International Politics*. Berkeley: University of California Press, 1990.

Faludi, Susan. *The Terror Dream: Myth and Misogyny in an Insecure America*. New York: Picador, 2007.

Gilmore, David. *Misogyny: The Male Malady*. Philadelphia: University of Pennsylvania Press, 2001.

hooks, bell. "Sexism and Misogyny: Who Takes the Rap? Misogyny, Gangsta Rap, and the Piano." *Z Magazine* (February 1994).

Jeffreys, Sheila. *Beauty and Misogyny*. New York: Routledge, 2005.

Johnson, Ann. "The Subtleties of Blatant Sexism." *Communication and Critical/Cultural Studies*, v.4/2 (2007).

Levy, Ariel. *Female Chauvanist Pigs: Women and the Rise of Raunch Culture*. New York: Free Press, 2005.

Messner, Michael. *Out of Play: Critical Essays on Gender and Sport*. Albany: State University of New York Press, 2007.

Modleski, Tania. *The Women Who Knew Too Much: Hitchcock and Feminist Theory*. New York: Methuen, 1988.

Wolf, Naomi. *The Beauty Myth: How Images of Beauty Are Used Against Women*. New York: William Morrow, 1991.

World Health Organization. "WHO Multi-Country Study on Women's Health and Domestic Violence Against Women." http://www.who.int/gender/violence/who_multicountry_study/en/ (Accessed October 2010).

Moyers, Bill

Bill Moyers (1934–), a native of Hugo, Oklahoma, is best known for his work as a news commentator on television. A major theme of his career is to examine democratic society by engaging voices and ideas on virtually every aspect of American political, economic, and social life. He focuses on issues of race, class, and gender on his shows while examining challenges facing American democratic society. In 1990, Moyers became president of the Schumann Center for Media Democracy, working tirelessly to address questions of media ownership and consolidation.

Moyers had an interest in journalism early in life, serving as a cub reporter for the *Marshall News Messenger* when he was 16 years old. While attending North Texas State College, Moyers interned for then U.S. senator Lyndon B. Johnson. Moyers later transferred to the University of Austin, where he graduated in 1956 with a degree in journalism. In 1959, Moyers earned his master of divinity degree from the Southwestern Baptist Theological Seminary.

When Johnson assumed the presidency after the assassination of John F. Kennedy, Moyers became a special assistant to Johnson, serving from 1963 to 1967. Moyers played a key role in organizing and supervising the 1964 Great Society legislative task force and was the chief architect of Johnson's 1964 presidential campaign. In the run-up to the 1964 election, Johnson ordered Moyers to request name checks from the Federal Bureau of Investigation (FBI) on 15 members of Senator Barry Goldwater's staff and White House staff to find "derogatory" material on their personal lives.

Moyers has had a long and varied career in broadcast journalism. From 1967 to 1970, he served as publisher for the Long Island, New York, daily newspaper *Newsday*. The conservative publication was struggling to survive when Moyers joined as publisher. Moyers successfully led the paper in a progressive direction. Although circulation increased and the publication won major journalism awards, the owner of the paper was a conservative and was disappointed with the liberal direction the paper had taken. The paper was eventually sold to the Times-Mirror Company, resulting in Moyers's departure from the paper.

In 1976, Moyers worked as editor and chief correspondent for *CBS Reports*, and from 1980 to 1986 he was a senior news analyst and commentator for the *CBS Evening News With Dan Rather*. During his last year with CBS, Moyers made public statements about the declining news standard at the network. In 1995, Moyers briefly joined NBC News as a senior analyst and commentator. In 1996, he became the first host of MSNBC's program *Insight*.

U.S. journalist and commentator Bill Moyers has examined issues of race, class, and gender and has explored nearly every aspect of American political, economic, and social life in his documentaries. (U.S. Congress image)

Moyers returned to the Public Broadcasting Service (PBS) in 2007 with *Bill Moyers' Journal*. The show had first aired on PBS from 1971 to 1981, with a break between 1976 and 1977. Other programs on PBS hosted by Moyers were *Now With Bill Moyers* (2002–04), *Faith and Reason* (2006), and *Bill Moyers in America* (2006). In 2005, Moyers announced to PBS that he would be retiring soon to complete writing a biography on Lyndon B. Johnson.

Moyers received more than 30 Emmy Awards and was the recipient of the 2006 Lifetime Emmy Award. Additionally, he has received virtually every major television journalism prize.

Teri Fair
Suffolk University, Boston

See also Federal Communications Commission; Jhally, Sut; McChesney, Robert; McLuhan, Marshall; Media Consolidation; Miller, Mark Crispin; Network News Anchor Desk; Newsrooms; Television

Further Readings

Burns, Ken. "'Moyers: A Second Look'—More Than Meets the Eye." *New York Times* (May 14, 1989).

Moyers, William. *Moyers on America: A Journalist and His Time*. New York: New Press, 2004.

Moyers, William. *Moyers on Democracy*. New York: Doubleday, 2008.

MULTI-USER DIMENSIONS

Multi-user dimensions, or MUDs, provide a unique opportunity to explore and express gender in media. MUDs are persistent, shared virtual worlds bound by rules in which users interact in real time through the use of characters or avatars. While online gaming is the primary use for MUDs, they have a variety of uses in online settings and will likely become more elaborate, ubiquitous, and immersive as technology advances.

MUD is generally accepted to stand for *multi-user dimension*, although it is not uncommon to encounter the terms *multi-user dungeon* and *multi-user domain*, depending on context. MUDs are virtual environments accessible by the Internet that allow for computer-mediated communication (CMC). In MUDs, multiple users can interact with one another. MUDs are also commonly understood as virtual communities or shared virtual worlds. Examples of popular MUDs include but are not limited to *World of Warcraft*, *EverQuest*, *The Sims*, and *Second Life*. MUDs are persistent, meaning that they exist continuously and exist even when no one is using the MUD. Users in MUDs interact in real time. The oldest and original form of interaction in MUDs is text-based chat. Text-based MUDs are still in use, but other forms of interaction are now available as well, such as graphical MUDs. In graphical MUDs, users can interact with virtual objects and may have the ability to add objects to the virtual world. MUDs should not be confused with chat rooms, nor should MUDs be confused with virtual reality, although MUDs can include chat rooms and elements of virtual reality.

Accessing one MUD places a user in a virtual world separate from any other MUD, making that user distinct from others. A user accesses a MUD by running a computer program on his or her personal computer. This computer program allows access to a server designed to facilitate a specific MUD. This server automatically manages the rules and feedback system of a MUD such that the server responds to the behaviors of its users through the computer program interface. Rules in a MUD are referred to as physics. While there are many different types of MUDs (AberMUD, TinyMUD, and LPMUD), the term *MUD* serves as a general category that encompasses all types of MUDs.

MUDs were originally created for the purpose of online gaming, and thus many MUDs are used primarily in this context, but they have been appropriated for many other purposes as well. For example, MUDs can be used for educational purposes, such as extending the classroom to a virtual environment to expose students to novel objects or events. The first multi-user dimension was a game called *MUD*, standing for multi-user dungeon. Roy Trubshaw and Richard Bartle created *MUD* in 1978. A common misconception about *MUD* is that it was based on the role-playing game (RPG) *Dungeons and Dragons*. However, there is an important connection between MUDs and RPGs such that in both forums each player assumes the role of a character within a fictional setting; players can fully assume the roles of these characters or simply act as decision makers for the characters by indicating what actions the character will take. The distinction is that RPGs do not necessarily need to take place in an online environment, whereas MUDs must occur in an online environment.

MUDs are relevant to gender in media because of the representations of gender they make available. Within MUDs, users are represented virtually, by characters or avatars. In most cases, users can customize the appearance of their characters. Users can control any number of characteristics, including gender, which determine how the character appears in a MUD. A character can appear as a male, female, and in some cases a gender-neutral being. Likewise, appearance in MUDs often does not reflect a character's attributes. Specifically, gender in MUDs is often superficial, meaning that the selection of gender has no bearing on what skills or abilities a character has. Users can uniquely shift identity in a MUD with regard to gender in ways that are not as flexible in the physical world. This aspect of MUDs offers interesting opportunities to explore gender and gender differences such that a man could experience a virtual world as a woman, a woman could experience a virtual world as a man, and anyone could experience a virtual world as someone who is gender-neutral. This practice is known as "gender swapping." An individual can explore personal gender in a virtual environment to escape his or her physical identity or to explore himself or herself in an alternate gender role. Despite this flexibility in gender, a MUD is still a social space and therefore the interactions between characters can be still be gendered. For example, female characters might receive unwanted attention or sexual advances from other characters regardless of the user's physical gender. Thus, MUDs offer a space to explore the influences of gender on social interaction. In virtual worlds gender is not intrinsic, but users and programmers alike often feel compelled to convey gender even if it is flexible.

MUDs currently provide a diverse set of interactions that will likely expand as they adopt and create new forms of technology. It is probable that MUDs will become common tools in business meetings, education, and any number of collaborative efforts. Through the adoption of virtual reality, MUDs can become more immersive environments in which people from all over the world can meet, interact, and work.

Ryan Rogers
University of North Carolina, Chapel Hill

See also Avatar; Cyberdating; Cyberpunk; Cyberspace and Cyberculture; Electronic Media and Social Inequality; Heroes: Action and Super Heroes; Identity; Massively Multiplayer Online Role-Playing Games; Misogyny; *Second Life*; Simulacra; Social Media; Video Gaming: Representations of Femininity; Video Gaming: Representations of Masculinity; Video Gaming: Violence; Virtual Community; Virtual Sex; Virtuality

Further Readings

Bartle, Richard. *Designing Virtual Worlds*. Indianapolis, IN: New Riders, 2003.

Cherny, Lynn. *Conversation and Community*. Stanford, CA: CSLI Publications, 1999.

Turkle, Sherry. "Constructions and Reconstructions of Self in Virtual Reality: Playing in the MUDs." *Mind, Culture, and Activity*, v.1/3 (1994).

MULVEY, LAURA

Laura Mulvey (1941–) is a feminist psychoanalytic film theorist and avant-garde filmmaker. She is most widely known in her field for her 1975 article in the film theory journal *Screen* called "Visual Pleasure and Narrative Cinema." She is famous for taking film theory in a new direction toward Freudian and Lacanian psychoanalysis and incorporating feminist theory into psychoanalytic film criticism. Mulvey argues for a political rather than an empirical reading of psychoanalysis and its relation to the cinema: specifically to the spectatorial position of the audience.

Psychoanalysis was previously seen as a justification for the status quo, both bourgeois and patriarchal. However, psychoanalysis can also be read not as a recommendation for a patriarchal society but as an analysis of one. Juliet Mitchell, another psychoanalytic feminist and author of *Psychoanalysis and Feminism*, states, "If we are interested in understanding and challenging the oppression of women, we cannot afford to neglect it." This conception of psychoanalysis helps to contextualize Mulvey's work as well as her point of departure into the world of psychoanalysis and its relation to gender in film.

Mulvey's years of study in Freudian and Lacanian psychoanalysis in relation to film allowed her to explore the concepts of pleasure, voyeurism, identification, scopophilia, and narcissism in relation to the role of women in cinema. For Mulvey, scopophilia, following Freud's analysis, comes from the pleasure of viewing another person as a sexual object. Delight can also be taken in knowing that one is being watched or is being seen as the object of someone else's sexual desire. Mulvey sought to explore the concept of scopophilia, the pleasure one may experience from being watched, and the pleasure that comes from watching another (in this case as a sexual object).

Mulvey was also particularly concerned with the "male gaze" that the Hollywood film industry constructs for its viewers. The pleasure of identification, the second pleasure in Freud's reading, stems from narcissism, and Mulvey explored this in her art and her analysis of the film industry as well. She plays with the idea of the pleasure of seeing oneself in representational forms, from identification with the image seen on the screen. In this sense it is formed with the constitution of the ego and makes sense in the Lacanian realm of the "mirror stage." Jacques Lacan posited that the exact moment when a child can realize his or her own self in the mirror is a crucial point in the development and constitution of the ego. A child cannot move into the Symbolic order (and into language as structure) and away from the Real (the realm of the mother's body) without this crucial realization.

Mulvey's work draws from Freudo-Lacanian readings/analyses and has often been of particular interest to feminist viewers and critics. If a woman's function (in the traditional psychoanalytic reading) is to raise her child into the Symbolic via the route of the Law of the Father, or to stand as a symbol of male castration (because she lacks a penis), then discovering how the woman is imaged as such in cinema and television helps women get closer to understanding the roots of their shared oppression. Mulvey suggests that women can take pleasure in the cinema only if they assume the role of the male spectator. This reading poses the ultimate challenge to feminist scholars and critics. Mulvey urges her readers and critics to accept her challenge, because she posits that these individuals prove that women can take pleasure in viewing the cinema not as a fetishized object, and not through dressing up ("the masquerade" or "transsexualism," as other gender and media scholars, such as Joan Riviere and Mary Ann Doane, suggest).

Scholars who have challenged Mulvey's reading of Hollywood cinema include Tania Modleski, who took issue with Mulvey's reading of Alfred Hitchcock's work. Mulvey had argued that Hitchcock films were voyeuristic and sadistic, while Modleski read them as more ambivalent. Modleski saw an expression of female desire in Hitchcock's films, even if it was quite limited. She also saw some resistance, however marginal, to the phallogocentric patriarchal order.

Gaylyn Studlar, in her work "Masochism and the Perverse Pleasures of the Cinema," has also contested Mulvey's assumption that the viewer either has to take a masculine spectatorial position and be a sadist or must take a feminine spectatorial position and be a masochist. For these critics, Mulvey's spectatorial positions are seen as too limited and binary. Thus Mulvey's work began a discourse about the many different spectatorial positions available to women and men who "read" and watch the cinema.

Her work made possible the multiplicity of meanings that viewers may take from certain cinematic experiences, and she also advocated for a new, alternative way to view the cinema.

Mulvey calls for a "new language of desire." She explains that the alternative (to the patriarchal order) includes "leaving the past behind without rejecting it, transcending outworn or oppressive forms, or daring to break with normal pleasurable expectations." She explains that cinema does this by making a mockery of empirical objectivity. The tension between the scopophilic pleasure (the pleasure of looking at, as well the pleasure of being looked at) and the desire for identification in representational cinematic forms results in both "indifference to perceptual reality" and an "imagined, eroticized concept of the world" that forms a "perception of the subject" that directly opposes, and makes a mockery of, the objective, "out there," empirical, observable world. It is this tension between the desire for identification in representational forms and the pleasure of watching (and of being watched) that creates the ultimate pleasure in viewing cinema or the television.

Mulvey has advocated for a new language of film and encourages women to challenge the patriarchal, phallogocentric order of cinema by creating avant-garde films that oppose the status quo in Hollywood cinema. Acting on her own call, she, along with her husband Peter Wollen, wrote and directed several independent films, including *Penthesilea, Queen of the Amazons* (1974), *Riddles of the Sphinx* (1977, often credited as their most influential film), *Amy!* (1980), *Crystal Gazing* (1982), *Frida Kahlo and Tina Modotti* (1982), and *The Bad Sister* (1980). In 1991, Mulvey returned to filmmaking, when she codirected *Disgraced Monuments* with Mark Lewis.

Judy E. Battaglia
Loyola Marymount University

See also Film: Hollywood; Film: Horror; Male Gaze; Patriarchy; Scopophilia

Further Readings

Doane, J. and D. Hodges. *Nostalgia and Sexual Difference.* New York: Methuen, 1987.

Doane, M. A. "Film and the Masquerade: Theorizing the Female Spectator." *Screen*, v.23/3–4 (1982).

Mitchell, J. and J. Rose. *Feminine Sexuality: Jacques Lacan and the École Freudienne.* New York: W. W. Norton, 1982.

Mulvey, L. *Visual and Other Pleasures.* Bloomington: Indiana University Press, 1989.

Mulvey, L. "Visual Pleasure and Narrative Cinema." *Screen*, v.16/3 (1975).

Riviere, J. "Womanliness as Masquerade." *The International Journal of Psychoanalysis (ILPA)*, v.10/1 (1929).

Strachey, J. *Sigmund Freud: Three Essays on the Theory of Sexuality.* London: Basic Books, 1975.

Turner, G. *Film as Social Practice*, 2nd ed. New York: Routledge, 1993.

MUSIC: UNDERREPRESENTATION OF WOMEN ARTISTS

The history of women's participation and representation in popular music reflects trends in the history of women's participation in all public occupations: As principals they have historically been pushed out of the limelight as soon as the viability of the industry as a mechanism for achieving financial and commercial success has been clearly established. This article considers the implications of women artists' underrepresentation by examining the history of women's engagement with popular music performance and recording. Although women have always been part of popular music performance and recording, they have historically been identified as niche or novelty performers and have been steered away from mainstage and dominant roles in the development of the popular music industry.

Women are traditionally associated with singing popular music—a limitation that has historically situated them in less powerful positions in the popular music industry as interpreters of music rather than as creators. Popular music recordings at the beginning of the 20th century focused on classical opera singers such as Enrico Caruso, but women singers were also included. Popular recording labels did not see a market until 1920, when General Phonographic's Okeh label recorded Perry Bradford's blues piece "Crazy Blues" with Mamie Smith, a popular stage singer in the Harlem neighborhood of New York City. A market for female blues singers became evident after Smith's recording sold 75,000 copies, which spawned a market for blues records by women in New York, Chicago, Philadelphia, Baltimore, and Atlanta. This was tempered by the social stigma against public performance by women in the early 20th century. Nevertheless, women singers became a staple on Tin Pan Alley and jazz recordings throughout the 1920s, 1930s, and 1940s. In the role of singers, women were marginalized as musicians—a role they have struggled to overcome throughout the history of contemporary popular music.

This social antagonism against women in public roles dominated the visible involvement of women in the popular music industry in anything but decorative roles, in the sense that, as singers, women contributed sex appeal to a band's performances, which might therefore draw larger audiences. The developing genres of popular music continued to reflect the biases of the music industry from the 1910s and 1920s forward in that industry officials did not recognize a market for women performers and hence were not supportive of women-fronted or women-run groups. Women's groups were consistently represented as novelty acts—ones that could be lucrative for a particular nightclub—but not as serious performers of music to be understood as mainstays of musical canons. A woman's body was and remains the most conspicuous element on the performance stage—her voice has historically taken second place and ability as a musician is placed last, because the dominant forces in the music industry have consistently assumed that pop music consumers are predominantly male.

This canonical connection between women and particular modes of performing continued through the development of blues into R&B and rock and roll in the 1950s and 1960s. Women could be seen, again predominantly as singers, performing pop music—but not jazz and not rock and roll. These genres were heavily troped as masculine spheres of performance. Niche categories such as R&B, bubble-gum pop, and the evolving sphere of singer-songwriter/Americana music became markets where women could become successful performers. Controversial pop performers like Madonna achieved marked levels of commercial success, though credit for creating Madonna's music consistently went to her producers and songwriters. In the late 1980s, with the meteoric success of Suzanne Vega's "Luka," women as rock performers were finally acknowledged as serious contributors to popular music as creators as well as interpreters.

As in rock and roll, women in country music have been categorized as singers; when they do achieve recognition, it is predominantly for their voices and sexuality, rather than their work as creators and musicians. Dolly Parton, arguably one of the most important figures in the latter half of 20th-century country music and an icon of classic country music, is perhaps the only woman to receive recognition in multiple spheres as businesswoman, songwriter, and performer.

The 1990s saw women performers moving into popular music in greater numbers, though they were still highly underrepresented. Many found the effort to gain major record deals insurmountably difficult and took different paths to pop music success through niche markets and self-production. Here, too, limits on their ability to break into the pop music market can be clearly seen with the development of a genre labeled "women's music," strongly associated with gay, lesbian, bisexual, transsexual/transgender (GLBT) culture and therefore not accepted as part of mainstream popular music.

As hip-hop continued its rise to visibility and achieved acceptance as a dominant form in contemporary popular music, the absence of women as central figures became more apparent. Women's roles in hip-hop have consistently been as backup singers and dancers in highly sexualized tropes of female representation in this heavily masculine genre. Similarly, women's roles in rock and roll are predominantly as backup singers and groupies. In contrast to most mediated genres of popular culture, in which men have retreated into hypermasculine representations as a reaction to increased female participation, in popular music women have continued to function within circumscribed roles and positions throughout the industry.

The consequences of women's underrepresentation in mainstream popular music are that women performers have been at the forefront of developing alternate means for creative exploration of popular music. Despite, or perhaps because of, the technological barrier whereby women have not developed representation in music production, particularly in the area of recording engineering, women performers have learned to utilize relationships with powerful members of the music industry to further their goals. Pop singer Madonna and Electronica singer/composer Björk, for example, have both been recognized for their work with producers and recording engineers to achieve their goals as performers.

Artists taking creative control of their musical production at the professional level have been an undercurrent in the music industry almost since its inception, especially after the development of the concept album in the 1960s, in particular the Beach Boys' 1966 *Pet Sounds* and the Beatles' 1967 *Sergeant Pepper's Lonely Hearts Club Band*. Marvin Gaye's 1970 *What's Going On* and Stevie Wonder's 1972 *Talking Book* both marked musicians taking control not just of performance but also of production. *Talking Book* is most important for being the first recording to identify supporting musicians in the liner notes, and Wonder himself both wrote and produced. These recordings, along with the developing recognition of the singer-songwriter in the 1960s, became vehicles by which women performers began to achieve recognition for their work. A notable example in this period was Carole King's 1971 recording *Tapestry*, the first platinum-rated pop music album, retaining its title until Michael Jackson's 1982 *Thriller*. Vega's 1987 single "Luka" represented another marker along a trajectory that has continued to mark an increase in musical and popular recognition for women's participation in the pop music industry.

By the mid-1990s, women performers across genres were critically recognized for their work, including Alanis Morrisette, Alison Krauss, Mary J. Blige, and Annie Lennox, among others, though they still represented only a fraction of overall music sales. The early 2000s have seen a continuation of this trend: Women have found niches and success in secondary markets such as Americana music as musicians and performers but still fight for recognition in the most lucrative pop music markets of rock and roll and hip-hop as anything more than interpreters of someone else's music.

J. Meryl Krieger
Indiana University–Purdue University
Indianapolis

See also Music Videos: Representations of Men; Music Videos: Representations of Women; Music Videos: Tropes

Further Readings

Bayton, Mavis. "How Women Became Musicians." In *On Record: Rock, Pop and the Written Word*, Simon Frith and Andrew Goodwin, eds. 1988. Reprint, New York: Routledge, 1990.

Biddle, Ian, and Freya Jarman-Ivens. "Introduction." In *Oh Boy! Masculinities and Popular Music*, Freya Jarman-Ivens and Ian Biddle, eds. New York: Routledge, 2007.

Bufwack, Mary A. and Robert K. Oermann. *Finding Her Voice: Women in Country Music 1800–2000*. Nashville, TN: The Country Music Foundation Press and Vanderbilt University Press, 2003.

Burnim, Mellonee V. and Portia K. Maultsby, eds. *African American Music: An Introduction*. New York: Routledge, 2006.

Burns, Lori and Mélisse Lafrance. *Disruptive Divas: Feminism, Identity, and Popular Music*. New York: Routledge, 2002.

Clawson, Mary Ann. "When Women Play the Bass: Instrument Specialization and Gender Interpretation in Alternative Rock Music." *Gender and Society*, v.13/2 (1999).

Gaar, Gillian G. *She's a Rebel: The History of Women in Rock and Roll*, Expanded 2nd ed., Preface by Yoko Ono. New York: Seal Press, 2002.

Light, Alan, ed. *The VIBE History of Hip Hop*. New York: Three Rivers Press, 1999.

Marsh, Charity and Melissa West. "The Nature/Technology Binary Opposition Dismantled in the Music of Madonna and Björk." In *Music and Technoculture*, Leslie C. Gay and René Lysloff, eds. Middletown, CT: Wesleyan University Press, 2003.

O'Brien, Lucy. *She Bop II: The Definitive History of Women in Rock, Pop and Soul*. New York: Continuum, 2002.

Simons, Dave. *Studio Stories: How the Great New York Records Were Made—From Miles to Madonna, Sinatra to the Ramones*. San Francisco: Backbeat Books, 2004.

Whiteley, Sheila. *Women and Popular Music: Sexuality, Identity and Subjectivity*. New York: Routledge, 2000.

MUSIC VIDEOS: REPRESENTATIONS OF MEN

Music videos have long been a site for exploring ideas about, and images of, men and masculinity. Although designed to promote artists and sell records, music videos also convey important cultural messages about what it means to be a man. Music videos rose in prominence after the introduction of the cable network MTV in 1981, although antecedents to modern music videos (such as experimental films, concert films, musical and variety television shows, and commercials) date back to much earlier eras of film and television production. Not unlike the controversies surrounding the televised performances of male artists such as Elvis Presley and Little Richard in the 1950s, music videos have been hotly debated in recent decades for their representations of gender, sexuality, race, and class as well as consumerism, violence, and misogyny.

In the early 1980s, MTV focused primarily on music videos by white male rock and pop artists from Australia, Britain, and the United States, prompting some to charge the network with racist business practices. MTV's nearly all-white programming strategy began to erode in 1983, when CBS Records allegedly threatened to pull its videos from the network if it did not show Michael Jackson's videos from the *Thriller* album. Ultimately, the overwhelming popularity of Jackson's videos paved the way for other nonwhite artists, including Prince, Lionel Richie, and Run-D.M.C., to receive airplay on MTV.

Sexual images have been used regularly in music videos to attract viewers' attention. Yet, as a great deal of historical and contemporary research has shown, sexual representations in music videos featuring male artists have tended to highlight unequal divisions of power between the sexes—often displaying a patriarchal visual landscape wherein images of authoritative, macho, and/or sexually assertive men are juxtaposed with images of highly sexualized and/or submissive women. In many such videos, men are represented as active agents in traditionally male-defined spaces (such as streets, bars, strip clubs, and concert stages dominated by male musicians), whereas women are depicted as objects to be gazed upon, consumed, and controlled by men. An early example of this kind is Duran Duran's 1981 video "Girls on Film," which depicts the group performing on an elevated stage while women dressed in costumes (as the naughty nurse, cowgirl, and swimsuit model) enact erotic vignettes in a boxing ring in front of them. Shots of the energetic and stylishly suited band members are intercut with shots of the women as they strut seductively in skimpy attire. Similarly, Whitesnake's "Here I Go Again" (1987) alternates between footage of the band wailing vigorously on musical instruments and into microphones and actress Tawny Kitaen writhing seductively on top of two luxury cars. Even more sexually explicit is Motley Crue's "Girls, Girls, Girls" (1987), which portrays the leather-clad metal

group's rowdy night at a strip club; the video cuts variously between images of the band riding around town on their motorcycles, performing in the strip joint, and surveying scantily clad women as they dance provocatively with a pole. While shots of male artists in these videos work to reinforce their "larger than life" status and seeming masculine prowess, shots of women emphasize their status as objects to be looked at, especially the close-ups of eroticized body parts and low-angle shots that offer glimpses between legs, underneath skirts, and inside blouses.

This pattern of representation was particularly popular in the 1980s, when bands such as ZZ Top, Whitesnake, Poison, Van Halen, and Aerosmith churned out countless videos depicting men as active inhabitants of a male-fantasy world where women held little power beyond looking "hot" and attracting the attention of men. Nevertheless, sexual images of male power and female subordination have persisted in contemporary fare. Prince's "Cream" (1991), for example, features the artist simulating sex with two female dancers—both of whom appear unfazed by his assertive antics, including pinning them down and pulling their hair. Kid Rock's "American Bad Ass" (2000) showcases the artist riding motorcycles, crashing cars, and rocking out with his boys while a bevy of beauties shimmy, mud-wrestle, and vie for his "bad boy" affections. Justin Timberlake's "My Love" (2006) features the singer, along with hip-hop artist T.I., intensely scrutinizing the bodies of several women; in one sequence, Timberlake aggressively tears off the pantyhose of one lingerie-clad temptress. Such images tend to equate male sexuality with physical forcefulness while also implying that such forcefulness is desired by women.

Despite their often sexually provocative nature, many pop and rock videos have fallen under the radar of popular criticism—perhaps because of their seeming tameness in relation to videos that feature exceptionally explicit sexual and misogynic imagery. For instance, rap artist Nelly's music video "Tip Drill" (2003), featuring the St. Lunatics, has been vehemently criticized for circulating harmful images of black masculinity and femininity. The term *tip drill* refers to an unattractive woman with a nice body whom men perceive to be good only for sex. This theme is reinforced in the video through images of Nelly and the other male rappers fondling, spanking, and gawking at half-naked women (many of them topless) as they engage in overtly sexual acts, poses, and dance moves. To highlight women's primary status as sexual commodities, several shots depict men throwing money at female dancers, and at the end of the video, Nelly enthusiastically swipes a credit card through one woman's G-stringed buttocks. While much of the controversy over "Tip Drill" centered on its demeaning representations of women, other critics have pointed out that it troublingly stereotypes black men as sexually oppressive and threatening.

Of course, images of hypermasculine "thugs" and overly sexual "playas" are modern incarnations of stereotypes about black men that have long circulated in popular culture. While some contemporary artists, such as 50 Cent, Nelly, and Snoop Dogg, have gained commercial success by adopting the thug and playa personas in music videos, such images tend to perpetuate white patriarchal notions of the Other while denying the social and economic factors that gave rise to hip-hop as a countercultural movement. Certainly, some rap and hip-hop artists have used their music as a political platform to speak out against social injustices, including N.W.A.'s "Fuck tha Police" (1988) and Body Count's "Cop Killer" (1992), both of which protest police brutality and racial profiling. However, in a media landscape dominated by corporate interests, songs and videos that do not deeply threaten white hegemony are those that typically win out in the marketplace. This is why, as many contemporary scholars have noted, it is necessary to interrogate the powerful social, economic, and political institutions that perpetuate troubling stereotypes and limit alternative representations of black masculinity.

Although some music-video representations of men and masculinity have circulated problematic sexual images, others have celebrated a loosening of sexual binaries. Many videos, for instance, showcase male artists who seem to defy markers of traditional masculinity via playful displays of androgyny. From Boy George and Twisted Sister's outlandish makeup to the big hair of glam/metal bands such as Poison and Motley Crue, from Michael Jackson's and Prince's high-pitched squeals and bejeweled pantsuits to their uber-macho dance moves, many male artists have productively critiqued the boundaries of masculinity and delightfully expanded its limits. With the tremendous popularity of the *Thriller* album and its corresponding music videos, Jackson was one of the first male artists of the MTV era to

use sexual ambiguity to great success. In the music video for "Thriller" (1983), for example, Jackson tries on a range of masculine personas. Although the video is framed within a traditional heterosexual narrative framework, chronicling a "date night" between Jackson and his girlfriend, it quickly gives way to alternative depictions of sexuality as Jackson morphs into one of the monsters that he sings about in the song. Whereas he dances aggressively with a bevy of ghouls and even menacingly hunts his girlfriend (first as a werewolf and later as a zombie), his red high-water hot pants, feminine squeals, and ethereal ballet spins—not to mention his painted eyes and processed hair—make him a pleasurable amalgamation of both masculine and feminine characteristics. Gender binaries cannot quite seem to fix on Jackson, thus enabling him to both question and resist masculine stereotypes. Although the lightening of Jackson's skin over the years prompted heated debates about the artist's racial allegiance, this, too, contributed to the artist's liminal status. Featuring Jackson as seemingly between black and white, male and female, and adult and child, Jackson's music videos—especially those from the *Thriller, Bad* (1987), and *Dangerous* (1991) albums—toyed with the star's sexual and racial ambiguities and, in the process, carved out a visual space wherein alternate masculine identities found expression.

Representations of androgyny still appear in music videos today, though often they are associated with adolescent boys whose androgyny seems more connected to their youth than other forms of political practice. Still, the music videos of boys and boy bands—from Lil' Bow Wow and Justin Bieber to the Backstreet Boys and 'N Sync—have been important for cultivating ideas about youthful masculinity. Not unlike their adult male counterparts, adolescents featured in music videos tend to engage in action (dancing, driving cars, and playing sports) and typically appear outdoors or in public spaces. Images of bars and strip clubs are replaced by images of airports, stadiums, schools, and shopping malls, but the message is still very much the same: Boys are free to go where they please—a pattern that variously taps into themes of independence, privilege, leisure, mobility, and consumerism. Today's modern commercial landscape is highlighted in Bieber's 2010 video "Baby," featuring Ludacris, which cuts between images of the artist hanging out with friends in a bowling alley and images of him singing outside as signs for popular stores and leisure establishments, such as Skechers and Hard Rock Café, swirl around him. As the artist disembarks an escalator with his female crush at the end of the video, a Starbucks sign gleams in the background—an image that seems to underscore the importance of commercial capitalism in the identities and lived experiences of male youth.

Considering the vast range in music video output over the past 30 years, perhaps it is unsurprising that some music video representations of male artists have offered liberating visions of masculinity while others have circulated troubling stereotypes. What remains consistent, however, is the power of music videos to capture our attention and provoke debate. Given their contemporary resurgence on Websites such as YouTube and Vevo—not to mention their sustained popularity on cable channels such as VH1 Classic, MTV Hits, and BET Hip Hop—it is likely that music videos will continue to be an important cultural form through which representations of men and masculinity are negotiated, interrogated, and explored.

Kirsten Pike
University College Dublin

See also Gender and Masculinity: Black Masculinity; Gender and Masculinity: Fatherhood; Gender and Masculinity: Metrosexual Male; Gender and Masculinity: White Masculinity; Music Videos: Representations of Women; Music Videos: Tropes

Further Readings

Austerlitz, Saul. *Money for Nothing: A History of the Music Video From the Beatles to the White Stripes*. New York: Continuum, 2007.

Balaji, Murali. "Owning Black Masculinity: The Intersection of Cultural Commodification and Self-Construction in Rap Music Videos." *Communication, Culture and Critique*, v.2 (2009).

Beebe, Roger and Jason Middleton, eds. *Medium Cool: Music Videos From Soundies to Cellphones*. Durham, NC: Duke University Press, 2007.

Frith, Simon, Andrew Goodwin, and Lawrence Grossberg, eds. *Sound and Vision: The Music Video Reader*. New York: Routledge, 1993.

Jhally, Sut. *Dreamworlds 3: Desire, Sex, and Power in Music Video*. Northhampton, MA: Media Education Foundation, 2007.

Lewis, Lisa A. *Gender Politics and MTV: Voicing the Difference*. Philadelphia, PA: Temple University Press, 1990.

Vernallis, Carol. *Experiencing Music Video: Aesthetics and Cultural Context*. New York: Columbia University Press, 2004.

MUSIC VIDEOS: REPRESENTATIONS OF WOMEN

In his *Dreamworlds* documentaries, Professor Satvider Jhally (known more commonly as "Sut" Jhally) examines the portrayal of women in music videos; his analysis has caused both tension and awareness, since he argues that music videos, in general, demean women and even encourage sexual violence. Patterns he noticed in the mid-1990s—such as women being thin, large-breasted, and sexy in music videos—continue in contemporary music videos. Some videos present women positively, but the majority (whether in the rap, hip-hop, rock, metal, or country genre) exploit women, capitalizing on their sexuality while insinuating that a woman's worth is based entirely on her physical appearance and sexual appeal.

The majority of music videos offer representations of women that focus on their sexuality or subservient status. Artists exist, however, who portray women positively, focusing on females having fun, taking pride in themselves, and serving as role models for viewers. One such artist includes country sensation Reba McEntire. Her videos, beloved by fans for the storytelling art utilized by McEntire and her video production team (nearly all of her videos supply an elaborate tale to supplement her lyrics, instead of simply showing her singing or dancing to the music), include women who dress respectfully and carry themselves with dignity. The focus of many of McEntire's videos remains the story and the accompanying lyrics, rather than the appearance of the people in the video. Another artist known for positive representation of women is Alicia Keys. She stars in her videos, like McEntire. Although Keys wears sexier costumes (sometimes tighter dresses, shorter skirts, or outfits that expose more skin), the focus of the video remains on Keys's musical abilities, as her videos show her singing and playing the instruments used in her songs. Hence, the stress on her sex appeal is balanced by an equal emphasis on her skills and role as a singer-songwriter and musician. These women do not disregard their physical attributes but choose to focus on their creative and musical talents instead of defining themselves in terms of their appearance.

Fans also roundly applaud Taylor Swift for her positive representation of women (herself) in her videos, earning her a respected place as a role model for young girls and adult women alike. Fans praise her for the respect she shows for herself both on the red carpet and in her videos; as a minor, she wore dresses and costumes that did not expose too much skin or present her as a sex object, and her appearance continues to reflect her identity as a spirited young woman who respects her body and herself enough not to reveal too much to her viewers. Swift finds a balance between sharing her fun, sexy side and upholding her self-respect. In videos such as "Our Song," Swift sports tiny pajama shorts while painting her toenails but wears layered tank tops so as not to expose too much skin on her torso—a choice disregarded by many young female artists.

Comparing McEntire, Keys, and Swift yields some useful patterns. To begin, two of them (McEntire and Keys) are adult women, evidently established and confident enough in their artistic abilities to create and perform in videos without buckling to the pressures imposed on younger artists, who may be more vulnerable to pressure to exploit sex appeal as a means of increasing their popularity. Swift remains an exception; as a young artist it would have been easier for her to recruit fans in the same manner as several of her pop-music contemporaries, but instead she showcases her voice and spirit in her videos, suggesting that women can be noticed for their talent and energy rather than for their bodies solely. A second notable similarity in these music videos is that they are for female artists. Few male artists who include females in their videos represent women in a respectful manner; rather, the videos of most male artists (and many female artists as well) stress and define a woman in terms of her sexuality.

Regardless of the genre, the vast majority of music videos objectify women. Music videos for songs in the rap, hip-hop, and rock genres do this most notoriously, but many videos for country artists' songs are also guilty of this pattern. Rap videos generate the most controversy concerning the representation of women. Viewers expect to see scantily clad women, gyrating against men and each other in rap videos, and this trope presents itself consistently within the genre. Rap artist 50 Cent's video "In Da Club" demonstrates this concept clearly; the majority of the video occurs in a club where women wearing tight or minimal clothing grind against men, who stare at the women's breasts instead of their faces. A similar situation presents itself in Mystikal's "Shake Ya Ass." Driving down the street, Mystikal happens upon three women; his attention focuses completely on their backsides and their breasts. The women approach him and provide him with an address and password for a private party. The party, in a mansion, is a house full of women rubbing themselves against their male grinding partners; women also dance on the tabletops, dancing and touching themselves. The women wear extremely tight, short clothing or skimpy bikinis. The video also cuts often to Mystikal singing, and in each scene a different woman grinds her behind into his crotch.

Hip-hop videos that exploit women even more than 50 Cent's and Mystikal's include "Thong Song" by Sisqó and "Superman" by Eminem. Sisqó's music video incorporates endless close-ups of women's breasts and behinds, and an opening scene in which a girl (no older than five) playing Sisqó's daughter enters and says, "Daddy, what's this?" as she holds up a red lace thong, indicating one of Sisqó's sexual conquests. In "Superman," Eminem brings a big-busted woman to his room. He rubs her breasts and then undresses as she lies gyrating her hips on the bed. As the line "won't put out, I'll put you out" plays, Eminem shoves the woman from his room and throws her clothes and belongings at her. Video producers also incorporate scenes of Eminem writhing in a swamp of women in skimpy lingerie between his confrontational scenes with the woman he threw out of his room earlier. The videos by 50 Cent, Mystikal, Sisqó, and Eminem provide striking examples of how artists and their production teams exploit women, encouraging their audiences to view women as sexual objects unworthy of respect.

Rock music videos also represent women as sex objects. An artist guilty of exploiting women through his decades-long career is Rod Stewart. One of the most powerful examples of Stewart's exploitation of women occurs in the video "Hot Legs." The video focuses on Stewart and his band, but pairs of female legs appear in many of the scenes (in one scene coming from the left of the screen); the rest of the woman's body, including her face, remains hidden. One iconic shot frames Stewart with a pair of women's legs—his face appears below the woman's crotch and then his body fills the space of the frame between her legs. By refusing to show the rest of the woman on whose legs the camera focuses, Stewart not only desensitizes his viewers toward women but also encourages his viewers to value women only for their bodies—their legs, specifically. Similarly, Robert Palmer's videos "Addicted to Love" and "Simply Irresistible" send messages about women as in secondary roles. Granted, Palmer is the singer and deserves the focus. Being surrounded by a large number of women, all in identical dress, hairstyles, and makeup, however, implies that women are indistinguishable and have only one trait: sex appeal. Like Stewart and Palmer, Billy Idol's "Rock the Cradle of Love" focuses on female sex appeal: In the video a young woman visits her single male neighbor, dances and strips, then kisses (and presumably becomes more physically intimate with) him. Idol's video indulges a stereotypical male sexual fantasy: having sex with a stranger, without any commitment.

Like their male counterparts, female rock artists are also guilty of portraying women as sex objects. In stark contrast to McEntire, Keys, and Swift, performers like Miley Cyrus and Britney Spears support and perpetuate female exploitation. In Cyrus's "Can't Be Tamed," Cyrus attempts to employ a metaphor: Dressed as a bird and trapped in a cage, she suggests that women are trapped. Cyrus simply steps through the bars of the cage, though, wearing a revealing, sexy, black costume. Although the video begins by suggesting that women are trapped, Cyrus then exploits herself by strutting around in little clothing and gyrating against both men and women, sometimes with more than one person, in the dark. Spears also freely exploits herself. In the music video "I'm a Slave for You," Spears, dripping with sweat, rubs her hands over her body while gyrating fiercely, both alone and then in a large group of people. Spears and Cyrus, unlike Swift in particular, do not hesitate to reveal their bodies and sexuality to viewers, encouraging viewers to place importance on a female's appearance instead of her talent or spirit.

Country music videos, often stereotyped as more wholesome than hip-hop or rock, also exploit women. Trace Adkins's "Honky Tonk Badonkadonk" shows Adkins in a bar, surrounded by friends—many of whom are attractive, scantily clad women, watching other women dancing while wearing short shorts. Toby Keith, much like Adkins, incorporates women in his videos but uses them to further sexual themes. In "Who's Your Daddy?" a woman splashes in a tub of bubbles, indulging in chocolate-covered strawberries, waiting for Keith to arrive home. Both Adkins and Keith exploit female sexuality in an effort to make their videos more appealing to male fans. Shania Twain also plays the role of sex object in her video "Man! I Feel Like a Woman," in which she turns the concept used by Palmer in both "Addicted to Love" and "Simply Irresistible" on its head. She stands in front of a group of men, all dressed alike, meant to imitate the women from Palmer's videos. Twain starts the video dressed in a long coat, but throughout the video she strips off items of clothing until she is left wearing a black corset, mini skirt, thigh-high boots, and a black choker. As she strips her clothes, Twain repeats that she "[feels] like a woman"; pairing these two elements in the video insinuates that to feel truly female, women need to wear as little clothing as possible. Like Cyrus and Spears in the rock genre, Twain exploits herself and encourages viewers to view women as sex objects.

In *Dreamworlds*, Jhally argues that sexual violence against women is, in part, encouraged by the negative presentation of women in music videos. By and large, most music videos, no matter the genre, impart messages that desensitize viewers to women as real and human; instead, audiences learn to associate women with sex and fantasy, thus supporting a negative representation of women.

Karley Adney
Butler University

See also Desensitization Effect; Gender and Femininity: Motherhood; Gender and Femininity: Single/Independent Girl; Gender and Masculinity: Black Masculinity; Gender and Masculinity: Fatherhood; Gender and Masculinity: Metrosexual Male; Gender and Masculinity: White Masculinity; Jhally, Sut; Mass Media; Media Rhetoric; Misogyny; Music Videos: Representations of Men; Music Videos: Tropes; Sexuality; Stereotypes; Tropes

Further Readings

Andsager, Julie L. "Contradictions in the Country: Rituals of Sexual Subordination and Strength in Music Video." In *Sexual Rhetoric: Media Perspectives on Sexuality, Gender, and Identity*. Westport, CT: Greenwood, 1999.

Austerlitz, Saul. *Money for Nothing: A History of the Music Video From the Beatles to the White Stripes*. New York: Continuum, 2007.

Cuklanz, Lisa M. and Sujata Moorti. *Local Violence, Global Media: Feminist Analyses of Gendered Representations*. New York: Peter Lang, 2009.

Jhally, Sut. *Dreamworlds 3: Desire, Sex, and Power in Music Video*. Northampton, MA: Media Education Foundation, 2007.

Roberts, Robin. *Ladies First: Women in Music Videos*. Jackson: University Press of Mississippi, 1996.

Seidman, S. A. "Revisiting Sex-Role Stereotyping in MTV Videos." *International Journal of Instructional Media*, v.26/1 (1999).

Taylor, Diane. "Attack the Rap." *The Guardian*. http://www.guardian.co.uk/music/2004/mar/08/popandrock.gender (Accessed October 2010).

Vernallis, Carol. *Experiencing Music Video: Aesthetics and Cultural Context*. New York: Columbia University Press, 2004.

Wilson, Janelle. "Women in Country Music Videos." *ETC: A Review of General Semantics*, v.57/3 (2000).

Music Videos: Tropes

Since the invention of the music video, certain tropes continue to appear regardless of the music genre, ranging from country to rock to hip-hop. Some of the most common themes include the sexualization of students and teacher–student fantasies; water imagery remains a common trope, often used to heighten the sensuality of a situation; another common theme is men hunting and taking advantage of women; and finally, there is the trope of an independent woman fulfilling her desires. These common tropes perpetuate and reinforce both negative and positive gender stereotypes for viewers.

One of the most common tropes concerns a sexualization of students and teachers. Perhaps the most famous example of this trope occurs in Van Halen's music video "Hot for Teacher." One teacher in the video enters her classroom in a bikini, walking on her desk. The video later shows a physical education teacher ripping off her clothes in the cafeteria, walking on a lunch table in a skimpy bathing suit. In a related example, in the video for her hit single "Hit Me Baby One More Time," Britney Spears sports a white blouse, tied to bare her midriff. She also wears the classic schoolgirl coif of pigtails and braids with pink bows. Costume designers complete her look with a short skirt, thigh-high stockings, and Mary Janes. Similarly, in the t.A.T.u video "All the Things She Said," the two band members wear schoolgirl uniforms of tight white blouses and very short skirts. The video also portrays the two young girls as lovers; they sit closely to one another, their fingers intertwined, smelling each other's necks, and even kissing. These examples perpetuate negative stereotypes about both men and women. Van Halen's video suggests that attractive female teachers are incapable of engaging students on an intellectual level and that students find them intriguing only for their physical appearance. This message reinforces a negative stereotype about men as well, implying that they are too distracted by a woman's appearance to appreciate her mental abilities. The other videos sexualize young women, encouraging viewers to value them for their sex appeal above all other characteristics.

The t.A.T.u. video uses another common music video trope: water. The image of girls standing alone in the rain emphasizes their vulnerability and makes their sopping-wet clothes cling to their flesh, almost making the women appear defenseless. The iconic video "What a Feeling," based on the film *Flashdance*, utilizes water somewhat differently. The most famous scene from this video shows a woman dancing on a stage in a club, then pulling a chain that releases water that falls over her taut body. The water, in this instance, adds to the dancer's already obvious sexuality. With her hair and body dripping, she appears animalistic. The videos "Water" (by Brad Paisley, a country artist) and "What's Your Fantasy" (by Ludacris, a hip-hop artist) both employ water. Although Paisley's entire song focuses on different activities in life that occur in the water, near the end of the video he highlights a man and woman getting physical in a pool. Similarly, Ludacris includes a scene in his video in which he takes a bath in a steel tub in a front yard with a nude, large-breasted woman. Video makers use the trope of water primarily to sexualize women, perpetuating the notion that women are sexiest when they are wet (as their clothes cling to them, or they wear no clothes at all).

While teacher-student fantasies and water emphasize a woman's sexuality, the trope of monstrous

Recurrent music video tropes include the sexualization of the schoolgirl image and student–teacher encounters, pouring water on women to create a revealing, defenseless look, and depicting men as hunters, hunting women instead of animals. (Photos.com)

men or men hunting women instead champions the idea of women as victims. In the German metal band Rammstein's video "Du Riechst So Gut" ("you smell so good"), a woman rides through the forest, her scent followed closely by a werewolf. Several men track her, and she eventually gives in to one of them. As the man undresses, several wolves jump from under his clothing; later people find the woman alone in her room, now a werewolf herself, with the other wolves running from the house. This suggests that multiple men ravished the woman and then left her to suffer. In the Type O Negative video for "Love You to Death," a girl, dressed like Little Red Riding Hood, has sex with a man who later abandons her. The video focuses on the young woman digging a toy doll out of the ground that she puts back in her basket, signifying that now her childhood and innocence are dead, no matter how she tries to preserve or cling to it. Videos incorporating this trope reinforce the negative stereotypes that men are more powerful than women and that women exist simply to fulfill a man's sexual desires.

Quite different are those videos that employ the trope of an independent woman who wreaks havoc by taking advantage of a man (or men). Some of the most famous examples of this trope occur in Aerosmith's videos, primarily in "Amazing" and "Crazy." In "Amazing," the video chronicles what appears to be a young, aroused teenage male who has created a virtual fantasy in which he and a girl share a sexual experience on a motorcycle. The end of the video reveals that the virtual fantasy is entirely the girl's creation; she addresses her own sexual desires by creating a world in which she dominates a man and fulfills her urges. "Crazy" follows the adventures of two young girls who rob from men and win a stripping contest. While some critics argue that these videos glorify women for their sexuality, others celebrate these videos as some of the first to depict women as independent, strong, and willing to do what is necessary to acquire happiness.

Music videos remain controversial for their tropes involving depictions of gender and for the messages these tropes send to their viewers about gender. Most often videos (of various genres) objectify women, but some videos turn gender stereotypes on their head, placing women in roles of power.

Karley Adney
Butler University

See also Jhally, Sut; Mass Media; Media Rhetoric; Misogyny; Music Videos: Representations of Men; Music Videos: Representations of Women; Sexuality; Stereotypes

Further Readings

Austerlitz, Saul. *Money for Nothing: A History of the Music Video From the Beatles to the White Stripes.* New York: Continuum, 2007.

Jhally, Sut. *Dreamworlds 3: Desire, Sex, and Power in Music Video.* Northampton, MA: Media Education Foundation Production, 2007.

Roberts, Robin. *Ladies First: Women in Music Videos.* Jackson: University Press of Mississippi, 1996.

NETWORK NEWS ANCHOR DESK

Network news is defined as the news programming produced by the traditional "Big Three" commercial broadcast networks: the American Broadcasting Company (ABC), the Columbia Broadcasting System (CBS), and the National Broadcasting Company (NBC). The focus here is on their 30-minute evening newscasts, whose format consists of a single anchor or commentator introducing pretaped video segments prepared by correspondents or reporters. The anchor traditionally is seated behind a desk or console table, often shown in a medium camera shot, and speaks while looking directly into the camera. The FOX network is excluded here because its national news is delivered via a 24-hour cable news channel in a format that differs from that of other national news programs.

History

The first television network newscasts appeared in the 1940s. Women contributed very little to these news programs until the 1970s and 1980s. The word *anchor* was not coined, according to CBS, until it was used to describe Walter Cronkite's role in the coverage of the 1952 presidential election. Prior to that event, the person in front of the camera was described as a newscaster, announcer, or commentator—all words borrowed from radio news. Researchers at the CBS Television Audience Research Institute recommended that people who delivered the news be suitable in dress and personality to be welcomed into the intimate setting of a family's living room. The news industry is a traditionally male business, and the nature of its subject matter—community, state, national, and world leaders leading change and restoring order—has dictated that men are featured in news stories. For many years, men were also telling stories that included comments from other men. Women in newsrooms are more likely to be assigned to cover "soft" news events or topics considered to be so-called women's issues. A female reporter promoted to the anchor desk would then have to struggle to convey the perception that she was qualified for that work, again reducing the number of women qualified to hold that position.

In the 1970s, women entered network news at significant rates after the Federal Communications Commission (FCC) ordered that all businesses making more than \$50,000 and employing 50 or more people match their employment demographics to the demographics of the community in which they were located. However, change at the anchor desk was slow. Carole Simpson, who was with ABC News, said when she started in network television in 1974 that if she had been asked if there would still be three white male anchors in 2001 she would have thought that was impossible. Only two years later, in 1976, Barbara Walters coanchored *ABC Evening News* with Harry Reasoner—a landmark event—but the pairing ended in 1978 because of Reasoner's disdain for Walters, which was almost palpable on air. CBS tried a similar pairing from 1993 to 1995, placing Connie Chung as coanchor with Dan Rather,

Women in early 20th-century newsrooms were more likely to be assigned to cover "soft" news events and did not appear at the anchor desk until the mid-1970s. Carole Simpson was the first African American woman to have anchor duties at a major network. (Photos.com)

with similar negative results. ABC paired Elizabeth Vargas with Bob Woodruff in 2004. Woodruff was injured in Iraq while Vargas was absent on family leave; that pairing was also short-lived.

Historically, the networks did not often change personnel. CBS news had only four main anchors between 1948 and 2005: Douglas Edwards, Walter Cronkite, Dan Rather, and Connie Chung (coanchor with Rather from 1993 to 1995). Cronkite was so popular that by the late 1960s and 1970s he was identified as the most trusted man in America. It was not until 2006 that a woman appeared as the solo anchor of a nightly network news program.

CBS predicted that Katie Couric would reinvent the evening news, but when the program remained in third place in the ratings, producers stopped experimenting with the format. Being named the first solo anchor proved notable for its novelty and mostly negative attention; Couric was described by sexualized and personalized frames, so much so that any commentary about her skills, preparation for the job, and recognition of the event as progress for women in the traditionally male-dominated world of journalism was overshadowed. She instead was described by her appearance (cute and perky) amid doubts that she could convey the sense of gravitas required by the "voice of God" intonation that had been a hallmark of decades of male anchors. Her wardrobe was even critiqued after her first broadcast. CBS itself framed her; it was discovered that the promotional department had digitally altered a photo to make her appear about 20 pounds lighter. As such, the mainstream media perpetuated hegemonic beliefs about women and authority. Diane Sawyer, who has had a career trajectory similar to Couric's, was named the sole anchor of ABC's *World News* at the end 2009. This time there was virtually no fanfare.

The Nature of News

Television is a visual medium. News reporters and anchors are judged on their physical characteristics, regardless of gender. However, research findings indicate that once women reach the age of 40, the number of them in on-camera roles begins to fall. Given that there was never equity with male numbers, this exacerbates gender differences.

While she was not working at the network level, Christine Craft was fired from an ABC affiliate in Kansas City in 1981; she was told that people did not want to watch her anchor because she was "too old, too unattractive, and not sufficiently deferential to men." The U.S. Supreme Court ultimately decided not to hear her sex discrimination case, after earlier court decisions in her favor were overturned.

The difficulty with this practice is that it comes at the price of experience. Younger women do not have as much, are not seasoned in the business of news, and therefore presumably do not produce stories of as high quality as women with more experience. Twenty years ago, a study commissioned by the Radio Television News Directors Association found that the average age of female reporters was 28; the average age of male reporters was 32. Another study indicated that female reporters said physical appearance was the top-rated career barrier for them. The quality of their work ranked 27th out of 34 other possible barriers. Often, broadcasters who aspire to be anchors must first pay their dues as reporters. Lifestyle choices may also be a factor in the phenomenon of the disappearing female news reporter or anchor. Many of these women leave the industry in their 30s or 40s to spend more time with family. Men rarely do, at least not in such a public way.

It may be reasonable to think that viewers would want to watch reporters and anchors near their own age; however, the age of someone who watches an evening network newscast continues to grow. That network evening news viewer is in his or her early 60s. In 2011, Diane Sawyer (ABC) was 65 years old, Katie Couric (CBS) was 54, and Brian Williams (NBC) was 52. In addition, viewing statistics show that women are more likely to watch network news, especially when gathering political news.

The death of network news has been predicted for the past 20 years, according to some industry observers. Their audience share has been cut in half since cable stations emerged in the 1980s. It is apparent that younger people now get their news from other sources—primarily the Internet, 24-hour cable news channels, and cell phones. Few working people are home to watch network news; they are more likely to check in with their favorite Internet news sources before the broadcasts. When a national crisis happens, the ratings numbers go up, but some believe that an older man who speaks in low, soothing tones is what viewers are tuning in to see—someone who reassures them.

As industry leaders struggle with falling ratings, it is clear that network news will have to reinvent itself in order to remain viable. The audience is changing, so the content must change. Each network has entered the digital realm, and anchors are now writing blogs and reading on streaming Webcasts.

Beth M. Olson
University of Houston

See also Beauty and Body Image: Beauty Myths; Hegemony; Newsrooms; Radio; Television

Further Readings

Alan, Jeff. *Anchoring America: The Changing Face of Network News*. Chicago: Bonus Books, 2003.

Craft, Christine. *Too Old, Too Ugly, and Not Deferential to Men*. Rocklin, CA: Prima, 1988.

Fensch, Thomas, ed. *Television News Anchors: An Anthology of Profiles of the Major Figures and Issues in United States Network Reporting*. Jefferson, NC: McFarland, 1993.

Holland, Patricia. "When a Woman Reads the News." In *Boxed In: Women and Television*, Helen Baehr and Gillian Dyer, eds. London: Pandora Press, 1987.

Matusow, Barbara. *The Evening Stars: The Making of the Network News Anchor*. Boston: Houghton Mifflin, 1983.

McGregor, Judy. "Stereotypes and Symbolic Annihilation: Press Constructions of Women at the Top." *Women in Management Review*, v.15 (2000).

Rakow, Lana F. and Kimberlie Kranich. "Women as a Sign in Television News." *Journal of Communication*, v.4/1 (1991).

Sanders, Marlene. "Television: The Face of the Network News Is Male." *Television Quarterly*, v.26 (1992).

Sanders, Marlene and Marcia Rock. *Waiting for Prime-Time: The Women of Television News*. Urbana: University of Illinois Press, 1994.

Walters, Barbara. *Audition: A Memoir*. New York: Knopf, 2008.

NEW MEDIA

New media is a fluid term. Today, it means the convergence of traditional media, including film, music, audio, and video, with the interactive power of the computer, cell phone, and other computer- and Internet-enabled gadgets. Tomorrow, the definition may shift as new technologies emerge and others fall from favor. The key element of new media is interactivity—the push-pull interaction of Web 2.0 and social media. With new media, people with access to the Internet and basic computer software has the ability to create, post, distribute, and consume information anywhere, anytime, on any digital device. In an ideal world, new media can be empowering, leading to the democratization of information. Many scholars see enormous possibilities in all this, but it is unclear if new media will ever live up to its potential. Gender has emerged as one issue that confronts the new media.

New media—as a term and as a technology—dates back to the 1990s when certain technological, economic, and social conditions coalesced to make these media possible. As media and cultural scholar Rosalind Gill points out, new media require certain conditions: the general affordability—and the widespread adoption—of personal computers with high-speed microprocessing capabilities, the pervasive accessibility of the World Wide Web to the general public, and the growth of dot-coms. Sociologist Saskia Sassen contends that those conditions did not exist until 1994.

The general public's embrace of new media did not take place until the 21st century, when certain Websites that encouraged interactivity emerged and gained popularity: Wikipedia, the online, collaboratively built encyclopedia, established in 2001; the social networking sites Myspace and Facebook, started in 2003 and 2004 respectively; and YouTube, the video-sharing Website that debuted in 2005. Each of these Websites was designed, built, and launched by men. Although there are feminist Websites online that encourage new media interactivity (for example, feministing.com, webgrrls.com, and feminist.com), they pale in comparison to the popularity of the Websites most commonly used by the general public: Wikipedia, Myspace, Facebook, and YouTube.

The involvement of women in new media has been the subject of much debate. New media scholars have built on the work of those who have studied women and computers in general. Those scholars found that males dominated the computer field and that women were seldom included in the design and development of computer technology and, therefore, lagged behind in the field.

Much the same could be said of the new media. Women have been excluded from the design and development of the computer hardware and software that make new media possible. Moreover, women have not been involved in the design and development of key new media Websites, specifically Myspace, Facebook, YouTube, and Wikipedia. However, over time, women have become central to new media—interacting, creating content, distributing and consuming it—and making it their own.

This did not happen overnight. Research into Internet usage (a key ingredient for the new media) in the early 1990s revealed a gender gap, with women significantly less likely than men to use the Internet and, therefore, unlikely to participate in the new media. Studies indicated that the gender gap vis-à-vis the Internet did not last long. The Pew Research Center found that the gender gap had virtually disappeared by 2000. Even then, however, men spent more time online, and today men remain the most common early technology adopters and seem more at ease with the Internet and computers than women.

Men and women use the Internet—and new media—in different ways. Deborah Fallows, working under the auspices of the Internet and American Life Project of the Pew Research Center, found men were more interested in technology and how gadgets, systems, and software work. They were more likely to be the technology innovators, trying new hardware and software and more adept and confident in the world of technology. Fallows also found that men were more avid consumers of online information, more likely to use the Internet (and new media) for recreation, and more tech-savvy. Men are more likely to pay bills online, gather information about hobbies, take informal classes, participate in fantasy sports leagues, download music, remix files, and listen to the radio.

In contrast, Fallows found that women approached the Internet—and, accordingly, new media—in a quite different manner. Women use the Internet and new media to deepen their connections with others. Accordingly, women outnumbered men on the social networking sites—an important portion of new media—reaching out to friends, making new connections, nurturing relationships, and interacting within their communities. However, women also found recreation in new media opportunities online. Fallows found they play games as much as men and listen to audio clips. They also share files, especially within their family, friend, and community networks. Fallows also discovered demographic shifts that suggest possible future changes in the new media picture. More and more younger women are online—and, accordingly, reaching out to new media—but older women (over the age of 65) continued to lag behind. Fallows also found African American women are more likely to be online—and have access to the new media—than African American men.

New media also offer opportunities for creative outlets for skilled amateurs—and professionals. With a flipcamera (camcorder for digital video), a cell phone, inexpensive audio equipment, and a little creativity, any person can become a filmmaker, a recording artist, or a citizen journalist in this new media world. Video can then be uploaded onto YouTube for all the world to see. In 2010, about 35 hours of video were uploaded every minute onto

YouTube. Heather Molyneaux and colleagues found a gender imbalance in the creation, uploading, and commenting on these vlogs (user-generated video texts) on YouTube. Men created and uploaded the greatest number of the videos and visited the site far more than women. When women did upload video, they had roughly the same level of technical expertise as the men. The Molyneaux study found that women participated in the vlog community in other ways. Women were more likely to ask questions, answer the questions of other vloggers, and provide suggestions in an information-sharing spirit. They were also far less likely to comment on videos or even watch them on YouTube, Molyneaux and her team found.

New media have also fostered a new information industry. Women who work in the new media industry have found that they often face a hostile environment. Although the new media have been characterized as "cool, creative and egalitarian" in news reports, women in the industry often face traditional patterns of gender inequality. In her study of 125 freelance new media workers in six European countries, Rosalind Gill found that the nonhierarchical, egalitarian workplace retains "old-fashioned patterns of gender inequality." The new media model of self-directed labor (self-employment, said to represent the future of work) has ramifications for women who work in the industry, but few scholars have examined the situation from a gender perspective. In her look at new media workers in Europe, Gill found that most new media workers were highly educated, were between the ages of 25 and 35, were white, and had two to six years of experience in the field. Women tended to be the newcomers to the field and faced inequalities at work. Gill found that women won far fewer work contracts than the men, and those that they did receive were more likely to be in the public sector or with volunteer organizations rather than in the more lucrative business sphere. Not surprisingly, women workers in new media earned less money. The informality and flexibility of the field posed other difficulties for women. Gill found that women often faced sexism when working in the male-dominated teams, had limited access to new contracts because of a kind of gendered exclusion, and were isolated in their workspaces, which limited their opportunities for networking and their prospects for future business. Gill also found what she called a "postfeminist problem": Men—and

women—were unable to see the disadvantages that females face in this work environment.

The future of new media—as a career or as a recreation (albeit a time-consuming one)—lies in the hands of a new generation who are undaunted by technology; adept at content creation, consumption, and distribution; excited about new ways of interacting with others; and willing to experiment with new ways of doing things.

Studies by the Pew Research Center's Internet and American Life Project suggest that teens and young adults are "digital natives," experienced users of the new technology, at ease on the Internet, and consumers of new media. Lee Rainie, founder and director of the Internet and American Life Project at Pew, made six generalizations about teens and college students in his study of "digital natives":

1. Media and gadgets are a part of their everyday life.

2. New gadgets allow these groups to interact with the media, gather information and communicate anywhere and anytime.

3. The Internet (especially broadband) is the center of their communication existence.

4. Teens and young adults are multitaskers.

5. This younger generation understands that ordinary citizens can be publishers, movie makers, artists and story tellers with relatively inexpensive equipment, a little technical expertise and creativity.

6. Everything is going to continue to change. This generation seems ready to adjust to the changes on the horizon.

In a more recent study by the Pew Center (2010), Amelia Lenhert and her colleagues charted media use by teens, young adults, and others. This study indicated that teens and young adults, especially, are already involved in new media and are experienced digital technology users. Among Lenhert et al.'s findings, which relate specifically to new media, are the following:

1. Almost seven of 10 teens (12 to 17) have access to computers.

2. Laptops are the computers of choice for those under the age of 30—and women and men have similar patterns of laptop usage.

3. Internet access is changing for teens and young adults, especially, with wireless the preferred method of access.

4. Teens and young adults are more likely to access the Internet through mobile gadgets (cell phone, game consoles and portable gaming devices) than other age groups.

5. Teens have greatly increased their usage of social networking—almost 75 percent use these Websites, with Facebook their favorite option.

6. Teens share self-created content online (photos, video, and artwork), often through social networking sites.

7. Cell phone usage is up (75 percent for teens and 93 percent for young adults—those 18 to 29 years of age).

8. The Internet is an information and economic "appliance" in the lives of young adults and teens.

No one can say with any certainty where the future of new media lies. Technological changes will tell only part of the story—and that is impossible to predict. The future of the field lies with the men and the women who see the new media as useful tools in their lives. Previous research indicates that women and men will use the new media in different ways. There is nothing to suggest that those patterns will change. The only thing certain about the future of new media is that it will be forever changing—and challenging.

Kathleen L. Endres
University of Akron

See also Blogs and Blogging; Cyberspace and Cyberculture; Social Media; Social Networking Sites: Facebook; Social Networking Sites: Myspace; Twitter; YouTube

Further Readings

Anderson, Janna and Lee Rainie. "The Future of the Internet." Pew Internet and American Life Project. http://www.pewinternet.org/~/media//Files/Reports/2008/PIP_FutureInternet3.pdf.pdf (Accessed February 2011).

Fallows, Deborah. "Women and Men Use the Internet." Pew Internet and American Life Project. http://www.pewinternet.org/Reports/2005/How-Women-and-Men-Use-the-Internet.aspx (Accessed February 2011).

Gill, Rosalind. "Cool, Creative and Egalitarian? Exploring Gender in Project-Based New Media Work in Europe." *Information, Communication and Society*, v.5 (2002).

Jackson, Linda, Kelly Ervin, Philip Gardner, and Neal Schmidt. "Gender and the Internet: Women Communicating and Men Searching." *Sex Roles*, v.44 (2001).

Lenhert, Amelia, Kristen Purcell, Aaron Smith, and Kathryn Zickuhr. "Social Media and Mobile Internet Use Among Teens and Young Adults." Pew Internet and American Life Project. http://www.pewinternet.org/Reports/2010/Social-Media-and-Young-Adults.aspx (Accessed February 2011).

Molyneaux, Heather, Susan O'Donnell, Kerri Gibson, and Janice Singer. "Exploring the Gender Divide on YouTube: An Analysis of the Creation of Reception of Vlogs." *American Communication Journal*, v.10 (2008) http://www.acjournal.org/holdings/vol10/01_Spring/articles/molyneaux_etal.php (Accessed February 2011).

Ona, Hiroshi and Madeline Zavodny. "Gender and the Internet." *Social Science Quarterly*, v.84 (2009).

Rainie, Lee. "The New Media Ecology: How the Marketplace of Ideas and Learning Is Different for 'Digital Natives.'" Pew Internet and American Life Project. http://www.pewinternet.org/Presentations/2007/The-New-Media-Ecology-of-Students.aspx (Accessed February 2011).

Sassen, Saskia. "New Media: Working Practices in the Electronic Arts Conference." Keynote address to New Media: Working Practices in the Electronic Arts conference (November 17, 1999).

Spilker, Hendrik and Knut H. Sorensen. "Women and Computers: From Exclusion to Gendered Design." *New Media and Society*, v.2 (2000).

NEWSROOMS

The newsroom is the hub of journalistic activity within any news-producing organization. The traditional configuration of the newsroom is a physical space shared by journalists, editors, and technicians engaged in gathering and editing information to be distributed through print, radio, television, and online news channels. Most of the prominent news organizations functioning today began producing news for one medium only and are transitioning to producing multimedia content. This has resulted in changes to traditional configurations of newsrooms. Along with charting technological and political economic shifts in the culture at large, newsrooms also provide rich sites of analysis for considering the shifts in the status of minorities in the workplace, including women. Scholarly research analyzing the role of gender in the production of media repeatedly looks to the newsroom to mark the presence or absence of ethnic, racial, and gender difference in the newsroom and its impact on what news is disseminated and how.

Traditionally, newsrooms catering to different media outlets have remained largely separate, but the recent trends in newsroom configuration emphasize a shared space where content is simultaneously produced for print, radio, television, and online outlets. This in large part is due to the conglomeration of news production and the desire of those conglomerates to reduce costs as revenue from news media continues to decline overall. In 2007, BBC News merged its radio, television, and online newsrooms in order to reduce the number of reporters dispatched to report on individual stories. While this was effective in reducing costs, interviews with BBC reporters suggest the merging provokes new dilemmas for journalists, who must prioritize producing content for each platform and produce content for multimedia channels with fewer personnel.

On the whole, newsrooms in the United States continue to be populated primarily by white males, despite the increase in ethnic, racial, and gender diversity in the newsroom in the latter half of the 20th century and the early 21st century. There is debate about how much of an impact racial and gender diversity in the newsroom has on the production of news itself. However, recent analyses suggest that the increased presence of women in the newsroom means greater attention to social issues. This could be a result of the history of women's segregation in the production of news, limiting their reporting to "women's issues," which initially excluded serious political content. As women's social movements gain traction in the fight for gender equality, reporting on "women's issues" increasingly moves content toward more traditional, serious content. Female reporters may also be inclined to incorporate feminist perspectives and lay people as sources in news reporting. Managerially, a lack of female editors in a newsroom does not result in a difference in the issues covered, but it does result in more traditional divisions of female and male reporters in the coverage of those issues. Male reporters are directed toward reporting on political and economic

News agencies have typically assigned political and economic issues to male reporters, while female reporters are often left to cover entertainment and human-interest stories and other "lighter" topics. (Photos.com)

issues, while female reporters are directed toward entertainment and human-interest stories, with an emphasis on "women's issues."

The introduction of women into U.S. newsrooms has increased since World War II, commensurate with the rise of women in the professional workplace on the whole. Census data and historical reviews show an initial growth in the number of women in newsrooms beginning in the 1950s and 1960s. This increase gained momentum in the 1970s as the second wave feminist social movement began disrupting traditional notions of femininity and argued that women were capable of succeeding in workplaces traditionally dominated by men. Both ethnographic studies and census data repeatedly characterize newsrooms on the whole as environments in which professional and social hierarchies reinforce a masculine hegemony. Historically newsrooms have been resistant to the full participation of women in all aspects of the production of news, which was evident in the segregation of the newsroom into areas producing women's pages and areas producing more substantive content. Female reporters and editors traditionally worked on pages or segments on fashion, health, beauty, entertainment, and human-interest stories. These realms of news production are considered of interest to female audiences and therefore the purview of female reporters and editors.

Since the 1970s, there has been little change in the numbers of women in American newsrooms. In the largest newsrooms, women make up just below 50 percent of the staff. Since the late 1990s the American Society of News Editors has included women in their census of minorities in newsrooms. While these data have failed to show a significant increase in the number of women present, they have shown a shift in the beats female reporters are assigned to cover and in the managerial and editorial positions women occupy in the newsroom. It was not until the 1990s that women began to occupy editorial positions for "hard" pages, such as sports, metro, and politics, and began to be a more significant presence in the photography and videography departments. Census data on today's newsroom show that the presence of women in these areas remains steady but has not increased as much as that of other minority groups.

Female pioneers in U.S. newsrooms include the reporter Nellie Bly (pen name of journalist Elizabeth Jane Cochran). Bly's first editor at the *Pittsburgh Dispatch* gave her the pen name, as was common for female reporters of the time. Driven to expand the scope of her reporting from women's pages, Bly took it upon herself to become a foreign correspondent by moving to Mexico. Eventually she worked her way into Joseph Pulitzer's newsroom at *The New York World*, where she conducted one of her most notorious journalistic endeavors: going undercover in an insane asylum to report on abuses of female patients. In the early 1960s, Charlayne Hunter-Gault became the first African American staff writer at *The New Yorker*. She went on to join the staff of the *New York Times*, eventually becoming the Harlem bureau chief. In 1978, Hunter-Gault joined the Public Broadcasting Service's television news program *The MacNeil/Lehrer Report* as a national correspondent; there she remained for the next two decades. Helen Thomas is another female journalist who overcame traditional notions of a woman's

place in the newsroom to become a White House chief correspondent. Thomas began her career as a staffer at United Press Radio in the 1930s, becoming a White House reporter for the United Press in 1943. She was the first woman to be accepted into the White House Press Corps.

The increasing number of women like these in the newsrooms of credible news agencies has gone a long way to changing the notion of what women are capable of accomplishing as journalists. News beats and assignments that were once thought to be entirely the domain of male interpreters are now also the purview of women, and their progress inside the newsroom has resulted in the increase of female reporters dispatched to cover stories on the ground. An increase in the number of women in the newsroom has meant an increase of women acting as foreign correspondents and has resulted in more women reporting from the front lines of combat. Other notable women include Judy Crichton, who was the first woman to work as a producer, director, and writer in the newsroom of *CBS Reports*, beginning in 1948.

The configuration of a newsroom depends largely on the size of the news organization, the size of the market to which it disseminates its content, and the medium for which it is producing content. Traditionally, reporters in the newsroom are assigned individual beats to be covered from the desk they occupy in the newsroom. Editors' offices are close to these desks, so that they are easily accessible to reporters and can communicate efficiently, fact-check, and quickly give feedback on stories reporters are preparing. Newsrooms as a whole are spaces where information is received, digested, and processed. Information is collected from newswires and by monitoring the news output of other news outlets. Additionally, newsrooms receive official reports from police and emergency authorities as well as government institutions and corporations. All this information must be prioritized. The newsroom is where decisions are made about which reporters will be dispatched to report on stories, and the newsroom is primarily where reporters receive their cues for what aspects of the story are most important to cover.

Processes of reporting, editing, and selection are located in the newsroom and dictate what content is disseminated to the audience. The organization of personnel and activities in the newsroom has far-reaching implications for the flow of information in the public sphere and for the state of journalism as a whole. On a day-to-day basis, individual reporters gather news from their position at the desk, conducting supplementary reporting from the scene if necessary. Reporters then fashion stories to submit to editors, who in engage in a system of checks before passing the story on for publication or broadcast. This includes the process of fact checking, as well as the manipulation of language, the addition of headlines and leads to frame the story, and ultimately the determination of how much of the information gathered will be included in the final product. Even in a free press, the exchange between reporter and editor in the newsroom can significantly narrow what information is actually related to the audience.

In its traditional configuration, the newsroom functions as a network of information exchange resulting in a set number of news stories for each production period. Each reporter and editor is assigned to a desk in the newsroom. Each desk covers a particular beat. Within the newsroom individuals pursue distinct stories while attempting to keep one another informed, and they deploy their resources in pursuing the story as efficiently as possible. Newsroom managers must supervise the deployment of reporters and their pursuit of stories while providing reporters with the freedom they require to report effectively. Recent studies suggest that gender can play a part in the effectiveness of newsroom communication and the exchange of information. Gender can also be a determinant of which personnel excel in leadership positions that require flexibility and adaptability as new technologies require the revision of usual routines of news production. More extensive research is needed to determine what specific factors contribute to the success of women in leadership positions in newsrooms.

There has been a growing acknowledgment among news producers and media watchdogs of the importance of increasing the presence of women in newsrooms globally. The status of women in newsrooms continues to be a strong indicator of the status of women in the public and professional sphere overall. As women have become more of a presence in newsrooms, the obstacles they still face have been illuminated. While the number of women training to be journalists has increased significantly in the United States and in African countries, reports show that male-dominated newsrooms are still reluctant to employ female journalists. The Al Jazeera network has employed a number of women to work as reporters, editors, producers, and anchors, but the departure of four female television anchors/reporters was said to be due to pressure from the organization to adhere to stricter dress codes.

In all newsrooms, the concern is that, while women occupy more managerial positions, they are a much smaller presence further up the executive ladder and almost nonexistent in the realm of media ownership, which has an impact on the orientation of the newsroom as well as its routines and practices. There is also concern that gender inequality may be replicated in the digital newsroom, where women are not represented enough in the occupation of Web development. At this stage in the history of the digital newsroom, it is difficult to foresee whether technological shifts affecting the production of news in the newsroom will result in a shift in the core gender dynamics of the newsroom.

Isra Ali
Rutgers University

See also Diversity; Hegemony; Media Consolidation; Media Convergence; Media Ethnography; Network News Anchor Desk; New Media; Television; Workforce

Further Readings

American Society of News Editors. "ASNE Newsroom Census." http://asne.org/key_initiatives/diversity/newsroom_census.aspx (Accessed February 2011).
De Bruin, Marjan and Karen Ross. *Gender and Newsroom Cultures: Identities at Work.* Cresskill, NJ: Hampton Press, 2004.
Hemmingway, Emma. *Into the Newsroom: Exploring the Digital Production of Regional Television News.* New York: Routledge, 2008.
North, Louise. *The Gendered Newsroom: How Journalists Experience the Changing World of Media.* Cresskill, NJ: Hampton Press, 2009.
Steiner, Linda. "Gender in the Newsroom." In *The Handbook of Journalism Studies*, Karin Wahl-Jorgensen and Thomas Hanitzsch, eds. New York: Taylor & Francis, 2009.

ONLINE NEW MEDIA: GLBTQ IDENTITY

Global access to cyber communication and mobile media has increased significantly, allowing usually silenced sexual minorities an opportunity to access and contribute to discourse. The widespread use of online communication and the anonymity it affords have had a large impact on discussions concerning sexual orientation and gender. Through tools such as YouTube, online messaging, and various other means of media convergence, users are able not only to broadcast their own personas but also to relate to and communicate with myriad audiences with little difficulty. Additionally, these media allow communicators to facilitate discussions they may not be comfortable having face to face in interpersonal communications. The disadvantage of the new online discourse, however, is that cyber-based communicative attacks have been easy to facilitate. Homo-, bi-, and transphobic messages have become increasingly common, resulting in a reconsideration of the efficacy of these media in reaching and positively affecting target audiences. These facets of mediated communication therefore present both positive and potentially invasive results.

In terms of global outreach and networking, online media have resulted in a number of positive efforts. Educational and social support service organizations related to the needs of the gay, lesbian, bisexual, transsexual/transgender, and queer/questioning (GLBTQ) community have been able to use online media to launch extensive online campaigns. The Gay, Lesbian, Straight Education Network (GLSEN), for example, supports effective programs for student inclusion, antibullying efforts, and references for educators on a number of levels. Additionally, educational lesson plans and best-practice procedures have been highlighted on online sources, as well as links to potential additional outreach organizations. These educational efforts have been paralleled by the online services of groups such as Parents, Families, and Friends of Lesbians and Gays (PFLAG), which focuses primarily on outreach to adolescents and their parents. Other organizations, such as the more recently developed Campus Pride, include online services marketed to GLBTQ college populations, as well as resources for college and university administrators, recruiters, and educators. In what is becoming a more common practice, GLBTQ college outreach efforts are being ranked and publicized online, including efforts taken by print publications, such as *The Advocate*, and through after-school services, such as those conducted at the Hetrick-Martin Institute, home of the Harvey Milk High School and part of a multistate educational services project.

The ability of online efforts to bolster the contributions of brick-and-mortar service centers has amplified the potential field of participants in such efforts considerably. Additionally, these online venues allow for anonymity and access from geographically disparate locations. As a result, efforts such as those undertaken through the suicide prevention organization the Trevor Project have reached new heights.

Examples include not only personal consultations through electronic communication but also personal outreach through online methods. The coupling of these electronic services with awareness campaigns structured across online media and through "real time" electronic productions has resulted in more awareness and participation, increasing knowledge of these services among the general public.

Similarly, online media such as videologs (vlogs) and weblogs (blogs) have proliferated, including anthologies and links to GLBTQ-focused YouTube channels on major, nationally syndicated blogs. Beyond the gossip focus of earlier blogs, such as Perez Hilton's ongoing contributions, contemporary blogs have addressed GLBTQ issues from a variety of perspectives. For example, Towleroad presents regular updates on GLBTQ concerns in politics, entertainment, social issues, and environmentalism. Typically, discussion items are presented and viewers' public contributions facilitate even more communication. A similar approach is taken by PamHouseBlend, which focuses on lesbian and racial identities and issues. The format of mixing political events with social and entertainment features is a common and even standard formula, with additional examples being taken from the supposedly left-leaning and occasionally snarky Queerty and the more conservative GayPatriot. Recent efforts have been undertaken to gauge public impacts and responses, including the introduction of Weblog awards, which since 2007 have constituted the largest format for tracking public awareness and public response. GLBTQ blog awards are given regularly and allow participants to vote on content related to material representing the needs of the GLBTQ community.

Online media have also been used to produce a number of socially oriented, GLBTQ-focused sites. Beyond facilitating organizations devoted to building romantic relationships, Internet usage targeted at social and entertainment functions has increased dramatically in recent years. Examples include blogs concerned with GLBTQ personal issues, such as the 2009 anticyberbullying project Big Fat Gay Collab, which featured the work of and links to 24 bloggers. The purpose of this project, which incorporated blogs specifically dedicated to raising awareness of GLBTQ youth issues, was to ensure that cyberbullying and other phobic methods were countered with positive images and personal reactions from GLBTQ youth. These earlier efforts have been fortified by more recent campaigns, such as the It Gets Better campaign, created in 2010 by Dan Savage as an Internet response to increased suicide rates among GLBTQ youth that have been associated with cyber bullying. The It Gets Better campaign was prompted by a rash of well-publicized suicides among GLBTQ youth, including those of a 13-year-old boy and college student Tyler Clementi, whose intimate encounters were filmed and subsequently broadcast through electronic communication. The project prompted videos that spotlighted the inclusion efforts and concerns of various groups and individuals throughout the United States, including President Barack Obama, Secretary of State Hillary Clinton, the head of the Democratic National Convention, and a great number of students and student groups.

Similarly, online media have been used to broadcast inclusive messages to GLBTQ bullied youth. Fort Worth, Texas, council member Joel Burns, for example, has issued impassioned pleas to thwart phobic bullying and youth suicide. The narrative project I'm From Driftwood has resulted in the creation of a series of online video depictions of GLBTQ youth; interviewers visit youth in a number of settings, record their experiences related to sexual orientation as well as personal stories, and broadcast these stories online. Visitors to the site are able to contribute their own online narratives, resulting in a greater cache of information related to the project. The contributions of viewers are also graphed on a map, not only illustrating the breadth of the GLBTQ community but also recording the project's expansion. The impacts of these initiatives remain unknown, although initial responses have been positive. For example, Burns received thousands of positive responses, including phone calls, after his statement, and an increasing number of media outlets are noting both the situations affecting GLBTQ youth and the efforts to increase their inclusion.

Conversely, online media have allowed users not only to attempt to thwart phobic efforts but also to campaign actively against them. For example, online campaigns were used extensively in elections leading to the passage of anti-GLBTQ measures, such as Maine Question 1 and California's Proposition 8. Phobic cyber messaging and broadcasts of personal information related to sexual orientation have also been noted as efforts have increased. Social networking sites such as Facebook and Twitter have allowed users to post anti-GLBTQ messages; when Arkansas school board member Clint McCance used strong homophobic slurs on his personal Twitter account, for example. The result was a national call for a public apology. McCance ultimately resigned, although his message continues to be recycled and reposted throughout myriad electronic communications outlets. Similarly, Andrew Shirvell, an assistant attorney general in Michigan, used his personal blog to harass gay University of Michigan student government president Chris Armstrong. Shirvell was ultimately temporarily suspended from his position, and there were plans to take him to court. In this case, as in many of the previous examples, Shirvell has invoked his right to free speech, including attacks over cyberspace. Currently, specific laws related to online harassment have not been fully developed, but legislation may emerge from these cases.

Beyond social and personal relations, online efforts undertaken by the GLBTQ population have blossomed in terms of political awareness campaigns and tactics. This outreach suggests that cyber communication is emerging as an important part of the fourth estate, potentially resulting in a greater amount of public engagement and participation in political and activist GLBTQ causes. The impacts of this method of political outreach are still being tested, but the inclusion of online new media in future efforts is a distinct certainty.

Scott Gratson
Temple University

See also Cultural Politics; Electronic Media and Social Inequality; Identity; Online New Media: Transgender Identity; Simulacra; Social Media; Social Networking Sites: Facebook; Social Networking Sites: Myspace; Viral Advertising and Marketing; Virtual Community

Further Readings

Dow, Bonnie J. *The Sage Handbook of Gender and Communication*. Thousand Oaks, CA: Sage, 2006.

O'Riordan, K. and P. J. Phillips, eds. *Queer Online: Media, Technology and Sexuality*. New York: Peter Lang, 2007.

Pullen, C. and C. Cooper. *LGBT Identity and Online New Media*. New York: Routledge, 2010.

ONLINE NEW MEDIA: TRANSGENDER IDENTITY

Transgender is usually defined as the status of a person's gender identity when that person's self-identification (as male, female, both, or neither) differs from the person's physiological sexual attributes. In other words, transgender people are those who feel that the gender assigned to them at birth does not match their inner gender identity. Transgender people do not identify with the gender they were assigned; in some cases, the gender assigned to them represents only part of their gender identity. In a broader definition, transgender includes transsexuals, transvestites, and cross-dressers.

In the field of gender studies, the term *transgender* has had a complex historical background. Even though "transgender" was also used to refer to people living a gender identity opposite to their biological gender, in the 1970s the emphasis was always on gender lifestyle rather than identity. With the development of politics of identity, "transgender" began to have two different functional meanings. On one hand, it is used as a generic term to describe individuals or certain groups who resist the existing social boundaries of gender. On the other hand, transgender is sometimes used to describe a person whose behavior does not comport with his or her biological gender or who has undergone a sex change by way of a surgical operation. These meanings also reflect the fact that transgender people usually face various social pressures and prejudices in their daily lives, since they challenge social gender norms. It is significant that the term *transgender* does not imply the sexual orientation of the person; in fact, a transgender person can be straight, homosexual, bisexual, or multisexual. Some people argue that the traditional categories of sexual orientation are insufficient to illustrate the sexuality of transgenders.

Different from the mass media, which often tend to present stereotypes that reinforce existing social norms of gender, new media are providing another way for those of transgender identity to find information and support groups and to flourish. Many new computer-mediated communication technologies enable their users to communicate by means of avatars or virtual bodies, which are considered an excellent way to present the transgender self.

The two most prevalent examples are the Internet and online gaming. Some scholars, such as Sherry Turkle, John Perry Barlow, and Manuel Castells, have suggested that the Internet has made it possible for users to be liberated from their bodies and from physical attributes and social categories. In addition to providing information about transgender identity, the Internet is seen as a medium that provides freedom for users to step outside the existing gender structure. Because identities on the Internet have no bodies, users are free to enter this world on equal terms and express themselves without limitations. The Internet is thus theorized as a place that enables the self-identity to be constructed and allows users to perform various characters.

Generally speaking, transgender in new media has two different meanings. The first is that non-transgender people who do not necessarily have strong desires to change gender identity in their daily lives perform different gender identities online. This type of online transgender gender performance is usually based on curiosity or other personal reasons. One famous example of a person whose disguising of gender online is unrelated to any real-world need to change gender identity is James Chartrand, who pretends to be a man in order to receive better remuneration as a blog writer. To overcome financial difficulty, she transformed her identity as a single mother into that of a male writer, aware that society often assumes that men are more knowledgeable than women about economic and technological issues. Not only did she attract fewer critics to her articles, but she also earned a better income because of her perceived gender role. The case of James Chartrand reveals that existing gender power politics are still effective on the Internet; she transformed her gender identity into that of a male professional writer in order to survive within this structure. This case reveals that some people transform their gender identities online not because of a desire to become another gender but because pretending to be another gender enables them to turn a real-life disadvantage into a more privileged status.

The other expression of transgender online occurs when real-world transgender people reveal their identities in the virtual world. The highly interactive nature of new media made these media into much more than places for downloading information—they have become relatively safe places to share and discuss issues that are difficult to approach in daily

life and to look for a support group. Not only do many online forums and Web pages address the issues of transgender identity, but transgender people can also express their true identities and find support groups in the virtual world. Many transgender-oriented groups build their sites online to raise awareness and to communicate with other users through forums or message boards. In the age of rising social media, the development of Web 2.0 and social networking Websites, such as Facebook and Myspace, has made it easier for transgender individuals and groups to spread their thoughts and have instant communication with other users interested in the issue. Plenty of groups related to transgender have pages on Facebook and encourage people with similar tendencies to join. Through instant messaging, posting wall, and other functions offered on social networking sites, communication within the group is facilitated and helps to form bonds between group members. Some transgender people, especially those who are younger, have also created videos to express their transgendered experiences. One famous example is Kyra Fisher, a young male-to-female transgender person, who created a video showing her taking an antiandrogen hormone pill. Kyra is one of many trans youths who have made online video logs (vlogs), raising questions about gender issues and sharing their transitional experiences. While growing up transgender can be a very isolating experience, the Internet provides resources to transgender children and teenagers to mitigate that impact. Vlogging may well have made transgenders like Kyra more confident and their worlds less frightening.

Online gaming is also often used to present transgender identity. Different from blogs, vlogs, and social media sites, where users often present their transgender identity through text and videos, online gaming provides a place for users/players to experience the transgender life by role playing the characters in the game. For example, massively multiplayer online role-playing games (MMORPGs) allow players to choose to represent characters of any gender (as in the game *World of Warcraft* or the virtual online world *Second Life*), within a universe where they can actually experience the lives and social interactions of being another gender. Transforming gender identity is very easy in these games, unlike real life. Players can choose a gender and appearance at the beginning of the game and not have to worry about whether the gender they chose matches their real gender identity; they can even change the gender of the role or create a new role if they are not completely satisfied with the gender and look they have in the game. The convenience of playing a transgender character has encouraged some people, even those who have never thought about being another sex in daily life, to try on this identity in online gaming environments.

One of the issues discussed in *Second Life*, as in most online games, concerns the lack of a specific option to be identified as transgender. A player can choose to be either male or female, but the possibility of being transgender is unavailable. This situation has drawn attention to the gender politics in the game. Some advocacy groups formed transgender communities in the game and argued that there was discrimination against transgender people in the game. The presentation of gender identity as a dichotomy in online games reflects the mainstream values of society and ignores the need for other gender identities, including transgender groups, to feel a sense of belonging in the game. Through advocacy by online communities, transgender issues were taken into consideration by the game, and awareness was raised.

Wei-Chun Victoria Wang
Ohio University

See also Cultural Politics; Cyberspace and Cyberculture; Electronic Media and Social Inequality; Identity; New Media; Online New Media: GLBTQ Identity; *Second Life*; Simulacra; Social Media; Social Networking Sites: Facebook; Social Networking Sites: Myspace; Transgender Studies; Virtual Community

Further Readings

Ho, Josephine Chuen-juei. "The Em(bodi)ment of Identity: Constructing Transgender." *Taiwan: A Radical Quarterly in Social Studies*, v.46 (2002).

Kennedy, Sarah. "TransTube." *The Advocate*, v.982 (2007).

Paasonen, Susanna. "Gender, Identity, and (the Limits of) Play on the Internet." In *Women's Everyday Uses of the Internet*, Mia Consalvo and Susanna Paasonen, eds. New York: Peter Lang, 2002.

Wacjman, Judy. "Virtual Gender." In *TechnoFeminism*. Cambridge, UK: Polity Press, 2004.

Patriarchy

The study of patriarchy has long extended beyond simply addressing the practice of economies being organized by male inheritance and descent. Cultural studies scholars have advanced feminist, Marxist, and postcolonial theories to critique the ways in which patriarchal norms structure gender norms and other facets of society. From interrogating the ways in which capitalism privileges male wealth to the tendency for science to pathologize women and from the male bias in legal codes to the normative products of popular culture that portray ideal femininity and masculinity, scholars have linked patriarchy to virtually every facet of cultural critique. Feminist theorists analyze patriarchal norms of masculinity and femininity; the connections between patriarchy, gender, and socioeconomic class; and the ways in which postcolonial theorists examine race, ethnicity, nationality, and gender in relation to patriarchy.

Feminist scholars argue that gender has a history that can be traced, has a structure that can be analyzed, and has changed over time in ways that can be documented. The historical investigation of how societies became organized by patriarchy and became invested in protecting patriarchy is one important aspect of understanding contemporary incarnations of patriarchal ideology. Gerda Lerner (1986) argues that the rise of private property is predicated on the subordination of women to men. In addition, she points out that reclaiming women's history is an important aspect of challenging patriarchal oppression, because history has been determined and written by men in a way that marginalizes women. Lerner contends that complete control over women's sexuality was crucial to the development of patriarchal dominance in ancient Mesopotamia. In addition to rendering women sexually and economically subordinate to men, patriarchy has systematically devalued women's spirituality by symbolically dethroning goddesses, promoting gods, punishing mythical women, and excluding women from valued spiritual roles in society. The prominent symbolic demonizing of women in creation myths and other religious texts constructs deep social myths of women being weak, incomplete, incompetent, and even evil, while upholding men as powerful and perfect. The widespread promotion of such patriarchal ideology may then be traced throughout secular aspects of society as well.

The social construction of gender creates individual and social expectations over time while structuring interactions. Patriarchal ideology becomes willingly internalized because it is incorporated into major social organizations, which in turn circulate it throughout societies. Challenges to patriarchal ideology by rejecting conventional gender roles are repressed through coercion and policing of boundaries throughout state institutions as well as cultural industries. Conceiving of gender as an institution similar to economics, for example, focuses attention on relations of power and interaction while also reinstating the body as part of institutions.

Feminists define power as "power over," most often exercised by patriarchy, as when power comes from being unmarked and therefore dominant. As Susan Bordo points out, particular hegemonic types of masculinity have been privileged by patriarchy, which marginalizes not only women but also feminine qualities expressed by men. Class, race, ethnicity, nationality, and religion also determine the hegemonic masculinity privileged in patriarchy. For example, heterosexual, white, Christian masculinity not only is normative in Western societies but has also been a dominant force in the shaping of colonized patriarchal societies. As colonialism circled the globe, enforcement of Western norms of sexuality, family life, and crime also resulted in the exportation of Western norms of citizenship and inclusion. Hierarchies that develop from patriarchal ideology can thus be examined throughout the world. However, the project of analyzing patriarchy in specific cultural contexts requires greater nuance than just conceiving of patriarchy as a colonial export. Uma Chakravarti builds on Lerner's examination of patriarchal control of female sexuality and reproduction to show that similar dynamics also exist in the caste systems of India, where women's purity determines caste purity.

Examinations of patriarchy include macro-social analyses as well as micro-level studies of family life and interpersonal relationships. Dorothy Smith and other scholars argue that families are key producers of gender norms and patriarchy. Smith's concept of "relations of ruling" is used to explain the material practices that produce power and dominance. Hierarchies develop around forms of knowledge, organized practices, and institutions, as well as questions of consciousness, experience, and agency. The concept of relations of ruling highlights the links between capitalism and patriarchy, race and colonialism, and other intersections. Smith also makes the case for studying organizational texts as well as popular texts, because any texts that people create and that organize their lives also build social structures, potentially sustaining or challenging patriarchy. When studying families, she advocates for analysis at the interpersonal and social levels, particularly stating that these structures may hold greater power to constrain and enable action than do people's personal beliefs or choices.

Feminist theory is grounded in overcoming the economic and cultural subordination of women to men. As a result, critiquing the dominant patriarchal economic and social orders is of foundational importance. French philosopher Simone de Beauvoir

Feminists define power as "power over," which is inherent in the patriarchal norms of masculinity and femininity. Simone de Beauvoir criticized women's complicit willingness to remain "enslaved" by a man to retain the privileges they gain from the male's economic position. (Wikimedia)

argues that conflicts between class and gender loyalty constitute a major cause of women's lack of power. In de Beauvoir's explication of the history of gender inequality (1952), it is class identification that leads to woman's complicity in her own subordination. Although de Beauvoir equates women with slaves throughout her writing, she is also careful to point out the ways in which women are complicit in their slavery. She argues that women share a bond with men beyond that of any other type of slave-master relationship, such that women have no basis for revolt against men. Women do not have a common history, religion, language, or culture apart from men, but share the history of men. Thus, it is because women identify more with the men of their own class, race, and cultural background than with the women of other classes, races, or cultural backgrounds that women are unable to unify and strive for significant social changes. It is difficult, de Beauvoir acknowledges, to rise against one's father, husband, or brother, knowing that to do so one will be forsaking the privileges that come from being associated with men. However, even while acknowledging the difficulties that women experience when seeking equality, de Beauvoir sharply criticizes women's willingness to remain complicit in their own enslavement in order to retain whatever privileges they gain from their economic positions.

On the practical level, she argues that women must gain economic freedom if they are to be able or willing to break away from patriarchal oppression. If women were economically independent, they would not be forced to rely on the privileges that come from associating with men.

Feminist cultural studies are characterized by a sustained attention to class and capitalism. Critics of patriarchy also draw on Marxist theories of politics, which call for the replacement of capitalism with socialism, a political economy in which workers are neither exploited nor alienated and through which communism—"the complete and conscious return of man himself as a social, that is, human being," as Rosemarie Tong put it—can be achieved. Contemporary Marxist feminists have drawn on these three aspects of Marxism to fight for women's liberation on several fronts, including advocating women's full-fledged entrance into the public workforce, payment for domestic labor, the socialization of domestic labor so that women no longer must work a "double shift" (that is, both inside and outside the home), and equal pay in the public workforce.

Developments in Marxist feminism have led to a more general socialist feminism. Socialist feminism argues that the strict Marxist focus on class does not pay sufficient attention to the oppression specifically of women by men. Socialist feminists still rely on Marxist theory and concepts but shift the primary emphasis from strictly class to the intersection of class and patriarchy. In 1990, Iris Young linked capitalism and patriarchy to argue that Marxism may theorize class and feminism may theorize gender, but it is far more productive to theorize gender-biased capitalist patriarchy as one concept. Such a theory recognizes that there is no gender-neutral economic order but that every aspect of capitalism is gendered. Socialist feminists argue that women of all classes, and indeed of both capitalist and communist economic structures, have been made subordinate to men. The challenge for understanding and dismantling patriarchy becomes accounting for why women have been confined to submissive roles in both public and private spheres.

Other socialist feminist critiques also focus on the ways in which patriarchy is reinforced in mainstream media and subculture media. For example, analyses of pornography find that patriarchy is upheld because women are represented as submissive and males are represented as dominant. Researchers have focused on content as well as production and reception in a manner that engages actively with socialist theory, rather than simply describing representations of women and girls.

Media analyses that contend that patriarchy symbolically eliminates women who become a threat to hegemony also relate to critiques of 19th-century literature that exalted the "cult of true womanhood" or the "cult of true domesticity." Such literature served the social purpose of instructing female readers in the fine art of being perfect women and then proceeded to ostracize, or kill off, any woman who defied the ideals of perfect womanhood. Prolifically represented in popular literature and early film, the 19th-century cult of true womanhood exalted purity, piety, passivity, and domesticity as the ideal and required attributes for "good" women to express. Throughout literature, those women who did not conform to expectation or who broke the codes of the cult that they be utterly submissive in religious practices, familial relationships, and social experiences were subjected to punishments including shunning, exile, and even death.

From literature that sought to contain women's roles within the home to contemporary mass-media representations that acknowledge and then punish female empowerment, popular culture is centrally involved in sustaining patriarchy. Competing explanations for the destruction of powerful female characters in the contemporary television action genre arose in the aftermath of many heroines' televised deaths, including several suicides. Sara Crosby (2004) argues that initial reactions interpreted the new heroines' suicides "as a patriarchal reaction to political threat: Patriarchy criminalizes and then violently eradicates the 'monstrous feminine' or metes out the ultimate punishment to women who have become just 'too tough or too strong.'" If the new heroines were, in fact, the victims of patriarchal retaliation, they were not the first women to be violently destroyed for threatening hegemony. However, Crosby disagrees with the interpretation that the new heroine suicides signified the retaliation of patriarchy against strong women. Rather, Crosby explains that the new suicidal heroines were not helpless victims of patriarchy but were entangled in a far more complex discourse than their antebellum sisters. In fact, Crosby asserts, "The tough women of 2001 died heroically, even admirably, and often with mystic trappings. . . . They did not simply fall victim to a misogyny that interprets women's aggressiveness as criminality to be punished."

In addition to calling for equality in economic, legal, and cultural realms, radical feminists have critiqued science as a male-biased institution. Feminist scholars contend that science has traditionally been identified with masculine values of objectivity, rationality, neutrality, and distance and that such associations make the practice of science biased against women. For example, feminist psychologist Carol Gilligan (1982) explores how the discipline of psychology has traditionally focused on the male life cycle, fashioning it as a norm against which women appear defective or lacking. Gilligan argues that women develop within the context of relationships and place a higher priority on the stability of relationships, whereas men form their identities based on independence from relationships and focus on work and competition to fulfill their lives. Thus, in the case of psychology, "A problem in theory became cast as a problem in women's development, and the problem in women's development was located in their experience of relationships." Gilligan believes that because research, as noted above, has focused primarily on the study of male psychology, the female voice has been ignored and researchers have concluded that the female sense of justice and morality is stunted and inadequate.

Spring-Serenity Duvall
University of South Carolina, Aiken

See also Beauty and Body Image: Beauty Myths; Bordo, Susan; Class Privilege; Cultural Politics; Douglas, Susan J.; Feminism; Feminist Theory: Liberal; Feminist Theory: Marxist; Feminist Theory: Postcolonial; Feminist Theory: Second Wave; Feminist Theory: Socialist; Feminist Theory: Third Wave; Feminist Theory: Women-of-Color and Multiracial Perspectives; Gender and Femininity: Motherhood; Gender and Femininity: Single/Independent Girl; Gender and Masculinity: White Masculinity; Hegemony; Misogyny; Radway, Janice; Sexism; Social Construction of Gender; Social Inequality

Further Readings

Beauvoir, Simone de. *The Second Sex*. New York: Alfred A. Knopf, 1952.

Bordo, Susan. *The Male Body: A New Look at Men in Public and in Private*. New York: Farrar, Straus, and Giroux, 1999.

Chakravarti, Uma. "Conceptualizing Brahmanical Patriarchy in Early India: Gender, Cast, Class and State." In *Class, Caste, Gender*, Manoranjan Mohanty, ed. Thousand Oaks, CA: Sage, 2004.

Crosby, Sara. "The Cruelest Season: Female Heroes Snapped Into Sacrificial Heroines." In *Action Chicks: New Images of Tough Women in Popular Culture*, Sherrie A. Inness, ed. New York: Palgrave Macmillan, 2004.

Lerner, Gerda. *The Creation of Patriarchy*. New York: Oxford University Press, 1986.

Lorber, Judith and Susan A. Farrell. *The Social Construction of Gender*. Thousand Oaks, CA: Sage, 1991.

Tong, Rosemarie. *Feminist Thought: A More Comprehensive Introduction*, 3rd. ed. Boulder, CO: Westview Press, 2009.

Young, Iris. "The Ideal of Community and the Politics of Difference." In *Feminism/Postmodernism*, Linda J. Nicholson, ed. New York: Routledge, 1990.

POLYSEMIC TEXT

Polysemic text refers to the idea that any text can have multiple meanings rather than a single meaning. Although the concept of polysemic text seems simple, researchers and theorists have examined and debated a number of questions regarding polysemy. For example, are the meanings of a text potentially endless? Are some texts more semiotically open than others (through the use of reflexivity, parody, or nonnarrative style)? Are some meanings more likely or commonsensical, given the impact of ideology on discourse and audiences? How active or free are audiences when interpreting texts? What method or methods are best for assessing the polysemic nature of texts? Do some variables, such as age, gender, race, and class, shape interpretation more than other variables? Scholars interested in semiotics, rhetoric, and reader-response theory, as well as those working within cultural and media studies, have examined these questions.

The catalyst for investigating the polysemic text emerged from three different scholarly strands: children and television reception research, research on

Challenging the thought that children's processing of media messages on television requires no interpretation, empirical research found that watching television teaches children to be visually literate in the same way that reading makes them book literate. (Photos.com)

media audiences' uses and gratifications, and reader-response theory.

The literature on children's interpretation of media messages challenged the notion that meaning, particularly in television, is commonsensical and requires no interpretation. Instead, empirical research demonstrated that children watching television learn to be visually literate, not unlike how they become book literate. Research in this tradition also examined how children's level of sophistication in interpretation grows with developmental age.

Empirical media scholarship in the area of uses and gratification also spurred inquiry regarding textual polysemy. This voluminous body of research repeatedly demonstrated how motivated and selective viewers—active audiences—make decisions about what to view and what it means in the light of

their needs and the gratifications they receive from these media choices.

Reader-response theory, a branch of literary studies, proved an additional influence. This paradigm criticized literary criticism's traditional focus on high culture, authorial intention, and the interpretation of canonical literary texts at the expense of popular literature and readers' responses to it. Challenging the notion that meaning exists in the text, critics asserted the importance of examining the text-audience interaction. Influenced by the work of Wolfgang Iser and Mikhail Bakhtin, particularly Bakhtin's idea of heteroglossia (referring to texts potentially speaking with "many voices"), this perspective influenced media studies by hastening the shift from a text-based or content-analytical approach to television to a focus on the moment of reception between text and audience.

These three strands of research led to a growth in the 1980s and 1990s of empirically based audience reception research, which emphasized the active viewer's partaking in a complex process of negotiating meaning. Suddenly media texts, no longer monolithic, were polysemic and open for interpretation. Some critical mass communication scholars argued that by focusing on the role of ideology and institutional power in shaping meaning, critics in this tradition minimized or ignored the audience's interpretive role and the potential openness of texts. Similarly, others criticized much of the work by media effects researchers, who, in attempting to account for the extent and magnitude of media impact on audiences' beliefs, attitudes, and behaviors, had increasingly relied on impoverished notions of media texts and the contexts in which they are interpreted.

Historically, many scholars point to Stuart Hall's 1974 "encoding/decoding" model of audience reception as a clarion call to examine this active audience. Seemingly offering some middle ground between ideological bound and completely open texts, Hall argued that although mainstream media encode "commonsensical" or "hegemonic" meanings that support the dominant cultural order (a nod to ideology theorists), audiences potentially engage in a range of interpretive positions vis-à-vis these messages. Viewers who make commonsensical readings are engaging in the "preferred reading," whereas those who subvert or systematically read the media text against the grain are engaged in oppositional decoding. Finally, others, falling somewhere in the middle, engage in "negotiated reading" of media texts. This middle position involves using a range of both "adaptive" and "oppositional" strategies to read texts. Audience members, given different contexts and confronted with different media messages, may shift between types of readings. For example, feminist "standpoint theory" might explain how a woman might examine an ad for her favorite brand of shoes and be interested in buying a pair, even though she has more shoes than she needs (an adaptive strategy supporting conspicuous consumption); she might be simultaneously aware of the ad's use of a highly objectified and sexualized model to create viewer desire, which, as a feminist, she resents (an oppositional perspective). The notion of the active audience introduced the idea that viewers, in constructing meaning—although responding to cues in the media message—make sense of media based on a number of factors, such as gender, race, age, class, nationality, and even more idiosyncratic variables, such as specific reception context and past experiences with the topic or event.

Much work in this active-audience, semiotically open text tradition has occurred in feminist media criticism. Most notable is the work on television, novels, and female audiences by Janice Radway, Ellen Seiter, Cathy Schwichtenberg, and Sonia Livingstone. Research in this vein intensified in rhetorical studies, semiotics, and cultural studies, notably in the work of Umberto Eco, John Fiske, and David Morley (particularly his landmark ethnographic study of British audiences' responses to the popular television show *Nationwide*). All of these scholars examine popular culture more broadly and television culture specifically in terms of audience pleasure, freedom, and textual polysemy. Research in media studies also increasingly called for or employed new or mixed methods in the analysis of audience interpretation. There was a marked increase in published work employing phenomenology, ethnography, in-depth interviews, focus groups, oral histories, and case studies, either together, alone, or in combination with critical media analysis and rhetorical criticism.

Starting roughly in the mid-1990s, although a few studies were published as early as 1989, a backlash developed against the notion of textual polysemy. Rhetorical critics such as Celeste Condit examined

"the rhetorical limits of polysemy," while others, particularly scholars in the Glasgow Media Group, charged that the reduced view of media effects—based, in part, on a simplified reading of the encoding/decoding model in Hall's seminal essay—led to a problematic blind spot regarding media power and the actual capacity of audiences to resist dominant ideological readings of media messages. Greg Philo, a member of the Glasgow Media Group, for example, argued that the support for polysemic texts—by cross-cultural studies of viewers' diverse interpretations of, for example, soap operas, and David Morley's focus on the impact of class, race, and gender on meaning—although important, resulted in critics' overestimation of viewers' interpretive ability. The Glasgow Media Group's empirically based research presents strong evidence that, although audiences can sometimes be active and critical, the media exert a powerful influence on audiences and potentially limit their interpretation. This occurs, in part, because, while audiences are always actively interpreting media in comparison to previously developed interpretive schemas, these frameworks have already been shaped by prior media exposure, thus ideologically limiting the range of potential meanings.

Susan Mackey-Kallis
Villanova University

See also Audiences: Producers of New Media; Audiences: Reception and Injection Models; Children's Programming: Cartoons; Children's Programming: Disney and Pixar; Discourse Analysis; Encoding and Decoding; Fiske, John; Hall, Stuart; Hegemony; Media Literacy; Media Rhetoric; Radway, Janice; Reception Theory; Semiotics; Television; Textual Analysis

Further Readings

Anderson, J. A. "Television Literacy and the Critical Viewer." In *Children's Understanding of Television*, J. Bryant and D. R. Anderson, eds. New York: Academic Press, 1983.

Bakhtin, M. *The dialogic imagination*. Austin: University of Texas Press, 1981.

Ceccarelli, L. "Polysemy: Multiple Meanings in Rhetorical Criticism." *Quarterly Journal of Speech*, v.84/4 (1998).

Condit, C. "The Rhetorical Limits of Polysemy." *Critical Studies in Mass Communication*, v.6/2 (1989).

Eco, U. "Introduction: The Role of the Reader." In *The Role of the Reader: Explorations in the Semiotics of Texts*. Bloomington: Indiana University Press, 1979.

Fejes, F. "Critical Mass Communications Research and Media Effects: The Problem of the Disappearing Audience." *Media, Culture and Society*, v.6/3 (1984).

Fiske, J. "Moments of Television: Neither the Text nor the Audience." In *Remote Control: Television Audiences and Cultural Power*, E. Seiter et al., eds. New York: Routledge, 1989.

Fiske, J. *Television Culture*. London: Methuen, 1987.

Hall, S. "Encoding/Decoding." In *Culture, Media, Language*, S. Hall et al., eds. London: Hutchinson, 1980.

Iser, W. "Interaction Between Text and Reader." In *The Reader in the Text: Essays on Audience and Interpretation*, S. R. Suleiman and I. Crosman, eds. Princeton, NJ: Princeton University Press, 1980.

Katz, E. "Viewers' Work." In *The Audience and Its Landscape*, J. Hay, L. Grossberg, and E. Wartella, eds. Boulder, CO: Westview Press, 1996.

Liebes, T. and E. Katz. *The Export of Meaning*. New York: Oxford University Press, 1990.

Livingstone, S. *Television and the Active Audience*. Manchester, UK: Manchester University Press, 2000.

Morley, D. *The* Nationwide *Audience: Structure and Decoding*. London: British Film Institute, 1980.

Philo, G. "Active Audiences and the Construction of Public Knowledge." *Journalism Studies*, v.9/4 (2008).

Radway, J. "Interpretive Communities and Variable Literacies: The Functions of Romance Reading." In *Mass Communication Review Yearbook*, M. Gurevitch and M. R. Levy, eds. Beverly Hills, CA: Sage, 1985.

Schwichtenberg, C. *The Madonna Connection: Representation, Political Subculture, Identities and Cultural Theory*, Boulder, CO: Westview Press, 1993.

Seiter, E., H. Borchers, G. Kreutzner, and E.-M. Warth. *Remote Control: Television Audiences and Cultural Power*. London: Routledge, 1989.

PORNIFICATION OF EVERYDAY LIFE

The "pornification of everyday life" is a term or concept used to describe what scholars, pundits, and journalists began noticing in the mid-1990s and later characterizing as the ways in which the gestures, styles, and aesthetics of pornographic media had entered into the nonpornographic landscape of the culture. Primarily expressed in media and language

use, pornification was characterized by the making public of what was previously a private concern. The use of pornographic terms or styles of photography in nonpornographic contexts made it clear that the rise and growth of pornography's consumption was no longer a small matter, relegated to a minority of the population. To understand the concept, it is important to understand the following interrelated aspects of the "pornosphere": (1) the changing nature of the media of pornography from writing to film to motion picture to videotape to DVD to CD-ROM and Internet files; (2) the increased consumption and use of pornographic media as these forms multiplied; (3) the normalizing of the perception of pornography consumption by the normative state of its consumption under changing media conditions; and (4) cultural, economic, political, and religious forces that also had an impact on these changes.

Pornography originally meant "writing about prostitutes" and was a form of cheap literature. As media evolved in the 19th and 20th centuries, the meaning of the term changed to include photographic pornography, film pornography, video pornography, and Internet (or digital) pornography. This evolution had key markers that were consonant with both the invention of and the mass mediation of a particular medium, with pornographic content often driving the medium's evolution. Thus, photography quickly became a medium for erotic and pornographic images, and the first pornographic film with motion was created in 1896, only one year after the film projection system invented by the Lumière brothers was perfected. By the 1960s, with advances in birth-control technology and loosening attitudes around sexuality thanks in part to television, European imported films, and the 1953 launch of *Playboy* magazine, pornography began to enter the culture in different ways. Several states changed their laws to allow for adult theaters. Throughout the 1970s, requiring the consumer to visit public theaters where filmed porn was being exhibited restricted access to pornography.

By the 1980s with the invention and mass mediation of the videocassette, pornography evolved in two significant ways: First, it entered the home and could be consumed privately, and second, it multiplied by virtue of the copyable nature of the medium. Throughout the 1980s, while *Playboy* and other magazines were able to be received in the home, they nevertheless only showed static photographs of women posing in a state of undress and were legally restrained from depicting explicit sex acts. Various legal cases attempted to define the distinctions between pornography and erotic art and between pornographic film actors and prostitutes, with the latter distinction coming down to the difference between "sex for hire" and "depictions of sex for hire."

In the 1990s, with the birth and rise of the Internet, pornography entered more American's homes. Many of the bandwidth and video-conferencing technologies that businesses use today were pioneered or perfected by the pornography industry, which is located in the heart of the San Fernando Valley in California (the backyard of the film industry in Hollywood, where thousands of young women go each year seeking success and, given the competition, where they quickly find themselves facing economic insecurity with nothing to offer the market but their youth, beauty, and acting skills). While Hollywood produces 350–400 wide-release films every year, the porn industry produces many hundreds of times that figure in X- to XXX-rated fare. In 2005, the number of porn films produced was 8,000. By 2009, the number had jumped to 11,000, or roughly 30 X-rated films per day. Under these conditions, it became nearly impossible to prevent porn from seeping into the mainstream culture. Not only was porn the thing that everyone had seen but did not want to talk about, but porn stars like Pamela Anderson and Jenny McCarthy were making "crossover" careers by leaving pornography and entering mainstream film and television careers. Since then, the strategically accidental release of the "sex tape" has helped launch the careers of several personalities, such as Paris Hilton and Kim Kardashian. Compared to 1988, when the release of a sex videotape could ruin or severely damage the career of someone like Rob Lowe, this deliberate and quasi-legitimate use of a form of porn to advance a "brand" heralded a sea change in the culture's attitude toward porn's ubiquity.

Pornification of everyday life, also called "porn creep" or just "pornification," is evident in most areas of public life now. In 2005, the cable channel Showtime produced a program called *Rated X: The True Story of America's Greatest Porn Kings*. In the same year, Playboy.com started advertising on public buses and billboards in Manhattan. One of the most consistent visual media tropes of pornification is advertising in which the female mouth is placed in sexually suggestive proximity to an item of food that is represented phallically. A 2009 Burger King print ad from Singapore for the "Super Seven Incher" showed a woman in profile with her mouth open to receive a chicken sandwich above the headline, "It'll Blow Your Mind Away." Other mainstream examples of pornification include Rated X liqueur, XXX Hot Sauce, XXX Mints, the clothing brand FCUK, Naked Juice, Naked Beer, Cumming cologne by Alan Cumming, the Fuddrucker's "Mother Fuddrucker" Cheeseburger, and American Apparel clothing's use of amateur porn stars as clothing models. Feminist critic Jean Kilbourne credits the "Got Milk?" campaign with mainstreaming the pornographic "money shot." Conservative commentator Laura Ingraham regularly features a "Pornification Alert" section in her radio show.

Read M. Schuchardt
Wheaton College

See also Advertising; Desensitization Effect; Film: Hollywood; Kilbourne, Jean; Male Gaze; Men's Magazines: Lad Magazines; Music Videos: Representations of Women; Music Videos: Tropes; Pornography: Gay and Lesbian; Pornography: Heterosexual; Pornography: Internet; Scopophilia; Sexuality; Virtual Sex

Further Readings

Corliss, Richard. "That Old Feeling: When Porno Was Chic." *Time* (March 29, 2005).

Durham, M. Gigi. *The Lolita Effect: The Media Sexualization of Young Girls and What We Can Do About It*. New York: Overlook, 2008.

Hans, Jason D., Martie Gillen, and Katrina Akande. "Sex Redefined: The Reclassification of Oral-Genital Contact." *Perspectives on Sexual and Reproductive Health*, v.42/2 (June 2010).

Levin, Diane and Jean Kilbourne. *So Sexy So Soon: The New Sexualized Childhood and What Parents Can Do to Protect Their Kids*. New York: Ballantine, 2008.

McNair, Brian. *Striptease Culture: Sex, Media and the Democratization of Desire*. New York: Routledge, 2002.

Ogunnaike, Lola. "Sex, Lawsuits, and Celebrities Caught on Tape." *New York Times* (March 19, 2006).

Paasonen, Susanna et al., eds. *Pornification: Sex and Sexuality in Media Culture*. Oxford, UK: Berg, 2007.

Schuchardt, Read Mercer. "Elephantiasis: How
Pornography Became as American as Apple Pie."
Breakpoint (April 10, 2006).

PORNOGRAPHY: GAY AND LESBIAN

Gay and lesbian pornographies, like their straight counterparts, are defined by whether they produce arousal and by often slippery legal categories such as obscenity. They are situated within evolving histories of communication media. Examples of same-sex pornography featuring men date from the late 19th century, and recent decades have seen an explosion of pornographic materials aimed at gay and lesbian audiences.

Gay and lesbian pornographies emerged with technologies of mass reproduction, including print media, photography, and film. However, moral unease and censorship laws constrained the production of pornographic materials. Other restrictions specifically aimed at same-sex desire, notably antisodomy laws, medical pathologization, and religious strictures, exerted an even more powerful force against same-sex pornographies. While printing presses enabled the production of pornographic texts, these texts, like any other materials related to sex, were subject to censorship and seizure. Many early pornographic novels were privately printed and carefully circulated within small social networks. *Teleny: Or, the Reverse of the Medal* is an example of such a novel. The novel underscores the ways same-sex-desiring men in the late 19th century already understood themselves to be a distinct cultural group with their own linguistic and sexual codes and styles, from the masculine "trade" (working-class men who sometimes prostituted themselves) to effeminate "fairies."

Early media put to pornographic use often did so under the alibi of art or fitness. Academic art photography provided anatomical references for painters and sculptors. Some of these images also conveyed erotic meanings. Wilhelm von Gloeden, his nephew Wilhelm von Plüschow, and a contemporary, Vincenzo Galdi, produced some of the first unmistakably gay photographs while living in southern Italy in the late 19th and early 20th centuries. The classical themes of their images made them appealing to a range of collectors. The images of nude or nearly nude young men and adolescents also attracted the patronage of gay men such as Oscar Wilde. While some art photography documented strong male types, von Gloeden's work anticipates another persistent gay type: the ephebe, the typically hairless young man at the threshold of adolescence and adulthood (and legal majority), who later evolved into the figure of the "twink." These images, and others like them, were subject to censorship—von Plüschow was briefly jailed, and Benito Mussolini's fascists destroyed some of von Gloeden's negatives and prints.

By the early 1900s, a range of physical culture magazines, ostensibly focused on health or body-building, became available either through mail order or on newsstands. Broadly promoting fitness and healthy lifestyles, they also featured photographs and illustrations of nearly nude men and some women. Within a few decades the eroticism of these images became obvious. Bob Mizer's Athletic Model Guild capitalized on the success of these magazines. In *Physique Pictorial*, the images of young men in skimpy posing straps or costumed as ancient Romans, cowboys, motorcyclists, and wrestlers made the gay themes explicit.

Lesbian pornography was less evident in early photographic and film media, but an analogue could be found in the mass-market paperbacks known as pulp novels that became popular after World War II, which often featured lesbian and gay themes. *Women's Barracks* (1950), by Tereska Torres, was the first and most popular such novel of its time. It told the story of women recruits in the Free French Army stationed in London during World War II. Despite its sensational cover, the matter-of-fact handling of these women's lives and their intimate affairs with one another is remarkably evenhanded. However, to conform to American censorship laws, the author was forced to alter her text to cast moral judgment on the women's lesbian love affairs when the novel was translated into English.

Largely regulated to gray and black markets for much of the 19th and 20th centuries, both straight and gay pornographic films saw a loosening of censorship laws in the 1960s (full frontal male nudity was not legal until 1962) and early 1970s, during which they were permitted a brief period of mainstream success. Early theatrical hardcore gay successes included Wakefield Poole's pivotal 1971 *Boys in the Sand*. This success was short-lived, however, as rising moral conservatism combined with the technological changes brought by home video, and, soon thereafter, fears about human immunodeficiency virus and acquired immune deficiency syndrome (HIV/AIDS) pressured most consumption of pornography into the private sphere of the home.

Although lesbian scenes became staples of heterosexual pornography in the 1970s, they largely served as a prelude to "real" (heterosexual) sex. This trend continues throughout much of the American mainstream heterosexual pornographic industry. By the 1980s and 1990s, however, lesbians were producing their own porn. Lesbian pornography emerged from the controversies of the feminist sex wars, in which feminists bitterly fought over sexual representations of women. Some feminists believed that sexually explicit images of women reproduced and embodied violence against women. Other feminists challenged calls to censor pornographic images, arguing that exploring and documenting sex were tied to feminist battles for equality in all spheres of life. Anticensorship and pro-sex feminists argued that pornographic images, although often misogynic, also permitted women's access to forms of sexual expression and pleasure and enabled broader conversations about sex and society. Whereas some early lesbian porn featured "natural" or egalitarian female sexuality, other pornographers explored themes, such as bondage and sadomasochism, that had been especially explosive during the sex wars. The lesbian erotica magazine *On Our Backs* appeared in 1984 as a direct challenge to *off our backs*, a feminist newsletter that featured the views of antipornography activists. The 1980s and 1990s also saw the development of several pornographic production companies led by women, including lesbians, among them Fatale Media and BLEU Productions.

Beginning in the late 1990s, the Internet facilitated a major porn boom. Tech-savvy Web entrepreneurs found the Web to be an ideal medium for the production and distribution of porn. The relatively low expense of hosting services and falling prices of digital recording technologies enabled the speedy mass production and dissemination of pornographic images. The Internet and other digital technologies have increasingly made pornography a do-it-yourself (DIY) phenomenon in which everyday consumers of pornography have become its producers. Websites such as Xtube, where users submit homemade pornographic content, have opened pornography to a participatory mode of cultural production. Because they are not necessarily constrained by the profit motive, DIY pornographers have contributed a vast archive of pornographic material that includes a range of body types, gender expressions, and sexual acts. Alternative (or "alt"), queer, and transgender porn draw on this DIY ethos and on the approaches of sex-positive lesbian pornographers by featuring transsexual performers and atypical sexual couplings (between trans men or between lesbians and gay men, for example). Alt and queer sites, performers such as female-to-male transsexual Buck Angel, and a range of DIY pornographers have offered self-consciously empowering images by and for gender dissidents.

Shaka McGlotten
Purchase College, State University of New York

See also Advertising; Audiences: Producers of New Media; Desensitization Effect; Film: Hollywood; Men's Magazines: Lad Magazines; Music Videos: Representations of Men; Music Videos: Representations of Women; Music Videos: Tropes; Pornification of Everyday Life; Pornography: Heterosexual; Pornography: Internet; Scopophilia; Sexuality; Virtual Sex

Further Readings

Faderman, Lilian. *Odd Girls and Twilight Lovers: A History of Lesbian Life in Twentieth-Century America.* New York: Columbia University Press, 1991.

Jacobs, Katrien. *Netporn: DIY Web Culture and Sexual Politics.* Lanham, MD: Rowman & Littlefield, 2007.

Waugh, Thomas. *Hard to Imagine: Gay Male Eroticism in Photography and Film From Their Beginnings to Stonewall.* New York: Columbia University Press, 1996.

PORNOGRAPHY: HETEROSEXUAL

Heterosexual pornography has long been the focus of heated debates, especially those concerning the portrayal of men, women, and physical intimacy. Though some viewers champion pornography for allowing people to experience pleasure and indulge in impossible fantasies, pornography furthers the theme of male domination and female suppression and exploitation.

Heterosexual pornography typically presents situations in which a man's desires and needs are met while the woman performs various sex acts, always enjoying herself while doing so. The scenarios in pornographic videos are endless but usually include some type of theme. Common tropes in heterosexual pornographic fantasies are teacher-student fantasies (wherein a woman plays a schoolteacher who has sex with her student, or vice versa) and babysitter fantasies (in which a young woman has sex with the father of the child she is babysitting or engages in a ménage à trois with both of the child's parents). Other common tropes are women dressed as nurses sexually servicing patients, women cheating on their husbands with a lover, or mature women sleeping with younger men. Some men also have fetishes that focus on certain body parts, such extremely large breasts, ample behinds, or feet.

Hundreds of sexual acts are featured in heterosexual pornography, but some of the most common (besides vaginal intercourse) include anal sex and oral sex, ending in a man ejaculating on a woman's face. The overwhelming presence of anal sex occurs, some scholars argue, because of its taboo nature. Similarly, oral sex is featured in most heterosexual pornography; in some cases, a porn film will consist only of a woman performing oral sex on a man. In many instances, after a woman performs oral sex, the man ejaculates on her face (in slang, this act is known as the "money shot"). The woman at the receiving end often smiles up at the camera, sometimes while licking her lips. Scholars have argued that this act valorizes and fetishizes sperm as a sign of male potency and power. Regardless of the theme, fetish, or sex act, these pornographic scenarios imply that women enjoy all sexual acts and that they should be valued only for their bodies (specifically, their genitalia). In this context, pornography is believed to desensitize men and to promote the view that women are passive and compliant sexual objects.

Other examples of heterosexual pornography encourage men to desensitize themselves with regard to women, especially examples that combine sex acts with violence. Sadomasochistic pornography showcases women in chains being whipped by men along with a variety of other violent acts, ranging from spankings to pinching to choking, almost to the point of suffocation. The most violent sexual act in pornography is rape, and scenes in which women are raped or gang-banged (raped by several men at once) remain common. Pornography provides viewers with a fantasy world, and in some fantasies physical abuse and rape become permissible, implying to readers that women are easy targets for both sexual advances and sexual violence.

Pornography catering to women or to people interested in engaging in sexual acts with people of ethnic groups other than their own also exists. Although less common than pornography created for male audiences, heterosexual pornography designed specifically for women likewise encourages women to value men for their sexual prowess. One of the most common scenarios in pornography for women is the ménage à trois, involving a single woman and two men. Another popular scenario in pornography for women is a black man having sex with a white woman; this scenario remains popular because of the common myth that black men are better endowed physically than any other ethnic group. Related to the situation of a black man with a white woman are common fantasies for white men, which include having sex with a black or Asian woman; these fantasies, in particular, suggest that black and Asian women should be subservient to white men. All of these examples misrepresent and exploit members of both genders, proving that pornography is one of the main sources for perpetuating gender (and racially based) myths.

Videos are the most common form of pornography, but sex toys are also popular and impart significant messages about gender. Dolls with orifices and fake vaginas allow men to simulate sex with a woman and pleasure themselves. Toys like these objectify women and encourage their users to view women in terms of their genitalia and other body parts. Likewise, sex toys for women (vibrators and dildos, in particular) encourage women to define men by their sexual organs. Sex toys do allow people to experience sexual pleasure without the risk of disease, embarrassment, or commitment, but the perception of who uses toys, coupled with gender, deserves more serious analysis. Men who use toys are considered simply to be sexual, or perhaps as having an insatiable sexual appetite. Some men who use toys are targeted as not being able to find or sustain a relationship with a real woman. Women who use sex toys can also be considered as having a healthy sexual appetite, but an unflattering stigma still persists for women who use toys. Since heterosexual pornography typically emphasizes men taking pleasure in having sex while women fulfill a man's needs, women who take control of pleasing themselves by substituting a dildo for a man's penis are considered dirty and aggressive; some men even find these women threatening.

Heterosexual pornography enables misrepresentations of gender while indulging sexual fantasies and desires for men and women. Various scenarios imply that members of either gender are willing to perform any and all sexual acts and experience pleasure while doing so. All heterosexual pornography, however, encourages men and women to value members of the opposite gender for their sexual organs and abilities.

Karley Adney
Butler University

See also Advertising; Audiences: Producers of New Media; Beauty and Body Image: Beauty Myths; Desensitization Effect; Film: Hollywood; Gender and Masculinity: White Masculinity; Heterosexism; Male Gaze; Media Rhetoric; Men's Magazines: Lad Magazines; Misogyny; Music Videos: Representations of Men; Music Videos: Representations of Women; Music Videos: Tropes; Patriarchy; Pornification of Everyday Life; Pornography: Gay and Lesbian; Pornography: Internet; Scopophilia; Sexism; Sexuality; Stereotypes; Violence and Aggression; Virtual Sex

Further Readings

Attwood, Feona, ed. *Mainstreaming Sex: The Sexualization of Western Culture*. London: I. B. Tauris, 2009.

Gibson, Pamela Church. *More Dirty Looks: Gender, Pornography, and Power*. London: British Film Institute, 2004.

Juffer, Jane. *At Home With Pornography: Women, Sex, and Everyday Life*. New York: New York University Press, 1998.

Kipnis, Laura. *Bound and Gagged: Pornography and the Politics of Fantasy in America*. Durham, NC: Duke University Press, 1996.

Lehman, Peter, ed. *Pornography: Film and Culture*. New Brunswick, NJ: Rutgers University Press, 2006.

Paul, Pamela. *Pornified: How Pornography Is Transforming Our Lives, Our Relationships, and Our Families*. New York: Times Books, 2005.

Slade, Joseph W. *Pornography and Sexual Representation*. Westport, CT: Greenwood, 2001.

Stoller, Robert J. *Porn: Myths for the Twentieth Century*. Binghamton, NY: Vail-Ballou Press, 1991.

Williams, Linda. *Hard Core: Power, Pleasure, and the Frenzy of the Visible*. Berkeley: University of California Press, 1989.

Williams, Linda, ed. *Porn Studies*. Durham, NC: Duke University Press, 2004.

PORNOGRAPHY: INTERNET

Erotic imagery has existed for 24,000 years. With the availability of high-speed Internet, sexuality explicit and erotic material is easily produced, viewed, distributed, and downloaded. Internet pornography is now a ubiquitous part of the media landscape. Genres of Internet pornography are virtually limitless. They include straight, gay, lesbian, and bisexual pornography, fetish, anime, and both professional and amateur videos and still photos. Internet pornography is considered free speech under the First Amendment of the U.S. Constitution. Pornography known as "hardcore," if found to be obscene, is not protected by the First Amendment. This material is subject to the three-pronged Miller test, established by the U.S. Supreme Court with *Miller v. California* (1973). Creating, owning, or distributing child pornography violates federal law.

Internet porn is a high-earning industry. The largest mainstream pornography producers include Vivid Entertainment Group, Adult Video News, Wicked Pictures, and Digital Playground. The Internet makes it possible to purchase or download pornography while maintaining a greater measure of privacy or anonymity than brick-and-mortar porn purchases or rentals allow. This contributes to vast industry growth. Professionals claim that the availability of amateur and free online porn cuts into business profit. However, consumers spend an estimated $3,000 every second on Internet pornography. In 2006, online pornography revenue reached $2.8 billion in the United States. There are approximately 370 million Internet porn sites, and industry revenues surpass the combined earnings of Microsoft, Google, Amazon, eBay, Yahoo, Apple, and Netflix.

Production and Consumption

Most Internet pornography is produced in the San Fernando Valley in southern California, where producers can take advantage of an available pool of actors from the Los Angeles entertainment industry along with state laws that are comparatively receptive to producing pornography. The California Supreme Court decision in *People v. Freeman* (1988) held that a person cannot be convicted of pandering if he or she is paid for producing an entertainment product rather than providing sexual gratification to a consumer. A New York district court came to a similar decision, yet there remain significant legal risks for producing pornography in all other states.

There is evidence that a wide cross-section of adults across the United States use Internet pornography, sometimes in contrast with self-reported conservative political affiliation or religious belief. Using anonymous credit-card receipts, a nationwide study of online pornography in the United States found little variation in use across the country. Where slight variations exist, the states with residents that consume the most porn tend to be more conservative and religious, compared to those in states with lower levels of porn consumption.

Sources such as comScore report that 36 percent of Internet users visit at least one porn Website each month. There are claims that one third of Internet porn users are women. Some data show that the average age of first exposure to porn is 11 years old for boys, whereas other research claims the average age of first exposure is 14.5 years old for boys and 14.8 years old for girls.

According to Nielsen/NetRatings from 2007, approximately one third of online porn users were women. However, this figure may be artificially low and difficult to assess accurately. Data from Hustler Video indicate that female consumers make up 56 percent of the company's video sales. Digital Playground reports that in 2004, 53 percent of their consumers were women. Data collection limitations are significant: Shared computers, shared credit cards, variabilities in tracking software, self-reporting bias, and the availability of free porn that is not linked to collectible online subscription information can skew research projects that attempt to determine who is using Internet porn.

Political Debates

There are competing arguments about Internet pornography regarding its value, the potential for causing harm, and issues regarding First Amendment free speech rights. These debates about Internet pornography constitute a continuation of the so-called sex wars that started in the 1970s. Andrea Dworkin and Catharine MacKinnon are two well-known antiporn figures from these earlier debates; other scholars, such as Elizabeth Wilson and Nadine Strossen, defend free-speech principles and oppose, as biased, the antiporn argument that presumes men are naturally predisposed to violence and visual stimulation.

While some research finds that pornography deters rape, other studies maintain that pornography causes its (male) users to emulate rape or sexual assault. Others are concerned that pornography neither deters nor causes sexual assault but instead creates a media genre in which sexual consent is blurry. Users may therefore be confused about the line between consensual, real-life sex and fantasy portrayals of domination, assault, or coercion. Research on young men in Sweden, however, finds that porn users are clearly able to distinguish between fantasy and reality.

Addiction models argue that, similar to alcoholism and drug abuse, use of pornography can become a dangerous addiction. Groups such as the Sexual Recovery Institute and sexual addiction experts such as Patrick Carnes believe that Internet pornography exacerbates the problem of compulsive sexual behaviors through easy access and a constant, streaming variety of pornography available through the Internet. However, the fourth edition of the *Diagnostic and Statistical Manual of Mental Disorders* does not identify pornography addiction in its list of addictions. The existence of pornography addiction as a condition is not universally accepted among professionals and is the subject of continuing debate.

Various scholars and activist groups oppose Internet pornography for political or moral reasons. These include members of the Christian right and specific feminist factions. Opponents argue that Internet pornography degrades and harms women and men, particularly people of color. Religious objections include biblically based opposition to nonprocreative sex outside heterosexual marriage. Radical feminist arguments are based on the idea that because we live in a culture that buys, sells, and trades women's bodies, online pornography perpetuates these violations. Feminist opponents claim that, as a media genre, Internet pornography eroticizes male supremacy and female subjugation, thereby further institutionalizing gender inequality.

Pornography supporters, civil libertarians, and self-described pro-sex feminists counter that Internet pornography is a legitimate source of pleasure and employment for women, men, transgender, and gender-queer adults. Civil libertarians argue that quashing the supply or distribution of online pornography amounts to censorship, which violates the U.S. Constitution. Others recognize the simultaneous potential for sexism, racism, and exploitation along with the ability to improve the industry and support the right of adults to make autonomous decisions about sexuality and employment. They identify the need for greater media literacy focusing on issues of gender, race, and sexuality in Internet pornography.

Shira Tarrant
California State University, Long Beach

See also Advertising; Audiences: Producers of New Media; Beauty and Body Image: Beauty Myths; Desensitization Effect; Film: Hollywood; Gender and Masculinity: White Masculinity; Heterosexism; Male Gaze; Media Literacy; Media Rhetoric; Men's Magazines: Lad Magazines; Misogyny; Music Videos: Representations of Men; Music Videos: Representations of Women; Music Videos: Tropes; Patriarchy; Pornification of Everyday Life; Pornography: Gay and Lesbian; Scopophilia; Sexism; Sexuality; Stereotypes; Violence and Aggression; Virtual Sex

Further Readings

Dines, Gail. *Pornland*. Boston: Beacon Press, 2010.
Edelman, Benjamin. "Red Light States: Who Buys Online Adult Entertainment?" *Journal of Economic Perspectives*, v.23/1 (2009).
Lust, Erika. *Good Porn: A Woman's Guide*. Berkeley, CA: Seal Press, 2010.
"National Survey of Sexual Health and Behavior." *The Journal of Sexual Medicine*, v.7, suppl. 5 (2010). http://www.nationalsexstudy.indiana.edu (Accessed October 2010).
Tarrant, Shira. "Pornography 101." AlterNet.org (September 15, 2010). http://www.alternet.org/media/148129/pornography_101:_why_college_kids_need_porn_literacy_training (Accessed October 2010).
Williams, Linda, ed. *Porn Studies*. Durham, NC: Duke University Press, 2004.

POSTFEMINISM

A common misconception regarding postfeminism is that it refers to a period "after the death of feminism," as if it constituted a postmortem on feminism and signaled that "we don't need feminism anymore." Postfeminism is a complex term that includes accounting for context, embracing multiple meanings, and reclaiming terms and concepts such as "girl culture." Some postfeminists embrace aspects of what it means to be a girl in contemporary Western societies and have championed "chick lit" and "chick flicks," literature and film produced for young-adult female audiences. Girl studies, fat studies, thin studies, and other scholarly fields that previously were not included in the academic canon have been linked to postfeminism. Many postfeminists are participants in larger girl and grrrl power movements. These movements are addressed in other entries in this encyclopedia. Many postfeminists challenge universalized and tacit standards of what it means to be a feminist. They continuously ask, "Feminist according to whom?"

Postfeminism is often linked to the third wave of feminism. The third wave of feminism is more dispersed because of the context in which it exists. It is more globalized and occurs in a sociopolitical environment of neoliberalism. It is often seen by earlier feminist theorists as more individualistic and more about consumption than prior waves of the feminist movements for solidarity. The third wave of feminism is indeed diverse and varied, and while many postfeminists are simultaneously anticapitalists, many also buy into the existing political and economic systems of the dominant culture.

Postmodern, post-structural, and postfeminist theories emerged as a response to their predecessors: modernism, structuralism, and feminism. Many postfeminists, like their feminist foremothers, were (and still are) fed up with the status quo and the existing system, which they believe do not address them. One of the major tenets of post-structuralism, often cited as a chief aspect of the theoretical grounding of postfeminism, adheres to the idea that the individual has the potential to bring the structure to crisis. Some elements of postmodernity that cannot be denied in postfeminism include the ideas of disassociation, technology, isolation, and globalization.

The term *postfeminism* is no longer used to express opposition to earlier feminist movements but rather has complex meanings and is linked to girl studies, "chick lit," girl and grrl power movements, and even drag performances. (Photos.com)

With each wave of feminism comes a backlash, as occurs with almost every successful social movement. Many argue that postfeminism emerged in the 1970s and 1980s, when journalists began declaring feminism dead. However, in an age when women still make 88 cents to a man's $1 and some tenure-track clocks stop for women who have babies, it would be extreme for any feminist to say that the movement is no longer needed or that feminists have achieved all that they set out to do. The prefix *post* can be seen as a misnomer (a declarative of the "true" death of feminism) or it can be seen as a way to separate the current context using an evolutionary perspective. It is not that as a society we are above and beyond feminism, just that the goals of new feminism look different from those of the past. Postfeminist women and men often see themselves as part of two unified movements for gender equality.

While many gender scholars trace the historical roots of postfeminism to post-structuralism and postmodernism, many also object to this outgrowth. The reason is that, as much as the post-structural theoretical feminist women agreed with this assessment of the emergence and development of postfeminism (see Luce Irigaray, Hélène Cixous, and Julia Kristeva), white academic postmodern men

with power and prestige also traced these origins (see Michel Foucault, Jacques Derrida, Jean Baudrillard, and Jean-François Lyotard). Just as women, people with disabilities, and other minorities found their voices, a new wave of academic European white men from the First World (and *Time* magazine) declared feminism, the author and the subject, dead.

Depending on the participant, some (such as Naomi Wolf and Camille Paglia) view postfeminists as inauthentic or "not real" feminists. It can be argued that within a postfeminist framework, what was once seen as rebellious, threatening, aggressive, and ominous is now seen as part of dominant culture: working within the feminist framework in order to move beyond it. Postfeminist feminists take for granted the "recuperation of résistance." As Foucault explains, as soon as something is shown to be actively challenging or resisting the dominant system, it becomes recuperated into the existing system, which makes the resistance less of a threat. However, within this Foucauldian model, power is also seen as arbolic and rhizomatic rather than hierarchical: existing in capillaries and not top-down. Therefore, there are more levels and possibilities for change and rupture.

Opponents of postfeminism see it as a factionalized, fragmented, and apolitical movement, buying into dominant ideologies and perpetuating hegemony (hidden domination, or domination by consent). Postfeminists, like some of their third wave counterparts, are not always visible in the streets marching or picketing. In the context of postfeminism and postmodernity, many young women's activism occurs online or through their discourse and consumptions. It is the context of feminism/postfeminism that has shifted and not necessarily the beliefs or the struggle. Postfeminists are fighting a different fight from feminists before them. Postfeminism is an embodied form of feminism. It emerged in a context of late capitalism and, as such, it embodies the corporeal and performative aspects of gender and sexuality. It plays with the notion of "play," and it is ludic and hyperbolic in the nature of its protests. In this way, postfeminism is similar to postmodernism and post-structuralism.

Examples of playful performances in the postfeminist context include drag shows. Drag shows bend and play with the idea of gender and are over-the-top. They point to the factitious nature of gendered performance, and through embodiment they show that gender is indeed enacted and uttered daily. The hyperbolic (exaggerated) aspect of drag shows is highlighted because in these performances the individuals who dress in drag are making fun of the way people perform and adhere to rigid notions of what it means to be a man or a woman in our society. As the process of "packing" and "tucking" show, there really is a person of the opposite gender "putting on" or "dressing up" as another gender. Gender is seen here as a cultural script. It is also viewed as a costume that one can put on and take off according to one's needs and the social context or environment in which the individual is participating at that particular moment in time. While some postfeminists realize this, many also understand that while gender is indeed a cultural script, and while sexuality is indeed fluid, there are also a limited number of gendered scripts to choose from and a limited number of gendered costumes to put on and take off. "Culture jamming," a form of radical street performance, is also often associated with postfeminism, as is "flash mobbing," choreographed routines meant to question hegemonic institutions in society. Along with drag shows, culture jamming and flash mobbing are important examples of postfeminist performance.

Postfeminism also understands the notion that multiple subjectivities are possible and that while feminist texts cannot be divorced from the time periods in which they occur, all theories are inherently intertextual—that is, they are self-referential and often work within a self-contained modality of operation. For these reasons, postfeminist theorists conduct readings of both mainstream and alternative texts from both mainstream and alternative subject positions. For postfeminists, culture consists of everyday (mundane) discursive and cultural practices, with these discursive practices both embodying and constructing a culture's ideology. Artifacts of popular culture "count" as legitimate data for critical analysis because they are places where struggles over meaning and ideologies occur. Postfeminists often do not distinguish between high and low culture and high and low art because they see the potential for political power and change existing on all levels of society, from classical paintings to comic books.

Judy E. Battaglia
Loyola Marymount University

See also Culture Jamming; Douglas, Susan J.; E-Zines: Riot Grrrl; E-Zines: Third Wave Feminist; Feminism; Feminist Theory: Liberal; Feminist Theory: Marxist;

Feminist Theory: Postcolonial; Feminist Theory: Second Wave; Feminist Theory: Socialist; Feminist Theory: Third Wave; Feminist Theory: Women-of-Color and Multiracial Perspectives; Gender and Femininity: Motherhood; Gender and Femininity: Single/Independent Girl; Guerrilla Girls; Hegemony; Identity; New Media; Postmodernism; Post-Structuralism; Sexism; Sexuality; Social Inequality; Women's Magazines: Feminist Magazines

Further Readings

Baudrillard, J. *Simulacra and Simulation. The Body, in Theory: Histories of Cultural Materialism.* Ann Arbor: University of Michigan Press, 1995.

Butler, J. *Gender Trouble: Feminism and the Subversion of Identity.* New York: Routledge, 1990.

Derrida, J. *Writing and Difference.* Chicago: University of Chicago Press, 1967.

Foss, S. J. *Rhetorical Criticism: Theory and Practice*, 4th ed. Long Grove, IL: Waveland Press, 2009.

Foucault, M. *A History of Sexuality.* Vol. 1, *An Introduction*, Robert Hurley, trans. New York: Vintage Books, 1980.

Lyotard, J. *Toward the Postmodern.* Atlantic Highlands, NJ: Humanities Press, 1993.

Paglia, C. *Sexual Personae: Art and Decadence From Nefertiti to Emily Dickinson.* New Haven, CT: Yale University Press, 1990.

Wolf, N. *The Beauty Myth: How Images of Beauty Are Used Against Women.* New York: William Morrow, 1991.

POSTMODERNISM

Postmodernism, as the term implies, refers to a decisive break that began during the 20th century away from the historical, philosophical, political, cultural, and aesthetic characteristics associated with modernism. In broad outline, modernism as an era spans the 400 years between humanism and the revival of classicism during the Renaissance in the early 1500s and the highly complex industrial societies of the mid-1900s. Modernism is rooted in the Enlightenment philosophies that spawned capitalism, nationalism, and modern science in western Europe in the 17th and 18th centuries, after the Renaissance. The rise of modernism is based on rationality as the key to human development, the accessibility of a universal and objective truth, a direct relationship between humans and nature, and a grand historical narrative of the progressive betterment of the quality of life through science and technology. Modernism also is associated with the rise of industrialization in the 19th century and the growth of the bureaucratic, hierarchical nation-state in the 20th century.

The idea of modernism has a different context in cultural and aesthetic realms, referring to art, literature, and architecture of the late 19th and early 20th centuries, which in some ways moved beyond representational, realistic styles and embraced an aesthetic of individualism, novelty, and universality. The term *postmodernism* was first used in 1917 by a German philosopher to describe the nihilism of 20th-century Western culture. It appeared prominently in literary criticism of the 1950s and 1960s in reaction to aesthetic modernism, and in architecture in the 1970s. In the 1980s, it came to refer in philosophy to French post-structuralism and in general to a reaction against modern rationalism in philosophy since René Descartes in the 1600s.

As a reaction against the general characteristics of modernism, whether in philosophy, politics, or culture, the term *postmodernism* is highly contested, leading to multiple interpretations of its nature and meaning, with scholarly debates about whether postmodernism actually exists or whether the tendencies it represents are simply another manifestation of modernism. Still, these contrary tendencies, or rejections of modernism, are identifiable and represent a definite shift in worldview and experience. Ruptures with each of the characteristics listed above point toward the sense that a decisive global change has occurred that is qualitatively different from modernism.

Both positive and negative readings of postmodernism show the centrality of new technologies to its definition. With a focus on negative qualities, postmodernism denies objective knowledge of the world as studied by science, the primary meaning of words and texts, and the unity of the individual self; in short, it rejects the basic intellectual assumptions and ideas of modern Western civilization. Various readings of postmodernism share some common themes. One is the recognition of pluralism and indeterminacy and an accompanying rejection of simplicity, completeness, and certainty. A second theme is the acceptance of playfulness in the cultural fields that previously were seriously searching for a realist truth. A third theme is a new focus on representation, images, information, and cultural signs as dominant in social life. The global changes signaling the rise of a postmodern world include the end of European colonization; the rise of mass culture; the modernization of the Third World; the shrinking of the globe by telecommunications, weapons, and marketing; and a shift from material-based production to information-based production.

The disappearance or decentering of the rational, individual subject, which is a mainstay of Enlightenment modernism, is a key idea in postmodern theory. Modernism assumes a universal human destination that considers history to be a linear process in which the modern is the endpoint. Postmodernism, by contrast, challenges this notion by undercutting the opposition of the modern, Western subject and the premodern, non-Western person. The postmodern is viewed as presenting many complex, contradictory forces with many conflicting subjective and cultural relationships. Postmodernism rejects the transcendentalist, universalistic sweep of Enlightenment thinking. Postmodernism challenges the veracity of scientific truth, promoting the notion that the belief in scientific truth is as "mystical" as religious revelation. The work of Michel Foucault pursues the central postmodern theme of discourse, proposing that social discourse is unconsciously founded in epistemic rules that change from era to era without a universal logic or continuity.

Brooding about a decisive, global change, the fading of modernism, and the emergence of a postmodern era in the mid-1970s, Fredric Jameson mentions "straws in the wind" of postmodern literary and art theory, and the rise of computers and information theory that supports the general impression that "modern times are now over" and a decisive change or "qualitative leap" has ushered in postmodernism in the mid-20th century. Jameson associates postmodern culture with postindustrial society, consumer society, media society, the information society, electronic society, and high technology. With the rise of global multinational capitalism after World War II, Jameson saw this postmodern shift as a cultural "dominant" affecting all social arenas. One central feature is the blurring of the boundaries between high culture and mass culture, opening the gates of critical interest in the mass media. John B. Thompson, on the other hand, sees little evidence of entering a new postmodern age that has closed the doors to modernity. He calls not for a theory of a new age but a new theory of an age whose broad outlines were set out beginning at the end of the Middle Ages and whose consequences have yet to be fully understood.

Art historian John Walker contrasts positive and negative responses. On the positive side, postmodernism recognizes a rich diversity and pluralism of cultural styles and forms globally, and it accepts a multitude of pasts and embraces tradition and history. It acknowledges that at a given moment, multiple pasts are alive and present. Conversely, negative interpretations include chaotic and anarchistic styles, an obsession with the past, shallowness, and omens of a debased society. In the arts, modernism and postmodernism are both tied to their relationship to the media. Walker offers a thematic typology of modernism as an aesthetic ideology that has dominated Western culture for 125 years until the 1960s. First, modernism embraces the new age of machines and technology and develops new forms of expression. Second, modernism completely breaks with the past to advocate the "tradition of the new," which values novelty and originality. Third, modernism rejects decoration and ornamentation, preferring geometric forms that suggest simplicity, uniformity, order, and rationality. Fourth, modernism rejects local styles, favoring a single universal style. Fifth, modernism describes itself as art of the future, frequently inspired by socialism. Artists perceive themselves as creators of a new world. Walker describes postmodernism in the arts, by contrast, as a midpoint, or "halfway house," between the past and an unclear future. Postmodernism rejects one universal style in favor of a plurality of styles and hybrids. Also, postmodernism revives historical and traditional styles in quotations and parodies. It permits ornament and decoration and values complexity, contradiction, and ambiguity, rejecting simplicity, order, and rationality. It blends high and low culture, and fine and popular art, offering multilayered readings. Finally, postmodern art references other works.

Architect Charles Jencks marks the beginning of postmodernism in the 1960s and defines it as paradoxical dualism, or double coding, which both extends modernism and transcends it. *Double coding* refers to combining modern techniques with traditional techniques in order to reach the public as well as a high-culture minority. Transcending modernism through the double coding of irony or humor symbolizes a loss of innocence and a desire to move beyond modernism's stylistic restrictions, as well as representing the failure of modernism. Indicators of postmodern art include symbolism,

ornamentation, humor, technology, and the relation of the artist to past cultures. The shift to postmodern culture is evidenced by other shifts, Jencks argues. Mass production is shifting to segmented production and mass culture to fragmented cultures. It is as easy to manufacture one-of-a-kind tailpipes instead of mass-produced tailpipes. In the media, network television's mass audience gave way to cable television's fragmented audiences. With a shift from centralized authority to decentralized pluralism in politics and the family, this pluralism leads to a shift from few styles to many genres. Stylistic pluralism and historical revivalism create a cultural framework that resembles the premodern era with the rejection of the idea of a single style. The postmodern era denotes an age of discontinuity and collision, which can be traced to cubism and James Joyce, as well as the daily newspaper. Postmodern artists incorporate incongruities and non sequiturs in their work because these elements appeal to their sense of reality.

Jencks devises a three-era history that begins with the premodern, which extends from prehistory to the Renaissance. This era was slow-changing, with a sense of reversible time that was repetitive and cyclical. Small-scale agriculture and handicrafts characterized production in a hierarchically structured peasant-priest-king social system. The second era, the modern world, arrived with the rise of capitalism and the industrial revolution. By the 19th century, the system had developed mass production and mass consumption. In the postmodern world from 1960 onward, information becomes more important than products. Traditional political models of liberal and conservatives and the two-party system become obsolete in the postmodern world. The media speed up our experiences of world events, and cultural systems change as more information is processed in less time.

A major figure in postmodernism's view of the media, Jean Baudrillard grants media tremendous power and social autonomy. The problem is that the media, according to Baudrillard in a theme shared with Frankfurt School theorist Max Horkheimer, foster noncommunication, or speech without response, or responsibility. The media prevent response, except for what Baudrillard calls response simulation, and the media extend social control and power. The solution Baudrillard puts forth is to restore the possibility of response to the media, but that would presuppose systemic change of media structures. The social control of the media stems from the fact that people are isolated in this system that prevents response. For Baudrillard, media have become a closed, mythological system that nothing can escape. In his pessimism, Baudrillard finds "mass mediatization" to be the essence of the media.

Baudrillard collapses the medium and the content into the simulations and simulacra of hyperreality. By the late 1970s, Baudrillard saw media, especially television, as simulation machines that reproduce images and signs that eventually constitute an independent world of hyperreality. In hyperreality, the media become more real than reality itself, subordinating the everyday reality to representation, dissolving it. In postmodern media, the medium and message collapse and the media are dissolved. Baudrillard expands on the idea to include not only the end of the message but also the end of the medium. There are no longer media operating between one reality and another; the medium and the real have imploded into a single state. Baudrillard concludes that the medium controls the process of meaning through its styles and techniques.

Paul Grosswiler
University of Maine

See also Critical Theory; Discourse Analysis; Hypermedia; Kellner, Douglas; Mass Media; Media Globalization; Post-Structuralism; Simulacra

Further Readings

Baudrillard, Jean. *For a Critique of the Political Economy of the Sign*. St. Louis, MO: Telos Press, 1974.

Baudrillard, Jean. *Simulations*. New York: Semiotext(e), 1983.

Brantlinger, Patrick. *Crusoe's Footprints*. New York: Routledge, 1990.

Jameson, Fredric. *The Ideologies of Theory: Essays 1971–1986*, Vol. 1. Minneapolis: University of Minnesota Press, 1988.

Jencks, Charles. *What Is Postmodernism?* New York: St. Martin's Press, 1986.

Kellner, Douglas. *Jean Baudrillard: From Marxism to Postmodernism and Beyond*. Stanford, CA: Stanford University Press, 1989.

Poster, Mark. *The Mode of Information: Post-Structuralism and Social Context*. Chicago: University of Chicago Press, 1990.

Thompson, John B. *The Media and Modernity: A Social Theory of the Media*. Stanford, CA: Stanford University Press, 1995.

Walker, John A. *Art in the Age of Mass Media*. London: Pluto Press, 1983.

POST-STRUCTURALISM

Post-structuralism is an intellectual movement that responds to and critiques structuralism. Post-structuralism has had an impact on a number of disciplines in humanities and social sciences, in particular literature, film studies, and media studies. Despite its influence, there is not a set of theories called post-structuralist theories and there is not a group of theorists called post-structuralists. In addition, post-structuralist theories intercept with postmodern theories, postcolonial theories, deconstruction theories, and psychoanalytic theories. Similarly, some of the key thinkers in post-structuralism, such as Roland Barthes, Jean Baudrillard, Jacques Derrida, Jacques Lacan, Julia Kristeva, and Luce Irigaray, are also neo-Marxist, postmodernist, structuralist, and psychoanalyst.

It is impossible to understand post-structuralism without understanding structuralism. Structuralism had a major impact on the development of theories in the 20th century in fields such as psychoanalysis, anthropology, and linguistics. The goal of structuralism is to understand the human world as systems. One key thinker of structuralism is the Swiss linguist Ferdinand de Saussure. Saussure wanted to understand languages as systems of signs. To Saussure, language is not limited to spoken and written language; it also includes signs (such as road signs), color, music, and so on. He proposed that there are two components to every sign: the signifier and the signified. The signifier can be a word (such as the word *tree*), a sound (the sound /tri/), or an image (a drawing of a tree or a picture of a tree). The signified is a concept elicited in the person's head. When an English speaker sees the word "tree," hears the sound /tri/, or sees an image of a tree, the concept of a perennial woody plant will be elicited in the head. Therefore, words, sounds, and images are all signs to Saussure. Saussure also coined the concepts of language (*langue*) and speech (*parole*). Language is a rule-governed system. Humans make speech according to linguistic rules. For example, in English, the sentence "I eat an apple" is a speech governed by several grammatical rules: there is only one subject; the verb follows the noun; and there is an article in front of the object. Using the same rules, speakers can make as many sentences as possible. Saussure's theory of semiology was later developed by Roland Barthes, who studied fashion, the Japanese culture, and images as systems of signs.

Structuralists believe that meanings are embedded in the systems and individuals simply obey the rules to make meanings. Structuralists also do not question if individuals have the power to make meanings or not. Post-structuralist theorists critique structuralists for failing to see the importance of language in meaning-making and for failing to realize the power of individuals to make meanings.

The later work of Barthes reflected his shift to post-structuralism from structuralism. In the essay "The Death of the Author" collected in *Image-Music-Text*, he argued that in traditional literary studies, the author is seen as the origin of meanings. Analysts and readers often ask, "What does the author mean?" This approach assumes that the author is the one who embeds meanings in a text. The meanings are later decoded by readers. Barthes had come to believe that the meanings of texts depend on the readers, not on the writers.

Post-structuralist thought also problematizes psychoanalysis. Psychoanalyst Jacques Lacan re-read Sigmund Freud's theory of child development by centralizing language in identity formation. He argued that a child only learns that he or she is not part of the mother when the child learns the meaning of "I." Feminist critics of Lacan such as Julia Kristeva and Luce Irigaray further emphasized the importance of language in the formulation of gender identity. Irigaray argues that because the French language is a masculine language, the female sex is linguistically effaced. For example, the male pronoun *ils* is used to refer to a group of people, even if only one of them is male. Feminist psychoanalysts argue that women's sense of inferiority is not rooted in their sense of lack, as Freud suggested, but is rooted in the secondary nature of the female sex in language.

Post-structuralism has a profound impact on feminism. Feminists question how meanings about gender are made through language. In the 1970s and the 1980s, feminist critique of the media focused on the unrealistic and biased portrayal of women.

There was an assumption that there was a reality "out there." Early feminists assumed that the media distort a reality. Post-structural feminists question if the boundary between the reality and the media is clear-cut at all. First, "real" people work in the media. Characters are played by actors who are real people. Second, people use language in daily lives to communicate. "Reality" is always represented by signs, be they written language or moving image. If the media are not about reality, neither are our daily lives. Therefore, post-structural feminists believe that reality is constructed by language. In this sense, daily lives are not more or less real than the media. Another implication of the notion that reality is constructed by language is that gender is not pre-given but negotiated. One is born either a male or a female, but it is through language that one constructs gender. For example, girl children are taught to talk and act differently from boy children; hence they learn to construct the female gender at an early age.

Post-structuralist feminists also problematize the notion of subjectivity. Enlightenment thought assumes that an individual is a unified, stable being; that is, the identity that individuals experience remains unchanged in different situations. Post-structuralist thought, on the other hand, suggests that an individual is a fragmented, unstable being; the identity that individuals experience changes under different circumstances. One is born either a female or a male, but one's sense of gender varies in different situations. For example, a woman who attends a sports game may experience her gender differently from the same woman who goes to a ball. To post-structuralist feminists, gender is fluid and playful. This is best exemplified at a drag performance in which biological males dress up as women and perform the other gender.

Last, post-structuralist feminists believe that meanings are not embedded in languages but are understood by individuals. Because each individual applies a different set of knowledge, repertoire, and competency to meaning-making, no one understands a text in exactly the same way. For example, whereas Americans may feel patriotic when seeing a U.S. flag, citizens of other countries probably see it only as a flag. Similarly, although some female audience may feel empowered by seeing "independent" women in *Sex and the City*, others may feel indifferent. Because meanings are not embedded in language but are understood by individuals, individuals may make new meanings of media texts by employing intertextuality. For example, satire is funny only if the audience has previous knowledge of particular texts. Satirical horror films such as *Scream* may appear to stereotype women as brainless, but they can also be read as a critique of gender conventions in the horror film genre.

Micky Lee
Suffolk University, Boston

See also Barthes, Roland; Identity; Polysemic Text; Postmodernism; Semiotics; Social Construction of Gender; Textual Analysis

Further Readings

Barthes, Roland. *Elements of Semiology*. London: Jonathan Cape, 1967.

Barthes, Roland. *Empire of Signs*. London: Jonathan Cape, 1983.

Barthes, Roland. *The Fashion System*. London: Jonathan Cape, 1985.

Barthes, Roland. *Image-Music-Text*. New York: Noonday, 1978.

Irigaray, Luce. *This Sex Which Is Not One*. Ithaca, NY: Cornell University Press, 1985.

Lacan, Jacques. *Ecrits: The First Complete Edition in English*. New York: W. W. Norton, 2007.

Lévi-Strauss, Claude. *The Savage Mind*. Chicago: University of Chicago Press, 1968.

Mori, Toril. *The Kristeva Reader*. New York: Wiley-Blackwell, 1991.

Propp, Vladamir. *Theory and History of Folklore*. Minneapolis: University of Minnesota Press, 1984.

Saussure, Ferdinand de. *Course in General Linguistics*. Peru, IL: Open Court, 1986.

PREJUDICE

Prejudice represents preconceived ideas or understandings about individuals or groups that are arrived at without full and adequate knowledge about the individuals or groups. Occurring across social categories, prejudice may involve making judgments regarding others based upon age, body size, disability, ethnicity, gender, homelessness, race, religion, sexual orientation, social class, or other characteristics. Prejudices regarding gender have been a particularly pernicious problem with regard to media portrayals of women and men. Women

Media representation has contributed to casting a prejudicial belief of women as physically weaker than men, less mentally stable, less in control of their emotions, less able to perform under pressure, and less able to function in high-stress settings. (Photos.com)

historically have suffered from prejudice in media representations as a result of representations that reinforce popular stereotypes. This includes showing women as physically weaker than men, more unstable mentally, more emotional, less able to put aside personal feelings, less able to perform under pressure, and less able to function in high-stress settings. To be sure, such prejudiced representations of gender have also proven damaging to many men and boys, but women and girls especially have been harmed. Prejudicial beliefs traffic through media content and production and have been present in many representations of women over the past few centuries and across various media.

Social Construction of Prejudice

Little thought was given, nor was much research conducted, regarding prejudice before the 1920s. Until that point, discussions regarding prejudice tended to center on attempts to prove white supremacy. Beginning in the 1930s, however, concerns about the anti-Semitism cultivated by the Nazis and other right-wing groups caused psychologists and sociologists to examine the pathological roots undergirding prejudice. These researchers began to explore whether certain personality syndromes could be linked to prejudice. Theodor Adorno posited that prejudice was a manifestation of an authoritarian personality. Those with authoritarian personalities represented rigid thinkers who approached the world as a series of black-and-white decisions, obeyed authority, and sought strict adherence to social hierarchies and rules. This authoritarian outlook caused its adherents to be more likely to be prejudiced against groups who displayed characteristics of lower status, whether those were demonstrated by gender, race, ethnicity, religion, or some other marker.

Building upon Adorno's findings, during the 1950s psychologist Gordon Allport linked prejudice to categorical thinking. Allport, one of the founders of the school of personality psychology, believed that prejudice was a normal process for humans, one of the ways in which individuals make sense of the world around them. As such, prejudice does not necessarily represent hatred for others but instead demonstrates favoritism toward one's own in-group. While categories are necessary for individuals to prejudge new situations, ultimate attribution error, first described by social psychologist Thomas Pettigrew, may also play a role in prejudice. Ultimate attribution error occurs when in-group members attribute negative behaviors in those from other groups (out-group members) to dispositional causes, whereas they attribute positive behaviors in that out-group to luck or special advantage, a fluke or an exception, high motivation and effort, or situational factors. Representations of out-groups, when perpetuated through beliefs of in-group members and reinforced through the media, can become very difficult to shake, and they buttress prejudice against out-group members. While prejudice can arise out of almost any topic, prejudices related to a person's ethnicity, gender, nationality, race, religious affiliation, sexual orientation, and socioeconomic status are especially difficult to disregard for individuals with a predisposition toward them.

Origins of Prejudice in Media

Prejudice often manifests itself in discrimination against members of the out-group by individuals and groups. Thus, prejudice against an individual of another race may result in racism, prejudice against one of a different gender as sexism, and prejudice against a member of a different socioeconomic group as classism. While media representations of gender prejudice in many ways merely reflect what exists in the world in which they are created, these representations also play a role in perpetuating

stereotypes and buttressing an inequitable distribution of power. The Bible, for example, is the most widely printed and read text globally. As early as the 19th century, however, the Bible was criticized for perpetuating the standard religious orthodoxy that women should be subservient to men. In an effort to address this perceived prejudice, a committee of approximately two dozen women, led by social activist and abolitionist Elizabeth Cady Stanton, published *The Women's Bible* in 1895. This two-volume work sought to challenge many of the prejudices against women that its authors believed were disseminated in the Bible as traditionally represented. In particular, Stanton and her colleagues believed that the Bible supported traditional Judeo-Christian teachings that women were the source of sin. Inspired by the Church of England's contemporaneous publication of the Revised Version of the Bible, Stanton and her group felt that an interpretation of the work that focused upon its true original form would support women's rights.

The Women's Bible was highly controversial when published. Although prejudices against women and other groups were present in many media forms, choosing to attack that perceived in the Bible was a contentious and divisive decision. The National American Woman Suffrage Association (NAWSA), of which Stanton was a founding member, voted to disassociate the NAWSA from *The Women's Bible* in 1898, and after this Stanton, 80 at the time, never again participated in the organization in any meaningful way. Stanton's longtime collaborator, Susan B. Anthony, had determined that focusing on the single issue of women's suffrage permitted the organization a better chance of success than focusing on the many other prejudices and inequities facing women. To that end, most of the group's focus went to achieving the vote for women, and instances of prejudice by religious bodies, financial institutions, and the media were largely ignored.

In dealing with media, women faced prejudicial challenges different from those of other groups. On one hand, women had published widely in a variety of fiction and nonfiction genres since the 18th century, unlike many racial minorities, whose voices were largely silenced up through the 20th century. On the other hand, a lack of control over the sources of dissemination, be it publishing, motion pictures, recorded music production, or radio or television broadcasting, placed groups that were the victims of prejudice in a relatively vulnerable position. How each of these media outlets promulgated prejudice, or fought to overcome it, varied greatly.

Prejudice in the Media Through 1960

By the start of the 20th century, increasing literacy and prosperity greatly expanded the scope and influence of the media. A group of women's magazines known as the Seven Sisters were extremely popular throughout the first half of the 20th century, helping to shape many of the tastes and preferences of the married women at whom they were targeted. The Seven Sisters—*Better Homes and Gardens* (first published in 1922), *Good Housekeeping* (1885), *Family Circle* (1932), *Ladies' Home Journal* (1883), *McCall's* (1897), *Redbook* (1903), and *Woman's Day* (1928)—featured diverse content that both played upon and challenged prejudices regarding women. Although the Seven Sisters focused on traditional values of home, family, and children, the magazines also offered literature by writers such as Virginia Woolf, Frances Parkinson Keyes, Edna St. Vincent Millay, Edith Wharton, Margaret Mead, Cynthia May Alden, and Mary Bass, among others. Although such magazines often built upon prejudicial stereotypes that women were chiefly interested in domestic matters, they also provided employment opportunities for women and an outlet for news and other areas of general interest. Controversial topics such as divorce and abortion were addressed by the Seven Sisters, although they were criticized for giving these issues less coverage than other outlets.

As radio programming became increasingly popular after 1920, broadcasters and advertisers sought to reach as wide an audience as possible through the use of a variety of genres and formats. As was typical of the era, many of the comedies, dramas, horror shows, musical variety programs, romances, mysteries, soap operas, and thrillers evidenced the prejudices that were common at the time. Most radio programming perpetuated prejudices and stereotypes against those out-groups that were neither male nor Caucasian, with the depictions of African Americans (*Amos 'n' Andy*, first broadcast in 1928), Asians (*The Adventures of Charlie Chan*, 1932), Hispanics (*The Cisco Kid*, 1942), the Irish (*The Life of Riley*, 1941), and Italians (*Life with Luigi*, 1948) on such shows being especially contentious today. Women, of course, were frequently depicted on radio. However, the depictions of women often relegated them to roles that reinforced traditional stereotypes, usually as weak, inefficient, or interested chiefly in domestic matters. Interestingly, it was the sensationalized and melodramatic soap operas that showcased strong female characters, women who had careers and were able to assert their rights. Such characters evidenced their ability to defy stereotypes and prejudices, including elderly Ma Perkins (on the show of the same name, which aired 1933–60), who ran a lumberyard; dressmaker Helen Trent (*The Romance of Helen Trent*, 1933–60); and the wife of a matinee idol, Mary Noble (*Backstage Wife*, 1935–59). Although the plots of these soap operas were often bizarre and unrealistic, this sort of fantasy allowed women to defy stereotypes and prejudices in ways that more mainstream programming did not.

Early television programming tended to perpetuate prejudices and stereotypes, especially with regard to women. Although Lucille Ball's character in *I Love Lucy* (1951–57), Lucy Ricardo, was the clear focus of the program, she was a housewife, depended upon her husband for support, and demonstrated an inability to make rational judgments. Film portrayals in the 1950s tended to reinforce prejudices and stereotypes that suggested women were mentally unstable and emotional. Doris Day, the number-one female performer at the box office during the 1950s, often appeared in roles that reinforced prejudices, including *Pillow Talk* (1959) and *Please Don't Eat the Daisies* (1960). Female characters who defied stereotypes and prejudices were most common in material aimed at children, including the *Wonder Woman* comic books (which first appeared in 1941) and children's book series featuring such characters as girl detective Nancy Drew (1930–), nurse Cherry Ames (1943–68), and stewardess Vicki Barr (1947–64).

Prejudice in the Media After 1960

Notions of gender and prejudice are intimately connected. Beginning in the 18th century, women and men fought for women's suffrage. This led to the passage of the 19th Amendment, which added women's right to vote to the U.S. Constitution. Reponses to this first wave of feminism developed into what is sometimes referred to as the second wave of feminism (1960–80). The first wave of feminism focused on access into full citizenship, including the rights to vote and to serve on juries. The central idea of this second wave, however, was to lessen discrimination, increase access and equality, and define the role of the body and reproductive rights through self-reflection and deeper engagement with the societal forces that led to lack of access. The slogan of this second wave, coined by Carol Hanisch, was "The Personal Is Political."

The notions that grounded the second wave of feminism were identified through various media venues during the period between 1960 and 1980. Texts such as Betty Friedan's *The Feminine Mystique* (1963), Simone de Beauvoir's *The Second Sex* (1949), and Gloria Steinem's work served as a foundation for the questions and approaches that media venues used to support or subvert these new visions. In addition to the aforementioned grounding questions, according to Friedan and de Beauvoir, womanhood required the opportunity to balance, if desired, one's public life with one's private life. Thus, television programs such as *Get Smart* (1965–70) and *The Nurses* (1962–65) provided strong female characters that were able to make life-and-death decisions regardless of genre, and *Julia* (1968–71) and *Good Times* (1974–79) also provided strong female characters who handled challenges and triumphs of raising a family and balancing work and family life. *Maude* (1972–78) encompassed the range of ideas central to second generation feminism. Played by Bea Arthur, Maude was once widowed and twice divorced. She was for abortion rights (the *Roe v. Wade* decision was delivered in 1973), had a daughter who was also divorced and portrayed as dating numerous men, and had a son who lived at home. The juxtaposition of the son and daughter is significant insofar as these were, in the early 1970s, new images. Maude served as an archetype for women in future television shows, such as reporter *Murphy Brown* (1988–98) and attorney *Ally McBeal* (1997–2002).

Television programs such as *The Brady Bunch* (1969–74) also forwarded important images and ideas to resist prejudice. Carol Brady, like Maude, was a divorced and remarried woman. Carol Brady had to balance her new and old children (her private life) and the work she and her husband did to provide for their children (her public life). *The Brady Bunch* led to shows such as *The Cosby Show* (1984–92), which contained characters who could enjoy, laugh, and struggle with their various professional and personal relationships.

The evolution of how women are presented on television has continued through the third wave of feminism, beginning in about 1990. Third wave feminism challenged what it saw as an overemphasis on upper-class white women by second wave feminists. Thus, the inclusion of perspectives that took the lives of lesbian women and women of color seriously is seen as important. Authors like bell hooks, Audre Lorde, Luisa Accati, and Maxine Hong Kingston are important thinkers in third wave feminism. Unlike second wave feminism, where media can more easily forward or subvert images of women, third wave feminism, with its emphasis on post-structural research methodologies (such as queer theory and autoethnographic approaches to research) uses current television programs and films as a springboard to demonstrate how the values, lives, and ideals of characters are conjoined with or fractured from the tenets of third wave feminism. Thus, shows like *Buffy the Vampire Slayer* and *The Bachelor* are lenses through which the lives of "differing others" can be viewed.

Concurrent with the way popular culture has represented the struggles against gender prejudice, organizations such as the National Organization for Women (NOW) developed to further the important causes initiated by the second wave of feminism. Founded in 1966, NOW has successfully confronted issues such as abortion rights, equality in hiring and the workplace, Title IX, and, most generally, the need for the larger culture to acknowledge the value of the multiplicity of work completed by women in their daily lives. Along with Gloria Steinem and Robin Morgan, Jane Fonda founded The Women's Media Center in 2005. Both of these organizations continue to support important aspects of first, second, and third wave feminism through political and activist agendas. In many ways, the ideas that are important to feminists in "speaking truth to power" are forwarded through the images presented in the media as well as the agendas of organizations such as NOW and The Women's Media Center.

Stephen T. Schroth
Jason A. Helfer
Jeffrey T. Wickman
Knox College

See also Advertising; Children's Programming: Cartoons; Diversity; Empowerment; Feminist Theory: Second Wave; Feminist Theory: Third Wave; Feminist Theory: Women-of-Color and Multiracial Perspectives; Film: Hollywood; Homophobia; Minority Rights; Misogyny; Patriarchy; Racism; Radio; Sexism; Social Construction of Gender; Stereotypes; Television; Tropes

Further Readings

Dunning, J. *On the Air: The Encyclopedia of Old-Time Radio.* New York: Oxford University Press, 1998.

MacDonald, J. F. *Blacks and White TV: African Americans in Television Since 1948,* 2nd ed. Chicago: Nelson-Hall, 1993.

Schroth, E. M. "*Camelot:* Contemporary Interpretation of Arthur in 'Sens' and 'Matiere.'" *The Journal of Popular Culture,* v.17/2 (1983).

Sears, D. O., J. Sidanius, and L. Bobo, eds. *Radicalized Politics: The Debate About Racism in America.* Chicago: University of Chicago Press, 2000.

Tucker, L. R. "Was the Revolution Televised? Professional Criticism About *The Cosby Show* and the Essentialization of Black Cultural Expression." *Journal of Broadcasting and Electronic Media,* 41 (1997).

Wilson, C. C., F. Gutierrez, and L. M. Chao. *Racism, Sexism, and the Media: The Rise of Class Communication in Multicultural America,* 3rd ed. Thousand Oaks, CA: Sage, 2003.

QUANTITATIVE CONTENT ANALYSIS

There are numerous useful definitions of the quantitative research method of content analysis as it pertains to the examination of media messages. One brief and particularly useful definition describes content analysis as a research methodology in which media messages are systematically examined, summarizing their characteristics by using procedures to categorize the content into carefully constructed types or groups. K. A. Neuendorf, a social scientist well-known for his work in this area, defines the method of content analysis as a summarizing, quantitative analysis of media messages that relies on the standards and procedures of the scientific method, which should not be limited either by the context in which messages are produced or distributed or by the types of variables that can be easily measured. Neuendorf's definition pays particular attention to the scientific method and the specific concerns that should be addressed when using the method of content analysis, with careful attention paid to determining the presence of specific message content in the categorized data. These aspects are crucial for conducting an analysis that is considered both credible and worthy of scholarly attention.

Another detailed definition of the method that should be considered when conducting research using this methodology includes the notion that quantitative content analysis should be both systematic and replicable in its examination of media messages. This is done through the assignment of numeric values to specific representations, which allows for the analysis of relationships using those values for statistical analysis. This procedure allows for the ability to describe the media messages and draw inferences about their meaning within the context in which the messages are produced and consumed. This definition addresses the necessity of relying on aspects of the scientific method and also emphasizes the importance of categorizing the data prior to analysis. Most notably, this definition includes the potential purposes or goals of conducting research using the method of content analysis. Not only is it necessary to offer a description of the content that is being examined, but also it should be the intent of researchers who rely on this method to make inferences about the meaning and potential impact of the content. This is a particularly important aspect of this definition, as one of the main criticisms of content analysis is its lack of theoretical grounding. This definition attempts to address such critiques and emphasizes the need for the inclusion of formal theorizing in relation to content analysis research. Quantitative content analysis differs from more qualitative methods of communication research in part because of its attempt to meet the standards of the scientific method, although qualitative research is also considered by many to be social scientific.

Objectivity-intersubjectivity is central to any research methodology attempting to meet the criteria for scientific research. Content analysis attempts to meet this requirement by providing descriptions of content that avoid bias by the researcher. Although objectivity would be the ultimate goal of such research, true objectivity is an impossible feat. According to this perspective, all social research is inherently subjective, making it all the more important to strive for consistency between researchers. Neuendorf uses the term *intersubjectivity* to describe the scholarly standard of agreement among researchers attempting to conduct scientific research. One way researchers meet the scientific requirement of objectivity-intersubjectivity is through an a priori research design. This requires that all decisions about the variables and the their measurement as well as the rules for coding must be decided and agreed upon before the observations of the media content can begin.

The concept of reliability is also necessary to address in all scientifically based content analysis research. In content analysis, reliability refers to the agreement among coders about how the content will be categorized. Specifically, reliability refers to the extent to which a study and its measurement techniques can be replicated by other researchers and still produce the same or similar results. The concept of *intercoder reliability* is used by researchers to address the level of agreement between two or more coders involved in a content analysis about the media representations in question through mathematical equations, in order to minimize the possibility of subjectivity.

Validity is another crucial factor when conducting content analysis research that purports to be scientifically grounded. In this context, validity can be thought of as the extent to which the variables being analyzed actually measure what the researcher claims and intends to measure. Validity is accomplished when a method of measurement represents the intended concept and nothing else. When validity is accomplished, researchers who use the method of content analysis can be confident that the claims being made about the data are legitimate and free of nonrandom error.

Generalizability and replicability are also essential features of any research that uses the scientific method as its basis. For a study to be generalizable, it must be able to be applied to other cases, often with a larger scope, likely similar to what the researcher has defined as the population from which the sample has been taken. In order to avoid overgeneralizing and making claims about a population that are inaccurate, it is crucial that a study be able to be replicated by either the same or other researchers. If similar results are obtained when a study has been repeated with either different cases or in a different context, then the condition of replicability has been satisfied. It is therefore necessary that researchers disclose their methodologies in full, so that other researchers have enough information to conduct replication studies to confirm the original findings.

Ample research data using the method of content analysis has been gathered in regard to the representation of gender in the media. Specifically in regard to television, content analysis research has determined that women have been consistently underrepresented since the onset of television and are more likely to be cast in minor roles than as major characters. Studies from the early 1970s reveal that only 18 percent of main characters were female at that time. More recent content analyses reveal that female characters now approach 40 percent of television characters.

Content analysis is also considered a scholarly research methodology in the humanities by which texts are examined in relation to meaning, underlying ideology, or authenticity. Additionally, disciplines such as sociology, anthropology, and political science make use of these qualitative techniques to study the lived experiences of their subjects through the analysis of the communication messages produced or consumed. Within the past few decades, this type of content analysis has also become a principal means of analyzing the success of corporations' public relations endeavors within the media landscape.

Andrea M. Bergstrom
Franklin Pierce University

See also Discourse Analysis; Gender Media Monitoring; Media Literacy; Textual Analysis

Further Readings

Elasmar, M., K. Hasegawa, and M. Brain. "The Portrayal of Women in U.S. Prime Time Television." *Journal of Broadcasting and Electronic Media*, v.43/1 (1999).

Krippendorff, K. *Content Analysis: An Introduction to Its Methodology.* Beverly Hills, CA: Sage, 1980.

Neuendorf, K. A. *The Content Analysis Guidebook.* Thousand Oaks, CA: Sage, 2002.

Riffe, D., S. Lacy, and F. G. Fico. *Analyzing Media Messages: Using Quantitative Content Analysis in Research.* Mahwah, NJ: Lawrence Erlbaum Associates, 1998.

Scharrer, E. "Content Analysis and Television." In *Encyclopedia of Social Measurement*, Kimberley Kempf-Leonard, ed. San Diego, CA: Academic Press, 2004.

QUEER THEORY

Queer theory is an interdisciplinary post-structural/ postmodern perspective on gender and sexuality. Judith Butler's notion of the performance of gender or "gender trouble," which she formulated in the early 1990s, is often considered the beginning of queer theory as a specific viewpoint. However, many scholars date queer theory to Michel Foucault's sociological study of the history of sexuality, published in the 1970s in France. In general, queer theorists challenge modernist notions of identity as coherent, stable, and natural, and subsequent categories and binaries such as gender/sex, masculinity/femininity, male/female, and heterosexuality/homosexuality, by positing the multiplicity, fluidity, and ambiguity of gender and sexuality. For most queer theorists, the term *queer* signifies something that is strange and sexual, as it has colloquially been understood. However, instead of also referring to something that is negative and used to abuse gays and lesbians, as has occurred in history, the term *queer* is considered positive by queer theorists. In this context, queer and the act of "queering" refer to productive strategies for the social acceptance and civil rights of people who do not fit into dominant perceptions of gender or sexuality or who in any way feel marginalized for their gender or sexuality. Moreover, academic definitions and uses of the term *queer* are intentionally slippery and still evolving. Toward this end, scholarship on queer theory usually seeks to identify and deconstruct contemporary cultural discourses that are more or less queer, ranging from medical definitions of homosexuality to mediated representations of transgender people. This scholarship often makes explicit connections to transgender studies, with which it has much in common.

Similar to other post-structural/postmodern perspectives, queer theory is a theoretical response to modernist bodies of knowledge such as Marxism, psychoanalysis, and structural linguistics. Given its focus on gender and sexuality, queer theory is also a theoretical and political response to first and second wave feminism and gay and lesbian studies, the latter of which grew out of the gay liberation movement that occurred in the 1970s in the United States. In addition, the epidemic of human immunodeficiency virus and acquired immune deficiency syndrome (HIV/AIDS) that occurred in the 1980s across Europe and in the United States contributed to the development of queer theory; for example, one group the disease significantly affected was men who had sex with men but who did not identify themselves as gay. The specific term "queer theory" is attributed to Teresa de Laurentis, who coined it in her introduction to a 1991 issue of *differences: A Journal of Feminist Cultural Studies*. Queer theory parts ways with modernist philosophies; the latter center on essentialist binary logics suggesting that identities are fixed and classify people, and that these identities are the means by which to organize social change. Exemplifying this modernist approach is the call by early women's rights activists for women to be included in universal conceptions of what it means to be human, as well as the critique by second wave feminists in the 1960s and 1970s of this universal concept of the human subject as being masculine. Both of these critiques rest on logics of placing men in a different category from, and in opposition, to women. Likewise, gay liberationist thinking and political action were (and still are) based in identity categories and binaries, such as homosexuality/heterosexuality and men/women, when its goal primarily concerns the attainment and defense of rights for gay men.

Although queer theorists are diverse and can disagree, they resemble one another in their challenge to the aforementioned identity-based modernist political agendas and philosophies of gender and/or sexuality. Foucault's and Butler's work is central to this postmodern perspective on gender and sexuality that is now known as queer theory. Specifically, Foucault documents how sexuality is a discursive construct that has changed across cultures and throughout history. In turn, Foucault shows how the beliefs that heterosexuality is the norm and natural and that homosexuality is an aberration are discursive effects and that the two states have nothing to do with the essence of being human. Furthermore, because Foucault theorizes a new model of power as a network of relations that are not simply made up of the rulers and those whom they rule, he also calls into question the political goal of liberation.

Influenced by Foucault and others, Butler later overturned feminist theory by deconstructing the identity category of woman and proposing an antifoundational politics of the "performance of gender." That is, gender is not something that people are or have but rather a set of repeated discursive

Academic uses of the term *queer* are still evolving. Among other things, scholarship on queer theory challenges the idea of identifying people by gender or sex, masculinity or femininity, being male or female, and heterosexuality or homosexuality. (Photos.com)

acts that are done, though not done by a subject who might be said to preexist the deed. For instance, Butler discusses how "gender trouble," such as a drag parody and other expressions of gender confusion, reveals that gender is permeable and plural in ways that do not fit the masculine/feminine dichotomy. These acts of destabilizing gender categories of identity constitute a political strategy, according to Butler, because their strangeness provides a way of seeing how a different society might be constructed.

A growing number of scholars across disciplines debate and deploy queer theory, especially in their studies of the politics of contemporary literature, newspapers and newsmagazines, film, television, and a range of other mediated and public discourses.

Eve Kosofsky Sedgwick's book *Epistemology of the Closet* (1990) influenced much of this scholarship. Sedgwick, a professor of English by training, analyzes landmark European and American novels and philosophical texts written by Henry James, Oscar Wilde, and Friedrich Nietzsche, among others, for their incoherent ideas on the division between homosexuality and heterosexuality. Sedgwick's attention to the role of words and speech acts in constructing the false dichotomy of homosexuality/heterosexuality and her observation that the gender of the person someone chooses to be with emerged as the defining characteristic for categorizing someone's sexual orientation align with Butler's queer theory of language and the performance of gender.

Michael Warner's edited collection on queer politics and social theory, published in 1993, illustrates how queer theory has not replaced earlier feminist and gay and lesbian studies but now exists alongside them. For instance, in his introduction, Warner discusses how the term queer has the effect of pointing out a wide field of normalization; essays in his collection explore social activism by ACT UP and Queer Nation as well as the new religious right, which vary in their claims and critiques about what is normal gender and/or sexuality.

In the fields of communication and critical/cultural studies specifically, Charles Morris and John Sloop analyze the proliferation and popularity of queer media, such as the cable television shows *Queer Eye for the Straight Guy* and *Queer as Folk*, and particular images of same-sex kissing that have appeared in films and in the wedding sections of newspapers. They trace how many of these celebrated contemporary queer media representations are still homophobic, heterosexist, or heteronormative, but also note that the visibility of man-on-man kissing has the potential for queer world-making when violating taboos and affirming sexual disruption.

Jamie Landau
Keene State College

See also Cultural Politics; Discourse Analysis; Feminism; Feminist Theory: Third Wave; Gay and Lesbian Portrayals on Television; Gender and Masculinity: Metrosexual Male; Gender and Masculinity: White Masculinity; Gender Embodiment; Gender Media Monitoring; Gender Schema Theory; Heterosexism; Homophobia; Identity; Ideology; Male Gaze; Online

New Media: GLBTQ Identity; Online New Media: Transgender Identity; Postfeminism; Postmodernism; Post-Structuralism; Sexuality; Social Construction of Gender; Social Learning Theory; Stereotypes; Transgender Studies; Transsexuality

Further Readings

Butler, Judith. *Gender Trouble: Feminism and the Subversion of Identity*. New York: Routledge, 1990.

de Laurentis, Teresa. "Queer Theory: Lesbian and Gay Sexualities—An Introduction." *differences: A Journal of Feminist Cultural Studies*, v.3/2 (1991).

Foucault, Michel. *A History of Sexuality*. Vol. 1, *An Introduction*. New York: Vintage Books, 1990.

Jagose, Annamarie. *Queer Theory: An Introduction*. New York: New York University Press, 1996.

Morris, Charles E., III and John M. Sloop. "'What Lips These Lips Have Kissed': Refiguring the Politics of Queer Public Kissing." *Communication and Critical/Cultural Studies*, v.3/1 (2006).

Sedgwick, Eve Kosofsky. *Epistemology of the Closet*. Berkeley: University of California Press, 1990.

Warner, Michael, ed. *Fear of a Queer Planet: Queer Politics and Social Theory*. Minneapolis: University of Minnesota Press, 1993.

RACISM

Much like gender, *racism* is a social construct that supports the belief that race causes inherent differences in an individual's traits and capacities, differences that moreover justify different treatment of individuals and groups. The practice of racism in media—print, radio, film, television, and video games—has resulted in different treatment of certain groups based on racial categories. These alternative treatments are rooted in a variety of causes, including popular stereotypes, the control of media production and ownership by whites, and the difficulties people of color have experienced trying to participate in the control of these images. Stereotypes, from minstrel shows to depictions of inner-city life, have perpetuated racism from the 19th century to the present day. While media portrayals of racism have certainly changed over the past half century, even contemporary media portrayals of certain ethnic groups bear the vestiges of stereotypes and prejudice.

Social Construction of Racism

Racial discrimination is often based on supposedly scientific taxonomic differences between different groups of people. *Race* itself is merely the classification of humans into distinct populations or groups based on indicators such as geographic origins and phenotypic characteristics. The term *phenotypic characteristics* refers to a person's observable traits, such as behavior, biochemical properties, development, physiological assets, and products of behavior. Morphology often plays a large role in the construction of race, dealing as it does with a person's outward appearance, including such variables as shape, color, structure, and pattern. Conceptions of race, however, are admittedly influenced by and correlated with other socially constructed traits, such as appearance, culture, ethnicity, and socioeconomic status. During the early 20th century, at the height of the eugenics movement, great efforts were made to establish biological differences between various races, to the extent that skeletal remains of individuals were examined to ascertain measurable differences, a process that is still used to some extent by anthropologists, biomedical researchers, and forensic scientists. Racism is the practice of treating individuals or groups differently based on these perceived differences.

The social construct of race is by no means universally accepted. While there are those who argue that inherent differences exist between different races, others maintain that such constructs are artificial and that allegations of such cultural, nonpersonal, and social distinctions are utilized only to justify different treatments of different groups. *Racism*, a term first used during the 1930s, refers to using race to justify disparate treatment of individuals or groups based on their race. Racism generally implies race-based discrimination, dislike, oppression, prejudice, or violence by one group or individual against another. Some prefer the term *racial discrimination*, which implies distinctions, exclusions, preferences, and restrictions based on race, to the term *racism*.

This preference is based on the way that "racial discrimination" more clearly delineates behaviors, whereas "racism" indicates attitudes that are harder to confirm or identify. Complicating matters further is the tendency of terms such as race, racism, and racial discrimination to change over time and to be used differently in different places. These differences influence media representations of racism and shape how certain groups or individuals are treated.

Origins of Racism in Media

The United States, with its history of forcibly bringing Africans to North America to serve as slaves, has long struggled to confront and deal with racism. Harriet Beecher Stowe's antislavery novel, *Uncle Tom's Cabin: Or, Life Among the Lowly*, first published in 1852, was enormously popular and helped shape many constructs regarding race that lasted into the 20th century. Stowe, a staunch abolitionist, sought to change public perceptions about slavery through her portrayal of the struggles and reality of slavery. Although often criticized by contemporary readers as overly sentimental and demeaning of African Americans, *Uncle Tom's Cabin* was the best-selling novel in the 19th century, outselling everything but the Bible. The novel, which also inspired several plays, not only was influential in changing attitudes toward slavery in the northern states but also helped to establish and solidify many of the stereotypes regarding African Americans, some of which persist to the present day. These stereotypes included the "mammy," a dark-skinned, affectionate maternal figure with a heart of gold; the "pickaninny," an unruly black child who is ill-behaved and who often engages in minor criminal activities; and the "Uncle Tom," a servile, dutiful, long-suffering domestic who is loyal to his white master or mistress. Written in response to the Fugitive Slave Act of 1850, which demanded that all runaway slaves be returned to their masters, even if they had reached a state where slavery was outlawed, *Uncle Tom's Cabin* helped many readers reach the conclusion that slavery was immoral and evil. The depictions of the book's African American characters, however, today often are seen as demeaning and condescending, with stereotypes regarding a lack of work ethic and immoral behavior among the slaves seen as especially damaging and influential on later works.

Minstrel shows—in which Caucasian performers would use burnt cork or other substances as makeup applied to their skin to make them appear black—are another source of the stereotypes that have perpetuated racism throughout media. Originating during the 1830s and 1840s, minstrel shows were one of the most popular forms of live entertainment during the 19th century, and the stereotypes regarding African Americans that developed in them persisted through radio, film, television, and amateur theater until the mid-20th century. Minstrel shows began as brief, unconnected skits but later developed into full performances, complete with music, dancing, and variety acts. Often parodying African Americans as buffoonish, ignorant, joyous, lazy, musical, and superstitious, minstrel shows were popular even in areas where few blacks lived. For this reason, stereotypes in minstrel shows were extremely influential in shaping the perceptions and reactions of many Caucasians to African Americans. Interestingly, although held in low esteem by almost all groups today, minstrel shows were opposed by many southerners before the Civil War, in the belief that they portrayed black characters in a sympathetic light and threatened slavery. Well-known composers such as Stephen Foster debuted many of their works as a part of minstrel shows, and after the Civil War it was not unknown for African Americans to appear in these shows. Minstrel shows were popular with African American audiences, although educated blacks disdained the genre as demeaning and racist. Although minstrel shows featured a variety of acts, two recurring characters had great influence in shaping stereotypes that buttressed racism in the United States: Jim Crow and Gumbo Chaff. Jim Crow represented a lazy and shiftless song-and-dance parody of African Americans, while Gumbo Chaff stood for a tall-tale-telling riverboatman who often appeared on stage with a prop raft. Both characters created stereotypes that lasted in other media for decades after the decline of minstrel shows.

Vaudeville and Film

After the decline of minstrel shows, blackface characters were kept alive in vaudeville and film. Vaudeville was a form of entertainment popular between the 1880s and 1930s that comprised separate, unrelated variety acts grouped together to form a bill of entertainment. Vaudeville featured comedians, singers, dancers, animal acts, magicians, and often performers in blackface. Vaudeville declined dramatically in popularity after the advent of motion pictures and radio, but its influence was felt for years on these newer media, in terms of both the transition of popular performers and the use of stereotypes established during its heyday.

Popular vaudeville blackface acts included the Two Black Crows and Al Jolson; other stars of the era, such as Eddie Cantor and George Jessel, also dabbled in the form. The Two Black Crows most famously comprised Charles Mack and George Moran, and the act focused primarily on well-worn, but generally nonracial, jokes and skits. The characters relied on then-prevalent stereotypes related to African Americans, with one being "naïve but practical" while the other was "lazy and shrewd." Major vaudeville shows featuring the Two Black Crows include the Ziegfeld Follies (1920) and Earl Carroll's Vanities (1924). The Two Black Crows' stage act was memorialized in several films, including *Two Flaming Youths* (1927) and *Why Bring That Up?* (1929). Jolson, an actor, comedian, and singer, was frequently hailed as the "world's greatest entertainer" during the course of his career, which spanned the years 1895 through 1950. Jolson enjoyed performing in blackface, which, it was felt, enhanced his performances of songs written or made popular by African Americans. Jolson is credited with introducing many African American songs to white Americans and was known for fighting for racial equality, permitting black artists such as Duke Ellington, Louis Armstrong, Fats Waller, Cab Calloway, and Ethel Waters the chance to play for Caucasian audiences. Jolson's first film, *The Jazz Singer* (1927), was the first feature-length motion picture with synchronized dialogue and musical sequences and highlighted Jolson performing in blackface. *The Jazz Singer* was astonishingly successful, ushering in the age of the "talkie" and almost singlehandedly destroying the market for silent films.

With the rise in popularity of the movies, African American performers found themselves offered marginalized roles or being excluded from the industry altogether. Since both the means of film production (the motion picture studios) and distribution (movie theaters) were owned almost exclusively by whites, there was little opportunity for African Americans to star in films, much less rise to managerial positions

such as directing or producing. Indeed, threats by theater owners and distributors in the southern United States made many producers leery of casting African Americans in films at all. The few roles offered to African Americans perpetuated stereotypes. When blacks were cast, it was often as domestic servants, such as Hattie McDaniel, who won an Academy Award for Best Supporting Actress for her portrayal of Mammy in *Gone With the Wind* (1939). Even when jazz greats such as Duke Ellington, Louis Armstrong, or Billie Holiday were allowed to perform in films, it was inevitably made clear that their character had a role as a domestic servant, a Pullman porter, or an entertainer, a role played by Ellington in *Murder at the Vanities* (1934), Armstrong in *High Society* (1958), and Holiday in *New Orleans* (1947). Only after 1960 did African American actors such as Sidney Poitier begin to obtain roles that were not based on negative stereotypes.

During the 1960s and 1970s, black performers used a series of blaxploitation movies to resist the notions forwarded through stereotypes. *Blaxploitation* films use stereotypes that have been inflicted upon African Americans in order to demonstrate how their commodification can, in fact, lead toward emancipation from the standard media viewpoints of blacks. Blaxploitation films developed stock characters such as the Spook, one who is afraid of others; the Sage, often an older person with the wisdom and experience to effect the outcome of the plot; the Seductress, a female character who would seduce others through words and actions; the Sidekick, one who is often presented as lazy and afraid; and the Stud, often the lead character who overcomes adversity and does so with the appearance of limited effort. The first movies to be considered blaxploitation were *Baadasssss Song* (1971) and *Shaft* (1971). While the heyday of blaxploitation films was the 1970s, various parodies occurred through the 1980s and 1990s, such as *I'm Gonna Git You Sucka* (1988), and continued in television shows such as *South Park* and *The Family Guy*. There is some controversy regarding whether these films have helped or hindered the causes important to black Americans.

Radio and Television

Radio became a popular medium during the 1920s, featuring comedies, dramatic shows, and mystery and suspense programs in addition to musical performances, news, and sports. One of the most popular early shows, *Amos 'n' Andy*, featured two Caucasian men, Freeman Gosden and Charles Correll, speaking in dialect as black characters. One of the original blockbusters of radio, *Amos 'n' Andy* aired on radio from 1928 through 1960, and a television version (starring African Americans) was aired from 1951 until 1966, both as original programming and in syndication. The radio program portrayed the lead characters as working-class African Americans who engaged in humorous situations, often based on misunderstandings or unfulfilled "get rich" schemes. Although the radio program drew few protests from African Americans, the 1953 premiere of the television program was vehemently protested as stereotypical by the National Association for the Advancement of Colored People (NAACP), causing the Columbia Broadcasting System (CBS) to cancel the series after 78 episodes were aired. Other early radio programs, including one featuring the Two Black Crows, featured adaptations of minstrel-type acts for the new medium. Few black actors appeared on radio, and those who did tended to be limited to roles as domestic servants.

As television became increasingly popular in the 1950s, it displaced radio as Americans' favorite source of home entertainment. Other than the *Amos 'n' Andy* program, however, few blacks appeared on television. Singer Nat "King" Cole broke many barriers when he was the first African American to host a network variety program, which the National Broadcasting Company (NBC) aired from 1956 until 1957. Although moderately popular, the program was unable to find a national sponsor, and Cole and NBC agreed to its cancellation after a year. Bill Cosby became the first African American to star in a dramatic role in a television drama when he was cast with Robert Culp in the *I Spy* series, which debuted in 1966 on NBC. Portraying a spy engaged in international espionage, Cosby was awarded three consecutive Emmys by the Academy of Television Arts and Sciences as outstanding lead actor in a dramatic series. Several NBC affiliates in the American South, however, refused to broadcast the show. After leaving the program in 1969, Cosby starred in a short-lived comedy program *The Bill Cosby Show*, which aired for two years, and also was involved in children's programming, including *The Electric Company* on the Public Broadcasting

System (PBS) and *Fat Albert and the Cosby Kids* on CBS. Cosby would later star in the groundbreaking television series *The Cosby Show*, which aired on NBC from 1984 through 1992. This program portrayed Cosby, as a physician, his lawyer wife, and their five children. Criticized by some as creating overidealized black characters (the family was clearly upper-middle-class, which some criticized as not reflecting the economic hardships faced by many if not most black families) and praised by others as breaking stereotypes by portraying intellectually and culturally sophisticated African Americans as the norm, *The Cosby Show* represented a breakthrough, remaining the number-one-ranked television program for five consecutive seasons. After the program aired, numerous other shows featuring African American actors appeared, featuring characters from all walks of life.

African Americans have also demonstrated their ability to set their own agenda using media through print, television, and movies. Magazines such as *Ebony* and *Jet* have provided positive role models for generations of African Americas. Television networks like Black Entertainment Television (BET), established in 1980, have also done much to provide strong visions for the African American community. Shows like *The Bernie Mac Show*, *The Steve Harvey Show*, and *The Jamie Fox Show* have provided outlets allowing for open subversion of those archetypes that initially stereotyped blacks.

Stephen T. Schroth
Jason A. Helfer
Jeffrey T. Wickman
Knox College

See also Advertising; Children's Programming: Cartoons; Diversity; Empowerment; Feminist Theory: Second Wave; Feminist Theory: Third Wave; Feminist Theory: Women-of-Color and Multiracial Perspectives; Film: Hollywood; Homophobia; Minority Rights; Misogyny; Patriarchy; Prejudice; Radio; Sexism; Social Construction of Gender; Stereotypes; Television; Tropes

Further Readings

Dunning, J. *On the Air: The Encyclopedia of Old-Time Radio.* New York: Oxford University Press, 1998.

MacDonald, J. F. *Blacks and White TV: African Americans in Television Since 1948,* 2nd ed. Chicago: Nelson-Hall, 1993.

Schroth, E. M. "*Camelot:* Contemporary Interpretation of Arthur in 'Sens' and 'Matiere.'" *The Journal of Popular Culture,* v.17/2 (1983).

Sears, D. O., J. Sidanius, and L. Bobo, eds. *Radicalized Politics: The Debate About Racism in America.* Chicago: University of Chicago Press, 2000.

Tucker, L. R. "Was the Revolution Televised? Professional Criticism About *The Cosby Show* and the Essentialization of Black Cultural Expression." *Journal of Broadcasting and Electronic Media,* 41 (1997).

Wilson, C. C., F. Gutierrez, and L. M. Chao. *Racism, Sexism, and the Media: The Rise of Class Communication in Multicultural America,* 3rd ed. Thousand Oaks, CA: Sage, 2003.

RADIO

Women have been a part of commercial radio since its inception in 1920. In radio's first four decades, the majority were either secretaries or entertainers, but even in that more traditional time in American history, a few women were station owners, sales managers, program directors, and occasionally news commentators or announcers. A major change occurred as a result of the women's movement of the 1960s and 1970s, and more women were able to enter areas of broadcasting previously closed to them; today it is not unusual to hear women as disc jockeys, news anchors, and talk show hosts, and a number of women are general managers or owners.

The first woman announcer was probably Sybil Herrold, the wife of early broadcast pioneer Charles "Doc" Herrold. As early as 1912, she hosted a weekly radio program on her husband's station at the Herrold College of Wireless in San Jose, California. When the first three commercial stations went on the air in 1920, most of their announcers, and all of their managers, were men, but at one station, 1XE (later called WGI) in Medford Hillside, Massachusetts, there was a female announcer, Eunice Randall. Randall not only announced some of the programs, but, as time passed, she read bedtime stories to the children, reported the news, and sometimes performed as a vocalist. In the early 1920s, when radio was still new, gender roles were not yet rigid; sometimes, it was a man who read the bedtime stories. A few other stations had a female announcer, and some had a female musical director, who arranged the programs. (Radio always needed live performers, since audiotape had not yet been invented.) Although some women were studio hostesses (the equivalent of a receptionist), just as many found work as vocalists. Some of the best-known opera singers, like Madame Louise Homer and Mary Garden, were heard on radio, as was African American blues singer Bessie Smith. The first woman to own a radio station was Marie Zimmerman, who began operating WIAE in Vinton, Iowa, in the summer of 1922; the next two women owners were preacher Aimee Semple McPherson (KFSG in Los Angeles in 1924) and theater owner Mary Costigan (KFXY in Flagstaff, Arizona, in 1925).

Now that women had the right to vote, members of the newly founded League of Women Voters sponsored informational radio programs, and female politicians took to the airwaves to campaign; some male journalists were surprised to discover that women did not automatically vote for someone just because she was female. Among the news makers heard on radio in the early 1920s were pioneering feminist Carrie Chapman Catt and Harvard astronomer Annie Jump Cannon, as well as a number of female movie stars, authors, and poets. Thanks to radio, the average person became more aware of women in nontraditional occupations, as women lawyers, business executives, and doctors also gave radio talks.

Despite early female radio station owners, program directors, and even at times news commentators or announcers, women did not enter the realm of disc jockeying until the 1960s and 1970s. Radio news has not progressed as far—21st-century radio stations usually use a team with a male anchor and a female coanchor to report the news. (Photos.com)

In 1926, commercial radio underwent a major change with the arrival of the first national network, the National Broadcasting Company (NBC), which was followed a year later by the Columbia Broadcasting System (CBS). Prior to this time, radio was noncommercial, and many performers and station personnel volunteered their time. Now, both networks chose a business model in which advertising paid for the entertainment, and advertising agencies began to select the talent. The sponsors became very powerful, and they were adamant about wanting only men (preferably white men with deep voices) to announce the programs, because it was believed that the male voice carried more authority. The women who had been announcers were taken off the air, unless they wanted to host a "women's show." (While many women of the 1920s were attending college or seeking careers, it was still a time when the societal expectation was for married women to be homemakers, and the women's shows were aimed at this audience.) The common wisdom was that women did not care much about politics or current events, so these programs focused on information that would be useful to the average housewife. One of the most popular hosts was Ida Bailey Allen, a home economist and author of many best-selling cookbooks. During her *National Radio Homemakers Club* on the CBS network, she not only offered helpful hints about cooking but also gave numerous testimonials about the products of her sponsors. Women's shows were very lucrative for advertisers, and the women who could do the most persuasive commercials were in great demand. Well into the 1950s, announcing a women's show was one of the few radio jobs for which women were encouraged to apply, and some became famous in this role, notably Mary Margaret McBride, whose on-air career began in the mid-1930s and continued for several decades. While her show had many sponsor testimonials and focused on traditional homemaking topics, McBride expanded the format of the program to include guest speakers: celebrities, political figures, and advocates for certain causes.

With the rise of the networks, sponsors now paid for the biggest names, which was good news for popular female vocalists such as Jessica Dragonette, Ireene Wicker, Kate Smith, and Ethel Waters. In the early 1920s, a few women had been program directors, but by the 1930s nearly all executives were men. During the Great Depression, the popular culture was very negative about women who worked, since it was believed that men, who had families to support, needed jobs more than women. There was also a common belief that men would not work for a woman boss. Yet despite these obstacles, a few women program directors with management experience achieved success, notably Bernice Judis of WNEW in New York and Corinne Jordan of KSTP in St. Paul, Minnesota. Several women also attained important positions with the networks. Bertha Brainard, whose radio career began in 1922, when she did theater reviews, became known for finding and guiding up-and-coming talent; she became NBC's first female executive when she was named national program manager in 1927. Another woman executive at NBC was Judith Waller, who was in charge of children's programming.

Despite the unofficial ban on women announcers, the 1930s saw several women news commentators. Print journalist Dorothy Thompson began broadcasting over the NBC radio network in the late 1930s, and former actress Kathryn Cravens became a commentator on CBS beginning in the mid-1930s. Cravens was probably the first person to produce "human interest" features, news stories meant both to inform and to create an emotional response from the audience. Despite the myth that a woman's voice did not sound credible when announcing news, both women earned favorable reviews and had large audiences. This did not stop male journalists from referring to female news reporters as "news hens," perhaps the precursor to calling females "chicks" in the 1960s.

The 1930s also saw the first First Lady have her own radio show: Eleanor Roosevelt began issuing a weekly program of commentary on current events in 1934. She was not the first to broadcast, however. President Herbert Hoover's wife, Louise, was a frequent guest speaker beginning in 1929. While today we take for granted the idea of a First Lady on radio or television, in the 1930s it was something new, and not everyone was comfortable with the idea of a First Lady having such a public role.

There were many famous women comedians during radio's Golden Age; some were part of a husband-and-wife team, such as Goodman Ace and his wife, Jane, and George Burns and Gracie Allen. Unfortunately, the roles the women played were often stereotypical, such as the Dumb Dora, a woman who is always getting into trouble and needing to be rescued. Another gendered role that welcomed women was as host of a children's program, and one of the best was Nila Mack's *Let's Pretend*, which won several awards. On the local level, some women, such as Boston's Louise Morgan, interviewed celebrities and gave listeners fashion and shopping tips; on the national level, gossip columnist turned radio host Hedda Hopper had a successful CBS program beginning in 1939 that continued through the 1940s.

During World War II, jobs previously closed to women, such as studio engineer or station manager, briefly opened up, but once the war was over, women were expected (and in some cases, ordered) to give their jobs to returning servicemen. Most did, and radio went back to being a predominantly male domain, with women relegated to women's shows or clerical work. As radio moved away from live performances in the 1950s and began playing records, even the jobs women once held as singers and comedians disappeared. Society remained very traditional throughout the 1950s, with women once again told by clergy, politicians, and magazines that their primary role should be as homemakers.

However, change was on the horizon. The 1960s saw the beginnings of second wave feminism, as the National Organization for Women was founded and some women began to speak out about what came to be called "sexism." Several years after the Civil Rights Act of 1964 passed, the Federal Communications Commission (FCC) decided to examine whether broadcasters were engaging in discriminatory practices in hiring and promotion. The FCC noted how few women and minorities were employed in jobs other than the stereotypical ones and concluded that broadcasters needed to promote diversity at their stations. By 1970, Equal Employment Opportunity (EEO) rules were in place, and suddenly it was mandatory for radio stations to seek out women for positions other than receptionist or women's show host. Gradually, more women were hired as announcers (although many stations hid them on the overnight shift at first), and a few were trained for positions in sales.

Music was also changing. Top 40 was the dominant format of the 1950s and 1960s, but the AM stations that played it were resistant to having women disc jockeys. The best a woman could hope for was to be music director, which meant she helped the program director select the music the station would air. When men were music director, they were often promoted to program director, but this rarely happened for women. Meanwhile, there were new opportunities on the FM band, which was gaining many new fans. A new format, album rock, was becoming popular with college-age listeners. Some stations began to play music that Top 40 would not play—antiwar songs, songs with drug-oriented lyrics, and long versions. Most FM rock stations had at least one "chick d.j." on the air. These women were expected to sound sexy, and many, like Alison Steele, "The Nightbird" at WNEW-FM in New York, held the late night shift.

Throughout the 1970s, a growing number of stations followed EEO guidelines and hired women as announcers or account executives. However, a few stereotypical jobs remained. Women seldom were allowed to host the station's top program, the morning show. They were hired mainly as sidekicks, and their role was to laugh at the jokes of the male announcer. However, some change occurred in the area of news. More women were working as reporters and news anchors, especially on National Public Radio (NPR), where women reporters like Linda Wertheimer, Susan Stamberg, and Nina Totenberg proved that women could cover the news as well as men; Stamberg was even the anchor of a program, *All Things Considered*, at a time when few women were news anchors. There were also a growing number of women in sales, some of whom became sales managers or general managers. An area where the lack of women persisted was sportscasting. Over the years, a few women, such as tennis star Alice Marble in the early 1940s, had broadcast women's sports, but men's sports remained off limits. However, in the early 1980s, this too began to change, and female voices such as that of Nanci Donnellan, the "Fabulous Sports Babe," were heard. By the early 1990s, women such as Suzyn Waldman were announcing major league sports or doing color commentary.

Today, even though the EEO rules were weakened in the 1990s, it is no longer unusual to find a woman reporting the news; the majority of news and news/talk stations have women reporters, and many stations have women anchors. While it remains customary for stations to have a team with a male anchor and a female coanchor, sometimes NPR uses an all-female team, when Michele Norris coanchors with Melissa Block. There are more women working in sales, and a growing number have risen to positions as managers. Although the heads of most major radio corporations remain male, a few women do own stations, notably Cathy Hughes, an African American entrepreneur whose company, Radio One, currently operates more than 50 stations throughout the United States. One other area where there were few women until fairly recently was talk radio, where mostly all of the hosts were male. In the 2000s, however, there are some women doing political talk—Laura Ingraham on the right, Stephanie Miller on the left—and Dr. Laura Schlessinger continues to do a sometimes controversial but very popular advice program.

While conditions for women in radio have improved greatly, media consolidation during the 1990s and early 2000s has resulted in fewer jobs at fewer stations. Some studies suggest that women managers still do not receive the same pay a male managers do, and sexism still persists, especially as a result of the rise of "shock jocks," disc jockeys (usually male) whose humor is crude and who regularly use crude stereotypes of women in their routines. As much progress as women have made, the fact remains that there is still an audience that does not object to women being insulted.

Donna L. Halper
Lesley University

See also Electronic Media and Social Inequality; Federal Communications Commission; Feminism; Mass Media; Media Consolidation; Media Convergence; Network News Anchor Desk; Newsrooms; Radio: Pirate; Talk Shows; Television

Further Readings

Butsch, Richard. "Crystal Sets and Scarf-Pin Radios: Gender, Technology, and the Construction of American Radio Listening in the 1920s." *Media, Culture and Society*, v.20/4 (October 1998).

Douglas, Susan J. *Listening In: Radio and the American Imagination*. Minneapolis: University of Minnesota Press, 1999.

Halper, Donna L. *Invisible Stars: A Social History of Women in American Broadcasting*. Stoneham, MA: M. E. Sharpe, 2001.

Hilmes, Michele. *Only Connect: A Cultural History of Broadcasting in the United States*, 2nd ed. Belmont, CA: Wadsworth\Thomson Learning, 2007.

Smulyan, Susan. "Radio Advertising to Women in Twenties America: 'A Latchkey to Every Home.'"

Historical Journal of Film, Radio and Television, v.13/3 (August 1993).

RADIO: PIRATE

Pirate radio stations are stations that defy the regulations of the Federal Communications Commission (FCC) and exist without a license to broadcast directly to the public. These stations, run by predominantly male hobbyists, provide alternatives to licensed stations, which in turn creates competition. Also known as free, bootleg, or microradio, pirate radio broadcasts on long-wave, medium-wave, and short-wave frequencies, as well as television and satellite bands. Today many pirate radio stations have turned to the Internet to avoid federal lawsuits. Pirate radio stations air everything from copyrighted music to sports to community-focused news and political views. Because of the illegal nature of pirate radio, some stations are short-lived, while others tend to move from place to place, making it difficult to estimate the number of existing pirate stations.

Pirate radio began with the start of wired communication and early radio-telephone experiments. At that time, there were no regulations limiting people from going on the air without a license. By the late 1920s, the Federal Radio Commission (the FCC's precursor) started to impose regulations and required licenses. These early stations were forced to close out after passage of the Communications Act of 1934. Nevertheless, pirate radio stations still managed to broadcast, sometimes from offshore ships equipped with powerful transmitters. Others were created by hobbyists who used low radio frequencies. When pirate radio operators were caught, they were usually fined and their equipment was confiscated.

The first true pirate station to hit U.S. airwaves was WUMS (the call sign stood for "We're Unknown Mysterious Station" or "We're Unlicensed Marine Station"), operated by David Thomas between 1924 and 1948 on the Ohio River banks. Although Thomas was fined $8,000 and sentenced to four years in prison, he managed to outsmart the FCC in 1938 and 1948 by building a secret transmitter into a table. Thomas tried to build another transmitter in 1983 to bring WUMS back on the air, but he died of cancer that year.

Pirate radio is different from clandestine, or guerrilla, stations because the majority of pirate stations are nonpolitical. Clandestine radio stations are more likely to support violent and radical change in their countries. Political pirates that border on the clandestine do not promote violent change, and they lack the support of powerful organizations that clandestine stations enjoy. Prominent political pirates include Berkeley Liberation Radio, Steal This Radio, and Black Liberation Radio.

An important phase in the history of pirate radio saw offshore pirates, which existed in Europe from the late 1950s to the early 1970s. These pirates offered European youth American-style Top 40 playlists, pop music, radio personalities, and news. Many of these stations were supported by American entrepreneurs and advertisers.

In 1958, Radio Mercur began its transmission into Copenhagen from a ship anchored in international waters. Radio Nord was a pirate station that broadcast from off the Swedish coast. In England, pirate stations threatened the monopoly of the British Broadcasting Corporation (BBC) by offering listeners American popular music, including rock and roll as well as ethnic music. Radio Caroline broadcast in England in 1964 and was known as England's premier rock station because it introduced to British youth new rock songs by The Beatles, The Who, and The Rolling Stones.

In 1967, the British government passed the Marine Broadcasting Offenses Act, which stipulated that British nationals who supported or aided offshore broadcasters would be punished by imprisonment and fines. Although this act destroyed most offshore broadcasting in Britain, it failed to destroy Radio Caroline, which existed until 1980, when its ship sank in bad weather. With the financial support of American advertisers, however, the station returned in 1983 with a larger ship and a stronger transmission signal. In the early 1990s, high costs forced the station off the air. Today, Radio Caroline can still be heard through a number of European satellites.

The United States, unlike Europe, did not see much offshore pirate radio. Pirates mainly sprang from teenage radio enthusiasts' bedrooms, basements, or attics. During the 1960s, U.S. pirate radio expanded on AM frequencies, and by the 1970s pirate radio was considered a full-time hobby, with a large audience dubbed "pirate radio listeners." In the late 1970s, pirate radio became "free radio," a movement that encompassed the free speech movement, hobby radio writing and production, and progressive music. Pirate radio continued to expand on the AM frequencies during the 1980s, with stations such as WFAT, Pirate Radio New England, and Free Radio 1615.

One of the prominent modern pirates is Radio Mutiny, a pirate station launched in the 1990s that was famous for its open resistance to regulations passed by the FCC and the National Association of Broadcasters. Radio Mutiny was known to transmit from public places such as the Liberty Bell and became famous for having a female announcer broadcast in the nude from the group's studio. Despite the group's flagrant resistance, the FCC took a long time to raid their studio, fearing negative coverage from the local media. When the FCC finally did raid the station, it did so during the night to avoid controversy.

Pirate radio continues to exist today, and thanks to the Internet, many broadcasters are now streaming their stations online. Websites such as pirate radio1250.com and blackcatsystems.com serve listeners by offering links to pirate Websites, broadcast listings, and program guides.

Nahed Eltantawy
High Point University

See also Blogs and Blogging; Culture Jamming; Electronic Media and Social Inequality; Federal Communications Commission; Mass Media; Media Consolidation; Media Convergence; Network News Anchor Desk; New Media; Newsrooms; Radio; Talk Shows; Television; YouTube

Further Readings

Adams, Michael H. and Steven Phipps. "Low-Power Radio/Microradio, Small Community Radio Stations." In *Encyclopedia of Radio*, Christopher Sterling, ed. New York: Fitzroy Dearborn, 2004.

Kemppainen, Pentti. "Pirates and the New Public Service Radio Paradigm." *The Radio Journal: International Studies in Broadcast and Audio Media*, v.7/2 (2009).

Robinson, K. G. "History of Pirate Radio." Associated Content, 2009. http://www.associatedcontent.com/article/1997412/history_of_pirate_radio.html (Accessed February 2011).

White, Thomas H. "United States: Early Radio History." http://earlyradiohistory.us/index.html (Accessed October 2011).

Yoder, Andrew. *Pirate Radio Stations: Tuning In to Underground Broadcasts in the Air and Online*. New York: McGraw-Hill, 2001.

RADWAY, JANICE

Janice Radway (1949–) is an American scholar in the fields of literature, American studies, and cultural studies. She has held teaching positions at the University of Pennsylvania, Duke University, and Northwestern University, where she is the Walter Dill Scott Professor of Communication Studies. Radway has written and coedited numerous publications but is best known for her 1984 book *Reading the Romance: Women, Patriarchy and Popular Literature*, a study of romance novels and their female readers in the United States. The book marked a significant intervention into reception studies and feminist cultural studies, as Radway studied not only the institutional and ideological structure of the romance novel but also, particularly, the ways in which a community of women turned to the act of reading romance fiction as a means of temporary escape from their assumed feminine roles. Radway's investigation into women's consumption of mass media has ultimately established her as a key contributor in the areas of feminist media criticism, feminist theory and practice, and cultural studies.

Reading the Romance has proven to be influential across multiple disciplines. In it, Radway presents her research on a community of women romance readers in a Midwestern town (for which she uses the fictional name Smithton), drawing on material she obtained through questionnaires, observations, and interviews with groups and individuals. The first chapter of her book provides an overview of the economic and publishing changes that contributed to the rise of the romance novel, and the final chapters analyze readers' characterizations of "ideal" and "failed" romance novels. Whereas romance novels are typically assumed to uphold patriarchal conventions, Radway postulates that the women's desire for romance-based narratives featuring a powerful heroine and a sensitive male hero can be conceived as women playing out their desire to reform failed heterosexual, monogamous marriages that did not satisfy their emotional needs.

The most notable aspects of the book are the chapters in which Radway analyzes the romance readers and their motivations for the voracious consumption of what is seen as predictably plotted, cheap, mass-produced fiction. Radway found that what was most significant about romance novels for the Smithton women—most of whom were married mothers—was not the quality or style of the content but rather the *act* of reading itself. For these women, reading books of this genre was a means by which they could escape into fantasy worlds of high drama and romance, providing a temporary relief from the constant physical and emotional demands of wife and mother. Radway argued that this act of reading could be construed as a form of resistance, a means for women to deny, if only temporarily, the patriarchal demand that they serve others before themselves. Her findings suggested that the act of reading the romance could best be viewed as a "declaration of independence," whereby women are able to free themselves momentarily from their typical routines in order to pursue their own individual pleasures. It is for these observations regarding gender and media consumption that Radway is best known.

Radway's approach to *Reading the Romance* and its findings helped to situate her as a pivotal voice in the areas of reception studies, feminist media studies, and cultural studies. Radway's emphasis on readers and reading experiences alludes to the encoding/decoding model, a cornerstone of the cultural studies approach, which emphasizes analysis not only of media content but also of its production and audience. Given Radway's emphasis on media consumption, she is often grouped alongside prominent reception theory scholars, many of whom are interested in the ways in which audiences construe meanings from media texts that may differ from their original encodings. What distinguishes Radway from other reception theorists is her additional emphasis on the motivations behind and processes of media consumption, as well as her focus on the romance novel, a women's medium traditionally thought to be one of the most degraded, mindless, and dismissible forms of mass culture. In addition, Radway has written reflectively on the process and value of media ethnography from a feminist perspective. She has advocated for ethnographers to be self-reflective about their own subject positions and how this may affect their interpretation of data and findings. Finally, Radway's work has helped to bridge academic analysis to actual practices of everyday people.

Much of Radway's subsequent research has turned more generally to the history and development of books and American literary culture. Her 1997 work *A Feeling for Books* examines the development of the Book-of-the-Month Club and the construction of "middlebrow" literary culture. Although she continues to be prolific in her examinations of literary history, it is Radway's investigation of the complex relationship between women and romance novels that has made an indelible impression in the landscape of gender and media studies.

Karen C. Pitcher

Eckerd College

See also Audiences: Reception and Injection Models; Encoding and Decoding; Feminism; Hall, Stuart; Media Ethnography; Patriarchy; Polysemic Text; Reception Theory; Romance Novels

Further Readings

Radway, Janice A. *A Feeling for Books: The Book-of-the-Month Club, Literary Taste and Middle Class Desire.* Chapel Hill: University of North Carolina Press, 1997.

Radway, Janice A. "Identifying Ideological Seams: Mass Culture, Analytical Method, and Political Practice." *Communication*, v.9 (1986).

Radway, Janice A. *Reading the Romance: Women, Patriarchy and Popular Literature*, 2nd ed. Chapel Hill: University of North Carolina Press, 1992.

REALITY-BASED TELEVISION: *AMERICA'S NEXT TOP MODEL*

America's Next Top Model (ANTM) is a fashion-themed, one-hour reality-based television program in which women compete in various modeling challenges for the chance to earn a contract with a major modeling agency, become a spokesperson for a well-known cosmetics company (CoverGirl), and be featured in a fashion photo spread in a national or international magazine. The program was created by former runway and Victoria's Secret model Tyra Banks, and it premiered on the United Paramount Network (UPN) on May 20, 2003. On September 20, 2006, ANTM began airing on the CW Network, a joint venture between Warner Bros. Entertainment and CBS Corporation. Since 2003, ANTM has had 15 cycles (or seasons), with each cycle lasting between 9 and 13 weeks. The program airs two cycles per year, usually in September and March. Like most reality programs, ANTM's seasons tend to be shorter than non-reality-based programs, which typically have seasons ranging between 20 and 24 episodes. Show participants are required to be 5 feet, 7 inches in height or taller, and between the ages of 18 and 27. The program tried a new approach in cycle 13, accepting only women shorter than 5 feet, 7 inches.

The format for ANTM has remained constant since the show began. The first episode highlights the audition process and features between 20 and 24 young women who compete with one another to win one of 14 coveted spots to be on the show. Once the participants are chosen, they move into a luxurious house or apartment together, usually in New York or Los Angeles. Each episode, which covers approximately one week of real time, features a modeling challenge and a photo shoot. Challenges are associated with a theme in the world of modeling, such as appearing in a runway show, learning how to pose, perfecting the runway walk, selling a commercial product, or visiting prospective employers in "go sees" (a "go see" is a visit to a designer who is looking to hire a model for his or her next fashion show). Models are critiqued on their portfolio pictures, how they look in and display clothes, and how they walk. Challenge winners usually receive a material prize, such as diamond jewelry, a night in a luxury hotel suite, or a designer gown. The second half of the show consists of a photo shoot, which usually involves a theme. Some past themes have included posing with animals (such as snakes, sheep, and horses), incorporating nature into a pose (standing next to a tree with leaves painted on the body), and beauty shots (close-up photos focusing on the face, usually used in cosmetics ads). At the end of each episode, all of the contestants appear before a panel of judges who critique each contestant's photo and comment on how well she performed in the photo shoot and other exercises. Tyra calls contestants individually, hands the models their photos, and tells each whether she is "still in the running to become America's next top model." The first person called is also the one voted best photo of the week. This woman has her photo displayed in the house for one week as digital art. One contestant is eliminated at the end of each episode.

ANTM has had a series of high-profile judges, well known in the fashion world. There are usually three permanent judges, including Tyra, and one guest judge each week. Among the permanent judges have been fashion photographer Nigel Barker (since cycle 2) and *Vogue* editor André Leon Talley (since cycle 14). Past judges have included former supermodel Janice Dickinson (cycles 1–4), former fashion editor for *Marie Claire* magazine Beau Quillian (cycle 1), fashion designer Kimora Lee Simmons (cycle 1), former *Jane* magazine editor Eric Nicholson (cycle 2), fashion stylist Nolé Marin (cycles 3–4), 1960s icon Twiggy (Lesley Hornby, cycles 5–9), runway coach J. Alexander (cycles 5–13), and former supermodel Paulina Porizkova (cycles 10–12).

The program has tackled issues about unhealthy body image, eating disorders, race and racism, sexuality, and gender. *ANTM* has featured models categorized as plus-size (those who typically wear sizes 8–12) and crowned a plus-size model, Whitney Thompson, in cycle 10. The show has also tackled issues of sexuality and gender and has had several lesbian and bisexual participants, who openly discuss their sexuality as it relates to the modeling world. The program was praised by the Gay and Lesbian Alliance Against Defamation (GLAAD), a lesbian, gay, bisexual, transsexual/transgender (LGBT) media advocacy group, and was heavily covered in the popular press during cycle 11, when the show featured a transgendered contestant. Isis King (born Darrell Walls) identified herself as a woman born physically male and used the show as a platform to discuss issues surrounding the transgender community. The program made headlines in cycle 15 when the judges let a contestant go for being too thin and sending what the producers said was the wrong message to young girls watching the show.

Although some in the press have praised *ANTM* for being passionate about deconstructing the way society defines beauty, the program has also received its share of criticism. Some feminist groups have accused the program of objectifying contestants by making them wear sexually revealing clothes or string bikinis during photo shoots. Others in the popular press have critiqued the judges for preaching female empowerment in one episode and humiliating contestants during the panel segment in another episode. Several qualitative studies in the academic press have analyzed race in *ANTM*, and although the show's host and creator is African American, the program has been accused of reifying racial difference by eroticizing some nonwhite contestants. Despite these criticisms, the show has an international fan base and continues to be one of the most highly rated shows on the CW Network.

ANTM is shown in 170 media markets worldwide and has been franchised in more than 40 countries, including Australia, Holland, Greece, Israel, and Vietnam. The show has earned its own *E! True Hollywood Story* episode, has garnered a onetime spin-off called *Modelville* (in which former *ANTM* contestants competed for the chance to be a national spokesperson for Carol's Daughter, a cosmetic and skin care line), and has sold cable rights to Oxygen Network, which created a series called *Top Model Obsessed*, a program that features an interactive fan-based Website along with *ANTM* marathons and behind-the-scenes vignettes of models and judges.

Lisa Pecot-Hebert
DePaul University

See also Audiences: Producers of New Media; Beauty and Body Image: Beauty Myths; Beauty and Body Image: Eating Disorders; Cultivation Theory; Feminist Theory: Women-of-Color and Multiracial Perspectives; Gender and Femininity: Single/Independent Girl; Reality-Based Television: Makeover Shows; Reality-Based Television: Wedding Shows; Televisuality; Women's Magazines: Fashion

Further Readings

Brennan, Steve. "Russians Love 'Model' Series." *Hollywood Reporter International Edition*, v.383/31 (2004).

Everett, Christa. "Tyra Banks 'Truly Sorry' for *America's Next Top Model* Promo Featuring Shockingly Thin Model." http://www.nydailynews.com/entertainment/tv/2010/08/16/2010-08-16_tyra_banks_truly_sorry_for_americas_next_top_model_promo_featuring_shockingly_th.html#ixzz13t6GBlxt (Accessed February 2011).

Hasinoff, Amy. "Fashioning Race for the Free Market on *America's Next Top Model*." *Critical Studies in Media Communication*, v.25/3 (2008).

Keller, Jessalynn. "Fiercely Real? Tyra Banks' Body Politics and Post-Feminist Branding." http://flowtv.org/2010/08/fiercely-real-tyra-banks (Accessed February 2011).

Marikar, Sheila. "America's Next Transgender Top Model?" http://abcnews.go.com/Entertainment/story?id=5629177 (Accessed February 2011).

Pozner, Jennifer. "Top Model's Beautiful Corpses: The Nexus of Reality TV Misogyny and Ad Industry Ideology." http://www.wimnonline.org/WIMNsVoicesBlog/?p=462 (Accessed February 2011).

Stack, Tim. "America's Next Top Mogul." *Entertainment Weekly*, v.979 (2008).

"Tyra's Next Top Model Struts Into Africa" *New African*, v.481 (2009).

REALITY-BASED TELEVISION: MAKEOVER SHOWS

Reality-based television (often called simply "reality television") has become one of the most influential genres in television programming. The popularity of the genre is reflected in the ratings of these shows and in the great advertising revenues they generate. As evidence of the popularity of reality television, the Website *Reality TV World* shows a list of more than 400 shows in this category produced in the United States. The success of reality television cannot be limited to its popularity among audiences; the genre provides a cheap production alternative to dramas. That is precisely why many scholars have abandoned the question of how factual reality television is. Instead, in recent years it has become clear that reality television shows are often scripted; thus, many argue the genre should be seen simply as a mode of production. Others argue that the key to reality television resides in the pleasure it brings to audiences. The viewers of the genre get their pleasure from the assumption that the characters are real people, just like them, which allows viewers to live vicariously through the characters.

The criticism from media scholars and many others has not stopped the rapid growth of the genre; in fact, the popularity of the genre has resulted in the formation of several subcategories within the format and a network. Some of the categories that make the genre are game, life, docu-soap, dating, drama, talk, hidden camera, law enforcement, and makeover shows. *The Swan* (FOX, 2004), *Queer Eye for the Straight Guy* (Bravo, 2003–07), and *What Not to Wear* (TLC, 2003–10) are examples of reality makeover shows.

Queer Eye for the Straight Guy aired between 2003 and 2007. The program made over mostly straight men in order to increase their appeal to their female partners. The recipient of the makeover sold access to his lifestyle and was taught new patterns of consumption to make him more desirable. The program incorporated product placements and countless endorsements that would fit into the new lifestyle of the participant.

Extreme Makeover was aired by the American Broadcasting Company (ABC) between 2002 and 2007. In this program, individuals, mostly women, volunteered to receive an extensive makeover that included plastic surgery, exercise for body toning and weight reduction, hair styling, and wardrobe changes. At the end of each episode the participants would reveal their new look to family and friends.

The Swan aired in 2004, on FOX. The concept of the show was similar to that of *Extreme Makeover*. This program, however, made reference to the story of the ugly duckling and offered several forms of surgery and access to a staff of professionals who included a coach, a therapist, a trainer, cosmetic surgeons, and a dentist. The show transformed "ugly" women during a period of three months and would conclude with a big reveal of the transformation.

The concept for *What Not to Wear* originated in the United Kingdom and has been adapted for audiences in several countries. In the United States its adaptation aired on The Learning Channel (TLC) starting in 2003. The show's participants are chosen for their bad fashion sense. They are flown to New York City, where they "learn" the secrets of dress for their body type and get a budget to buy new clothing. The show ends with a big event during which the participant appears in the new clothing and hairstyle before friends and family members. Although early episodes featured both men and women, eventually most episodes featured women.

Other makeover shows include *How Do I Look?* which aired in 2004 on the Style Network; *How to Look Good Naked*, another British showed adapted for U.S. audiences, which aired in 2008 on Lifetime Television; and *Ambush Makeover*, which aired on the Style Network from 2004 to 2005.

Makeover reality television shows recruit people who are willing to work for nothing or very little in the hope of receiving free clothing, accessories, and in some cases plastic surgery. Central to the format is the idea that participants in this genre will do and submit themselves to almost anything, including exposing their lives and sacrificing their privacy, for cash, services, and prizes. The main goal of makeover shows, which are designed to encourage the desire to attain an ideal of physical beauty through the consumption of goods, is to sell products and services. It follows that the main premise behind makeover shows is that consumption is the route to self-improvement. These shows effect superficial physical changes in their participants and ignore the reasons those participants may feel a need to alter their appearance. Moreover, the participants are presented through individual stories that inspire empathy, becoming case examples for goods and services the target of the makeover could not afford.

Critics of makeover shows argue that the shows link superficial self-improvement with happiness. These scholars state that makeover shows advance the notion that the route to success—happier and better life—is in changing the way one looks, even to the extent of making radical changes. Second, critics explain that many shows contribute to the normalization of plastic surgery. Shows like *Extreme Makeover* and *The Swan* ignore or diminish the risks of plastic surgery and present it as desirable. Third, the shows present a limited understanding of beauty, eliminate diversity, and reinforce stereotypes. Finally, makeover shows depict consumption as a desirable "skill." Many of the shows create needs by teaching participants to learn how to select brands and use goods and services. Makeover shows suggest that participants can achieve success and move up the social ladder through consumerism and consumption.

Yarma Velázquez Vargas
California State University, Northridge

See also Advertising; Audiences: Producers of New Media; Beauty and Body Image: Beauty Myths; Beauty and Body Image: Eating Disorders; Cultivation Theory; Gender and Femininity: Single/Independent Girl; Gender and Masculinity: Metrosexual Male; Men's Magazines: Lifestyle and Health; Reality-Based Television: *America's Next Top Model*; Reality-Based Television: Wedding Shows; Social Construction of Gender; Women's Magazines: Fashion

Further Readings

Andrejevic, Mark. *Reality TV: The Work of Being Watched*. Lanham, MD: Rowman & Littlefield, 2004.
Deery, June. "Trading Faces: The Makeover Show as Prime-Time Informertial." *Feminist Media Studies*, v.4/2 (2004).
Lancioni, Judith. "Fix Me Up." In *Essays on Television Dating and Makeover Shows*. Jefferson, NC: McFarland, 2010.

REALITY-BASED TELEVISION: WEDDING SHOWS

The 2009 creation and debut of Wedding Central, a channel devoted entirely to wedding-related programming, exemplifies the popularity of reality television shows such as *Bridezillas*, *Bridalplasty*, *Say Yes to the Dress*, *Platinum Weddings*, and *My Fair Wedding With David Tutera*. Nearly every one of these programs focuses on the woman, her interests, and her needs, while almost dismissing the man entirely from any conversations about the impending marriage. This pattern conforms to the stereotypical ideology that a wedding is more about the bride's wishes than the groom's (few, if any of these programs showcase same-sex marriages). These shows, however popular, reinforce very traditional stereotypes about gender, romance, and weddings.

Bridezillas and *Bridalplasty* examine some of the most troubling gender stereotypes of brides. *Bridezillas*, as the name implies, highlights demanding, self-centered, and at times cruel brides-to-be. In one episode, a child goes missing and the bride begins to cry. When asked if she is worried about the missing boy, the bride says she is crying because the child took the attention from her on her special day. This example, like so many others on *Bridezillas*, plays on the show's focus on extreme and atypical emotions; most women would show compassion for a missing child, regardless of circumstances. *Bridezillas* capitalizes on the behavior of a particular type of stereotypical bride, the selfish bride who believes that the wedding is a celebration of her alone, rather than a celebration of the love between partners.

The show *Bridalplasty* also conveys messages about stereotypical brides, in this case related specifically to their physical appearance. *Bridalplasty* follows a group of brides-to-be living in the same house who compete against one another. In each episode, one girl loses her place in the house. The winner receives as much plastic surgery as she desires, so she can look perfect for her wedding day.

The behavior of the women on the reality show *Bridezillas* reinforces the image of the selfish bride who believes that her upcoming wedding is "her day" rather than a celebration of the love between her and her future husband. The popularity of wedding-related programming led to the debut of the channel Wedding Central. (Photos.com)

When the popular tabloid *Life and Style* ran a story on the show, one contestant, Alexandra, commented that she wanted to win so she could have a tummy tuck, because "Women need to look good for their man." This show perpetuates the stereotype that women care more about their physical appearance than more important issues and that men care more about their partner's appearance than her character or intelligence.

Reality-based wedding shows such as *Say Yes to the Dress* and *Platinum Weddings* also imply that brides-to-be are more concerned about their attire, flowers, meals, jewelry, and wedding favors than they are about their partner. *Say Yes to the Dress*'s slogan, "More Drama, More Weddings, More Dresses," implies that weddings are not meant to

be peaceful times of celebration but occasions during which women resort to primal survival strategies to obtain the dream wedding gown. Episodes of this show include women who typically use phrases like "I want to look like a perfect princess" and "This is my special day." These brides refuse to view or acknowledge the wedding as a shared celebration in which both the bride and groom star. *Say Yes to the Dress* also emphasizes the gender stereotype that brides care little (if at all) about what a wedding costs while grooms are concerned about cost, in this case the cost of the dress. In the episode "Time to Cut the Cord," future bride Sarah says that her fiancé thinks only about how much things cost, which the wedding dress consultant says "kills the mood and kills the sale." Another bride-to-be, Diana, shops for dresses with her mother. When the salesperson asks Diana's mother how much she would be willing to spend on her daughter's gown, the woman answers, "I can't put a price on my daughter." This example reinforces the notion that women in general (not just future brides) do not worry about costs associated with a wedding; instead, beauty remains their top priority. In addition, the mother's equation of the cost of a dress with care for her daughter underscores the program's main message: that material acquisition supports or leads to intangible goods such as love and happiness.

The future brides and grooms starring in episodes of *Platinum Weddings* rarely concern themselves with building or following a budget; furthermore, the show perpetuates gender stereotypes about romance and weddings. In the episode "Katherine and Eddy," Katherine regales viewers with the tale of her perfect courtship with and proposal from Eddy, followed by their extravagant wedding. This program emphasizes the gender stereotype that a wedding day should be designed entirely around the bride, with little if any concern for the groom's wishes. Although Eddy appears in many segments of the episode, the rhetoric of the show implies that Katherine's ideas and feelings are much more important than Eddy's. For instance, the wedding cake is referred to as "Katherine's Cake," and caterers plan the $137,000 meal around her tastes, which include seafood and the color pink; in another example, the desserts for a bridal tea party are embellished with 24-karat gold flakes.

The popular show *My Fair Wedding With David Tutera* suggests that, while women can be overly concerned with wedding preparations, grooms feel little anxiety about their forthcoming nuptials and often choose to remain uninvolved in the planning of the wedding. In the episode "Zen Bride," Jessica Munger tells David Tutera that planning the wedding has been very stressful and that her future husband, Namid Nolan, has been of little help with the preparations. Like "Katherine and Eddy" of *Platinum Weddings*, the "Zen Bride" features rhetoric that perpetuates the gender stereotype of women valuing weddings as opportunities to be the center of attention, while the groom remains in the shadows. Munger repeatedly uses the phrase "my wedding." In one instance, when Tutera speaks with both Munger and Nolan, he turns to Munger and suggests that they begin discussing wedding plans while he simply dismisses Nolan, referring to him as a "sweet guy" for showing interest in the wedding planning. Tutera also supports gender stereotypes by excusing the groom and asking only for the bride-to-be's input on decisions related to the wedding.

Critics often attack reality-based television programs for not portraying reality. Reality-based programming such as *Bridezillas*, *Bridalplasty*, *Say Yes to the Dress*, *Platinum Weddings*, and *My Fair Wedding With David Tutera* all capture and reinforce real gender stereotypes concerning wedding planning. These programs often depict women as selfish and obsessed with physical appearance and men as uninterested, uninvolved, and unimportant. In real life, however, many people work together with their partners to create a marriage celebration reflecting both people's interests and passions. By contrast, most reality-based wedding programs distort this concept and instead showcase gender stereotypes in relation to wedding planning.

Karley Adney
Butler University

See also Advertising; Audiences: Producers of New Media; Beauty and Body Image: Beauty Myths; Beauty and Body Image: Eating Disorders; Cyberdating; Film: Hollywood; Media Rhetoric; Reality-Based Television: *America's Next Top Model*; Reality-Based Television: Makeover Shows; Sexism; Social Construction of Gender; Stereotypes; Toys and Games: Gender Socialization; Tropes; Women's Magazines: Fashion; Women's Magazines: Lifestyle and Health

Further Readings

Andrejevic, Mark. *Reality TV: The Work of Being Watched.* Lanham, MD: Rowman & Littlefield, 2004.

Dubrofsky, Rachel. "Therapeutics of the Self." *Television and New Media*, v.8/4 (2007).

Engstrom, Erika and Beth Semic. "Portrayal of Religion in Reality TV Programming: Hegemony and the Contemporary American Wedding." *Journal of Media and Religion*, v.2/3 (2003).

"Falling to Pieces." *Bridalplasty*. The Entertainment Channel. December 5, 2010.

Holmes, Su and Deborah Jermyn. *Understanding Reality Television*. New York: Routledge, 2004.

"Katherine and Eddy." *Platinum Weddings*. Women's Entertainment Channel. September 12, 2010.

"Sara and Natalie." *Bridezillas*. Women's Entertainment Channel. August 13, 2010.

"Shandra and Sara." *Bridezillas*. Women's Entertainment Channel. August 13, 2010.

"Time to Cut the Cord." *Say Yes to the Dress*. The Learning Channel. August 14, 2010.

"Why We Want Plastic Surgery for Our Wedding." *Life and Style* (November 22, 2010).

"Zen Bride." *My Fair Wedding With David Tutera*. Women's Entertainment Channel. August 14, 2010.

RECEPTION THEORY

Reception theory focuses on the relationship between media and receiver and considers how individual audiences use and make meaning of texts, which can be in the form of television, film, books, or other types of popular culture. The key question for reception studies is whether the audiences are seen as active or passive in their media consumption. The starting point for reception theory is that the ways the spectator defines herself or himself as a person and as a member of a larger society affect the ways she or he will view the media material. Reception theory emphasizes the study of audiences as sets of people with unique, though often shared, experiences who are in charge of their own lives. It looks at the ways individuals receive and interpret a text and how their specific circumstances (gender, class, age, ethnicity, and so forth) affect their reading. Audiences for particular genres often comprise "interpretative communities," which share many of the same experiences, forms of discourse, and frameworks for making sense of media. Studies of audience reception investigate how mass media work on audiences' perceptions of themselves and of the world outside; how they reconcile, accept, or resist the conflicting media messages; and how they identify with or distance themselves from multiple forms of representation.

The encoding/decoding model promulgated by British cultural studies theorist Stuart Hall suggests three ideological positions of audience members situated in a society in which the mass media serve the status quo. The model describes three hypothetical interpretation codes for audiences of the text: dominant, negotiated, and oppositional readings. Hall argues that the dominant, or mainstream, ideology is generally the preferred reading in a media text but that not all readers automatically adopt that reading. The social situations of readers, viewers, and listeners may lead them to adopt different stances. Negotiated readings are produced by those who inflect the preferred reading to take account of their social position. Oppositional readings are produced by those whose social position places them in direct conflict with the preferred reading.

Communication scholar John Fiske believes that for a television program to be popular, it needs to have multiple sets of meanings to appeal to viewers at different places in the social structure. The pleasure of viewing for subordinate groups is produced by the assertion of one's social identity, such as the assertion of gender identities, subcultural identities, class identification, and racial solidarity. Fiske uses the concept of "popular cultural capital" to discuss the resistance potential of television viewing. This is a reworking of Pierre Bourdieu's metaphor of cultural capital, a concept to illustrate that a society's culture is as unequally distributed as its material wealth. Fiske argues that the metaphor of cultural capital should be extended to include that of popular cultural capital, which includes meanings that validate the social experience of the subordinates, but not their subordination. The competence of such popular cultural capital involves a constant negotiation and renegotiation of the relationship between the textual and the social, with an understanding of the textual conventions based on the viewers' media and social experience.

Studies have found that audiences of various groups confront the same text with their own traditions and their own experiences, bringing different angles of vision to the same program. The resistant activities of the audience are demonstrated in the ethnographic studies of women viewers, who use fandom to form their own subculture. For example, in a study of soap opera fans by Mary Ellen Brown, the viewers' pleasure of resistance comes through a recognition by these women of themselves as belonging to a subordinated group that is oppressed by the dominant culture. It affirms their connection to a women's culture, the culture of home and of women's concerns, recognized but devalued in patriarchal terms, that provides a notion of identity that values women's traditional expertise. Studies of audience reception also examine the specific environment in which the audience consumes the media text. Janice Radway's ethnographic study of female romance readers is an important breakthrough in audience research, highlighting the issues of the context of reception and the agency of audience. In her research, Radway pays much attention to the social and material situations within which the activity of romance reading occurs, instead of looking only at the responses of the women to the messages in the novels.

Empirical studies of television viewing in the domestic context have indicated the unequal distribution of pleasures between men and women viewers and between viewers of different ethnicities. According to Ellen Seiter, the interpretation of viewing as active is not equally available to all; it depends on one's fears for the future, the degree and nature of social aspiration, and one's moral or religious judgment of popular media and consumer culture. To ignore demonstrations of power relations in the practices of television viewing runs the risk of validating the status quo. On the issue of audience autonomy based on the multiple meanings of texts, critics point out that the ability of audiences to shape their own readings, and hence their social lives, is constrained by a variety of factors in any given rhetorical situation, which include audience members' access to oppositional codes, the ratio between the work required and pleasures produced in decoding a text, the repertoire of available texts, and the particular historical occasion.

Janice Hua Xu
Cabrini College

See also Audiences: Producers of New Media; Audiences: Reception and Injection Models; Class Privilege; Encoding and Decoding; Fiske, John; Hall, Stuart; Identity; Ideology; Media Ethnography; Polysemic Text; Radway, Janice; Soap Operas

Further Readings

Ang, Ien. *Living Room Wars: Rethinking Media Audiences for a Postmodern World*. New York: Routledge, 1996.

Brooker, Will and Deborah Jermyn, eds. *The Audience Studies Reader*. Abingdon, UK: Routledge, 2003.

Brown, Mary Ellen. *Soap Opera and Women's Talk: The Pleasure of Resistance*. Thousand Oaks, CA: Sage, 1994.

Hall, Stuart. "Encoding/Decoding." In *Culture, Media, Language*, Stuart Hall et al., eds. London: Routledge, 2002.

Morley, David. *Television, Audiences, and Cultural Studies*. New York: Routledge, 1994.

Radway, Janice A. *Reading the Romance: Women, Patriarchy, and Popular Literature*. Chapel Hill: University of North Carolina Press, 1984.

Seiter, Ellen. *Television and New Media Audiences*. New York: Clarendon Press, 1998.

Seiter, E., H. Borchers, G. Kreutzner, and E.-M. Warth. *Remote Control: Television Audiences and Cultural Power*. London: Routledge, 1989.

ROMANCE NOVELS

Romance novels remain one of the best-selling genres of mass-market fiction. Articles in both *Bloomberg Businessweek* and the *New York Times* have noted that the romance novel industry continues to thrive—even in times of economic hardship—because readers enjoy the escapism the genre (and its many subgenres) provide. As their luscious cover illustrations indicate, many romance novels focus on stories about beautiful women being saved and loved by strong, handsome, bare-chested men. The vast majority of romance novel writers are female, and the majority of romance novel readers are female. Therefore, notions these female authors hold about gender influence their female reading public as well, and these ideas most often uphold traditional notions about love, sex, women, and men.

Scores of subgenres of romance novels exist, and all of them make significant, though general, statements about gender. Some of the most popular subcategories of the romance novel include historical romance, science fiction and fantasy romance, and erotic romance. By definition, historical romance concerns events occurring prior to World War II. Many of these novels, set in the 19th century, involve relationships with a member of the aristocracy or royalty. For instance, in Julia Quinn's *The Duke and I* (2000), a woman tries not to fall in love with the man to whom she is engaged, a duke, since their engagement is meant to be a sham. Instead, the two do fall in love. Another well-known historical romance, Lisa Kleypas's *The Devil in Winter* (2006), chronicles the story of a woman, Evangeline, who proposes to a society scoundrel, needing to marry in order to obtain her inheritance. The man to whom she proposes has a horrible reputation and is known for his dalliances with many women, so Evangeline states that she will marry the scoundrel only for her convenience but will not consummate the marriage. Eventually, love grows between the characters. In Sarah MacLean's *Nine Rules to Break When Romancing a Rake* (2010), Calpurnia Hartwell feels unsatisfied with life, as she has not yet been able to find a husband. She decides to blatantly break the rules set for women by society, with the help of a roguish man. As he helps her break the rules, however, she begins to fall in love with him. Similarly, Johanna Lindsey's *Gentle Rogue* (1991) follows the story of a woman (Georgina Anderson) who, after sneaking onto a ship dressed as a man, is forced to serve the captain, a man who thought he would never marry. Georgina entices the captain, though, and their love blossoms. These examples of historical romance novels uphold traditional stereotypes about gender. The women in these novels (even if rebellious like MacLean's Calpurnia) seek status as a wife or higher social standing tied to marriage. Likewise, these novels reinforce ideas about the male gender, suggesting that men are roguish, unfaithful, and commitment-phobic.

Science fiction and fantasy romance novels incorporate various galaxies, species, spaceships, and plots concerning galactic war in their stories, but one of the most popular contemporary trends involves vampires. Perhaps because of the success of Stephenie Meyer's *Twilight* series (often referred to as romance novels for teens), romance novels with women who are vampires or women who fall in love with vampires are common. Some examples of this trend include Karen Chance's *Touch the Dark* (2008), in which lead character Cassandra Palmer deals with vampires; Patricia Briggs's *Moon Called* (2008), which tells the story of Mercy Thompson and her encounters with werewolves, vampires, and even gremlins; and Kim Harrison's popular *Dead Witch Walking* (2004), about a vampire bounty hunter. These examples experiment with gender roles by placing women in positions of power and authority but also stress the fantasy of being bitten by a vampire, an act that (as in Bram Stoker's novel *Dracula*, 1897) places women in subordinate positions and awards men great power.

A subgenre that typically grants women power is the erotic romance novel. The novel *Claudia's Men* (2010), by Louisa Neil, tells the story of a woman involved with two vampire men (Neil's work also fits the fantasy subgenre). The novel bears a tag of M/M/F, indicating that the story involves a ménage à trois with two men and one woman, a pattern seen in other erotic romance novels. Melissa Schroeder's *Mele Kalikimaka, Baby* (2011) is about a woman who has intense simultaneous sexual experiences with two cousins she meets in Hawaii. The same trope appears in Michele Zurlo's *Two Masters for Samantha* (2011), in which Samantha shares a night with two brothers. An example of an erotic romance novel that surpasses the fantasy of a threesome involving two men and one woman is Destiny Blaine's *Breakfast by the Sea* (2011). In the novel, a group of men sent to kill a woman fall in love with her instead. Publishers describe the book as M/F/M/M/M/M, indicating that one woman engages in sexual acts with five men at the same time. Erotic romances seem to assign women power because men swoon over them (and are willing to participate in sexual ménages just to indulge in the woman's body), but they actually reinforce stereotypes about gender more than most romance subgenres, because the power of the female protagonists originates entirely from their bodies and sexual appeal. Novels like those by Neil, Schroeder, Zurlo, and Blaine also imply that men can become so addled by a woman's appearance that they are willing to participate in orgies to fulfill a strong sexual desire for a woman. Similarly, most erotic romance novels suggest that a woman's ultimate sexual fantasy is to be ravished by multiple men at the same time (reinforcing men's stereotypical fantasy of having sex with two or more women at once).

Thousands of romance novel writers find success and develop loyal fan followings, regardless of the subgenres in which they work. Each of these writers may develop distinct plotlines and characters, but certain tropes appear in every genre, tropes that usually confirm gender stereotypes for their readers.

Karley Adney
Butler University

See also Advertising; Beauty and Body Image: Beauty Myths; Gender and Femininity: Single/Independent Girl; Gender and Masculinity: White Masculinity; Heterosexism; Male Gaze; Radway, Janice; Reality-Based Television: Wedding Shows; Sexuality; Soap Operas; Stereotypes; Tropes

Further Readings

Gill, Rosalind and Elena Herdieckerhoff. "Rewriting the Romance? New Femininities in Chick Lit?" *Feminist Media Studies*, v.6/4 (2006).

Goade, Sally, ed. *Empowerment Versus Oppression: Twenty-First Century Views of Popular Romance Novels*. Newcastle Upon Tyne, UK: Cambridge Scholars, 2007.

Markert, John. "Romance Publishing and the Production of Culture." *Poetics: International Review for the Theory of Literature*, v.14/1–2 (1985).

Morgan, Spencer. "Getting Dirty in Dutch Country." *Bloomberg Businessweek* (July 26–August 1, 2010).

Motoko, Rick. "Recession Fuels Readers' Escapist Urges." *New York Times*. http://www.nytimes.com/2009/04/08/books/08roma.html (Accessed November 2010).

Radway, Janice A. *Reading the Romance: Women, Patriarchy, and Popular Literature*. Chapel Hill: University of North Carolina Press, 1984.

Saunders, Corinne, ed. *A Companion to Romance: From Classical to Contemporary*. London: Wiley-Blackwell, 2007.

Selinger, Eric Murphy. "Rereading the Romance." *Contemporary Literature*, v.48/2 (2007).

Weisser, Susan Ostrov. "The Wonderful-Terrible Bitch Figure in Harlequin Novels." In *Feminist Nightmares, Women at Odds: Feminism and the Problem of Sisterhood*, Susan Ostrov Weisser and Jennifer Fleischner, eds. New York: New York University Press, 1994.

RUSHKOFF, DOUGLAS

Douglas Rushkoff (1961–) is an award-winning author and analyst of new media as it relates to popular culture. He is a prolific media theorist, writer, and documentarian. He teaches media studies at

New York University and the New School in Manhattan. Rushkoff has written several books, *Cyberia: Life in the Trenches of Hyperspace* (1994), *Media Virus* (1995), *Playing the Future* (1996), *Coercion* (1999; winner of the Media Ecology Association's Marshall McLuhan Award), *Get Back in the Box: Innovation From the Inside Out* (2005), *Life, Inc.* (2009), and *Program or Be Programmed* (2010). He is a regular commentator for National Public Radio's *All Things Considered, Talk of the Nation*, and *Fresh Air*. He has also written and hosted three Frontline documentaries, *The Merchants of Cool* (2001), *The Persuaders* (2004), and *Digital Nation* (2009–10). Because of his contributions to the field of media ecology, he is often distinguished as the most influential and widely read American cyberculture and new media analyst to emerge during the 1990s.

Rushkoff has written about new media since the 1990s. He has been one of the leaders at the forefront of the movement. His constant involvement in the field allows him to witness the development, growth, and proliferation of new media and the building of a digital society. As new media progressed and matured, so did Rushkoff. In the beginning, he had a techno-utopian view of new media, one bursting with emancipatory and egalitarian potential. Over the years, Rushkoff has refined his utopian view into a nuanced critique of cyberculture

A leader in the study of new media and winner of the first Neil Postman Award for Career Achievement in Public Intellectual Activity, Douglas Rushkoff is an author, teacher, and documentarian. (Wikimedia)

discourse and the impact of media on society. His development and commitment to the study of new media have earned him an international reputation and make him one of the most influential media theorists in America.

For his scholarship, Rushkoff has received numerous honors, including the first Neil Postman Award for Career Achievement in Public Intellectual Activity (2004). He is one of 12 founding members of Technorealism (a continuous critical examination of how technologies could help or hinder people in the struggle to improve the quality of their lives); he serves on the board of directors of both the Media Ecology Association and the Center for Cognitive Liberty and Ethics; and he is a member of the advisory board for both the National Association for Media Literacy Education and HyperWords.

Rushkoff's research focuses on the ways that people, cultures, and institutions create, share, and influence one another's values. How the elements of media, culture, and people intersect determines the influence of new media on the intersections. Additionally, Rushkoff helps individuals to question and analyze their media consumption and highlights the need to regain control; he sees children as an especially vulnerable population.

For Rushkoff, the Internet and new media have created a potentially limitless world, one that could be free from the constraints of appearance and prejudice, time and space, and gender and power. Given this, the Internet has been described as promoting a do-it-yourself (DIY) type of mentality, a space that provides the individual with the opportunity to design her or his world on her or his own terms. For critical scholars such as Rushkoff, the Internet represents a decentralized reality that they believe could penetrate and exist within every level of society. In their view, new media constitute a catalyst for the emergence of a holistic society. Within this boundless space, humans would no longer be controlled and divided by ideology, socioeconomic status, ethnicity, or gender.

Michelle Millard
Wayne State University

See also Cyberpunk; McLuhan, Marshall; Media Literacy; New Media; Social Media; Viral Advertising and Marketing

Further Readings

Rushkoff, Douglas. *Coercion: Why We Listen to What "They" Say*. New York: Riverhead Books, 1999.

Rushkoff, Douglas. *Get Back in the Box: Innovation From the Inside Out*. New York: Collins, 2005.

Rushkoff, Douglas. *Life, Inc.: How the World Became a Corporation and How to Take It Back*. New York: Random House, 2009.

Rushkoff, Douglas. *Program or Be Programmed: Ten Commands for a Digital Age*. New York: O/R Books, 2010.

S

SCOPOPHILIA

Scopophilia is erotic pleasure related to seeing. Often cited as a basic feature of our experience of visual media, its unique quality is fascination, an experience that combines attraction and fear. Gender differences have been suggested in connection with the intensity of scopophilia in males and females. These are the basis for many decisions made by producers of advertisements, films, television, and Internet presentations.

Scopophilia originally referred to sexual pleasure in both looking at and being looked at by someone. The word is a translation of the German *Schaulust* (literally, lust for looking), a term introduced into psychology, in 1910, by Sigmund Freud. When only being looked at can bring about sexual arousal, scopophilia is termed exhibitionism, and when only looking at someone (while not being observed doing so) leads to sexual excitement, it is termed voyeurism. The form of scopophilia most relevant to media studies is voyeurism.

Currently, among psychiatrists exhibitionism and voyeurism are understood as sexual disorders termed *paraphilias*, unusual forms of sexuality originally called perversions, since the exhibitionist and voyeur do not desire heterosexual genital contact with the person who is the source of sexual arousal and only one of the forms of scopophilia can bring this about. Both paraphilias have been reported almost exclusively in males. Most adult sexuality includes an element of scopophilia (termed a partial instinct) that initiates the sex act. Sexual interest in other people nearly always begins with pleasure in looking at them, often with concurrent pleasure in being looked at.

According to Jean Piaget, at the beginning of life, our first cognitive experiences are indistinguishable from the physical actions of looking at, reaching for, and grasping objects. Looking at the mothering figure's face is an essential component of bonding emotionally with her (or him). As the term suggests, eye contact with another person is a kind of touching, but at a distance. All seeing has a quasi-tactile quality. Being looked at may produce the same sort of response as being touched. Looking at people and things is also the basis of orienting ourselves in space. The activity soon becomes pleasurable for its own sake (functional pleasure). For most people, looking at the faces, bodies, and actions of other human beings is more compelling than looking at other things.

Scopophilia has been associated with pornography, but nearly everyone is sexually excited to some degree by images of nongenital parts of the bodies of other human beings. Sometimes the stimulation of looking at does not lead to genital arousal. This speaks to its more general erotic meaning and its relation to our aesthetic sensibility.

Direct observation of infants has determined that males prefer looking at moving objects whereas infant females prefer looking at faces. There may also be preferences for certain colors and shapes that are typical for most males and most females. After the sexual awakening of puberty, boys are said to look at bodies more than faces, whereas girls tend to focus more on facial features. It is not clear that this is based on innate differences between the sexes. Similarly, males are generally said to take greater pleasure than females in looking at people, but it is difficult to be certain whether this generalization is justified. Postpubescent females are said to be more exhibitionistic than males. This would lead us to expect young males to be more modest than girls, and that may be the case. It is difficult to know the extent to which attitudes toward one's body and the desire to display it are the result of encouraging or inhibiting (even prohibiting) certain tendencies that are common to both sexes. With respect to these preferences, the formation of habits of social response (and therefore preferences) begins early in life and so much of it is preverbal that, short of ethically irresponsible experiments in upbringing, we are likely never to know which tendencies are sex-specific and which are socially constructed.

Painting and, eventually, photography and video have allowed us to look at representations of people without their immediate awareness that we are doing so. This has led to relating scopophilia to experiencing visual media, because a basic source of voyeuristic excitement is remaining hidden from and unknown to the person or persons being watched at the time they are been viewed. As consumers of visual media, we are all therefore in a sense voyeurs. The sexual voyeur typically masturbates alone to orgasm, unseen by the object of his or her gaze. The viewer of a photograph, film, or video can arrange to be alone when looking at an image. Because cinema is experienced in the dark, sexual self-stimulation undetected by others is possible. Alone in front of a television or other video screen, we are permitted unlimited opportunities for sexual self-stimulation.

Assumptions about the visual sensibility of males and females have influenced marketing strategies for selling clothing and other merchandise as well as filmmakers' strategies in creating movies that are more likely to attract the interest of males or females. If women are less voyeuristic than men, they nevertheless respond intensely to images of things. Perhaps this is related to the infantile preference, cited earlier, for looking at things that are not moving. Certain television channels now program exclusively for women (for example, Lifetime) and men (for example, Spike). Programming for women typically includes themes related to relationships, while men's programming features sports, action, and adventure. Clothing, comestibles, and cosmetics are marketed to females. Vehicles and alcoholic beverages are marketed to male audiences. For decades, subliminal marketing has been common in advertising. For example, shapes of naked bodies are worked into the configuration of ice in a glass containing an alcoholic beverage, or a message a few milliseconds long may be flashed several times in a film or video sequence. Initially, males were targeted more than females for purchasing expensive or luxury items. As women have become independent wage earners, television channels (for example, the shopping channels HSN and QVC) now target exclusively female consumers.

Children are known to be very susceptible to the impact of television and to computer display images. This is especially important as the culture becomes less of a reading culture (which requires a long attention span and concentrated looking) and more of a scanning culture (which demands rapidly shifting one's attention from one byte of visual information to another). The editing of most television shows does not permit viewers to become too absorbed by one image. There are no dead or empty visual intervals that permit time for reflection.

Miles Groth
Wagner College

See also Doane, Mary Ann; Male Gaze; McLuhan, Marshall; Men's Magazines: Lifestyle and Health; Mulvey, Laura; Pornification of Everyday Life; Pornography: Gay and Lesbian; Pornography: Heterosexual; Pornography: Internet; Sexuality; Virtual Sex

Further Readings

Damon, William, ed. *Handbook of Child Development,* 6th ed. New York: John Wiley and Sons, 2006.

Freud, Sigmund. *Five Lectures on Psychoanalysis.* 1909. Reprint, New York: W. W. Norton, 1990.

McLuhan, Marshall. *Understanding Media.* New York: McGraw-Hill, 1964.

Piaget, Jean and Bärbel Inhelder. *The Psychology of the Child.* New York: Basic Books, 1969.

SECOND LIFE

Second Life, or *SL*, is a massively multiplayer online role-playing game (MMORPG) that was developed by Linden Labs in 2003. *SL* is home to business ventures, educational laboratories, dance clubs, art shows, and role-playing games. *SL* is for adults over the age of 18 but exists in a teen version for those between the ages of 13 and 17. *SL* is unique in that it cannot be classified as a traditional game, nor does it compare to platforms such as *World of Warcraft*. *SL* has no objective and is entirely open to the users' choices and experiences.

When users sign up for *SL*, the first step is to create an avatar. An avatar is a digital representation of the user. Avatars in *SL* are three-dimensional (3-D) characters that will be the mode by which the user interacts within the virtual environment. Gender plays a crucial role in *SL* avatar development. Upon entering *SL*, one chooses a gender, which unlike a screen name can be changed at any time. The female body is smaller and comes with animations in which women sit with their legs closer together than their male counterparts. At the same time, *SL* residents have the freedom to choose their gender, an option that allows for possibilities of new forms of gender realization. This can be seen as liberating one from the restrictions of biological gender designations. Users will often role-play as other genders in order to experience an expanded notion of gender. Beauty standards from the real world appear to realize themselves within the virtual world, despite possibilities for new conceptions of body politics. This can be seen in the large breasts and highly sexualized avatars that dominate the landscape of *SL*.

Users often create multiple avatars known as alts. Someone may use different avatars to express different parts of their personality or desires. This provides the possibility for experiencing the world from a different set of eyes but also leads to "identity tourism." Identity tourism is a concept that describes the dangers of trying on different identities as a way to understand other cultures. While there are potentially positive uses of such experimentation, it also can lead to unrealistic understandings of the consequences and realities of lived experiences of people from marginalized positions. When people engage in identity tourism, they often attempt to "pass" as the chosen identity by displaying stereotypical markers of identification. Identities become aesthetic consumer choices within such a setting and, as critics point out, can lead to a false sense of understanding between cultures when in fact they are working to increase negative stereotypes.

Although users have the option of creating avatars that are completely customized, users generally create avatars that follow traditional gender divides. Users also tend to create or buy avatars that represent idealized versions of the human body. Female avatars reflect unrealistic beauty standards that tend to reinforce aesthetic ideals of female beauty. Gender remains, as it is in real life, an essential characteristic in initial interactions among avatars. The practices of everyday gender performances are formed through social interactions within the virtual world.

MMORPGs such as *SL* bring up issues of embodiment, which are essential to feminist studies. Embodiment is a performative act that is related to the feeling of presence and interaction within a setting. Users are embodied within their avatars, and the experience of virtual embodiment provides new experiences of identity. As one experiences oneself as both a virtual and a real person, one's identity is shaped by these feelings. The avatar becomes the home in which the user's identity is embodied through careful crafting. The ability to control one's appearance completely provides new opportunities for embodied experiences that differ from those possible in the real world, where people are limited by the physical world.

Sex represents a large market within *SL*. Users can engage in multiple forms of role-playing and sexual fantasies, ranging from bondage/domination sadomasochism (BDSM) to rape reenactments. Users can purchase prostitutes, and often female avatars are portrayed as submissive within these sexual games. Users can create female prostitute avatars that they then can exploit to make real-world money. The ability for users to generate real-world revenue from *SL* sexual exploits posits new challenges for understanding the dynamics of sexuality and its relationship to capitalism.

There are, however, positive uses for women within the commerce of *SL*. Because *SL* is user-generated, the opportunities available are open and rely on the ingenuity of those who use it. Users can create real estate, clothing, skins, custom homes, and whatever else they desire and then sell these commodities for real money. As a result, women users can generate new identities in a way that is impossible in the physical world. The first *SL* millionaire, Anshe Chung, was a woman. She achieved financial success through her virtual real estate business.

Megan Jean Harlow
European Graduate School, Switzerland

See also Avatar; Beauty and Body Image: Beauty Myths; Cyberdating; Cyberpunk; Cyberspace and Cyberculture; Cyborg; Electronic Media and Social Inequality; Gender Embodiment; Massively Multiplayer Online Role-Playing Games; Multi-User Dimensions; Social Construction of Gender; Video Gaming: Representations of Femininity; Video Gaming: Representations of Masculinity; Video Gaming: Violence; Viral Advertising and Marketing; Virtual Community; Virtual Sex; Virtuality; Web 2.0

Further Readings

Boellstorff, Tom. *Coming of Age in* Second Life: *An Anthropologist Explores the Virtually Human.* Princeton, NJ: Princeton University Press, 2008.

Brookey, Robert Alan and Kristopher L. Cannon. "Sex Lives in *Second Life.*" *Critical Studies in Media Communication,* v.26/2 (June 2009).

Nakamura, Lisa. "Race in/for Cyberspace: Identity Tourism and Racial Passing on the Internet." *Works and Days,* v.13/1–2 (1995).

Stone, Allecquere Rosanne. "In Novel Conditions: The Cross-Dressing Psychiatrist." In *The War of Desire and Technology at the Close of the Mechanical Age.* Cambridge, MA: MIT Press, 1995.

SEMIOTICS

Semiotics (or semiology) is the study of signs. Although people use semiotics to interpret and understand symbolic meanings every day, the semiotic tradition was founded on the work of several important scholars. Beginning in the late 19th and early 20th centuries, it was not until the second half of the 20th century that semiotics became influential in the study of culture and media. It was adopted by scholars and critics as a way to examine relationships of power, cultural meanings, and values. Based on the idea that all meanings are socially constructed, semiotic analysis provides cultural critics a way to deconstruct how meaning is made and how ideology is created and circulated. The semiotic tradition has been important to gender studies because it is a tool used to address how ideas about gender are created and circulated through various media texts.

Although semiotics uses a specific set of terms, or vocabulary, most people are already experts at understanding signs. In this way, semiotics can be seen as a process of interpreting the symbols that people come across in their everyday lives. For instance, people interpret traffic signs to navigate intersections. People also infer information about others based on signs related to personal appearance, such as clothing and hairstyle. Each is a sign sending a message to be interpreted or analyzed by others. For example, the way a person wears his or her hair sends a message about that person's identity. A mohawk may signify youth or rebellion, whereas a chignon may signify modesty or decorum. These meanings are, of course, socially constructed, culturally specific, and thoroughly gendered. For instance, if a man chooses not to shave, it sends one kind of message about gender conformity and his identity. If a woman chooses not to shave, it sends a very different message about gender conformity and her identity. Fundamentally, people understand each of these meanings because they are actively interpreting signs. While semiotics is widespread in its use, most people do not stop to think about the process of creating and interpreting signs. Semiotics, on the other hand, is devoted to explaining this process.

Foundations in Semiotics

Swiss linguist Ferdinand de Saussure and American philosopher Charles Saunders Peirce were both influential figures in developing semiotics. Peirce first coined the term *semiotics*, and Saussure's work became the foundation for *semiology*. Today, the two terms can be used interchangeably to refer to the study of signs. Saussure specifically set out to develop a science of signs. He defined a sign as anything that carries meaning. He considered signs to be the most basic units of meaning. They can consist of words, images, sounds, or objects that have symbolic value. Saussure divided the sign into two parts: the signifier and the signified. The signifier is the form that the sign takes, whether printed word or sound. For example, the words *red rose* constitute a signifier. In contrast, the signified is the meaning that is associated with the signifier, the concept—here, of a red flower—that is triggered in a person's head in response to the signifier. Semiotics would explore what a red rose might signify. Semiotics would question if it means something different from, for example, a yellow rose. In many cultures, a red rose means not only a flower but also romantic love, whereas a yellow rose means friendship. Thus, in certain contexts, the words red rose or an image of a red rose (the signifier) equates with romantic love (the signified). At base, all signifieds are mental representations. According to Stuart Hall, mental representations are never purely individual but are conceptual maps shared by a culture or community. Conceptual maps are common reference points that enable people to interpret and understand one another.

Saussure was also concerned with the relationship between the signifier and the signified. He would consider why romantic love, instead of friendship, is associated with the red rose. He would answer this question by stating that the relationship between a signifier and a signified is arbitrary. In other words, there is no natural or essential connection between the parts of a sign. Semiotics does not look to the world of nature to discover how meaning is made. Instead, it looks to the world of culture, because meaning is socially constructed. Meaning is not inherent in a sign. However, to say that there is no natural relationship between signifier and signified is not to say that there is no relationship at all. Instead, it is to say that the connection between signifier and signified is a culturally specific, socially constructed relationship. In other words, the connection between signifier and signified is socially, not naturally, determined.

If all meanings are associations, then they are also always relational. People understand meanings based on both similarities to and differences from other signs. Another example, also used by Hall, would be the language of a traffic light. Green is associated with *go*, whereas red is associated with *stop*. People can successfully navigate traffic intersections because they understand signs through their differences. Green is not red, just as go is not stop. There is nothing inherent in the color red that means stop. The color purple could just as easily designate stop. Semiotics contends that the connection between red

and stop is a symbolic, not a natural, connection. Additionally, two of the foregoing examples use the color red. In the language of flowers, red means romantic love, but in the language of traffic signs, red means stop. This fact points out that there is no inherent meaning in the color red. Instead, the meaning depends on its context. People fundamentally understand signs based on their relationship to other signs, like other roses or other traffic signals. Furthermore, signs may have different meanings and even different interpretations. In semiotics, this phenomenon is called polysemy. Derived from the Greek term *polysemos*, it translates as "many meanings." Polysemy refers to the idea that signs are never fully fixed but have a certain degree of flexibility and the ability to signify a diversity of meanings.

Semiotics and Cultural Criticism

Semiotics gained popularity in the second half of the 20th century. Prominent figures in this movement were Italian scholar Umberto Eco and French scholar Roland Barthes. They both assert that signs are deceptive. Because there is no inherent meaning in a sign, Eco believed that all signs lie. He also thought that if signs can lie, then they cannot be trusted to tell the truth. For him, signs always present an ideological view of the world, not a natural truth. Likewise, Barthes was most interested in signs that seemed to be simple or straightforward but contained subtle messages that perpetuate dominant values in society. Like Saussure, Barthes wanted to take signs apart, not only to see what they mean but also to see how they carry ideology. Ideology consists of ideas, values, and beliefs that reflect the interests of those in power and work to legitimate social inequalities. Barthes famously studied images of race and masculinity in *Paris Match* magazine and professional wrestling, respectively. In these studies, he sketched out a method for uncovering levels of meaning that can be easily applied to a range of other images in order to explore their ideological content.

The first level of meaning is denotation. Denotation is the most basic layer of meaning, simply describing what is depicted. This layer of meaning is without ideological content and consists of a basic description of the signs presented in an image. Where denotation is concerned, people would most likely agree on what is depicted in a specific image.

The next level of meaning is connotation. Connotative meanings are the ideas, beliefs, and values associated with what is depicted. This layer of meaning deals with ideological content. Connotative meaning is concerned with what ideologies are being promoted in an image. Because signs are polysemic, people may not interpret them similarly or come to a consensus regarding the connotations of a specific image.

The next level of meaning is myth. Myth does not consist of simple stories or fables. Instead, myth makes a statement about what is natural, good, or just. Myth goes beyond simply identifying the ideas and interests of dominant groups via connotations. The work of myth is to transform history into nature, or to detach meaning from its historical, social, and political context. When myth is detached from history, it becomes depoliticized speech. Stripped of its context, myth makes specific ideologies appear to be normal and natural. The aim of the semiotic approach is to repoliticize speech, or to return nature to history. Semiotics can be a powerful tool for gender studies because it enables the view that constructs such as patriarchy or sexism are social, historical, political phenomena rather than effects of nature.

Semiotics and Gender Studies

This type of semiotic interpretation has been widely used to critique a variety of media and cultural texts. Advertising, fashion, television news, film, music video, Websites, and comics are among the texts that have been analyzed in this tradition. Based on the assumption that they carry gendered ideologies, these areas provide a rich and fertile field for analyzing concepts of femininity, masculinity, and sexuality. This type of analysis is aimed at deconstructing the myths surrounding these constructs and working for more equality between genders. Consequently, advertising has been a particularly important site for semiotic analysis. Because advertising images are ever present, scholars in this area believe that special attention should be paid to how they communicate gendered values and ideologies. Judith Williamson conducted a classic semiotic study focusing on how social differences are constructed in advertisements. Gillian Dyer conducted semiotic analyses in this same tradition. Concerned with how people make symbolic associations, she focused on

the juxtaposition of signs, or how certain product signifiers become associated with preexisting cultural signifieds. For instance, an advertisement may juxtapose a certain beverage with a famous athlete or a fragrance with erotic or sexual images. Semiotic juxtaposition creates mythic connections between the product (signifier) and values presented in the image (signified). The signifier, the beverage, becomes associated with exceptional and successful athletes. Likewise, a fragrance comes to signify sexual desire and satisfaction. Advertisements like these exploit the process of semiotic associations between signifier and signified and create powerful cultural myths.

Dyer also identified several important areas to consider when conducting a semiotic analysis. When analyzing advertisements, she noted, it is important to pay attention to these key features: representations of bodies (age, gender, race, hair, body, size, looks); representations of manner (expression, eye contact, pose); representations of activity (touch, movement, spatial arrangements); and setting (props, location, surroundings). In the process of conducting a semiotic analysis, it is also useful to consider what is absent. Because semiotics holds that people make meaning based on both similarities and differences, what is not depicted can also mean a great deal. When conducting a semiotic analysis, scholars also believe that it is important to imagine what else could have been depicted. Because images are motivated by ideology, they are necessarily promoting a particular view of the world by including certain things and excluding others. Semiotics holds that promoting certain ideas about concepts such as masculinity or femininity can limit not only our roles in society but also the human imagination itself. By imagining alternatives, semiotics emphasizes that these ideologies are historically, politically, and socially situated. Ultimately, the aim of semiotic analysis is to identify and critique the structures of myth in order to uncover aspects of power, ideology, and inequality in advertising and a variety of other media texts.

Amy M. Corey
Gonzaga University

See also Advertising; Audiences: Producers of New Media; Audiences: Reception and Injection Models; Barthes, Roland; Critical Theory; Cultivation Theory; Cultural Politics; Encoding and Decoding; Feminism;

Feminist Theory: Liberal; Feminist Theory: Marxist; Feminist Theory: Socialist; Hall, Stuart; Hegemony; Ideology; Media Rhetoric; New Media; Patriarchy; Polysemic Text; Postmodernism; Post-Structuralism; Quantitative Content Analysis; Radway, Janice; Reception Theory; Romance Novels; Social Inequality; Stereotypes; Television; Textual Analysis

Further Readings

Barthes, Roland. *Mythologies*. New York: Hill & Wang, 1972.

Dyer, Gillian. *Advertising as Communication*. London: Methuen, 1982.

Eco, Umberto. *A Theory of Semiotics*. Bloomington: Indiana University Press, 1978.

Hall, Stuart, ed. *Representation: Cultural Representation and Signifying Practices*. London: Sage, 1997.

Saussure, Ferdinand de. *Course in General Linguistics*. New York: McGraw-Hill, 1966.

Williamson, Judith. *Decoding Advertisements: Ideology and Meaning in Advertising*. London: Marion Boyars, 1978.

SEXISM

In recent years, some individuals have questioned whether sexism is dead in the Western world. On March 8, 2011, for example, the International Women's Day organization released the results of a poll that revealed that most women do not believe that Britain is a sexist place. Despite this rhetoric, most scholars agree that blatant and subtle forms of sexism still exist. In fact, some media scholars and social commentators, such as Susan J. Douglas, Rebecca Traister, Diana B. Carlin, and Kelly L. Winfrey, point to the 2008 U.S. elections as an example of just how sexist Western culture remains.

Origins

Sexism, according to *Merriam-Webster's Collegiate Dictionary*, is "prejudice or discrimination based on sex, especially discrimination against women" or "behaviors, conditions, or attitudes that foster stereotypes of social roles based on sex." Although now a household word, the term *sexism* was actually coined during the 1960s women's movement. According to gender historian Fred R. Shapiro, the term most likely originated during Pauline M. Leet's

address, "Women and the Undergraduate," to the Student-Faculty Forum at Franklin and Marshall College in 1965. At the forum, Leet described the "sexist" mentality of individuals within the literary community. The term later appeared in print in Caroline Bird's "On Being Born Female" (1968) and Sheldon Vanauken's "Freedom for Movement Girls—Now" (1968). By 1968, Bird and Vanauken had used the term to denote the general tendency to judge women as inferior on the basis of sex.

In Education and the Workplace

After the release in October 1963 of *The Presidential Report on American Women*, by the Presidential Commission on the Status of Women, individuals like Betty Friedan, author of *The Feminine Mystique* (1963), and groups like the National Organization for Women (established in 1966) fought sexism in all aspects of society. However, they focused the brunt of their early attention on eliminating "sexism," "sex bias," and "sexual discrimination" in education and the workplace.

Their efforts led to the passage of Title IX (originally part of the 1964 Civil Rights Act and later amended in the Education Amendments of 1972), which guaranteed that "no person shall, on the basis of sex, be excluded from participation in, be denied the benefits of, or be subject to discrimination under any educational program or activity receiving federal funds," and the Equal Rights Amendment (proposed in 1972), which would have amended the U.S. Constitution by guaranteeing equal rights on the basis of sex. Although the Equal Rights Amendment was never ratified by the requisite number of states, laws like Title IX and (once prodded by NOW) enforcement agencies like the Equal Employment Opportunity Commission (EEOC) allowed women to gain considerable ground in education and the workplace.

Women have made huge strides in education since the passage of Title IX. According to the U.S. census, in 2008 women made up 55 percent of all college undergraduates, compared to just 44 percent in 1972. Likewise, women entered historically male-dominated disciplines, such as engineering, medicine, and law, in greater numbers. In 1972, women earned less than 10 percent of all medical and law degrees and 0.7 percent of all engineering degrees; by 2009, women made up approximately

In the early 21st century, women still composed the majority of pink-collar workers—occupations stereotypically considered women's work. Susan J. Douglas found that the top five careers for women were secretaries, registered nurses, elementary- and middle-school teachers, cashiers, and retail salespersons. (Photos.com)

45 percent of all medical and law students and 20 percent of all engineering students. With greater access to education, women have advanced to an extent in the workplace. For instance, following the passage of Title IX, in the first half of the 1970s, the number of women lawyers doubled. In 2009, women composed a little more than 30 percent of practicing lawyers and physicians and 12 percent of all practicing engineers.

Despite these achievements, women still face sexual bias and discrimination in the workplace. At the dawn of the 21st century, women still are working in more lower-level, lower-paying positions than men. Although women have gained some ground in traditionally male-dominated fields, they continue to compose the bulk of pink-collar workers. For instance, in 2007, as media scholar Susan J. Douglas notes, the top five careers for women were secretaries, registered nurses, elementary and middle-school teachers, cashiers, and retail salespersons. Nearly half of women are confined to pink-collar positions, where the median income is approximately $27,000 per year.

Disturbing pay disparities remain a reality for women—a year out of college, women earn only 80 percent of what men make, and a decade out of college, the gap widens, with women earning just 69 percent of what men receive. In many industries, the "glass ceiling" appears to be firmly in place. Although nearly half of all medical and law graduates in the United States are women, they make up only about 15 percent of partners at law firms and 20 percent of new surgeons across the nation. Moreover, although the number of suits filed with the EEOC has declined in the last decade, women continue to face sexual harassment in the workplace, especially in male-dominated fields. In fact, a study released in a 2010 issue of *Springer's Journal of Law and Human Behavior* revealed that nine out of 10 women in legal and military jobs reported experiencing gender harassment. In addition, as Douglas contends, women in the United States remain at an unfair disadvantage in terms of the costs associated with child and aging-parent care. The result: The United States has the largest gap in poverty rates between men and women of any country in the Western world.

In the Media Industry

Sexism persists in the media industry. Although women compose nearly two thirds of journalism and mass communication graduates and one third of the U.S. media workforce (up from one fifth in the early 1970s), the majority of women are confined to the *pink ghetto*, the term used to describe the relegation of women to lower-paying, lower-level positions within an organization. Globally, women are not faring much better. Although women represent anywhere from approximately one fourth to almost one half of the media workforce in foreign countries, they still report experiencing discrimination and marginalization to certain positions based on gender roles.

Today, women hold approximately one third to one fifth of all leadership positions in print, radio, television, and film; still, most of these women hold jobs in middle management. Some scholars have argued that the key to overcoming the "glass ceiling" lies in solving issues associated with work-home conflicts and the "friendliness trap." Many scholars agree that traditional feminine values like cooperation, respect, honesty, fairness, and loyalty, which serve as an advantage in acquiring and maintaining entry-level and middle-management positions, serve as an obstacle to career advancement for women.

Pay disparities also remain. Pay gaps within the media industry mirror national trends; thus, women in the media industry earn approximately 80 percent of their male counterparts' salaries. Even in sectors like public relations, where women have reportedly shattered the glass ceiling, women continue to earn a fraction (63 percent) of what their male colleagues receive. For instance, in 2006, the average male salary in public relations was $123,310, compared to $80,940 for women.

Other evidence suggests that sex bias is still pervasive in the media industry. For instance, many women continue to admit to experiencing harassment in media careers, according to scholars David Weaver and Karen Ross. Women are still funneled into positions marked as "feminine." For example, in sports broadcasting, women continue to be relegated to positions as sideline reporters instead of more lucrative positions as play-by-play announcers. Likewise, female war correspondents in traditional "machismo" roles expressed concerns about lingering sexism in interviews with media scholars. In particular, they reported that their bosses were reluctant to send women into combat zones as opposed to their male counterparts.

Trends like these may shed light on why some scholars have found that women tend to flee jobs in journalism after a few years, a result of burnout in the male-centered newsroom. In 2009, Scott Reinardy's survey of 715 U.S. newspaper journalists revealed that women suffer from higher levels of burnout than their male counterparts, and 30 percent of women under the age of 27 say that they plan on leaving the field. Women listed differences in perceived organizational support and differing job expectations based on gender as reasons for feeling overburdened.

In the Media

Many scholars agree that sexism in the media operates through stereotypes—social constructions about gender roles and norms. Media stereotypes continue to portray women as submissive, less intelligent than men, sexual objects, and preoccupied with their roles as "sexy" wives and mothers. Sexist stereotypes in the media have a long history, and these images continue to help constitute cultural constructions about women. For instance, at the dawn of the 21st century, the beauty standard for

women perpetuated by the media remains white and abnormally skinny. Although some media coverage portrays women in alternative ways, the cumulative effect of the media landscape remains harmful for women's advancement in society.

At the dawn of the television age in the 1950s, the media portrayed women as the perfect housewives and mothers. During World War II, more than six million women had gained newfound economic independence in wartime jobs; the media helped usher these same women back into the kitchen. Popular television characters like June Cleaver, Harriet Nelson, and Donna Reed normalized women's roles as loving, patient, demure homemakers. Likewise, women's magazines portrayed women as reveling in their motherly duties. Media images reinforced Victorian ideologies of true womanhood and the cult of domesticity. Under these ideologies, women were constructed as beautiful, passive, and pure creatures. When women were seen in the workplace, the media represented them in stereotypical women's roles as secretaries (Alice from the *Jack Benny Program*) or bartenders (Miss Kitty from *Gunsmoke*). During this era, mediated images of men reinforced the idea, extolled in the television series of the same name, that "father knows best." Men were in control in the public and private spheres—in the boardroom, the bedroom, and every room in between. The media constructed a type of virulent masculinity that men should strive to enact.

During the height of the women's movement in the 1960s and 1970s, the media fed American women mixed messages—from newspaper and magazine articles that questioned the treatment of women in the workplace (alongside gender-segregated want ads and sexist advertisements such as Eastern Airlines' "Fly Me" Campaign), to magical, sexually liberated female television characters (such as Jeannie in *I Dream of Jeannie*, 1965–70) who, as Douglas contends, if not properly contained (as Jeannie was in her bottle) could wreak havoc on the man's world of business, to the single working woman (as portrayed by Mary Tyler Moore) who was seemingly liberated from patriarchal stereotypes of husband-hunting and widow-dom but, as Bonnie Dow points out, eventually domesticated into traditional gender-role constructs. Naomi Wolf contends that as women gained vestiges of power in mainstream culture, the media began constructing ideals of feminine beauty to which many women felt increasing pressure to conform. For instance, in the 1970s, the media gave viewers images of the first supermodels and television characters, such as Charlie's Angels and the bionic woman. In addition to reinforcing the beauty myth, the media largely ridiculed the feminist movement and provided images of submissive women, who functioned primarily as objects of the male gaze.

Although elements of the mainstream media contested the feminist movement in the 1970s, the media began portraying successful career women in the 1980s. Television producers gave the world women like Clair Huxtable and Angela Bauer, who were successful professionals and mothers. In advertisements, women were represented as liberated individuals who deserved to reward themselves—and indulge in extravagant (mostly beauty) products. Women's magazines such as Helen Gurley Brown's *Cosmopolitan* offered women career advice, alongside sex tips and health advice.

By the early 1990s, the media portrayed women as having achieved sexual equality with men. Powerful female television characters like Murphy Brown and Roseanne, constituted in part by the feminist movement, offered viewers images of strong, successful women who could exert control in the boardroom and the family room without necessarily ascribing to society's pervasive "beauty myth." Publishers developed magazines, like *Sassy*, that offered young women alternatives to the mainstream media's image of bone-skinny, sex- and beauty-obsessed teens. *Sassy* and independent zines offered young women serious journalism about important social issues such as racism, eating disorders, and suicide. The media seemed to offer women "girl power" in ample supply.

However, as a number of media scholars have noted, sexism was not absent from the 1990s media landscape. Instead, it cropped up in a new form. Television shows like *Beverly Hills, 90210* and *Melrose Place* and women's magazines from *Seventeen* to *Cosmo* encouraged women to ascribe wholeheartedly to the beauty myth and "commodity feminism," which refers to the way in which feminist ideas are (re)appropriated into mainstream culture for commercial purposes. Media producers offered girls and women feminist messages stripped of their political significance and at the same time encouraged women to embrace a brand of girl power that entailed purchasing unlimited amounts of beauty products to look the "sexy" part. By the dawn of the 21st century, many scholars argued that feminism had been co-opted further by the media and refashioned into a form of "new" sexism.

"New" (and Old-Fashioned) Sexism

At the beginning of the 21st century, some media scholars argue, sexism reared its ugly head in a new way. "New" sexism, or "enlightened sexism"—as Douglas dubs it, refers to the resurgence of sexist images and stereotypes in the alleged age of postfeminism. New or enlightened sexism operates through the deployment of irony and humor—through the slippery multiaccentuality of a text that offers multiple readings. For instance, media scholar Bethan Benwell argues that "new lad" magazines like *Maxim* incorporate the use of irony to undermine feminist politics. Douglas contends that enlightened sexism functions in similar ways in programs like *The Man Show* and *The Bachelor*. Media-savvy female viewers are expected to wink or smirk at the resurrection of sexist images that objectify women's bodies, knowing that they have already achieved full sexual equality. The media reinforce the notion that for women the secret to true power lies not in personal achievement or economic independence but in the guise of beauty—the strategic deployment of one's body. As British scholar Angela McRobbie argues, the key in the equation of new sexism is the negation of feminism as an "old-fashioned" movement that has already been won. Mediated images of female chief executive officers, presidential candidates, and anchors, as well as female television presidents, attorneys, surgeons, and judges, reinforce the notion that feminism is no longer needed in society. As a whole, Douglas argues, these mediated images offer women "fantasies of power." Ultimately, however, enlightened sexism serves to support the status quo of patriarchy and masculine hegemony (the term used to refer to dominant constructions about masculinity in society).

Other scholars suggest that more blatant forms of sexism are still alive and well in our society, especially in the media. They point to images in advertising and pornography, as well as the sports and news media, to support their argument that sexism is pervasive in Western culture. Scholars like Rosalind Gill argue that "it's time to get angry again" about the ways in which sexism still permeates Western media.

Although some advertisers have presented women as liberated and independent since the 1980s, evidence suggests that many advertisers still portray women as sex objects, whose place is within the home. Media scholars like Jean Kilbourne argue that the cumulative effect of the advertising landscape is a cultural obsession with beauty and sexiness. The graphic sexual messages serve not only to objectify women, but also to idealize narcissism, instant gratification, arousal, and romanticism, instead of intimacy and commitment. Other scholars argue that advertising messages continue to portray women as less intelligent, less active, and less instrumental than men. The cultural pressures to conform to advertising messages extend to even the youngest members of society.

The cumulative result of pornography remains dangerous to women. For the satisfaction of the *male gaze*, which refers to the term coined by Laura Mulvey to denote the objectification of women in film, producers continue to fragment the female body through close-ups. These fragmentary images serve to reduce and objectify women. Meanwhile, downward-looking camera angles enhance the image of the submissive female object of male desire and domination. African American women continue to be depicted as animals, while Asian women are portrayed as sweet and docile. A number of scholars have suggested that these increasingly pervasive images on the Internet and in traditional media outlets serve to encourage sexual violence toward women.

In the historically male domain of sports, male athletes still receive the bulk of media coverage. Although there is some evidence that journalists are beginning to provide more responsible coverage of women's sports than they have in the past, female athletes are often portrayed in stereotypical ways—as mothers, wives, and fashion models in a still homophobic sports media landscape. Sports media personnel are also portrayed in sexist manners by the media. The voice of the sports "authority"—the play-by-play announcer and color commentator—remains virtually all male, especially in traditionally masculine sports like football and baseball. Likewise, female sports broadcasters primarily are relegated to the sidelines—where they are objectified, hypersexualized, and commodified. Many scholars argue that mediated images like these serve to reproduce hegemonic masculinity.

Although women like Katie Couric and Rachel Maddow have reached positions as news and political show anchors, the voice of authority in news coverage remains predominantly male. For example, women are shown in the position of expert source only 15 percent of the time. Likewise, female candidates still receive less coverage than male candidates, and the coverage that they do receive remains primarily focused on their appearance, personality, and family. When their stance on political issues warrants coverage, the issue is often framed as "feminine."

A number of scholars have documented the pervasive sexism present in the 2008 election. Diana B. Carlin and Kelly L. Winfrey argue that the media represented Hillary Clinton and Sarah Palin through the use of traditional women's stereotypes of sex object, mother, pet, and iron maiden. For instance, Palin was portrayed as John McCain's childlike pet in the mainstream media, and Clinton was vilified as an overly ambitious, cold, calculating iron maiden with a cackle and cankles. Both women were subjected to and delegitimized by the media's pervasive beauty and mommy myths. Carlin and Winfrey suggest that the mainstream media used Clinton's failure to conform to cultural beauty ideals and the image of Clinton as a bad mother willing to "pimp out" her daughter on the campaign trail to undermine her candidacy. The portrayal of female candidates in the 2008 elections by the mainstream media, scholars argue, suggests that sexism is still prevalent in U.S. culture and that problematic images of women as "too emotional" to hold political office remain.

Bending Traditional Stereotypes?

Some research suggests that not all of the images of women in the media are negative. As Victoria Nagy contends, in some popular television shows such as *South Park*, traditional stereotypes about women and families are inverted. The result: The image of the perfect American mother is questioned and trivialized, and new images of women that once were seen as outside the realm of normality are shown to be socially acceptable. Likewise, scholars such as Sherrie Inness contend that the media have given us new, tough female heroes like Buffy the Vampire Slayer and Xena and successful women like Carrie Heffernan on *The King of Queens*. Still, other scholars argue that many of these images subtly reinforce patriarchy. They point out that many of these tough action chicks must conform to cultural ideals of beauty. In addition to reinforcing the beauty myth, superheroes like Claire Bennett in *Heroes* have passive superpowers and are often portrayed as victims. Likewise, shows such as *The King of Queens*, Kimberly Walsh argues, although appearing to represent women as physically and intellectually superior to men, ultimately reaffirm male dominance.

Combating Sexism

Research on sexism in the media tends to fall into one of two categories: quantitative studies that compare portrayals of men and women and critical cultural analyses that critique one particular character, show, or the entire media landscape. Although educating the public and providing relevant critiques about sexism, many of these studies have failed to provide approaches to combat sexism in society.

Feminists have actively attempted to combat sexism in the media and mainstream society since the 1960s and 1970s. They have argued for both individual and collective approaches to systematically annihilate sexism in the workplace and in the media. Many second wave feminists contended that placing women in positions of power would drastically transform the sexist culture of the media world. Others argued that even if women gained positions of power, structural pressures would ultimately serve to reproduce the status quo. Some radical feminists have advocated a transformative approach, calling for the creation of grassroots movements such as Women in Media and News, the establishment of women's news agencies like Unnati Features, and the implementation of feminist approaches to media production, like feminist filmmaking, which contests the traditional male gaze. Most scholars, however, agree that to change the sexist media climate, it is necessary to enlist a combination of approaches, which includes school curricula, to advocate for gender equity in the media workforce and to reinvigorate a grassroots feminist movement that can be at the center of progressive politics for generations to come.

Lori Amber Roessner
University of Tennessee

See also Affirmative Action; Empowerment; Equal Employment Opportunity Commission; Feminism; Gender and Femininity: Motherhood; Gender and Femininity: Single/Independent Girl; Gender Media Monitoring; Gender Schema Theory; Hegemony; Identity; Ideology; Male Gaze; Mass Media; Minority Rights; Misogyny; Network News Anchor Desk; Newsrooms; Patriarchy; Pornification of Everyday Life; Pornography: Heterosexual; Pornography: Internet; Postfeminism; Prejudice; Racism; Scopophilia; Sexuality; Stereotypes; Workforce

Further Readings

Andrews, Emily. "90% of Women 'Sexually Harassed in the Workplace.'" Mail Online. http://www.dailymail.co.uk/news/article-1302016/90-women-sexually-harassed-workplace.html (Accessed May 2011).

Banet-Weiser, Sarah. "Girl's Rule! Gender, Feminism and Nickelodeon." *Critical Studies in Media Communication*, v.21/2 (2004).

Benwell, Bethan. "New Sexism? Readers' Responses to the Use of Irony in Men's Magazines." *Journalism Studies*, v.8/4 (2007).

Berg, Barbara J. *Sexism in America: Alive, Well, and Ruining Our Future*. Chicago: Lawrence Hill Books, 2009.

Byerly, Carolyn M. and Karen Ross, eds. *Women and Media: A Critical Introduction*. Malden, MA: Blackwell, 2006.

Carlin, Diana B. and Kelly L. Winfrey. "Have You Come a Long Way, Baby? Hillary Clinton, Sarah Palin, and Sexism in 2008 Campaign Coverage." *Communication Studies*, v.60/4 (2009).

Creedon, Pamela and Judith Cramer, eds. *Women in Mass Communication*, 3rd ed. Thousand Oaks, CA: Sage, 2007.

De Bruin, Marjan and Karen Ross, eds. *Gender and Newsroom Cultures: Identities at Work*. Cresskill, NJ: Hampton Press, 2004.

Desjardins, Mary. "Gender and Television." Museum of Broadcast Communications. http://www.museum.tv/archives/etv/G/htmlG/genderandte/genderandte.htm (Accessed May 2011).

Douglas, Susan J. *Enlightened Sexism: The Seductive Message That Feminism's Work Is Done*. New York: Times Books, 2010.

Douglas, Susan J. *Where the Girls Are: Growing Up Female With the Mass Media*. New York: Random House, 1995.

Dow, Bonnie. *Prime-Time Feminism: Television, Media Culture, and the Women's Movement Since 1970*. Philadelphia: University of Pennsylvania Press, 1996.

Durham, M. Gigi. *The Lolita Effect: The Media Sexualization of Young Girls and What We Can Do About It*. Woodstock, N.Y.: Overlook Press, 2009.

Gill, Rosalind. "Sexism Reloaded, or It's Time to Get Angry Again!" *Feminist Media Studies*, v.11/1 (2011).

Inness, Sherrie, ed. *Action Chicks: New Images of Tough Women in Popular Culture*. New York: Macmillan, 2004.

McRobbie, Angela. "New Times in Cultural Studies." In *Feminist Cultural Studies II*, T. Lovell, ed. Brookfield, VT: Edward Elgar, 1995.

Nagy, Victoria. "Motherhood, Stereotypes, and South Park." *Women's Studies*, v.39/1 (2010).

Reinardy, Scott. "Female Journalists More Likely to Leave Newspapers." *Newspaper Research Journal*, v.30/3 (2009).

Shapiro, Fred R. "Historical Notes on the Vocabulary of the Women's Movement." *American Speech*, v.60/1 (1985).

Stabile, Carol. "'Sweetheart, This Ain't Gender Studies': Sexism and Superheroes." *Communication and Critical/ Cultural Studies*, v.6.1 (2009).

Traister, Rebecca. *Big Girls Don't Cry: The Election That Changed Everything for American Women*. New York: Free Press, 2010.

Walsh, Kimberly, Elfriede Fürsich, and Bonnie Jefferson. "Beauty and the Patriarchal Beast: Gender Role Portrayals in Sitcoms Featuring Mismatched Couples." *Journal of Popular Film and Television*, v.36/3 (2008).

Weaver, David H. and G. Cleveland Wilhoit. *The American Journalist in the 1990s: U.S. News People at the End of an Era*. Mahwah, NJ: Lawrence Erlbaum Associates, 1996.

Wolf, Naomi. *The Beauty Myth: How Images of Beauty Are Used Against Women*. New York: HarperCollins, 2002.

SEXUALITY

The representation of sexuality in the media is a hotly debated topic among both scholars and audiences. Over the course of the 20th and early 21st centuries, analysis of the media's depiction of sex has come from many different sectors. The purview of this essay is limited to the academic discussion of sex in the media over approximately the last 50 years. It examines several major perspectives on media and sexuality in both thematic and approximate chronological order, looking at the philosophical contributions, methodological innovations, and sociological insights offered by each approach. Feminism, in its many forms, plays a central role, but other schools of thought, including psychoanalytic film theory,

queer theory, intersectionality, postfeminism, and recently media studies, have also put forward novel perspectives for understanding media representations of sexuality. The sexualized representations considered throughout this entry range from mainstream film and television shows to magazines and beauty contests to pornography. Pornography is an especially important category of sexual representation and its near-omnipresence at the beginning of the 21st century is discussed at length at the close of this article.

Radical and Marxist Feminism

It would be impossible to provide a well-informed overview of sexuality in the media without granting substantial attention to the influence of second wave feminism. Beginning in the late 1960s, feminists have provided incisive critiques of representations of sexuality in a variety of media, including literature, the visual arts, television, film, romance novels, and a variety of other popular-culture texts. Radical feminists, who believed that women needed to be "liberated" from the constraints of patriarchy and capitalism, demanded many changes in the mass media's depiction of gender and sexuality. In the late 1960s and early 1970s, second wave feminists inaugurated a new era of media critique with sit-ins at women's fashion magazines and guerrilla theater at beauty pageants, where in one case they crowned a live sheep the contest's "queen." Feminists challenged television, magazine, film, and advertisements' depiction of women as passive, irrational, and innately domestic, calling for more realistic and diverse representations. They rejected the dualistic portrayal of women as sex objects or demure housewives, which reinforced a virgin/whore dichotomy with classist and racist overtones. The prevalence of simplistic and denigrating representations of women and female sexuality helped fuel second wave feminists' suspicions of sexualized representations generally. This wariness, combined with a long-standing American suspicion of sex generally, paved the way for a stance that was hostile not only to "negative" depictions of sex but to all other forms of erotic representation as well.

The period from the late 1970s through the 1980s was a time of growing fragmentation and polarization within feminism and the larger American culture; theories that emerged during this era necessarily reflected prevailing tensions and concerns. Catharine MacKinnon, a lawyer and scholar who pioneered the field of sex discrimination law, turned her attention to what she perceived to be the inherently discriminatory nature of pornography. MacKinnon identified herself as a Marxist feminist, and her commitment to Marxism is demonstrated in her understanding of sexual representation. Marxism argues that members of the working class accept an unfair social order because they are brainwashed into supporting capitalism. Analogously, women who defend or enjoy pornography are dupes complicit with patriarchy. Although other feminists had decried the objectification of women in pornography, MacKinnon went further than those before her. She argued that pornography did not simply represent the objectification of women; it was an act of violence against them. MacKinnon and her supporters believed that pornography caused damages to women that should be actionable under the law; in other words, women should be able to receive restitution for the psychological damages of pornography as well as the discrimination they inevitably faced from men conditioned by the "dehumanizing" effects of porn.

MacKinnon's arguments were influential—some cities enacted ordinances based on her legal theories—but many critiqued her work. Some argued from a civil liberties position, defending sexualized representations as free speech. Many feminists declared themselves "prosex" and called for a more nuanced, empirically sound, and sophisticated account of how men and women actually experience pornography. The strongest arguments against pornography as a form of sexual discrimination and sexual abuse noted that MacKinnon's theory relied on a one-dimensional view of human (male) sexuality. Many complexities of sexual identity and sexual activities were not, and could not be, acknowledged within her framework. Male and female homosexuality were written off or subsumed under an overarching framework of heterosexual (that is, aggressive male) desire. Female sexual agency was redefined as false consciousness. An inability to engage seriously with contradictory information, combined with the ubiquity of pornography and its growing acceptance, weakened the hold MacKinnon's theories had on the scholarly and public imagination.

Psychoanalytic Film Theory

During the 1970s, film theorists influenced by Freudian and Lacanian psychoanalysis developed new perspectives for thinking about sexual representations. Laura Mulvey's work was particularly influential in the way it utilized both psychoanalysis and feminism. Focusing on movies from Hollywood's "classic" era (approximately from the 1930s through the early 1960s), Mulvey theorized that these films were composed of three "looks" or "gazes": the camera's gaze at the characters, the characters' views of one another, and the audiences' view of the characters on the movie screen. All three of these gazes were constructed as masculine, meaning that the viewer was meant to identify with a heterosexual male perspective. Within the psychoanalytic paradigm, the masculine gaze could be either voyeuristic or fetishistic. A voyeuristic gaze was sadistic, delighting in a woman's humiliation. The fetishistic gaze was worshipful and suppressed the sexual urge to dominate. Female characters were "to-be-looked-at." Women in these films were not protagonists who moved the plot forward but instead props that provided the male characters with motivation. Other film scholars, many of whom were influenced by second wave feminism, criticized the theory of the "male gaze" because it seemed to collude with, rather than challenge, the phallogocentricity of psychoanalytic thought. Additionally, a more sophisticated critique questioned whether real viewers inhabited the limited subjectivities classic Hollywood film supposedly proffered. Mulvey argued that her schema was meant to be provocative; she never meant for her theory to be the final word on how film represented women and sexuality.

Queer Scholarship and Intersectionality

In the 1980s, queer theorists began questioning the heterosexism that shaped so many of the academic writings on sexual representation. As is clear with some of the approaches described above, the heterosexuality of media producers and audiences is simply assumed. Little attention is given to the fact that many media viewers are not straight or that representations of sexuality can be complex and open to many interpretations. Gay and lesbian writers argued that scholars needed to recognize the possibility of diverse audiences' identifications, as well as the richness of cinematic and other texts' representations of sexuality.

Throughout most of the 20th century, representations of sexuality and sexual politics in the mainstream media might contain a homosexual subtext. This means that, along with the heterosexual story line that was clear to all viewers, there was fodder for a queer reading. For example, the sharp-tongued maiden aunt or the lifelong bachelor could easily be interpreted as homosexual, meaning that gay men and lesbians were not entirely erased from popular culture. The "camp" aesthetic (associated much more with gay men than with lesbians) provides another example of how queer culture influenced representations of sexuality. Camp is a way of viewing the world that derives from an ambivalent identification, that is, the strongly mixed feelings many gay men had toward their homosexuality. Camp manages to be at once ironic, sentimental, celebratory, and able to take pleasure in the absurd. For a long time, a camp reading could be superimposed on a subject—for example, Judy Garland or Joan Crawford—perhaps in the glamorous yet raunchy figure of the drag queen. Now, however, camp has become integrated with the postmodern aesthetic, with its special affection for mismatched elements, particularly high-low culture pairings.

Intersectionality refers to the ways that different identities overlap in the same person. Within intersectionality, there is a particular concern with how different conjunctions of race, gender, and sexual orientation combine in people's lives. For example, an analysis of a sexualized representation of a lesbian Latina not only would consider homosexuality or gender but also would attempt to think through several features at once. Scholars of intersectionality do not tend to focus on mass-media representations of sexuality. However, their work points to the ways that race, gender, sexual orientation, class, physical ability, and other factors influence how of people are depicted across a wide range of disciplines—particularly the law and public policy—as well as texts.

Postfeminism and the "Pornification of Everyday Life"

In the last several years, there has been a backlash against feminism's perceived tendency to downplay women's agency and sexual pleasure and focus only on women's sexual victimization. This is one factor among several that helped fuel the emergence of what Rosalind Gill identifies as the "postfeminist sensibility." Postfeminism accepts many of the tenets of second wave feminism—such as women's substantive equality with men and their right to self-determination—but it emphasizes women's sexual agency and pleasure while rarely, if ever, turning a critical eye to media representations of female sexuality. Though postfeminism's emphasis on women's empowerment is welcome, the reluctance of many postfeminists to think rigorously about sex in the media is problematic and unhelpful at a time when sexual representations are becoming ever more numerous and pervasive.

Since the mid-1990s, when the commercial Internet began to take off in the United States, millions of men, women, and children have accessed Internet pornography or other kinds of sexual representation on the World Wide Web. Every year, new technologies present Internet users with novel opportunities for representing sexuality; in addition to streaming or still-image pornography, chat rooms, online dating sites, and interactive sex-themed games all provide opportunities for representing sex. The new ubiquity of Internet pornography and an increasing number of graphic depictions of sex in mainstream film, movies, and magazines have led to what some observers have termed "the pornification of everyday life." The incredible variety and endless cornucopia of visual representations of sex have challenged long-standing shibboleths about the impact of sexualized media. For decades, not only feminists but also quantitative researchers in the social sciences argued that pornography and other sexual representations of women increased male heterosexual violence. However, the natural experiment facilitated by the explosion of Internet pornography does not appear to have borne out this theory.

Instead of focusing on the damages ostensibly caused by pornography, a new generation of academics is thinking about pornography as part of a larger cultural matrix, connecting sexual representations not only to gender and race but also to issues of economics and politics. Brian McNair has argued that the wealth, diversity, and accessibility of sexual representations signal a new "democratization of desire." Not everyone shares McNair's easy optimism about pornography, however. For instance, Laura Kipnis views the sexual fantasies found in pornography as examples of carnivalesque inversion. In other words, pornography provides the opportunity for people symbolically to violate social taboos. Instead of simply labeling pornography as "good" or "bad," Kipnis, and other scholars like her, are pushing thoughtful consumers of sexual representations to reflect on the role of sexualized media in society, as well as what different sexual representations might tell viewers about themselves.

Brittany N. Griebling
University of Pennsylvania

See also Feminism; Feminist Theory: Marxist; Feminist Theory: Third Wave; Film: Hollywood; Heterosexism; Homophobia; Intersectionality; Male Gaze; Mulvey, Laura; Pornification of Everyday Life; Pornography: Gay and Lesbian; Pornography: Heterosexual; Pornography: Internet; Postfeminism; Queer Theory; Scopophilia; Sexism; Virtual Sex

Further Readings

Gross, Larry. *Up From Invisibility: Lesbians, Gay Men, and the Media in America.* New York: Columbia University Press, 2002.

Kipnis, Laura. *Gagged and Bound: Pornography and the Politics of Pleasure in America.* Durham, NC: Duke University Press, 1998.

MacKinnon, Catharine. *Feminism Unmodified: Discourses on Life and Law.* Cambridge, MA: Harvard University Press, 1988.

McNair, Brian. *Striptease Culture: Sex, Media and the Democratization of Desire.* New York: Routledge, 2002.

Mulvey, Laura. *Visual and Other Pleasures.* London: Palgrave Macmillan, 2009.

SIMULACRA

Simulacra are representations that have no direct relation to the referent system. In its original meaning, the Latin word *simulacrum* means "likeness" and "similarity." A simulacrum is a representation of an object or a person that may or may not exist. For example, a painting of a dragon and the statue of Venus de Milo are both simulacra. The term was made popular by French postmodernist Jean Baudrillard, who argued that simulacra in hyperreality have come to replace real objects and people

in reality. Baudrillard used the term to explain the pervasiveness and primacy of images in a media-saturated consumer society. The concept has been applied in studies of media, film, arts, and culture in general.

Baudrillard's earliest writings were grounded in the philosophy of Karl Marx, but he later criticized Marxist thought for emphasizing the materialist nature of the social world. For example, in his essay "For a Critique of the Political Economy of Sign," he critiqued Marx for failing to see the use value and exchange value of symbols. In Marxist thought, a basic-necessity good like a loaf of bread has a use value and an exchange value. The use value is the need to reduce hunger; the exchange value is the cost to buy a loaf of bread. To Baudrillard, the use value (which he called symbolic exchange) and the exchange value of signs (which he called sign value) in a consumer society work in different ways. For example, an advertisement of designer perfume often shows a glamorous woman in a fancy setting. The images signify to consumers that perfume brings joy, love, romance, and sex. Baudrillard believed that the symbols (the images of a glamorous woman, the perfume, and so on) determine the sign value, which is an abstract, fetishized social relation (such as romantic/sexual attraction). The images created the need of use, in this case the need to be in a romantic/ sexual relationship.

Baudrillard's interests in the primacy of images in a consumer society are also reflected in his work *Simulacra and Simulation* (1994). He asserts that there are four different types of simulacra, each corresponding to a historical period. The first kind is a faithful representation of "reality." Portraits and sculptures before the Industrial Revolution were examples of these simulacra. Artists documented a person, an object, or a landscape as closely as possible. A good artist was one who could reproduce reality in the most precise way.

The second kind is associated with mass-produced images in the Industrial Revolution era and with the advancement of technologies such as photography. To Baudrillard, a photograph may hint at the existence of reality, but it shows only part of the reality. For example, family portraits taken in the late 19th century often showed a well-dressed, middle-class family. These portraits, however, failed to show the preparation the family had to undertake before the photograph was taken. Nevertheless, the

French postmodernist Jean Baudrillard wrote about simulacra used to market items like designer perfume. He stated that the symbols used, such as images of a glamorous woman using perfume, determined the sign value, which is an abstract ideal such as a romantic involvement, and that the images created the belief that one needed to use the product to obtain the relationship. (Photos.com)

image in the photograph has come to represent the family.

The third kind of simulacrum is associated with a media-rich consumer society in which images dominate daily life. To Baudrillard, the simulacrum pretends to be a faithful representation of reality, yet that reality does not exist. For example, in Cindy Sherman's collection *Untitled Film Stills* (1990), the photographs are like film stills from old Hollywood movies. However, those images were only made to look like film stills; they were actually created by the artist who is also the model in the photos. Reality television shows exemplify this kind of simulacrum as well. Reality shows do not document reality, but they create a "reality" that has no relation to the daily life of the viewers and the participants.

The fourth kind of simulacrum is one that does not refer to reality at all. Such simulacra have their own referent system. Baudrillard used the examples of Disneyland and Las Vegas to illustrate these simulacra. The architecture of Disneyland does not bear resemblance to any actual place. It is impossible to find a place where a castle is next door to a tropical jungle. Visitors to Disneyland can enjoy the park only if they do not make reference to daily life. For example, children may know that fairy tales are only stories, but they are not to question the realness of the Disney princesses in the park.

Baudrillard's neo-Marxist stance on simulacra was criticized by Marxists for failing to pay attention to the materialist nature of social relations and reality. His suggestion that the United States is a simulacrum attracted criticism of his French superiority. Finally, his comments on the Gulf War attracted ridicule in France and abroad.

Micky Lee
Suffolk University, Boston

See also Postfeminism; Postmodernism; Post-Structuralism

Further Readings

Baudrillard, Jean. *America*. New York: Verso, 2010.

Baudillard, Jean. *Simulacra and Simulation*. Ann Arbor: University of Michigan Press, 1994.

Baudrillard, Jean. *Symbolic Exchange and Death*. London: Sage, 1993.

Kellner, Douglas. *Jean Baudrillard: From Marxism to Postmodernism and Beyond*. Cambridge, UK: Polity Press, 1989.

Poster, Mark. *Jean Baudrillard: Selected Writings*, 2nd ed. Stanford, CA: Stanford University Press, 2001.

Sitcoms

Broadcast television established itself as a cultural stronghold in the 1950s. Many predicted television to be a temporary fad, but it soon proved to be anything but. Its rapid expansion clogged the airwaves, resulting in a temporary freeze by the Federal Communications Commission (FCC). Initially, broadcast television imitated programming that had already been established in radio, but television programming soon expanded to include drama anthologies, news programs, quiz shows, and the weekly, half-hour situational comedy, known as the sitcom.

As opposed to stand-up or sketch comedy, a situational comedy has a story line and often comprises a series of shows or episodes with ongoing characters. The situation is usually that of a family, workplace, or group of friends. Early sitcoms reflected the postwar cultural shift toward a white, suburban audience by featuring white, middle-age suburban couples with families. These shows idealized nuclear families and derived their humor from trivial everyday situations with problems that were easily resolved. The overriding themes of a sitcom are comedic. While some story lines might involve serious issues or carry a moral, laughter is always an objective. Sitcom humor tends to be character-driven and relies heavily on one-liner jokes. These shows feature broadly drawn characters who seldom have major personality changes, although they may marry, divorce, have children, change jobs, or switch romantic partners. Sitcoms are designed to encourage viewers to form long-term relationships with the characters and return to view them repeatedly. Writers use characters and situations that are immediately recognizable to a majority of viewers. With time, the definitions of domestic comedy and roles adapted by family members have changed and expanded. However, the typical sitcom formula remains constant, with a pattern of establishment, complication, confusion, and resolution.

Families portrayed on television have provided a historical record of gender roles. Though obviously fictional, these families enact examples of family interactions that may be used as indicators of changing societal attitudes about gender roles within the family. The overall message is one of familial stability and support. Sitcom story lines are believed to carry with them implicit lessons about family life. Television is credited with being the great socializer in American society. While it is generally agreed that television contributes to our notion of what is believed to be important and how we are to behave in a variety of settings, research is less conclusive with regard to sex-role stereotyping and television. The situational comedy format has particular ramifications for Albert Bandura's social learning theory. Social learning theory is often used to examine the media effects on individuals, particularly on children and adolescents. It is applied to gender roles and sitcoms with the notion that viewers may vicariously learn life lessons by viewing these types of programs and modeling the familial roles portrayed in the shows, especially if the characters receive positive rewards for their behavior.

Early Sitcoms: 1950s–1970s

The early years of television are often referred to as the Golden Age. Shows during this time were characterized by white, middle-class, intact, suburban families. It is interesting to note that these television appearances were in much higher percentages than they occurred in actuality. The commercial nature of television is credited with featuring a middle-class ambiance, to closely identify with the audience members and the products that formed its commercial basis. Therefore, a proliferation of middle-class family images characterized most situation comedy programming of American television's prime-time from the mid-1950s through the late 1960s. Women in these families overwhelmingly did not work outside the home and were shown primarily in the activities associated with their roles as wives and mothers, which were shown to be the center of their lives and identities. Thus 1950s programs like *Leave It to Beaver* (1957–63), *The Donna Reed Show* (1958–66), and *The Adventures of Ozzie and Harriet* (1952–66) are considered seminal examples. The Beaver, Mary, or Ricky experienced some sort of minor dilemma, and then Ward, Donna, or Ozzie administered some parental wisdom with words of advice. The child learned the moral lesson, only to be confronted with a new predicament the following week.

One sitcom that broke the mold of white suburbia was created by Lucille Ball and Desi Arnaz in the early 1950s with the hit show *I Love Lucy* (1951–57). It was the first sitcom to portray a mixed marriage between a white woman and a Latino male. The show featured Ricky Ricardo as a Cuban bandleader and Lucy as an inept housewife continually trying to break into show business. *I Love Lucy* incorporated both professional and domestic settings as well as the use of zany, physical humor. Within four months of its premiere, it became a top-rated show and remained number one for four years. *I Love Lucy* is still aired today and continues to make people laugh. The success of *I Love Lucy* led to a profusion of sitcoms and cemented the sitcom genre as a mainstay in television programming.

By the 1960s, the domestic comedy was expanding beyond the nuclear family or married couple. Television families began to change on prime-time television in the late 1960s as alternative images of women in the workplace, as well as in the family, slowly began to proliferate. For example, the television situation comedy *That Girl* (1966–71), starring Marlo Thomas, was the first show of the period to feature a young, unmarried girl living on her own. Her character, who wants to become an actress, leaves her family's home in Brewster, New York, to occupy her own apartment in Manhattan while she searches for fame and fortune in the entertainment business. Although her father and boyfriend are portrayed as protectors in the show, this sitcom presented a new image for single women in the big city. During this period, the sitcom also portrayed more diverse roles that went beyond the traditional home and conventional family value system. Some of the more popular shows of the time include *Gilligan's Island* (1964–67), about seven stranded castaways, men and women from different classes and walks of life, surviving together on an island; and *The Andy Griffith Show* (1960–68) and *My Three Sons* (1960–72), featuring widowers fathering their children. Sitcom producers also began adding more fantastical elements, including monsters, genies, and witches. This new character base led to shows such as *The Munsters* (1964–66), *I Dream of Jeannie* (1965–70), and *Bewitched* (1964–72).

Domestic comedies of the 1970s began to address controversial issues in a serious way with diverse casts. Norman Lear produced some of this decade's more popular shows, including the milestone comedy *All in the Family* (1971–79), featuring the famous Archie Bunker (played by Carroll O'Connor) as a working-class father whose obtuse bigotry, selfishness, and sexism are usually if begrudgingly overcome by his genuine impulses for kindness and fairness, especially under the pressure of changing social values as represented by his hippie daughter and son-in-law as well as a wife whose submissiveness masks her inner strength. The program highlights the "generation gap" and the dying mores and prejudices of the 1950s and early 1960s, intentionally undercutting those values by placing hypocrisies on full display. Problems addressed in these sitcoms included taboo topics such as abortion, racism, the women's movement, and antiwar sentiment. In addition to addressing new content, these 1970s sitcoms began to acknowledge different types of families when *The Brady Bunch* (1969–74) focused on the issues faced by a blended family. Many 1970s shows successfully abandoned the traditional family setting altogether for work settings. On-air professional relationships transformed business relationships into familial ones by assigning certain familial roles to the office workers—the cranky boss became the father, the ditzy newsman took the place of the wild brother, and so on. One of the more popular shows to accomplish this was *The Mary Tyler Moore Show* (1970–77). In this sitcom, viewers were introduced to what is perhaps television's first true career woman, Mary Richards, the product of a broken

engagement who has determined to make it on her own, without husband or family. The show revolves around what becomes her workplace family and her apartment neighbors Rhoda and Phyllis.

Later Sitcoms: 1980s–Present

Sitcoms in the 1980s reflect different themes—a return to a familial comedy as well as a continuation of stronger women's roles in a variety of settings. Programs that bridged the 1970s and 1980s began to feature the single mother. Notable single television moms of this time include Ann Romano as a feisty, hardworking divorced mom with teenage daughters on *One Day at a Time* (1975–84) and the hardworking waitress and single mom of *Alice* (1976–85), an independent and logical person who continually faced problems but handled them in a level-headed manner. *Kate and Allie* (1984–89) featured two single-mother friends sharing a household, and *Who's the Boss?* (1984–92) focused on a single mother and her male household helper, whose platonic friendship carried undertones of attraction. Sitcoms such as *Family Ties* (1982–89), *Growing Pains* (1985–92), *The Cosby Show* (1984–92), and the later *Full House* (1987–95) returned to themes of family life and parent-child relationships and centered less on the social issues that had defined many 1970s sitcoms.

By the mid-1980s, the growth of cable television, additional broadcast networks, and the success of first-run syndication had fractured the mass audience into smaller, niche markets. Programming could now be targeted to specific audiences rather than a general audience, and this capacity extended to sitcoms. By the end of the decade, a backlash against the dominance of family-oriented sitcoms was emerging, with producers creating sharper takes on working-class family life in the satirical *Married With Children* (1987–97) and the animated series *The Simpsons* (1989–). There was also a return to adult programs, such as *Seinfeld* (1989–98), that focused largely on relationships among single adults. Other shows, including *Roseanne* (1988–97) and *Murphy Brown* (1988–98), appeared to be portraying more assertive women in both the domestic and working worlds.

In the 1990s, sitcoms began to incorporate aspects of domestic comedy and family melodrama. Both *Roseanne* (whose content evolved significantly under star Roseanne Barr's influence) and *Grace Under Fire* (1993–98), for example, tackled the topics of incest, spousal abuse, alcoholism, masturbation, and unemployment within the context of the family sitcom. The sarcasm and cynicism of the central characters diffused any seriousness associated with these problems, keeping their treatment comedic. The programs often inserted situation comedy routines (drunkenness, mistaken identity, extravagant production numbers) in the middle of an episode. Two of the more popular sitcoms to achieve top-ten ratings include *Everybody Loves Raymond* (1996–2005) and *Two and a Half Men* (2003–). Another distinct change in sitcoms during this time is the use of a pseudodocumentary style of filming as seen in *The Office* (2005–) and *Modern Family* (2009–).

Sitcom Influence on Gender Construction

Television is an integral part of American culture. As it takes up a great deal of time and attention, it is important to assess and study how television and mass media depict the roles of men and women. Access to mass media has increased, and television for many people has become part of their daily lives. Individuals learn social norms, including what it is like to be a male or female, in part by watching television. Television displays and maintains societal norms and values as well as exposing individuals to alternative choices. Definitions of what is considered to be acceptable behavior for men and women are provided on television. Stereotypes offer generalizations about people on the basis of their group membership and often help to maintain and reinforce the power of the status quo. Many scholars study the influence of viewing these types of roles found on television and what effect they might have on individuals' concepts of gender.

Early television offered a rather restricted set of images, confining women to the home and family setting. The increase in working women in the 1960s and 1970s gave rise to television images of working women and women living nontraditional family lives. Studies of sitcom fathers show males originally being cast as smart, wise, and to some extent sensitive. Over time, the sitcom father lost his authority as sitcoms began to feature strong, independent mothers. More recent sitcoms continue to perpetuate traditional gender stereotypes, but a

number of them have begun to show smart, witty, and attractive women married to inept, overweight, and immature men.

Traditional gender roles are based on idealized masculinity and femininity, which provide prescriptions for the way that males and females are to behave. Traditional gender roles would include expectations for women to be family-oriented and men to be career-oriented. In the early days of television, men and women were typically portrayed in traditional gender roles. These traditional gender roles involved women being actively involved in household and domestic chores. They were always in roles that were passive and mild-mannered. Married women were rarely portrayed as employed outside the home because a man's role was to work and provide for his family. Television reinforced traditional gender roles of women by casting them as characters in parts that performed typical household duties and childcare in the role of homemakers. Traditionally domestic and household duties were considered women's work and women's responsibility. Mothering and caring for others were natural and expected responses for women. Television shows like *Leave It to Beaver* (1957–63), *Father Knows Best* (1954–63), and *The Brady Bunch* (1969–74) emphasized traditional women as women who enjoyed staying home and who were content having little power. The fathers on those shows held power within the family and typically were the decision makers. Traditional gender roles depicted women as relationship-oriented and family-oriented. Women on television generally did not venture into men's public world of work. Early sitcoms clearly reinforced traditional gender roles.

Research on gender roles concludes that sitcoms still depict these traditional roles for men and women, but not as prevalently as in earlier years of programming. Today's sitcoms reflect a wider range of lifestyles. While approaches to research vary, consistent findings include that younger, sexier, and more independent female roles are cast, humor is used to disparage men and women, men predominate as leading characters, and women are acted upon while men are actors. There also appears to be a correlation between increased levels of television watching and adherence to sexist views and traditional roles for men and women. Gender stereotyping continues to promote masculinity as a heterosexual given, portrayed as natural and universal.

Sitcom femininity traits are associated with emotion and prudence.

The 21st century has seen broadcast television lose its audience members to cable, television on demand, and the Internet. While the sitcom is still evident on prime time, it does not dominate the airwaves as it once did. Hollywood producers and network executives continue to look to create programs that are edgy and different, while mass audiences are drawn to contemporary material that tweaks the safe and familiar. However, sitcoms still serve a prime-time purpose, because they present modern problems in a variety of contexts that entertain us. By playing on current issues in a humorous way, sitcoms also give viewers the chance to laugh at themselves, laugh at society, and laugh at the actors and the show. Sitcoms can, therefore, effectively confront issues yet soften the pain of confronting them at the same time. Sitcoms provide us with a unique, although somewhat distorted, mirror in which to view ourselves and our world.

Laura Barnes Ashley
University of Houston

See also Advertising; Audiences: Reception and Injection Models; Children's Programming: Cartoons; Children's Programming: Disney and Pixar; Gay and Lesbian Portrayals on Television; Mass Media; Patriarchy; Radio; Sexism; Soap Operas; Social Learning Theory; Stereotypes; Television; Televisuality.

Further Readings

Archive of American Television. http://www .emmytvlegends.org (Accessed February 2011).

Douglas, William and Beth Olson. "Beyond Family Structure: The Family in Domestic Comedy." *Journal of Broadcasting and Electronic Media*, v.39 (1995).

Morreale, Joanne. *Critiquing the Sitcom: A Reader.* Syracuse, NY: Syracuse University Press, 2003.

Olson, Beth and William Douglas. "The Family on Television: Evaluation of Gender Roles in Situation Comedy." *Sex Roles*, v.36 (1997).

Scharrer, Erica. "From Wise to Foolish: The Portrayal of the Sitcom Father, 1950s–1990s." *Journal of Broadcasting and Electronic Media*, v.45 (2001).

Spigel, Lynn. *Make Room for TV: Television and the Family Ideal in Postwar America.* Chicago: University of Chicago Press, 1992.

Taylor, Ella. *Prime-Time Families: Television Culture in Postwar America.* Berkeley: University of California Press, 1989.

Walsh, Kimberly, Elfriede Fürsich, and Bonnie Jefferson. "Beauty and the Patriarchal Beast: Gender Role Portrayals in Sitcoms Featuring Mismatched Couples." *Journal of Popular Film and Television*, v.36/3 (2008).

SOAP OPERAS

Soap operas are often referred to as a "women's genre." The term *soap operas* is used to describe daytime radio and television dramas because of their advertising sponsors, which marketed detergents and other household products to homebound female listeners and viewers. The genre's marketing strategies reinforce the notion that women are soap operas' primary audience, which is based on patriarchal stereotypes (hypothetical male ideals) about what constitutes appropriate female behavior. The gender roles presented in soap operas are shaped by these perceptions. Patriarchal assumptions about women's desire for dialogue, fantasy, romance, and intimacy influenced the way soap operas evolved.

Women and Early Radio Serials

Daytime soap operas became a successful form of daytime radio entertainment in the early 1930s, following the success of evening serials airing at the time. *Painted Dreams* (1930–43), written by radio actress Irna Phillips, is considered the first American soap opera. It featured Irish-American widow Mother Moynihan running a boardinghouse and raising a large family. The daytime serial introduced many of the structural conventions for which soap operas are known today, including the serial narrative and open-ended cliff-hanger endings. Its themes, including domestic life, family, personal relationships, and morality, created the foundation for the modern daytime drama.

Advertising copywriters Frank and Anne Hummert developed a plot-driven assembly-line approach to writing and producing serial dramas that is still followed today. Their sensationalist romantic adventures and fantasy stories incorporated such themes as deceit, jealousy, infidelity, and murder. Their stories appealed to America's desire to mentally escape the difficulties of the Great Depression while conveying traditional American ideals: working hard, saving money, prioritizing family life, and punishing bad behavior. Stable female characters living in the Midwest mostly articulated these values. Hummert radio serials such as *Ma Perkins* (1933–60) and *Young Widder Brown* (1938–56) featured heroines who were wives, mothers, and widows struggling to take care of their families. They also cared for their injured or diseased husbands and sons if and when they returned from the war. Most of the Hummert plots also attempted to bridge the gap between the wealthy and the aspiring middle class in their mythic story worlds. Soap operas like *Stella Dallas* (1937–55) and *Our Gal Sunday* (1934–59) feature poor or orphaned young heroines who successfully marry above their station and maintain happy, stable lives.

Daytime Television Dramas

Radio soap operas aired until 1960. By this time, most major daytime advertising sponsors had stopped backing dramatic radio programming in favor of television shows. The DuMont network produced and aired television adaptations of the radio soap operas *Big Sister* (1936–52) and *Aunt Jenny's True Life Stories* (1937–56) in 1944. In 1946, DuMont created the short-lived daytime drama *Faraway Hill* (October–December 1946), in which techniques such as the offscreen voice (a narration that verbally articulates a character's thoughts) were developed to allow housewives to continue to tune in to the drama without having to stop their domestic activities to watch it unfold. Early successful long-term television soap operas such as *Search for Tomorrow* (1951–86) and Irna Phillips's adaptation of the radio serial *The Guiding Light* (1937–2009) assimilated these techniques while adapting the traditional female radio heroine to television.

The modern television soap opera was born with the 1956 launch of Phillips's *As the World Turns* (1956–2010). Episodes were extended from 15- to 30-minute (and later 60-minute) segments, allowing for multiple plotlines, increased character development, and more opportunities for writers to incorporate real-life social issues into the narratives. Phillips also adapted cinematographic devices, such as close-up shots, to create visually and emotionally intimate relationships between soap characters and female viewers. In the 1960s, soap writers such as Agnes Nixon and Bill Bell continued to incorporate contemporary social issues into soap opera plots as well as salacious themes similar to those made popular by Hummert radio soaps. In soap operas like *One Life to Live* (1968–2012), Nixon addressed nontraditional issues such as women's health and preventive gynecological care. She also developed ways to use videotape to visually enhance fantasy sequences by highlighting characters' private desires. Bell's first serial drama, *The Young and the Restless* (1973–), reflected the social changes brought on by the sexual revolution by moving scenes into the bedroom. He also had model-type actresses play lead roles and used lighting techniques to enhance characters' sensuality. The Nixon-Bell tradition also led to the creation of the archetype of the female soap opera villain, who has become a driving force in the modern soap narrative.

Prime-Time Soap Operas

The controversial television evening serial drama *Peyton Place* (1964–69), which focused on the lives of three women in a small New England town, became the model for what came to be known in the 1980s as the prime-time soap opera. The show's sensational plotlines, as well as its attention to timely issues such as teen pregnancy, are reflected in later prime-time series such as *Dallas* (1978–91), *Knots Landing* (1979–93), and *Dynasty* (1981–89). These stories revolved around feuding wealthy families, moral excess, and strong ambitious female types made popular by the Nixon-Bell tradition.

Teen-oriented series like *Beverly Hills, 90210* (1990–2000) and *Melrose Place* (1992–99) gave a modern, youthful context to the soap opera genre when they examined issues like sex, drug addiction, and homosexuality, topics that have since been adopted by 21st-century traditional soap operas. (Photos.com)

Prime-time programs that combine soap opera conventions with other generic formats are also common. A popular example of this is *Desperate Housewives* (2006–), a show that draws heavily on the themes and conventions featured in *Peyton Place* while using humor to tell the stories of the women living on a private suburban street. Teen-oriented series like *Beverly Hills, 90210* (1990–2000) and *Melrose Place* (1992–99) also incorporate themes of family and romance made popular by early daytime dramas. These themes are offered in a modern context that expands on notions of family, including social groups, and that reflects changing social attitudes about sex, homosexuality, and other issues among the youth culture.

Soap Operas and Gender Roles

The gender roles portrayed in soap operas combine mythic representations of men and women with images that reflect the real-life cultural norms and values of the time period in which they appear. The thoughts and actions of early radio and television soap opera heroines reflect female gender roles that were widely accepted at the time and were dictated by patriarchal ideals. Lead male characters were strong and humble, leading simple lives. Unwed heroines passively waited for men to marry them, while those who were married or widowed were committed to taking care of their families. Women lucky enough to marry well often found themselves protecting their marriages from vampy seductresses trying to usurp their positions. These sexually aggressive women were eventually punished for their actions and disappeared. Despite Irna Phillips's introduction of a few career women, most female characters negotiated their role within the domestic sphere of the home. It was common for early male soap opera characters to play the role of the sensitive, polite listener, who understood the female heroines as they talked about their concerns. The small number of male soap opera heroes of the time, such as town barber Bill Davidson in *Just Plain Bill* (1932–55), actively solved problems. Boyfriends and husbands not killed in the war often returned with severe physical injuries or suffering emotional traumas that left them emasculated and in need of a woman's care. Occasional plots brought in male villains to seduce a female heroine, but these efforts ultimately ended in failure.

Between the 1950s and early 1960s, television soap operas introduced characters that fulfilled the gender roles outlined in early radio daytime serials. These roles began to change once soap operas began to address the real-life cultural changes brought on by social movements like the sexual revolution and feminism. By the early 1970s, both male and female characters were evolving into more sophisticated and complex personality types. Along with the traditional family-oriented female characters, soap operas began introducing educated and professional suburban women into their story worlds. Some of these characters, like Marlena Brady of *Days of Our Lives* (1965–), reflect this contemporary female image while fulfilling the traditional role of loving wife and mother. Doting grandmothers were also introduced as upper-class socialites. The central sexy female villain archetype, introduced in the late 1960s, is the modern embodiment of the Hummert tradition of fantasy and scandal. These women, often referred to as "soap bitches," directly contradict the roles of early passive and moral heroines. They are strong, assertive, ambitious, and comfortable with their sexuality. They openly covet power and privilege, and their sense of morality is guided by this desire. They will often stop at nothing to get what they want and will selfishly use sex and marriage to achieve their goals if necessary. Many of these characters, like *All My Children* (1970–2011) villain Erica Kane and *Dynasty* schemer Alexis Colby, are characterized as egotistical, overambitious, and vengeful, much like the seductive vixens of early radio. Unlike the early radio vamps, however, they are permanent fixtures in the modern soap opera story world and pose a continual threat to the stable world of traditional marriage and family.

Soap operas situate men as women's objects of focus. Central male soap characters reinforce the idea that women desire men and are therefore developed to reflect social perceptions of the kind of men female audiences privately yearn for. Early female soap opera heroines and villains were largely motivated by their desire to marry them. Married women were dedicated to holding on to their spouses and taking care of them. Women consistently knew more than they did and often manipulated them to achieve their desired goals. The introduction of strong, ambitious, and sexualized female characters in the 1970s led to the creation of lead male characters who were stronger, sexier, and more violent than their early counterparts. Characters like Max Holden of *One Life to Live* (1968–2012) and Luke Spencer of *General Hospital* (1963–) fulfilled the role of the strong, handsome, action-hero male archetype, which is based on patriarchally defined gender roles, to satisfy the perceived sexual fantasies of female audiences and to challenge the strong female characters with whom they were interacting. Far from perfect, these men also exhibited villainous traits that led to the punishment of strong and ambitious women through actions like rape and kidnapping. In the 1990s, male soap opera characters, including Holden and Spencer, began to negotiate their macho image to appeal to the political correctness of the time. Today's leading men fulfill the roles of protector and villain but also exhibit a level of sensitivity and understanding characteristic of their roles in early radio serials.

The introduction in 1982 of lesbian Dr. Lynn Carson in *All My Children* and the 1987 story line about gay character Hank Elliott in *As the World Turns* initiated the presence of significant lesbian, gay, bisexual, and transgendered characters in daytime soaps. These characters are often portrayed as victims who are paying a price for their sexual orientation. They often lead lives that are loveless and sexless, lacking the dramatic complexity of their heterosexual counterparts' lives. Their roles are often short-lived.

Soaps and Contemporary Social Themes

Serial dramas, particularly daytime dramas, are continually adapted to reflect industry and social changes. Irna Phillips's radio serials reflected real-world events of the time, addressing social themes such as alcoholism, war-induced stress, and other mental disorders. Hummert soap operas produced story lines reflecting wartime events, like sending heroine Stella Dallas to work in a munitions factory and featuring the death of one of Ma Perkins's sons in battle.

Over the years, modern television soap operas have integrated socially relevant narratives that explore issues like domestic violence, birth control, sexual assault, abortion, and various forms of cancer. It is usually female characters who are directly confronted with these issues, the impact of which is discussed within the context of traditional soap opera narratives like romance and marriage. The effect these issues have on individual women is often overshadowed by their impact on the community at large.

In the mid-1990s, soap operas began introducing story lines about human immunodeficiency virus and acquired immune deficiency syndrome (HIV/AIDS). These narratives focused primarily on how the disease was affecting heterosexual Caucasian women rather than African Americans and homosexuals, which were the populations most affected by the disease at that time. Later episodes featured gay characters like Hank Elliott, who had loved ones dying from the disease who were rarely featured on camera.

Plotlines involving the gay, lesbian, bisexual, and transgendered community have been largely limited to subjects like coming out, homophobia, gay bashing, and AIDS. By 1992, soap operas like *One Life to Live* and *All My Children* began introducing teen-oriented story lines designed to address some of the struggles faced by real-life gay teens. In 2000, *All My Children* began chronicling the life of Bianca Montgomery, the first openly lesbian teenager to be featured in a daytime soap opera. Her 2003 romance with Lena Kundera, a bisexual teen, led to the first lesbian kiss on daytime television. However, Bianca's subsequent rape and resulting pregnancy by Kundera's ex-boyfriend placed her character within a largely heteronormative context (cultural bias in favor of heterosexual values) and drew attention away from her promising romantic life as a lesbian woman. Three years later, *All My Children* introduced Zarf, daytime drama's first transgendered character to transition from male to female on broadcast television. *As the World Turns* featured daytime drama's first gay male couple, Luke Snyder and Noah Mayer, in 2007. Following a highly publicized on-screen kiss in August 2007, the pair failed to exhibit any kind sexual intimacy. Mayer's later marriage to a woman in order to help her secure a green card moved the attention away from the gay relationship. His struggles with coming out to his homophobic father also reflect daytime dramas' resistance to expanding the roles of homosexual characters beyond perceived homosexual-oriented themes.

Soap Opera Imports

Soap operas exported from other countries, such as the popular telenovelas from Central and South America, are mostly targeted to immigrant women residing in the United States. Despite their localized focus, they remain popular among female audiences thanks to their universally appealing stories about romance and fantasy. The characters introduced in these programs traditionally reflect patriarchal gender roles. One of the most successful international imports, the Colombian soap opera *Yo soy Betty, la fea* (1991–2001), centers on a young, intelligent but unattractive economist who takes a secretarial position in the EcoModa fashion company and is secretly in love with the company's president. It combines the dramatic elements of the soap opera with slapstick-like humor. The successful U.S. adaptation of the show, *Ugly Betty* (2006–10), mixed sensational plotlines reminiscent of the Hummert serials with humor created by Betty's awkward inadequacies, often brought to light while she yearns for her various male colleagues.

Melissa Camacho
San Francisco State University

See also Advertising; Audiences: Reception and Injection Models; Children's Programming: Cartoons; Children's Programming: Disney and Pixar; Gay and Lesbian Portrayals on Television; Mass Media; Patriarchy; Radio; Sexism; Sitcoms; Stereotypes; Television; Televisuality

Further Readings

Cassata, Mary B. *Life on Daytime Television: Tuning-in American Serial Drama*. Norwood, NJ: Ablex, 1983.

Matelski, Marilyn J. *The Soap Opera Evolution*. Jefferson, NC: McFarland, 1988.

Museum of Television and Radio. *Worlds Without End: The Art and History of the Soap Opera*. New York: Harry N. Abrams, 1997.

Williams, Carol T. "Soap Opera Men in the '90's." *Journal of Popular Film and Television*, v.22/3 (1994).

SOCIAL COMPARISON THEORY

Social comparison is a theoretical model that examines psychological phenomena when an individual compares some aspect of the self—body image, for example—to that of others who may be actual, imagined, or implied. Leon Festinger, who is well known for developing cognitive dissonance theory, developed the theory of social comparison in 1954. Much research has taken place based on social comparison theory since Festinger first suggested that comparing oneself to another was a basic human need. Over the years, the theory has been expanded and revised to go beyond self-evaluation to include self-improvement or enhancement, varying degrees of interest regarding social comparison among individuals, and consideration of an individual's social environment. With regard to the latter, social comparisons are influenced by social environment when one makes upward (someone is better off), downward (someone is worse off), or lateral comparisons (someone is like me). Considering an idealized image—celebrity or sports figure—prevalent in advertising, one would expect that comparisons would be made in the upward direction, although it is clearly possible that the individual will evaluate the idealized image as one that is unattainable and may feel threatened in a way that affects the individual's self-esteem. Research has shown that viewing images of those less fortunate, however, directs comparison downward. Complexity grows when one considers that evaluation of an inferior other as beneath or worse off might lead to self-enhancement.

In the mid-1990s, feminist author Jean Kilbourne, among others, brought focus to the social costs extracted through young women's social comparison with ultra-thin models. She argues that the repetition of ideals that are unattainable by most women fuels a crisis rooted in eating disorders and low self-esteem, among other social issues. It was not until 2000 that research began to give full consideration to the implications for social comparison of idealized images on masculine gender identity. With regard to cross-sex comparisons, research indicates that when a male looks at the image of a very attractive female and evaluates her as someone with whom he would have no chance of developing a relationship, his self-esteem may be threatened. Sociologist Michael Kimmel, author of several books on masculinity, suggests that in American culture a successful male will adhere to standards including rugged individualism, adventurous spirit, risk taking, displays of physical prowess, and having a high degree of personal autonomy. However, research has shown that when men determine, after viewing such attributes in media, that they cannot attain those standards, they become depressed and dissatisfied with their bodies. Such research findings assume that the ideal muscular image of traditional masculinity is one that males desire to emulate but perhaps cannot. In fact, the basis for social comparison theory is the idea of emulation.

A unique twist on social comparison theory takes place when less than ideal images appear in media. Less than ideal images began to proliferate in U.S. and U.K. advertising during the mid-1990s, a trend that may be rooted in societal changes regarding men's roles, as traditional masculinity gave way to a more shifting gender identity that wavers between the traditional and the new. Also, advertisers have grown weary of utilizing sports figures, many of whom in recent years have fallen from grace: Tiger Woods, Andre Agassi, Michael Vick, Marion Jones, and Kobe Bryant are among them. Perhaps in response, some advertisers have opted to use less than ideal images, such as the cavemen who appeared in a long-running U.S. advertising campaign for GEICO insurance. The cavemen transcended their advertising platform when in 2007 the American Broadcasting Company (ABC) television network aired a short-lived sitcom based on these characters. With regard to social comparison theory, it is interesting to consider what happens when less than ideal images, like the cavemen, are presented in the media. Advertisers have also depicted men as wolves and werewolves and in a variety of socially awkward and perhaps humiliating positions, such as being caught in public without their pants. Based on social comparison theory, if looking at unattainable idealized images is depressing, then looking at less than ideal images would be uplifting or at least provide relief from the feeling of having to live up to the idealized other.

In contemporary society, several standards regarding gender identity coexist; in the case of males, they range from the traditional to the "new" male. Because of the complexity of gender identity, advertisers, in particular, push boundaries in order to develop creative deviations that invite elaborations on the part of consumers. In the case of females, for example, the Dove company's Campaign for Real Beauty depicted women in a realistic manner. A number of female celebrities are also beginning to appear on the covers of popular magazines without makeup or digital alterations, inviting lateral and downward comparisons. Such representational complexity renders gender identity problematic. In the case of male consumers, they must work through various images that range from the ideal, which traditionally constituted their strength and thus legitimized their hegemonic status, to the less than ideal, which may be indicative of an acutely troubled psychology of the male.

Social comparison theory has grown increasingly complex, along with contemporary constructions of gender identity. The traditional male might see his reflection in an advertisement and evaluate the traditional image of masculinity in a positive manner, whereas a "stay-at-home dad" might confront the same image and feel inadequate. Therefore, the route to self-enhancement that social comparison theory initially put forth is not as straightforward as the theory initially suggested. Less than ideal media images counterbalance traditional constructions of gender identity that operate in everyday life, making interpretation of those images tenable. To make sense of the less than ideal image, the individual must understand the implausibility of the visual depiction. With regard to the GEICO advertising mentioned above, for example, the following question may be raised: If a caveman is not a man, what is a man? Within this rhetorical complexity the viewer replaces the meaning conventionally linked to the visual/verbal expression—men lack intelligence or men have not evolved—with a meaning that is more in comparison with the individual's own evaluation of himself. The multiple ways in which media depict gender identity that ranges from idealized images to less than ideal images destabilize potential meanings for those who compare themselves to those images. Therefore, processing media images requires work on the part of the individual: move in the direction of the less than ideal image, for example, empathizing with the image's low status and lack of respect; isolate and identify with only one aspect of the less than ideal image; discard or partially disassociate from that aspect of the image found distasteful; or reject the image based on the comfort derived from the fact that the image is not a self-reflection of the viewer.

Repetition is an important part of the social comparison process. The more the individual encounters multifarious representations of gender identity—ideal and less than ideal—the more effective media is at dislodging the self. In other words, the motivation toward interpreting the rhetorical figures is the little effort it takes to process the metaphor. Additionally, there is pleasure to be had in processing media content that is incongruous and deviates from expectation. With regard to advertising, less than ideal and idealized images serve the purpose of metaphorically "spreading the word" about gender identity—an unintended consequence of advertising. The fluidity of gender identity is made increasingly possible because of the multiple ways in which images are visualized in media and the ways in which individuals compare themselves to those images; one way in which we make sense of our world is through comparing ourselves to others.

The mixing of idealized images and less than ideal images, along with other representations, opens gender identity to the multiple pathways through which individuals subjectively interpret and compare themselves to images depicted in media. As such, masculinity or femininity is not one thing. As is the case with race and class, masculine gender identity may not be defined simply as that which is not feminine, and feminine gender identity may not be defined simply as that which is not masculine. It is through social comparison with the multifarious images that are represented in media that individuals contend with various cultural meanings and their significance.

Neil M. Alperstein
Loyola University Maryland

See also Beauty and Body Image: Beauty Myths; Beauty and Body Image: Eating Disorders; Gender and Femininity: Motherhood; Gender and Femininity: Single/Independent Girl; Gender and Masculinity: Black Masculinity; Gender and Masculinity: Fatherhood; Gender and Masculinity: Metrosexual Male; Gender and Masculinity: White Masculinity; Gender Embodiment; Gender Media Monitoring; Gender Schema Theory; Kilbourne, Jean; Media Literacy; Social Construction of Gender

Further Readings

Agliata, Daniel and Stacey Tangleff-Dunn. "The Impact of Media Exposure on Males' Body Image." *Journal of Social and Clinical Psychology*, v.23/1 (2004).

Alperstein, Neil M. "Disciplining the Carnivore: Pop Primitivism in Contemporary Advertising." In *Gender and Consumer Behavior*, Vol. 8, Lorna Stevens and Janet Borgerson, eds. Edinburgh, UK: Association for Consumer Research, 2006. http://www.acrWebsite .org/.../CP%20paper%2012%20Neil%20M%20 Alperstein.pdf (Accessed February 2011).

Festinger, Leon. "A Theory of Social Comparison Processes." *Human Relations*, v.7 (1954).

Gulas, Charles and Kim McKeage. "Extending Social Comparison: An Examination of the Unintended Consequences of Idealized Advertising Imagery." *Journal of Advertising*, v.29/2 (2000).

Ritson, Mark and Marsha Richins. "Social Comparison and the Idealized Images of Advertising." *Journal of Consumer Research*, v.18 (1991).

Taylor, Shelley and Marci Lobel. "Social Comparison Activity Under Threat: Downward Evaluation and Upward Contacts." *Psychological Review*, v.96/4 (1989).

Social Construction of Gender

Society creates categories for simplifying information, serving as institutions commonly understood and practiced within the culture. These categories include age, race, ethnicity, and gender, and one's understanding of these categories is co-constructed through social interaction. The first category a child learns is sex-linked: People are boys or girls. Early in development, children may confuse who may be placed in these categories, but the categories eventually become fixed as children come to understand that individual persons fit into only one category and their placement in that category does not change. Children then learn, from social interaction, attributes connected to these sex-linked categories: those that are characteristic of boys (males) and those that are characteristic of girls (females). Among those attributes are norms, social roles, expectations, and stereotypes. Social construction theory is a socialization theory explaining the process whereby society structures these sex-linked categories and combines them with the commonly held perceptions about the accompanying psychological, physical, and behavioral attributes associated with the gender categories. A contrasting view to the notion that gender is equivalent to observable biological sex differences, categorized into sex-linked groups, distinguishes the observable biological/physiological attributes acquired from "nature" from those acquired through socialization (that is, those acquired through "nurture").

The study of gender from a social constructivist perspective steps beyond observation of sex differences from within the static categories of "male" and "female" by focusing on the influences of social interaction in the acquisition of beliefs and attitudes associated with sex role stereotypes. Persons from Western cultures commonly believe particular attributes, roles, and behaviors are linked directly to masculinity or femininity; therefore, information becomes co-constructed through persons' social interaction into dichotomously organized categories of what is typical of males or females. Gender labeling results in forcing people to think in terms of polarities (either male/masculine or female/feminine) without accounting for individual differences not attributable to gender.

People receive social reinforcement for perpetuating culturally held beliefs about males and females into gendered stereotypes. This tends to govern their templates for their own enactment of being male or female and their expectations about the gender-appropriateness of the beliefs, roles, and actions of others. They conform to societal expectations and encourage others to do so as well, thus perpetuating gender-based stereotypes. A continuous renegotiation of gender-role expectations occurs within relationships as the partners co-construct the parameters of their relationships.

In confronting social situations involving persons of ambiguous gender, many people are uncomfortable and resolve this discomfort by taking mental shortcuts that allow for the framework through which they know how to interact. Thus, it becomes easy to connect sex to gender. Categorization occurs as a means of making mental shortcuts. These shortcuts enable persons to better understand information attained in their social world. Individuals are confronted with new information routinely. Information is acquired from strangers, often gleaned from increasing amounts of interaction with an acquaintance or a close relational partner, or by receiving inconsistent information. People must make sense of each piece of newly discovered information, which must be housed into some meaningful place. What is most noticeable and simplest to categorize about a person is biological sex.

Closely related to views about persons of a particular sex are those psychological characteristics so often stereotyped into categories linked to gender. Social construction of gender occurs when persons engage in gendered behavior while interacting with others and may be noticed in a number of ways. A person's own interaction style is heavily influenced by what is learned from observing persons from within each sex. Males may display certain mannerisms while in conversation with other males and different mannerisms with females. The same may be true for females in conversation. Any differences would be associated with what members of the particular sex groups are perceived to do. Persons' patterning of their own behaviors after those of others of their same sex group would then receive social reinforcement. Inconsistent patterns may receive negative responses, discouraging the continuation of those behaviors. Thus, views about sex-linked appropriateness of behavior would result from the co-construction of persons' own gendered identity through continued social interaction. Similar results would occur regarding learning linguistic rules, language choice, and means of engaging in self-presentation. Gendering begins in social relationships, is maintained in social relationships, and is done unconsciously. Therefore, although one is a member of a particular sex, one engages in ongoing dialogue with relational partners, *enacting gender* as opposed to *being a member of a gender group*.

Gendering begins before the birth of a child. Advanced medical technology provides the opportunity to learn the baby's sex before birth. Parents, family members, and friends want to know the child's sex as soon as possible, and many parents elect to discover the sex before birth. Parents envision welcoming a boy or a girl. Within those categories are perceptions of appropriate names: John or Joan? Regardless of the baby's sex, the unborn child is discussed in reference to "he" or "she" or by the name to be given upon birth. The social construction of the child's gender has begun.

Parents then imagine life with that child. If a boy, will he be athletic, outgoing, and a peer leader? If a girl, will she be attractive, social, and nurturing? These simple stereotypes are commonly held in many cultures, along with the expectations that children ultimately will possess the socially appropriate attributes according to their sex. Planning for a new child brings excitement. Parents prepare for the child's impending birth by decorating a place for the child to sleep. The room may be filled with images of airplanes, sporting equipment, teddy bears, or trains. It may be a vision of pink and offer the delights of dolls, flowers, and bows. Family members and friends share the enthusiasm by purchasing clothing and toys distinctly suited to their culturally shared perceptions of what is appropriate for girls and for boys.

Upon arrival in the world, the baby is described according to physical attributes, but these often are linked to stereotypical perceptions of gender. Attributes of newborns such as "strong," "robust," or "big" typically are perceived as masculine. Thus, they are socially constructed descriptions for boys. Others, such as "dainty," "sweet," and "precious," are more "girl-like" and typical of being feminine. The baby is dressed for the first trip home in clothing suitable for a boy or for a girl. Gendering continues with each interaction the child experiences throughout his or her lifetime. Once a child's sex is identified, whoever comes in contact with the child potentially influences that child's views of his or her masculinity or femininity.

Children notice biological differences in males and females. Ray Birdwhistell describes these as tertiary sex differences. Labeling children according to these differences is extended to dress and toy choice as children learn to associate sex differences with these other nonverbal devices. They may attribute sexual categorization to socially appropriate dress or play: Boys wear blue and girls wear pink; boys play with trucks and girls play with dolls. They learn to associate these nonverbal devices and behaviors with their own sex label. A child has trucks to play with, so he is a boy. He generalizes this understanding to other children who also have trucks; they must be boys as well. His sister plays with dolls; therefore, she cannot be a boy so she must be a girl.

Gender construction continues as children view the actions of role models with whom they either identify or not. Among the first models children identify are those of the primary caregiver. They imitate these models and through their interactions with others learn the behaviors deemed appropriate, or not appropriate, for persons of their sex; they then are encouraged, or discouraged, to perform these behaviors. Once children have acquired the understanding that males and females are different, they typically behave in ways more characteristic of their same sex role models. They may repeat the behaviors associated with persons of the opposite sex, but eventually they are socialized to behave in ways more consistent

of those of their same sex. Children want to please others and gain approval; therefore, they respond by adjusting their behavior. Socialization also occurs by observing other role models: siblings, teachers, peers, adult family members, and mediated images. Social interaction in the family impacts gender socialization through parenting practices. For example, boys often have larger physical boundaries for exploration than do girls; as a result, a greater sense of independence tends to be instilled in boys. Gender socialization also is evident in the games children play. Games more typical of boys focus on team play and competition, whereas girls' play evidences collaborative, one-on-one role play.

Alice Eagly's social role theory suggests that society teaches particular roles according to sex. Boys reject those roles associated with being female, and girls reject those roles associated with being male. Females tend to be placed in caregiving or nurturing roles; thus it is inferred that females naturally are more nurturing. Males tend to be placed in more competitive roles, perpetuating the notion that males are more assertive. Awareness of sex roles begins as early as age two, with sex and sex role stereotypes observable as early as two and a half years of age. Parents and teachers use direct messages perpetuating sex-linked stereotypes. Evidence of stereotypical influence on children has been identified. Boys are less likely to be smiled at, touched, or spoken directly to in a positive manner than are girls. Boys are more likely to be instructed to perform stereotypically male household chores, whereas girls are more likely to assume more stereotypically female household activities. Fathers have been shown to interact with their sons differently from the way they interact with their daughters, thereby instilling more sex-stereotypical attitudes in their children.

Caregivers often direct children to sex-appropriate toy choices and activities. Research suggests that girls are rewarded for behaviors and toy choices that encourage noncompetitiveness and being deferential, nurturing, obedient, quiet, loving, and emotionally expressive. Conversely, they are discouraged from those behaviors fostering independence, boisterousness, a lack of concern for others, and competitiveness—all characteristics associated with being masculine/male. Gender creation continues throughout the lifetime as roles are renegotiated and internalized into one's self-image while others are rejected.

Gendering is ever-present in interpersonal relationships. Socially constructed expectations greatly influence the ways males and females conduct their same-sex and cross-sex relationships and how they communicate within their relationships. Gendered communication cultures are created when children adhere to gendered stereotypes. The presence of gender stereotypes about communication may be viewed according to the perceived level of prominence communication holds in relational maintenance and in the actual communication strategies males and females employ. Deborah Tannen and Julia Wood described two distinctly different communication cultures where communication focuses on the accomplishment of particular types of goals. Males generally interact using a style of communication focused on attaining instrumental goals characterized by the presence of social hierarchies and one's placement within the hierarchies, the pursuit of individual goals, and competition. Feminine communication cultures generally focus on a more democratic and collectivistic organizational structure and cooperative means of speaking. The importance of communication from within the framework of masculine culture is for *doing* something—acquisition of a tangible and instrumental goal. From a feminine standpoint, communication serves as a way of creating and maintaining a relational bond. Therefore, persons sharing feminine culture communicate as a way of *being*.

Mediated role models play a particularly important part in children's acquisition of gender labels and gender identity. Children consume mass quantities of mediated messages in Western cultures. Roles influence persons' behaviors, attitudes, self-concepts, and self-presentation regardless of age. Advertising often is directed to audiences segmented according to gendered groups perpetuating culturally based stereotypes; for example, products are framed as promoting masculinity or femininity. Mediated images also reflect societal views of roles and behaviors deemed appropriate for one or another gender (such as parenting roles or occupational choices and their associated behaviors) and also provide societal standards for conducting personal relationships and sexuality.

Patricia Amason
University of Arkansas

See also Gender and Femininity: Motherhood; Gender and Femininity: Single/Independent Girl; Gender and Masculinity: Black Masculinity; Gender and Masculinity: Fatherhood; Gender and Masculinity: Metrosexual Male; Gender and Masculinity: White Masculinity; Gender Embodiment; Gender Media Monitoring; Gender Schema Theory; Heterosexism; Identity; Intersectionality; Mediation; Queer Theory; Sexuality; Social Comparison Theory; Social Learning Theory; Stereotypes; Transgender Studies; Transsexuality

Further Readings

Birdwhistell, R. L. *Kinesics and Context: Essays on Body Motion Communication*. Philadelphia: University of Pennsylvania Press, 1970.

Deaux, K. "From Individual Differences to Social Categories." *American Psychologist*, v.39 (1984).

Eagly, Alice Hendrickson, et al. *The Psychology of Gender*. New York: Guilford Press, 2004.

Fagot, B. I., M. D. Leinbach, and R. Hagan. "Gender Labeling and Adoption of Sex-Typed Behaviors." *Developmental Psychology*, v.22 (1996).

Lorber, J. *Paradoxes of Gender*. New Haven, CT: Yale University Press, 1994.

Tannen, D. *You Just Don't Understand: Women and Men in Conversation*. New York: HarperCollins, 1990.

West, C. and D. Zimmerman. "Doing Gender." *Gender and Society*, v.1 (1987).

Wood, J. *Gendered Lives*, 8th ed. Florence, KY: Cengage Wadsworth, 2009.

SOCIAL INEQUALITY

Social inequality refers to the observed inequalities that are generated by social institutions. The institutional processes in society determine resources as more or less valuable and allocate resources across various services and positions in society, connecting individuals to those services and positions. These institutional processes therefore result in unequal control of valued resources. For example, in the airline industry, a higher level of economic resources (in this case payment) is allocated to the position of airline pilot as compared to the position of flight attendant. Social institutional processes are more likely to connect men than women to airline pilots and are more likely to connect women than men to flight attendants. As a result, when women are connected

The male-dominated field of piloting an airplane is likely to be designed by and for men. Women who wish to work as airline pilots have to overcome the obstacles imposed by gender, which can only be achieved with societal changes in the definition of social position. (Photos.com)

to the occupation of flight attendant, social inequality by gender is generated, because as flight attendants, women are paid less. Although remarkable progress has been made to reduce social inequality of all types, it persists. Social inequality by gender, as the foregoing example suggests, is no exception.

Definition and Dynamics of Social Inequality

In society, there is a constant flux of incumbents in social positions, and individual members change. However, the positions themselves and the resources allocated to them remain relatively static and change only gradually. That is, both men and women can assume the position of airline pilot, but because it is a male-dominated occupation, the definition of

airline pilot is likely to be designed by and for men, and changes or modifications to the position are most likely to be perpetuated by men. Therefore, women who wish to work as airline pilots have to overcome the obstacles imposed by gender, which in this example are disguised by the male-influenced criteria for becoming an airline pilot. Women's efforts to secure such male-influenced social positions therefore face more obstacles than do men's. Without enough women influencing the definition of airline pilot, the social position tends to remain unchanged, and women continue to be discouraged from occupying the position. However, as more women occupy this position, the definition of airline pilot can eventually be renegotiated and redesigned to reflect the interests of both men and women. With the changed definition of social position that accommodates both men and women, the opportunities for women to become airline pilots may become equal to those for men and may in turn lead to more women occupying the position.

Valued resources need not be only economic. A variety of resources are allocated to social positions. In general, resources can be broadly categorized in eight groups: economic (such as property ownership, monetary compensation, and liquid assets), political (societal authority), cultural (privileged lifestyles), social (valued social networks), honorific (prestige), civil (civil rights), human (expertise), and physical (health). Although each type of resource is important on its own, social inequality is multidimensional, and eliminating one form of inequality (resource deficit) will not eliminate all. Some argue that a subset of resources, such as economic and political, can determine the overall degree of social inequality; others argue that overall social inequality can be synthesized into a measure that covers a wide range of resources simultaneously (for example, social position can be a synthetic measure, for it covers almost all types of rewards).

Despite the argument over whether overall social inequality is reducible to a subset of resources or is synthesized into a measure that reflects most of the inequalities across different resources, it is generally agreed that two mechanisms generate social inequality. One is the unequal distribution of social resources across social positions. The other is the unequal distribution of opportunities to secure social resources. The unequal distribution of social resources refers to the different amounts of resources that are attached to different social positions (airline pilots, for example, are rewarded more than flight attendants). One would argue that this seems to be reasonable. If piloting a commercial airplane is more important and requires more investment in training and experience than attending to passengers on the airplane, then airline pilots should be compensated accordingly. From a functionalist perspective, societies must have some mechanisms that motivate the most qualified people to assume the most important and difficult social positions.

This argument, however, has been criticized for neglecting the cumulative power of unequal rewards. Put simply, the incumbents of the valued social positions not only have the power to demand the expected resources attached to the social positions, but cumulatively they can even insist on increasing the amount of resources attached to the social positions. As they receive more and more resources, the power of the incumbents also becomes larger and larger, which enables them to demand more resources in turn. Therefore, this self-perpetuating system may lead to a social position's institutionalized value exceeding its true value to society. If one subscribes to the functionalist view, it is essential to define the minimum necessary level of differentiating resources allocated and effectively redistribute resources to maintain the complex division of social roles without creating stratification among individuals.

The unequal distribution of opportunities to secure resources is another mechanism of social inequality. This relates to the institutional processes through which individuals are connected to various social positions to which different amounts of resources are attached. In the United States, a typical individual will probably tolerate a substantial amount of difference in resource allocation across different social positions as long as the opportunity to secure the resources is equal to each individual. For instance, although the presidency of the United States has substantially more resources than many other positions in the United States, the differences in resources are acceptable as long as everyone has the same opportunity to become the president. However, the opportunity to become president is not equal for everyone. A physically able, white, heterosexual, rich man is more likely to become president than a physically disabled, black, homosexual, poor woman. The example is extreme, but the point is clear: The opportunity to secure resources is not equally distributed across individuals.

In social inequality research, several core concepts are important. One is the overall amount of inequality. This refers to the dispersion of any given resource among individuals in society. Some scholars have used single measures as a reflection of overall amount of inequality, but one needs to acknowledge that some resources are distributed more equally than others. For example, between men and women, civil rights are distributed more equally than are economic or political resources.

Another core concept in examining social inequality is the rigidity of inequality. This refers to the continuity of social inequality across individuals in society. The more rigid the inequality is, the more likely inequality will persist. In other words, the current social standing of individuals is largely predicted by the prior social standing of individuals. However, one also needs to realize that the degree of persistence may differ across types of inequalities. Different types of inequalities can also correlate with each other. This is referred to as the crystallization of inequalities. If inequalities of different types are highly correlated, then individuals who experience inequality in one resource are likely to experience inequality in other resources as well.

Furthermore, ascriptive processes, which refer to conditions at birth, influence the likelihood of securing social resources and constitute another core concept in social inequality research. In contemporary societies, ascription is generally perceived as discriminatory, and much effort has been directed at reducing social inequality that grows out of ascription.

Social Inequality by Gender

Social inequality by gender (referred to hereafter as gender inequality) is a result of ascription. Sex, which is assigned at birth, influences the likelihood of securing social resources when sex differences transform into gender inequality. Men tend to be favored over women in society. Although gender inequality has been greatly reduced, what remains is considerable. Examination of gender inequality across different types of resources will illustrate the persistence of the problem (although it is important to bear in mind that this examination is not meant to be exhaustive).

There was a time when women had very limited economic resources. They could neither work nor own property legally. Nowadays, women have the right to own property and can work in all occupations, but there is still a pay gap by gender, with men being paid more than women. The pay gap between women and men has been decreasing, but the gap is still substantial and the rate of decrease has slowed in recent years. Two sources can generate the pay gap. One is pay differences within an occupation; when this occurs, women are paid less for the same work men do. Another is pay differences across occupations; when this occurs, women are paid less for an occupation that is similar to (or at a level similar to) that required of another occupation performed by men. In this type, regardless of the similar level of skills and investment, the male-dominated occupation receives greater payment than the female-dominated occupation. For example, comparing nurses (a female-dominated occupation) with fire-truck mechanics (a male-dominated occupation) reveals that the two occupations require similar levels of training and human capital investment, but the male-dominated occupation is paid more.

In regard to political rewards, although women in the late 20th and early 21st centuries have participated in politics more than ever before, high-status political positions are still held disproportionately by men. For example, in the United Kingdom, women consist of about 50 percent of the population, but on average they constitute only 15.7 percent of the members of Parliament. A similar situation persists for honorific resources. Women make up about half of the labor force in the United Kingdom, but high-status positions are disproportionately occupied by men. Gender inequality exists in human resources, too. Although significant progress has been made to reduce gender inequality in higher education (a form of human resources), gender inequality prevails in other forms of human resources. For example, women who are in positions of motherhood are less likely than men in positions of fatherhood to be recommended for occupational training and are less likely than men to receive promotions. All these situations resonate with the cultural images (a form of cultural resources) surrounding men and women. In general, men are perceived as dominant, rational, career-centered, and goal- and action-oriented, whereas women are perceived as submissive, emotional, relational, and family-centered. Given that such cultural expectations are associated with men and women, it is not surprising that gender inequality prevails in other areas as well, and the existing gender inequality in turn reinforces and perpetuates inequality in cultural images and expectations.

Social inequality in physical resources has been gaining attention in recent years. For example, gender inequality is observed in access to health resources, a form of physical resource. Compared to men, women experience higher mortality rates from heart disease, and this may be attributable to gender inequality. Historically, the male body has been considered the standard in biomedical research, and the results from research based on male bodies are assumed to be true (or at least have become prescriptive) for females as well. This has led to misdiagnoses and failures to detect heart disease in women, because men and women have different presenting symptoms and those symptoms typical of males have been used as the standard. Indeed, women themselves may subscribe to this conventional wisdom and thus may fail to push their doctors to follow up on serious symptoms. Having been assumed to be at greater risk for heart attacks, men have had greater access to the physical resources of healthcare for the disease, whereas women have been more likely to be overlooked when it comes to diagnostic tests and preventive care. The result may explain the high mortality rate that women suffer from heart disease.

Media and Gender Inequality

As a social institution that constructs and reconstructs social reality, media certainly play a role in gender inequality. On one hand, the portrayal of men and women in media may contribute to gender inequality by communicating to audiences what is "reality." Even though women consist of roughly half the population, media tend to feature more portrayals of men than women and are more likely to depict men than women in leading social roles. Media images also present men as having more financial responsibility, more political power, higher-status occupations, greater commitment to their careers, and less commitment to family activities than women. These portrayals tend to result in greater rewards for men than for women, including all types of resources: economic, political, honorific, human, and cultural. Although the content of media cannot be directly translated into the effects of media, media images at least convey what men and women should be to the audiences, and that warrants the investigation of media effects on gender inequality. Indeed, research has shown that exposure to the ideal body images portrayed in media—which often target girls—can lead to eating disorders in girls and not boys. This is one example of how media can contribute to gender inequality in the physical resource of health.

Moreover, media content is controlled and produced by the media industry, which exhibits gender inequality within itself. For example, in broadcasting news, women made up about 40 percent of the workforce in 2010, but they accounted for only about 28 percent of news directors. The representation of women is even less equal in other areas of the media industry. Only 24 percent of producers, 19 percent of editors, 14 percent of writers, and 11 percent of directors were women in 250 top-grossing domestic films in 2000. Furthermore, because these high-status positions are largely dominated by men, it is possible that women who are incumbents of those positions may have to adopt the standards designed by and for men, which may limit women's ability and willingness to facilitate changes in media content to reduce gender inequality. Therefore, even with women in positions of power, the institution continues to produce content that largely reflects men's interests. In turn, media content that features gender inequality reinforces gendered social life.

Media as a social institution supports gender inequality, both within itself and in society at large through production of content that perpetuates gender inequality. Despite the fact that these forms of social inequality have been reduced over the years, substantial gender inequality still exists across all media platforms.

Ming Lei
Washington State University

See also Beauty and Body Image: Beauty Myths; Beauty and Body Image: Eating Disorders; Electronic Media and Social Inequality; Feminism; Gender Embodiment; Gender Media Monitoring; Gender Schema Theory; Minority Rights; Network News Anchor Desk; Newsrooms; Patriarchy; Postfeminism; Sexism; Workforce

Further Readings

Croteau, David and William Hoynes. *Media Society: Industries, Images, and Audiences*. Thousand Oaks, CA: Pine Forge Press, 2003.

Dines, Gail and Jean M. Humez, eds. *Gender, Race, and Class in Media: A Text-Reader*. Thousand Oaks, CA: Sage, 2003.

Grusky, David B., ed. *Social Stratification: Class, Race, and Gender in Sociological Perspective*. Boulder, CO: Westview Press, 2008.

Satow, Roberta, ed. *Gender and Social Life*. Boston: Allyn and Bacon, 2001.

SOCIAL LEARNING THEORY

To be a "model housewife," do we imitate June Cleaver or Bree Vandekamp? To be a "perfect doctor," do we strive to become like Dr. Miranda Bailey or Dr. Gregory House?

Social learning theory's major premise is that we can and do learn by observing others. The vicarious experience of observing other human beings and their behavior is a typical way that an individual will model his or her own behavior. Modeling and role-playing can have as much impact on a person's behavior as direct experience. Albert Bandura's social learning theory is a general theory of human behavior, and some researchers have used it to explain media effects. Bandura suggested that children and adults acquire attitudes, emotional responses, and new styles of conduct through filmed and televised modeling. He cautioned parents that television created a violent reality that was worth fearing.

Society plays a significant role in molding the attitudes and behaviors of all of its members. Humans are social beings who are overloaded with information from the environment that shapes our perceptions of the world and our attitudes and beliefs. Slowly, we are molded into "acceptable" members of the society in which we live. Our perceptions are believed to be created by experiences, community, family, and school. However, today these influences have decreased as our changing society adapts to a more technological age. The growth of the mass media has had a huge impact on the lives of everyone, with specifically television becoming a dominant medium.

Observational Learning and Media

Observational learning via media pertains to how learning is facilitated through the mere observation of the attitudes and behaviors of television characters. For example, popular television shows portraying lead actors engaging in sexual activity that the youth culture finds favorable may result in youth mimicking that behavior in an attempt to be perceived favorably by their peer groups. In 1977, Bandura conducted an experiment that involved children observing adults displaying aggressive behavior toward a doll named Bobo. The adults punched, kicked, and verbally insulted the doll in the children's presence. The results of the experiment showed a marked increase in aggressive behavior from the children toward Bobo the doll. These results support the social learning theory.

Social learning theory in media and the Bobo experiment are similar in significant ways. Mass media's influence on human behavior in societies is real. In society today, the television set is not only a means of entertainment but also an important source of information. With recent research indicating that, on average, children spend four hours per day in front of the television, it seems inevitable that, as a learning source, it plays an important role in helping the impressionable minds of children to develop certain social roles and behaviors.

Gender, Media, and Social Learning

Social learning theory is learning by modeling and observing. Females make up 50 percent of the U.S. population, but they are underrepresented in film and television, so (in these media) they have fewer people to mimic and observe than do males. In a study conducted in 2006 by Stacy Smith and Amy Granados, it was found that males appeared almost three times as frequently as females in 400 top-grossing films released between 1990 and 2006. In another study conducted by the same researchers, children's programs were found to have a 2:1 ratio of male to female characters.

The media show many girls and women in a traditional and stereotypical light. Across G-rated films and children's television shows, females are more likely than males to be caregivers and in a committed relationship. Women are in emotionally centered roles, and males are less frequently shown acting as fathers and loving partners. Television shows and G-rated films tend to depict more working males than females, which distorts the reality that women now comprise about half of the American workforce.

Physical appearance also reigns in television and film. Females are more likely than males to be younger and sexier. Interestingly, females in G-rated films are nearly as likely to be shown in sexually revealing clothing as females in R-rated films: 20.3 percent versus 23.5 percent. Also in G-rated movies, animated females are more likely than live-action ones to be shown with small waists and large chests—the ideal body of the Disney princess posse. One must ask, then, if children really have an accurate perception of their gender role in today's society.

Television can teach children about how men and women act in society and mold their views of what is expected of them. Because males dominate the television medium, female role models are few. In television, movies, and advertisements, males are depicted as having authority and control in the world. When a female is depicted, she is placed in a position where she is made to feel inferior to men. This may be displayed in a physical representation, such as when a man stands over a woman. This sends an implicit message to young and impressionable viewers: that men are superior and authoritative whereas women are inferior and submissive.

Television also sends out explicit messages regarding how men and women should behave in society. The media adopt a traditional or stereotypical view of gender roles. They present women as caregivers, nurturers, emotional, and dependent, whereas men are the strong, authoritative breadwinners of society. Displaying gender in this fashion has disturbing implications for the type of society in which our children are living. Learning from these media depictions affects a child's choice in toys, clothes, activities, future work, and sense of pride and self-respect. Children are influenced by gender-role stereotyping from television shows and advertisements. Advertisements appeal to children's short attention span and therefore may have more appeal and influence on them. For example, when a child sees a commercial in which a woman appears to be excited about laundry detergent and discusses nothing else, the image makes an impression on the child's unconscious mind. Such images give female children cues as to how to act and behave, even though they may be unaware that they are observing a biased depiction.

Some researchers have found that children are likely to imitate same-sex behaviors they view in the media, even when the behavior is seen as inappropriate. This indicates that gender rather than behavior is an identifying factor in the learning process. Other researchers indicate that children imitate behavior appropriate to their own gender regardless of the gender of the actor, relying on the fact that children have already learned gender-appropriate behavior. This body of research reinforces social learning of gender roles in the media.

Gayle M. Pohl
University of Northern Iowa

See also Children's Programming: Cartoons; Children's Programming: Disney and Pixar; Cognitive Script Theory; Gender Schema Theory; Media Literacy; Sitcoms; Social Comparison Theory; Social Construction of Gender; Television; Toys and Games: Gender Socialization; Violence and Aggression

Further Readings

Bandura, A. *Social Learning Theory*. Englewood Cliffs, NJ: Prentice-Hall, 1977.

Beasley, Elena. "Children, Television and Gender Roles." 1997. http://www.aber.ac.uk/media/Students/elb9501 .html (Accessed February 2011).

Gerbner, G. "Reclaiming Our Cultural Mythology: Television's Global Marketing Strategy Creates a Damaging and Alienated Window on the World." *The Ecology of Justice*, IC 38 (Spring 1994).

Liebert, R. and J. Sprafkin. "The Surgeon General's Report." In *The Early Window: Effects of Television on Children and Youth*, 3rd ed. New York: Pergamon, 1988.

Smith, S. and A. Granados. "Gender and the Media." *PTA Magazine* (December/January 2010).

Smith, S. L., K. Pieper, A. D. Granados, and M. Choueiti. "Equity or Eye Candy: Exploring the Nature of Sex-Roles in Children's Television Programming." Executive Summary prepared for Dads and Daughters, Duluth, MN, 2006.

SOCIAL MEDIA

The term *social media* commonly refers to forms of digital communication technologies that allow users to create personalized networks, share information and knowledge, and collectively solve problems. While traditional mass media offer a one-way form of communication, from the sender to the receiver, social media facilitate a two-way form of communication that encourages interactivity. Social media allow users to become active producers of media by enabling activities such as documenting and sharing experiences and selecting and rating information that they find relevant. Social media tend to be a defining characteristic for Web 2.0. Web 2.0 refers to the many ways in which individuals control the flow of information or produce information on the Internet. Social media are distinguished by the activities in which they allow users to engage. Types of social media include blogs (Blogger, WordPress), social networking sites (Myspace, LinkedIn, Facebook), social news sites (Digg, Reddit), and location-based social media (FourSquare). The availability of smart phones, which allow users to access the Internet from mobile communication devices, has accelerated the adoption of social media.

Social media are used for both personal and commercial purposes and have had a significant impact on many aspects of social, political, and economic life. Socially, social media provide opportunities for people to keep in touch and create personalized networks to share information. Politically, social media have been integrated into the democratic process, not only by providing increased opportunities for politicians to keep in touch with their constituents but also by increasing access of citizens to politicians. Economically, social media have led to the creation of new jobs and have expanded opportunities for businesses to market information about their products to potential customers. While many celebrate social media for their ability to democratize information, encouraging participation among citizens, researchers warn that it is important to be cautious and critical of social media, especially regarding their implications for privacy (the protection of personal information), negative social behaviors (such as cyberbullying and hate speech), and the trend toward commercialization and consolidation.

Early Social Media

While the term social media is used to refer to the current offerings of online technologies, social interaction has always been a goal of computer-mediated communication. Precursors of the current forms of social media include Bulletin Board Systems (BBS) and Usenets, both of which originated in 1979. Both BBSes and Usenets were designed to encourage social interaction and provide specialized knowledge to the public. BBSes consisted of small servers powered by personal computers. Individuals would access a BBS through the use of a telephone modem. Often, BBSes were accessed by only one person at a time and were moderated by a facilitator. BBS content consisted of social discussion, community-contributed downloads, and online games. Unlike BBSes, Usenets did not have a central server or dedicated administrator. Usenets allowed users to post articles to topical categories, also called newsgroups. Individual users could access newsfeeds or read and post messages to a local server.

Both BBSes and Usenets were offered free to the public. The first online commercial services that tried to encourage social interaction were Prodigy and Compuserve. Compuserve instituted an online chat system in 1980. America Online (AOL), launched in 1983, quickly emerged as the most popular service for social interaction with its instant messaging (IM) services. In a controversial merger, Time Warner acquired AOL in 2000, signaling the media industry's trend toward convergence, or the merging of previously separate media platforms.

In addition to online technologies that allowed users to communicate with one another, other technologies allowed for the sharing of files among users. Napster, which used peer-to-peer file-sharing applications, emerged in 1999. Napster was an important development in social media because it provided the means through which users could share music. The technology of Napster shifted the distribution power from record companies to individuals, challenging the gatekeeping function of the music industry. Other online services, such as Limewire and BitTorrent, also developed. File-sharing services are controversial, because there is some debate over whether these services facilitate copyright infringement.

Today, social media are distinguished by the different functions they offer for users. The most popular social media include social networking sites, video- and file-sharing sites, social news sites, wikis, and blogs.

Social Networking

In general, social networking sites allow users to share information with selected groups of people. Users can determine whom they want to invite into their network to access their personal information. Social networking sites allow users to interact by commenting on statuses, joining groups, and engaging in discussion. Additionally, social networking

sites allow users to share their networks with others. This form of networking can result in a type of synergy in which new relationships are formed. This is especially important with businesses that are interested in marketing their products to consumers or creating loyalty among customers.

The first social networking site was SixDegrees, launched in 1997. Other sites, including Friendster, Myspace, and Facebook, followed. Facebook began in 2004 and was originally marketed as an exclusive site for college students. However, the rise in popularity of Facebook led to the opening of the site to the general population in September 2005. Facebook is ranked as one of the most often visited Websites on the Internet. Many researchers argue that Facebook has had a huge influence on how people use the Internet and engage with others. For example, there are many stories of people reuniting with lost family members and friends. The groups function of Facebook has enabled the formation of political groups that have organized and enacted social change. For example, a Facebook page was created for organizing the protests in Egypt in 2011. These protests led to the resignation of the Egyptian president, Hosni Mubarak.

Although Facebook is a popular and influential form of social media, some argue that it is important to be critical of Facebook, especially in the areas of commercialism and privacy. Facebook relies on advertising revenue to support its business model. As a result, some of Facebook users' personal information is provided to advertisers, which can lead to data mining, or the use of personal information to market products. Others critique social networking sites for increased emphasis on commercialization. For example, News Corporation purchased Myspace in 2005. News Corporation is one of the largest media conglomerates in the world. The concern is that media conglomerates may threaten competition and innovation.

Video- and Photo-Sharing Sites

In addition to social networking sites, social media include video- and photo-sharing sites such as YouTube and Flickr. These sites allow users to share personal photos and videos for selected users. Additionally, these sites often allow users to leave comments on videos, which can enhance and expand communities.

YouTube was launched in 2005. YouTube made it possible for people with little technical knowledge of video editing to post videos that can reach a mass audience. YouTube has had an enormous impact on how users access and consume information. The intent of YouTube is to post original content, but one of the main critiques of YouTube is that users upload material without securing the appropriate copyrights to do so. Media companies such as Viacom have pursued litigation against YouTube for not enforcing copyright laws.

Social News Sites

Social news Websites allow users to select and recommend published news stories. Slashdot, started in 1997, was one of the first social news sites. Slashdot is focused primarily on science and technology news stories. Another popular social news site, Digg, gained popularity in 2006. One common feature of social news sites is a section that allows users to comment on news stories. These comment sections allow for interactivity, a key feature of social media. In addition to social news sites, which allow users to rate the popularity of news stories, sites such as Del.icio.us, allow for social bookmarking. Social bookmarking enables users to tag Websites based on commonly used keywords and search through Websites bookmarked by others. Tags allow users to share information based on agreed-upon key terms.

Both social news sites and social bookmarking sites change the traditional flow of information from the producer of media content to the audience. Because these sites allow users to recommend articles to others and organize information, users can customize information in which they are interested, challenging the gatekeeping function of traditional media outlets. Users can pick and choose the information they are interested in and select how they want to receive it.

Wikis

A wiki is a collaborative Website in which users can create and edit Web pages that are hyperlinked. Users interact by adding articles and editing existing articles. One of the strengths of wikis is that they allow users to create associations between topics. In a sense, wikis allow users to design databases that create, browse, and search information.

Wikipedia is the most famous wiki. Wikipedia is a multilingual online encyclopedia in which users contribute content. Other popular wikis include Wikimedia Commons, a Website that contains free images, sound, and videos, and Wikileaks, an international nonprofit organization that publishes classified documents.

Blogs

Blogs refer to Web logs where users can publish information on a range of topics. Blogs are an outgrowth of online diaries, where people kept track of their personal lives. Most blogs are interactive and allow users to leave comments. Blogs differ in content and delivery. For example, personal blogs allow users to provide their viewpoints and perspectives. In addition to personal blogs, many organizations have developed business-oriented blogs. Blogs also vary in genre and can include political blogs, travel blogs, music blogs, and fashion blogs. Finally, blogs can contain multimedia content. A vlog (video log) comprises video content, and photoblogs contain pictures. Common blog sites include Blogger, Tumblr, and WordPress. News blogs, such as the *Huffington Post*, a collection of a variety of news-related content posts, have been influential in breaking important news stories and swaying public opinion on particular topics. In this way, blogs have challenged mainstream models of news gathering and distribution.

A relatively new form of blogging is microblogging. Twitter, created in 2006, is the most popular microblogging site. Twitter allows users to create "tweets" or text-based posts of up to 140 characters. Users can send and receive tweets from their mobile phones. Users have the opportunity to follow different users. Additionally, "hashtags," or words and phrases that are denoted by a # sign, allow users to post tweets by topics.

Social Impact

Researchers and policy makers have debated the positive and negative impacts of social media. On one hand, social media can allow people to make new connections, expand their networks, and maintain relationships. Social media have been instrumental in creating what Howard Rheingold terms "smart mobs," to which users can announce social protest for the purpose of enacting social change.

Additionally, social media have created new jobs and contributed to economic development by allowing companies to better market to their publics. On the other hand, critics point out some of the negative impacts of social media. For example, there is an increase in reports of youth who report being victims of cyberbullying or cyberstalking. These forms of harassment can lead to depression, low self-esteem, and anxiety. Others worry about the impact of forming and maintaining relationships in online environments and the loss of face-to-face communication.

Finally, recent research looks at gender differences in social media usage. Research suggests that women are heavier users of social networking sites, such as Facebook, than men. This finding supports communication scholarship that suggests that women tend to use online communication technologies for relationship building, whereas men tend to use these technologies for searching out information. This research has found that women's and girls' activity online is different from that of men and boys because women are more interested in building relationships, communicating with friends, and making new friends. Thus, there have been many attempts to market to them. However, outside social networking sites, women are the minority of producers of social media content. For example, according to a survey by the Wikimedia Foundation, only 13 percent of Wikipedia contributors were female. This research suggests the need to better understand how different categories of social media allow for different forms of participation.

In addition to studying the production of social media content, research examines how social media have altered the way that individuals identify. For example, in a December 2010 TED talk titled "Social Media and the End of Gender," Johanna Blakley argued that social media allow individuals to identify by their likes and interests rather than by gender or racial identity.

Carolyn Cunningham
Gonzaga University

See also Audiences: Producers of New Media; Blogs and Blogging; Cyberspace and Cyberculture; Media Consolidation; Media Convergence; New Media; Online New Media: GLBTQ Identity; Online New Media: Transgender Identity; Social Networking Sites: Facebook; Social Networking Sites: Myspace; Twitter; Viral Advertising and Marketing; Virtual Community; Web 2.0; Wiki; YouTube

Further Readings

Blakley, Johanna. "Social Media and the End of Gender." http://www.ted.com/talks/johanna_blakley_social_media_and_the_end_of_gender.html (Accessed May 2011).

boyd, danah m. and Nicole B. Ellison. "Social Network Sites: Definition, History, and Scholarship." *Journal of Computer-Mediated Communication*, v.13/1 (2007). http://jcmc.indiana.edu/vol13/issue1/boyd.ellison.html (Accessed February 2011).

Burgess, Jean E. and Joshua B. Green. *YouTube: Online Video and Participatory Culture*. Cambridge, UK: Polity Press, 2009.

Jones, Steven G., ed. *CyberSociety: Computer-Mediated Communication and Community*. Thousand Oaks, CA: Sage, 1995.

Rheingold, Howard. *Smart Mobs: The Next Social Revolution*. New York: Basic Books, 2002.

Shirky, Clay. *Here Comes Everybody: The Power of Organizing Without Organizations*. New York: Penguin, 2008.

Surowiecki, James. *The Wisdom of Crowds*. New York: Anchor Books, 2004.

SOCIAL NETWORKING SITES: FACEBOOK

Online social networks and face-to-face social networks form for similar reasons: like-minded individuals associate for mutual gain and the greater good. Currently the most popular online social networking Website, Facebook began as a Website exclusively for college students but is now available to the public worldwide. Facebook claims more than 500 million active users. Approximately 150 million users access their accounts via mobile telephone. Many scholars recognize that Facebook provides "social space" for the formation of conversations, relationships, groups, and social networks.

Unlike other social networking Websites, such as Myspace, Facebook provides a template to assist each new user to develop a Facebook homepage, also called the user's profile. The template provides a series of standard questions about demographic information (such as name, birth date, sex, and job), questions concerning popular culture (such as favorite television shows, movies, and quotations), and questions related to personal information (such as relational goals—to make friends and/or to meet

A laptop user in the Czech Republic posting a photo of his or her computer screen while browsing Facebook reinforces the company's claim that it has over 500 million active users in over 200 countries. In most countries as of early 2011, Facebook was either the first, second, or third most popular Website. (Photos.com)

potential dating partners). However, the new user is never asked information about nationality, ethnicity, or race. The user may answer as many or as few of these questions as desired. After completing the template, users can elect to personalize their profiles further by displaying a profile photograph, a personal Website, or selected applications available via the Facebook Website.

Applications range from informational (for example, to display "bumper stickers" that represent users' philosophies) to serious (for example, to display charities and political candidates that the user supports financially and thus to encourage others to do so) to frivolous (for example, to take the quiz "What kind of chocolate are you?"). Facebook now claims to display 550,000 active applications offered by independent developers for the Facebook Website.

Networking on Facebook

A user's individual Facebook network consists of the user and the "friends" listed on his or her profile. Users acquire friends by employing Facebook's search function to discover known associates by entering their names and/or e-mail addresses. After locating an associate's profile, the user sends a friend request. When the recipient confirms the request, the Facebook friendship is established and each party is listed on the other's profile page as a friend. According to Facebook, the average user has 130 friends.

Facebook friendships can be formed online or, as is more often the case, as a supplement to offline relationships. Users typically "interact" on Facebook by posting brief updates about their lives ("had a great dinner with friends tonight") as well as displaying photographs (perhaps a picture of the dinner itself) and links to YouTube sites to display typically music videos they recommend. Friends can read these posts and respond either by clicking the "like" button or by posting comments about them. Updates are often "twittered" to the Facebook accounts, as the software programs link and users can update both accounts simultaneously. According to Facebook, about half of its active users log on to Facebook in any given day.

In addition to individual social networks, Facebook users come together to discuss their common interests via Facebook groups. Groups are an open technology, and any user can form a group. Groups range from the serious (professional groups such as the Southern States Communication Association) to the frivolous (April 1st Birthdays). Similarly, multiple users can "like" (by clicking the like button) a posted page (such as the page of a celebrity), forming a fan network. Via groups and pages, Facebook users can participate in a wide range of activities, including political discussions as well as spiritual networks based on common religious beliefs. Research examining online groups has documented that group members attend to social cues from other group members; they can form face-to-face (FtF) relationships with members of their online networks, though such relationships tend to develop at a slower pace than relationships initiated FtF.

Facebook allows users to announce their relational goals on their profiles. To achieve relational goals, users may attempt to manage the way others view them through careful construction of their profiles. Additionally, users may "look up" people on Facebook after meeting them in FtF venues, as a means of gathering information about the individual. Such information can inform the user's decision about whether to escalate the relationship and can assist the user in shaping future discourse with the individual.

Users may also employ Facebook's extensive and complex privacy settings. Many users find it advantageous to select privacy settings that permit their information to be seen by certain readers or viewers but not by others. Such privacy controls may allow users to feel more comfortable self-disclosing at higher levels in both posts and chat.

Gender and Networking

Some feminist commentators praise the rise of social media, including Websites such as Facebook, because these tools privilege expressiveness and social skills, traits often considered feminine. Furthermore, some feminist commentators speculate that the negative press about Facebook may be, in part, because the site's success is associated with feminine communication skills. Surveys among college students indicate that women are more likely than men to use social networking Websites—in one study four or five times more likely. However, another study reported no significant differences between the numbers of college men versus women who used the specific social networking site Facebook.

Men and women may differ in how they use Facebook. Studies indicated that women spend more online time engaged in social networking. A recent study found that female college students spend more time communicating with others on social networking sites than male college students; also, women received and accepted more friendship requests than men. Another study revealed that college men tended to view Facebook friends as acquaintances or instrumental associates, whereas college women tended to see them as "real" friends. Furthermore, college men reported using Facebook to locate and initiate relationships with potential dating partners, whereas college women reported using Facebook to maintain existing relationships. Among college students, both men and women were more likely to initiate Facebook friendships with opposite-sex users with attractive versus unattractive profile pictures.

Men and women also may differ in how they design and interpret profiles. In an analysis of profiles of 13- to 30-year-old users, males and females were equally likely to provide basic profile information, such as name, e-mail address, hometown, and a profile picture. However, perhaps for safety reasons, women were less likely to reveal locator information such as a home address and mobile telephone number.

How do strangers interpret the comments that friends write on users' profiles? Both male and female college students viewed negative comments by friends on a user's profile about the user's moral behavior as influencing the profile owner's attractiveness. Specifically, the negative comments decreased the attractiveness of female profile owners and increased the attractiveness of male profile owners.

Any user can elect to create a sex-free or gender-neutral Facebook profile. In such situations, users must choose their language carefully, because their talk style could reveal their gender. A line of research has documented that male versus female language differs in multiple online venues, including instant messaging, online support communities, and home pages. Men tend to employ competitive, factual, emotionless language, whereas feminine language tends to be expressive, inclusive, passive, cooperative, and accommodating.

Furthermore, stereotypical content of messages also leads to deconstructions and assignments of online gender. For example, a user discussing cooking and childcare is likely to be decoded as female, whereas a user discussing boxing and auto repair is likely to be decoded as male. Users are more likely to use gender-stereotypical language when discussing gender-stereotypical content rather than general content. In one experiment, almost two thirds of the college-student participants reported guessing the sex of an online gender-neutral interactant. Once manifest, gender can play a role in user relationships on Facebook. However, the full extent of the influence of sex and gender on Facebook interactions remains unknown and awaits further study, especially among the population beyond U.S. college students.

Lynne M. Webb
University of Arkansas

See also Audiences: Producers of New Media; Blogs and Blogging; Cyberspace and Cyberculture; Media Consolidation; Media Convergence; New Media; Online New Media: GLBTQ Identity; Online New Media: Transgender Identity; Social Media; Social Networking Sites: Myspace; Twitter; Viral Advertising and Marketing; Virtual Community; Web 2.0; Wiki; YouTube

Further Readings

Sheldon, Pavica. "Maintain or Develop New Relationships? Gender Differences in Facebook Use." *Rocky Mountain Communication Review*, v.6/1 (2009).

Taraszow, Tatjana, Elena Aristodemou, Georgina Shitta, Yiannis Laouris, and Aysu Arsoy. "Disclosure of Personal and Contact Information by Young People in Social Networking Sites: An Analysis Using Facebook Profiles as an Example." *International Journal of Media and Cultural Politics*, v.6/1 (2010).

Walther, Joseph B., Brandon Van Der Heide, Sang-Yeon Kim, David Westerman, and Stephanie Tom Tong. "The Role of Friends' Appearance and Behavior on Evaluations of Individuals on Facebook: Are We Known by the Company We Keep?" *Human Communication Research*, v.34/1 (2008).

Wang, Shaojung Sharon, Shin-Il Moon, Kyounghee Hazel Kwon, Carolyn A. Evans, and Michael A. Stefanone. "Face Off: Implications of Visual Cues on Initiating Friendship on Facebook." *Computers in Human Behavior*, v.26/2 (2010).

Social Networking Sites: Myspace

Myspace was once the dominant social networking site. Millions of women, especially young women, turned to Myspace to define (and redefine) themselves, to reach out to old friends, to make new friends, and to participate in and develop communities. Today, Myspace, now owned by Rupert Murdoch's media conglomerate News Corporation, is a shadow of what it once was, overtaken in popularity by newer social networking sites, notably Facebook. In response, Myspace has redefined itself and now specializes in social entertainment, an area that it has always emphasized.

Myspace was not the first social networking site online. Researchers danah boyd and Nicole Ellison (2007), who have written one of the most comprehensive histories of the early rough-and-tumble days of the social networking sites, explain that Myspace started in 2003 to compete with Friendster, Xanga, and AsianAvenue. Specifically, Myspace was designed to attract Friendster's disgruntled users, who had been put off by rumors that Friendster planned to charge for services and by that site's decision to expel indie-rock music groups who failed to follow profile rules. These two groups—but especially the bands and their fans—explained the initial growth of Myspace. Few, however, could have predicted what was going to happen to social networking next.

Like most social networking sites, Myspace was started by men, Chris DeWolfe, Tom Anderson, Brad Greenspan, Josh Berman, and a skilled team of programmers, all employees of eUniverse, headquartered in California. The launch of Myspace in 2003 was fortuitous, for the mainstream Web-surfing population was about to discover the benefits of social networking. Myspace soon became an Internet and media sensation. Mainstream newspapers and broadcast outlets began to report on the social networking phenomena—and Myspace, in particular. That, in turn, further increased traffic and drove more users to Myspace. Myspace had become not only the leading social networking site but an Internet giant as well. In 2005, Rupert Murdoch's News Corporation acquired Intermix Media, formerly known as eUniverse and the owner of Myspace, for $580 million. For several years, Myspace remained the dominant social networking site, but competitor Facebook was gaining ground. In 2008, Facebook overtook Myspace in unique monthly visitors. Thereafter, Myspace was unable to catch up. In 2010, Myspace redefined itself with a social entertainment focus. Myspace would "complement" Facebook rather than compete against it.

Within Myspace, women—especially young women, aged 13 to 35 (the so-called Generation Y)—have found a welcoming home. In 2010, women made up 64 percent of Myspace's almost 60 million users. Indeed, according to Rapleaf, the social media data company, women are more likely to engage in, be involved with, post to, and consult social networking sites than men—women being more relationship-driven than men. Indeed, Auren Hoffman, Rapleaf's chief executive officer, concluded that the future of social media is women.

Men, women, and children (13 years of age or older for Myspace) must join a social networking site (SNS) before participating. Nonmembers, however, are able to search Myspace and see materials accessible to the public. On Myspace, an individual must provide the following information to participate: his or her e-mail address (which must be confirmed to activate the account), a password, full name (which may be fictitious and can be hidden once the account is created), date of birth (which does not necessarily have to be accurate), and gender (which also is not confirmed). Once the account is activated, a profile, a personal Website within Myspace, is generated with the registration information provided.

That information is only the starting point, however. Myspace members may share as much information as they wish on their profiles. Some Myspace profiles are a cacophony of sights and sounds—video, audio, photographs, and art. Some offer questionable material, including sexually suggestive photographs, drinking and partying plans, and details of a sexual nature. (News reports have noted that school administrators and police in certain communities patrol Myspace and other social networking sites for reports of illegal activity, especially underage drinking.) Many Myspace participants, especially women, block their profiles from casual browsers and provide access only to "friends," individuals acknowledged by the SNS participant. One of the benefits of Myspace—and all the other social networking sites—is the ability to reach out to old friends, make new friends, and connect with communities.

In 2010, Myspace was one of the most extensively researched social networking sites, primarily because of its long history (by Internet standards). Researchers from a variety of disciplines have been especially interested in the social networking behavior of adolescents and "emerging adults," young people between the ages of 18 and 24. These two groups remain important populations of Myspace.

In her examination of Myspace profiles, Tamyra Pierce found that women and girls were central to the interactive nature of this Website. Women and girls posted more, provided more personal information, offered more sexual pictures, and were more likely to link to sexual communities than men and boys. Younger adolescents were also more likely to post personal contact information on Myspace than older adolescents. (This type of disclosure has been especially problematic for Myspace and other social networking sites. Indeed, Myspace, in its Myspace Safety Tips, warns its teenage users to be careful about what they post: "Don't post anything you wouldn't want the world to know. . . . Avoid posting anything that would make it easy for a stranger to find you.")

A 2008 study by Adriana Manago and colleagues focused on "emerging adults" and how their profiles constructed their social identity. The researchers found that these profiles reflected mainstream U.S. culture; women were "affiliative and attractive," men, "strong and powerful." The researchers also found a pervasive "sexualized female presentation" in profiles but believed that this reflected the general sexualization of the female body in the media and the culture as a whole. The researchers also emphasized that Myspace—and by implication all social networking sites—did not lead to a fragmentation of social identity. Both offline and online identities worked in tandem and complemented each other.

Myspace may no longer be the dominant social networking site it once was. However, it remains an important forum for millions of women who wish to reconnect with old friends, make new friends, and create communities. It also represents a locale for unmediated voices of women who are discussing everything from their day-to-day routines to their views on social and political issues, from their hopes to their dreams. As such, Myspace provides a unique perspective on women in the 21st century, providing insights into their realities and fantasies, their evolving communities, and trends in shifting communication styles.

Kathleen L. Endres
University of Akron

See also Audiences: Producers of New Media; Blogs and Blogging; Cyberspace and Cyberculture; Media Consolidation; Media Convergence; New Media; Online New Media: GLBTQ Identity; Online New Media: Transgender Identity; Social Media; Social Networking Sites: Facebook; Twitter; Viral Advertising and Marketing; Virtual Community; Web 2.0; Wiki; YouTube

Further Readings

Bonds-Raacke, Jennifer and John Raacke. "Myspace and Facebook: Identifying Dimensions of Uses and Gratifications for Friend Networking Sites." *Individual Differences Research*, v.8 (2010).
boyd, danah m. and Nicole B. Ellison. "Social Network Sites: Definition, History, and Scholarship." *Journal of Computer-Mediated Communication*, v.13 (2007). http://jcmc.indiana.edu/vol13/issue1/boyd.ellison.html (Accessed October 2010).
Hoffman, Auren. "The Social Media Gender Gap." *Bloomberg Businessweek*. May 19, 2008. http://www .businessweek.com/technology/content/may2008/ tc20080516_580743.htm (Accessed October 2010).

Koppelman, Alex. "MySpace or OurSpace?" *Salon* (June 8, 2008). http://www.salon.com/life/feature/2006/06/08/my_space/print.html (Accessed October 2010).

Manago, Adriana M., Michael B. Graham, Patricia M. Greenfield, and Goldie Salimkhan. "Self-Preservation and Gender on Myspace." *Journal of Applied Developmental Psychology*, v.29 (2008).

Myspace.com. "Myspace Safety Tips and Settings." http://www.myspace.com/index.cfm?fuseaction=cms.viewpage&placement=safety_pagetips (Accessed October 2010).

Pierce, Tamyra A. "X-Posed on MySpace: A Content Analysis of 'Myspace' Social Networking Sites." *Journal of Media Psychology*, v.12 (2007). http://www.calstatela.edu/faculty/sfischo/X-posed_on_%20MySpace.htm (Accessed October 2010).

Van Doorn, Niels. "The Ties That Bind: The Networked Performance of Gender, Sexuality and Friendship on Myspace." *New Media and Society*, v.12 (2010).

Walker, Kathleen, Michelle Krehbiel, and Leslie Knoyer. "'Hey You! Just Stopping By to Say Hi!' Communicating With Friends and Family on Myspace." *Marriage and Family Review*, v.45 (2009).

Sports Media: Extreme Sports and Masculinity

Extreme sports is a catchphrase for a range of activities that tend to share a high degree of risk taking, a celebration of style and flair, a desire to push limits, and a carefully cultivated sense of "outsider" status. While any attempt to catalog extreme sports (also known as lifestyle sports) would inevitably be open to debate, some of the more traditional extreme sports include mountain biking, snowboarding, bungee jumping, skydiving, ski jumping, ultra marathons, ultimate fighting (or mixed martial arts), and aggressive forms of skateboarding, inline skating, and climbing. Less recognized extreme sports include activities like B.A.S.E. jumping, mountain boarding, and sky surfing.

While it has long been acknowledged that sports and athletics intentionally and unintentionally cultivate masculinities, extreme sports by their very nature have developed a masculine ethos. This is not to suggest that girls and women are not active and successful participants in many extreme sports or that such female competitors sacrifice their femininity as they play and compete. Rather, extreme sports celebrate and extol many of the same attributes traditionally associated with masculinity. However, extreme sports also provide some unique challenges to traditional constructions of what it means to be masculine.

The origins of extreme sports are most often traced back to surfing. The antiestablishment sensibilities of surfing, along with the focus on individual accomplishment and performance (rather than belonging to a team or engaging in head-to-head competition), became hallmarks of most extreme sports. In the past two decades the popularity of extreme sports has grown exponentially, frequently dwarfing the popularity of more established sports. Ultimate fighting consistently draws larger audiences than boxing; snowboarders outnumber skiers on the slopes; and new events like ski cross and moguls (as well as snowboarding) have become crowd favorites at the Olympics.

Some of the most readily identifiable aspects of extreme sports are emblematic of attributes typically identified with hegemonic masculinity. The sense of "pushing limits" that is at the heart of making extreme sports extreme, for example, makes the risk-taking and recklessness characteristic of hegemonic masculinity an important part of the extreme sports culture. Numerous academic and popular writers have also identified toughness, specifically an ability to fight through or ignore pain, as an important part of extreme sports. Traits such as these have for decades been recognized as qualities of a hegemonic masculinity typically associated with traditional sports such as football and hockey. The ease and frequency with which contestants, reporters, and spectators alike celebrate these qualities help to foster a very traditional form of masculinity within these very nontraditional sports.

Although the high mortality rates associated with sports like B.A.S.E. jumping and the numerous injuries required in order to master the aggressive jumps and flips associated with many of the sports illustrate the more traditional masculine attributes present in extreme sports, there are other, less dramatic forms of masculinity present in extreme sports. Researchers and reporters have noted that participants of extreme sports frequently identify masculine and feminine styles of competition within their respective sports. Climbers, for example, will refer to the more masculine style of climbing that relies on strength (such as climbing an inverted rock absence of teammates who rely on one another thus amplifies the centrality of independence to the various sports.

The wide discrepancy between male and female participation in extreme sports also reinforces the masculine identity associated with extreme sports. Far more men than women compete in extreme sports contests; women make up roughly one third of official competitors. Although there are no official records of nonprofessional participants, most accounts suggest that male competitors outpace females by a large margin. Thus, at some level, for both viewers and participants, extreme sports constitute, by and large, a man's world.

There are thus clear and compelling reasons for why extreme sports may be thought of as a masculine activity, yet there are equally compelling reasons that extreme sports may be considered as challenging, or at least complicating, masculinity. The participation rate for females mentioned above, for example, can alternately be viewed as a significant challenge to thinking of any sports, let alone extreme sports, as a masculine enterprise. There are very few opportunities for men and women to compete or play alongside each other, let alone for women to potentially outperform or beat men in open competition. Extreme sports, outside most organized competitions, are practiced in a mixed-sex setting, thus allowing women to participate as equals with men. Even the organized competitions offer a format that alternates coverage of men's events with coverage of women's events, so that the attention given to women as athletes is much more considerable than other broadcast opportunities for female athletes.

Likewise, the individualism of so many extreme sports mitigates the hegemonic masculinity of more traditional team sports, such as football, basketball, baseball, and hockey. The group pressure to conform and join a team, the pervasive sense that being on a team is what boys should do, has been disrupted by the numerous options to be athletic and active that extreme sports provide. The lack of a team structure allows participants, both male and female, to compete at their own level and to develop a style that reflects their individual interests and tastes. Moreover, the antiestablishment ethos of extreme sports lends itself to a critique of the tough-guy posturing often associated with other sports.

A young, male skateboarder performs at Yoyogi Park in Tokyo, Japan. "Pushing the limit" and risk-taking are at the heart of extreme sports, characteristics traditionally assigned to masculinity. (Wikimedia/Tsutomu Takasu)

face) versus the more feminine style of climbing that relies on finesse (such as crossing a ledge). Such gendered styles have been found in participants and media reports across a range of extreme sports and demonstrate that social stereotypes of traditional masculine and feminine attributes are still used to create a heavily gendered sporting experience.

The fact that most extreme sports are individual activities rather than team events means that there is a pervasive sense of independence attached to extreme sports. The self-reliance that such activities require is consistently cited as a draw for participants. This self-reliance parallels the type of aloofness and disconnection that is a hallmark of hegemonic masculinity, the kind glorified by the action heroes and cowboys of Hollywood. The

Finally, the dominant research methodology used to study extreme sports has been ethnographic—interviewing and following a set of dedicated participants in a particular extreme sport. It has been suggested that this approach may overemphasize the beliefs and practices of an exceptionally dedicated core group and that the attitudes noted may not be representative of the broader range of less hardcore participants. This means that the masculine attitudes detected by scholars who have studied extreme sports may not be as pervasive or as strongly committed as many studies might suggest. It has been suggested, in fact, that extreme sports competitors may be much more tolerant of nontraditional constructions and performances of gender than the general population is.

The relationship between extreme sports and masculinities is thus not an easy one to characterize, nor is it devoid of ambiguities and contradictions. Extreme sports are ultimately a symbol capable of allowing participants and spectators alike to construct, modify, or deconstruct what it means to be masculine.

Shane Miller
St. John's University

See also Gender and Masculinity: Black Masculinity; Gender and Masculinity: Fatherhood; Gender and Masculinity: Metrosexual Male; Gender and Masculinity: White Masculinity; Social Construction of Gender; Sports Media: Olympics; Sports Media: Transgender; Toys and Games: Gender Socialization

Further Readings

Kusz, Kyle. *Revolt of the White Athlete: Race, Media and the Emergence of Extreme Athletes in America.* New York: Lang, 2007.

Messner, M. A., M. Dunbar, and D. Hunt. "The Televised Sports Manhood Formula." *Journal of Sport and Social Issues*, v.24/4 (2000).

Robinson, Victoria. *Everyday Masculinities and Extreme Sport: Male Identity and Rock Climbing.* New York: Berg, 2008.

Sweeny, Robert W. "'This Performance Art Is for the Birds': 'Jackass,' 'Extreme' Sports, and the De(con)struction of Gender." *Studies in Art Education: A Journal of Issues and Research in Art Education*, v.49/2 (2008).

Wellard, Ian. *Sport, Masculinities and the Body.* New York: Routledge, 2009.

SPORTS MEDIA: OLYMPICS

The Olympic Games attract thousands of athletes representing myriad countries whose athletes compete to become Olympic champions in 33 sports that include archery, curling, volleyball, skating, and wrestling. The Olympic Games are managed and controlled by the 115-member International Olympic Committee and are held every two years alternating between the Summer and Winter Olympics.

The modern Olympics include both male and female sporting events, but women have not always been accepted as Olympic competitors. In the ancient Greek games, women were largely excluded from participation. Similarly, women participated in only a limited capacity in the early modern Olympic Games (1900–28). After 1928, women began to become more involved in the event, and by the end of World War II, female athletes had made significant advances in the Olympics. Since 1960, the women's Olympic program has expanded considerably to include women's cycling, rhythmic gymnastics, tennis, and beach volleyball.

Media coverage of the Olympic Games, which can include as many as 17 nights of prime-time coverage and hundreds of broadcast hours, is unparalleled in the sporting world. Over the last few decades, media coverage of the event has become more commercialized, and the media have paid great amounts for the right to broadcast the games. To profit from their investment, the media create a program that will garner the viewer's interest. Media coverage highlights dramatic stories about the athletes or the event to create greater interest among viewers. Therefore, the Olympic media event is often quite different from the actual sporting event. In fact, some critics have argued that the televised event more closely resembles a soap opera than a sporting event.

The 2008 Beijing Olympic Summer Games garnered close to 4.7 billion television viewers, which was a 20 percent increase in the number of viewers who had tuned in to watch the 2004 Athens games. Media coverage of the 2010 Vancouver Olympics was unprecedented for the Winter Games, as it was broadcast in more than 220 territories and reached a potential audience of 3.8 billion people worldwide. These televised broadcasts of the Olympics are most popular among women and older adults.

Media depictions of Olympic athletes' personas and physical prowess differ by gender. Male success is often attributed to superior strength and intelligence, whereas female success is often attributed to experience. The amount of television coverage devoted to male and female Olympic athletes can also be highly skewed toward covering males. (Photos.com)

For decades, scholars have been interested in how the media portray female athletes and how this may affect viewers. In 2000, Michael Messner, Michele Dunbar, and Darnell Hunt identified a consistent "televised sports manhood formula" in sports programming (including sports events, news programs, and commercials) that promoted and reinforced the hegemonic masculine ideals of male domination and female sexual objectification. A considerable body of scholarship has noted that media coverage of the Olympic Games is based on this formula and privileges male athletes by devoting more time to them and their events, which undermines gender equity by promoting traditional gender stereotypes.

The media's decisions to focus on certain sports, to include live or scripted telecasts, and to use certain production techniques result in opportunities for gender disparity in media coverage. Although the majority, if not all, Olympic sporting events are shown in media coverage, the greatest amount of prime-time coverage focuses on a handful of highly popular events, such as gymnastics, track and field, swimming, and diving. Furthermore, research has shown that live coverage, which is less scripted than packaged programs, contains more gender-stereotypical language. At least one study has found that a male sporting event (track and field) was produced with more variation in point of view, more slow-motion spots, and more special effects than the production of the same female sporting event (track and field).

With few exceptions, analyses of Olympic coverage have found that most of the actual "clock time" is devoted to male athletes. Furthermore, mentions of male athletes outnumber those of female athletes. Media coverage is more equitable during the Summer Games, when, on average, 48 percent of the coverage is devoted to women. By 2008, however, the gender disparity in media coverage of the summer events was growing, as men were portrayed 8.4 percent more often than women. In comparison, media coverage of the Winter Games is significantly inequitable in regard to gender. Male athletes, on average, are portrayed 20 percent to 30 percent more often than women during the Winter Games. In the 2002 Salt Lake City Winter Games, male athletes received six and a half more hours of media coverage than female athletes. Researchers have also compared media coverage devoted to specific events. A comparison of clock time devoted to men and women competing in track-and-field events, typically considered a gender-neutral sport, found that men received 55 percent more coverage than women.

The omission of female athletes is fairly common in mediated sports programs and results in what Gail Tuchman in 1978 referred to as symbolic annihilation. Tuchman argued that media portray individuals in acceptable roles based on societal values, and the absence of women in the media indicated that they had few acceptable, noteworthy roles that contribute to society.

The way men's and women's events are covered also may lead to greater gender bias. This body of research is founded primarily on agenda setting and framing theory. According to these theories, the media suggest what is important and include frames that help audience members define reality. Thus, media portrayals of the Olympic Games may guide audience members' perceptions of what it means to be a male or female athlete, specifically, and what it means to be a successful man or woman, broadly.

The media coverage of the Olympics emphasizes traditional gender stereotypes based on physicality, personality, and sexuality. Male Olympians are portrayed as physically strong and muscular, and commentary often focuses on their physical size. In comparison, female Olympians are portrayed as fit and elegant, and commentary often focuses on their physical attractiveness. Women Olympians' bodies and actions are often sexualized.

Media coverage of the Olympics, like coverage of other sports, privileges heterosexuality. Stories about female Olympians often focus on their backgrounds, including their relationships with men or lack thereof. In media coverage, female athletes are likely to be identified as girlfriends, wives, or mothers. Single female athletes either are portrayed as available sexual objects or are questioned with regard to their heterosexuality. Homosexual athletes (both men and women) face tremendous obstacles as Olympians and are largely absent from media coverage.

Researchers have found that in most media coverage of men's sporting events the winner is decided via objective means (such as a stopwatch). In contrast, female sporting events covered by the media tend to be based on subjectivity, with the winner chosen by an external judge. Research indicates that events with subjective assessments contained more gender bias than sports with objective assessments. It is possible that the judge's assessment of the sporting event may increase opportunities for commentators to make assessments of their own, thus increasing an opportunity for gendered language.

Descriptions of athletes' personalities and physicality differ by gender. Male athletes' success is often attributed to their superior strength and intelligence, whereas female athletes' success is often attributed to their experience. Essentially this coverage suggests that men work for their success but that successful women athletes are innately talented.

Although women athletes have made considerable gains in gender equity in the Olympics, the media coverage of the Games still promotes a dichotomy of male hegemony and female submission. Further increases in one aspect of equity may result in increasing disparity in other aspects. For example, although media coverage of beach volleyball is on the rise, which may result in greater media coverage devoted to women Olympians, the nature of the sport provides more opportunity for sexualized portrayals of female athletes.

Stacey J. T. Hust
Washington State University, Pullman

See also Gender and Masculinity: Black Masculinity; Gender and Masculinity: Fatherhood; Gender and Masculinity: Metrosexual Male; Gender and Masculinity: White Masculinity; Social Construction of Gender; Sports Media: Extreme Sports and Masculinity; Sports Media: Transgender; Toys and Games: Gender Socialization

Further Readings

Billings, A. C. "Clocking Gender Differences: Televised Olympic Clock Time in the 1996–2006 Summer and Winter Olympics." *Television and New Media,* v.9/5 (2008).

Billings, Andrew and Susan Eastman. "Selective Representation of Gender, Ethnicity, and Nationality in American Television Coverage of the 2000 Summer Olympics." *International Review for the Sociology of Sport,* v.37/3–4 (2002).

Cavanagh, Sheila and Heather Sykes. "Transsexual Bodies at the Olympics: The International Olympic Committee's Policy on Transsexual Athletes at the 2004 Athens Summer Games." *Body and Society,* v.12/3 (2006).

Denham, Bryan E. and April L. Cook. "Byline Gender and News Source Selection: Coverage of the 2004 Summer Olympics." *Journal of Sports Media,* v.1/1 (2008).

Eastman, Susan Tyler and Andrew C. Billings. "Gender Parity in the Olympics: Hyping Women Athletes, Favoring Men Athletes." *Journal of Sport and Social Issues,* v.23/2 (1999).

Martinez, D. P. "Documenting the Beijing Olympics: An Introduction." *Sport in Society,* v.13/5 (2010).

Mayeda, David. "Characterizing Gender and Race in the 2000 Summer Olympics: NBC's Coverage of Maurice Greene, Michael Johnson, Marion Jones, and Cathy Freeman." *Social Thought and Research,* v.24, parts 1/2 (2001).

Messner, Michael A., Michele Dunbar, and Darnell Hunt. "Masculinity as Portrayed on Sports Television." In *Professional Sports,* James D. Torr, ed. San Diego, CA: Greenhaven Press, 2003.

Sports Media: Transgender

Media sources strongly impact our ideas and beliefs about gender. In some instances the media have been used to challenge and expand notions of gender, and at other times media have reinforced a gender binary. Homophobic attitudes and misinformation are often reinforced in media coverage. Traditionally, the media have presented biased and discriminatory images and articles sensationalizing transgender athletes, adding to misperceptions and stereotypical views. However, some changes have been made as media personnel have become more educated on relevant topics. Sports media and journalists are in a unique position to help shape public perceptions of transgender athletes.

The National Center for Transgender Equality estimates that about 3 million people in the United States identify themselves as transgender people. This organization offers information to journalists to help promote sensitive, fair media coverage and positive portrayals of transgender people. In 2007, major broadcast and cable networks doubled their coverage of transgender issues over that of 2006. The explosion of coverage in 2007 was due, in part, to the public announcement that *Los Angeles Times* sports writer Mike Penner had transitioned and would be writing as Christine Daniels.

Heated debate has occurred over the issue of transgender, transsexual, and intersex inclusion in sporting events. Many argue that, on the basis of fair play, transgender athletes should be kept out of sporting competitions. Several key athletes have received media attention for their gender status as well as for their political struggles for inclusion. Former tennis player Renee Richards and, more recently, golfer Mianne Bagger, track cyclist Kristen Worley, and mountain biker Michelle Dumaresq have helped to increase public awareness of transgender issues. Included in this debate is the controversy over the way in which transgender, transsexual, and intersex are defined. In sport, determination of participation is largely made along the male/female dichotomy. Gender policies have been created by sports-governing bodies to attempt to define sex for the purposes of sports participation.

In 2004, the International Olympic Committee (IOC) introduced the Stockholm Consensus to regulate the inclusion of, primarily, male-to-female transsexual athletes in Olympic Games. Individuals undergoing sex reassignment after puberty would be eligible to compete, under the following conditions: (a) surgical anatomical changes were completed, (b) legal recognition of the assigned sex had been conferred by the appropriate official authorities, and (c) hormonal therapy appropriate for the assigned sex had been administered in a verifiable manner and for a sufficient length of time. It was further recommended that eligibility should begin no sooner than two years after surgery. In 2010, Worley, cofounder of the Coalition of Athletes for Inclusion in Sport, working with the Transitioning/Transitioned Athletes in Sport project, developed an alternative policy.

The Federation of Gay Games (FGG) and other organizations have struggled to develop inclusive gender policies. FGG policy defined a transgender person as "someone who was born anatomically male or female, but has a strong and persistent, bona fide identification with the gender role other than that assigned at birth." A transgender person may or may not have had medical treatment to transition to the chosen or self-identified gender. Intersex is also specifically defined: "Persons with intersex conditions may have one of many long-established biological conditions where a person is born with reproductive organs and/or sex chromosomes that are not exclusively male or female. . . . A person with an intersex condition may identify as male, female, both or as intersex." Other organizations have used different definitions in their policies. For example, the World Outgames' policy distinguishes between transitioned athletes and transgender athletes, but not intersexed.

Information on gender policies and individual athletes who have been questioned was covered in the media with varying impacts on societal views. Castor Semenya, a South African who won the 800-meter run in the 2009 World Championship, was scrutinized in the media. In 2006, Indian runner Santhi Soundarajan attempted suicide after similar humiliating media attention. It was reported that an official became "suspicious" while observing Soundarajan's voiding of urine during a drug-testing procedure. Media attention over the sex of both athletes became public, violating their privacy.

The media play an important role in building public understanding of important medical and legal issues surrounding transgender issues. The Sports Media Program of the Gay and Lesbian Alliance Against Defamation (GLAAD) works with gay and transgender athletes and sports media outlets to support and educate. The goal is for media outlets to present fair, accurate, and inclusive images, combating stereotypical views. Media outlets have benefited from the information presented by GLAAD. For example, contrary to popular belief, there is little to no empirical evidence supporting the assumption that transitioned athletes compete with an advantage over "physically born" females and males.

Some news outlets are beginning to make further significant changes. The Associated Press, the

New York Times, and the *Washington Post* have developed style guides educating reporters on how to refer to transgender people, such as using their preferred name and pronoun rather than relying on anatomical status. People from transgender organizations contend that the quality of news stories could improve with better communication between reporters and experts who can provide advice on definitions and terminology.

Claire F. Sullivan
University of Maine

See also Gender and Masculinity: Black Masculinity; Gender and Masculinity: Fatherhood; Gender and Masculinity: Metrosexual Male; Gender and Masculinity: White Masculinity; Social Construction of Gender; Sports Media: Extreme Sports and Masculinity; Sports Media: Olympics; Toys and Games: Gender Socialization; Transgender Studies; Transsexuality

Further Readings

Cavanagh, Shelia and Heather Sykes. "Transsexual Bodies at the Olympics: The International Olympic Committee's Policy on Transsexual Athletes at the 2004 Athens Summer Games." *Body and Society*, v.12/3 (2006).

Federation of Gay Games. "Gender Policy." http://www .gaygameschicago.org/registration/gender.php (Accessed April 2010).

Gay and Lesbian Alliance Against Defamation. *Media Resource Guide*, 8th ed. New York: Author, 2010. http://www.glaad.org/document.doc?id=99 (Accessed October 2010).

Hollar, Julie. "Transforming Coverage: Transgender Issues Get Greater Respect—but Anatomy Remains Destiny." *Extra!* (November/December 2007). http://www.fair.org/ index.php?page=3216 (Accessed October 2010).

International Olympic Committee. "IOC Approves Consensus With Regard to Athletes Who Have Changed Sex." May 17, 2004. http://www.olympic.org (Accessed April 2010).

National Center for Transgender Equality. "Understanding Transgender." http://transequality.org/resources/NCTE_ UnderstandingTrans.pdf (Accessed October 2010).

Sykes, Heather. "Transexual and Transgender Policies in Sport." *Women in Sport and Physical-Activity Journal*, v.15 (2006).

Worley, Kristen. "An Alternative to the IOC's Gender Testing Policy." *World Sports Law Report*, v.8 (March 1, 2010). http://kristenworley.ca/wp-content/ uploads/2010/02/WSLRfeb10worley.pdf (Accessed October 2010).

STEINEM, GLORIA

Gloria Marie Steinem (1934–), feminist journalist, activist, writer, and lecturer, was born to parents Leo and Ruth Steinem in Toledo, Ohio. After her parents divorced when she was still a child, Steinem cared for her ailing mother, who was plagued by mental illness and poverty. Steinem enrolled in government courses at Smith College in the early 1950s, a time when most women were either enrolled in home economics classes or simply not attending college and anticipating motherhood. Steinem was famously quoted as stating, "A woman needs a man like a fish needs a bicycle." While at Smith, Steinem noticed major differences in the privileges of men and women, also noting the subjugation of women. Therefore, she became adamantly opposed to the idea of a woman being dependent on a man for financial support. Steinem excelled in her studies and graduated with honors.

Set on a journalistic and politically engaged career, Steinem took a job at *Help!* magazine as the publication's first employee. She became a major proponent for the second wave of the feminist movement and wrote for *New York* magazine. In 1972, she cofounded *Ms.* magazine, which grew out of an article she wrote for *New York* magazine. In this article, Steinem shed light on the situation that forced women to choose between motherhood and a career outside the home, and she emphasized points that would later be noted in major works, such as Betty Friedan's *The Feminine Mystique* (1963) and Arlie Russell Hochschild's work on the idea of the "second shift." Steinem alluded to this double-dutied second shift by explaining the idea that a woman's shift is never done, that even if a woman is able to work in the public sphere she is still the one held responsible for the household chores. Steinem's article also preceded Friedan's canonical text by one year. While her work in journalism was heralded, her work in other arenas also received attention.

Steinem actively campaigned for the Equal Rights Amendment (ERA) and also founded or cofounded many other women's and social justice groups and organizations, including the Women's Action Alliance, the National Women's Political Caucus (NWPC), the Coalition of Labor Union Women, the *Ms.* Foundation for Women, Choice USA, and the Women's Media Center.

American feminist and cofounder of *Ms.* magazine and the Women's Media Center, Gloria Steinem has been an activist for over 40 years. She continues to speak to young people at high schools and on college campuses. (Wikimedia)

Always returning to journalism, Steinem complemented her activism with her writing. In 1969, she and Dorothy Pitman Hughes published an article titled "After Black Power, Women's Liberation." Steinem, Hughes, and other second wave feminists soon realized that while they were able to participate in civil rights and New Left movements, they were still the ones responsible for typing the letters and making the coffee. In other words, they were campaigning for equal rights for others while their rights were still being abrogated. In this article, Steinem and Hughes discussed such inequalities but also took on the challenging fact that second wave feminism tended to have a "white face" and was understood by mass publics and lay audiences to be largely a white women's movement. Steinem, a Jewish American, struggled to include the voices of all women regardless of race, socioeconomic status, religion, creed, national origin, or ethnicity in the liberation movement. She would go on to write many texts to address these issues. Some of them include *A Thousand Indias* (1957), *The*

Beach Book (1963), *Outrageous Acts and Everyday Rebellions* (1983), *Marilyn* (1986), *Revolution From Within* (1992), *Moving Beyond Words* (1994), and *Doing Sixty and Seventy* (2006).

Continuing with the cause, Steinem explored gender roles and gender exploitation, infiltrating the "granddaddy" of gender subjugation and control, the Playboy empire. She conducted an investigative journalistic reporting piece on how Playboy bunnies were treated and trained: to perch and never sit, bend a certain way, deliver drinks and flirt with the patrons in a specific manner, and so forth. In 1985, the piece was adapted for the film *A Bunny's Tale*. Already an ethnographer and autoethnographer, Steinem continued to tell tales of injustice based on socioeconomic status, gender, age, ability, sexuality, race, religion, and national origin.

Steinem's life and work have been dedicated to exposing and recognizing the intersectional component of all arbitrary markers of identity and thus their overlapping nodes of oppression and discrimination. She has worked to make sure that taken-forgranted assumptions do not go unquestioned and that privileges do not go perpetually unexamined. She has sought to make these privileges nameable and visible through her work. As a result, she has garnered attention as a pivotal yet somewhat controversial icon of the second wave of the women's movement in the United States. As the "face" of second wave feminism, she has experienced criticism as well as recognition. In fact, many second wave feminist women believed that Steinem played into the media's fascination with her and that she became a hyperglamorized feminist figure.

Although the sensationalism died down, Steinem continued to work, writing texts and getting involved with several causes and organizations. In the year 2000, she married David Bale (actor Christian Bale's father), who died of brain cancer in 2003. Steinem remains engaged with the organizations she helped to found. She speaks at college campuses and political events and has worked with leaders on Democratic campaigns and movements for social justice.

Judy E. Battaglia
Loyola Marymount University

See also Feminism; Feminist Theory: Second Wave; Gender and Femininity: Motherhood; Gender and Femininity: Single/Independent Girl; Gender Media Monitoring; Hanna, Kathleen; Sexism; Women's Magazines: Feminist Magazines

Further Readings

Friedan, B. *The Feminine Mystique.* New York: W. W. Norton, 1963.

Heilbrun, C. G. *The Education of a Woman: The Life and Times of Gloria Steinem.* New York: Ballantine, 1996.

Hochschild, A. *The Second Shift.* New York: Penguin, 1989.

Stern, S. L. *Gloria Steinem: Her Passions, Politics, and Mystique.* Secaucus, NJ: Carol, 1997.

STEREOTYPES

Stereotypes are overly simplified conceptions, images, or beliefs about individuals and specific social groups. Popular stereotypes rely on assumptions, are often mistaken for reality, and usually have negative connotations. The term *stereotype* was first coined in 1798 in the field of typography. It originally meant "duplicate impression" and described the process of casting a print mold. In 1922, American journalist Walter Lippmann redefined the term as a perpetual "picture in our heads." The power of the image in our heads is its ability to perpetuate without change. Unfortunately, that image, the stereotype, is usually negative and constricts individual identities to preconceived group characteristics.

Theories of Stereotypes

Perspectives on the development of stereotypes vary; views range from a belief that stereotypes help to frame an individual's experience with different groups of people to a belief that stereotypes are patterns of communication that are, by definition, inaccurate representations and projections of one to another. Early studies suggested that stereotypes were used only by repressed authoritarians as a form of prejudicial thinking. More recent theories acknowledge the complexity of stereotypes and stereotyping and conclude that both are commonplace.

Social psychologists attribute the stereotyping process to the human need for mental categorizing. There are two generally agreed-upon perspectives about stereotypes and how they operate. The first perspective suggests that stereotypes are automatic (subconscious) and explicit (conscious). Automatic stereotyping is the stereotyping everyone does without notice and is accompanied by an explicit stereotype, which creates more concrete ideas in the mind. In this case, stereotypes act first as mental categories with which to contain new information (people, groups, places, and so forth) and then as a set of perceptions about the new information. For example, the stereotype of people from New Jersey as loud and obnoxious, with a taste for ostentatious clothing and usually Italian-American, will cast all state residents in such a light even though the state's population is quite diverse. The power of stereotypes is reinforced when the stereotype is mass-produced in the media, as in shows like *The Real House Wives of New Jersey*, *The Jersey Shore*, and *Jerseylicious*.

The second perspective on stereotypes relies on the notion of in-groups and out-groups. In-groups are perceived as normal and thus the superior group of which to be a member, whereas out-groups are simply all other, less desirable groups. In this second perspective on stereotypes, the members of the in-group are not stereotyped because they are seen as normal individuals with distinct identities. Members of the out-group are treated en masse and are ascribed few discernible or notable differences. In the United States, heterosexuals are an in-group, leaving all other sexual orientations to be stereotyped as deviant. There are no stereotypes about heterosexuals, because heterosexuality is the nonstereotypical in-group.

In general, stereotypes are constructed for people and groups of people with whom individuals have little to no contact. Lack of familiarity encourages the lumping together of unknown people. Most often, the lack of distinction combined with the lack of specific knowledge results in stereotypes that are largely negative assumptions about a group or individual person within that group. However, social scientists and psychologists tend to agree that stereotypes help humans manage the complexities of other people as individuals. Even though stereotyping can be problematic, it is an efficient way to organize large blocks of information. The need to categorize is an essential human characteristic that allows people to simplify and operate within the world. By assigning general traits to members of groups, humans are more apt to avoid processing new information and are better able to predict the social world in a general sense.

A very different view of stereotypes suggests that the reason people stereotype is that they need to feel good about themselves. Stereotypes enhance self-esteem and protect people from feelings of anxiety by designating one's own group as normal and superior and making all other groups abnormal and inferior. In other words, stereotypes can help provide people with a sense of worth and pride in their identity. It is important to note that groups that are negatively stereotyped can, over time, enact the labels that are placed on them and assume, even if subconsciously, that a negative stereotype applied to them by a dominant group is a norm to emulate. Furthermore, stereotypes can prevent or discourage members of an in-group from forming any emotional identification with members of an out-group, leading to erroneous judgments and scapegoating. Characteristics subject to stereotyping range from age and gender to race and religion, always with the idea that there is one ideal way to be and all other identities can be lumped together and stereotyped.

In media, the recognizable nature of stereotypes has assured their use in contemporary advertising and comedy. Moreover, throughout history, literature and art have relied on stereotyped stock characters. Storytellers have used clichéd or predictable characters and situations in order to quickly connect with readers and audiences.

Gender and Sexual Stereotypes

Stereotypes about gender and sexuality are the most prolific form of stereotyping. Stereotypes about sexuality work to maintain society's strict notion of a gender binary. That is, male and female stereotypes perpetuate the idea that only male and female genders exist. Common gender stereotypes claim that men are promiscuous whereas women are sexually repressed, men are aggressive and brutish whereas women are demure and passive, and men are insensitive and detached whereas women are naturally caring and nurturing. These stereotypical gender roles place women at home, raising children and completely satisfied by their husbands, and men away at work, with few emotional ties to their families and eyes for every woman who passes them by. Gender stereotypes assume that all men must act stereotypically male, all women must act stereotypically female, and any deviation from the norm is intensely problematic. Living up to sexual stereotypes is damaging for people and creates ideas about one gender being better than another, leading to the notion of one person being better simply because of

the person's biological reproductive capabilities or genitalia.

Sexual stereotypes also affect how we conceive of hetero-, homo-, and bisexuality. Heterosexuality is often considered the norm, or in-group, which causes all other sexual orientations to be stereotyped as out-groups and thus deviant and abnormal. Sexual stereotypes are damaging to nonheterosexual people and often result in the denial or limitation of civil rights, as well as violence and discrimination. Some sexual stereotypes suggest that lesbians are unrefined, unattractive, and overweight (similar to heterosexual men) and that gay men are stereotypically thin, effeminate, and vain (similar to heterosexual women).

Racial and Ethnic Stereotypes

In the United States, some of the longest-held and potentially most detrimental stereotypes are those about African Americans. Stereotypes about African American people date back to the colonial years of settlement, particularly after slavery became a racial institution. Blacks have been stereotyped as lazy, primitive, religious, and violent. They have been depicted as loving fried chicken, Kool-Aid, and watermelon. The archetypal African American image comes primarily from the minstrel shows of the 19th century. In these shows, white people wore blackface makeup and performed African Americans as buffoonish and ignorant characters. Some of the most well-known black stereotypes are the Sambo (a trickster), the Mammy (a large, dark-skinned woman who raises white folks' babies), the Uncle Tom (an African American man who acquiesces in everything white people want), the Magical Black Man (a character who saves white people from their own mistakes), and the Welfare Queen (an African American woman who has babies only to get money from the government). In news media today, the stereotype of angry, violent black men and women has led to some of the most racist images seen in American culture. Sports are the one place where African American stereotypes are somewhat positive, but the assumption that all black people are natural-born athletes can still be damaging and limiting: The more positive image is only made negative by the resulting stereotype that assumes that black communities place a low priority on education.

Similarly, Hispanics are cast as a group of people uninterested in education. Rather, the stereotypical Hispanic person cares only for his or her family and having more and more children—especially because the most prominent stereotype of Hispanic people is that they all hail from a common country of origin. In the United States, Hispanic and Latino people are incorrectly given racial identities and are often depicted as part of one homogeneous culture or ethnic group with no defining characteristics. If a country of origin is specified, it is invariably Puerto Rico or Mexico, regardless of an individual's actual home country.

Recently, a rise in stereotypes about Middle Eastern, Arab, and Muslim people has occurred. Although a fascination with the Near East has long existed in literature and film and characters have long been depicted as billionaires on camels or belly dancers in tents, the more common stereotype today is of a bomber or terrorist. After the September 11, 2001, attacks on the World Trade Center in New York City, a wave of anti-Arab images and stereotypes emerged. Racial profiling done at airports has become a common form of stereotyping and another example of the ways in which out-groups are demeaned and degraded by stereotypes.

Stereotyping people from "the Orient" has long been a cultural fascination of Americans. A major stereotype of East Asia is its exotic and mysterious nature compared to the bland, ordinary aspect of Western culture and customs. An interestingly detrimental effect of the East's mystique places all Asian cultures in a perpetual state of ancient timelessness, whereas the West is seen as constantly emerging, innovating, and reconstructing itself. In the late 19th century, a fear of the "Yellow Peril" overwhelmed Western countries, including the United States, where anti-Asian sentiments were readily expressed on the West Coast as Chinese, Japanese, and other Asians began immigrating to America. Since then, Asians have been stereotyped as the "model minority"; that is, positive traits have been ascribed to all Asian individuals as part of their stereotype. Asians are seen as studious, productive, intelligent, and inoffensive people who have elevated their social standing through diligence and hard work. Asians are also stereotyped by their choice of professions: as dry cleaners, grocery store owners, and scientists. When Asians are not performing a stereotypical job or operating as part of an ideal minority, then they fall into one of these even more limiting roles: the Fu Manchu (an evil, Satan-like character), the Charlie Chan (a "good" Asian who has good manners), the Dragon Lady (a hypersexual woman manifested in the war bride as well as the prostitute), and the China Doll (a subservient maiden).

Another minority that has been subjected to both positive and negative stereotypes are Jews. Throughout the centuries, Jewish people have been made scapegoats for a multitude of societal problems. However, they are also praised for their ability to survive and be successful. Jews have been cast as greedy, cheap, loud, and obnoxious. They are often depicted counting money or diamonds. Jewish female stereotypes include guilt-inflicting mothers and spoiled, materialistic daughters (the Jewish American "princess"). Caricatures of Jews show them as having curly hair, large hook noses, thick lips, and olive-brown skin. Usually somewhere in the picture is also an image of a bagel, yarmulke, or menorah, and the character is often playing the violin, haggling with a customer, or undergoing circumcision. One of the most famous Jewish stereotypes is William Shakespeare's character Shylock from *The Merchant of Venice*. Shylock is a moneylender who insists on being repaid in full and attempts to claim his "pound of flesh" when Antonio (the lead character and clearly a member of society's in-group) is unable to repay him with money.

The gendered specificity of ethnic and cultural stereotypes adds a layer to the process whereby groups are belittled through stereotypes. In the United States, because the ideal in-group woman displays the characteristics of attractive, demure, and nurturing, stereotypes of nonwhite women are the opposite. For example, the African American Mammy may take care of children, but they are not her own and she is usually depicted as obese and thus unattractive. The China Doll may be demure, but too much so; white men cannot take her seriously enough to consider her worthy of marriage. Nonwhite stereotypical women are never pretty and almost always overly sexual if not completely asexual. Likewise, the stereotypical nonwhite male is also always "too much" or "not enough"; he is either too weak, like the Uncle Tom; too aggressive, like the Fu Manchu; too smart and cunning, like the Jewish Shylock; or too lazy and unintelligent, like African American and Hispanic men. Particularly damaging nonwhite male stereotypes have marked many minority males as not only defective but also completely nonhuman, as animals to be handled.

Because stereotypes affect at least one aspect of everyone's identity, the potential damaging or limiting impact of stereotyping is endless. However, awareness of and education about stereotypes, and of how they are proliferated in various media depictions, can work to mitigate, if not fully correct, that damage. With that awareness and a fuller personal experience with people different from ourselves, how we as individuals choose to use stereotypes—whether as guides and mental frameworks about large quantities of information or as distinctive and determinative knowledge about individuals in groups—is up to us.

Rachel E. Silverman
Embry Riddle Aeronautical University

See also Affirmative Action; Class Privilege; Cultural Politics; Diversity; Empowerment; Gender and Femininity: Motherhood; Gender and Femininity: Single/Independent Girl; Gender and Masculinity: Black Masculinity; Gender and Masculinity: Fatherhood; Gender and Masculinity: Metrosexual Male; Gender and Masculinity: White Masculinity; Hegemony; Heterosexism; Homophobia; Identity; Ideology; Intersectionality; Minority Rights; Misogyny; Patriarchy; Prejudice; Queer Theory; Racism; Sexism; Social Construction of Gender; Transgender Studies; Tropes

Further Readings

Foxman, Abraham. *Jews and Money: The Story of a Stereotype*. New York: Palgrave Macmillan, 2010.

Lee, Stacey J. *Unraveling the "Model Minority" Stereotype: Listening to Asian American Youth*. New York: Teachers College Press, 2009.

Macrae, C. N., C. Stangor, and M. Hewstone, eds. *Stereotypes and Stereotyping*. New York: Guilford Press, 1996.

Said, Edward. *Orientalism*. New York: Pantheon Books, 1978.

Steele, Claude M. *Whistling Vivaldi: How Stereotypes Affect Us and What We Can Do*. New York: W. W. Norton, 2011.

Turner, Patricia A. *Ceramic Uncles and Celluloid Mammies: Black Images and Their Influence on Culture*. New York: Anchor Books, 1994.

TALK SHOWS

Since their inception in 1935, talk shows have had a profound influence on American life. The term *talk show* generally refers to a program, whether on radio or television, that has a host (or hosts), guests, and some audience participation—whether listeners call in on radio or a television host interacts with a studio audience. Historically, although some women were guests on these shows, stereotypes prevented women from being hosts for many years.

There were fledgling attempts as far back as the 1920s to allow listeners to interact with radio hosts, but the technology of that time made it difficult. Guest "experts," the majority of whom were male, gave radio talks, but there was no easy way to interact with the speakers in real time. In the mid-1930s, a new radio program tried to change that: *America's Town Meeting of the Air*. It had a live studio audience and "listening rooms" throughout the country; audience members could step up to the microphone and ask questions of the week's guests. Mirroring the common wisdom of the day that expertise on current events and politics was something only men possessed, the majority of the guests were male. However, *Town Meeting* did include some women: among those heard in the 1930s were commentator Dorothy Thompson; U.S. Secretary of Labor Frances Perkins; Lena Madison Phillips, president of the International Federation of Business and Professional Women; and Mary McLeod Bethune,

vice president of the National Association for the Advancement of Colored People (NAACP).

From the 1930s through the 1950s, there were also many women who hosted "women's shows," one of the few domains that welcomed women announcers. Although these programs focused on what society believed were the interests of housewives, sometimes hosts would invite guests to address subjects like the arts, politics, or science. Among the best-known women's show hosts on radio was Mary Margaret McBride, who spoke with such news makers as First Lady Eleanor Roosevelt, novelist (and feminist) Fannie Hurst, photographer Margaret Bourke-White, and African American folklorist Zora Neale Hurston. The majority of the guests, even on the most progressive women's shows, tended to be white, but in the late 1940s that began to change when the first black-formatted radio stations went on the air. Continuing the same cultural stereotypes, the black stations too had women's shows that focused on homemaking: the first was probably Willa Monroe's; she hosted the *Tan Town Homemakers*, a program on WDIA in Memphis, in 1949.

One popular talk radio program was on the air at KDKA in Pittsburgh. *Party Line* was hosted by a husband-and-wife team, Ed and Wendy King; it began in 1951 and had great success for nearly two decades. Meanwhile, some of radio's women's show hosts began their careers on radio and then moved to the new medium of television. A good example is Cincinnati's Ruth Lyons, who began her career on WLW radio with *The 50 Club* (named for the number of people in her studio audience) and then moved to television during the 1950s, where it was renamed *The 50/50 Club*, after the studio audience was expanded. Lyons was known for her philanthropy and used her program to raise money for worthy causes as well as to interview a wide range of celebrity guests.

With only a few exceptions, television talk shows consigned women to the same stereotypical roles as radio. Hosts of talk shows in the 1950s and 1960s were generally men, and women either appeared in commercials, selling items for the home, or were glamorous studio hostesses. Like radio talk shows, television talk programs sometimes invited women news makers, such as Maine senator Margaret Chase Smith, but most of the guests continued to be male. The only female television hosts were seen on programs aimed at women, such as *Home*, which starred actress Arlene Francis. It debuted in 1954 on NBC-TV but lasted only three years.

When the Federal Communications Commission (FCC) issued a ruling in the late 1960s that broadcasters were required to hire more women and minorities, a number of women reporters were hired (on both radio and television), and several women became announcers on radio, but talk shows remained an all-male preserve well into the 1970s and early 1980s. Interestingly, one woman who would go on to become a great success in television talk was making her debut as a radio news reporter in 1973—Oprah Winfrey. She worked for WVOL in Nashville and was then hired by a Nashville television station, WTVF, where she became the station's first African American news anchor. Her career took her next to Baltimore, where in 1977 she became the cohost of *People Are Talking*, a local talk show on WJZ-TV. She was then hired in Chicago to be part of the morning show on WLS-TV. By 1984, she had become the host of her own local talk show, and by the late 1980s, she was hosting a very successful syndicated program. An updated version of the "women's show," her program was a combination of interviews with celebrities, news makers, and experts on relationships, fashion, or cooking and segments about dieting or health. Oprah's success refuted two myths: that white viewers would not watch a show hosted by a black woman and that as a woman and as an African American she would be unable to command sufficient ratings. Instead, her appeal transcended race, and she garnered and maintained excellent ratings. Moreover, she did not look like a model; in fact, she struggled with weight, yet fans felt better able to relate to her as a result. By the 1990s, Winfrey was known as the queen of daytime television talk, and her successful career would extend well beyond the first decade of the 2000s.

On radio, one of the first women to gain success as a talk host was Dr. Laura Schlessinger. Her doctorate degree was in physiology, but many listeners came to believe she was a medical doctor. Her radio career began accidentally, after she called a controversial Los Angeles talk show host, Bill Ballance, to answer his question of the day. (Critics said programs like Ballance's exploited women, because he got them to discuss intimate topics on the air, in a format dubbed "topless radio.") Dr. Laura quickly developed a good rapport with Ballance, and he invited her to call again, not to discuss her sex life but rather to be his relationship expert; she gave advice to some of his callers. By 1976, Dr. Laura had her own talk show on a small station in Santa Ana, California. At that time, she was simply offering encouragement and guidance to callers; the role of the helpful advice giver was one that women had traditionally played on radio in the past. After taking a hiatus to marry and to raise a child, she returned to radio in 1990 at KFI in Los Angeles, and this time she had a much different persona, more conservative and (her critics said) more judgmental. Nevertheless, her ratings grew and her fame as a talk show host increased throughout the 1990s. By the early 2000s, she was among the top five most listened-to talk show hosts, according to *Talkers* magazine.

Another pioneering woman in talk radio was Sally Jessy Raphael, who got her start in broadcasting in Puerto Rico and then worked at a number of stations in the eastern United States, as a disc jockey, a news reporter, and even the host of a television cooking show. By 1981, she finally found a niche as a syndicated talk radio host, when she was hired by NBC's Talknet. By 1983, she was also hosting a syndicated television talk show. On both radio and television, she tended to avoid politics, preferring to focus on relationships, romance, and human interest stories. By the early 1990s, her television show had become more controversial; critics accused her of hosting a lowbrow, trashy television show that was reminiscent of Jerry Springer's show, but she maintained a loyal fan base throughout the 1990s.

In 2002, *Talkers* magazine named her as one of the top five radio hosts of all time, and she made the list of all-time top television hosts as well, coming in at number 11.

Raphael was not the only one accused of "going lowbrow" to get ratings: another syndicated daytime talk host, Jenny Jones, made headlines after the taping of a 1995 program about "same sex secret crushes." The show's focus was on guest Scott Amedure, who was homosexual and admitted that he had a crush on a friend, Jonathan Schmitz, who was straight. Schmitz believed he had been humiliated on national television; he claimed that he had not been told that the person with the secret crush on him was a gay man, and he came on the show unaware that the premise was a same-sex crush. Several days later, he killed Amedure. Amedure's family sued and won, but the verdict was overturned on appeal.

Although it was heartening to see more female talk show hosts, they generally remained mired in the "women's show" genre. Men hosted talk shows on a wide range of topics, while most of the women's talk shows, even the controversial ones, still emphasized stereotypical subjects like fashion or relationships. Political talk continued to be dominated by men, both on radio and on television, until the 1990s. One of the few women to work in this format was Randi Rhodes, at one time a disc jockey at album rock stations in several states. In 1992, the brash and outspoken Rhodes began doing "hot talk" at WIOD in Miami, Florida. The format was not political, but it did touch on current events and anything else she and the callers wanted to discuss. At a time when women were still hosting programs that only gave advice or focused on stereotypical women's topics, Rhodes was unique; she gained a reputation for being unafraid to discuss any topic. Despite her excellent ratings, however, she discovered that she was not being paid equally with the male announcers at WIOD and left to work at WJNO, a radio station in West Palm Beach. As current events such as the O. J. Simpson trial dominated the news, she found callers wanting to talk about news. She also began to take stands on politics, inspired by what she believed were partisan attacks on President Bill Clinton and his wife, Hillary Rodham Clinton. By this time, the majority of political talk shows on radio were hosted by conservative white males. Rhodes carved out a niche as a liberal (and female) political talker, and by the late 1990s, that was what she was known for. By the early 2000s, her program was being syndicated, giving her an audience in other cities.

Another trailblazing woman talk show host was on the air in the Spanish-language market. Cristina Saralegui, a well-known magazine journalist, carved out a successful television career beginning in 1989. *El Show de Cristina* earned her a reputation as the Latina Oprah Winfrey. On a talk show that lasted several decades, she addressed the traditional women's show topics, fashion, food, and celebrity interviews, but she also discussed issues previously taboo in the Spanish-language media, including the negative effect of machismo on relationships as well as hot-button issues such as gay marriage and birth control. She also took a strong stand against domestic violence, another topic rarely discussed on Spanish-language television at that time. As she got older, she took on another taboo subject: the idea that once women reach a certain age, viewers find them undesirable as hosts. She became very outspoken on the topic of ageism on television, and in 2006 she was named a spokesperson for the American Association of Retired Persons (AARP), an organization that advocates for people over the age of 50.

In the 2000s, Randi Rhodes is no longer alone in the landscape of political talk radio. Although most of the best-known talk hosts remain men, more women have broken through. On the left are syndicated hosts such as Laura Flanders and Stephanie Miller; on the right are syndicated hosts such as Laura Ingraham and Monica Crowley. They are joined by women who have local programs in a number of cities, including conservative Heidi Harris in Las Vegas and liberal Shannyn Moore in Anchorage, Alaska. One woman who began her career as a political talk show host on radio, Rachel Maddow, is now a highly regarded liberal commentator and host of her own program on the cable network MSNBC.

On television, in addition to Oprah Winfrey, there are a number of successful women hosting their own program, including Ellen DeGeneres, one of the first openly lesbian talk show hosts.

Donna L. Halper
Lesley University

See also Advertising; Blogs and Blogging; Children's Programming: Cartoons; Cyberspace and Cyberculture; Diversity; Fairness Doctrine; Federal Communications Commission; Film: Hollywood;

Film: Independent; Gamson, Joshua; Gay and Lesbian Portrayals on Television; Gender Media Monitoring; Mass Media; Media Consolidation; Media Rhetoric; Network News Anchor Desk; Newsrooms; Radio; Radio: Pirate; Soap Operas; Social Media; Telecommunications Act of 1996; Television

Further Readings

Halper, Donna L. *Invisible Stars: A Social History of Women in American Broadcasting.* Armonk, NY: M. E. Sharpe, 2001.

Hilmes, Michele. *Only Connect: A Cultural History of Broadcasting in the United States,* 2nd ed. Belmont, CA: Thomson-Wadsworth, 2007.

Ware, Susan. *It's One O'Clock and Here Is Mary Margaret McBride.* New York: New York University Press, 2005.

TELECOMMUNICATIONS ACT OF 1996

The Telecommunications Act of 1996 was the first successful overhaul of the Communications Act of 1934. The act deregulated media ownership and regulated sexual, violent, and obscene media content. One profound consequence of the act has been the increased concentration of media ownership.

President Clinton signed the Telecommunications Act of 1996 after Congress passed it by a large margin. The objectives of the Act are to promote competition, to reduce regulation, to provide low-cost and high-quality services for the consumers, and to encourage the spread of new telecommunications technologies. Because the advancement of digital technology facilitates convergence, media companies and politicians both saw that the act would lead the United States to a new "information age." Media and telecommunications companies criticized previous regulations as outdated and obsolete. The act also helped the administration of President Bill Clinton to promote the concept of the "information highway."

The act affected five major areas of regulation: (1) telecommunications services, (2) broadcast services, (3) cable services, (4) regulatory reform, and (5) obscenity and violence. With regard to telecommunications services, digital technology allows the transmission of data and video as well as voice. Before the act, local telephone companies had monopolistic control of the domestic market. The

act requested local telephone companies to share the market with other companies. On the other hand, local telephone companies were allowed to enter the long-distance service market. It was believed that the telecommunications service cost for consumers would drop because of competition.

With regard to broadcast television, before the act a television company could not reach more than 25 percent of television households, it could not own more than 12 television stations, it could not own cable television, and its broadcast license lasted for only five years. Now that the act is law, a television company can reach up to 35 percent of television households, there is no limit on the number of television stations a company can own, a television company can own cable television, and a broadcast license lasts for eight years. With regard to radio, before the act a radio station could not own more than 40 stations, and it could not have more than four stations in a single market. Now that the act is law, there is no limit on how many stations a radio company can own, and it can now own up to eight radio stations in a local market. The removal of limits and the increase of possible market share were expected to increase competition in the broadcast market.

With regard to cable services, the act abolished all regulation on rates for nonbasic services. The act allows broadcast television companies to own cable companies, and it permits telecommunications companies to provide cable services. The act also prohibits local cable franchising authorities from making certain demands of cable companies. For example, local franchises are not allowed to set technical standards for cable companies. The deregulation of cross-ownership was expected to increase opportunity and flexibility for broadcast, cable, and telecommunications companies. It was also believed that consumers would have more choices of media content and cable service providers.

With regard to regulatory reform, a broadcast license allows a television company to use the analog spectrum for free. Before passage of the act, the National Association of Broadcasters lobbied Congress to allocate the digital spectrum for the implementation of high-definition television.

With regard to obscenity and violence, the act included the Communications Decency Act of 1996. This part of the law regulated indecent, obscene, and violent content in broadcast television, cable television, and the Internet. The Communications Decency Act mandated that a V-chip (the V is for "violence") be installed in all television sets sold in the United States. This chip can automatically block out content that is deemed unsuitable for children.

Public interest groups and critical scholars criticize the Telecommunications Act for increasing media ownership concentration, decreasing market competition, limiting consumer choices, increasing costs for consumers, and ignoring the public interest. Public advocacy group Common Cause published a report, *The Fallout From the Telecommunications Act of 1996: Unintended Consequences and Lessons Learned*, that documents the new ownership landscape after the act. The report found that, since passage of the act, the biggest media and telecommunications companies now oligopolistically control the markets for broadcast television, cable television, radio, and telecommunications. Companies have merged to create mega-firms, or conglomerates. One early merger took place between America Online (AOL) and Time Warner in 2001. According to the report, because the main objective of companies is to make money, the content and services that they provide are of dubious quality.

The act may not appear to have a direct relation to women's and gender issues, but it has some significant implications. First, a less competitive market may prohibit minority- and women-owned companies from entering a concentrated market. Second, a concentrated media market may provide and promote less diverse or even potentially harmful media content (such as images that degrade women). Third, the blocking of indecent materials may stigmatize issues such as acquired immune deficiency syndrome (AIDS) and sexual health.

Micky Lee
Suffolk University, Boston

See also Advertising; Cultivation Theory; Fairness Doctrine; Federal Communications Commission; Mass Media; Media Consolidation; Media Convergence; Network News Anchor Desk; New Media; Pornification of Everyday Life; Radio: Pirate; Talk Shows

Further Readings

Common Cause. *The Fallout From the Telecommunications Act of 1996: Unintended*

Consequences and Lessons Learned. Washington, DC: Author, 2005.
Federal Communications Commission. "Telecommunications Act of 1996." http://www.fcc.gov/telecom.html#fcc (Accessed February 2011).
Library of Congress. "Bill Text 104th Congress (1995–1996) S.652.ENR Telecommunications Act of 1996." http://thomas.loc.gov/cgi-bin/query/z?c104:s.652.enr: (Accessed February 2011).

TELEVISION

Television, arguably the most important communication technology of the 20th century, has a rich history. Distinguished from previous media by its ability to receive moving images and broadcast them over the airwaves and for its ubiquity, television as a medium remains a central part of contemporary culture in the United States.

The Early Years: 1930s–50s

Although proof-of-concept television broadcasts occurred in the late 1920s and throughout the 1930s, many historians point to television's unveiling at the 1939 World's Fair in New York City as the beginning of the technology as a mass medium. At the fair, Radio Corporation of America (RCA) president David Sarnoff championed the new technology by broadcasting the events of the fair and launching televised content on the National Broadcasting Company (NBC) network. These earliest televisions displayed images in black and white on five-inch screens, were prohibitively expensive, and were able to receive only a small amount of programming. Television met with a mixture of curiosity and enthusiasm, but widespread production and adoption of the new technology did not occur in the United States until the late 1940s and early 1950s, following the end of World War II. Television programming during this period borrowed heavily from popular radio and stage acts, and variety shows and news dominated the airwaves. Milton Berle's *Texaco Star Theater*, *Meet the Press*, Ed Sullivan's *Toast of the Town*, and the *Howdy Doody Show* were some of the most popular shows during the early years of television.

Early televisions from the 1930s and 1940s displayed images on small black-and-white screens, cost hundreds of dollars (the equivalent of around $4,000 today), and could receive a minimal amount of programming. (Photos.com)

The Golden Age: 1950s–70s

From the early 1950s through the 1970s, television cemented its place in homes in the United States and around the world as its programming branched out from its vaudeville and radio roots to include shows that took full advantage of the immensely popular, in-demand medium. The situation comedy, the artfully directed drama, the news magazine show, and most other staples of contemporary television programming are grounded in this era. Most of the programs during the Golden Age were broadcast by the three major television networks, the American Broadcasting Company (ABC), the National Broadcasting Company (NBC), and the Columbia Broadcasting System (CBS).

Television saw some important technological changes during this era. Not only did television sets become larger, cheaper, and more dependable, but the amount and technical quality of programming increased as well. In the mid-1960s consumers started purchasing color televisions, and by the end of the decade it was common to find many homes with multiple sets.

As television adoption became widespread, many sectors of public life had to learn how to adapt. High-interest sporting events were aired during prime television viewing hours, press releases were timed to coincide with the television news cycle, and anyone interested in selling a product or idea had to learn how to best utilize the medium. For example, among the many important "firsts" for television during this period, the presidential debate between a perspiring and ill-prepared Richard Nixon and a television-primed John F. Kennedy in 1960 is seen by many as a turning point in American political life. Popular programming of the era included shows such as *I Love Lucy* (1951–57), *Leave It to Beaver* (1957–63), *I Dream of Jeannie* (1965–70), *All in the Family* (1971–79), and *M*A*S*H* (1972–83).

The Cable Era: 1980s–90s

During this era, the amount of television programming available grew significantly as the influence of the three major networks subsided. In addition to increased competition from UHF broadcast networks such as FOX and UPN, consumers were presented with a wealth of channels that could be provided by paid subscription and delivered via a cable connection. Unlike broadcast television stations, which focused on a variety of programming, many cable channels were dedicated to specific subjects, such as news, weather, music videos, children's programming, sports, or movies. During this era, both broadcast and cable television also faced competition for screen time from the growing home video market (which allowed consumers to purchase feature films, television specials, or other forms of video entertainment) and from video games (which could deliver interactive, arcade-like experiences on preexisting television sets).

Despite the penetration of cable service (and, to a lesser extent, satellite television), the most popular shows of the era continued to be those that aired on network television. Popular programming of the era included shows such as *Dallas* (1978–91), *The A-Team* (1983–87), *Full House* (1987–95), *Friends* (1994–2004), and *Seinfeld* (1989–98).

Television in the 21st Century

Television in the 21st century has continued to expand, often in ways that move television programming into new contexts. While rates of television adoption, network creation, and program development have all continued to increase, the television industry has had to grapple with a new competitor: new media technology. Most significantly, networks have had to develop programming that competes with the wealth of video content available on the Web on sites like YouTube. The low cost barrier to online content dispersal has made it possible for individuals to find mass audiences that can easily access their programming. Television networks have responded in several ways.

For one, many networks have moved to make their premier programming accessible via official Websites and other channels of digital distribution, such as Apple's iTunes store. Much of this content is free, provided with limited commercial interruption, and available immediately after broadcast. This shift to online digital distribution was predated by a widespread trend of publishing both older and contemporary series to consumer DVDs, a practice that met with only limited adoption on previous home video formats.

In addition, network programming has increasingly been reflective of the personal nature of many videos found on the Web. Some of the most popular programs of the early 21st century have been reality television shows, shows that reinforce the potential that "regular people" might one day become a celebrity. Popular programming of this era has included shows such as *Survivor, CSI, Grey's Anatomy, The Office, Lost,* and *American Idol.*

David S. Heineman
Bloomsburg University of Pennsylvania

See also Advertising; Audiences: Producers of New Media; Audiences: Reception and Injection Models; Children's Programming: Cartoons; Federal Communications Commission; Mass Media; New Media; Reality-Based Television: *America's Next Top Model*; Reality-Based Television: Makeover Shows; Reality-Based Television: Wedding Shows; Sitcoms; Soap Operas; Televisuality; YouTube

Further Readings

Gillespie, Marie. *Television, Ethnicity, and Cultural Change.* London: Routledge, 1995.
Hilmes, Michele and Jason Jacobs, eds. *The Television History Book.* London: British Film Institute, 2008.
Spigel, Lynn. *Make Room for TV: Television and the Family Ideal in Postwar America.* Chicago: University of Chicago Press, 1992.
Wheatley, Helen. *Re-Viewing Television History: Critical Issues in Television Historiography.* London: I. B. Tauris, 2007.

Televisuality

Televisuality is a theoretical term coined by John Caldwell in the mid-1990s to characterize a change in the look and practice of television programming. This change began around 1980 and continues to the present day. Describing and discussing television through the lens of televisuality requires one to consider television as a mode of mass communication reliant on popularity with viewers and created in an industrial context whose labor relations affect how shows are produced. Overall, the main identifying feature of "the televisual" is "an excess of style." Thus, programs produced from the 1980s onward are likely to break with traditional "invisible" production styles and to innovate in ways that call the viewer's attention to the constructedness of the show—that it is a televisual text and that the viewer is watching (or, in a best-case scenario, participating) in the construction of meaning through attraction to or investment in the style of the televisual text.

This excess of style can manifest itself in a multiplicity of ways. On one end of this spectrum are the swooping, highly stylized opening credits and graphic displays of *Entertainment Tonight* or *Access Hollywood*, which have been increasingly co-opted by sports programming and certain unscripted program forms (such as *American Idol*). The other includes cinematic visual forms utilized first by Steven Bochco in the 1980s series *Hill Street Blues* and *St. Elsewhere*. This one-camera, film-inspired form continued into the 1990s and beyond with Dick Wolf's *Law & Order* franchise and also has been used in the production of genres that were traditionally studio-bound, such as the one-camera sitcoms *Sex and the City*, *Arrested Development*, and *Malcolm in the Middle*. A more recent development is the conflation of these stylistic innovations in programs such as *CSI*. This would lead one to conclude, rightly, that a further marker of the "televisual" signaled, but not directly addressed by Caldwell, is that it is dynamic—as an activity and an evolutionary strategy, one can expect to see stylistic innovations continue to evolve as television programs continue to seek spectacularity and thus attract viewers with these innovations.

As a theoretical concept, televisuality is useful in that it accounts for the industrial production of television and the economic factors that affect the construction of television shows. It also addresses the consumption of these shows within a culture whose central mass media, until the rise of Internet-based media forms in the late 1990s, was television and whose collective history and experience of events of historical importance had been mediated through this form. Thus televisuality recognizes that the television industry is an industry and subject to the same market fluctuations and demands as other product-producing economic endeavors. It further acknowledges the characteristics that are peculiar to the television industry—that it is a culture industry and that its products differentiate themselves in ways that are much more complex and variant than merely "new model years." In accounting for the many behind-the-scenes relationships that may have an effect on style, televisuality suggests that a movement toward the spectacular or heightened aesthetic presentation of meaning is a continuing trope and goal.

Caldwell identifies six principles which inhere in televisuality: stylistic performance, structural inversion, industrial product, programming phenomenon, audience participation, and a reaction to an economic crisis facing the industry.

Of these, style is the main attribute that has garnered attention and has been most influential to subsequent scholars. Caldwell discusses the "excess of style" that is televisuality's most observable and obvious marker as an activity, as opposed to a look. It is expansive enough to encompass the increase in digitally processed chyrons and other graphics in news and news-entertainment shows as well as an increasing self-reflexivity (or "structural inversion")

in the performance of fictional shows. This structural inversion highlights elements that may have formerly been backgrounded—in terms of either production or narrative. Thus, a sitcom might call attention to its construction and the artificiality of its proscenium-based three-camera design. The interior thoughts or fantasies of a character might be visualized for the viewer, as in *Arrested Development* and *Malcolm in the Middle*. Characters might engage in direct address to the audience, either in an unmediated breaking of the fourth wall (in the early seasons of *Sex and the City*) or as part of an unexplained interview sequence with a nameless, faceless interviewer (in *Modern Family*). All of these signal to the audience that the producers and even the characters in the show know that these are constructed performances, manufactured within an industrial structure of labor relations, cultural, and economic needs, for the television audience. A recent example in which the character Liz Lemon (Tina Fey) acknowledges the effect of industrial conditions of production on content from within a fiction about the television industry can be found in the Verizon-sponsored episode of *30 Rock*. After a verbal exchange about a Verizon product with Jack Donagy (Alec Baldwin), Lemon/Fey turns to the camera and breaks the fourth wall, asking, "Can we have our money now?"

The other three principles of televisuality (programming phenomenon, audience participation, and economic crisis facing the industry) describe different aspects of the challenges that faced traditional broadcast networks (the Big Three, ABC, CBS, and NBC) in the early 1980s as a result of the growing popularity of cable in American homes. Cable brought with it the multichannel environment and a multiplicity of viewing options to subscribers, which resulted in an erosion of the viewing audience for the over-the-air (OTA) broadcasters. Beyond simply competing with one another's first-run dramas and sitcoms, the networks were now competing with the niche programming of specialized cable networks, such as CNN (1980) and MTV (1981). As a result of exposure to innovative television styles, such as MTV's music videos, audience members not only watched programs that were more stylistically excessive and self-reflexive but also came to expect (and accept) these modes of address across genres. Narrowcasting reconfigured the audience as niche programming became more popular and allowed for demographic-specific styles and looks to become acceptable and even sought after. Last, the stylistic excesses of televisuality can be viewed as a defensive strategy utilized by mainstream television networks and producers to address and (one hopes) ameliorate the growing threat that cable networks were posing to their market shares. It was, in other words, an attempt at product differentiation and innovation in an increasingly multichannel viewing environment.

Because the phenomenon of televisuality is a response to the industrial reconfiguration of the audience brought about by narrowcasting and niche programming (particularly observable in the growth of interest-specific cable networks such as the Food Network, HGTV, WE, and Lifetime), it also allows for different and innovative modes of address. Thus shows often utilize cultural-, ethnic-, and even gender-specific styles and aesthetics. Therefore, while it has been utilized by scholars of particular genres (Jeremy Butler's *Television Style* focuses on the sitcom, James Friedman addresses unscripted programming), a focus on televisuality also allows for the interrogation of how these particular stylistic innovations and strategies are aimed at particular types of ethnic- or gender-specific audiences: how *America's Next Top Model*'s excess of televisual style and innovation are particularly constructed and calibrated to be attractive to female viewers, for instance. More recent considerations of the televisual address the development of multiple digital platforms and screens on which television can be viewed and the explosion of do-it-yourself (DIY) digital video camcorders, editing software, and Internet distribution in the construction and aesthetics of television programs. These new means of reception and production are forcing the expansion of previous conceptions of televisuality while also challenging the very definition of television itself as an industrial category of media production and form of mass media.

MJ Robinson
Marymount Manhattan College

See also Advertising; Audiences: Producers of New Media; Audiences: Reception and Injection Models; Children's Programming: Cartoons; Federal Communications Commission; Mass Media; New Media; Reality-Based Television: *America's Next Top Model*; Reality-Based Television: Makeover Shows; Reality-Based Television: Wedding Shows; Sitcoms; Soap Operas; Television; YouTube

Further Readings

Butler, Jeremy. *Television Style*. New York: Routledge, 2010.

Caldwell, John T. *Televisuality: Style, Crisis and Authority in American Television*. New Brunswick, NJ: Rutgers University Press, 1995.

Friedman, James, ed. *Reality Squared: Televisual Discourse on the Real*. New Brunswick, NJ: Rutgers University Press, 2002.

Hartley, John. *Tele-ology: Studies in Television*. London: Routledge, 1992.

Newcomb, Horace, ed. *Television: The Critical View*, 6th ed. New York: Oxford University Press, 2000.

Spigel, Lynn. *Make Room for TV: Television and the Family Ideal in Postwar America*. Chicago: University of Chicago Press, 1992.

TEXTBOOKS

Education is a system in which social values and cultural attitudes are transmitted, and textbooks are an important part of this socialization process. Gender representations in textbooks have received significant scholarly attention over the past four decades, beginning after the rise of the women's movement. Since Title IX of the Education Amendments of 1972, which prohibited sex discrimination against students and employees in any federally funded program, issues of equality in education have received national attention. As Title IX applies to all aspects of student life, including sports, testing conditions, and school rules and policies, textbooks' stereotypical and limiting portrayals of the sexes also came under scrutiny. Publishers also began to recognize the importance of ensuring equal representation in their textbooks, and by the mid-1970s most publishers had issued guidebooks for authors, noting the potential impact that textbooks can have on students. By 1975, major textbook publisher Macmillan issued the statement (quoted by G. E. Britton and M. C. Lumpkin in a 1977 article) that "children are not simply being taught mathematics and reading; they are also learning, sometimes subliminally, how society regards certain groups of people." McGraw-Hill Book Company also issued guidelines to help ensure equal treatment of the sexes in their publications and called for the elimination of sexism and sexist language from all McGraw-Hill publications. Their guidelines included directives such as that characteristics traditionally praised in males, specifically assertiveness and boldness, should also be praised in females. Yet, while textbook publishers have noted the importance of equitable representation of both males and females in their books since the passage of Title IX, analyses of these publications have continued to find unequal portrayals of the sexes.

In most studies of textbook representations prior to the 1980s such content remained highly stereotypical in its portrayals of male and female characters. According to a 1984 review of the existing literature in this area, conducted by scholars C. G. Schau and K. P. Scott, most instructional materials for students remained sexist. In their meta-analysis of the research to date, which included textbooks targeted at audiences from preschool to college age, the authors concluded that the equitable representations of the sexes had not yet been attained. Importantly, the authors noted, students' exposure to sex-equitable materials results in more flexible sex-role attitudes for both males and females, but exposure to sexist material contributed to more sex-typed attitudes, with students' attitudes directly related to amount of exposure. Based on these findings, Schau and Scott argued that in order for students to fulfill their learning potential, a flexible gender-role attitude is needed, and therefore equitable, nonstereotypical representations of males and females within educational materials are necessary.

In 1992, the American Association of University Women (AAUW) released a report that the organization had commissioned from the Wellesley College Center for Research on Women that received national attention. This report synthesized the research to date on gendered performance in schools. The report found that many inequalities still existed within U.S. school systems, including sex discrimination and sex stereotyping, inadequate teacher training in issues related to gender and learning styles, and the absence of curricular materials that fairly represented females and avoided sex stereotyping. The report also found that the historical and social contributions, as well as the experiences, of girls and women were still marginalized or ignored entirely in many of the textbooks used in schools across the country. Related findings noted in the report were that girls did not emerge from public schools with the same degree of confidence and self-esteem as did boys, with a loss of

Scholars concluded from a 2000 analysis of elementary-school textbooks and their depictions of gender traits that, despite increasing awareness of gender issues and stereotypes, male characters were still largely portrayed as competitive, aggressive, and argumentative. (Photos.com)

self-confidence in girls twice that for boys as they shifted from childhood into their adolescent years. Classroom experiences played a crucial part in challenging and changing gender-role expectations that undermined the self-confidence and achievement of girls. In a 1998 follow-up report, the AAUW noted that teaching materials such as textbooks still needed improvement. Although many textbook authors and publishers had become more conscious of gender representations, many continued to portray female characters in stereotypical roles that reinforced gender biases. Critics, however, took issue with the AAUW findings, citing the expanded coverage of topics such as women's history and broader treatment and inclusion of gender in textbooks by the end of the 1970s. While the AAUW report criticized the lack of balanced treatment of the sexes and highlighted the rare inclusion of women's perspectives within textbooks, critics questioned the desire for a new social history and responded that it was almost exclusively men who held positions of political and economic power. Concerns were voiced about what aspects of the standard history could be left out of textbooks if space continued to be allocated to what was framed by opponents as personal issues, such as sexism and racism. Advocates for more inclusive and equality-based textbook coverage of gender issues argued that this would be an improvement over the elitist and patriarchal sequence of events usually taught to students.

Numerous studies examining textbooks within a variety of disciplines continue to find evidence of gender bias through the images and language used in these learning materials, which is rather ironic, since these educational tools may actually hinder successful learning. For instance, a 1994 review of U.S. history textbooks found that in a commonly used text, there were four men for every one woman mentioned and fewer than 3 percent of the historical accounts within the textbook included women. Common complaints about foreign-language textbooks were that women were frequently depicted as sex objects or homemakers and that gender imbalance occurred in the textbook dialogues, serving to alienate female students. In a 1992 examination of the content within science textbooks, researchers found that these texts included minimal information about the accomplishments of women within the fields of science or about medical or scientific topics pertaining to women's lives, such as childbirth and menopause. Images included within educational materials also reveal ample evidence of gender biases. In a 1985 analysis of gender representations within 80 textbooks used across elementary and secondary schools, more than 85 percent of occupations pictured included only men. More recently, a 2006 review of seven high school chemistry textbooks found that only one of seven textbooks achieved gender balance within images, while the other books clearly pictured significantly more men than women.

Beyond simply examining the frequency with which males and females are represented in textbooks, researchers have also examined the stereotypical ways women are portrayed when they are in fact included. For instance, in a 1992 review of introductory-level psychology and human development textbooks, researchers found that males were significantly more likely to be depicted as active and in leadership roles than females, who were more likely to be depicted as passive. Not without consequence, such stereotypical representations have been found to have a negative impact on female learning. For instance, researchers found in 2010 that chemistry lessons with counter-stereotypical images of female scientists were significantly related to higher comprehension of lesson material by female students than were lessons with stereotypical images.

Beginning in the 1990s, the study of gender was expanded to examine the representation of males with consideration to stereotypical images and language within textbooks, following larger trends in academic research. Until this point, most of the research on textbooks' representation of gender focused on female roles and characteristics. Other noteworthy findings in 1990 were that male characters were more often depicted as more imaginative and adventurous than female characters. In a 2000 analysis of elementary school reading textbooks and their depictions of traits related to masculine and feminine stereotypes, L. Evan and K. Davies concluded that, despite increasing awareness of gender issues and stereotypes, male characters were still mainly portrayed in a stereotypical manner. Males were consistently represented as competitive, aggressive, and argumentative. Moreover, male characters acting in socially acceptable ways almost never displayed personality traits considered to be feminine, whereas gendered behaviors as displayed by female characters appeared to be less static, with a wider range of traits considered to be appropriate.

While recent research may indicate a greater numerical equality among male and female characters depicted in textbooks across various subject matters than in earlier decades, the ways in which males and females are portrayed in textbooks through their actions and personality traits remain sexist. Questions concerning the internalization of sexist stereotypes among pupils—as well as the effectiveness, for both male and female students, of learning from textbooks that include gender-biased information—still need further examination across disciplines.

Andrea M. Bergstrom
Franklin Pierce University

See also Media Literacy; Prejudice; Sexism; Social Construction of Gender; Stereotypes

Further Readings

American Association of University Women. *Gender Gaps: Where Schools Still Fail Our Children*. New York: Marlowe, 1999.

American Association of University Women. *How Schools Shortchange Girls*. Washington, DC: Author, 1992.

Britton, G. E. and M. C. Lumpkin. "For Sale: Subliminal Bias in Textbooks." *Reading Teacher*, v.31 (1977).

Evan, L. and K. Davies. "No Sissy Boys Here: A Content Analysis of Representation of Masculinity in Elementary School Reading Textbooks." *Sex Roles*, v.42/3–4 (2000).

Schau, C. G. and K. P. Scott. "Review of 21 Cause and Effect Studies." *Psychological Documents*, v.76 (1984).

Sewall, G. T. "How Textbooks Shortchange Girls: A Study of Major Findings on Girls and Education." *Society*, v.94–96 (1993).

TEXTUAL ANALYSIS

Textual analysis is an interdisciplinary qualitative method used to critique cultural artifacts, most commonly media texts. Though textual analysis has historically been associated with cultural studies, the method has increasingly been utilized in mass communication research to expose power dynamics in media representation, reception, and production. Textual analysis is grounded in a critical or interpretive research perspective that views reality as constructed through interaction and discourse. In the critical paradigm, the researcher is the primary instrument of analysis because she is understood as an active, subjective part of the knowledge-building process. Carrying a postmodern disillusionment with truth claims, critical perspectives interrogate power hierarchies and inequity. Textual analysis has been identified as an ideal method for analyzing hegemonic representations of gender, race, class, and sexuality, as well as illuminating subversive messages embedded in dominant texts.

The very use of the word *text* illustrates a certain post-structuralist perspective at the root of textual analysis. In the practice of textual analysis, there is an understanding that people from different cultures experience reality differently and that there is no right or wrong way to interpret texts such as films, advertising, books, and fashion. As Alan McKee argues, the meanings of texts are culturally specific, and researchers must be aware of the ways in which language, culture, values, and relationships change over time and place. Understanding the diversity of possible interpretations and experiences, researchers may turn the same critical lens on their own culture and begin to dissect and discuss the meaning embedded in texts. Textual analysis often focuses on the geographically and temporally specific nature of texts but situates the texts historically. Illuminating themes in texts requires an understanding of the culture that produces and consumes them: the myths, embedded norms, and stereotypes that underlie the texts.

Textual analysis is an effort to decode the latent meanings that exist in texts. In a sense, it is taking a given text (such as an advertisement) and working backward to try to understand the cultural values and norms that would have informed the production of the text. Researchers may ask, What stereotypes are present? What cultural norms would have informed the reproduction of those stereotypes? There is less concern with determining how the text may or may not "match" a given "reality" and more effort to understand the ways that texts represent the embodiment of producers' own notions of what reality is and then how the texts may further construct or influence what *consumers* believe about reality. Texts therefore provide insight into the intentions, beliefs, values, and norms of any given culture. Textual analysis requires an examination of those cultural norms that have become so ubiquitous as to be considered invisible, inconsequential, or "normal" and to question why those norms exist and how they are reproduced in text as unquestioned realities.

Furthermore, researchers often discuss a range of possible interpretations based on the audiences' subject positions. One of the foundations of textual analysis is a concern with the fluidity of meanings in any given cultural artifact. Cultural theorist Stuart Hall argues that every text carries traces of dominant ideology but that all texts are also polysemous and may incorporate embedded meanings that allow for oppositional or negotiated interpretations. Thus, a major consideration of textual analysis is the variety of possible interpretations of meaning and the role that the consumer plays in decoding texts. Therefore, there is also an onus on researchers who use textual analysis to be self-reflective by explaining their own subject positions and experiences with the texts.

Textual analysis can draw intertextual meaning from a range of media genres across which dominant themes may be exposed. Intertextuality refers to the ways in which texts reference previous texts, requiring the consumer to rely on culturally specific knowledge to decode the messages. Advertising in particular has been the subject of extensive textual analyses. The minutely produced nature of advertising makes it a potent site for the production of cultural norms, so textual analysis is ideal for deconstructing such complex texts. Journalism is also ripe for textual analysis, because it is a complex media genre that straddles conventions for highbrow and lowbrow culture. Textual analysis, in other words, has been utilized in virtually every medium and genre, not only producing insight into specific programs, publications, images, and narratives but also illuminating the ways in which cultural texts are interconnected and carry cultural norms throughout societies.

Textual analysis often includes an engagement with the modes of production as well as audience understandings of texts. However, Elfriede Fürsich argues that texts themselves represent specific moments of intersection between the encoding of meaning by producers and the decoding by consumers and therefore requires special consideration by researchers. She contends that for all the possible insights that may be gained from quantitative content analyses, experiments, or reception studies, there is unique knowledge to be gained by analyzing the narratives and ideologies embedded in texts, specifically media texts such as journalism.

Textual analysis may be inspired by semiotic analysis, in which close readings of cultural texts require exploring the relationship between media texts (signs) and their socially constructed, arbitrary meanings (signifiers). By its very nature, semiotic analysis is subjective; its value lies in its explanatory and heuristic possibilities. According to Jonathan Bignell, the semiotic approach considers media texts both as *products* of specific sociohistorical contexts and as simultaneously *constructing* reality as sign systems that give structure and meaning to the world by reinforcing hegemonic values as commonsensical or natural realities. Textual analysis shares with semiotics an understanding that language and culture are the foundation of how people understand the world around them and therefore how they engage with texts that both reflect and construct reality.

Because textual analysis is subjective, the method has been criticized as a simple interpretation on the part of the researcher. However, decades of theoretical developments and application have produced sophisticated guidance for conducting rigorous textual analyses. There is no one method for conducting textual analysis, but the process may be summed up as the systematic asking and answering of a series of progressively more detailed questions. The qualitative and interpretative practice of textual analysis must be systematically carried out in order to account for the complexity of sign systems, including those of mass media.

McKee argues that one system for carrying out textual analysis includes forming a question, selecting the texts that may provide answers to that question, and then placing the text in context. Doing so may include considering the time, place, and culture that produces and consumes the text, the genre in which the text is situated, and the nature of the cultural industry in which the text circulates (the economy, language, and institutional structure of the industry). Researchers must also select "intertexts," or related texts that will offer insight into how audiences interpret the primary text. For example, a textual analysis of a book may also take into account the meanings produced in fan fiction, magazine reviews, literary critiques, and so on.

Although textual analysis is most commonly qualitative in nature, it is not always devoid of numeric coding. Researchers may find it useful to track specific instances of a recurring theme, set of words or phrases, images, or other phenomena. In this way, the researcher's focus remains on interpretation but may use some numeric data to show patterns in representations or to organize the reporting of data.

One significant contribution that textual analysis makes to media studies is to establish an alternative mode of critique to the traditional social science methods that form the foundation of mass communication research. Quantitative methods provide crucial insights into media production, content, and reception, yet in the application of textual analysis, there may also be a political motivation for using critical methodology. Feminist scholars in particular have established the necessity of illuminating dissonance in discursive formations of gender, race, sexuality, and class by exposing binary oppositions in texts. Much of feminist methodological exploration grew from the radical feminist perspective that science is male-biased and that women are uniquely suited to studying women's issues. Traditional science has historically been identified with masculine values of objectivity, rationality, neutrality, and distance, and such associations make the practice of science biased against women.

Spring-Serenity Duvall
University of South Carolina, Aiken

See also Audiences: Producers of New Media; Cultural Politics; Discourse Analysis; Encoding and Decoding; Hall, Stuart; Media Literacy; New Media; Polysemic Text; Postmodernism; Post-Structuralism; Quantitative Content Analysis; Reception Theory; Semiotics

Further Readings

Bignell, Jonathan. *Media Semiotics: An Introduction.* New York: St. Martin's Press, 1997.

Fürsich, Elfriede. "In Defense of Textual Analysis: Restoring a Challenged Method for Journalism and Media Studies." *Journalism Studies*, v.10 (2009).

McKee, Alan. *Textual Analysis: A Beginner's Guide.* Thousand Oaks, CA: Sage, 2003.

TOYS AND GAMES: GENDER SOCIALIZATION

Although often disregarded as simple playthings created for children's amusement, toys constitute a microcosm of society, reflecting gender ideology, status, and roles enacted in the adult world. As artifacts of socialization, Susan Kahlenberg and Michelle Hein note, toys serve five purposes suitable for critical examination: Toys allow children to develop a shared culture with playmates; they prepare children for adult roles and concerns; they foster children's imagination and creativity; they serve as conduits for children to acquire solitary behavior; and they serve as cherished items, for both children and adults. Rather than miniature items used in adult work, toys encourage play while simultaneously teaching children the demarcation between appropriate and inappropriate gender behavior, practices, and values. In this manner, toys also reflect power relations regarding gender in a given society in a certain historical period.

The modern toy industry finds its roots in 16th-century Europe, while the foundation for modern ideas about childhood as requiring a sheltered environment and special activities for educating them (not necessarily playtime) goes back to the late 17th century, notes Gary Cross in his 1997 book *Kids' Stuff.* During the 18th and 19th centuries, toys served as intellectual and moral training tools. In the United States, by 1900 toys as playthings in and of themselves had become commonplace. At the start of the 20th century and by the 1930s, Cross notes, toys were clearly demarcating boys' and girls' gender roles: "The boys' toybox mirrored the world of science and industrial production, the girls' a consumerism of modern homemaking and personal vitality." Boys' toys, such as trains, cars, and other mechanized objects, dealt with technology and innovation, whereas girls' toys, such as dolls and household items, trained them to become housewives and nurturers. Research during the 1970s on the toys and decorations present in boys' and girls' rooms found that boys tended to have more "spatial temporal" toys used actively and reflective of movement and motor skills, such as sports equipment, vehicles, toy garages, animals, machines, and military toys; "dolls" for boys were of cowboys or soldiers. Girls' rooms tended to have more dolls and domestic items, as well as floral furnishings that embodied a feminine appeal. These also correspond to findings regarding toy requests, as research based on holiday and Christmas wish lists has found a socialization pattern based on the work and home spheres associated with men and women. A review of this literature by Kahlenberg and Hein revealed that girls' requests for toys are associated with the inner sphere of family, the home, and childcare: baby dolls, dollhouses, clothes such as ballerina costumes, and stuffed animals. Girls also were more likely to ask for cross-gender brands of toys. Boys typically asked for vehicles, sports equipment, space toys, and machines, reflecting the male world of the outer sphere related to the public world of work, careers, and civic participation.

Studies on the origins of children's toy requests and preferences note the influence of parents' choices for their children, in terms of decor and providing certain toys based on a child's sex, children's versus parents' choices in toys, and evidence for evolutionary or biological factors. Judith Blakemore and Renee Centers find of interest that children tend to ask for more gender-stereotyped toys than gender-neutral toys chosen by parents, such as educational or artistic materials suitable for either sex. Kay Bussey and Albert Bandura note that even before children attain gender constancy (the realization that one's sex is a permanent attribute not dependent on superficial characteristics), which occurs in stages between the ages of two and seven, they prefer to play with toys traditionally associated with their gender and reward peers for gender-appropriate behavior. Gerianne Alexander offers an evolutionary explanation for this preference for toys associated with one's own gender, based in part on studies of day-old infants' visual preferences (moving objects for male infants, and female faces for female infants). Visual-processing biases resulting from selection pressures (spatial skills required for hunting in males, and identifying shapes and colors required for foraging and infant care in females) thus may explain toy choices: Boys appear to give interest and attention to toys that allow for active movement and propulsion, whereas girls show greater interest in form and color, with dolls providing opportunities for nurturance.

Children are taught which styles of play correspond to gender roles and expectations, as gender typing begins from the moment of birth and becomes instilled in children not only by parents and their choice of gender-typing artifacts but also in terms of what kinds of play behavior parents encourage or discourage. Fathers encourage physically active play for sons rather than daughters, and cross-gender conduct is more negatively rewarded for boys than it is in girls. Given the number of studies on children's and parents' toy preferences and those that have found clear distinctions between what people identity as masculine and feminine toys, Blakemore and Centers find surprising how little research has actually been devoted to determining the impact of toys on children's cognitive and social skills and behavior. For example, they note that although dolls have been given to girls for centuries, little direct evidence shows that doll play actually increases the nurturing behavior of girls toward younger children.

Dolls represent both female and male persons and serve as texts by which gender roles, expectations, and paradigms become "real," either in terms of preferred (dominant and intentional) meanings or as conduits for alternate play, used by children in ways other than those cast by manufacturers. The very term "action figure" for male dolls reflects a gendered meaning, indicative of the active, outdoor-oriented play of boys. Carmen Caldas-Coulthard and Theo van Leeuwen note how kinetic design, text in the form of product descriptions on packaging

and names, and visual attributes of dolls all reinforce gender roles and stereotypes. Kinetic design, which allows for manipulation of legs, hands, and heads, denotes masculine or feminine "movement." Female dolls, such as Barbie, are designed more for posing and viewing, while male action figures, such as G.I. Joe (known as Action Man in Great Britain) and his "kung-fu" grip are made for action, movement, and articulating. The adventure-oriented G.I. Joe doll, introduced by Hasbro in 1963, served as the toy industry's male counterpart to the popular Barbie, first released in 1959 by Mattel. G.I. Joe's marketing plan was based on the slogan "America's Moveable Fighting Man" and the "accessories sold separately" paradigm of toy making; outfits and equipment were needed for children to create Joe's different adventures. Representing the average soldier and evoking in fathers their experiences of World War II and the Korean War, G.I. Joe appealed to the toy owner's self-identity with the doll in an all-male world that featured conventional play in which boys bonded through adventure; "this was a womanless world," notes Cross. As an example of an unsuccessful cross-gender attempt in the toy world, the female G.I. Joe Nurse, released in 1967, was unpopular among boys *and* girls (which ironically made it a rare collectible several decades later).

Texts of doll and action-figure packaging emphasize the active nature of male dolls and the passive, romanticized nature of female dolls, and visuals in the form of images tend to show male figures in outdoor, "on the go" settings and use darker colors, in contrast to the domestic settings and more rigid, posed style of fashion dolls, which feature the familiar pink color associated with femininity. The Barbie doll, notes Cross, comes from a long history of fashion and paper dolls that were used to display the latest women's fashions as well as figures of royalty. Barbie served as a three-dimensional paper doll, an adult woman rather than a child dressed in children's fashions. The appeal of feminine interests, such as fashion and appearance, coupled with the marketing of Barbie accessories (clothes, dollhouses, cars, a beauty shop, and the like), create a female-centered world in which young girls are taught consumerism. Barbie's image represents an "emphatic femininity," notes Mary Rogers, that feminizes and maternalizes the multitude of careers that Barbie takes on—whether baby doctor, teacher, astronaut (first released in 1965), amorphous "career woman," veterinarian, paleontologist, soldier, or U.S. president (which by the 2008 edition came in white, African American, Hispanic, and Asian American versions). Barbie's form-fitting outfits (including business suits that can be transformed into dresses for after-hours parties), pink packaging, and text describing her proper demeanor teach young girls that a female's physical appearance serves as the central defining element of femininity. By 2010, Barbie product lines included the "i can be" career series (the lowercase "i" used as actual text; the line included careers such as rock star, race-car driver, and the perennial bride), "Fashion Fairytale," "Sparkle Lights Fairy," and "Fashionistas."

Incursions into Barbie's world have taken several forms. In 1999, Smartees, a limited-released line of individually named fashion dolls (such as Jessica the Journalist and Ashley the Attorney), designed to teach girls career requirements and responsibilities, served as a short-lived counter to Barbie and received some media attention, notably in the *New York Times*. The early 2000s saw a threat to Barbie's hold on the fashion doll market in the form of the Bratz line of hip, ethnically diverse teenage dolls, which furthered the message of consumerism and material wealth to its targeted girl audience. Bratz dolls were different, observes Lisa Guerrero, because unlike Barbie, whose racial and ethnic diversity came in the form of different versions of Barbie herself, the Bratz dolls made racial difference cool and desirable.

One can consider toys themselves as three-dimensional "sign-vehicles" created within a cultural circuit of meanings as described by Stuart Hall, with advertising furthering the ideologies inherent and imbued in them. Researchers investigating the gender-role stereotypes in toy commercials theorize that the socialization process combined with television exposure may affect children's toy preferences, because toy manufacturers design, package, and market products to align with target audiences' gender identities. For example, in their analysis of the content of 455 toy commercials aired in 2004 on the U.S. children's television network Nickelodeon, Kahlenberg and Hein found differential background settings and activities for boys and girls, reflecting traditional gender roles and spheres. Girls-only commercials tended to be set in a home or other indoor setting, such as a shopping mall or dance studio. Outdoor settings for girls included backyards, gardens, or shopping centers, which the authors described as mere backdrops for traditional female activities such as gossiping, courting, or caretaking. In contrast, outdoor settings of boys-only commercials were more diversified or nondescript, suggesting the wider range of social roles and opportunities representative of the masculine world. As an example of the gendered nature of activities that include both boys and girls, the authors pointed out that a commercial for a bowling game depicted boys playing while the girls watched and cheered. They concluded that while the programming on Nickelodeon may feature girls in leading roles, the toy ads still forward gender stereotyping, with girls more likely engaged in cooperative play indoors and boys playing competitively outdoors.

A summary of findings regarding gender display communicated through and by toys and games shows that boys' toys and play promote action, adventure, competition, and displays of aggression, whereas girls' toys and games encourage and foster more socially oriented activities, cooperation, and domestic-oriented play styles. Rather than mere "child's play," the ideology embodied by gendered toys and games, and further disseminated and reinforced by mass media, helps to perpetuate a cultural hegemony that upholds traditional ideals of masculinity and femininity. Computer and video games continue these modes of gender socialization as well. Some researchers, such as Bussey and Bandura, have pointed to the negative effects of limited and gender-typed play that result in boys being socialized into avoiding housework and childcare in adult life. Similarly, the girls' games movement, as documented by studies compiled by Justine Cassell and Henry Jenkins, has forwarded the need for more computer games that appeal to both boys and girls, as computer literacy has become a vital aspect of contemporary work life.

Erika Engstrom
University of Nevada, Las Vegas

See also Advertising; Children's Programming: Cartoons; Children's Programming: Disney and Pixar; Encoding and Decoding; Hall, Stuart; Heroes: Action and Super Heroes; Social Construction of Gender; Toys and Games: Racial Stereotypes and Identity; Video Gaming: Violence

Further Readings

Alexander, Gerianne. "An Evolutionary Perspective of Sex-Typed Toy Preferences: Pink, Blue, and the Brain." *Archives of Sexual Behavior*, v.32 (2003).

Blakemore, Judith and Renee Centers. "Characteristics of Boys' and Girls' Toys." *Sex Roles*, v.53 (2005).

Bussey, Kay and Albert Bandura. "Social Cognitive Theory of Gender Development and Differentiation." *Psychological Review*, v.106 (1999).

Caldas-Coulthard, Carmen and Theo van Leeuwen. "Stunning, Shimmering, Iridescent: Toys as the Representation of Gendered Social Actors." In *Gender Identity and Discourse Analysis*, Lia Litosseliti and Jane Sunderland, eds. Philadelphia: John Benjamins, 2002.

Cassell, Justine and Henry Jenkins. *From Barbie to Mortal Kombat: Gender and Computer Games*. Cambridge, MA: MIT Press, 1998.

Cross, Gary. *Kids' Stuff: Toys and the Changing World of American Childhood*. Cambridge, MA: Harvard University Press, 1997.

Guerrero, Lisa. "Can the Subaltern Shop? The Commodification of Difference in the Bratz Dolls." *Cultural Studies <=> Critical Methodologies*, v.9 (2009).

Hays, Constance. "A Role Model's New Clothes." *New York Times* (April 1, 2000).

Kahlenberg, Susan and Michelle Hein. "Progression on Nickelodeon? Gender-Role Stereotypes in Toy Commercials." *Sex Roles*, v.62 (2010).

Rogers, Mary. *Barbie Culture*. Thousand Oaks, CA: Sage, 1999.

Toys and Games: Racial Stereotypes and Identity

Aside from their role as children's playthings, toys serve as tangible reflections of a society's values as well as markers of a historical period's treatment of gender and of minorities. As such, toys—especially dolls—provide a means of studying commonplace and popular notions regarding ethnicity, standards of beauty, and status. As Doris Wilkinson noted in her 1987 article "The Doll Exhibit," toys and games serve as play artifacts that provide "historical repertoires of shared beliefs." Historically, toy manufacturers have imbued their products with racial and racist stereotypes. Gary Cross noted in his 1997 book *Kids' Stuff* that during the post–Civil War period in the United States, racist toys in the form of mechanical windup figures and other toys offered demeaning caricatures of "foreigners" but especially targeted blacks with racial stereotypes. Although, as Cross observed, such toys reflected racist attitudes, they also signified the exotic and unknown and were grouped with character toys, such as those based on popular cartoons. Cross noted that racist toys and dolls, which lasted into the 20th century, "were designed to prompt negative emotions, feelings of power at abusing an outcast character, who was pictured as uncivilized, insignificant, and foolish," reflecting indirectly Stuart Hall's notion of the Other. Regarding gender specifically, female-figured toys such as "Old Aunt Chloe, the Negro Washerwoman" or "Negro Nurse" not only framed women of color as holding subservient roles in society but also conveyed a patronizing tone.

In her 1987 study of the history of black dolls in the United States and the stereotypes they embodied, Wilkinson examined descriptions and labels of black female dolls in department store catalogs from the early 1890s through the Great Depression of the 1930s; such dolls were marketed through World War II. Titles of dolls from this decades-long period incorporated derogatory terms of the times; stereotypes of the "Mammy" and "the good Negro woman" domestic became reified as the Aunt Jemima doll, portrayed as a fat, round-faced woman in servant's attire, which appeared frequently from the 1890s until the 1920s. Wilkinson noted how language communicated negative perceptions of African American women, with dolls targeted to children sustaining such perceptions. Furthermore, Wilkinson reported that she was unable to find any positive role models among the black dolls in her sample of catalogs, which included those from well-known retailers such as Sears and Montgomery Ward. Wilkinson observed that most early dolls were created for the upper class and targeted "young aristocrats." She found racial and class differences even more apparent when comparing descriptions of black and white female dolls: Titles of white dolls included descriptors such as "sweet," "countess," and "society belle," while those for black dolls contained terms such as "darky head" and other phrases today considered as overt racial slurs, not only reinforcing racial difference and awareness but also indicating class and status preferences on a wider societal level.

As instructional tools, dolls thus capture a society's beliefs and in turn normalize and make acceptable attitudes regarding race and ethnicity. A line of research examining the effects of racism has utilized dolls to test the racial preferences of children, which this approach assumes also serve as indicators of racial self-perception. The "Dolls Test" method, originating in the 1930s (with the most well-known study published in 1947), used samples of young children to test their preferences for white and black (or brown) dolls. In the 1947 study, examiners presented children ranging from three to seven years old with a brown doll and a white doll, identical except for color. The examiners asked the children which doll they thought was the "nice" doll, which one looked "bad," and other questions regarding the race of each doll, as well as which doll they thought looked most like them. Based on their findings—which demonstrated that the majority of both black and white children from Arkansas (South) and Massachusetts (North) indicated preferences for the white doll in terms of the good-or-bad valence—the researchers concluded that rejection of the brown doll indicated similar perceptions regarding racial self-perception.

Authors of subsequent studies in this vein (including Myrna Burnett and Kimberly Sisson, and Phyllis Katz and Sue Zalk) have pointed out several methodological problems of the Dolls Test, such as social desirability on the part of children based on whether or not the examiner was white or black, reliability and validity of the data (such as whether doll preference actually indicated preference for one race over another), consideration of children's age and cognitive development, and the assumption that dolls' skin color (as opposed to hair or eye color) served as the only basis for children's preference for a certain doll. Indeed, when considering a child's age as a factor, research findings indicate that older African American children tend to show decreasing preference for white dolls. Katz and Zalk further pointed out that, if the race served as the only cue of difference for children, the strength of race over a child's own gender may be overestimated. In their own study using dolls of different skin colors and genders, they found that for girls, gender tended to serve as a stronger preference cue than did race.

Racial features of dolls tended to be confined to variations in skin color; for example, the difference between a white or "colored" doll has typically resided in different colors of vinyl or paint. Racial differences in girls' dolls and boys' "action figures" of the latter 20th century were literally skin deep, since all had basically the same body and face molds. The G.I. Joe doll, first introduced to the toy market in 1964, was issued in an African American version in 1965. Though its maker, Hasbro, produced G.I. Joe with varying skin, eye, and hair coloring during the later 1960s, he had the same head and body molds. In 1970, Hasbro retooled Joe following years of lagging sales; this makeover included diversifying his appearance, and African American G.I. Joe got his own head sculpts and facial features, which, Karen Hall has observed, reflected heightened racial awareness during this period.

One of the most popular and best-selling toys in the United States, and indeed the world, the Barbie doll has seen efforts to diversify her appearance, with varying degrees of success. Barbie, the blond or brunette white teenage fashion model, was introduced to the toy market in 1959 at the Toy Fair in New York City. In 1967, Mattel issued a black version of Barbie's cousin Francie, naming her Colored Francie. Colored Francie was simply a white Francie in brown vinyl with straight hair and Caucasian features; it did not sell well. Mattel then introduced Christie, an African American "friend" of Barbie in 1968. Christie's skin color was dark brown, and, as Janine Fennick reports, she sported a "modified afro" hairstyle. Talking Christie was released that same year, along with a slew of other new Barbie friends, including Stacey, who came from the exotic land of Great Britain. The company also produced a black version of Ken named Brad; according to Fennick, Christie and Brad were two of the first African American dolls to be produced as "friends" by any doll company. It was not until 1980 that a Black Barbie (not a friend) appeared. During the mid-1980s, Asian and Hispanic friends of Barbie appeared, and Quinceañera Teresa appeared in the mid-1990s. The early 1990s saw the introduction of the Shani line of dolls, intended for the African American community; these came with their own clothing line inspired by African *kente* fabric patterns, but the line did not sell as well as expected. By 2000, the Barbie for President doll came in Caucasian (blond), African American, and Hispanic versions, with an Asian version added in 2008.

Critics of Barbie's "diversified" appearance noted that essentially these were the white Barbie with little in the way of true racial difference. Indiscernible skin tones, which demarcated "white" only by extreme paleness when compared to other variations, and long, straight, "combable" hair betrayed Barbie's labeled ethnicities. As a cultural signifier, straight hair serves as a white-based, Eurocentric beauty standard, especially among African American women, and serves as what Ann Ducille

Bratz dolls are an example of changing mores about representing multiethnicity in toys. In 2004, Bratz became the best-selling fashion dolls in Great Britain, eclipsing even the evergreen Barbie doll. (Photos.com)

has termed a "site of difference." The contention regarding the authenticity of African American versions of Barbie became the center of media attention in 2009 with a new line of Barbies called So In Style. Designed by an African American woman, Barbie's new friends had face molds featuring wider noses, fuller lips, a range of skin tones, and thick, off-the-shoulder, curly hairstyles described by Katie Engelhart as "Afro puffs." The So In Style friends even had their own story line, which began when one, a best friend of Barbie, moved to Chicago. In addition to various racially based versions of Barbie and her friends, Mattel's Dolls of the World/ Princess line of collectible dolls began in 1980 as the International Series, featuring Parisian, "Royal," and Italian dolls dressed in "native" costume and packaging text describing their lives in their respective countries. By the mid-2000s, Dolls of the World featured Barbie presented as being from 50 countries, representing Europe, Africa, Asia, and North and South America. Ducille observed that, rather

than color or facial features, the site of difference had become the dolls' costuming, which provided "the face of cultural diversity without the particulars of racial difference." Otherwise, all were essentially the same doll, regardless of nation or culture. The packaging text, describing cultural history and language lessons, was also used to mark difference, conveying the impression of diversity yet still marking otherness as exotic. As a signifier, dress functions not only to establish but also to reaffirm boundaries, as noted by Carol Magee, who saw the nature of the collectible doll—which disallows removal from the box or of the costuming—as symbolic of keeping the cultural difference and Otherness within the confines of the packaging. Thus, a doll such as Ghanian Barbie must remain in the costume and, by extension, her culture and country—"forever in *kente*." Even as the dolls presumably represent a variety of nations and cultures, the largest market for these "international" or ethnic dolls is the United States.

Among Barbie's competitors, the Bratz line of multiethnic teen dolls based itself on the notion of globalization, with difference and diversity serving as cornerstones of its doll design and marketing approach. While Barbie, even with her various iterations, represents "normal" beauty based on white standards, the Bratz girls challenge the Euro- and Anglocentric version of womanhood by opening up "a space in the popular imaginary for the normalization of multiracial identities," according to Lisa Guerrero. The ambiguity of racial/ethnic identities of the various Bratz characters further allows for their owners to self-identify with them. After only two years on the market, in 2003 Bratz owned 30 percent of the fashion doll market; in 2004, it became the best-selling fashion doll in Great Britain, overthrowing Barbie. As illustrative of the Other, then, the Bratz dolls provide an example of what Guerrero called the "browning of America," illustrating the success of toys that hinge their appeal on representing racial difference as desirable.

Erika Engstrom
University of Nevada, Las Vegas

See also Advertising; Beauty and Body Image: Beauty Myths; Children's Programming: Cartoons; Children's Programming: Disney and Pixar; Encoding and Decoding; Hall, Stuart; Heroes: Action and Super Heroes; Social Construction of Gender; Toys and Games: Gender Socialization

Further Readings

Burnett, Myrna and Kimberly Sisson. "Doll Studies Revisited: A Question of Validity." *Journal of Black Psychology*, v.21 (1995).

Cross, Gary. *Kids' Stuff: Toys and the Changing World of American Childhood*. Cambridge, MA: Harvard University Press, 1997.

Ducille, Ann. "Dyes and Dolls: Multicultural Barbie and the Merchandising of Difference." *Differences: A Journal of Feminist Cultural Studies*, v.6 (1994).

Engelhart, Katie. "There's a New Black Barbie in Town." *Maclean's*, v.122 (August 17, 2009).

Fennick, Janine. *The Collectible Barbie*. Philadelphia: Courage Books, 1996.

Guerrero, Lisa. "Can the Subaltern Shop? The Commodification of Difference in the Bratz Dolls." *Cultural Studies <=> Critical Methodologies*, v.9 (2009).

Hall, Karen. "A Soldier's Body: G.I. Joe, Hasbro's Great American Hero, and the Symptoms of Empire." *Journal of Popular Culture*, v.28 (2004).

Katz, Phyllis and Sue Zalk. "Doll Preferences: An Index of Racial Attitudes." *Journal of Educational Psychology*, v.66 (1974).

Magee, Carol. "Forever in *Kente*: Ghanian Barbie and Fashioning of Identity." *Social Identities*, v.11 (2005).

Wilkinson, Doris. "The Doll Exhibit: A Psycho-Cultural Analysis of Black Female Role Stereotypes." *Journal of Popular Culture*, v.21 (1987).

Transgender Studies

Transgender studies as an area of interdisciplinary research is relatively new and is still evolving. It was not until the early 1990s that the term *transgender* even appeared in scholarship. In general, transgender studies focus on people who are medically deemed ambiguous in sex at birth or later, on the surgical reassignment or changing of identity categories of gender and sex that a person is assigned at birth, and/or on how media and society perceive people who transition gender, sex, or both. Transgender persons include people who have been called, at various times throughout history, the following names: hermaphrodites, intersex persons, transsexuals, females-to-males (FTMs), males-to-females (MTFs), transvestites, transgenders, cross-dressers, drag kings or drag queens, and queers, among other names. In turn, transgender studies seek to explain, evaluate, and challenge medical, legal, media, and public discourses about people transgressing gender, sex, and sexuality. Political activism that advocates for the social acceptance and civil rights of this diverse group of people is typically another major goal of this area of research.

Transgender studies have roots in feminist studies of gender and sex and in gay and lesbian studies of sexuality. Traditionally, the main subjects of feminist scholarship are the oppression of heterosexual women and the social construction of femininity and the female body, while the main subjects of gay and lesbian scholarship are the oppression of gay men and lesbian women and the social construction of homosexuality. Both research traditions highlight the influence of mass media (ranging from artwork and print media to moving pictures on film, television, and online media) on public perceptions and legal policies about women, on one hand, and about gays and lesbians, on the other hand. Furthermore, these scholarly traditions are activist in aim, due in a large part to their origins in the struggle for women's civil rights (in the late 1800s and the early to mid-1900s in the United Kingdom and the United States) and in the gay liberation movement (which began in the 1970s in the United States). Transgender studies share many of these same concerns about the problems of mass-mediated representations of gender and sexuality, and likewise advocate for social and political change.

However, transgender studies can be differentiated from feminist and gay and lesbian scholarship because transgender studies are also a direct response to two other bodies of knowledge: medical conceptions of transsexuals and queer theory. For much of the 20th century, transsexuality was a medicalized term for the pathologization of gender deviance, such as when a person cross-dressed or modified the body through sex reassignment surgery. This line of thinking was problematic for a number of reasons, including how it biologically reinforced and made normal the identity categories of being heterosexual and male/masculine or female/feminine, while denouncing anything other as a disease. Thus, transgender studies explicitly developed as a counter to these initial oppressive medical conceptions of transsexuals. For example, Sandy Stone deployed the term *posttranssexual* in her early activism and scholarship to resist the medical establishment's pathological terminology and treatment of people, such as herself, who changed the gender and/or sex that they had been assigned at birth. Eventually "transgender" became the preferred and nonpejorative umbrella term used by scholars and social activists for anyone who does not fit the gender binary that for the most part is still maintained in medicine and legislation, as well as in media messages and society at large. Transgender studies was named as such on similar grounds.

Transgender studies are also a response to queer theory. Although transgender studies most often align with queer thinking, sometimes they are not queer enough or not queer at all. In general, queer theory is a post-structural/postmodern perspective that, like transgender studies, arose out of gay and lesbian scholarship and political activism and feminist scholarship and political activism during the latter half of the 20th century. Queer theory was articulated as a specific viewpoint in the 1990s, but some scholars date it to the 1970s when referencing influential work by the French philosopher, sociologist, and historian Michel Foucault, for instance. Queer theory stands apart from earlier feminist and gay and lesbian scholarship by displacing the identity categories and binaries that grounded these traditions, including gender/sex, masculinity/femininity, male/female, and heterosexuality/homosexuality. As a result, the concern is with the plurality, permeability, and ambiguity of gender and sexual identities and how to promote them in medical, legal, media, and public discourses in place of minority status groupings and the political agenda of liberation. Exemplifying this stream of scholarship is Judith Butler's theory of the performance of gender and her endorsement of drag, since she says it has the potential to disturb normal categories of bodily sex, gender, and sexuality. The majority of transgender studies likewise attend to and affirm these categories as social constructions that can change, are ambiguous, and in many senses refer to both/neither rather than either man or woman, for instance. Nonetheless, a number of transgender scholars and activists question some identity categories and politics while reasserting others, thereby limiting the extent to which they are queer. For example, transgender psychologist Pat Califia stays invested in masculinity and sexual minority identities such as sadomasochist butch lesbianism even while critiquing society for permitting only two genders and keeping them polarized. When people express that they feel trapped in the wrong body since birth and have sex reassignment surgery as a result, they are also in many ways fitting back into the traditional two gender/sex model instead of transgressing or in other ways displacing it.

Given that mass media strongly influence public perceptions and performances of gender and sexual identity in the late 20th- and early 21st-century United States, it is common for transgender scholars to turn to popular literature, newspapers and newsmagazines, film, television, the Internet, and a range of other verbal and visual media for their case studies. To illustrate her argument that a person's gender expression is not exclusively a product of either biology or culture and that there is not only one way to look like a man or a woman, transgender activist Leslie Feinberg included in her book *Transgender Warriors* (1996) photographs from around the world that depicted the depth and breadth of sex and gender identities, such as images of the cross-dressing American basketball player Dennis Rodman. In addition, English literature professor Judith Halberstam's work on female masculinity examines the history of butches in cinema, such as M, the boss in the James Bond action films, and characters played by actresses Linda Hamilton and Sigourney Weaver for the Hollywood blockbuster movies *Terminator* and *Alien*, respectively. In the field of communication specifically, John M. Sloop rhetorically analyzes mainstream news media representations of five much-publicized cases that involved people with gender ambiguity, whether the person was medically deemed ambiguous in sex at birth, underwent sex reassignment surgery, or did not appear to the public to fit dominant norms of gender and sexuality: John/Joan or David Reimer, Brandon Teena, k. d. lang, Janet Reno, and Barry Winchell/Calpernia Addams.

Jamie Landau
Keene State College

See also Online New Media: Transgender Identity; Queer Theory; Sexuality; Social Construction of Gender; Sports Media: Transgender; Transsexuality

Further Readings

Bornstein, Kate. *Gender Outlaw: On Men, Women, and the Rest of Us*. New York: Vintage Books, 1994.

Butler, Judith. *Gender Trouble: Feminism and the Subversion of Identity*. New York: Routledge, 1990.

Califia, Pat. *Sex Changes: The Politics of Transgenderism.* San Francisco: Cleis Press, 1997.

Feinberg, Leslie. *Transgender Warriors: Making History From Joan of Arc to Dennis Rodman.* Boston: Beacon Press, 1996.

Halberstam, Judith. *Female Masculinity.* Durham, NC: Duke University Press, 1998.

Sloop, John M. *Disciplining Gender: Rhetorics of Sex Identity in Contemporary U.S. Culture.* Amherst: University of Massachusetts Press, 2004.

TRANSSEXUALITY

Transsexuality is a term that has a problematic history and, as a result, many scholars of media and gender have stopped using it. However, countless researchers, social activists, and everyday people proudly self-identify as transsexuals still today. In general, transsexuals are people who are born with what medical professionals deem normal male or female bodies, but psychologically they identify with the opposite sex. For example, feeling trapped in the wrong body is a common theme in discourse coming from transsexual people and in media coverage and medical reports about them. As a result, many transsexuals not only dress up as the opposite sex but also change their bodies to align with the opposite sex by undergoing hormone therapy and/or sex reassignment surgery. *Transvestite* is an older name for transsexuals who did not physically modify their bodies, whereas pre-operative or post-operative females-to-males (FTMs) or males-to-females (MTFs) have become more common names for them in recent decades as a result, in a large part, of advancements in medical treatment and an increase in its accessibility. Sometimes transsexual people refer to themselves as (or are referred to as) cross-dressers, drag queens or drag kings, or queer. These people are rarely called hermaphrodites or intersex, since they are not born with ambiguous gonads or external genitalia.

Transsexuality did not emerge as an identity category until the 20th century, when social scientists started studying gender-crossing in dress and body modification that occurred in various cultures across the world. As people in Western cultures sought medical and legal aid to transform the sex they had been assigned at birth, the modern medical establishment began to recognize and name them

transsexuals as well. Initially, then, transsexuality was a medicalized term for the pathologization of a person who cross-dressed, underwent hormonal therapy, and/or had a sex-change operation. Specifically known as "gender dysphoria syndrome" in the 1960s and classified by the American Psychiatric Association in 1980 as an "official disorder," transsexuality was considered a pathology of someone's psyche in particular, because transsexuals usually expressed, and were diagnosed by their physicians as, having a body that did not properly conform to what they thought was their real gender. This concept of transsexuality is problematic for a number of reasons, foremost because it conceives of people who transition gender as diseased, or at least sees them as unhealthy until they make physical modifications to the exteriors and/or interiors of their bodies. Even when transsexuality is celebrated instead of denigrated, underlying this belief in a real gender and the desire for a person's bodily sex to align with it is the reinforcement of the gender/sex binary, a traditional two-gender/sex system, and an authentically gendered self. Exemplifying this latter line of thinking is Jay Prosser, a female-to-male scholar of transsexuality, who argues that transsexual people have a right to have "gender homes," as he terms them. For Prosser, gender homes are recognized if and when transsexuals are accepted as real men and women, get health insurance coverage for sex reassignment surgery, and/or are legally allowed to change to the opposite sex on their birth certificates. Another leading transsexual theorist is Janice Raymond, who similarly suggests that transsexuality involves social conformity yet disagrees that it is an authentic gender identity. Media messages about transsexuals successfully passing in or blending into society as normal males or normal females also fit within these assimilative conceptions of transsexuality.

Given the problematic history of the term *transsexual*, a growing number of scholars, social activists, medical and media professionals, and people who identify with this group use other terms, ranging from posttranssexual to pre-operation MTF. To date, the most accepted term is *transgender* (though this term has also become an umbrella term that includes intersex people). The post-structural/postmodern perspective of queer theory is regularly cited as influencing this new terminology. As a result, transitioning gender is not considered pathological,

A common theme arising among transsexual people is a sense of feeling trapped in the wrong body. To remedy this, transsexuals may dress as the opposite sex and/or may undergo hormone therapy or sex reassignment surgery. (Photos.com)

nor is it about the search for true gender identity and social conformity. In fact, transgender studies argue that transgenderism (what was once called transsexuality) has the sociopolitical possibility to challenge norms of gender, sex, and sexuality and can even displace the gender/sex binary itself. Media messages that celebrate people who come out as neither male nor female in a traditional sense, or in other ways are always transitioning gender, fit within these queer conceptions of transsexuality.

Jamie Landau
Keene State College

See also Online New Media: Transgender Identity; Queer Theory; Sexuality; Social Construction of Gender; Sports Media: Transgender; Transgender Studies

Further Readings

Fausto-Sterling, Anne. *Sexing the Body: Gender Politics and the Construction of Sexuality*. New York: Basic Books, 2000.
Garber, Marjorie. *Vested Interests: Cross-Dressing and Cultural Anxiety*. New York: Routledge, 1992.
Hausman, Bernice L. *Changing Sex: Transsexualism, Technology and the Idea of Gender in the 20th Century*. Durham, NC: Duke University Press, 1995.
Prosser, Jay. *Second Skins: The Body Narratives of Transsexuality*. New York: Columbia University Press, 1998.
Raymond, Janice. *The Transsexual Empire: The Making of the She-Male*. Boston: Beacon Press, 1979.
Stone, Sandy. "The 'Empire' Strikes Back: A Posttranssexual Manifesto." In *Body Guards: The Cultural Politics of Gender Ambiguity*, Kristina Straub and Julia Epstein, eds. New York: Routledge, 1991.

TROPES

Tropes are rhetorical devices or units of metaphor. They are gendered in the same ways that other forms of human communication are gendered. Dominant communicative categories are verbal and nonverbal, visual and aural, and are evident in all parts of the world. Tropes in a gendered sense can be seen as culturally determined narratives, visual stereotypes, and aural gestures, and they are commonly understood as mechanisms to deliver meaning in literature, film and television, and music. This entry reviews the historical framework from which Western culture has historically used tropes and reflects on their uses and ubiquity in a gendered and mediated sense.

Tropes began as mechanisms in music, as texts added to the Catholic liturgy attaching literary meanings and images to established components of the Mass, dating back to the 10th century. Over time, these were performed as independent dramas. Tropes as gendered images have a complex history, the language of their connection being complicated by the use of gendered imagery throughout recorded human history and the concept of the trope being tied to the study of literary traditions. The concept of trope is heavily tied to genre; indeed, genres are frequently demonstrated through the use of characteristic tropes. The use of a trope within any narrative locates that narrative within a cultural framing that contextualizes any individual or specific meanings that may be generated by that text's creator/composer. Studies of semiotic, or nonverbal, communication systems (according to Hayden White) view tropes as a mechanism for understanding the different forms of linguistic/articulated and visual communication modes in terms of the cultural conceptions each set of images expresses through such mechanisms as metaphor, synecdoche, irony, and metonymy.

In traditional media such as storytelling, gender tropes dominate folklore and fairy tales. Classic images of the "hero," "damsel in distress," "evil stepmother," and helper categories of "fairy godmother" and "seven dwarfs" are juxtaposed with tropes of storytelling, such as "the quest," with devices that represent cultural norms, such as the poisoned apple of Snow White, naming the villain such as Rumpelstiltskin, and so on. Such images have been transformed over time to reflect shifting cultural norms and have transferred to newer modes of media transmission, beginning with Eleanor of Aquitaine in 13th-century France and going on to Sir Thomas Malory's depiction of the Arthurian legends, the Grimm brothers' collection of 19th-century Germanic fairy tales, and the Disney Studios' transformation of these into representations shown in contemporary media.

As a mechanism of contemporary media, tropes are utilized in a variety of ways to depict both cultural norms and transgressive images of gendered action, behavior, and being. War, historically troped with masculine imagery, is an early entry in the arena of electronic media representation, particularly in film reels of World War I beginning in 1914. Within the past century, film and recorded sound have expanded the scope whereby tropes are applied, enmeshing tropes even further into genres of mediated representation—to the point where tropes have become inseparable from genres. As in all types of gendered language use, gendered tropes represent cultural values and norms, making them fundamental to especially visual forms of communication. Cultural stereotypes of gender as metaphors of positive and negative human behavior are clearly presented in film and television as well as displayed in all forms of advertising. Tropes such as bisexuality, while in themselves not dominant tropes of discourse or representation, when they do appear are used to critique mainstream representations of gender and sexuality, as for example in the 2005 film *Brokeback Mountain*.

Gendered masculine tropes can function at levels as basic as the "sensitive man" of chick flicks to the "everyday guy" construction of Joe the Plumber as seen during the U.S. presidential election cycle of 2008. Gendered feminine tropes also vary, from the highly sexualized backup singers/dancers of music videos (who are invariably shapely bodies dancing around the charismatic male rapper or vocalist) to the female action hero who balances out her role as powerful and independent with more conventional feminine presentations in traditional, sexually objectified modes (as in the *Charlie's Angels* films). Tropes vary by genre but always are the mechanism by which an audience can accept a story line. It is a basic assumption in mediated storytelling that what is directed at men (action/adventure, coarse comedy) is not what is directed at women (romantic comedy, soap opera). Male characters are strong and heroic, whereas female characters are emotional and sexual; women listen, whereas men do.

Of the traditional masculine and feminine tropes, the most stereotypical are currently presented in video games, pornography, and extreme sports and sports-oriented programming. Professional wrestling, for example, has become a male-focused soap opera containing toxic, also known as extreme, masculine imagery that is directed almost exclusively at a homosocial male, 18- to 35-year-old audience. Both masculine and feminine tropes are cartoonlike in their depiction of gender norms, and representations of other modes of gender behavior are similarly presented.

Gender tropes are heavily applied on the Internet on social networking and dating sites. Personal descriptions, photos, and questionnaires all are geared toward representing a party within a particular gender norm. Photos are particularly relevant, displaying the "good parent," the "adventurous guy" doing some type of outdoor activity, the "outgoing girl" at a party with friends, the "sensitive guy" with his girlfriend or wife, the "good mom" with her children, or children as a primary picture to represent the "good mom."

Similarly, popular music is heavily troped, from musical genres to vocal style. A female singer-songwriter is usually a long-haired, waif-like girl with a guitar, generally with a light, high voice if she is singing mainstream popular music or else with a midrange soprano if she sings in a niche category, such as Americana or folk rock. Male singer-songwriters have a wider range of available tropes, again heavily tied to musical genre. Rock-and-roll singers generally have long hair, play guitar, and wear jeans. Hip-hop or rap singers are frequently tattooed, often shirtless or with bared arms, frequently wearing heavy jewelry, and often depicted with numerous scantily clad women around them. Race and ethnicity also are factored into tropes in such displays: The rock-and-roll singer is troped as white, while the hip-hop singer is generally troped as African American. Men are generally photographed in active poses and are often outdoors, whereas women are generally photographed in passive or off-balance poses, often leaning against either men or other women. Visual tropes within the gay, lesbian, bisexual, transsexual/transgender (GLBT) music community reflect many of the images from the heterosexual, mainstream perspective. Gay tropes are often exaggerated representations of heterosexual images, particularly in the drag community, where the markers of femininity, such as sexually provocative clothing, high heels, and extensive amounts of theatrically applied makeup, are commonly seen. The lesbian community frequently plays to either the "butch" or the "androgynous" image, with lesbian women wearing short, masculine-looking hairstyles, clothing that is highly masculine in cut and style, and body postures that adopt traditional, heterosexually male, active poses.

Classical music is troped by role, genre, and performance style. Conductors are white, European or American men; so are composers. Similar to those of popular musicians, such roles, because they are active, creative, and performative, are consistently troped as masculine. Vocal performances are troped as feminine. Amateur musical performance is troped as feminine and middle- to upper-class, and both categories are troped as white. Virtuosity is troped as Asian, particularly for the piano and the violin, but musicality is troped as European or American. Positive tropes for musical or theatrical performances are always positioned as heterosexual: GLBT imagery is rarely positively portrayed and invariably positioned against mainstream culture.

The function of tropes remains that of communicating social and cultural norms in abbreviated forms that can be easily understood by audiences and other media producers. While the historical tropes remain grounded in language and visual codes, contemporary uses of troping frequently take advantage of this communicative shorthand to present complex messages about culturally appropriate and inappropriate behavior.

J. Meryl Krieger
Indiana University–Purdue University
Indianapolis

See also Music Videos: Representations of Men; Music Videos: Representations of Women; Music Videos: Tropes; Pornography: Gay and Lesbian; Pornography: Heterosexual; Stereotypes; Video Gaming: Representations of Femininity; Video Gaming: Representations of Masculinity; Video Gaming: Violence

Further Readings

Alexander, Jonathan and Keith Dorwick. "Introduction: Where the Bisexuals Are . . . or Not. . . ." *Journal of Bisexuality*, v.7/1–2 (2007).

Chandler, Daniel. *Semiotics for Beginners: The Basics.* New York: Routledge, 2002.

De Lauretis, Teresa. *Technologies of Gender: Essays on Theory, Film, and Fiction.* Bloomington: Indiana University Press, 1987.

Jhally, Sut, producer and director. *The Codes of Gender: Identity + Performance in Pop Culture.* Northampton, MA: Media Education Foundation, 2009.

Lakoff, George and Mark Johnson. "Conceptual Metaphor in Everyday Language." *Journal of Philosophy*, v.77/8 (1980).

Orenstein, Catherine. "Fairy Tales and a Dose of Reality." *New York Times* (March 3, 2003). http://www.nytimes.com/2003/03/03/opinion/03OREN.html (Accessed October 2010).

Pranger, Brian. *The Arena of Masculinity*. London: GMP, 1990.

Williamson, Judith. *Decoding Advertisements*. London: Marion Boyars, 1978.

TWEEN MAGAZINES

Written for young children between the ages of 8 and 14, "tween" magazines are produced by magazine publishers seeking to extend their marketing, advertising, and branding to children in this age bracket, part of a demographic whose size and disposable income have earned them the "tween" moniker. Representing $10.1 billion in the United States alone, this industry is the fastest-growing global market, including the United Kingdom, Australia, and Korea (according to Just-Style.com). In addition to using their own disposable income, tweens use their "pestering power" to influence household purchases of products such as toys, clothing, and food. Because tweens are increasingly accessible through mobile phones, the Internet, and magazines, media companies have strategically recast their nets to profit from this emerging demographic.

In the quest to materialize earnings, tween magazines strive to inculcate a new breed of teenage and young adult consumers through targeted media content. While magazines produced for this youth market reach both sexes with stories about pop stars, music, sports, and entertainment, girls are a highly sought-after demographic. According to an article in the May 28, 2007, online edition of the *New York Times*, by Elizabeth Olson, among the most popular commercial magazines targeting girls ages 8–14 in the United States are *J-14*, *M*, and *Nickelodeon Magazine*, with roughly 30 percent of preteens reading or looking at each. Disney and Nickelodeon are the dominant media companies that drive the tween magazine market. By marketing young stars across their media channels and outlets through a strategy known as synergy, these media companies have been credited with bolstering the success of other popular tween magazines, including *Twist*, *Tiger Beat*, *Bop*, and *Popstar*. Disney-created stars, such as Zac Efron and Corbin Bleu from the 2006 movie *High School Musical* and Miley Cyrus from the television series *Hannah Montana*, have helped boost the circulation of tween magazines by as much as 25 percent.

Young girls are regarded by the tween magazine industry as a key segment of the economy and powerful market for advertisers seeking to develop brand loyalty. Using an economic formula similar to other popular girl magazines, such as *Seventeen*, tween magazines feature stories about pop stars, dating, and growing up to lure readers to polling quizzes and advertisements for beauty and fashion. Tween magazines have proliferated, in part, because they allow clothing companies to profit from girls seeking to look older than they are. By exposing girls to the realm of beauty and fashion at a young age, the industry believes that they can create a desire among girls to consume new products to improve their image, leading to future narcissistic tendencies that can be exploited well beyond the teenage years.

Debate about tween magazines centers around whether young girls are becoming empowered by their content or whether reading these magazines encourages them to act and dress older than their age, taking advantage of their developing and impressionable minds. (Photos.com)

Publishers of commercial tween magazines contend that their business empowers young girls, through reading age-related content, to make their own independent choices in social activities, entertainment, quizzes, and contests. Coining phrases such as "girl power," proponents claim to have founded the industry so that young girls can have a place of their own within the culture, allowing them to relate to issues and topics that they find interesting as they grow up. Likewise, the fashion industry defends tween magazines as allowing girls to make their own clothing choices and other purchases by offering them miniature versions of items targeted to older girls and women.

In contrast, critics point out the dangers associated with commercial tween magazines. Psychologists, parents, educators, and religious figures contend that marketing adult content to children pressures them to grow up too fast and takes advantage of them at a time when they are still developing and impressionable. Concerns over the influence of popular culture and the commercial exploitation of childhood persist among parents as they try to retain their authority and autonomy while raising their children in a heavily mediated environment. By exposing girls to adult themes alongside celebrities and models who overtly flaunt their sexuality, tween magazines pressure young girls to accept the ideals associated with developing sex appeal without understanding all of the consequences. Examples of the content aimed at these girls include "Does Teen Mom Glamorize Teen Pregnancy?" "Give Us Your Kissing Stories!" "Is It Okay to Get Married in Your Teens?" "Plastic Surgery: Are You for or Against It?" "Do You Feel Pressure About Your Weight or Appearance?" and "Do You Feel Like Drinking Affects Your Judgment?" (available on the "Hot Topic" page of the *J-14* Website). Subsequently, parents are left in a vulnerable position, forced prematurely to explain to their young daughters why certain fashions, topics, and behaviors are inappropriate. Peer pressure to conform to style, taste, and behaviors as dictated by these magazines exacerbate the problem, leaving parents with the difficult choice of either resisting or acquiescing to capitalistic pressures.

Such concerns were voiced in protest against *Vogue Girl* when it launched publications in Australia and South Korea. After receiving criticism for its depictions of girls in objectified or provocative ad campaigns, such as one in which a young girl was depicted as a toy doll in a toy box, the publication ceased operations. Notwithstanding, ad-driven tween magazines, such as *Trendy Tween*, continue to proffer online content that targets girls as young as six years of age with fashion and beauty content. Despite claiming that it does not contain articles inappropriate for its targeted age group, *Trendy Tween* offers photo contests driven by the modeling aesthetic associated with beauty pageants and the sexualization of young girls.

Some magazines that produce content for this age group refrain from including advertising or tailor their content to issues written by and for girls in the realm of art, education, and self-esteem. For example, *New Moon Girls* (http://www.newmoon .com) explains that it promotes a "fully-moderated, educational environment designed to build self-esteem and positive body image" without ads through "an online community and magazine where girls create and share poetry, artwork, videos, and more; chat together; and learn." Each issue contains stories about girl activities, adventures, and athletics, global travel and service, careers for girls to aspire to, historical female role models, fiction, accurate

health and body information, inspirational messages from successful girls and women, book reviews, and cartoons. Although it accepts limited select ads approved by their editorial board, *Teen Voices Magazine* (http://www.teenvoices.com/about-us/ mission-vision-and-values) explains that it "supports and educates teen girls to amplify their voices and create social change through media." It envisions equality and opportunities for girls by featuring stories that they write and contribute that affect their lives personally and politically outside commercial culture. *American Girl* and *Hopscotch for Girls* fall within a similar classification, in that their stories embody the development of girls' self-esteem and success outside commercial media and the beauty myth. Unlike their commercial counterparts, these tween magazines do not cull market trends through contests and quizzes or reduce the identity of girls to "fashionistas."

Despite the problems associated with girls' magazines, some feminist scholars have argued that tween, teen, and women's magazines provide an important cultural space for young girls and women to discuss sexual desires, pleasures, and problems directly in complicated ways. Angela McRobbie suggests that there are discernible shifts within the normative ways in which girlhood and womanhood are understood in these magazines as public debates about sex and acquired immune deficiency syndrome (AIDS) offer more nuanced, more knowledgeable, and less normative forms of sexuality. She suggests that magazines targeted at girls and women are more overt, more complex, and less prescriptive than the liberated *Cosmopolitan* of the 1970s and 1980s.

Julie Frechette
Worcester State University

See also Advertising; Beauty and Body Image: Beauty Myths; Beauty and Body Image: Eating Disorders; Children's Programming: Cartoons; Children's Programming: Disney and Pixar; E-Zines: Riot Grrrl; E-Zines: Third Wave Feminist; Reality-Based Television: *America's Next Top Model*; Women's Magazines: Fashion; Women's Magazines: Lifestyle and Health

Further Readings

Brooks, Katherine. "Daughter of *Vogue* Sells More With Less Flesh." *The Courier Mail* [Queensland, Australia] (May 11, 2005).

Children's Review. "Magazines for Tween Girls." *Feminist Collections: A Quarterly of Women's Studies Resources,* v.30/1 (2009).

"Girls Grow Up Before Time With 'Tween' Mags." *Hobart Mercury* [Australia] (April 13, 2009).

Holroyd, Jane. "At $1.3bn a Year, Tweens Are Vogue." *Sunday Age* [Melbourne, Australia] (April 10, 2005).

Hutchinson, Jane. "Bringing Up Barbie." *Sunday Telegraph Magazine* [Australia] (November 12, 2006).

Lawson, Valerie. "Tween Dreams." *The Age* [Melbourne, Australia] (January 6, 2007).

Linn, Susan. *Consuming Kids: The Hostile Takeover of Childhood.* New York: New Press, 2004.

Schor, Juliet B. *Born to Buy: The Commercialized Child and the New Consumer Culture.* New York: Scribner, 2005.

TWITTER

Twitter is a social networking and microblogging site that allows its users to send and receive text-based messages, called "tweets," that can be no more than 140 characters in length. Tweets are posted publicly on the user's profile page, which resembles a blog consisting only of short messages. Twitter is a type of social networking site because its users can choose to subscribe to (or follow) another author's tweets and any given tweet will reach only the parties that have subscribed unless it is a comment that is "retweeted" by a person the user follows. By late 2010, Twitter.com was one of the top 10 most visited sites on the Internet and had more than 165 million registered users worldwide. Like other forms of social media (Facebook or Myspace, for example), Twitter has experienced a tremendous amount of expansion and has exerted significant influence as both a social networking site and a type of real-time information network utilized by organizations, businesses, and mainstream media outlets. In its short history, Twitter not only has established a new type of social networking platform for individuals but also has proven to be a unique information tool with great potential to impact many facets of social life, including journalism, business, politics, and popular culture.

The Twitter Website is run by Twitter, Inc., a San Francisco–based company that launched the service in mid-2006. During a brainstorming session, its founders conceptualized the idea of a site that enabled individuals to send real-time messages via short message service (SMS, also known as text messages or texting) to groups of people. Given that the typical SMS message was capped at 160 characters, the creators decided to limit the length of a tweet to 140 characters, allowing room for the username and colon in front of the message. The original name for the service was "twitch," reminiscent of a vibrating cell phone. The team later determined that "twitter" was a more appropriate word for branding purposes and best described what they considered the primary function of the site: to provide short, fleeting bursts of information.

While Twitter generated buzz among early adopters and trendsetters, the service saw its biggest surge in popularity during 2009, probably because of its increased accessibility and growing consumer use. First, the widespread adoption of text messaging and Facebook (with its status update feature) meant that many users were already adept at formats similar to the tweet. Twitter moved beyond computers by improving its mobile applications for smart phones, a technology of media convergence that was also gaining popularity around this time. The mobile applications no longer required users to own or have access to a computer and enabled reporting or updating information in real time. Second, Twitter's popularity and rise in membership spiked when popular-culture icons began using the service, effectively ushering Twitter out of the technology world and into mainstream culture. In April 2009, actor Ashton Kutcher declared a "race" to gather 1 million Twitter followers before cable news station CNN did; he succeeded within a matter of a few days. Nearly simultaneously, talk show host Oprah Winfrey posted her first tweet, resulting in a spike of visitors to Twitter.com and new account registrations. Twitter also received significant media attention in June 2009, following the unexpected death of singer Michael Jackson. Jackson's death was cited as a notable "trending topic" (frequently tweeted phrase, word, or name) in the days after his death. The onslaught of users crashed the site as they went to Twitter to express their grief or search for real-time, breaking news updates.

Twitter has proven to be an effective journalistic tool in such breaking news situations, where information is changing so quickly that mainstream media cannot assemble all the facts at once. Tweets can serve as a type of tip sheet for reporters and sites that track trending topics and hashtags (Twitter-speak for a set of tweets about the same topic,

Part of the appeal of Twitter for both those in the public eye and the general public is that celebrities can use Twitter to directly communicate with fans, giving celebrities more control over their image than the coverage offered up by gossip media and the paparazzi. (Photos.com)

person, or event, indicated by a # sign before a topic word) function as a type of collective intelligence providing early warnings about trends, people, and news. Twitter was cited as a key tool for breaking eyewitness accounts during the Mumbai terrorist bombings in November 2008 and the Haitian earthquake in 2010. Twitter was also an important news source during the disputed Iranian presidential elections in June 2009. After the Iranian government banned journalists from covering the election protests, it was for a time one of the only means of news transmission out of Iran. In this way, Twitter can serve as a reciprocal medium between news organizations and the general public, where one has the potential to inform the other.

Similar to blogs, Twitter is a democratic medium, allowing its individual users a "voice" within a larger media network. This type of message control enables new types of public relations tactics between businesses, celebrities, and politicians. Businesses and organizations are able to use Twitter as a marketing channel and specifically connect with consumers by sending messages to followers and by targeting users based on their history of tweets. Celebrities use Twitter as a means to directly communicate with fans, taking back some control over their image from the paparazzi and gossip media. Politicians and political movements such as the Tea Party movement have effectively used Twitter as a

means of direct communication with voters and as a type of digital insurgence. Former vice presidential nominee Sarah Palin has been notable in evoking Twitter as a medium of choice to bypass mainstream media and break news about herself or to quickly share her opinions on other public matters. The simultaneously public yet individualized platform of Twitter fosters a new, perhaps more direct, mode of communication between specific people or organizations and a greater audience, allowing for new types of targeted messaging and public relations.

As of 2011, Twitter remained in its infancy, and although signs pointed to increased usage over time, it was hard to predict exactly in what ways it would continue to manifest. The service has existed long enough for the emergence of some distinct patterns, however. A Harvard Business School study noted that, although women comprised 55 percent of Twitter users and men and women tweeted at the same rates, men tended overwhelmingly to follow other men. In addition, the study indicated that the median number of lifetime tweets per user is one—suggesting that only a small minority of Twitter users are highly active. It therefore appears that Twitter may be transitioning from a peer-to-peer social networking site to a one-to-many, real-time information service. Given the dynamic shifts and growth of Twitter in its infancy, only time will tell whether the site will decline in the wake of new technological innovations—or continue to transform the way people, organizations, businesses, and news outlets connect to the world and one another.

Karen C. Pitcher
Eckerd College

See also Blogs and Blogging; Cyberspace and Cyberculture; Media Convergence; New Media; Social Media; Social Networking Sites: Facebook; Social Networking Sites: Myspace; YouTube

Further Readings

Ahmad, Ali Noble. "Is Twitter a Useful Tool for Journalists?" *Journal of Media Practice*, v.11/2 (2010).

Farhi, Paul. "The Twitter Explosion." *American Journalism Review*, v.313 (June/July 2009).

Heil, Bill and Mikolaj Piskorski. "HBR Blog Network: New Twitter Research: Men Follow Men and Nobody Tweets." *Harvard Business Review* (June 1, 2009). http://blogs.hbr.org/cs/2009/06/new_twitter_research_men_follo.html (Accessed October 2010).

VIDEO GAMING: REPRESENTATIONS OF FEMININITY

Since the 1980s, researchers have examined femininity in video games, in terms of both the physical representations of female characters and the roles female characters occupy within video games. Video games are important symbolic sites for conveying messages about appropriate gender roles and perceptions of social reality. Additionally, video games increasingly are used in educational settings and are important for developing children's media literacy and digital skills. In general, researchers have examined femininity in video games through both quantitative and qualitative research methods. Content analyses of female characters show that the most popular available video games tend to portray negative representations of femininity. Female characters are highly sexualized, represented with overly exaggerated feminine features (such as large breasts and small waists), and wear revealing clothing to draw attention to these features. Female characters also tend to play passive roles within the games, as submissive characters, victims of violence, or damsels in distress. In the 1990s, several female-owned video game companies marketed games to a female, primarily youth, audience as a strategy for challenging the dominant representations of female characters in video games. These "girl games" offered different types of stories and female characters. Despite progress in marketing video games to a female audience, the most popular video games available continue to have negative portrayals of femininity.

The history of female characters in video games can be traced back to the 1980s, with the development of the arcade game *Ms. Pac-Man*. Designed to attract female players, this maze game emphasized hand-eye coordination. The only feminine feature of Ms. Pac-Man was a red bow on her head. Advancements in graphics technology in the 1980s led to games that featured human characters. While female characters were noticeably absent from early video games, the introduction of Chun-Li in *Streetfighter 2* helped to popularize the practice of providing a range of female characters that players could select to play.

Research on video games stresses the importance of how representations differ by video delivery system and genre. Video delivery systems include personal computers (PC), video game consoles, arcades, and handheld devices. The rise of the Internet in the 1990s led to online gaming that included interactivity among players. Massively multiplayer online role-playing games (MMORPGs), such as *World of Warcraft* and *Second Life*, allow users to create their own avatars and interact in constructed spaces with other players. MMORPGs offer a range of female characters from which players can choose. However, many of the female characters tend to be hypersexualized. Video games also differ in their content. Video game genres are distinguished by the method of game play and the set of challenges presented to the player. Some of the most popular genres include action, adventure, role-playing, simulation, and strategy games. Despite differences in genres, the most violent games tend to be the best-selling.

Most of the research on representations of femininity in video games tends to focus on violent video games. Quantitative content analyses of popular mainstream video games suggest that female characters are underrepresented in video games. When female characters do appear, their appearance is characterized by "hyperfemininity," typified by traits such as overly large breasts, small waists, and revealing clothing. Not only are female characters physically represented in stereotypical ways; their roles within video games tend to be passive. Female characters are often victims of violence, submissive "damsels in distress" who are rescued by male protagonists. For example, in the controversial video game *Grand Theft Auto: Sin City*, players can have sex with a prostitute, then kill her and take their money back. Finally, the sexualized representations of female characters tend to appeal to male players, who often rate female characters in video games by their sex appeal.

In addition to the noticeable absence of female characters in video games, there is a lack of ethnic and racial diversity among female characters. The majority of female characters are white, and the racial representation of female characters does not mirror the broader demographics of the United States. When nonwhite characters do appear, they are likely to be victims of violence or represented by racial and ethnic stereotypes. Research has found that many of the nonwhite characters in video games remain in the background and are unplayable. This lack of representation of minorities in video games sends the message that their identities are not valued.

Negative portrayals of females in violent video games can reinforce stereotypes of women as submissive and valued for their beauty over their intellect. These representations can lead to a low self-image among girls and women and discourage them from becoming video game players. Additionally, qualitative research has found that girls and women do not identify with female characters in video games and do not like the aggressive and highly competitive nature of available games.

Women and girls do like playing video games, just not the ones that are generally available. Statistics from the Entertainment Software Group suggest that women make up about 40 percent of video game players. To counter the negative stereotypes of femininity, there was a rise in girl-oriented video games in the 1990s. The first game marketed to girls was titled *Hawaii High: The Mystery of the Tikki*, designed by Trina Roberts and distributed by Sanctuary Woods. This adventure-based game featured two female characters. The game was significant for inspiring the development of a new genre of video games marketed to girls. Female-run game companies such as HerInteractive, Girl Games, Girltech, and Purple Moon developed games for girls that included narrative development and a range of female characters with which girls could identify. In general, there were two main strategies developed to reach the girl audience. The first strategy included game play centered on gender-specific activities, such as cooking and clothing. *Barbie Fashion Designer* was the most successful. In this PC game, players designed clothing and accessories for their Barbie dolls. Girl-themed games tend to feature character-centered plots, narratives that involve social relationships, and colorful graphics. Girl-oriented games also feature popular female fictional characters, such as Disney princesses or Dora the Explorer. Nintendo's *Cooking Mama* is an example of a popular video game marketed to girls.

Many are critical of gender-specific games for highlighting stereotypical feminine behavior. These games may reinforce cultural messages that males and females occupy separate domains. However, proponents of gender-specific games argue that it is important to develop games that reflect girls' cultural tastes and interests. Additionally, playing video games is important for developing girls' digital literacy skills. Playing video games encourages skills such as multitasking, visual learning, and problem solving, which are crucial for computer programming. If girls and women do not develop an interest in playing video games, they may be less likely to enter science, technology, engineering, and math (STEM) fields.

A second strategy to attract a female audience was to introduce stronger female characters into available games. In 1996, the British company Core Design launched *Tomb Raider*, which featured the female protagonist Lara Croft, an archaeologist who ventures into ancient tombs and ruins. Instead of being submissive, Croft is portrayed as tough, competent, and dominant. She is also depicted as an athletic woman, and her outfit consists of a sleeveless tank top, shorts, combat boots, a utility belt, and a backpack. While Croft's design did challenge dominant representations of femininity, she is still sexualized, because she has exaggerated breasts and a small waist. Critics argue that Croft is conceived in terms of male, rather than female, pleasure. Additionally, Croft has become a worldwide sex symbol marketed in terms of her attractiveness.

Available research is critiqued on the basis of sample size and generalizabilty. Researchers argue that the sampling of video games needs to be improved; most available research examines only the most violent video games and thus findings do not accurately reflect representations of femininity in other genres. Finally, there is a need to look at how game players respond to video game content to better understand the impact of representations of femininity.

Carolyn Cunningham
Gonzaga University

See also Avatar; Beauty and Body Image: Beauty Myths; Beauty and Body Image: Eating Disorders; Comics; Film: Horror; Gender and Femininity: Motherhood; Gender and Femininity: Single/Independent Girl; Gender and Masculinity: Black Masculinity; Gender and Masculinity: Fatherhood; Gender and Masculinity: Metrosexual Male; Gender and Masculinity: White Masculinity; Heroes: Action and Super Heroes; Massively Multiplayer Online Role-Playing Games; Multi-User Dimensions; *Second Life*; Sports Media: Extreme Sports and Masculinity; Video Gaming: Representations of Masculinity; Video Gaming: Violence; Virtual Community; Virtual Sex; Virtuality; Web 2.0; Wiki; Women's Magazines: Fashion; Women's Magazines: Lifestyle and Health

Further Readings

Cassell, Justine and Henry Jenkins, eds. *From Barbie to Mortal Kombat: Gender and Computer Games.* Cambridge, MA: MIT Press, 1998.

Dietz, Tracy. "An Examination of Violence and Gender Role Portrayals in Video Games: Implications for Gender Socialization and Aggressive Behavior." *Sex Roles*, v.38/5–6 (1998).

Entertainment Software Group. "2010 Essential Facts About the Computer and Video Game Industry." http://www.theesa.com/facts/gameplayer.asp (Accessed October 2010).

Gee, James Paul. *What Video Games Have to Teach Us About Learning and Literacy.* New York: Palgrave Macmillan, 2003.

Vorderer, Peter and Jennings Bryant, eds. *Playing Video Games: Motives, Responses, and Consequences.* Mahwah, NJ: Lawrence Erlbaum Associates, 2006.

Walkderdine, Valerie. *Children, Gender, Video Games: Toward a Relational Approach to Multimedia.* New York: Palgrave Macmillan, 2009.

Williams, Dmitri, Nicole Martins, Mia Consalvo, and James D. Ivory. "The Virtual Census: Representations of Gender, Race and Age in Video Games." *New Media and Society*, v.11/5 (2009).

VIDEO GAMING: REPRESENTATIONS OF MASCULINITY

The research on the representation of masculinity in video games reveals a preponderance of violent and militaristic characters in terms of action and game-play activity. In terms of body image, representations of men in video games tend to emphasize bodybuilder physiques over other types of muscle tonality. However, there are important differences in representations of masculinity when different video game genres are examined. Role-playing games, first-person shooting games, sports games, and strategy games have developed somewhat different kinds of representations of masculinity.

The history of video games as a medium is rooted in military applications of computer technology developed during the Cold War. There is still a relationship between the video game industry and the U.S. military in terms of simulation and computer hardware research and development. Many of the most popular games that have been created have had military-inspired themes because of these historical and cultural roots of video game development. The dominant representation in these types of military-inspired games has come to be known as militarized masculinity. Militarized masculinity is a form of representation in which video game characters perform violent action through combat with the intent to conquer and defeat enemies. These representations are tied to military principles of honor, sacrifice, and heroism when they are associated with a player's avatar. Additionally, militaristic and other uses of violent force are the dominant ways to accomplish goals, such as defeating violent enemies, to progress through many video games and ultimately win them.

Digital artists who create militaristic masculine characters use the aesthetic style that is representative of hypermuscular or "hard" bodies. This style was originally developed in Hollywood action films in the 1980s, often associated with characters played by actors such as Arnold Schwarzenegger, Bruce Willis, and Sylvester Stallone. The aesthetic is also similar to superhero body types found in mainstream comic books produced by such publishers as DC Comics and Marvel. One example of a militarized masculine representation in video games is Chris Redfield, the paramilitary hero of the *Resident Evil* video game franchise. Redfield has huge biceps and forearms, with pectoral muscles that are barely contained by his tight-fitting, army-green shirt. He has a strong jaw and the close-cut, brown hair associated with the military. Most of the franchise games situate Redfield among a horde of infected mutant creatures, and he must use military-developed weapons to survive. The various weapons he uses adorn his hypermuscular body. He carries pistols in side holsters, while a rifle, machine gun, shotgun, and machete are slung over his back. This combination of the hypermuscular body and the weapons used to kill and otherwise perform physically violent acts creates the dominant representation of masculinity in video games. Militarized masculinity is also tied to heterosexuality, although many games do not feature romantic story lines.

Not all video games are alike, however. Video games are categorized into genres, and there are in many cases differences in the representation of masculinity based on these genre distinctions. Most first-person shooter (FPS) games involve representations of militarized masculinity. Two of the most influential and best-selling video game franchises in this genre, *Call of Duty* and *Halo*, rely on militaristic representations of men in combat. In genres that simulate sports, the type of masculine representation in video games is typically carried over from the culture of the sport being simulated. In wrestling games and ultimate fighting games, the representation of masculinity is based on the extreme forms of macho behavior developed by World Wrestling Entertainment. These representations also emphasize the use of hypermuscular bodies as weapons. In the racing games, representations of masculinity are tied to the cultural notion that cars, motorbikes, all-terrain vehicles (ATVs), snowmobiles, and off-road vehicles (ORVs) are associated with men who race but also practice mechanics by fixing, upgrading, overhauling, and tinkering with their racing

Video game characters often perform violent action through combat and with the intent to conquer and defeat enemies, representations tied to militarized masculinity. Studies have shown that, when a male avatar is chosen, if the player faces a female opponent within the game, it significantly decreases aggressive thoughts toward the character. (Photos.com)

machines. Thus, in video game franchises such as *Midnight Club* and later releases in the *Need for Speed* franchise about street racing, most of the main characters are men who compete to have the fastest, flashiest, and most exotic cars with the best engines, shocks, tires, and transmissions. Electronic Arts develops and publishes a number of games based on the world's professional sporting leagues, such as the National Football League, National Basketball Association, Major League Baseball, and leagues that are part of Féderation Inernationale de Football Association (FIFA). The major trend of representation in these video games is to make the video game characters look exactly like sports figures in terms of facial features and body physique. The representation of masculinity in professional sports video games is associated through ultrarealism with actual sports stars such as Tiger Woods, Tom Brady, Christiano Ronaldo, and LeBron James, to name a few. Furthermore, representations of men playing professional sports involving physical contact can be seen as offering condoned and sanctioned forms of competitive violence among men.

Fantasy role-playing games (RPGs) constitute another popular video game genre. Most RPGs allow players to select either a male or a female character at the onset of play. Throughout the game, the player's avatar gains experience points for performing tasks. Thus, players choosing a male character can gain traits such as strength and agility that help them complete goals within the game. Many RPGs encourage collective game play with many different characters working together to defeat a common enemy. In these games, players explore masculine roles, such as being a respectable man who is strong-willed and helpful. Many RPGs also promote a representation of masculinity that is tied to the notion of the eternal boy, who is playful and carefree in nature rather than a militarized action hero. Some RPGs allow the player to make different choices that place a character on a scale between good and evil. These choices affect whether violent masculinity is represented as just or unjust. One particularly well-known game development studio, BioWare, creates these types of games. For example, in the popular and critically acclaimed science fiction series *Mass Effect*, the player makes a series of choices for the avatar throughout the game that determine whether the character is a paragon of virtue or a hostile renegade. There are motivating factors in consistently pursuing one or the other, such as extra dialogue between characters or the ability to intimidate or charm artificial intelligence (AI) characters.

Video games are an interactive medium that requires the user to participate in the mediated experience. Because the player is involved in the actions of an avatar, how gender is performed through the player's action is an important element in the study of representations of masculinity in video games. For example, avatars in action-adventure video games are created with distinct gendered identities. The repeated gendered performances of the player through the character lead to advancement through a game. *Grand Theft Auto: San Andreas*, an action-adventure game, provides one example of how gender representation is performance-based in the gaining of experience. The player interacts with the game through the main character, CJ, an African American male character. The narrative of the game is about CJ's return to his hometown of Los Santos to investigate and take violent revenge on the people responsible for killing his mother. The player performs what the game creators consider to be an archetype of African American masculinity: the tough, streetwise black man who hustles for money and women. To gain experience points that make the avatar more effective in completing goals in the game, the player performs activities associated

with this stereotyped African American masculinity. Experience points can be gained by doing bodybuilding exercises, training to acquire fighting and weapons skills, taking women out on dates and engaging in sex, garnering respect through gang warfare, and increasing sex appeal by purchasing expensive clothing and cars.

In video games based on strategy and simulation, the representation of masculinity is less about the specific characters or avatars on screen. Instead, masculinity is tied to the types of activities performed by the player. In video games such as those in the *Civilization* franchise, a bureaucratic masculinity is represented through the player's ability to organize, manage, and manipulate information such as city resources and growth, diplomatic relations among nations, the use and development of technologies, and the movement and strategic deployment of armies.

Robin Johnson
Sam Houston State University

See also Avatar; Beauty and Body Image: Beauty Myths; Beauty and Body Image: Eating Disorders; Comics; Film: Horror; Gender and Femininity: Motherhood; Gender and Femininity: Single/Independent Girl; Gender and Masculinity: Black Masculinity; Gender and Masculinity: Fatherhood; Gender and Masculinity: Metrosexual Male; Gender and Masculinity: White Masculinity; Heroes: Action and Super Heroes; Massively Multiplayer Online Role-Playing Games; Multi-User Dimensions; *Second Life*; Sports Media: Extreme Sports and Masculinity; Video Gaming: Representations of Femininity; Video Gaming: Violence; Virtual Community; Virtual Sex; Virtuality; Web 2.0; Wiki; Women's Magazines: Fashion; Women's Magazines: Lifestyle and Health

Further Readings

Alloway, Nola and Pam Gilbert. "Video Game Culture: Playing With Masculinity, Violence and Pleasure." In *Wired-Up: Young People and Electronic Media*, Sue Howard, ed. New York: Routledge, 1998.

Burrill, Derek. *Die Tryin': Video games, Masculinity, Culture*. New York: Peter Lang, 2008.

Kirkland, Ewan. "Masculinity in Video Games: The Gendered Gameplay of *Silent Hill*." *Camera Obscura*, v.24/2 (2009).

Kline, Stephen, Nick Dyer-Witheford, and Greig de Peuter. *Digital Play: The Interaction of Technology, Culture and Marketing*. Montreal, QB: McGill-Queen's University Press, 2003.

VIDEO GAMING: VIOLENCE

Since the 1980s, a primarily quantitative body of literature on gender and video game violence has explored both gender portrayals in violent video games and gender differences in the effects of violent games on players. In terms of textual analysis of story narratives in games, studies have assessed the relationship between character gender and violent behavior, on one hand, and character gender and the violence committed against them, on the other. In the media effects tradition, studies have examined gender differences in the impact of violent content on players' arousal, perceptions, attitudes, and aggressive or violent behaviors. Studies have also examined gender differences in choices to play violent games and in the actual aggressiveness of violent video game play. Because of the relative newness of video-gaming popularity, the effects research in gender and video game violence is still in its infancy, and results regarding violence effects and gender differences in effects remain inconclusive. This may be due both to the rapid changes in gaming technology and to the increasing sophistication of video-gaming research design. Because of these developments, some critics argue that it is unhelpful even to compare effects studies from the 1980s and 1990s to more recent research in this area.

Several content analyses have examined gender stereotyping in relation to violence in video games. A summary of the findings indicates that male characters, representing the majority of available characters in games, overwhelmingly are heroic leads, are more muscular and powerful than female characters, and have a greater number of weapons at their disposal. Female characters tend to be secondary characters and are depicted as weaker, more highly sexualized, and more scantily clothed. In filmed scenes (predominantly found at the beginnings of games), when female characters are violent, their violence is often linked to sexuality, whereas male characters' violence is visually dominated by muscularity.

Gender stereotypes abound in violent video games. Female characters are represented as highly sexualized; male characters possess exaggerated strength, are hypermasculine, are aggressive, and, with the exception of showing hostility, lack emotion. They are also less likely to display helping or nurturing qualities. One study found that the central role for male characters was "competitor," whereas females' central roles were "victim," "damsel in distress," or "evil obstacle" for the hero to overcome. The findings of these violent video game content analyses have remained fairly consistent over time and have been shown to be perceived by audiences. The findings regarding gender and violent representations in video games have also been consistently demonstrated in content analyses of gaming magazines, advertisements, and Websites.

As the popularity of video games and the level of their realistic violence have increased, so have the number of studies examining the effects of game violence. Findings are similar to results regarding the violent effects of other mass media. Some researchers have argued for strong effects, with repeated exposure to violent games linked to severe aggression and violence. Other studies have argued for limited, short-term, or no apparent behavioral effects. Gender differences in violent effects also remain inconclusive.

Studies have examined the short-term impact of gender and age on aggression, with studies finding that male college students become more aggressive after playing violent games than those watching nonviolent games, children who play violent games more likely to imitate those behaviors later in play settings, and adolescents with greater exposure to violent games generally are more hostile than those with lower levels of exposure. Playing violent games, as opposed to simply watching them, increases the impact level.

Other studies have concluded that playing violent video games, regardless of gender, was not in itself predictive of aggressive behavior in a laboratory setting. Thus, these studies question the premise that violent video game exposure causes violence. One meta-analysis of violent video effects studies, while unable to confirm a causal link, did show evidence of a correlation between aggression and violent game play. One study that examined correlations between violent acts, trait aggression, exposure to violent games, and family violence found that playing violent video games was not predictive of violent crime, whereas trait aggression, male gender, and a history of family violence were.

More recently, in order to account for inconclusive results regarding violent effects, studies have increasingly employed the General Aggression Model (GAM) to explain and explore the potential effects of violence in video games on gamers. This model examines media effects as a result of preexisting activated "scripts" or "schemas" that may shape both single-exposure, short-term effects and long-term effects on players' personalities or behaviors.

Although males, particularly adolescents, still make up the majority of gamers, females now make up 40 percent of the gamer audience. Studies on the impact of violent videos on female gamers is less well developed; however, some studies have replicated the link between exposure and increased levels of aggression in female gamers, with one meta-analysis finding no gender difference for aggressive outcomes. Studies have begun to examine the multiple pleasures female gamers experience in gaming in a way that begins to expand definitions of gender. Other studies examining the relationship between gender and aggressive video game play have found that male players tend to be more aggressive gamers than females. One study, however—which combined survey and behavioral data on more than 7,000 users of the massive multiple online (MMO) game *EverQuest* in order to examine gaming motivations, in-game behaviors, and offline characteristics—found results that defied common gender stereotypes, even those related to in-game aggression.

Effects research has also grown increasingly discriminate in research design. One study, for example, examining the relationship among user and opponent gender, opponent type, presence, and aggressive thoughts from violent video game play found that "females experience greater presence and more aggressive thoughts from game play when a gender match between self and game character exists" and when playing against a human versus a computer-generated opponent. Additionally, "playing as a female against a male opponent increases aggressive thoughts," whereas "playing as a male against a female opponent consistently and significantly decreases aggressive thoughts."

The body of gender and violence effects research that has explored the impact of first- versus third-person perspective suggests that, regardless of gender, first-person violent video games (first-person shooter, or FPS, games) are more likely to increase levels of aggressive thoughts in gamers than are third-person violent games. First-person violent games allow the player to embody and play as the character and are thus more likely to impact a player's aggressive feelings and thoughts. Studies have shown that technological advancements in modern video games also increase players' sense of "involvement" (physiological and self-reported arousal) and "presence" (the sense of moving through a nonmediated world and the ability to interact with objects in that world). These qualities are increased when playing as a character (first person) rather than playing with a character (third person). The results of these studies of higher-involvement or greater-presence games, however, although linked with increasing levels of arousal regardless of gender, have not been definitively linked either with greater levels of aggression or with gender differences in aggression.

Although a less examined area of video game research, at least one study of the effect of video game violence against women demonstrated that male players with short-term exposure to this content were more tolerant of real-life instances of sexual harassment than those not exposed. Long-term exposure of male players to video game violence was correlated both with greater tolerance of sexual harassment and with greater acceptance of the rape myth.

Susan Mackey-Kallis
Villanova University

See also Avatar; Desensitization Effect; Film: Horror; Gender and Masculinity: Black Masculinity; Gender and Masculinity: Fatherhood; Gender and Masculinity: Metrosexual Male; Gender and Masculinity: White Masculinity; Heroes: Action and Super Heroes; Massively Multiplayer Online Role-Playing Games; Multi-User Dimensions; Sports Media: Extreme Sports and Masculinity; Video Gaming: Representations of Femininity; Video Gaming: Representations of Masculinity; Violence and Aggression

Further Readings

Dill, K., B. Brown, and M. Collins. "Effects of Exposure to Sex-Stereotyped Video Game Characters on Tolerance of Sexual Harassment." *Journal of Experimental Social Psychology*, v.44/5 (2008).

Eastin, M. "Video Game Violence and the Female Game Player: Self- and Opponent Gender Effects on Presence and Aggressive Thoughts." *Human Communication Research*, v.32/3 (2006).

Eastin, M. S., R. Griffiths, and J. Lerch. "Beyond Shooter Games: How Game Environment, Game Type, and Competitor Influence Presence, Arousal and Aggression." Paper presented to the Communication and Technology Division of the Annual International Communication Association, New York, 2005.

Ferguson, C., S. Rueda, and A. Cruz. "Violent Video Games and Aggression: Causal Relationship or Byproduct of Family Violence and Intrinsic Violence Motivation?" *Criminal Justice and Behavior*, v.35/3 (2008).

Hutchinson, R. "Performing the Self: Subverting the Binary in Combat Games." *Games and Culture*, v.2/4 (2007).

Robinson, T., M. Callister, B. Clark, and J. Phillips. "Violence, Sexuality, and Gender Stereotyping: A Content Analysis of Official Video Game Web Sites." *Web Journal of Mass Communication Research*, v.131/17 (2008).

Scharrer, E. "Virtual Violence: Gender and Aggression in Video Game Advertisements." *Mass Communication and Society*, v.7/4 (2004).

Taylor, T. "Multiple Pleasures: Women and Online Gaming." *Convergence: The Journal of Research Into New Media Technologies*, v.9/1 (2003).

Williams, D., N. Yee, and S. Caplan. "Who Plays, How Much, and Why? Debunking the Stereotypical Gamer Profile." *Journal of Computer-Mediated Communication*, v.13/4 (2008).

VIOLENCE AND AGGRESSION

The extensive literature on gender differences in aggression and violence in media examines these differences both in media portrayals and in potential impact on audiences. These broad areas have been developed using a wide diversity of methods and theoretical perspectives and have examined a number of media formats and industries, including film, television, video games, magazines, Websites, advertising, entertainment programming, and journalism. Research into the effects of media violence and aggression has most often drawn on the following theoretical paradigms; the general aggression model (GAM), cultivation theory, uses and gratifications, priming, social learning theory, presumed influence theory, and third-person effects. Specifically in regard to gender issues in media effects, scholars have also used masculine ideology theory. A good deal of this research has focused on violent media's effects on children and adolescents due to evidence of their developmental vulnerability and the increased likelihood that they will seek out such media, particularly in the case of adolescent males and video gamers. Content analyses of gender differences in media portrayals of violence and aggression often draw on cultivation theory. In qualitative studies of gender and media portrayals of violence and aggression, theoretical frameworks used range from feminist backlash theory to masculinity ideology theory, Julia Kristeva's work on horror and the abject, Laura Mulvey's "male gaze" in cinema, Freudian and Lacanian psychoanalysis, and feminist film theory generally. Analyses of media portrayals have focused on gender differences in violence and aggressive behaviors and attitudes, as well as the gender of the victim and victimizer with special attention paid to violence against women, rape, the linking of sex and violence, and, more recently, scenarios of revenge upon or punishment of aggressive, violent, and/or sexual women.

The media effects literature related to violence has demonstrated that exposure to violent media influences aggression and violent behavior as well as aggressive thoughts, while increasing viewers' desensitization to violence. Research also shows that aggressive and violent individuals are more likely to seek out violent media and that viewers selectively expose themselves to violent and aggressive media. The research in this area has focused on both short-term and long-term effects. Short-term effects studies have examined (separately and together) the impact of priming (prior exposure to media violence and aggression) and the level of arousal (physiological response to stimulus media) on both imitation of aggressive behavior in post exposure settings and self-reported desensitization to violence. Research indicates that priming increases the short-term effects and that level of arousal from the stimulus media also impacts short-term effects, with more highly engaging or arousing violent or aggressive media increasing effects (as indicated in postexposure imitation and in postexposure self-reports). In the area of long-term exposure, effects have been demonstrated in the areas of desensitization and observational learning. Research indicates that repeated observational learning, where the media role models are rewarded for violent or aggressive behavior, results in self-reported aggressive imitation, behavioral intention, or attitudes that indicate that violence and/or aggression are effective for problem solving and conflict management. Research also indicates that heavy (as opposed to light) viewing of media violence also increases self-reported desensitization to violence and the overestimation of both

Media viewers who identify with characters who use violence to solve problems or who are rewarded or experience no penalty for violent behavior are more likely to develop beliefs that violence and aggression are effective problem solving tools in their real lives. (Photos.com)

real-life violence and the likelihood of becoming a victim of violence.

Results regarding gender differences in short-term and long-term effects of exposure to media violence and aggression are mixed; some studies show greater increase in short-term effects for males, while other studies show no difference. Selective exposure research indicates that some people, particularly males and especially adolescent males, are more likely to seek out violent or aggressive media content. Thus males, who are generally more likely to seek out violent media than females, are more likely to be primed for subsequent exposure. A number of studies have also found that contributing nonmedia factors, all of which are experiences by both males and females (although in varying degrees), such as real-life experience with violence, incarceration, and a history of family violence, correlate with observed imitative violence and self-reported violent and aggressive intentions, beliefs, and attitudes.

A summary of the media research in this area indicates that blanket statements about the strong effects of media violence and aggression are unwarranted. Instead, the research indicates limited effects in specific contexts, with specific audiences. Some audiences are more susceptible to media influence

based on such factors as gender, heavy media use, self-selection of violent and aggressive media, priming, level of arousal, and real-life exposure to violence and aggression. Thus, media depictions of violence vary in the level of risk they represent for shaping antisocial attitudes and behaviors, and gender is only one of a number of factors shaping effects.

Theoretical Models: Media Violence Affects Research

Researchers draw on several models and theoretical paradigms when examining gender difference in media effects. Although the general aggression model (GAM) was developed to account for human aggression generally, it has increasingly become employed in media effects research, because it explains both short- and long-term effects of violence and aggression by arguing that a variety of aggression "scripts" are potentially activated after viewing violent media and that these scripts are used by viewers to interpret the appropriateness or effectiveness of the violence portrayed. According to the theory, children and adolescents are particularly vulnerable to violent media effects, because scripts for interpreting violence are not as well developed in young people as they are in adults. Exposure to violent and aggressive media is thus more likely to influence their aggressive thoughts and behaviors. Regarding gender differences in media effects, to the extent that male viewers, particularly adolescents, are more likely to self-select violent or aggressive media, they are more likely to have highly developed scripts related to violence and aggression. What is not clear from the literature, however, is whether these scripts act as priming agents in each new exposure (thereby increasing the impact of violence or aggressive media on attitudes and behaviors) or, because their scripts are more highly developed, ultimately act to decrease the impact of violent media on males.

Another often cited theory applied to violent media content is Albert Bandura's social learning theory. This theory asserts that imitation and observational learning can lead to long-term effects from exposure to media violence. For example, viewers who identify with characters who use violence to solve problems or who are rewarded for violent or aggressive behavior are more likely to develop beliefs that violence and aggression are effective for real-life problem solving and that characters who are the recipients of violent behaviors deserve their fate. This impact, through observational learning, is increased when the aggressive or violent character is portrayed as popular, attractive, or powerful. The findings in this area are particularly troubling when coupled with content analyses of media portrayals that overwhelming demonstrate that, while males are predominantly both the aggressors and the victims, females are predominantly the victims of male violence and aggression.

Presumed influence theory and third-person effects theory argue that mass media have powerful, albeit indirect, effects on behaviors and attitudes. The third-person effect contends that people invoke a self-serving bias that views them in the most favorable light. Because of this bias, negative media messages are perceived as having a greater impact on others. Similarly, the presumed influence theory argues that each individual tends to believe that the media influence others but have no effect on him- or herself. Despite this, the theory explains why individuals, after viewing media content, will subsequently change attitudes or behaviors because of the presumed influence this content has on peers and society as a whole. For example, a male video gamer might believe that others will view the masculine and aggressive male video game characters as normative and ideal and may then attempt to adopt that personality, not because he or she believes it is ideal, but because others do.

Cultivation theory, developed by George Gerbner, argues that heavy media users (defined as those with more than four hours of exposure per day) are more likely to develop the "mean and scary world" syndrome and that increased levels of exposure to media violence increases desensitization to violence. Heavy viewers overestimate the level of violence in society (even when controlled for demographics regarding levels of crime activity in their own neighborhood) and overestimate the likelihood that they will be a victim of violence or aggression. In terms of violence desensitization, males who are heavy viewers of media violence, for example, are more likely to report believing in the rape myth—the idea that "she had it coming" or that "she asked for it"—and are more likely to perceive aggression as an acceptable, even an effective, conflict management tool.

Masculinity ideology theory explains that males, who internalize cultural standards for masculinity, draw on these standards in shaping their own behaviors and attitudes. In American society, these norms include toughness, independence, and sexual virility. Exposure to sexually promiscuous and aggressive media portrayals, for males, results in viewing these portrayals as normative while increasing the likelihood of adopting them. Research has demonstrated that heavy media users are more likely to exhibit traditional masculinist ideology. One experimental study that examined "the effects of exposure to television programming that contains both violent actions and macho portrayals of male characters on subsequent self-reports of aggression and hostility" showed that "those exposed to a violent and hypermasculine television program had a larger increase in reports of aggression and hostility compared to those exposed to a nonviolent, hypermasculine television program. Self-reports of higher levels of hypermasculinity prior to exposure led to larger increases in aggression and hostility after exposure."

Uses and gratification research, which attempts to understand how audiences use media and the gratifications they receive from it, argues that viewers' media uses and gratifications may mediate the impact of media exposure. Using this paradigm, for example, one study of gender differences in the impact of violent and aggressive media examined how individual viewer characteristics—such as locus of control, experience with crime, involvement, perceived realism, and prior exposure to television violence—interacted with motivation to explain these gender differences. They found that for males, motivation was a much more important predictor of aggression, whereas for women background factors such as locus of control and experience with crime predicted aggression.

Theoretical Frameworks: Gendered and Sexual Violence in Media Research

Various theoretical paradigms have been used in qualitative analyses of portrayals of gendered violence and aggression in mass media, predominantly film.

Freudian and Lacanian psychoanalytical theory has been a central theoretical paradigm for the analysis of gendered and sexual violence in cinema. The work of both Sigmund Freud and Jacques Lacan has been used by Laura Mulvey, in her development of the idea of the "male gaze" in cinema, and by Christian Metz, in his development of a general theory of film spectatorship. Lacan postulates that the child (male or female) experiences himself simultaneously as an individual and as an object of others' gaze when, for the first time, he recognizes himself in the mirror as separate from the mother. This mirror phase, and the newfound object/subject relationship, shapes the child's experience with looking for the rest of his life. In cinema, Metz argues, the child's (male's or female's) act of identification with herself as subject is replaced in film viewing by the act of identifying not with the protagonist of the film directly but with herself (the ego) in the pure act of perception. Mulvey argued that in mainstream cinema this looking, regardless of the sex of the spectator or the film protagonist, is a "male looking," which drives the narrative of the film. She argued that there are actually three gazes operative in cinema: the camera shooting the profilmic event, the characters' gazes at each other in the film, and the spectator's gaze at the film. All of these are coded "male," with the "male" spectator/camera/characters as active and the female characters as passive or coded for strong erotic pleasure as the object of the male gaze, which is either voyeuristic (a distant look) or fetishistic (an intimate look). In the Lacanian mirror phase, as the male child realizes his separation from the mother, he also simultaneously realizes the need to compete with the father for her love and fears castration by the father for this illicit love (Freud's Oedipal complex). Freud explains that as the male child learns to identify with the father, patriarchy, and the symbolic order, he also learns to reject the mother. In doing so, his fear of father castration is projected onto the feminine because, by lacking a phallus, she is already castrated, thus representing loss. To assuage or cover over the fear of this loss and the fear of the feminine as potentially castrating, the woman in film either is punished or becomes an object of either fetishized or voyeuristic desire.

Many critics assert that Alfred Hitchcock exploits this Freudian complex brilliantly in such films as *Rear Window* (1954), *Psycho* (1960), and *Marnie* (1964). Critics argue that it is also a central element of film noir and detective films from the 1930s and 1940s, which often portray a castrating or femme

fatale figure who is an object of fear and voyeuristic or fetishistic desire but who ultimately must be punished, contained, or killed. Modern noir examples include *Fatal Attraction* (1987) and *Basic Instinct* (1992). Other manifestations of this framework are the "rape revenge dramas" prevalent in hardcore pornography and soft-core male adolescent action adventure films, in which a woman avenging her rape drives the narrative. This revenge, however, links sex and violence in problematic ways, because she first lures her victim with sexual overtures and then often kills him savagely during the act of sex. Examples of films that employ this strategy are *Monster* (2003), based on the real-life female serial killer Aileen Wuornos, Clint Eastwood's *Sudden Impact* (1983), and the film *I Spit on Your Grave* (2010).

Examining the violence against women in detective and slasher film genres, critics have also often drawn on feminist theorist Julia Kristeva's notion of the abject and the "clean a proper body." In the slasher film and detective genres, and often in the science fiction and the television crime genre as well, women, gays, and minorities are associated with the nonsymbolic and possess "messy" or "unclean" bodies, whereas white males, aligned with patriarchy, law, and the symbolic, are associated with clean and proper bodies. The horror genre articulates our repulsion and fascination when "insides come out" (bodies as the abject), while at the same time presenting sexually active women needing to be punished by horrific violation of their bodies (women as abject). The male killer in the slasher films is associated with the abject feminine and is ultimately, like them, punished, whereas the virginal last girl, "the hero," becomes associated with the masculine and is a source of identification and triumph, particularly for adolescent males. Examples of films that employ versions of this script are *The Silence of the Lambs* (1991), *Psycho*, *Dressed to Kill* (1980), and Clint Eastwood's *Dirty Harry* films. In the science fiction genre, the female monster is often presented as castrating, all-consuming, a "toothed vagina," and dangerous in both her procreative and sexual power. Examples are the *Alien* and *Aliens* film series. One critic, examining the prime-time television show *Law & Order: Special Victims Unit*, demonstrated how this show, because of its focus on crimes of sexual assault, provides a contradictory blend of feminist messages while remaining squarely within the historically masculine detective genre. In particular, in the analysis of episodes centered on the family and crimes committed by women, it is argued that depictions of female criminals and "feminine" qualities in other characters re-create the idea of the "monstrous maternal."

Feminist backlash theory employs a sociological rather than a psychological framework to understand violence against women in film and television. The theory argues that the 1960s civil rights, feminist, and gay movements led to white heterosexual men increasingly imagining themselves as the victims of a system designed to reward these marginalized groups at their expense. Media critics have examined how this "crisis in white masculinity" has been portrayed in popular media, with particular attention to white characters' misogyny and backlash violence against women, gays, and minorities. Some recent films that have spoken to the idea of white masculinity in crisis include Clint Eastwood's *Dirty Harry* films, Michael Douglas's character in *Falling Down* (1993), and *Fight Club* (1999). This ideology is also exhibited in the rap lyrics of Eminem and the "white boy pain" of singers such as Ben Folds.

Film critics have argued that there is a backlash in contemporary films against the "crisis in masculinity" and the feminist backlash articulated in media in the 1970s and 1980s. Since the early 1990s, a growing number of films present female protagonists who seek justice or revenge against men or against patriarchy more generally. Examples include *Thelma and Louise* (1991) and *Blue Steel* (1989). Despite the empowering quality of these films for women, critics argue that the female protagonists' violence or aggression is contained and that they are demonized, destroyed, captured, or killed. Although these films move into territories traditionally reserved for the masculine (the road trip/buddy film and the outlaw and crime genre) and provide challenges to the "male gaze" in cinema, they remain deeply controversial and problematic as answers to the unending cycle of media portrayals of violence against women.

Susan Mackey-Kallis
Villanova University

See also Avatar; Cultivation Theory; Desensitization Effect; Film: Horror; Gender and Masculinity: Black Masculinity; Gender and Masculinity: Fatherhood; Gender and Masculinity: Metrosexual Male; Gender and Masculinity: White Masculinity; Heroes: Action and Super Heroes; Male Gaze; Massively Multiplayer Online Role-Playing Games; Multi-User Dimensions; Mulvey, Laura; Quantitative Content Analysis; Social Learning Theory; Sports Media: Extreme Sports and Masculinity; Video Gaming: Representations of Femininity; Video Gaming: Representations of Masculinity; Video Gaming: Violence

Further Readings

Carl, E. "News Portrayal of Violence and Women." *American Behavioral Scientist*, v.46/12 (2003).

Cooper, Brenda. "'Chicks Flicks' as Feminist Texts: The Appropriation of the Male Gaze in *Thelma and Louise*." *Women's Studies in Communication*, v.23/3 (2000).

Cuklanz, L. and S. Moorti. "Television's 'New' Feminism: Prime-Time Representations of Women and Victimization." *Critical Studies in Media Communication*, v.23/4 (2006).

Franco, Judith. "Gender, Genre and Female Pleasure in the Contemporary Revenge Narrative: *Baise Moi* and *What It Feels Like for a Girl*." *Quarterly Review of Film and Video*, v.21/1 (2004).

Gunter, Barrie. "Media Violence." *American Behavioral Scientist*, v.51/8 (2008).

Haridakis, Paul. "Men, Women, and Televised Violence: Predicting Viewer Aggression in Male and Female Television Viewers." *Communication Quarterly*, v.54/2 (2006).

Johnson, Merri Lisa. "Gangster Feminism: The Feminist Cultural Work of HBO's *The Sopranos*." *Feminist Studies*, v.33/2 (2007).

Kilker, Robert. "All Roads Lead to the Abject: The Monstrous Feminine and Gender Boundaries in Stanley Kubrick's *The Shining*." *Literature Film Quarterly*, v.34/1 (2006).

Paige, Linda. "Wanted Dead or Alive: The Female Outlaw and Callie Khouri's *Thelma and Louise*." *American Studies Journal*, v.50 (2007).

Reich, Nina. "Towards a Rearticulation of Women-as-Victims: A Thematic Analysis of the Construction of Women's Identities Surrounding Gendered Violence." *Communication Quarterly*, v.50/3–4 (2002).

Scharrer, Eric. "Men, Muscles, and Machismo: The Relationship Between Television Violence Exposure and Aggression and Hostility in the Presence of Hypermasculinity." *Media Psychology*, v.3/2 (2001).

Ta, Lynn. "Hurt So Good: *Fight Club*, Masculine Violence, and the Crisis of Capitalism." *The Journal of American Culture*, v.29/3 (2006).

VIRAL ADVERTISING AND MARKETING

Viral advertising and marketing constitute a fast-growing phenomenon that can cast light on communication and media. It is generally agreed that the term *viral marketing* was coined by two venture capitalists Steve Jurvetson and Tim Draper in 1996 when they described the marketing strategy for Hotmail's free e-mail service. The tactic was that every e-mail originated from a Hotmail e-mail account would have a message and link tagged at the end to encourage recipients to open a free Hotmail e-mail account. Hotmail's subscribers grew exponentially. After one and a half years, Hotmail had more than 12 million subscribers. The result was remarkable, considering that Hotmail had spent only $500,000 on advertising for two years. Another company, Juno, spent $20 million to recruit a third as many subscribers.

Because the field of advertising and viral marketing is relatively new and rapidly developing, several definitions exist. Broadly, viral marketing is defined as a word-of-mouth communication that is disseminated from consumers to those within their social networks, such as acquaintances, colleagues, friends, and family. Network effects, another component, refer to the benefits consumers gain by passing on a communication that attracts others. For example, a consumer passing along information about Skype (a software program that allows economical phone calls over the Internet) to other potential consumers can have positive network effects, because the original consumer can benefit from the growth of Skype (for example, by becoming able to connect with more people through Skype). With this component, viral marketing is defined as word-of-mouth communication disseminated from consumers to consumers that generates positive network effects. Additionally, computer-mediated communications have been used to qualify viral marketing as word-of-mouth communication from consumers to consumers through computer-mediated communications and online environments.

Although the advertising component in viral marketing was suggested shortly after the term *viral marketing* was coined, the academic definition of viral advertising did not appear until 2006. Viral advertising can be different from viral marketing, with viral marketing a more comprehensive marketing strategy that consists of multiple components and viral advertising a more specific, online distribution method for advertisements. In particular, viral advertising as a distribution method emphasizes identifiable sponsors (originators of the content can be identified by consumers), the nature of the viral content (provocative to evoke consumers' motivation to pass along the viral content), and the online environment. In addition, viral advertising is defined as unpaid peer-to-peer communication. Even though the original viral content may be created with a budget, the viral distribution of the content should be largely unpaid.

A variety of viral advertising and marketing formats have emerged, including e-mails, social networking Websites such as Facebook and Myspace, video-sharing Websites such as YouTube, blogs, and microblogs such as Twitter. The strategy has been adopted by companies across industries (ranging from the food and beverage industry to nonprofit organizations) and companies of different sizes (both Fortune 500 companies and non–Fortune 500 companies). The majority of viral advertising seems to use sex appeal, nudity, and violence, more so than traditional advertising. Also, the nature of viral content differs by industry; the pharmaceutical industry, for example, uses more sex appeal and nudity but less violence. In addition, non–Fortune 500 companies seem to apply viral advertising more often than Fortune 500 companies.

Viral advertising and marketing have been perceived as effective. In 2002, BMW created a series of short films promoting its products. The films were strictly distributed through viral marketing via the online environment. They attracted nearly 55 million viewers and averaged 80,000 daily downloads two years after release. In 2006, Unilever initiated a 75-second viral video online titled *Dove Evolution*. Within 10 days, it had generated 2.3 million views, which was three times more than the 30-second advertisement aired during the Super Bowl had garnered.

Viral advertising and marketing have advantages over traditional methods. From a financial perspective, viral advertising and marketing are inexpensive compared to traditional advertising and marketing, because the product is promoted voluntarily, from consumer to consumer. Also, the diffusion can be exponential, reaching a large number of audiences within a short period of time. Furthermore, the viral method may make it possible to reach more target audiences, because advertising is disseminated through consumers' own social networks. The audiences reached through personal channels may be more interested in the product than those who are reached through mass media. Additionally, the volunteer, peer-to-peer transmission may enhance the effects of the marketing and advertising because it is perceived as more trustworthy, personal, and relevant.

However, viral advertising and marketing have risks and disadvantages. One of them is the relative lack of control compared to traditional marketing and advertising. Once the viral distribution starts, marketers and advertisers lose control over where the content is distributed. Moreover, the viral content can be distorted and filtered. It can be misused and abused relatively easily to generate negative impacts, and the negativity can be distributed exponentially as well. Additionally, viral advertising and marketing heavily depend on consumers' motivation to disseminate the viral content. If consumers lack motivation to distribute the content, the content can die through lack of distribution. Finally, there are legal and ethical concerns about viral advertising and marketing, such as content regulation, consumer exploitation, and privacy invasion.

To have a successful viral advertising and marketing effort, several elements should be considered. First, the viral content should be free to consumers; for example, the short films from BMW and Dove are free to download, and the e-mail service provided by Hotmail is free to register. Second, the transmission from consumers to consumers should be easy; it takes only a click of a button to pass videos from BMW and Dove to another person. Third, the content should evoke common motivations that facilitate viral distribution; the BMV videos were perceived as cool and desirable to share with others. Also, the content of viral advertising should be provocative, to the extent the advertisement itself becomes a desirable product. Fourth, it should take advantage of consumers' social networks; Hotmail embedded its promotion in their e-mails, which were sent through and among consumers' social networks. Fifth, viral content should use others' resources; the Dove video was uploaded to the video-sharing Website YouTube for dissemination. Last, viral advertising and marketing should have scalability, meaning that the marketers and advertisers should be prepared for the potential exponential growth; for example, Hotmail's e-mail server had to be able to handle the rapid growth of its subscribers to prevent the e-mail service from becoming slow and unstable.

Gender has been an influential factor in media representations, uses, and effects, but investigations into the role of gender in viral advertising and marketing are scarce. Extant research examining the role of gender in viral advertising and marketing indicates that gender is a factor that warrants investigation. Research has revealed that, although there are no differences between men and women in terms of the number of e-mails they receive, women are more likely to pass along received e-mails than men. Furthermore, gender differences in the likelihood of forwarding e-mails are affected by the type of viral content, the source of that viral content, and the context of the viral content. It has been shown that when viral content evokes fear and disgust, men are more likely than women to forward the viral content to others. However, research also suggests that the emotional responses of fear felt by women are stronger than those felt by men. As a result, women are more likely to forward the fear-evoking viral content to other women in an attempt to alert them about the perceived danger.

Gender differences are also discovered in effects of the viral content source. Research indicates that men are more likely to forward viral content that comes from a negative source (a source that is not necessarily attractive or trustworthy but is perceived to be credible through the source's experience) than a positive source (a source that is perceived to be trustworthy but not necessarily expert). Conversely, women are more likely to pass along viral content that comes from a positive source than content from a negative source. When it comes to the context of viral content, women are more likely to forward viral content that is high in emotions as opposed to content low in emotions; no such difference is observed for men.

Additionally, research on the content of viral advertising suggests that it is more likely to use sex appeal, nudity, and violence than television advertising is. Given the history of women's sexual objectification, victim portrayals in violence, men's perpetrator portrayals in violence, and preferences for violent and sexual media content, it is possible that the amount of sex, nudity, and violence in viral advertising will contribute to gender differences in the content, usage, and effects of viral advertising and marketing. Future research should keep examining how gender is represented in viral advertising and marketing, how gender influences consumers' participation in viral advertising and marketing, and how gender interacts with the effects of viral advertising and marketing. Also, research needs to investigate how viral advertising and marketing, in turn, influence, construct, and maintain gender in society.

Ming Lei
Washington State University

See also Advertising; Audiences: Producers of New Media; Blogs and Blogging; New Media; Social Media; Social Networking Sites: Facebook; Social Networking Sites: Myspace; Tropes; Twitter; Virtual Community; Web 2.0; Wiki; YouTube

Further Readings

Chiu, Hung-Chang, et al. "Viral Marketing: A Study of E-Mail Spreading Behavior Across Gender." *Journal of Website Promotion*, v.2/3 (2007).

Dobele, Angela, et al. "Why Pass on Viral Messages? Because They Connect Emotionally." *Business Horizons*, v.50 (2007).

Phelps, Joseph E, et al. "Viral Marketing or Electronic Word-of-Mouth Advertising: Examining Consumer Responses and Motivations to Pass Along Email." *Journal of Advertising Research*, v.44/4 (2004).

Porter, Lance and Guy Golan. "From Subservient Chickens to Brawny Men: A Comparison of Viral Advertising to Television Advertising." *Journal of Interactive Advertising*, v.6/2 (2006).

Vilpponen, Antti, et al. "Electronic Word-of-Mouth in Online Environments: Exploring Referral Network Structure and Adoption Behavior." *Journal of Interactive Advertising*, v.6/2 (2006).

Wilson, Ralph F. "The Six Simple Principles of Viral Marketing." *Web Marketing Today* (February 1, 2005). http://www.wilsonweb.com/wmt5/viral-principles-clean.htm (Accessed November 2010).

Woerndl, Maria, et al. "Internet-Induced Marketing Techniques: Critical Factors in Viral Marketing Campaigns." *International Journal of Business Science and Applied Management*, v.3/1 (2008).

VIRTUAL COMMUNITY

The concept of *virtual community* uses the metaphor of a community of interaction that exists in geographically delineated space to describe a relationship between collectives (groups of individuals) who are physically based in unrelated geographical locations, although there is no consensus beyond this among Internet scholars regarding the actual meaning of the term. Indeed, there is dispute over whether the term is a viable description for the kinds of interactions that occur between individuals in virtual space, particularly with the word *community*. Virtual communities can have social, professional, and political dimensions and frequently combine various aspects of two or more dimensions in their application, existing within imaginary or asynchronous spaces in the public sphere of discourse.

Since the development of the Internet and its subsequent commercialization in the 1990s, virtual communities have flourished most effectively online. As a result, the definition of a virtual community itself is considered problematic, and hence the current association with online interactions between individuals and/or groups of individuals. The term *virtual community* has frequently been interchanged since 1990 with the related term *online communities*. This entry will outline the history and definitions understood by the term *virtual communities*, from a practical as well as a theoretical perspective. It examines the major arenas of virtual community relevant to gender and media, with emphasis on the kinds of gender representation and community use that have become prevalent in the early 21st century. This article also differentiates between gender use and gender representation in male and female uses of virtual communities in terms of mainstream and gay, lesbian, bisexual, transsexual/transgender, queer/questioning (GLBTQ) usage of virtual spaces.

Definition and Theoretical Models

Virtual communities were identified before 1980 by a number of different scholars and social analysts, including Barry Wellman, whose 1979 term *nonlocal communities* identified social support networks that existed outside the immediate physical space of a geographically defined community. Virtual communities accessible through Usenet newsgroups in 1979, along with The WELL, started in 1985, are the first identifiable communities that existed in early cyberspace. The term *virtual community* itself was becoming active in the discourse around such communities. In 1993, Howard Rheingold defined virtual communities as social networks that interact through computer-mediated communications (CMCs). Through the work of Benedict Anderson, they also were frequently linked to concepts of national and other "imagined" community groupings. Virtual communities, while always bonded by some variety of social ties, are frequently based on work or other formal group activities. This has been particularly true since the late 1990s, when telecommuting became a viable option for corporations wanting to give their employees flexibility in their work/family and work/home lives. This also has become important not just for working mothers but also for fathers desiring more face-to-face time with their children.

A term that is often used in place of the problematic *virtual* is *Web community*, which, like online community, situates the relationship between participants on an Internet site. Virtual communities by any name, however, frequently involve offline interaction among members in addition to their online relationships—one of the reasons remote or home office options in corporate settings will often require some manner of synchronous communication, either through regular online or face-to-face meetings between remote employees. Similarly, online education courses and online business ventures construct aspects of virtual communities into their design to promote feelings of attachment and commitment both among participants and between participants and the organization or Website.

Social groupings in virtual communities form in the metaphorically named virtual spaces of the Internet and can consist of synchronous groups (whose communication occurs at the same time) or asynchronous groups (whose communication does not occur at the same time) or combinations of the two. In 2001 Greg Urban discussed interpretive communities and social imaginaries linked by modes of circulation forming communities, and in 2002 Michael Warner took those communities one step further, using the term *public* to address the relationship of members of a collective through a text. Both of these approaches to online communication provide yet another avenue to understanding the kinds of asynchronous relationships intended by the early use of the term *virtual community*, and both focus on the role of text as central to the relationships of members of these communities. For the remainder of this entry, virtual community will be used predominantly in the sense of an online community, though this is done with the understanding that a virtual community can exist in spheres beyond the Internet and the identities of members of such communities share aspects of all of these concepts of communities and publics.

Business-Focused Virtual Communities and Web 2.0

An inevitable dimension of virtual communities has been their potential for producing income for a particular business interest. Online communities, therefore, are frequently constructed for many businesses, often taking the form of online forums for interactions between consumers of particular products, or focused on members of specific industries. Connections between members of such communities can be very loosely based, as in online forums for interacting with customer support departments or online job-searching forums where members share industry information about, for example, the status of job searches within a particular industry. By the early 2000s, the label of Web 2.0 began to be applied to online forums of interaction where the members themselves could shape the content and direction of interaction.

Web 2.0, first identified in 2002, has been identified with a transition in CMC technology to a phase whereby the participants shape the space far beyond the designs of the site designers. Prime examples of Web 2.0 sites of interaction include Friendster, founded in 2002; LinkedIn and Facebook, both founded in 2003; and Myspace and YouTube, both founded in 2006. The interactive nature of all these sites has created spaces where smaller communities can host themselves, though a focus on popular culture or other specific social categories functions as a common denominator tying members of the community together.

Anonymity

The potential for anonymity has always been an important constituent in participation in online communities. Chat rooms and bulletin boards dominated early virtual interactions, primarily because of limitations in bandwidth and online technology. The best-known chat rooms for social interaction during the 1990s were those situated in the America Online (AOL) network. These virtual rooms were an active place for the meeting of persons in an anonymous setting for social interaction, as popularized by films such as *You've Got Mail* (1998), which featured Tom Hanks and Meg Ryan as New York City residents who meet in an AOL chat room and develop a romantic relationship. Participants in chat-room sessions could use whatever identifiers they chose as their online identities, which also allowed them to identify themselves as anyone and anything they chose, including alternative ages, genders, sexualities, and other culturally identifying features. Studies of chat-room interactions in the 1990s often focused on, or at least noted, the importance of anonymity in constructing an identity for social interactions, investigating the degree to which individuals could pass as members of the opposite sex as a result. Such virtual communities can be placed under the general category of social support communities.

Like business-focused virtual communities, social support communities tend to focus on something the participants have in common, ranging from illnesses such as cancer to parenting to mainstream and GLBTQ social interactions. Hence, dating sites like Match.com fall under this category. Virtual and online communities are acknowledged to be major resources for queer and GLBTQ communities, particularly for individuals who live in rural or secluded areas. Social support communities have existed in virtual connection far longer than the Internet has been in existence, but they consolidated in online formats by the early 1990s using the chat-room format.

By the early 2000s, chat rooms had given way to virtual worlds, the best known of which has been *Second Life*, where participants design an avatar, or virtual personality, through which they interact with other *Second Life* participants. *Second Life* has been called a massively multiplayer online role-playing game (MMORPG), though it differs in its lack of structured game play from more traditional MMORPGs, such as *World of Warcraft*, in a number of respects. Notably, *Second Life* encourages participants to change the virtual environment to suit their own interests (including adding buildings, for example).

Virtual Interactions and Relationships

As asynchronous Internet-based communication and communities grew during the late 1990s, it became a question whether such interactions and virtual relationships would become a central aspect of public interaction among residents of technologically developed countries. Predictions from recent studies conclude that the degree to which people are interconnected in this way is going to increase substantially. Not only adults but also children and teens, across the United States and the European Union, are actively participating in online and virtual worlds at a rate of approximately 17 percent, according to Sonia Livingstone and her colleagues. Participants frequently choose personas or avatars to represent themselves in some visual form. These visual representations range from symbols and iconography to digital photographs of themselves or some aspect of their personal lives. Depending on the nature of the community, members can be either named and known to one another or, at the other extreme, be entirely anonymous. One representation of anonymous interaction is the type that takes place in chat rooms, social spaces defined by specific common interests or goals where participants can meet others with similar interests or goals. Interactions in the chat room tend to be bound by "netiquette," the unofficial rules of courtesy that guide virtual communication in much the same way that norms of communication guide interactions between members of a community in face-to-face interactions.

Much like face-to-face interactions and communities, virtual interactions and communities are inflected and bounded by gender stereotypes and assumptions. In the earliest days of the Internet, the masculine associations of technology and computer programming meant that women were not assumed to have the vocabulary or technological skills to interact online when part of the requirement for active participation meant having the knowledge to use computer languages and coding. The association of women's modes of communication with emotional expression also created, and continues to create (although to a much lesser degree today), a social barrier to women's participation in public forums. Similar constraints and stereotypes of gendered discourse place barriers on women's participation, where in order to participate successfully women, in mixed gender groups, must adopt masculine modes of communication.

Despite such barriers, by the mid-1990s women began to take advantage of the opportunities for interaction in order to support women's issues. Similarly, GLBT groups found that they could create virtual niche communities that supported the formation of virtual support groups. Such communities have particular importance in rural communities, where access to support networks can be difficult to obtain, but gender differences in communication are as relevant to virtual relationships and interactions as they are to face-to-face relationships and interactions.

Gender Differences in Virtual Community

Because of the association of technology, particularly computer-related technology, with masculine stereotypes and associations, it is necessary to consider the role that gender differences play in the use, and construction, of virtual communities. Research into gender differences across virtual community platforms, particularly social networking and e-mail, has shown consistent differences in both use of and comfort level with Internet communication. This is representative of similar trends that have been found in face-to-face and other synchronous communication forms.

Women, acculturated more than men to respond to nonverbal cues and having higher degrees of differentiation in emotional responses within communication behaviors, write far longer e-mails and have generally been found to be less comfortable communicating asynchronously. Men, who are acculturated to more instrumentally driven and less emotional expression in their verbal and written communication, and who are trained to have more sophisticated vocabularies involving technology, tend to have higher comfort zones and higher levels of use of virtual, asynchronous communication. Such communication differences are also mirrored in the use of online communication and virtual communities among children and teens: Although there is little overall difference between boys and girls in children's and teens' use of the Internet, boys are seen to participate in a wider range of online activities, including creating avatars and using social networking sites, than are girls, according to Livingstone.

Online groups formed around diseases or health concerns constitute one of the most common types of communities where adults seek support. Data from research on online health communities seem to support a lower level of gender difference in this online communication, but such findings need to be approached with caution, given that men and women are known to use the Internet differently, which in turn affects their participation and interaction levels in virtual and online communities. This caution is supported by a study of teen and adolescent use of online communities and communication strategies conducted by Justine Cassell and colleagues in 2006, which supports a widely held view that men and women, and boys and girls, communicate, both online and offline, using gendered modalities, but that in mixed interaction, not attending to cultural differences, gender is not a predictor of power dynamics and leadership roles. Despite the more positive connotations of the potential for self-construction in virtual space, both the fear and the reality of misrepresentation of age and gender indicators have been raised. The possibility of abuse of minors, particularly sexual abuse and manipulation, has highlighted potential dangers in online encounters, and parental controls over Internet use have thus become an important social issue.

J. Meryl Krieger
Indiana University–Purdue University
Indianapolis

See also Avatar; Blogs and Blogging; Cyberdating; Cyberspace and Cyberculture; Cyborg; Massively Multiplayer Online Role-Playing Games; Multi-User Dimensions; Online New Media: GLBTQ Identity; Online New Media: Transgender Identity; *Second Life*; Social Media; Social Networking Sites: Facebook; Social Networking Sites: Myspace; Web 2.0; Wiki; YouTube

Further Readings

Anderson, Benedict. *Imagined Communities: Reflections on the Origin and Spread of Nationalism*, Rev. ed. London: Verso, 1991.

Cassell, Justine, David Huffaker, Dona Tversky, and Kim Ferriman. "The Language of Online Leadership: Gender and Youth Engagement on the Internet." *Developmental Psychology*, v.42/3 (2006).

Gray, Mary L. *Out in the Country: Youth, Media, and Queer Visibility in Rural America.* New York: New York University Press, 2009.

Horrigan, John B. *Online Communities: Networks That Nurture Long-Distance Relationships and Local Ties.* Washington, DC: Pew Internet and American Life Project, 2001.

Lenhart, Amanda, Kristen Purcell, Aaron Smith, and Kathryn Zickuhr. *Social Media and Mobile Internet Use Among Teens and Young Adults.* Washington, DC: Pew Research Center, 2010. http://www.pewinternet.org/Reports/2010/Social-Media-and-Young-Adults.aspx (Accessed November 2010).

Livingstone, Sonia, Leslie Haddon, Anke Görzig, and Kjartan Ólafsson. *Risks and Safety on the Internet: The Perspective of European Children.* London: EU Kids Online Project/London School of Economics and Political Science, 2010.

Powazek, Derek M. *Designing for Community: The Art of Connecting Real People in Virtual Places.* Indianapolis, IN: New Riders, 2002.

Preece, Jenny. *Online Communities: Designing Usability, Supporting Sociability.* West Sussex, UK: Wiley & Sons, 2000.

Rainie, Lee and Janna Quitney Anderson. *The Future of the Internet IV Report: The Future of Social Relations.* Washington, DC: Pew Research Center/Elon University, 2010. http://www.elon.edu/e-web/predictions/expertsurveys/2010survey/default.xhtml (Accessed November 2010).

Rainie, Lee and Janna Quitney Anderson. *The Future of the Internet IV Report: Millennials Expected to Make Online Sharing in Networks a Lifelong Habit.* Washington, DC: Pew Research Center/Elon University, 2010. http://www.elon.edu/e-web/predictions/expertsurveys/2010survey/default.xhtml (Accessed November 2010).

Rheingold, Howard. *The Virtual Community: Homesteading on the Electronic Frontier,* Rev. ed. Cambridge, MA: MIT Press, 2000.

Ridings, Catherine M. and David Gefen. "Virtual Community Attraction: Why People Hang Out Online." *Journal of Computer-Mediated Communication,* v.10/1 (2004/2006 online).

Shade, Leslie Regan. *Gender and Community in the Social Construction of the Internet.* Digital Formations Series 1, Steve Jones, ed. New York: Peter Lang, 2002.

Urban, Greg. *Metaculture: How Culture Moves Through the World.* Foreword by Benjamin Lee. Minneapolis: University of Minnesota Press, 2001.

Warner, Michael. *Publics and Counterpublics.* New York: Zone Books, 2002.

Wellman, Barry and Barry Leighton. "Networks, Neighborhoods, and Communities: Approaches to the Study of the Community Question." *Urban Affairs Quarterly,* v.14/3 (1979).

VIRTUAL SEX

Sex and technology have likely been intertwined since humans recognized that they could use tools on themselves. Yet with the advent of new communication technologies, people have, unsurprisingly, devoted considerable interest to the notion of virtual sex. Despite its seeming simplicity of definition, virtual sex encompasses a wide variety of practices, ranging from simple masturbation with an accompanying fantasy to the use of sex robots. However, when most speak of virtual sex, they are describing the practice of sex mediated through machinery or software. There are three main modes of virtual sex: textual/image-based, mechanical, and interface-driven.

Textual/Image-Based Virtual Sex

It is often said that the largest sexual organ is the human brain. One can stimulate another through the imagination and therefore through words, and when this occurs it is known as cybersex. There have long been Internet chat rooms dedicated to cybersex. In such rooms, individuals describe what they would be doing to the other if he or she were present. There are other types of virtual sex that bridge the textual elements of cybersex with "point of view" (POV) pornography. One such program is VirtualFem, which incorporates artificial intelligence with sexual commands and video. However, compared to textual cybersex with an actual person, the artificial intelligence seems stilted and uninteresting.

Another aspect of virtual sex is a practice referred to as "sexting," or sending sexually explicit texts and images to another individual, generally through cell phones. This has recently been in the media because teenagers have been sending images of themselves to others, making them subject to child pornography laws. Also included in image-based virtual sex are sexual activities that take place between avatars in virtual reality environments such as *Second Life*, which can also incorporate voice-over-IP chat as well as text-based chat.

At its heart, these forms of cybersex retain their roots in the love letters and phone sex lines of previous generations. What distinguishes cybersex from its predecessors is the ability to participate anonymously with one or more individuals who are likewise seeking similar sexual stimulation. While phone sex lines are generally operated on a pay-per-call basis and the exchange of love letters generally necessitated a relationship, digital cybersex can circumvent these barriers. Moreover, a major draw for practitioners of cybersex is that they need not be who they are in real life. For example, a male can have virtual sex as a female, animal, or mythical creature in the digital realm.

Mechanical Virtual Sex

Another strand of virtual sex focuses on tricking the body into thinking that it is participating in sexual activity through the use of machinery and POV pornography. Some of these programs include the Virtual Sex Machine and Real Touch. However, all of this could just as easily be accomplished using a dildo, vibrator, or synthetic vaginal sleeve while watching POV pornography. Because of the ubiquity of digital cameras and camcorders, POV pornography is hardly novel anymore, and there are countless amateur POV videos online.

While the Virtual Sex Machine and Real Touch rely on the illusion of an active participant in the sexual encounter, other forms of virtual sex take a more strictly mechanical approach. Synthetic sex dolls have a long history, although mainly as gag gifts. However, these have become more sophisticated and expensive, costing thousands of dollars. Some, such as the RealDoll, are equipped for both men and women, while others, such as the CybOrgasMatrix, are only female. These synthetic sex dolls come equipped with functional genitalia and other orifices. There are sex machines geared toward women, which consist of a dildo attached to an oscillating machine that can be controlled by wireless access or remote control. However, both the sex dolls and these sex machines simply offer methods of technologically enhanced masturbation as opposed to true virtual sex.

Interface-Driven Virtual Sex

Despite the previous advancements that fall under the general rubric of virtual sex, those that come closest to embodying the idea of virtual sex are interface-driven models that allow for a more direct mediation between two (or more) individuals, such as interface-based products like Sinulator and HighJoy. For example, Sinulator allows control of a vibrator that is connected over the Internet to a synthetic vagina, while HighJoy simply allows an individual to control another's vibrator online. The vibrator is given a name, and anyone with that name can connect and control the vibrator. This is often the case with women who perform sexual acts on webcam. There are also simpler remote control vibrators that can be used anywhere (within range) but are not controlled through the Internet. Because the vibrator is connected to the remote control, there is no anonymity involved, as can be the case with the other interface-driven systems.

Like all sexual activities, virtual sex has its advantages and disadvantages. Perhaps chief among the advantages is the fact that such practices carry little or no chance of contracting sexually transmitted diseases or becoming pregnant. Virtual sex also allows individuals to engage in alternative sexual practices, effectively "trying on" a different sexuality, including engaging in sexual behavior as the other sex, homosexuality, and fringe behaviors such as bondage/domination sadomasochism (BDSM). Because many participants view virtual sex as not real, they perceive their participation as harmless pleasure. Moreover, participants are able to engage in high-risk sexual activities, such as fetish play, with less bodily risk. Related to this benefit is the relative ease with which one can find a willing partner or even a community built around such activities. This can be especially useful in finding offline sexual partners who share a particular fetish or affinity for less common sexual practices. Finally, there are reported benefits in communicating about sexuality. Despite the fact that virtual sex is taking place in the online or mechanical plane, practitioners still must learn to articulate their desires, especially in cybersex and interface-driven virtual sex, which, according to some, can be a liberating experience.

A major disadvantage to virtual sex comes when one or both partners in the interaction are married to or otherwise involved with someone else. When the unincluded partner finds out about the virtual liaison, he or she can feel a deep sense of betrayal, despite the fact that no physical contact with the virtual partner has taken place. Such concerns have raised questions about the ethics of virtual sex in the face of cyberinfidelity. This may be especially problematic if the online sexual behavior becomes compulsive, leading to problems in the primary offline relationship. Related to this issue is the potential for unwanted emotional attachments to form; where one participant may view the activity as harmless fun, the other participant may believe that a relationship is being created.

There are other, more troubling dangers in virtual sex. With the advantage that virtual sex makes it easier to find willing participants in less common sexual practices comes the potential to bring into the open more dangerous and damaging practices, such as bestiality, pedophilia and age play, rape fantasies, virtual child pornography through the use of child-like avatars, and other forms of edge play (sexual acts that push the boundaries of safety). There is also the possibility that one or both of the individuals involved in the virtual sex act may be an underage person. This has been especially problematic in the case of sexting.

Overall, virtual sex has forced people to redefine what falls under the rubric of sex when no physical contact has taken place. It seems clear that in virtual sex, something has taken place, even if it is not sex in the traditional manner. Indeed, the power of virtual sex is that the act takes place mainly in the mind of the individual or individuals involved. Moreover, by mediating the sexual act, virtual sex also calls into question how men and women interact sexually when one can "be" the other, at least in virtual space. One thing seems certain: Because sexuality is such a core aspect of the human experience, as long as technology continues to evolve, people will continue to find new ways to express themselves sexually.

Brett Lunceford
University of South Alabama

See also Avatar; Cyberdating; Cyberspace and Cyberculture; Pornification of Everyday Life; Pornography: Gay and Lesbian; Pornography: Heterosexual; Pornography: Internet; Sexuality; Transsexuality; Virtual Community; Virtuality

Further Readings

Döring, Nicola M. "The Internet's Impact on Sexuality: A Critical Review of 15 Years of Research." *Computers in Human Behavior*, v.25/5 (2009).

Kibby, Marjorie and Brigid Costello. "Between the Image and the Act: Interactive Sex Entertainment on the Internet." *Sexualities*, v.4/3 (2001).

Lunceford, Brett. "The New Pornographers: Legal and Ethical Considerations of Sexting." In *The Ethics of Emerging Media: Information, Social Norms, and New Media Technology*, Bruce Drushel and Kathleen M. German, eds. New York: Continuum, 2011.

Lynn, Regina. *The Sexual Revolution 2.0: Getting Connected, Upgrading Your Sex Life, and Finding True Love—or at Least a Dinner Date—in the Internet Age.* Berkeley, CA: Ulysses Press, 2005.

Mileham, Beatriz Lia Avila. "Online Infidelity in Internet Chat Rooms: An Ethnographic Exploration." *Computers in Human Behavior*, v.23/1 (2007).

Rheingold, Howard. *Virtual Reality*. New York: Summit Books, 1991.

VIRTUALITY

At the most basic level, *virtuality* refers to a condition or location outside the real; it is usually understood as the opposite of *reality*. The term has a rich history of usage in media studies scholarship, in the popular press, in traditional and interactive fiction, and in many other contexts. Virtuality may refer to simulations, to processes of imagination, or to any other kind of activity that takes place at least partially outside the physical world. Although it is a term most often associated with new media technologies, the term *virtual* predates digital technologies and has a long history in philosophy and literature, among other fields.

Outside electronic contexts, virtual might refer to something being either "in effect" or "almost" real (as in "Beatlemania is a virtual cult" or "That cubic zirconia ring is virtually as beautiful as a diamond ring"). It may also refer to something being created mentally ("I can imagine myself virtually sitting on a park bench"). However, the term *virtuality* almost always refers to simulation of reality through the use of digital technologies. Common examples of virtuality would include video games (especially titles that employ virtual reality), Web-based communities, online libraries, online storefronts, or online classrooms.

Scholarship on virtuality in digital contexts is wide-ranging in that it covers instances of virtuality as they occur in practice, the philosophy of virtuality, the technologies that make virtuality possible, and the effects of virtuality on real-world experiences and interactions. Across this scholarship certain trends have emerged that, collectively, create a better

New media technologies have changed how we think about everything from relationships to politics to entertainment. The term *virtuality* is used to refer to a simulated reality through the use of digital technology, including video games, Web-based communities, or virtual classrooms. (Photos.com)

understanding of how the term *virtuality* might be understood in specific contexts. For example, in politics, virtuality might refer to the ability of voters to engage with candidates via social networking technology, to vote for a candidate through an online system, to share opinions and organize through Web-based communities, or otherwise to use technology in order to participate in political affairs. In romantic relationships, virtuality might refer to practices as wide-ranging as real world couples sending one another digital gifts via social networking sites to cybersex to developing a relationship with a graphical manifestation of artificial intelligence software. These activities are "virtual" because they have a historical, actual counterpart in material, physical practices of political or social engagement.

Because of the scope of the study of virtuality, there is widespread debate about its impact both in specific arenas such as those mentioned above and on public and private culture more broadly. Specifically, it is useful to consider virtuality from the perspectives offered by several leading thinkers on the subject so as to get a sense of the critical landscape.

Virtuality and Technology

A number of technologies have been designed to provide complete or partial virtual experiences for users. Early (predigital) examples would include the first military and commercial vehicle simulation machines in the mid-20th century, pioneering three-dimensional (3-D) cinema technologies, and late 19th- and early 20th-century art designed to stimulate multiple senses. As digital imaging technologies expanded in the 1980s and early 1990s, virtuality experiences could be found in some video games, in training software for professional vehicle operators (such as pilots), and in interactive art. During this period, the idea that technology would be able to provide consumers with "virtual reality" experiences increasingly captured the public imagination, and virtuality became a recurrent theme in science fiction films (such as *Blade Runner*, *Total Recall*, *Altered States*, and *The Matrix*) and gaming (such as Sega's arcade games *Virtua Fighter* and *Virtua Racing* and Nintendo's *Virtual Boy* console). More recently, the 2010 documentary *Digital Nation: Life on the Virtual Frontier* suggested that virtuality technologies are currently in use to help soldiers cope with post-traumatic stress disorder and to create sensory-focused experiences for the disabled. Themes of virtuality also continue to be explored in films like *Avatar* (2009) and in popular science fiction.

A recurring design found across many of the (fictional or actual) technologies for experiencing virtuality is computer hardware that encompasses the head (virtual reality helmets) or the body as a whole (sensory deprivation or immersion machines). However, because the idea of what counts as virtuality is contested, the means for physically accessing and entering into a virtual world are potentially wide-ranging and could include less invasive devices, such as a keyboard and mouse (as in games such as *Second Life*) or even a specialized camera (as in Microsoft's *Kinect* technology).

Virtuality and the Body

Some of the earliest ideas of how a body may enter into a virtual, digital world were expressed in the fiction of William Gibson, and most notably in his early cyberpunk novel *Neuromancer* (1984). In this work, Gibson differentiated between the "bodiless exultation of cyberspace" and the nonvirtual realm, where bodies are "meat . . . the prison of the flesh." Thus, Gibson set the tone for an ongoing debate about the role of the body in cyberspace from this earliest of formulations. For him, the body itself is no longer what matters in cyberspace, where one is detached, freed from the trappings of the physical realm; the body is left behind, the mind reigns. In the virtual world is, instead, a mind/body split of a new order: The virtual is a template for new realities. Words and images become the material substance of the everyday; they ground the mode of existence in the plane of cyberspace. Gibson's idea is often translated into scholarship that addresses the avatar, scholarship that is concerned with Web identity and, broadly, with gendered representations online. His is a perspective that posits the body as malleable and personal identity itself as fluid.

However, even *Neuromancer* acknowledges the messiness of this split; for Gibson's protagonists, there is always a trace of the body within the virtual. This bodily trace is the same one that is the focus of Julian Dibbell's famous essay "A Rape in Cyberspace." Dibbell's essay discusses how virtual sex crimes, especially when they take place within virtual communities, can leave lasting impressions on the physical, emotional bodies behind an avatar. Hence, even though Gibson suggests that cyberspace is the place where the body can be left behind (if only temporarily), Dibbell and others have argued that we often choose to bring it with us anyway and that in virtuality the "ghost in the machine" is material—it is not spirit, but flesh.

Critics who pursue questions of the body in virtual space grapple with how humans succeed and fail at replicating physical-world activities (as well as what those successes and failures might teach us); how virtuality may enable or constrain transcendence of markers such as race, class, and gender; how technologies of virtual reality function to interface with the body; and how the promise of convincing, immersive simulation drives the kinds of actions in which people participate in virtual landscapes.

Virtuality's Impact on the Real

While some scholarship on virtuality has focused on what happens to the physical body or mind when it enters into the cyberspatial realm, other work has turned to understanding the ways in which the concepts of cyberspace and virtuality have begun to shape physical-world behaviors and interactions. In other words, critics have suggested that, just as any engagement with the virtual requires one to bring at least part of the physical body into the virtual world, so too does a return to the physical world bring with it something of the virtual.

Much of N. Katherine Hayles's work, for example, considers how our engagement with new media technologies has considerably changed how we think about everything from relationships to politics to entertainment. In virtual space, everything that appears physical can be understood as information; the world consists of discrete but linked, hypertextual components. For Hayles and others interested in how the physical world is shaped by our engagement with virtuality, the material world becomes something that we sometimes think of through a digital framework.

Jean Baudrillard's famous essay "The Gulf War Did Not Take Place" (included in his book of the same name) shares an affinity with Hayles's work in that both suggest that we often miss the material, physical consequences of decisions made in what appear to be detached virtual spaces. For Baudrillard, the virtual has significantly displaced the real, and those once well-defined barriers between the simulation and the actual have deteriorated. This framework is especially intriguing when it is applied to warfare. When war is presented to the public as a technological marvel in which calculated, strategic actions are accomplished via computer screens controlled by operators thousands of miles away, we can see the specter of virtuality in the physical world.

The notion that bringing the body online has consequences not only for the virtual but also for the physical informs the work of Donna Haraway, who suggests that the result is the cyborg, "a cybernetic organism, a hybrid of machine and organism, a creature of social reality as well as a creature of fiction." For Haraway, the physical body's articulation with the virtual results in a change to the political potential of the body and the creation of the cyborg. The teleos of virtuality is that replication usurps reproduction, labor is replaced by robotics, and the cyborg transcends biopolitics to instead "simulate politics, a much more potent field of operations." The cyborg figure illustrates that in postmodernity the body (both inside and outside cyberspace) still matters for the creation of subject positions, identities, and political agency.

David S. Heineman
Bloomsburg University of Pennsylvania

See also Avatar; Cyberdating; Cyberpunk; Cyberspace and Cyberculture; Cyborg; Simulacra; Virtual Community; Virtual Sex

Further Readings

Baudrillard, Jean. *The Gulf War Did Not Take Place.* Bloomington: Indiana University Press, 1995.

Dibbell, Julian. "A Rape in Cyberspace; or, How an Evil Clown, a Haitian Trickster Spirit, Two Wizards, and a Cast of Dozens Turned a Database Into a Society." In *Reading Digital Culture*, David Trend, ed. Malden, MA: Blackwell, 2001.

Gibson, William. *Neuromancer.* New York: Ace Books, 1984.

Haraway, Donna. "A Manifesto for Cyborgs: Science, Technology, and Socialist Feminism in the 1980s." In *The Norton Anthology of Theory and Criticism*, Vincent B. Leitch, ed. New York: W. W. Norton, 1985.

WEB 2.0

Web 2.0 refers to a large range of Web applications and advancements within Internet technology. Encompassing a shift from earlier versions of the Web, where users went to the Internet simply to obtain information, Web 2.0 allows for users to engage in the creation and sharing of information. The term refers to Web applications that are user-centered and allow for information sharing and collaboration online. Examples include social networking sites such as Facebook and Myspace, blogs, wikis, and video-sharing sites such as YouTube. Web 2.0 has led to the advancement of women within the traditionally male-dominated world of technology.

Web 2.0 is of unique interest to those studying gender because of shifts in notions of the public and private spheres. Often it has been argued by academics that women's roles throughout history have been limited to the private sphere, whereas men operate within the public sphere. This separation between public and private has been detrimental to women's ability to obtain equality. Work done in the private sphere is often disregarded as less important than the work done by men in the public sphere. Cooking, cleaning, caring for children and other, most often unpaid, forms of labor are not valued as highly as work in the public sphere, such as the business world. Often denied a public voice in the male-dominated publishing world, women who have blogged online have discovered a voice in the public sphere. Women account for a large portion of active posting on blogging Websites. Blogging in many ways is similar to journal writing, which has historically been a site for feminist expression.

The focus on production within the Web 2.0 world challenges binaries directly related to gender, such as production/consumption and male/female. This provides unique and interesting opportunities for a future transgendered public sphere. Web 2.0 provides a challenge to the public/private dichotomy through its inherent changing of many dichotomous relations between production and consumption. As many feminist scholars have argued, the dichotomous relationship between male and female is fundamental to the oppression of women. Web 2.0 is making it possible for people to create new identities for themselves that expand our notions of a gender dichotomy. Participating in and generating content for spaces without having to identify oneself as physically female or male present unique opportunities. Through anonymity or the guise of a screen name, many people are contributing to and influencing new knowledge centers, such as Wikipedia.

As people increasingly put their private lives in the public domain through Web 2.0 technologies, the strict boundaries between a private sphere and a public sphere no longer hold. In some ways this change is positive, as seen through the increasing number of women who are publishing their work online and the ability for women to come together and support one another, as seen in pregnancy forums. Wikis offer tools for collaboration and editing that open doors for new forms of feminist collaboration. Wikis allow for the participation of women from different locations and positions to contribute equally to the creation and distribution of information.

There are also detrimental effects to the blending of public and private that uniquely affect young women and young men. In particular, social networking sites have been problematic. Many teens and young adults have felt the negative effects of posting inappropriate pictures when they are denied jobs or fired by their employers. Young adults who are digital natives often have a different idea of what should be kept private and what should be public. This can clash with the attitudes of those who did not grow up with such technologies. Many older people view Facebook and such sites as public places where one is publishing and creating a certain persona. Gender is often an important part in the creation and use of Web 2.0 sites. Sites such as Facebook require users to generate a profile that offers gender as an option in the creation of identity. Advertising is thus aimed at specific genders reinforcing stereotypes. Gender norms are often re-created in virtual environments, reflecting the nature of gender roles in the "real" world.

Censorship is a key issue in the Web 2.0 world. Whereas in previous modes of communication censorship came from above, censorship now lies in the hands of the users. Businesses are taking a more active role in watching the use of social media by their employees. The information posted by individual users of Web 2.0 communities becomes public, and issues of privacy are raised. As the world begins to deal with the challenges of increased access to personal information, users must take privacy into their own hands.

New forms of social activism become possible in Web 2.0 as users connect despite geographical and ideological differences. Groups of people can collaborate and create networks that were previously unthinkable. Student protesters can upload videos to YouTube and update Twitter before any form of government censorship can intervene. This provides new opportunities for political activism.

Web 2.0 permits a positive expression of gender and identity through formulating alternatives. Instead of only obtaining information from mainstream media outlets, where information is communicated in a top-down model, users can actively participate in the creation of positive media environments. Whereas traditional media such as television, newspapers, and broadcast journalism are in the control of an elite few whose information is then widely distributed, Web 2.0 provides a new means of expression. The future of Web 2.0 is in the hands of its users, who will generate and distribute its content. As women take the production of media into their own hands, the Internet becomes a space where women's agency can be asserted and new, inclusive viewpoints can take hold.

Web 2.0 opens new doors in education and provides tools that can help today's students. Through the use of Web 2.0 technologies, students can create and share information in exciting ways. Educators and students can now collaborate in new forms and must come to terms with the vast changes in the technological environment. What is needed now is collaboration that integrates teaching strategies into Web 2.0 learning.

Megan Jean Harlow
European Graduate School, Switzerland

See also Audiences: Producers of New Media; Blogs and Blogging; Cyberdating; Cyberpunk; Cyberspace and Cyberculture; Cyborg; Electronic Media and Social Inequality; Identity; Mass Media; New Media; Social Media; Social Networking Sites: Facebook; Social Networking Sites: Myspace; Tropes; Twitter; Virtual Community; Wiki; YouTube

Further Readings

Chaudhuri, Saabira. "Most Influential Women in Web 2.0." Fastcompany (November 6, 2008). http://www.fastcompany.com/articles/2008/11/influential-women-web.html (Accessed February 2011).

Hoffman, Auren. "The Social Media Gender Gap." *Business Week* (May 19, 2008). http://www.businessweek.com/technology/content/may2008/tc20080516_580743.htm (Accessed February 2011).

Kapin, Allyson. "Cracking the Boys Club: 10 Pioneers in Tech and Web 2.0." *Huffington Post* (November 14, 2008). http://www.huffingtonpost.com/allyson-kapin/cracking-the-boys-club-10_b_143826.html (Accessed February 2011).

Lai, Linda S. L. "Impacts of Web 2.0 Based Social Networks: The Good, the Bad and the Ugly." *Conference on Information Management and Internet Research*. Edith Cowan University, Joondalup, Western Australia (November 2007).

WIKI

Wikis have become important information-gathering and collaboration-building tools. Coined in the mid-1990s by Ward Cunningham, the term *wiki* means an Internet composition system or database space designed to function as a repository of written information that can be viewed and edited by anyone who has access. The term was inspired by the Hawaiian word for "quick." Wikis have been described as Web pages with an edit button.

The idea of the wiki developed from FLOSS (Free, Libre, and open source software programs) that enable the modification and redistribution of source code. Some wiki templates or software programs are completely open on the Internet and available for customization, and others are housed in school or business content management systems or in-house spaces used for human resources management, such as group discussion and collaboration in the workplace. Some wikis take the form of encyclopedia Web "documents," while others work more as social experiments. Many wikis can be designed using "open source" software that is easily made available and customized through a WYSIWYG ("what you see is what you get") interface to display content under construction so users can visualize the display after editing is complete. Most wiki content is considered to be "user-generated content," which means that anyone with access to the content management type container can generate materials for the wiki.

The Internet has dethroned the traditional publishing paradigm of content in a wide variety of media, and wikis play a significant role in this media revolution. They allow citizen journalists and activists to create alternative histories to a variety of world experiences and to update and/or correct knowledge. A variety of gender-based wikis have been produced, including Wikigender. The collaborative and fluid nature wiki content means that inaccuracies and misrepresentations can be posted but then altered by an ever-growing stream of new content creators and re-creators.

Wiki pioneers have called on women to make more online contributions to current popular wiki media and also to create new spaces for collaboration. Users come to the wiki environment with their own languages, cultures, politics, perceptions of gender, and social norms. The wiki framework allows users to cross boundaries of time and place to create a collective intelligence, negotiate discourse and meaning, take action on issues, reflect experience, and organize and develop as a group. The most important aspect of a wiki is the content that is housed on the wiki "site." Promising learning opportunities can be opened through online learning communities fostered by wikis. The tool can provide contributors with diverse resources, information, and social and emotional support. Collaborators can learn about important and complex scenarios and experiences through the new networked mind-set, fostering fundamental shifts in the way people think, form groups, and work collaboratively. This in turn allows users to do new things with old content and build completely new approaches to solving problems. The users' ability to quantify contributions to a project and share work and learning builds potentially strong teams.

Like other kinds of Internet media, wikis are almost always unmoderated. Some wikis have disclaimers, some allow anyone to write something, and some reserve the right to remove, change, or further develop content. Wikis keep a record of changes, and previous content can be easily reintroduced to the wiki without any review of content. The use of nonsexist and inclusive language in educational and informational wikis is often discussed and always encouraged. Almost all wikis allow anyone with access the chance to modify content quickly and easily. Increased access and user friendliness promise increased participation and new forms of discussion, collaboration, and networking.

The collaborative nature of a wiki means that it is not always the correct tool for every project. If no single person or group is in charge, the content can become confusing and disorganized. Creative and intellectual ideas can be gathered and acted on elsewhere without the wiki contributor's knowing about it. People who are not tech-savvy might not feel comfortable about writing on a "public" space, and those with learning challenges such as dyslexia and dysgraphia may find it hard to collaborate in a text-based environment. If keeping the ideas a secret is a main concern, then a wiki is not an appropriate environment for content because it can easily be transferred. Additionally, wikis may pose concerns about the presence of vandals, trolls, and hackers, who may be motivated to take advantage of a wiki's weakness and damage the wiki or the content it holds. In some cases this results from ideological disagreements and in others vandalism.

As the Web becomes increasingly interactive—with information sharing, interoperability, and user-centered design—its use becomes more popular and integrated into everyday life. The co-construction of gender and body can have far-reaching effects on the use of wikis as catalysts for gender relations and gender politics. Gender content on sites like Wikipedia is consistently under revision, and gender-based content is consistently debated, defended, and opposed. Notions about what sources constitute a "seminal" work are often challenged in the wiki environment, which seeks, through the design of the tool, to collaborate and disseminate information instead of protecting it or housing it in passworded spaces.

The prominence of the wiki has created a variety of active gender, feminist, and mothering wikis, activity that promotes solidarity and increased communication, research, and discussion. Wikis foster the creation of online identities and online voices. This potential of the Internet as a tool for increased collaboration in the areas of gender, mothering, and feminism has made some strides, and the potential for increased participation is even greater.

Stacey O. Irwin
Millersville University

See also Audiences: Producers of New Media; Blogs and Blogging; Cyberdating; Cyberpunk; Cyberspace and Cyberculture; Cyborg; Electronic Media and Social Inequality; Identity; Mass Media; New Media; Social Media; Social Networking Sites: Facebook; Social Networking Sites: Myspace; Tropes; Twitter; Virtual Community; Web 2.0; YouTube

Further Readings

Carstensen, Tanja. "Gender Trouble in Web 2.0: Gender Relations in Social Network Sites." *International Journal of Gender, Science and Technology*, v.1/1 (2009).

Gunawardena, Charlotte N., Mary Beth Hermans, Damien Sanchez, Carol Richmond, Maribeth Bohley, and Rebekah Tuttle. "A Theoretical Framework for Building Online Communities of Practice With Social Networking Tools." *Educational Media International*, v.46/1 (2009).

Scearce, Diana, Gabriel Kasper, and Heather McLeod Grant. "Working Wikily." *Stanford Social Innovation Review*, Summer 2010.

Shachaf, Pnina and Noriko Hara. "Beyond Vandalism: Wikipedia Trolls." *Journal of Information Science*, v.36/3 (2010).

Wei, Zhang and Chéris Kramarae. "Feminist Invitational Collaboration in a Digital Age: Looking Over Disciplinary and National Borders." *Women and Language*, v.31/2 (2008).

WOMEN'S MAGAZINES: FASHION

For almost 200 years, American fashion magazines have advised their readers on what to buy, how to look, and the proper way to act. These beautifully produced periodicals showcased lavish illustrations and the finest photography as well as serialized novels, short stories, and essays by some of the best writers of the day. In the process, these magazines crafted images of women that transformed American culture—and, many have argued, scarred generations of women, endangering their health, damaging their bodies, and ruining their self-esteem. In addition, these magazines brought enormous power and wealth to the women and men who edited them and fortunes in advertising and circulation revenues to their publishers.

American Fashion Magazines: The First Generation

The history of fashion magazines in America traditionally begins with the launch of *Godey's Lady's Book* in 1830. *Godey's* was a general women's magazine that featured fashion in its beautiful hand-colored fashion plates, which are still treasured by collectors across the country. The magazine also featured instructions on how readers, primarily middle-class women, could make bonnets, dresses, and undergarments in the latest style. The fashion industry in Antebellum, Civil War, and Reconstruction America was still in a primitive state.

Godey's spurred a host of imitators, the most successful of which was *Peterson's Magazine*. The fashion magazines of this early period shared certain characteristics: a large circulation for the day (both *Godey's* and *Peterson's* had circulations in excess of 100,000) and editorial content that included short stories, essays, and poetry in addition to fashion. Women always figured prominently at these publications. *Godey's* was edited by Sarah Josepha Hale for almost 50 years; Ann S. Stephens, a well-known novelist, served as coeditor of *Peterson's* for a time. In addition, both *Godey's* and *Peterson's* published the work of women writers when few other magazines would.

These magazines are also credited with developing and reinforcing the "cult of true womanhood," also known as the "cult of domesticity." Through their short stories, poetry, essays, advice, and illustrations, these magazines emphasized the characteristics commonly associated with the 19th-century "lady": piety, purity, domesticity, and submissiveness. The fashion plates, illustrations, and instructions showed how the middle-class woman should dress, which was not necessarily healthful. As women's rights

Companies advertising in women's fashion magazines nearly always use photographs of women who are young, beautiful, and the image of physical perfection in their quest to create more young consumers striving to be young, beautiful, and physically perfect. (Photos.com)

activists, feminists, physical culture enthusiasts, and contemporary physicians emphasized, the heavy, long skirts and corsets were health hazards. Corsets, particularly, were maiming women and curtailing their physical ability to exercise, carry out their household responsibilities, and obtain employment outside the home, these critics argued.

The decline of *Godey's* and *Peterson's* coincided with the development of two different types of fashion magazines, each with its own distinct editorial flare. One type of magazine was created to promote dress patterns so women could make their own clothing at home. The other type was established to showcase the work of designers from across the world.

Fashion Magazines and the Dress-Pattern Industry

Women entrepreneurs and editors were central to the creation of the magazines that featured dress patterns as their fashion bedrock. Ellen Louise Curtis (Nell) Demorest invented the mass-produced (albeit uncopyrighted) tissue-paper dressmaking patterns, and Ellen Augusta Pollard Butterick improved on Demorest's invention by developing (and marketing) paper patterns in a variety of standard sizes. These two women also figured in the two magazines that came to dominate this genre: *The Delineator*, which showcased the Butterick paper patterns, and the much smaller (and less widely circulated) *Demorest's Monthly Magazine and Mme. Demorest's Mirror of Fashions*, which featured Nell Demorest's tissue patterns. Nell served as coeditor of the latter magazine. Ellen Butterick died shortly after her pattern company made its first foray into fashion magazine publishing. These two magazines shared one other characteristic. Both came to be known for municipal housekeeping, a reform of the late 19th and early 20th centuries that encouraged women to take their housekeeping responsibilities into the community and clean up cities, organize women's clubs, and bring about reforms that would protect underrepresented populations, especially children.

Of the two magazines, *The Delineator* was the dominant publication. *Demorest's* started earlier (in 1860), had a shorter life (about 40 years), and had a smaller circulation (120,000 at the time the periodical ceased publishing in 1899). In contrast, *The Delineator* started in 1863. *The Delineator* reached a circulation in excess of two million and died in 1937, at the depth of the Great Depression. Of the two magazines, *Demorest's* was probably the most fashion-forward. The Demorests (Nell partnered with husband William) hired consultants in Europe, who reported on the latest fashion trends. Then Nell and her sister Kate Curtis tailored the designs to American needs and demands. *Demorest's* started as a quarterly, *Mme. Demorest's Mirror of Fashions*. Certainly, Nell had the design credentials to launch such a magazine. A milliner by training and an inventor by creativity, she introduced a line of comfortable corsets and affordable hoopskirts in addition to the tissue-paper dress patterns.

The Demorests brought a unique perspective to fashion magazine publishing. The wife and husband believed that fashion could, and should, mix with reform. The magazine, the shop (Madame Demorest's Emporium of Fashion on Broadway in New York City), and the pattern-manufacturing facility reflected that vision. Fashion was obvious in the patterns, the premiums, and the magazine, but so too was reform. The Demorests believed in women's rights and employed more than 200 women in the pattern-manufacturing shop. The magazine included the newest styles but also incorporated reform. Coedited by Jane "Jennie June" Cunningham Croly, one of the founders of the women's club movement in America, *Demorest's* embraced women's rights in many different ways, urging colleges to admit women, publicizing the success of women in the professions, encouraging women to seek employment outside the home, and applauding the work of women's organizations across the nation. Croly even added dress reform to her column in the magazine. In response, the Demorests made changes to their fashion patterns—lifting hemlines on skirts so they were less dangerous and tailoring clothes so they were more comfortable to wear.

The grind of putting out a magazine and running a fashion empire wore on the Demorests. By 1887, the couple had sold their fashion business and turned the magazine over to their sons. The couple wanted to spend their remaining years working for social reform: he in temperance, she in women's rights. *Demorest's* continued, but its creative spark and energy were gone. (After the Demorests left, longtime coeditor Croly departed as well.) The magazine, which melded fashion with reform, passed into history in 1899.

The Delineator had long before eclipsed *Demorest's*. *The Delineator* would never have existed if Ellen Butterick, with her husband Ebenezer, had not begun merchandising their clothing patterns. The couple and their newly formed Butterick Pattern Co. saw magazine publishing as a means of merchandising their clothing patterns, not as an end in itself. In 1863, Butterick started the *Ladies' Quarterly of Broadway Fashions* and, in 1868, the *Metropolitan*. Each offered fashion news and advice—and mail-order services for the company's patterns. In 1873, two years after Ellen Butterick's death, the pattern company merged the two magazines to create *The Delineator*, which quickly developed editorial fare that appealed to a growing number of middle-class women subscribers: 30,000 in 1876, 500,000 in 1900, more than 1 million in 1920, and more than 2 million in 1930.

The increased circulation coincided with changes in the editorial content and graphic design of *The Delineator*—and the corporate structure of the Butterick company. In its earliest days, circulation was small; under editors Jonas Warren Wilder and R. S. O'Loughlin, the magazine was little more than an inexpensive black-and-white advertising premium for Butterick designs and patterns. New editor Charles Dwyer transformed the cheap little publication into a fashion magazine worthy of its genre. Dwyer added editorials and fiction (primarily short stories)—and color, which complemented the more sophisticated Butterick designs of the early 20th century. The improvements to the magazine accelerated once the Butterick corporation split the pattern company from the publishing house.

Dwyer, especially, was responsible for the municipal housekeeping of the late 19th and early 20th centuries. *The Delineator* came to be known for three campaigns: a push to improve public schools based on the investigative work of Rheta Childe Dorr; an attempt to reform state laws that limited legal rights of women, which was spearheaded by William Hard; and an investigation of orphan asylums and an attempt to enact the Child Rescue Law. Male editors directed the municipal housekeeping campaigns. In addition to Dwyer, the great American novelist Theodore Dreiser and the social reformer and reporter William Hard served as *Delineator* editors, respectively, from 1907 to 1910 and from 1910 to 1913. By 1913, municipal housekeeping had ebbed in the pages of *The Delineator*—and nationally.

Women editors guided the magazine from 1917 to 1927, its zenith, in fashion, design, and editorial content. These editors—Honore Willsie Morrow, Mrs. William Brown Meloney, and Mary Day Winn—redefined fashion to include the home, and *The Delineator* increased the number of articles on home decorating and homemaking. For example, the magazine's "Better Homes Campaign" in the 1920s offered a room-by-room guide to decor, which stood in sharp contrast to the clutter of the Victorian period.

At its height, *The Delineator* was chock-full of advertising for products that every middle-class woman consumer should want and need—from women's clothing products (undergarments to hosiery, belts to hairpieces, shoes to dresses) to home-decorating needs (drapes to linoleum, furniture to appliances) and daily household products (polish to cleaners).

The Depression hit *The Delineator* (by then edited by Oscar Graeve), and Butterick, hard. The magazine's circulation plummeted, and advertising revenue decreased in 1936 and 1937. In April 1937, with little warning, *The Delineator* ceased publication, merging into William Randolph Hearst's *Pictorial Review*. With that, a fashion icon for generations of American women passed into history.

The fashion magazines, which helped to build the paper pattern manufacturing industry, can be seen on three different levels. First, as part of the nascent American fashion industry, these magazines built an awareness of changing fashion trends on the part of their middle-class women readers and, through the inexpensive paper patterns, helped nurture a demand for the latest fashions. As Helen Woodward observed, paper patterns—and by implication the fashion magazines that merchandised them—helped level fashion among American women. Because of the inexpensive, widely available paper patterns, along with the home sewing machine, the latest fashions were no longer the purview of the very rich. *The Delineator* and *Demorest's* played their part in fostering those changes. Second, like the fashion magazines that came before and those that followed, *The Delineator* and *Demorest's* helped create images of women that imposed unrealistic expectations on the readers—and set impossibly high standards

for consuming. The beautiful illustrations, which showcased flawless, thin women modeling the latest elegantly appointed fashions, set a beauty standard. The advertising, the feature stories, and the fiction all complemented the message: The reader needed to dress in the latest fashions (made possible with the inexpensive paper patterns and the home sewing machine) and achieve the highest standards for furnishing her home and maintaining her household. As if those expectations were not high enough, these two magazines also helped foster the municipal housekeeping movement so popular in the late 19th and early 20th centuries. Not only should readers follow the latest fashion trends, keep an immaculate house, and raise well-behaved children; they also should extend their household responsibilities to their communities, work to correct social ills, protect less fortunate women and children, and get involved in the women's clubs so popular at the time.

A Modern Model for Fashion Magazines

In 1867, the stodgy Harper and Brothers entered the lucrative, albeit crowded, fashion publishing niche. The new launch drew on what the Harper brothers did best: etchings and news in a weekly publication cycle. The new weekly, *Harper's Bazar* (spelled with only one *a* in a nod to the German fashion magazine *Bazar*), looked like the other Harper properties (notably *Harper's Weekly*), with etchings on the front page of the tabloid, which was printed on coarse newsprint paper stock. The content was quite different, however. This new periodical was devoted to things that were under the jurisdiction of women in the gender-defined (and gender-divided) spheres of 19th-century America. (Women were responsible for all things within the home, including child rearing; the male sphere was outside the home, in the world of business, industry, and politics.) The new tabloid was devoted to things under the jurisdiction of women: dress, household matters, and, especially, fashion. Although the magazine faced formidable competition in the fashion niche, the weekly had a healthy circulation of 80,000 within 10 years of its launch. Women editors—Mary L. Booth (1867–89), Margaret Sangster (1889–99), and Elizabeth Jordan (1900–13), each a well-known writer before her association with the magazine—ran the periodical when it was owned by the Harper brothers. By 1913, *Harper's Bazar* was a monthly printed on better-quality paper stock with fashion illustrations and photographs of society matrons. That year, Hearst acquired the publication and added it to his International Magazine stable of properties. It has been within the Hearst family of magazines ever since. *Harper's Bazaar* (today with another *a*) is the oldest continuously published fashion magazine in the nation.

In 1913, however, the likelihood of *Harper's Bazar* (with or without its *a*) gaining such a title seemed remote. *Harper's* was facing formidable competition from an upstart Condé Nast property called *Vogue*. Launched in 1892 by Arthur Baldwin Turnure, this magazine was initially started to cover New York City society. After Turnure's death, the debonair Condé Nast, who had been an advertising executive for the tremendously successful general interest magazine *Collier's*, bought *Vogue* in 1909 and transformed it into a fashion magazine, a book of unparalleled artistic grandeur featuring the work of the finest illustrators and photographers. If *Harper's Bazar* was going to survive, it would need to join a publishing house that could afford to provide the resources needed to face *Vogue*, its imaginative editorial and graphic content, and the upscale Condé Nast publishing house. Clearly, the enormous wealth of Hearst and his publishing empire could meet the challenge.

For almost a century, Hearst and Condé Nast have jockeyed for the fashion magazine crown. It is a crown worth the battle. Although other publications, notably *Elle*, *Allure*, *Marie Claire*, and *W*, have gained a share of the lucrative fashion magazine market, *Vogue* and *Harper's Bazaar* remain fashion queens—for good or ill. It was *Vogue* and *Harper's* that transformed the fashion magazine genre from hand-colored fashion plates, paper patterns, and etchings on newsprint to fine art, showcasing the finest illustrators, the greatest artists, and the best photographers of the nation, indeed of the world. More recently, these magazines have imposed on American women an image of a young, gaunt model who is physically perfect and chronically underweight.

A look at the history of *Vogue* and *Harper's* illustrates how these two magazines influenced fashion, American art, literature, culture—and women. Of the two, *Vogue* has relied primarily on women editors to define the editorial direction of the magazine. Edna Woolman Chase (1914–52), Jessica Daves

(1952–62), Diana Vreeland (1963–71), Grace Mirabella (1971–88), and Anna Wintour (1989–) each brought change to the fashion and magazine industries.

During her long tenure with the magazine, Chase revolutionized *Vogue*'s look and editorial content—and, in the process, helped create the U.S. fashion industry. When the French fashion industry shut down during World War I, Chase—with the power of *Vogue* magazine behind her—organized the first fashion shows in New York City, which showcased American designers. Chase's *Vogue* was a literary and artistic cornucopia. The magazine featured the works of Thomas Wolfe, William Saroyan, Bertrand Russell, Jean-Paul Sartre, and Margaret Mead and showcased such modern artists as surrealist artist Salvador Dalí and post-Impressionist painter Vincent van Gogh. Bankrolled by *Vogue*'s enormous advertising revenue, Chase hired some of the greatest photographers in the world, including Edward Steichen, Cecil Beaton, and Irving Penn, to transform fashion photography into fine art.

Chase also discovered and trained the great fashion editor Carmel Snow, who deserted *Vogue* for *Harper's Bazaar* in 1934. Snow transformed *Harper's* into a worthy adversary for *Vogue*. Like Chase, Snow showcased great writers, including Virginia Woolf, Eudora Welty, and Truman Capote, and introduced readers to the modern art of Pablo Picasso, Marc Chagall, and Georges Braque. The surrealist artist Salvadore Dalí even contributed fashion sketches to *Harper's*. Snow also transformed fashion photography. She used socialites instead of models and encouraged photographers to get out of their studios for their fashion shoots. Snow changed fashion photography in other ways as well. No admirer of the static fashion shot, Snow wanted photographs that featured models running, laughing, walking, and jumping. It was a trend that would influence fashion photography for generations.

Today, all fashion magazines look similar on the newsstand. The cover of the print magazine usually features some celebrity, the fashion genre having succumbed to the nation's fixation with fame. A glimpse inside reveals painfully thin, young models showing off the latest fashions. (Since the late 1960s, fashion magazines have preferred waiflike models.) Advertisements emphasize the young, the beautiful, the physically perfect. The prevailing message throughout the magazines is to consume—to be young, successful, physically attractive, and socially pleasing. These messages are not isolated to printed fashion magazines; they now permeate the Internet. Every fashion magazine has a strong online presence, but the mantra of consumption and the idealized image of women remain the same.

For almost 200 years, fashion magazines have been a staple of American publishing. Millions of American women have been exposed to their advertising, which repeats call to consume, and fashion photography, which idealizes young, and now gaunt, models—images that are neither realistic nor healthy. Over those same years, however, fashion magazines have offered remarkable opportunities for women writers, editors, illustrators, and artists. These magazines published the work of women when others refused to do so. The magazines have offered their readers short stories, poetry, essays, feature stories, and journalism, which were often thought-provoking—and occasionally important. Over the decades, these magazines became almost art books, offering not just the fashions of the day but also the great artistic trends of the day. The front covers of *Harper's* and *Vogue* particularly remain hallmarks of great graphic design. Although modern fashion magazines have succumbed to the nation's preoccupation with celebrities and too seldom provide noteworthy commentary, some issues do capture the imagination and energy of an earlier time. At their best, today's fashion magazines are an imaginative blend of illustration, photography, and design.

Kathleen L. Endres
University of Akron

See also Advertising; Beauty and Body Image: Beauty Myths; Beauty and Body Image: Eating Disorders; Bordo, Susan; E-Zines: Riot Grrrl; E-Zines: Third Wave Feminist; Gender and Femininity: Motherhood; Gender and Femininity: Single/Independent Girl; Gender Media Monitoring; Men's Magazines: Lad Magazines; Men's Magazines: Lifestyle and Health; Steinem, Gloria; Tween Magazines; Women's Magazines: Feminist Magazines; Women's Magazines: Lifestyle and Health

Further Readings

Chase, Edna W. and Ilka Chase. *Always in Vogue*. Garden City, NY: Doubleday, 1954.

Endres, Kathleen and Therese Lueck, eds. *Women's Periodicals in the United States: Consumer Magazines*. Westport, CT: Greenwood, 1995.

Gottlieb, Agnes H. *Women Journalists and the Municipal Housekeeping Movement, 1868–1914*. Lewiston, NY: Edwin Mellen Press, 2001.

Kitch, Carolyn. *The Girl on the Magazine Cover: The Origins of Visual Stereotypes in American Mass Media*. Chapel Hill: University of North Carolina Press, 2001.

Mott, Frank L. *A History of American Magazines*. Cambridge, MA: Harvard University Press, 1938–68.

Peterson, Theodore. *Magazines in the Twentieth Century*. Urbana: University of Illinois Press, 1956.

Seebohm, Caroline. *The Man Who Was Vogue: The Life and Times of Conde Nast*. New York: Viking, 1982.

Sypeck, Mia, James J. Gray, and Anthony H. Ahrens. "No Longer Just a Pretty Face: Fashion Magazines' Depiction of Ideal Female Beauty From 1959 to 1999." *International Journal of Eating Disorders*, v.36 (2004).

Welter, Barbara. "The Cult of True Womanhood: 1820–1860." *American Quarterly*, v.80 (1966).

Woodward, Helen. *The Lady Persuaders*. New York: Ivan Obonlensky, 1960.

WOMEN'S MAGAZINES: FEMINIST MAGAZINES

While the majority of today's women's magazines tend to be driven by consumer culture and focus mainly on product sales while reinforcing unrealistic standards of beauty, there are notable alternatives to this format. The most widely recognized feminist magazine is *Ms.*, cofounded in 1972 by feminist activist Gloria Steinem, which continues to produce serious investigative reports on issues of importance to women as well as in-depth feminist analyses of a wide range of national and global issues. More recently, the creation of other feminist magazines, including *Bust* and *Bitch: Feminist Response to Pop Culture*, has added to the array of reading materials available to readers with a feminist bent. The intent of *Bust*, launched in 1993, is to provide an uncensored response to the experience of being female in today's world, including women's personal lives and popular culture. *Bitch* commenced in 1996 as a means of responding to the antifeminist messages targeted at young adults in the mainstream media. These publications provide alternative perspectives for the feminist reader, in contrast to the traditional women's magazine.

The history of *Ms.* begins with a group of women meeting in their living rooms. They wanted to create a publication in which readers could find information on the women's movement without having to join an organization, though initially the founders had difficulty generating the necessary capital to realize their vision. However, when the first issue reached the newsstand, all 300,000 copies sold out in a mere 10 days, generating more than 30,000 subscriptions. These sales generated the financial support the magazine needed to begin regular publication. The early years of *Ms.* were filled with consciousness-raising articles that focused on women's lives and women's problems, including the pay inequity between the genders, inadequate maternity leave policies, women's limited reproductive freedoms (including lack of access to safe and legal abortions), and wife battering and domestic abuse. Articles also named the epidemics of date and acquaintance rape and sexual harassment that plagued women around the nation. The magazine resonated with readers, and by the end of 1973, *Ms.* was receiving more than 200 letters from readers every day.

By the end of the 1970s, the enthusiasm and support for the first publication to openly identify and discuss women's issues began to waiver, as *Ms.* tried to appeal to an increasingly fractured audience. The concerns of the women's movement and the various groups of feminists it contained had become significantly more diverse and difficult to represent within each issue of the magazine. By the early 1980s, conservative politics came to dominate national offices, and younger women struggled with whether to identify with the term *feminist*, which was often believed to be associated with an earlier generation of women. However, even as national politics shifted, *Ms.* remained the only magazine to place value on substantive content over aesthetics and to foster the presence of alternative voices within mainstream markets.

This did not make *Ms.* an ideal environment for advertisers, the driving force behind the magazine industry. Advertisers have been known to shy away from the controversial topics often covered within the pages of *Ms.*, which do not meld well with fashion and cosmetics ads. As a result, the staff at *Ms.* sustained a great deal of financial pressure. The majority of ads that *Ms.* was able to attract were for cars, hard liquor, and cigarettes, and this influenced the coverage of the magazine when it reluctantly had to limit its coverage of smoking and fetal alcohol syndrome. Financial pressures led to the sale of *Ms.*

in 1987 to Fairfax, and the founders hoped the new publisher would carry on their mission. *Ms.* had been published as a nonprofit magazine from 1978 to 1987 through the *Ms.* Foundation for Education and Communication; during this transition and through the following decade and a half, *Ms.* had four different owners, which eventually resulted in the adoption of a radical advertising-free publication model.

The new editors brought in by Fairfax in 1987 tried to carry on the work of Steinem, Andrea Dworkin, and others involved in the original vision of the magazine, yet they also wanted to incorporate a more traditional, mainstream feel into the magazine with the hope of attracting a wider range of readers and creating financial stability. When Fairfax sold its control over *Ms.* to Matilda Publications, controversial sections on gardening and fashion were added to the magazine's content under this new leadership. Early in its management era, Matilda encountered its own financial difficulties, and the new editors struggled to maintain control of *Ms.* as well as *Sassy*, a teen magazine that balanced fashion with feminist issues, which they had hoped would support the original publication. However, as *Sassy* came under attack from conservative Christian groups for its coverage of teen condom use and acquired immune deficiency syndrome (AIDS) education, advertisers began to withdraw their support, and this put both publications in jeopardy. *Ms.* continued to struggle financially, and in order to keep its much needed advertising base, editorial decisions concerning the magazine's contents were compromised. Citicorp bought both *Ms.* and *Sassy* in 1989 as the publications' tenuous relationships with advertisers began to recover. Later that same year, Dale Lang announced his intentions to purchase *Ms.* along with a percentage of *Sassy*. Once control over the magazine was turned over to Lang—the first male in its ownership history—he immediately suspended its publication. *Ms.* was eventually relaunched under the editorial leadership of feminist Robin Morgan at the end of 1989 as an advertising-free magazine rededicated to the pursuit of gender equality and women's issues, this time without the pressure to conform to the constraints of advertisers. This is the model that *Ms.* maintains today.

In 1998 *Ms.* began being published under Liberty Media for Women, LLC, run by a group of feminists, including Marcia Gillespie and Steinem, as well as a board of businesswomen, students, and activists.

Today, the magazine maintains a diverse readership of women who are simultaneously engaged with one another and with world issues. The modern version of *Ms.* includes extensive coverage of international women's issues, more so than any other magazine available in the United States. The magazine's traditions of investigative reporting and feminist political analysis, as well as its Women of the Year Awards and the well-known "No Comment" section, have been enhanced by the discussion of environmental feminism, women's work styles, and the politics of emerging technologies with the mission of working toward the feminism of the future.

Ms. is no longer the only magazine to claim the domain of feminist publication. Both *Bust* and *Bitch* were established in the 1990s, and each maintains a stable following today. *Bust*, written in an ironic and flippant tone, primarily targets young women and includes coverage on various topics, such as popular culture and music, arts and crafts, fashion and beauty, books, movies and television, food, health, and sex. *Bitch: Feminist Response to Pop Culture* was created by friends Lisa Jervis and Andi Zeisler, popular-culture enthusiasts who had both interned at *Sassy* in the early 1990s. These self-proclaimed feminists created a magazine that specializes in witty analyses of the sexist representations embedded in media, specifically movies, television, and advertising. In 2009, *Bitch* renamed itself Bitch Media in order to emphasize its redirected focus as a nonprofit multimedia organization rather than just a print magazine.

Andrea M. Bergstrom
Franklin Pierce University

See also Advertising; Beauty and Body Image: Beauty Myths; Beauty and Body Image: Eating Disorders; Bordo, Susan; E-Zines: Riot Grrrl; E-Zines: Third Wave Feminist; Gender and Femininity: Motherhood; Gender and Femininity: Single/Independent Girl; Gender Media Monitoring; Jervis, Lisa; Men's Magazines: Lad Magazines; Men's Magazines: Lifestyle and Health; Steinem, Gloria; Tween Magazines; Women's Magazines: Fashion; Women's Magazines: Lifestyle and Health

Further Readings

Bitch Magazine. http://www.bitchmagazine.org (Accessed February 2011).
Bust Magazine. http://www.bust.org (Accessed February 2011).
Freedman, E. B. *No Turning Back: The History of Feminism and the Future of Women*. New York: Ballantine Books, 2002.
Ms. Magazine. http://www.msmagazine.org (Accessed February 2011).
Orenstein, P. and M. Grimes. "*Ms.* Fights for Its Life." *Mother Jones*, v.15/7 (1990).
Perlstein, R. "*Ms.* Magazine: Feminist Fighter." *Columbia Journalism Review*, v.40/4 (2001).

WOMEN'S MAGAZINES: LIFESTYLE AND HEALTH

Women's magazines have a rich history that has been instrumental in forming a social network among their readers. These magazines helped women fill their times of isolation as stay-at-home wives and enabled them to make sense of a woman's place in the "new workplace" beginning in the 1970s. The history of these magazines emphasizes their power to remain relevant for the modern woman. Despite their similar purpose, many of these magazines have different emphases, ranging from sports and fitness to lifestyle. Women's lifestyle magazines can be assigned to various categories: mainstream lifestyle, bridal, pregnancy and motherhood, ethnic-based, and cooking magazines.

History

The first women's magazine was the *Lady's Magazine*, which was published in 1792. This magazine and several others released during that time targeted the elite population and were focused on fiction, etiquette, and fashion. One of the best-known magazines was *Godey's Lady's Book*, which focused on fashion and manners. These magazines experienced similar barriers: distribution problems, delinquent subscribers, lack of interest, and inadequate production methods.

After the Civil War, several women's magazines appeared, perpetuated by advances in printing technology, refined methods of mass production, and an increased level of distribution that enabled publishers to print and distribute magazines in unprecedented numbers. These magazines were referred to as the "big six": *Ladies' Home Journal, McCall's, The Delineator, Woman's Home Companion, Pictorial Review,* and *Good Housekeeping*. These new magazines were characterized by their affordable price, high circulation, bountiful advertising, and appealing content. Two of these magazines, *Ladies' Home Journal* and *Good Housekeeping*, are still published today.

The prices of these magazines were relatively low (between 5 and 15 cents) and placed these publications within economic reach of the working class. These magazines experienced a circulation higher than their general-magazine predecessors. In 1891, the *Ladies' Home Journal* had a circulation of 600,000, *The Delineator* had a circulation of 393,000, and *Woman's Home Companion* had a circulation of 125,000. With their growing circulation numbers, women's magazines experienced a growth in advertising revenues and the magazines' publishers took a lead in marketing their journals by differentiating their product and utilizing sophisticated promotional strategies.

Magazine publishers had to respond to readers' preferences and tastes to maintain their livelihoods. Some publishers decided to form strategies to create and maintain two-way communication between writers and readers. These publishers accomplished their task by printing readers' letters and providing responses. In this magazine-based forum, women asked questions and received answers focused on public and private aspects of their lives. In addition to sponsoring question-and-answer forums, publishers distributed surveys and provided incentives for the respondents. Edward Bok, one of the earliest editors of *Ladies' Home Journal*, included questions on his survey based on the readers' preferences. These questions ranged from "What in the magazine do you like least?" to "What do you like best?" and "What new features would you like to see started?" This survey technique yielded thousands of answers, allowing Bok to address many of his readers' concerns.

Sports and Fitness

In 1972, Title IX was signed into law and provided women and girls with equal opportunities regarding participation in sports, from elementary school to the university. When Title IX was adopted, only one out of 27 girls participated in high school sports. By 1998, the participation rate had increased dramatically, with one in three girls participating in high school sports. The 1996 Olympics fueled an interest in women's sports leagues, featuring volleyball, softball, basketball, and soccer. Despite this increased interest, women's sports struggled to maintain sponsorships of their teams and spectators of their events. Traditionally, magazine and newspaper sports sections covered only a small portion of women's sports (a situation that continues).

In the early 1980s, *Shape*, a women's magazine, was launched to address the needs of fitness-oriented women. This magazine offers workout, fitness, diet, and beauty tips to its readers. *Shape* does not usually report on sports events, but it often includes coverage of female athletes. With a circulation of 1.5 million readers, *Shape* contains articles with titles such as "Celebrities Work Their Abs" and "Wine Country Cycling." In the mid- to late 1990s, the increasing amount of interest in the women's sports movement in the United States perpetuated the creation of magazines focused on women's sports and fitness. Most of these magazines featured titles like *Real Sports*, *Sports Illustrated for Women* (or *SI Women*), and *Women's Sports and Fitness*. *SI Women* and *Women's Sports and Fitness* included material focused on beauty, fitness, and women's sports. In the early 2000s, *SI Women* featured articles focused on Women's National Basketball Association (WNBA) athletes, fashion and fitness tips, and a male and female swimsuit edition. *Women's Sports and Fitness* and *SI Women* did not survive past 2005, and *Real Sports* became an online publication.

Women's fitness magazines have been criticized for reinforcing male perceptions of American culture through their emphasis on the sexual differences between males and females. In addition, these magazines have been accused of promoting images of women that might not seem as empowering as those in women's sports magazines. Critics state that these nonempowering images do not encourage women to step outside the sexy, stylish, and fashionable boundaries of gender-stereotyped womanhood. Researchers found that each of these magazines also contains advertising that features stereotypical images of women.

Mainstream Publications

Between the 1950s and the 1980s, traditional women's magazines experienced a shift in the number of articles focused on the typical woman. Magazines like *Good Housekeeping* and *Ladies' Home Journal* decreased the number of articles focused on women's traditional roles as wives, mothers, and homemakers. At the same time, these magazines increased the number of articles focused on new roles for women, which included occupations in the workplace. These articles were more focused on politics, social concerns, and economic issues.

One of the books that may have perpetuated this movement was *The Feminine Mystique*, written by Betty Friedan and published in 1963. This book challenged traditional female roles and introduced women to new perspectives on attractiveness and gender. In addition to Friedan's work, *Ladies' Home Journal* featured an entire section titled "The New Feminism," which appeared six months after an 11-hour takeover of the magazine's offices by a group of protesters. Subsequent articles in *Ladies' Home Journal* had similar themes, ranging from subjects focused on a confrontation between revolutionary blacks and wealthy whites to an article focused on the death of Allison Krause, a Kent State University protester.

In the late 1980s, women's magazines featured stories about birth control and work options for women. Other prominent magazine articles during this period focused on women who had decided to delay childbearing until their 30s or 40s.

Today, women's lifestyle magazines such as *Cosmopolitan* and *Marie Clarie* continue to feature articles focused on clothing fashions and hairstyles; since the 1990s, however, topics have expanded to include once taboo subjects such as advice about men, dating, and sex. Other magazines, such as *Family Circle*, *Redbook*, *Woman's Day*, and *O, The Oprah Magazine*, focus on the 25- to 45-year-old demographic.

Women's magazine covers and advertisements often feature photos of models wearing the latest fashions. Most of the photos on mainstream women's magazine (fitness, sports, and lifestyle) usually feature one woman dressed in clothing from the latest season. Most of the women on the magazine covers are white celebrities (although women featured on ethnic magazine covers reflect the magazine's predominant ethnic demographic). Many women's magazines have the same advertisements, which often focus on cooking, cleaning, and child-care products. Some researchers believe that women's magazine editors are less likely than are editors of other magazines to publish articles that contradict their advertisers' messages. With the economic recession in 2008, many mainstream women's magazines began to feature coupons in their advertisements.

Bridal, Pregnancy, and Motherhood Magazines

Some of the women's magazines with the most pages per issue are bridal magazines, which feature a wealth of information focused on wedding proposals, ceremonies, and honeymoons. Filled with advertisements for wedding dresses, honeymoon destinations, and wedding favors, these magazines are usually purchased by recently engaged women. Some of the titles include *Modern Bride* and *Brides*.

Women's magazines focused on pregnancy and motherhood were some of the first how-to guides for aspiring mothers, mothers-to-be, and mothers of small children. These magazines feature various articles on subjects ranging from hospital birthing rooms and baby nursery decorations to a baby's first day at day care and tips for mothers who are transitioning back to the workplace. Prominent among this group are *Pregnancy*, *Parenting*, *Parents*, *Working Mother*, and *Family Fun*.

Ethnic Magazines

Several women's magazines are focused on women of a specific ethnicity. Some of these include *Latina* magazine and *Essence* magazine. *Latina* was founded in the late 1990s and was one of the first magazines to focus specifically on the interests of the diverse Latina population. *Essence* was founded in the late 1960s and is one of the only magazines for African American women. *Essence* sponsors an annual music festival, the *Essence* Music Festival, every year in New Orleans. Both these magazines focus on lifestyles of ethnic women. Common articles cover topics typical of other women's magazines, such as beauty and fashion, career, celebrities, and health, but with a specific emphasis on the issues and topics unique to the ethnicity. This targeting extends to advertising; ads in both *Latina* and *Essence* focus on ethnic women and tout commodities from hair-care products to fast-food restaurants (with advertisements featuring ethnic models).

Lifestyle and Cooking Magazines

Some women's magazines focus on women's traditional roles in the household, which include cook, decorator, and housekeeper. These domestically focused magazines raise such tasks to an art in order to increase the attractiveness of these activities and the products that support them. Such magazines include *Martha Stewart Living*, *Southern Living*, and *Every Day With Rachel Ray* magazine. *Martha Stewart Living* focuses on decorating the home and planning home-based events. *Southern Living* emphasizes the differences between the seasons and the impact these seasons may have on cooking, gardening, decorating, and travel. The *Rachael Ray* magazine primarily focuses on cooking for the busy household and emphasizes quick and easy decorating tips.

Jennifer T. Edwards
Tarleton State University

See also Advertising; Beauty and Body Image: Beauty Myths; Beauty and Body Image: Eating Disorders; Bordo, Susan; E-Zines: Riot Grrrl; E-Zines: Third Wave Feminist; Gender and Femininity: Motherhood; Gender and Femininity: Single/Independent Girl; Gender Media Monitoring; Men's Magazines: Lad Magazines; Men's Magazines: Lifestyle and Health; Steinem, Gloria; Tween Magazines; Women's Magazines: Fashion; Women's Magazines: Feminist Magazines

Further Readings

Gough-Yates, Anna. *Understanding Women's Magazines: Publishing, Markets, and Readerships*. New York: Routledge, 2003.

Munnien, Needee. *Which Masculinity? Which Femininity? Gender Representations in Men['s] and Women['s] Lifestyle Magazines*. Leicester, UK: University of Leicester, 2002.

Palmer, Gianna Marshall. *Mixed Signals: Sexuality in Men's and Women's Lifestyle Magazines*. Honors Thesis, Wesleyan University. http://wesscholar.wesleyan.edu (April 15, 2010).

Walker, Nancy A. *Women's Magazines, 1940–1960: Gender Roles and the Popular Press*. Boston: Bedford/St. Martin's, 1998.

WORKFORCE

In 2010, women comprised approximately one third of the U.S. media workforce, up from about one fifth in the early 1970s. Despite the overall increase in the number of women employed in the industry since then, gains have been incremental and at times nonexistent. For instance, since the mid-1980s in the United States, the number of women working in media fields has stalled at approximately 30 percent, and the *glass ceiling* seems still to be firmly in place. Women hold only about one fifth of all upper management positions and continue to experience pay disparities in most industry segments. Women also still report experiencing sexual discrimination and are relegated to traditional workplace roles based on gender. Globally, women are not faring much better. They represent roughly between one fourth and almost one half of the media workforce. They also report experiencing discrimination and marginalization to certain positions based on gender roles.

Although women continue to take two steps forward and one step back in many segments of the media, the news is not bleak on all fronts. Women have made strides in certain fields, such as the magazine and film industries. In these two industries, women such as Cathleen Black, chair of Hearst Corporation, and DreamWorks Studios chief executive officer Stacey Snider have earned positions as executives in film production companies and media conglomerates. Historically, a number of media scholars have argued that as women gain positions of authority, they will create a more welcoming environment for women in the workplace and will begin to portray women in a more responsible manner in the media. However, scholars hoping for transformative change in the media industry have been frustrated by lackluster strides toward gender equity. In fact, some scholars angered by the apparent backlash toward women in the industry are advocating for more than reforming the existing system. These scholars argue that the issue goes beyond one of numbers and must include a shift in the culture of the media workplace.

By the Numbers

The ratio of women to men in the media industry has remained relatively stagnant since the 1980s at approximately 1:3. These numbers, however, vary by media field. Historically, women have been best represented in the magazine and public relations industries. Since the early 1800s, women have claimed positions as writers, editors, and publishers of prominent national magazines. It is difficult to determine the current percentage of women in the magazine industry, because no statistical data are kept by a central clearinghouse; however, magazine scholar Sammye Johnson argues that the industry appears to have achieved gender parity. Likewise, in 2009, the U.S. Bureau of Labor Statistics reported that women made up 60 percent of public relations professionals (women constitute 47 percent of the overall American workforce). Women also have made strides in television and film since the early 1970s. For instance, the percentage of women in television news operations increased from 11 percent in 1971 to approximately 40 percent in 2010, according to the Radio Television Digital News Association.

Nevertheless, the numbers are not positive. In 2009, Martha Lauzen, the executive director of the Center for the Study of Women in Television and Film at San Diego State University, found that women made up only 16 percent of all directors, producers, writers, cinematographers, and editors involved in the top-grossing U.S. films, representing a 3 percent decrease since 2001. Research conducted by Lauzen in 2002 revealed similar statistics about the number of women working in a creative capacity in entertainment television. Women have not fared much better in newspapers and online news media. In its 2010 annual newsroom census, the American Society of Newspaper Editors found that women made up approximately 37 percent of all news workers, even though more women than men have entered the journalism profession in the last three decades. (The 2009 Annual Survey of Journalism and Mass Communication Graduates revealed that women remain the overwhelming majority enrolling in undergraduate journalism and mass communication programs.) Research shows that the gender composition of online media mirrors traditional news media. Perhaps the most disheartening research for gender activists comes from the radio industry, where, after the elimination of Equal Employment Opportunity rules in 1999, the number of women working in radio news declined from 37 percent in 2000 to 29 percent in 2010, according to the Radio Television Digital News Association.

Power and Pay

At the dawn of the 21st century, women still are working in lower-level, lower-paying positions than men in the media industry. The American Society of

Women have made strides in the workforce, but in most professions, women are still working in lower-level, lower-paying positions than men and are more likely to encounter harassment and discrimination. (Photos.com)

Newspaper Editors reports that in 2010 approximately 33 percent of women worked in supervisory capacities in newsrooms across the nation. These numbers mirror the 2006 *Women in Media* report released by the Media Management Center at Northwestern University. This group found that the number of female publishers at newspapers with circulations greater than 85,000 had stalled at 25 since 2003, and the percentage of female managing editors remained around 39 percent. Women hold approximately one fifth of all leadership positions in radio, television, and film, a proportion that has remained relatively consistent throughout the decade. The majority of women within these media industries remain in middle-management or lower-level positions. Meanwhile, women in public relations and magazine industries have broken out of the *pink ghetto* (the term used to describe the relegation of women to lower-level positions within an organization). Women made up 53 percent of public relations managers in 2009, the U.S. Bureau of Labor Statistics reports, and *Folio: The Magazine for Magazine Management* reported in 2000 that 60 percent of all managing editors at U.S. magazines were women. Still, the total number of female supervisors in media continues to lag behind that of the overall U.S. workforce, where women comprise approximately half of all individuals in management roles. Overseas, female media practitioners encounter similar conditions. In 1996, Margret Lunenborg reported that women comprised only 12 percent of all editorial management positions.

Within most media sectors, women continue to earn less than their male counterparts. On average, female media workers earned approximately 80 percent of what men earned in 2006, which was equivalent to the ratio of the overall U.S. workforce. Even in fields such as public relations, where women have earned positions of power, pay disparities remain. In 2002, female public relations managers made only 63 percent of what men earned, according to the U.S. Bureau of Labor Statistics. In the magazine industry, however, women have lessened the gender pay gap. In 2002, *Folio* reported that female editorial directors actually made more than men. However, the magazine industry still serves as the exception for women instead of the rule. A number of scholars argue that male-owned media conglomerates contribute to continuing power and pay disparities. Since the 1980s, more than 50 media companies have merged into six multinational media conglomerates: Time Warner, Bertelsmann, Viacom, Vivendi, News Corporation, and the Walt Disney Company, all owned by men. Some scholars argue that the goal of these media empires is to (re)produce capital by maintaining the status quo. Other scholars have theorized that, as women flood certain media sectors, all salaries will be suppressed, creating a "velvet ghetto."

Discrimination and Marginalization

Women are not just earning less than men; they also are suffering from discrimination and marginalization. A number of studies in the 1990s and 2000s reported that women still experience harassment and discrimination. Research by David Weaver in the mid-1990s revealed that approximately half of the women who participated in his study had experienced some form of harassment. Likewise, in 2001, a majority of the women Karen Ross interviewed admitted to experiencing discrimination in the newsroom. Qualitative scholarship has revealed that women still experience blatant harassment. One woman interviewed for Carolyn Byerly and Karen Ross's 2006 book *Women and Media* reported that a colleague gave her a jock strap.

Women also have been marginalized to certain positions. Historically, female journalists have been placed primarily in "soft news" positions, such as gossip columnist, while their male counterparts covered "hard news," such as crime. This still holds true today. In 2006, the Associated Press Sports Editors (ASPE) released its first race and gender report card, revealing that only 12.6 percent of the total sports staffs of ASPE members were women; of those women in sports departments, more than 20 percent were in the low-ranking positions of support staff such as clerks. Likewise, relatively few women in sports broadcasting work in lucrative positions, such as play-by-play announcer or color commentator; instead, many women are relegated to positions as sideline reporters. Some scholars argue that female sideline reporters are objectified and serve to reproduce *hegemonic masculinity*, a term used to refer to dominant constructions about masculinity in society.

Although women make up approximately two thirds of journalism and mass communication graduates, some scholars have found that women tend to flee jobs in journalism after a few years, as a result of burnout from male-centered newsrooms. In 2009, Scott Reinardy's survey of 715 U.S. newspaper journalists revealed that women suffer from higher levels of burnout than their male counterparts; 30 percent of women under the age of 27 said that they planned on leaving the field. Women listed differences in perceived organizational support and differing job expectations based on gender as reasons for feeling overburdened. In addition to the pay disparities, sexism, and discrimination that some women face, many also encounter work/life balance issues in a male-driven newsroom. Some scholars argue that newsrooms have been historically constructed as a male sphere; therefore, men are perceived as the norm and women are "otherized." In a male-ordered domain, women must work harder to achieve respect from colleagues by becoming more aggressive or relying on other strategies to succeed, such as forming alliances with other marginalized groups. Within the male culture of the newsroom, editors are less likely to rely on women as expert sources or to report on topics perceived as women's issues, such as health, child abuse, and rape.

Theory and Practice

Second wave feminists (the name given to feminists active in the 1960s and 1970s) focused on achieving gender equity in the media workforce. As illustrated above, at the dawn of the 21st century, despite some incremental gains, women still lag behind men in the media workplace not only in numbers employed but also in power and pay. Some scholars argue that as women gain positions of authority in media fields, more women will follow and pay disparities will disappear. Little quantitative evidence exists to support this notion. However, some evidence does exist to support the notion that women in positions of power can change the culture of the workplace.

For instance, in 2004, Wayne Wanta suggested that female editors change the "macho" culture of the newsroom. Female editors tend to place female reporters on traditionally male-dominated beats such as crime and politics. Still, for some scholars and activists change has not moved swiftly enough. Some radical feminists advocate for the creation of grassroots movements such as Women in Media and News; the establishment of women's news agencies, such as Unnati Features; and the implementation of feminist approaches to media production, such as feminist filmmaking, which contests the traditional *male gaze* (a term coined by Laura Mulvey). In addition to these strategies, scholars and activists hoping to reform the current media system suggest actively campaigning for change, encouraging existing media corporations to provide mentors and resources for women in the workforce, and advocating for more flexible work environments with on-site day care, telecommuting, and flex time to ease work/life balance issues.

Lori Amber Roessner
University of Tennessee

See also Diversity; Empowerment; Equal Employment Opportunity Commission; Federal Communications Commission; Feminist Theory: Third Wave; Film: Hollywood; Hegemony; Male Gaze; Minority Rights; Misogyny; Mulvey, Laura; Network News Anchor Desk; Newsrooms; Patriarchy; Sexism; Social Inequality; Stereotypes; Talk Shows; Television

Further Readings

American Society of News Editors. "Newsroom Census." 2010. http://asne.org/key_initiatives/diversity/newsroom_census.aspx (Accessed December 2010).

Arnold, Mary and Mary Nesbit. "Women in Media 2006: Finding the Leader in You." Media Management Center at Northwestern University. http://www.mediamanagementcenter.org/research/wim2006.asp (Accessed December 2010).

Beck, Lee, Tudor Vlad, Paris Desnoes, and Devora Olin. "2009 Annual Survey of Journalism and Mass Communication Graduates." James M. Cox Jr. Center for International Mass Communication Training and Research, Grady College of Journalism and Mass Communication. http://www.grady.uga.edu/annualsurveys/Graduate_Survey/Graduate_2009/Grad2009MergedColor.pdf (Accessed December 2010).

Byerly, Carolyn M. and Karen Ross, eds. *Women and Media: A Critical Introduction*. Malden, MA: Blackwell, 2006.

Creedon, Pamela and Judith Cramer, eds. *Women in Mass Communication*, 3rd ed. Thousand Oaks, CA: Sage, 2007.

De Bruin, Marjan and Karen Ross, eds. *Gender and Newsroom Cultures: Identities at Work*. Cresskill, NJ: Hampton Press, 2004.

Lapchick, Richard, Jenny Brenden, and Brian Wright. "The 2006 Racial and Gender Report Card of the Associated Press Sports Editors." DeVos Sports Business Management Program at the University of Central Florida. http://web.bus.ucf.edu/documents/sport/2006_racial_gender_report_card_associated_press_sports_editors.pdf (Accessed December 2010).

Lauzen, Martha M. "The Celluloid Ceiling: Behind-the-Scenes Employment of Women on the Top 250 Films of 2009." http://womenintvfilm.sdsu.edu/research.html (Accessed December 2010).

Papper, Bob. "2010 Women and Minorities Data." Radio Television Digital News Association/Hofstra University Survey. http://www.rtdna.org/media/women_minorities_survey_final.pdf (Accessed December 2010).

Reinardy, Scott. "Female Journalists More Likely to Leave Newspapers." *Newspaper Research Journal*, v.30/3 (2009).

Wanta, Wayne and Stephanie Craft. "Women in the Newsroom: Influences of Female Editors and Reporters on the News Agenda." *Journalism and Mass Communication Quarterly*, v.81/1 (2004).

Weaver, David H. and G. Cleveland Wilhoit. *The American Journalist in the 1990s: U.S. News People at the End of an Era*. Mahwah, NJ: Lawrence Erlbaum Associates, 1996.

YOUTUBE

YouTube LLC began in 2005 as a Web-based platform for storing and delivering home movies and music. It has grown into a billion-dollar venture owned by Google Inc. since 2006, and it also distributes professionally produced entertainment and news. Now the world's most popular video Website, YouTube was started by three employees of PayPal who apparently were attempting to share personal videos unsuccessfully. The first YouTube video in 2005 was "Me at the Zoo," in which one of the business's cofounders said the two elephants behind him had long trunks. A year later, 3 million viewers watched "A Message from Chad and Steve," announcing that Google had bought YouTube. The sale of YouTube to Google made all three male YouTube founders billionaires.

Before the acquisition, YouTube had grown larger than its competitors, including Google Video, and promoted itself as a vehicle producing no video itself but offering a platform for the public to share amateur videos, with the claim that it was the world's leading online video community. YouTube provided a simple Internet interface that allowed people without much technical background to share videos. In general, the interface allows anyone to view videos for free, but only registered members may add videos, and they are assigned to a channel similar to a Facebook page. For a fee, members are provided other privileges. YouTube may delete videos without notice, a reminder that it is a private company, not a public service. Viewers may comment on videos in writing or with another video. Viewers can flag perceived copyright infringements, which YouTube employees check.

YouTube has grown exponentially since its inception. In 2006, the audience was 70 percent American, which declined to 30 percent in 2008. By the end of 2006, YouTube was receiving more than 100 million viewers daily. By November 2007, YouTube was the most popular entertainment Website in Britain, followed by the British Broadcasting Corporation. In 2008, YouTube was in the top 10 most popular Websites globally, accounting for 37 percent of all online videos watched in the United States; Fox was second with 4 percent. In March 2009, YouTube recorded more than 90 million visitors, a total more than 10 times greater than its closest competitor. In fall 2009, YouTube served 1 billion people globally, and amateurs produced 80 percent of its videos. By the end of 2009, 80 percent of Internet users had watched some video online, with a strong possibility that those videos were on YouTube, which garnered 40 percent of audience share. YouTube has hosted more than 150 million videos, which themselves sometimes make news. During the 2008 presidential election, several endorsements were announced on YouTube. In the Iraq War, both American soldiers and Iraqi opposition fighters documented the killing of enemies on YouTube.

Notwithstanding, YouTube has also distributed countless videos of people's cute pets. YouTube's success has been linked to various features, including a list of video recommendations, an e-mail link for video sharing, comments, and an embedded video player. Another reason for its success has been mainstream media attention. A *Saturday Night Live* skit posted on YouTube in 2005 reached 1.2 million hits and attracted the attention of the press. YouTube reached a milestone when it announced receiving 24 hours of video per minute in March 2010. In December 2010, the Website reported adding 35 hours of video per minute globally. YouTube has become the second most used Web search engine after its parent company.

Google bought YouTube in 2006 for $1.65 billion. Although an industry analyst predicted that YouTube would become profitable in 2010 with $700 million in revenues, the video publisher had yet to become profitable at the end of 2010. In the fiscal quarter ending in September 2010, YouTube ads were part of the $625 million Google earned in display advertising, but that is a small percentage of the $7.3 billion Google earned in that time. YouTube has experimented with various advertising strategies, including home-page ads for entertainment advertisers and deals with video and music production studios for television movies and music videos. Most amateur videos are without advertiser support to help turn a profit from the site's $700 million (2009) operating cost, half of which was from bandwidth cost. YouTube invites popular members to become partners and add advertising, and some make a living from their YouTube channels. YouTube has formed partnerships with traditional media, such as the National Broadcasting Company (NBC), the Columbia Broadcasting System (CBS), Universal Music, Sony BMG, and Warner Music, as well as the BBC, to provide material. News stations have used YouTube to encourage audiences to file videos and images with their news operations, setting up their own news sites on YouTube. In the 2008 presidential election, YouTube partnered with CNN to host debates in which audiences could file their questions via videos for candidates to answer. One debate succeeded in attracting a younger audience of 18- to 34-year-olds to such programming.

In 2010, YouTube reportedly was offering 2 billion videos a day. It has become a model for other video-sharing Websites, such as Kyte, Revver, and Radar, but YouTube still is the leading site of its type. YouTube's global presence also has been increasing; its videos are getting longer; viewers are spending more time on YouTube; and its videos are being shared across the Internet. In addition to viewing and sharing videos, consumers can embed videos in weblogs, as well as video logs (vlogs) and social media sites, such as Myspace and Facebook. YouTube also functions as a so-called social media forum, where consumers are able to comment, rate, and share information. As a cultural technology, online digital video is different from the film home movies of the mid-1900s. YouTube represents new media practices of displaying domestic everyday life. Video diaries are characteristic of YouTube as a social medium, creating a hybrid domain of self-expression, community, and marketing. More than a collection of millions of home videos, YouTube also constitutes an emotional and social space, as well as a space for virtual community and cultural politics. Within YouTube, viewers may find racist, sexist, violent debates over politics, religion, and war.

In what may become a post-television era, amateur videos are a media force to be reckoned with, which fragments audiences, concerns advertisers, and erodes traditional corporate media. As an emerging cultural medium, YouTube reflects a symbiotic relationship between amateur cultural products and commercial cultural products. It must deliver audiences to advertisers yet provide alternatives to television. YouTube may therefore be described as a new hybrid cultural medium. It is both an industry and a pastime or hobby. It has been noted to follow the 90–9–1 rule of online communities: 90 percent of the audience does not interact; 9 percent do, sometimes; and 1 percent interact often. YouTube is also characterized by its multiple metaphors: as a library, an archive, a laboratory, and a mass medium. From a computer technology perspective, YouTube is a database, nothing more. Its hybridity of metaphors raises problems and questions about issues such as open access, legal constraints, traditional media distribution, aesthetics, and media careers. As a sign of hybridity, YouTube video providers include television stations, sports enterprises, advertisers, cultural organizations, artists, advocates, and amateurs, an amalgam of participatory culture. Not producing video itself, YouTube has been termed a meta-business, which offers information created by others, much like Apple's iTunes store.

YouTube is an important research topic, because there is not yet a shared understanding of YouTube's form and function as a business and popular-culture product. Therefore, as of 2011, there was no comprehensive research on YouTube as an industry, archive, and cultural form. However, some media and gender research has examined YouTube. One study in 2008 found that both consumers and producers were more likely to be male than female. A Canadian study of gender difference found that most YouTube video logs, or vlogs, had a single participant, and 58 percent of the time that participant was a man. The average participant age was 23 years old, with 21 the average for females and 24 for males. A majority of the vlogs were young men in the United States. Female vloggers were more likely to focus on personal matters. Males created more entertainment, public, and technology vlogs. Viewing instances ranged from none to more than 150,000, although less than 10 percent had 1,000 or more views, and 68 percent had fewer than 100. Gender and topic were the best predictors of view, as vlogs featuring females averaged 7,000 views and those featuring men averaged 150. More than a third of the vlogs featured a woman as the primary character. Males were more likely to post videos and comments, although females were more likely to interact with other vloggers.

Paul Grosswiler
University of Maine

See also Audiences: Producers of New Media; Audiences: Reception and Injection Models; Blogs and Blogging; Cyberspace and Cyberculture; Electronic Media and Social Inequality; Media Convergence; New Media; Reality-Based Television: *America's Next Top Model*; Reality-Based Television: Makeover Shows; Reality-Based Television: Wedding Shows; Social Media; Social Networking Sites: Facebook; Social Networking Sites: Myspace; Twitter; Viral Advertising and Marketing; Virtual Community; Web 2.0; Wiki

Further Readings

Burgess, Jean and Joshua Green. *YouTube: Online Video and Participatory Culture.* Cambridge, UK: Polity Press, 2009.

Molyneaux, Heather, Susan O'Donnell, and Kerri Gibson. "YouTube Vlogs: An Analysis of the Gender Divide." *Media Report to Women*, v.37/2 (Spring 2009).

Snickars, Pelle and Patrick Vondreau, eds. *The YouTube Reader.* Stockholm: National Library of Sweden, 2009.

Strangelove, Michael. *Watching YouTube: Extraordinary Videos by Ordinary People.* Toronto, ON: University of Toronto Press, 2010.

Glossary

The Beauty Myth: A 1991 book by Naomi Wolf, which charges than an ideal of female beauty has been used to oppress women and maintain the patriarchal system.

Body image: An individual's perception of his or her physical appearance. Some theorists believe that promotion of idealized body types in the media has led to widespread dissatisfaction with bodies that are in fact normal, leading in turn to unhealthy practices such as extreme dieting, bulimia, or excessive plastic surgery.

Bridezilla: A pejorative term (combining "bride" and "Godzilla") coined in the 1990s to denote a demanding and difficult bride; it was adopted in 2001 for the television reality program *Bridezillas*, which followed a number of women from engagement to wedding, reinforcing gender stereotypes about women as more concerned than men with their weddings and also emphasizing the self-centeredness of the female characters.

Culture jamming: Resistance to cultural practices and media messages through activities such as ad parodies (e.g., of "Joe Camel" as "Joe Chemo"), defacement of billboards (e.g., adding an antismoking message to a cigarette advertisement), and pranks (e.g., switching the voice boxes of Barbie and G.I. Joe dolls and then returning them to store shelves).

Cyberculture: The technologies, attitudes, values, and modes of thought developed by people who take part in cyberspace. Practices associated with cyberculture include social networking, cloud computing, mass collaboration, social bookmarking, and distributed creation.

Cyberspace: A term coined by science fiction writer William Gibson in his 1984 novel *Neuromancer* and currently used to describe the nonphysical world created by computer systems and their users.

Desensitization: An effect of continual exposure to something that results in diminished emotional, cognitive, biological, or behavioral response to it. With regard to the media, the term is most often used to refer to the effects of repeated exposure to violence on television or other media, such as video games or films, which may make audiences more accepting of violence in real life.

Encoding/decoding model: A theory of audience reception developed by Stuart Hall that states that media producers encode messages in the mass media, which are then decoded by the audience. This model envisions the audience as active rather than passive and describes four ways in which a message may be decoded: professional, dominant, negotiated, and oppositional.

Ethnography: A method of research and cultural practice based on long periods of participant observation in order to explore aspects of human social processes.

Facebook: A social networking service created in 2004 by Mark Zuckerberg, Eduardo Saverin, Chris Hughes, and Dustin Moskovitz, which as of 2010 claimed to have more than 500 million active users.

Fairness doctrine: A policy introduced by the Federal Communications Commission (FCC) in 1949 that required fair and equitable presentation of controversial issues to license holders (e.g., radio and television stations). The fairness doctrine was upheld in a 1969 U.S. Supreme Court decision, but in 1987 a court decided that the FCC did not have to continue enforcing the doctrine.

Federal Communications Commission (FCC): An agency of the U.S. government established in 1934 to regulate nongovernmental use of the radio spectrum, including radio and television broadcasting and interstate telecommunications.

First-person shooter: A video game such as *Call of Duty* or *Halo* in which the player experiences simulated combat through the point of view of the game's protagonist (i.e., in the first person).

Frankfurt School: A group of European scholars originally affiliated with the School of Social Research in Frankfurt, Germany, who were concerned with the philosophical and political analysis of culture. Prominent members of the Frankfurt School (many of whom immigrated to the United States around the time of World War II) include Theodor Adorno, Max Horkheimer, and Herbert Marcuse.

Gender inequality: Social inequality due to gender.

Gender-specific advertising: Advertising that uses persuasive messages created specifically to address men or women.

Gold farming: A practice in some massively multiplayer online role-playing games (MMORPGs) of playing a game for the purpose of acquiring virtual currency, which is then sold to other players. Most typically, a gold farmer lives in a low-wage country such as China, whereas those who purchase the currency live in higher-wage countries such as the United States; users purchase currency to advance quickly in the game without investing large amounts of time playing it.

Hacking: Unauthorized entry into a computer or computer system or use of a computer for unauthorized purposes; if performed as part of a political or social protest, this activity may be termed *hacktivism*. Examples of hacking include Website defacement, denial-of-service attacks, and e-mail bombing.

Hashtag: A set of tweets (messages sent on Twitter) on a particular topic, identified by the # sign before the topic word.

Hegemony: A term, popularized by the Marxist theorist Antonio Gramsci, referring to the process whereby the beliefs, practices, and values of a particular class become dominant in a society to the point where alternative beliefs are excluded.

Hypermedia: Media in which information (including words and images) is connected in a web, allowing for construction of a nonlinear narrative.

Injection model of audience reception: A theory of audience reception popular in the early 20th century. Also known as the "magic bullet" or "hypodermic needle" model, it hypothesizes that a mass communication medium such as radio or television simply inserts its messages into the consciousness of the audience and that all audience members respond in the same way to a given message.

Intersectionality: A feminist theory that deemphasizes the common experience of women and emphasizes instead the different experiences of, for instance, poor versus middle-class or white versus black women; this theory argued that black women's identity was holistic and not separable into aspects informed by race and other aspects informed by gender.

Male gaze: A concept explicated by Laura Mulvey in her 1975 essay "Visual Pleasure and Narrative Cinema" that states that conventional Hollywood movies are created as if all audience members were male, with story lines and shot selections designed to appeal to a male point of view.

Massively multiplayer online role-playing game (MMORPG): A type of computer game developed in the 1990s characterized by virtual narrative environments and in which users create avatars and interact with other users through them. MMORPGs developed from real-world role-playing games, and there is some debate about what constitutes a MMORPG: Some would include virtual communities such as *Second Life* (which does not involve gaming), whereas others would restrict the definition to games such as *Ultima Online* and *World of Warcraft*.

Media convergence: A term describing changes brought about by digital technologies, including the merging of different types of media (e.g., video, audio, and text) onto a single platform and the merging of media industries (e.g. Time Warner and America Online in 2000) as well. Convergence has increased the ability of users to create and use media but has also led to consolidation of ownership and greater horizontal and vertical integration in the media industry.

Media Education Foundation (MEF): An organization based in Massachusetts that produces and distributes educational resources, including documentary films, which encourage critical reflection on the American mass media and its social, political, and cultural impact. Topics covered by MEF materials include gender, sexual orientation, consumerism, violence, media ownership, and media consolidation.

Metrosexual: A term coined around 2000 to refer to heterosexual men who adopt cultural practices formerly identified more with gay men, such as close attention to grooming and fashion.

Misogyny: Hatred of, dislike of, or prejudice against women.

Multi-User dimensions (MUDs): Shared virtual worlds used in online gaming and similar contexts, in which users can interact in real time through the use of avatars. Examples of MUDs include *Second Life*, *The Sims*, and *World of Warcraft*.

Myspace: A social networking site, created in 2003, that became the most popular networking site in the United States in 2006 but was overtaken in 2008 by the rival site Facebook.

Pathologizing: A technique used in advertising in which normal human conditions, particularly those associated with aging (such as graying hair or loss of skin tone), are presented as problems that need correction or that can be overcome through purchasing the product being advertised.

Polysemic text: A text having multiple meanings.

Pornification: A term coined in the 1990s by scholars to describe what they saw as the aesthetics of pornography entering the general culture; an associated term is *porn creep*.

Reception theory: A method of analysis that focuses on the relationship between media and the person or audience receiving it and emphasizes that texts or other media are interpreted by people (rather than being passively received by them). British theorist Stuart Hall describes three interpretation codes audiences may apply to a text: dominant (the preferred reading, reflecting mainstream ideology), negotiated (in which the preferred reading is inflected to take into account the audience's own experience), and oppositional (which is when the audience's reading is in direct conflict with the preferred reading).

Semiotics: The study of signs, a field of philosophical inquiry begun in the 19th century by Ferdinand de Saussure and Charles Saunders Peirce. Semiotics was applied to the field of gender studies by, among others, Gillian Dyer and Judith Williamson, who focused on advertising and how it constructs social difference.

Sexism: A term in existence since the 1930s but that came into common use in the 1960s to refer to discrimination against men or women based on their biological sex.

Short message service (SMS): A communication service that allows short text messages to be sent between fixed or mobile phones.

Sitcom: Situation comedy, a type of television program with ongoing characters and a story line, usually set in a situation such as a workplace, family, or group of friends.

Soap opera: A fictional serial program on television or radio. The name derives from the fact that some of the early programs were sponsored by soap companies and, as the programs were broadcast during the daytime, the programming was intended to appeal to women, particularly housewives.

Social comparison theory: A theory, first developed by Leon Festinger in the 1950s, that argues that people tend to make comparisons between themselves and others and also against idealized images, such as are often presented in advertising.

Social inequality: Inequalities generated by social institutions and leading to unequal control of valued resources.

Social role theory: A theory put forward by Alice Eagly that posits that society assigns or teaches roles depending on gender and that by playing those roles people acquire or renounce certain attributes. For instance, females are more often placed in nurturing roles and thus develop caregiving and nurturing qualities (which are also associated in the public mind with femininity), whereas boys are placed in competitive roles and thus develop qualities such as independence and aggression, both traits identified in the public mind as masculine.

Stereotype: A generalization about people or groups of people, often based on characteristics such as gender or race. Stereotypes are pervasive in popular media (arrogant Americans, lazy African Americans, vain women, obsessed and violent Arabs), and thus the media can reinforce and perpetuate incorrect or biased beliefs.

Televisuality: A term coined in the mid-1990s by John Caldwell to denote a new visual style in television programming that calls attention to itself and contrasts with the previous ideal of the "invisible" style.

Textual analysis: An approach to cultural artifacts, including media texts, that emphasizes the fluid and multiple interpretations possible and the possibility that multiple meanings are encoded in any text.

Traditional media: Types of mass communication such as television, radio, and newspapers in which professionals (e.g., writers and producers) create and implement programming, while the participation of audience members is restricted to consuming the finished product.

Trope: Rhetorical devices or units of metaphor that reflect cultural norms and are used to facilitate communication. Common gendered tropes in folklore include the hero (for men) and the damsel in distress, evil stepmother, and fairy godmother (for women).

Tween: A young person between the ages of 8 and 14, an age group that has been identified as a demographic with specific tastes and sufficient disposable income to make them a useful target for marketing.

Twitter: A social networking and microblogging site, created in 2006 by the San Francisco–based company Twitter, Inc., which allows users to communicate through "tweets" or text-based messages of up to 140 characters.

Usenet: An Internet discussion system created in 1979 by Tom Truscott and Jim Ellis that allows users to post messages, organized around topics, to newsgroups.

Virtual community: A community created through the interactions of individuals or groups of people who may be distant from one another geographically. Among the early Internet-based virtual communities were those formed by people through Usenet newsgroups (beginning in 1979) and the Internet forum The WELL (founded in 1985).

Virtuality: A socially constructed world that does not exist in reality (as does the physical world) but is created through the interaction of users. Virtual worlds are key to role-playing games (RPGs), in which users create avatars that interact with one another in the context of the game.

Web 2.0: Web applications that allow users to create and share information: examples include wikis, video-sharing sites such as YouTube, and social networking sites such as Facebook and Myspace.

Wiki: An Internet composition system and particular Websites or other repositories of information created in using such a system. The defining characteristic of wikis is their collaborative nature: The wiki is created by its users, and generally anyone with access can contribute, view, and edit the information. Major wikis devoted to gender issues include Wikigender.

Sarah E. Boslaugh
Kennesaw State University

Resource Guide

Books

Alan, Jeff. *Anchoring America: The Changing Face of Network News*. Chicago: Bonus Books, 2003.

Alasuutari, Petri. *Rethinking the Media Audience: The New Agenda*. Thousand Oaks, CA: Sage, 1999.

Austerlitz, Saul. *Money for Nothing: A History of the Music Video From the Beatles to the White Stripes*. New York: Continuum, 2008.

Barthes, Roland. *Camera Lucida: Reflections on Photography*. London: Jonathan Cape, 1982.

Barthes, Roland. *Elements of Semiology*. London: Jonathan Cape, 1967.

Barthes, Roland. *Empire of Signs*. London: Jonathan Cape, 1983.

Barthes, Roland. *The Fashion System*. London: Jonathan Cape, 1985.

Barthes, Roland. *Image-Music-Text*. New York: Noonday, 1978.

Barthes, Roland. *Mythologies*. London: Jonathan Cape, 1972.

Bell, Elizabeth, Lynda Haas, and Laura Sells, eds. *From Mouse to Mermaid: The Politics of Film, Gender, and Culture*. Bloomington: Indiana University Press, 1995.

Bongco, Mila. *Reading Comics: Language, Culture, and the Concept of the Superhero in Comic Books*. New York: Garland Publishing, 2000.

Bordo, Susan. *The Male Body: A Look at Men in Public and in Private*. New York: Farrar, Straus and Giroux, 1999.

Bordo, Susan. *Twilight Zones: The Hidden Life of Cultural Images From Plato to O.J.* Berkeley: University of California Press, 1997.

Bordo, Susan. *Unbearable Weight: Feminism, Western Culture, and the Body, Tenth Anniversary Edition*, 2nd ed. Berkeley: University of California Press, 2004.

Brooker, Will and Deborah Jermyn. *The Audience Studies Reader*. New York: Routledge, 2003.

Burrill, Derek. *Die Tryin': Videogames, Masculinity, Culture*. New York: Peter Lang, 2008.

Butler, Jeremy. *Television Style*. New York: Routledge, 2010.

Byerly, Carolyn M. and Karen Ross, eds. *Women and Media: A Critical Introduction*. Malden, MA: Blackwell, 2006.

Caldwell, John T. *Televisuality: Style, Crisis and Authority in American Television*. New Brunswick, NJ: Rutgers University Press, 1995.

Carroll, John and John Payne, eds. *Cognition and Social Behavior*. New York: Lawrence Erlbaum Associates, 1976.

Cassell, Justine and Henry Jenkins, eds. *From Barbie to Mortal Kombat: Gender and Computer Games*. Cambridge, MA: MIT Press, 1998.

Castel, Davis and Katherine Phillips. *Disorders of Body Image*. Petersfield, UK: Wrightson Biomedical Publishing, 2002.

Craft, Christine. *Too Old, Too Ugly, and Not Deferential to Men*. Rocklin, CA: Prima, 1988.

Creedon, Pamela and Judith Cramer, eds. *Women in Mass Communication*, 3rd ed. Thousand Oaks, CA: Sage, 2006.

Cuklanz, Lisa M. and Sujata Moorti. *Local Violence, Global Media: Feminist Analyses of Gendered Representations*. New York: Peter Lang, 2009.

De Bruin, Marjan and Karen Ross, eds. *Gender and Newsroom Cultures: Identities at Work*. Cresskill, NJ: Hampton Press, 2004.

de Lauretis, Teresa. *Technologies of Gender: Essays on Theory, Film, and Fiction*. Bloomington: Indiana University Press, 1987.

Douglas, Susan J. *Where the Girls Are: Growing Up Female With the Mass Media*. 1994. Reprint, New York: Three Rivers Press, 1995.

Friedman, James, ed. *Reality Squared: Televisual Discourse on the Real*. New Brunswick, NJ: Rutgers University Press, 2002.

Gee, James Paul. *What Video Games Have to Teach Us About Learning and Literacy*. New York: Palgrave Macmillan, 2003.

Giroux, Henry. *The Mouse That Roared: Disney and the End of Innocence*. Lanham, MD: Rowman & Littlefield, 1999.

Goade, Sally, ed. *Empowerment Versus Oppression: Twenty-First Century Views of Popular Romance*

Novels. Newcastle Upon Tyne, UK: Cambridge Scholars, 2007.

Hartley, John. *Tele-ology: Studies in Television*. London: Routledge, 1992.

Heaton, Jeanne and Claudia Strauss. *Talking to Eating Disorders: Simple Ways to Support Someone With Anorexia, Bulimia, Binge Eating, or Body Image Issues*. New York: New American Libraries, 2005.

hooks, bell. *Ain't I a Woman: Black Women and Feminism*. Boston: South End Press, 1981.

hooks, bell. *Feminist Theory From Margin to Centre*. Boston: South End Press, 1984.

Horrigan, John B. *Online Communities: Networks That Nurture Long-Distance Relationships and Local Ties*. Washington, DC: Pew Internet and American Life Project, 2001.

Jaggar, Alison M. and Susan Bordo, eds. *Gender/Body/Knowledge: Feminist Reconstructions of Being and Knowledge*. Rutgers, NJ: Rutgers University Press, 1989.

Kilbourne, Jean. *Can't Buy My Love: How Advertising Changes the Way We Think and Feel*. New York: Free Press, 2000.

Kline, Stephen, Nick Dyer-Witheford, and Greig de Peuter. *Digital Play: The Interaction of Technology, Culture and Marketing*. Montreal, QB: McGill-Queen's University Press, 2003.

Linn, Susan. *Consuming Kids: The Hostile Takeover of Childhood*. New York: New Press, 2004.

Lynn, Regina. *The Sexual Revolution 2.0: Getting Connected, Upgrading Your Sex Life, and Finding True Love—or at Least a Dinner Date—in the Internet Age*. Berkeley, CA: Ulysses Press, 2005.

Marlane, Judith. *Women in Television News Revisited: Into the Twenty-First Century*. Austin: University of Texas Press, 1999.

McRobbie, Angela. *Jackie: An Ideology of Adolescent Femininity*. Birmingham, UK: Centre for Contemporary Cultural Studies, University of Birmingham, 1977.

Morgan, John. *The Invisible Man: A Self-Help Guide for Men With Eating Disorders, Compulsive Exercise and Bigorexia*. London: Routledge, 2008.

Morreale, Joanne. *Critiquing the Sitcom: A Reader*. Syracuse, NY: Syracuse University Press, 2003.

Nakamura, Lisa. *Cybertypes: Race, Ethnicity, and Identity on the Internet*. New York: Routledge, 2002.

Newcomb, Horace, ed. *Television: The Critical View*, 6th ed. New York: Oxford University Press, 2000.

Paul, Pamela. *Pornified: How Pornography Is Damaging Our Lives, Our Relationships, and Our Families*. New York: Owl Books, 2006.

Pipher, Mary. *Reviving Ophelia: Saving the Selves of Adolescent Girls*. Boston: Riverhead Trade, 2005.

Porter, David, ed. *Internet Culture*. New York: Routledge, 1997.

Powazek, Derek M. *Designing for Community: The Art of Connecting Real People in Virtual Places*. Indianapolis, IN: New Riders, 2002.

Preece, Jenny. *Online Communities: Designing Usability, Supporting Sociability*. West Sussex, UK: Wiley & Sons, 2000.

Propp, Vladamir. *Theory and History of Folklore*. Minneapolis: University of Minnesota Press, 1984.

Pustz, Matthew. J. *Comic Book Culture: Fanboys and True Believers*. Jackson: University Press of Mississippi, 1999.

Reynolds, Richard. *Superheroes: A Modern Mythology*. Jackson: University Press of Mississippi, 1994.

Rhode, Deborah. *The Beauty Bias: The Injustice of Appearance in Life and Law*. New York: Oxford University Press, 2010.

Robbins, Trina. *The Great Women Superheroes*. Northampton, MA: Kitchen Sink Press, 1996.

Roberts, Robin. *Ladies First: Women in Music Videos*. Jackson: University Press of Mississippi, 1996.

Rushkoff, Douglas. *Coercion: Why We Listen to What "They" Say*. New York: Riverhead Books, 2000.

Rushkoff, Douglas. *Get Back in the Box: Innovation From the Inside Out*. New York: Collins, 2005.

Rushkoff, Douglas. *Life, Inc.: How the World Became a Corporation and How to Take It Back*. New York: Random House, 2009.

Rushkoff, Douglas. *Program or Be Programmed: Ten Commands for a Digital Age*. New York: O/R Books, 2010.

Saunders, Corinne, ed. *A Companion to Romance: From Classical to Contemporary*. London: Wiley-Blackwell, 2007.

Schank, Roger and Robert Abelson. *Scripts, Plans, Goals and Understanding: An Inquiry Into Human Knowledge Structures*. Hillsdale, NJ: Lawrence Erlbaum Associates, 1977.

Schor, Juliet B. *Born to Buy: The Commercialized Child and the New Consumer Culture*. New York: Scribner, 2005.

Spigel, Lynn. *Make Room for TV: Television and the Family Ideal in Postwar America*. Chicago: University of Chicago Press, 1992.

Vorderer, Peter and Jennings Bryant, eds. *Playing Video Games: Motives, Responses, and Consequences*. Mahwah, NJ: Lawrence Erlbaum Associates, 2006.

Walkderdine, Valerie. *Children, Gender, Video Games: Toward a Relational Approach to Multimedia*. New York: Palgrave Macmillan, 2009.

Warner, Michael. *Publics and Counterpublics*. New York: Zone Books, 2002.

Wasko, Janet. *Understanding Disney: The Manufacture of Fantasy*. Malden, MA: Blackwell, 2001.

Weaver, David H. and G. Cleveland Wilhoit. *The American Journalist in the 1990s: U.S. News People at the End of an Era*. Mahwah, NJ: Lawrence Erlbaum Associates, 1996.

Williamson, Judith. *Decoding Advertisements*. London: Marion Boyars, 1978.

Wolf, Naomi. *The Beauty Myth: How Images of Beauty Are Used Against Women*. New York: William Morrow, 1991.

Wright, Bradford W. *Comic Book Nation: The Transformation of Youth Culture in America*. Baltimore, MD: Johns Hopkins University Press, 2001.

Journals

American Journalism Review
American Psychologist
Archives of Sexual Behavior
Columbia Journalism Review
Computers in Human Behavior
Critical Studies in Media Communication
CyberPsychology & Behavior
Developmental Review
Educational Media International
Feminist Collections: A Quarterly of Women's Studies Resources
Feminist Media Studies
Human Communication Research
Information, Communication and Society
International Journal of Business Science and Applied Management
International Journal of Eating Disorders
International Journal of Electronic Commerce
International Journal of Gender, Science and Technology
Journal of Advertising Research
Journal of Aesthetics and Art Criticism
Journal of Bisexuality
Journal of Black Psychology
Journal of Broadcasting & Electronic Media
Journal of Computer-Mediated Communication
Journal of Consulting and Clinical Psychology
Journal of Counseling Psychology
Journal of Experimental Social Psychology
Journal of Information Science
Journal of Interactive Advertising
Journal of Media Practice
The Journal of Philosophy
Journal of Popular Film and Television
The Journal of Research into New Media Technologies
Journal of Website Promotion

Journal of Women in Culture & Society
Journalism and Mass Communication Quarterly
New Media & Society
Newspaper Research Journal
Sex Roles
Sexualities
Social Identities
Stanford Social Innovation Review
Television Quarterly
Urban Affairs Quarterly
Web Journal of Mass Communication Research
Women and Language
Women's Studies in Communication

Internet

American Society of News Editors: http://asne.org
Annenberg School for Communication, University of Pennsylvania: http://www.asc.upenn.edu
Annenberg School for Communication, University of Southern California: http://annenberg.usc.edu
Archive of American Television: http://www.emmytvlegends.org
Bitch Magazine: http://www.bitchmagazine.org
Bust Magazine: http://www.bust.org
Center for the Study of Women in Television and Film: http://womenintvfilm.sdsu.edu
danah boyd Blog—Apophenia: http://www.zephoria.org/thoughts
danah boyd Website: http://www.danah.org
Federal Communications Commission: http://www.fcc.gov
Gay and Lesbian Alliance Against Defamation: http://www.glaad.org
Geena Davis Institute on Gender in Media: http://www.thegeenadavisinstitute.org
Gender, Media and Politics: http://www.gendermediaandpolitics.org
Grady College of Journalism and Mass Communication: http://www.grady.uga.edu
HealthyPlace: http://www.healthyplace.com
International Network for Gender Media Watchdogs: http://www.mediawatchdogs.gendersquare.org
Jean Kilbourne Website: http://www.jeankilbourne.com
Mark Crispin Miller Website: http://markcrispinmiller.com
Media and Gender Justice: mediaactioncenter.org/gender
Media Education Foundation: http://www.mediaed.org
Media Management Center at Northwestern University: http://www.mediamanagementcenter.org
Media Report to Women: http://www.mediareporttowomen.com
Media Watch: http://www.mediawatch.com
Ms. Magazine: http://www.msmagazine.org

Museum of Broadcast Communications: http://www
.museum.tv

National Center for Transgender Equality: http://
transequality.org

National Organization for Women: http://www.now.org

National Telemedia Council: http://
nationaltelemediacouncil.org

Pew Research Center, Internet and American Life Project:
http://www.pewinternet.org

Radio Television Digital News Association: http://www
.rtdna.org

Robert McChesney Website: http://www.robertmcchesney
.com

2010 Essential Facts About the Computer and Video Game
Industry: http://www.theesa.com/facts/gameplayer.asp

Women in Media and News: http://www.wimnonline.org

Women's Media Center: http://www.womensmediacenter
.org

Appendix

The following selected Websites, along with editorial commentary, are provided for further research on gender in media.

American Psychological Association: Sexualization of Girls

http://www.apa.org/pi/women/programs/girls

The American Psychological Association (APA) has been involved in issues related to children and media content since the 1990s, including the representation of violence in media (including television, video games, and interactive media) and the effects of advertising aimed at children. In 2007, the Women's Programs Office of the Public Interest Directorate Task Force on the Sexualization of Girls released a report that summarized the evidence for the sexualization of girls in mass media and other societal influences (from magazines and television programs to dolls and clothing) and the psychological consequences of this sexualization. This Website includes a downloadable copy of this report and an executive summary of it, press releases related to it, and a number of ancillary materials.

The APA's report concluded that almost every type of media studied (including television, music lyrics and music videos, movies, magazines, video games, and the Internet) sexualized women, that women were more likely to be portrayed in a sexual manner than were men, and that an unrealistic standard of physical beauty was emphasized in women. An extensive study of the sexualization of children in advertising found that although such images were rare (occurring in about 1.5 percent of the advertisements studied), when children were presented in a sexual manner they were almost always (85 percent of the time) images of girls rather than boys. The study also concluded that sexualization had negative effects on girls' cognitive functioning, mental and physical health, and sexual well-being. Materials, available in HTML and PDF format, added to the Website to follow up the information contained in this report include suggestions on what parents and other adults can do to combat this sexualization of girls, what girls can do to challenge these images, and a collection of links to organizations that promote media literacy and improved images of girls and women in the media.

Gay & Lesbian Alliance Against Defamation

www.glaad.org

The Gay & Lesbian Alliance Against Defamation (GLAAD) was founded in 1985 to monitor media representation of GLBT (gay, lesbian, bisexual, and transgender) issues and people. Today GLAAD sees itself as an "amplifier" of the voice of the GLBT community and works with many local organizations to build support for equality while also continuing to monitor the media, advocate change, and conduct educational and outreach activities. The Website includes a form for reporting unfair and defamatory coverage in the news media, and such incidents are reported on the Website (including the original material, date and source, and reasons the material is objectionable).

GLAAD organizes its activities into 10 program areas: advertising media; entertainment media; field work and community media; national news; religion, faith, and values; Spanish-language media; Spirit Day (October 20, a day designated for showing support of GLBT youth); sports advocacy; transgender voices; and voices of color. The entertainment media program monitors film, television, music, and related media; speaks out against anti-GLBT content; and works with television and film executives, script writers, and producers to advocate the inclusion of GLBT material in popular media and to provide consulting services to ensure the authenticity of that content. GLAAD publishes two reports in this area, the "Network Responsibility

Index," which ranks the networks according to their inclusion of GLBT content, and the annual "Where We Are on TV," which measures the number of GLBT characters in television programming.

The GLAAD Website includes a number of informational materials that can be downloaded for free or viewed on the Website. These include the "Where We Are on TV" reports, the Network Responsibility Indexes, a Media Reference Guide to transgender issues (including information about Chaz Bono), a Spanish-language guide to GLBT terminology (*Guía de terminologia gay, lebiana, bisexual y transgénero*), the GLAAD Media Reference Guide, and resource guides to issues and topics ranging from the film *The Kids Are All Right* to adoption and gay parenting. Publications in the "Talking About" series are also available for free download. These publications are guides intended to help open discussions on sensitive topics such as gay marriage or transgender protections in the workplace and suggest language that may help keep the discussion usefully focused on the issues at stake.

The GLAAD Advertising Media Program (www.commercialcloset.org) was founded in 1996 as the Commercial Closet Association to scrutinize the portrayal of GLBT people in advertising and to advocate appropriate inclusion as a means to fight homophobia and discrimination. The program maintains a searchable online library of over 4,000 television and print ads from all over the world; many of these ads are available for viewing on the Website. The Website offers breakdowns by year, region, type of product (e.g., computers), target, medium, company, brand, and agency. The Website also offers a number of resources related to the GLBT presence in advertising, including links to scholarly materials, marketing resources, lesson plans, and an explanation of the "respect score" and how it is calculated.

The GLAAD Website includes a blog carrying news relevant to GLAAD's mission and can be sorted by topic or searched. The Website also includes press releases and information about GLAAD events, including the annual GLAAD Media Awards.

Geena Davis Institute on Gender in Media

www.thegeenadavisinstitute.org

The Geena Davis Institute on Gender in Media was founded in 2004 by actress Geena Davis to research gender roles in children's media (media aimed at ages 11 and younger), educate the general public as well as decision makers about this issue, and advocate for more balanced portrayals of both boys and girls in children's media. Davis's motivation for founding the institute, according to its Website, was her realization while watching children's media with her daughter that there were almost no female characters. She commissioned a study on gender in film and television, authored by Dr. Stacy Smith of the University of Southern California Annenberg School for Communication and Journalism. The study found that in family films male characters outnumber females 3:1, and in group scenes 83 percent of the characters are male.

The goal of the institute is to change the portrayal of female characters and gender stereotypes in children's media. The Geena Davis Institute holds a biennial Symposium on Gender in Media attended by over 300 industry professionals, has amassed a large body of research on gender in children's media, performs outreach with media creators and the general public, and is regularly cited by educational and governmental institutions and major media outlets.

Two of the institute's research reports—"Gender Disparity on Screen and Behind the Camera in Family Films" and "Gender Stereotypes: An Analysis of Popular Films and TV"—are available for download in PDF format from the institute's Website. Executive summaries and key findings from three reports are also available for download: the "Gender Disparity on Screen" report cited above plus "Changing the Status Quo: Industry Leaders' Perceptions of Gender in Family Films" and "Occupational Aspirations: What Are G-Rated Films Teaching Children About the World of Work." The Website also presents basic facts about gender disparity in children's media and information to debunk common myths about gender in children's and family media and provides links to other research and to organizational Websites that are concerned with issues of gender roles in children's media.

The programming arm of the Geena Davis Institute is See Jane, which works with professionals and students in the media industry to challenge gender stereotypes presented in children's television, to provide media training to students in middle school and high school, and to produce educational media. See Jane, in conjunction with college media producers, created the video series "Guess Who?" to educate children ages six to nine about gender stereotypes. This program appeared on Channel One and may be viewed on the Website also.

The "Press" section of this Website includes press releases from the Geena Davis Institute, video interviews and keynote addresses, and links to press coverage of the institute's research and work. A number of other videos and photo galleries relating to the Geena Davis Institute's work are also available in the "Resources & Media" section of the Website. The institute also publishes a weekly e-mail newsletter, "The Geena Davis Institute SmartBrief," which compiles relevant news from industry sources; the Website includes an interface to subscribe to this newsletter.

Media Education Foundation

www.mediaed.org

The Media Education Foundation (MEF), located in Northampton, Massachusetts, produces and distributes educational resources, including documentary films, intended to motivate viewers to reflect on the cultural impact of American mass media. The MEF is motivated by the belief that language and image define the limits and possibilities of thought and imagination and that it is crucial to teach students to think critically about the media they consume and which forms a large part of their environment.

Gender issues are one of the major categories covered by MEF media, with specific topics that include male and female sex roles, body image, homosexuality, sexual violence, and body image as well as how these and other issues are portrayed in the mass media. The MEF was founded by Sut Jhally, a professor of communication at the University of Massachusetts, Amherst; it is governed by a board of directors and a board of advisers.

MEF videos may be ordered from the site, and many may be screened in part or in whole on the Internet; when the entire video is available for preview screening on the Internet, the streamed video is low resolution and is intended only for purchase consideration. A description of each film, including information about the filmmakers, is available from the Website. Examples of gender-related titles available from MEF include *The Bro Code: How Contemporary Culture Creates Sexist Men*, *The Codes of Gender: Identity and Performance in Pop Culture*, *Date Rape Backlash: Media & the Denial of Rape*, and *Playing Unfair: The Media Image of the Female Athlete*.

A number of other educational materials addressing issues of concern to MEF are available for free from the Website. For many of the films, specific materials such as study guides, transcripts for some films, and links to related information are included. In addition, the Website offers a number of free downloadable resources related to media education, including handouts, articles, and classroom activity suggestions (e.g., a poster titled "10 Reasons Why Media Education Matters," guides to deconstructing advertisements, and fact sheets on topics such as the advertising industry and media ownership and regulation).

Media Stereotyping: Media Awareness Network

http://www.media-awareness.ca/english/issues/ stereotyping/index.cfm

The Media Awareness Network (MNet), founded in 1996, is a Canadian nonprofit organization dedicated to promoting media and digital literacy, conducting research, and producing programs and resources to increase awareness and education of media issues. The main focus of MNet, according to its Website, is "equipping adults with information and tools to help young people understand how the media work, how the media may affect their lifestyle choices and the extent to which they, as consumers and citizens, are being well informed."

Most of MNet's materials are freely available from the Website in French and English. The section "Media Stereotyping" briefly explains what media stereotypes are, their effects on the audience, and why they are problematic. The Website then treats the following issues in separate sections: ethnic and visible minorities, aboriginal people, girls and women, men and masculinity, gays and lesbians, whiteness and white privilege, and persons with disabilities. Each issue is further broken down into subtopics, with summaries of the relevant topics within each, and links to further information and related Websites. For instance, the "Girls and Women" section includes the following subtopics: "Beauty and Body Image in the Media"; "Sex and Relationships in the Media"; "Media Coverage of Women and Women's Issues"; "Media and Girls"; "Economics of Gender Stereotyping"; "Women Working in the Media"; and "Resisting Stereotypes and Working for Change."

MNet's Website provides access to its press releases, fact sheets, newsletters, annual reports, public service announcements (videos viewable online with QuickTime), and other reports and publications. The site also includes materials meant specifically for teachers and for parents. In the former case, these include materials designed for classroom use, professional development materials, information about media education initiatives in the Canadian provinces, a number of free games for student use, and a catalog of resources available to schools. Materials focused on parents include advice and information about children's Internet use, a public education program on Web safety, and games designed to teach children how to use the Internet safely.

Sarah E. Boslaugh
Kennesaw State University

Index